Adam Nathan

Windows® 8 Apps with XAML and C# Unleashed

 800 East 96th Street, Indianapolis, Indiana 46240 USA

Windows® 8 Apps with XAML and C# Unleashed

Copyright © 2013 by Pearson Education

ISBN-13: 978-0-672-33601-0
ISBN-10: 0-672-33601-4

Library of Congress Cataloging-in-Publication Data is on file.

Printed in the United States of America

First Printing December 2012

Trademarks

All terms mentioned in this book that are known to be trademarks or service marks have been appropriately capitalized. Sams Publishing cannot attest to the accuracy of this information. Use of a term in this book should not be regarded as affecting the validity of any trademark or service mark.

Warning and Disclaimer

Every effort has been made to make this book as complete and as accurate as possi-ble, but no warranty or fitness is implied. The information provided is on an "as is" basis. The author(s) and the publisher shall have neither liability nor responsibility to any person or entity with respect to any loss or damages arising from the information contained in this book or from the use of the programs accompanying it.

Bulk Sales

Sams Publishing offers excellent discounts on this book when ordered in quantity for bulk purchases or special sales. For more information, please contact

U.S. Corporate and Government Sales

1-800-382-3419

corpsales@pearsontechgroup.com

For sales outside of the U.S., please contact

International Sales

international@pearsoned.com

EDITOR-IN-CHIEF
Greg Wiegand

EXECUTIVE EDITOR
Neil Rowe

DEVELOPMENT EDITOR
Mark Renfrow

MANAGING EDITOR
Kristy Hart

PROJECT EDITOR
Deadline Driven
Publishing

COPY EDITOR
Kelly Maish

INDEXER
Angie Martin

PROOFREADER
Deadline Driven
Publishing

TECHNICAL EDITOR
Ashish Shetty

**PUBLISHING
COORDINATOR**
Cindy Teeters

COVER DESIGNER
Mark Shirar

COMPOSITOR
Bronkella Publishing

Contents at a Glance

Table of Contents

About the Author

Adam Nathan is a principal software architect for Microsoft, a best-selling technical author, and arguably the world's most prolific developer for Windows Phone. He introduced XAML to countless developers through his books on a variety of Microsoft technologies. Currently a part of Microsoft's Startup Business Group, Adam has previously worked on Visual Studio and the Common Language Runtime. He was the founding developer and architect of Popfly, Microsoft's first Silverlight-based product, named by *PCWorld* as one of its year's most innovative products. He is also the founder of PINVOKE.NET, the online resource for .NET developers who need to access Win32. His apps have been featured on Lifehacker, Gizmodo, ZDNet, ParentMap, and other enthusiast sites.

Adam's books are considered required reading by many inside Microsoft and throughout the industry. Adam is the author of *101 Windows Phone 7 Apps* (Sams, 2011), *Silverlight 1.0 Unleashed* (Sams, 2008), *WPF Unleashed* (Sams, 2006), *WPF 4 Unleashed* (Sams, 2010), and *.NET and COM: The Complete Interoperability Guide* (Sams, 2002); a coauthor of *ASP.NET: Tips, Tutorials, and Code* (Sams, 2001); and a contributor to books including *.NET Framework Standard Library Annotated Reference, Volume 2* (Addison-Wesley, 2005) and *Windows Developer Power Tools* (O'Reilly, 2006). You can find Adam online at www.adamnathan.net, or @adamnathan on Twitter.

Dedication

To Tyler and Ryan.

Acknowledgments

First, I thank Lindsay Nathan for making this possible. Words fail to describe my gratitude.

I'd like to give special thanks to Ashish Shetty, Tim Heuer, Mark Rideout, Jonathan Russ, Joe Duffy, Chris Brumme, Eric Rudder, Neil Rowe, Betsy Harris, Ginny Munroe, Eileen Chan, and Valery Sarkisov. As always, I thank my parents for having the foresight to introduce me to Basic programming on our IBM PCjr when I was in elementary school.

Finally, I thank *you* for picking up a copy of this book! I don't think you'll regret it!

We Want to Hear from You!

As the reader of this book, *you* are our most important critic and commentator. We value your opinion and want to know what we're doing right, what we could do better, what areas you'd like to see us publish in, and any other words of wisdom you're willing to pass our way.

You can email or write me directly to let me know what you did or didn't like about this book—as well as what we can do to make our books stronger.

Please note that I cannot help you with technical problems related to the topic of this book, and that due to the high volume of mail I receive, I might not be able to reply to every message.

When you write, please be sure to include this book's title and author as well as your name and phone or email address. I will carefully review your comments and share them with the author and editors who worked on the book.

E-mail: feedback@samspublishing.com

Mail: Neil Rowe
            Executive Editor
            Sams Publishing
            800 East 96th Street
            Indianapolis, IN 46240 USA

Reader Services

Visit our website and register this book at informit.com/register for convenient access to any updates, downloads, or errata that might be available for this book.

Introduction

If you ask me, it has never been a better time to be a software developer. Not only are programmers in high demand—due in part to an astonishingly low number of computer science graduates each year—but app stores make it easier than ever to broadly distribute your own software and even make money from it!

I remember releasing a few shareware games in junior high school and asking for $5 donations. I earned $15. One of the three donations was from my grandmother, who didn't even own a computer! These days, of course, adults and kids alike can make money on simple apps and games without relying on kind and generous individuals going to the trouble of mailing a check!

The Windows Store is an app store like no other. When you consider the number of people who use Windows 8 (and Windows RT) compared to the number of people who use any other operating system on the planet, you realize what a unique and enormous opportunity the Windows Store provides.

When you write a Windows Store app, you can work with whichever language and technology is most comfortable for you: JavaScript with an HTML user interface, or C#/Visual Basic/C++ with a XAML or raw DirectX user interface. (You can also componentize code to get different mixtures, such as using C# with HTML or some JavaScript in a XAML app.) Besides familiarity, your choice can have other benefits. Outside of the core Windows platform, each language and technology has different sets of reusable libraries and components. C++ has features for high-performance algorithms, for example. However, regardless of which choice you make, the Windows APIs are the same, and the graphics are hardware accelerated.

The key to the multiple-language support is the Windows Runtime, or WinRT for short. You can think of it like .NET's Common Language Runtime, except it spans both managed and unmanaged languages. To enable this, WinRT is COM-based. Most of the time, you can't tell when you interact with WinRT, however. This is a new, friendlier version of COM that is more amenable to *automatic* correct usage from environments such as .NET or JavaScript. (Contrast this to over a decade ago, when I wrote a book about mixing COM with .NET. This topic alone required over 1,600 pages!)

WinRT APIs are automatically *projected* into the programming language you use, so they look natural for that language. Projections are more than just exposing the raw APIs, however. Core WinRT data types such as `string`, collection types, and a few others are mapped to appropriate data types for the target environment. For C# or other .NET languages, this means exposing them as

> Although WinRT APIs are not .NET APIs, they have metadata in the standardized format used by .NET. Therefore, you can browse them directly with familiar .NET tools, such as the IL Disassembler (ILDASM). You can find these on your computer as .winmd files. Visual Studio's "Object Browser" is also a convenient way to search and browse WinRT APIs.

`System.String, System.Collections.Generic.IList<T>`, and so on. To match conventions, member names are even morphed to be Camel-cased for JavaScript and Pascal-cased for other languages, which makes the MSDN reference documentation occasionally look goofy.

In the set of APIs exposed by Windows, everything under the `Windows.UI.Xaml` namespace is XAML-specific, everything under the `Windows.UI.WebUI` namespace is for HTML apps, everything under `System` is .NET-specific, and everything else (which is under `Windows`) is general-purpose WinRT functionality. As you dig into the framework, you notice that the XAML-specific and .NET-specific APIs are indeed the most natural to use from C# and XAML. General-purpose WinRT APIs follow slightly different conventions and can sometimes look a little odd to developers familiar with .NET. For example, they tend to be exception-heavy for situations that normally don't warrant an exception (such as the user cancelling an action). Artifacts like this are caused by the projection mechanism mapping HRESULTs (COM error codes) into .NET exceptions.

I wrote this book with the following goals in mind:

➜ To provide a solid grounding in the underlying concepts, in a practical and approachable fashion

➜ To answer the questions most people have when learning how to write Windows Store apps and to show how commonly desired tasks are accomplished

➜ To be an authoritative source, thanks to input from members of the team who designed, implemented, and tested Windows 8 and Visual Studio

➜ To be clear about where the technology falls short rather than blindly singing its praises

➜ To optimize for concise, easy-to-understand code rather than enforcing architectural patterns that can be impractical or increase the number of concepts to understand

➜ To be an easily navigated reference that you can constantly come back to

To elaborate on the second-to-last point: You won't find examples of patterns such as Model-View-ViewModel (MVVM) in this book. I *am* a fan of applying such patterns to code, but I don't want to distract from the core lessons in each chapter.

Whether you're new to XAML or a long-time XAML developer, I hope you find this book to exhibit all these attributes.

Who Should Read This Book?

This book is for software developers who are interested in creating apps for the Windows Store, whether they are for tablets, laptops, or desktops. It does not teach you how to program, nor does it teach the basics of the C# language. However, it is designed to be understandable even for folks who are new to .NET, and does not require previous experience with XAML. And if you are already well versed in XAML, I'm confident that this book still has a lot of helpful information for you. At the very least, it should be an invaluable reference for your bookshelf.

Software Requirements

This book targets Windows 8, Windows RT, and the corresponding developer tools. The tools can be downloaded for free at the Windows Dev Center: s. The download includes the Windows 8 SDK, a version of Visual Studio Express specifically for Windows Store apps, and Blend. It's worth noting that although this book almost exclusively refers to Windows 8, the content also applies to Windows RT.

Although it's not required, I recommend PAINT.NET, a free download at http://getpaint.net, for creating and editing graphics, such as the set of icons needed by apps.

Code Examples

Source code for examples in this book can be downloaded from www.samspublishing.com.

How This Book Is Organized

This book is arranged into five parts, representing the progression of feature areas that you typically need to understand. But if you want to jump ahead and learn about a topic such animation or live tiles, the book is set up to allow for nonlinear journeys as well. The following sections provide a summary of each part.

Part I: Getting Started

This part includes the following chapters:

→ Chapter 1, "Anatomy of a Windows Store App"

→ Chapter 2, "Mastering XAML"

This part provides the foundation for the rest of the book. If you have previously created Windows Phone apps or worked with XAML in the context of other Microsoft technologies, a lot of this should be familiar to you. There are still several unique aspects for Windows 8 and the Windows Store, however.

Part II: Building an App

This part includes the following chapters:

→ Chapter 3, "Sizing, Positioning, and Transforming Elements"

→ Chapter 4, "Layout"

→ Chapter 5, "Interactivity"

→ Chapter 6, "Handling Input: Touch, Mouse, Pen, and Keyboard"

→ Chapter 7, "App Model"

Part II equips you with the knowledge of how to place things on the screen, how to make them adjust to the wide variety of screen types, and how to interact with the user. It also digs into the app model for Windows Store apps, which is significantly different from the app model for desktop applications in a number of ways.

Part III: Understanding Controls

This part includes the following chapters:

→ Chapter 8, "Content Controls"

→ Chapter 9, "Items Controls"

→ Chapter 10, "Text"

→ Chapter 11, "Images"

→ Chapter 12, "Audio and Video"

→ Chapter 13, "Other Controls"

Part III provides a tour of the controls built into the XAML UI Framework. There are many controls that you expect to have available, plus several that you might not expect.

Part IV: Leveraging the Richness of XAML

This part includes the following chapters:

→ Chapter 14, "Vector Graphics"

→ Chapter 15, "Animation"

→ Chapter 16, "Styles, Templates, and Visual States"

→ Chapter 17, "Data Binding"

The features covered in Part IV are areas in which XAML really shines. Although previous parts of the book expose some XAML richness (applying transforms to any elements, the composability of controls, and so on), these features push the richness to the next level.

Part V: Exploiting Windows 8

This part includes the following chapters:

→ Chapter 18, "Data"

→ Chapter 19, "Charms"

→ Chapter 20, "Extensions"

→ Chapter 21, "Sensors and Other Devices"

→ Chapter 22, "Thinking Outside the App: Live Tiles, Toast Notifications, and the Lock Screen"

This part of the book can just as easily appear in a book about JavaScript or C++ Windows Store apps, with the exception of its code snippets. It covers unique and powerful Windows 8 features that are not specific to XAML or C#, but they are things that all Windows Store app developers should know.

Conventions Used in This Book

Various typefaces in this book identify new terms and other special items. These typefaces include the following:

Typeface	Meaning
Italic	Italic is used for new terms or phrases when they are initially defined and occasionally for emphasis.
Monospace	Monospace is used for screen messages, code listings, and filenames. In code listings, *italic monospace type* is used for placeholder text.
	Code listings are colorized similarly to the way they are colorized in Visual Studio. Blue monospace type is used for XML elements and C# keywords, brown monospace type is used for XML element names and C# strings, green monospace type is used for comments, red monospace type is used for XML attributes, and teal monospace type is used for type names in C#.
Bold	When appropriate, bold is used for code directly related to the main lesson(s) in a chapter.

Throughout this book, and even in this introduction, you find a number of sidebar elements:

What is a FAQ sidebar?

A Frequently Asked Question (FAQ) sidebar presents a question you might have about the subject matter in a particular spot in the book—and then provides a concise answer.

Digging Deeper Sidebars

A Digging Deeper sidebar presents advanced or more detailed information on a subject than is provided in the surrounding text. Think of Digging Deeper material as something you can look into if you're curious but can ignore if you're not.

A tip offers information about design guidelines, shortcuts, or alternative approaches to produce better results, or something that makes a task easier.

Warning!

A warning alerts you to an action or a condition that can lead to an unexpected or unpredictable result—and then tells you how to avoid it.

Chapter 1

ANATOMY OF A WINDOWS STORE APP

To get acquainted with Windows Store apps, this chapter takes you on a tour of the project you get when you create a new C# Windows Store app in Visual Studio. No matter what programming language you choose, when you select "New Project" in Visual Studio, you get the following three options (among others) under the "Windows Store" category:

- → Blank App
- → Grid App
- → Split App

The latter two are multipage apps with a lot of prebuilt behaviors based on features covered in later chapters. The Blank App choice is the simplest, and it's also the type of project you're most likely to start with, so this chapter looks at a Blank App project to drive the discussion.

> No matter which type of Windows Store project you create, Visual Studio provides a long list of sophisticated items you can add to your project: pages, templates for supporting various Windows 8 contracts, and more. For example, you can individually add a Split Page and an Items Page that are just like the ones you would get if you created a Split App. Other pages can be added that are just like the ones you would get if you created a Grid App.

Launching a New App

When you create a Blank App, you get a project that's ready to compile and run. Although pressing F5 (or clicking the "Start Debugging" button) in Visual Studio launches your app locally, you've got three slick options to choose from via the button's dropdown menu, shown in Figure 1.1 under Visual Studio's light theme (used throughout this book).

FIGURE 1.1   The three ways to launch your app in Visual Studio

With the "Remote Machine" option, you can deploy and debug to any other Windows 8 computer reachable on your network (although not over the Internet). This is extremely handy for testing things on a Surface or other tablets. The target device must have the Remote Tools for Visual Studio installed and running, which you can download from microsoft.com.

The "Simulator" option is the next best thing to having a real tablet, as it provides mechanisms to simulate touch input, different device orientations, location services, and more. The simulator is shown in Figure 1.2. In fact, it has one huge advantage over testing on a physical device: It enables you to experience your app in a number of different resolutions and virtual screen sizes, including different aspect ratios. Given the wide variety of shapes and sizes of screens out there that run Windows 8, testing your app in this fashion is a must.

Once your app is finished, you can submit it to the Windows Store via items on the Store menu in Visual Studio Express for Windows 8, or via the Project menu in other editions of Visual Studio.

FIGURE 1.2   Testing your app on the simulator is like testing it on an army of different-sized devices.

> **⚠ The simulator is your actual computer!**
>
> Although the simulator simulates several things, what you see on the virtual device is your real "host" computer running with your actual user account, apps, files, and so on. (Running the simulator is like initiating a special kind of remote desktop connection to yourself!) Changes you make inside the simulator affect your computer just as if you made them outside the simulator.

> **❓ What's the minimum resolution that a Windows Store app needs to support?**
>
> 1024x768 (or 768x1024 in portrait mode). Because Windows disallows snapping a Windows Store app at this low resolution, which would force your app to share the screen with another app and therefore get fewer pixels, your app's normal user interface is guaranteed to get at least 768 pixels of width and at least 768 pixels of height. The one exception is when your app is snapped to the side of the screen. In this case, it gets only 320 pixels of width. The best thing to do is to support a special snapped view of your user interface, which is covered in Chapter 4, "Layout."

> **❓ How do I run my app outside of Visual Studio?**
>
> Although compiling your app produces an `.exe` file in the `bin\Debug` or `bin\Release` subfolder, you can't simply double-click it from the Windows desktop to run it. If you try, you get an error that explains, "This application can only run in the context of an app container." (An "app container" refers to the sandbox in which all Windows Store apps run.)
>
> Like all Windows Store apps, you must launch it from the Start screen. Visual Studio automatically installs your app the first time you launch it, and it also pins it to the Start screen for convenience.

When you run a Blank App project without any changes, you'll see that it lives up to its name. The app doesn't actually *do* anything other than fill the screen with darkness. It does, however, set up a lot of infrastructure that would be difficult and tedious to create from scratch. The project contains the following items:

→ The package manifest, a temporary certificate used to sign it, and some images

→ The main page (`MainPage.xaml` and `MainPage.xaml.cs`)

→ The application definition and related files: `App.xaml`, `App.xaml.cs`, `StandardStyles.xaml`, and `AssemblyInfo.cs`

The Package Manifest

The *package manifest* is a file called `Package.appxmanifest`. ("AppX" is a term sometimes used within Microsoft for Windows Store app packages that stuck around in the file-name.) This manifest describes your app to Windows as well as the Windows Store—its name, what it looks like, what it's allowed to do, and more. It's an XML file, although you have to tell Visual Studio to "View Source" in order to see the XML. There's usually no need to view and edit the XML directly, however. The default view is a tabbed set of forms to fill out, which is the easiest way to populate all the information. There are four tabs:

→ Application UI

→ Capabilities

→ Declarations

→ Packaging

Application UI

On the Application UI tab, you can set the app's name and description, characteristics of its tile and splash screen, and notification settings (if your app supports them). Notifications are covered in the last chapter of this book. You can even restrict the preferred of your app if you'd rather not have it automatically rotate to all four of them:

→ **Landscape (horizontal)**

→ **Landscape-flipped (horizontal but upside down)**

→ **Portrait (vertical, with the hardware Start button on the left)**

→ **Portrait-flipped (vertical, with the hardware Start button on the right)**

Disabling the *flipped* orientations would be an odd thing to do, but disabling some orientations can make sense for certain types of games that wish to be landscape only. Note that this is just a *preference*, not a guarantee, because not all devices support rotation. For example, a portrait-only app launched on a typical desktop PC must accept the one-and-only landscape orientation. However, if a device that *does* support rotation is currently locked to a landscape orientation, a portrait-only app will actually run in the portrait orientation, ignoring the lock setting.

Customizing Your Splash Screen

To ensure that every app's splash screen can be displayed practically instantaneously (before your app even gets loaded), you have little control over it. You can specify a 620x300 image, and a background color for the screen. That's it. Visual Studio gives you an appropriately sized placeholder SplashScreen.png file in an Assets subfolder, intentionally made ugly to practically guarantee you won't forget to change it before submitting your app to the Windows Store.

When your splash screen is shown, the image is displayed centered on top of your chosen background color. Figure 1.3 shows an example SplashScreen.png containing a Pixelwinks logo, and Figure 1.4 shows what this looks like on the simulator with a 768x1024 resolution. The splash screen was given a yellow background for demonstration purposes. A real app should make the background color match the background of the image or simply make the image's background transparent.

FIGURE 1.3   An example `SplashScreen.png` with a nontransparent background for demonstration purposes

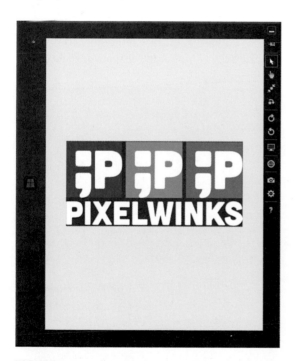

FIGURE 1.4   A live splash screen shown inside the simulator at a resolution of 768x1024 with a garish yellow background to clearly show the bounds of the image

When your app is launched, the splash screen automatically animates in and automatically fades out once your app has loaded and has made a call to `Window.Current.Activate`. This gives you the flexibility to do arbitrarily complex logic before the splash screen goes away, although you should avoid doing a lot of work here. (Your app is given only five seconds to show the splash screen before Windows terminates it.)

Customizing Your Tile

In the "Tile" section, you can specify three logo images:

→ **Logo**—A 150x150 image used on your tile

→ **Wide logo**—A 310x150 image used on your tile in its "double-wide" configuration, if you want to support that

→ **Small logo**—A 30x30 image used wherever a tiny icon is needed, such as in the searchable "All apps" view on the Start screen

 How do I get my app to support a wide tile?

Supporting a wide tile is as simple as including a 310x150 image in your project and then specifying that image for the wide logo in the package manifest. When you do this, your app not only *supports* a wide tile, but it displays it by default when installed. If you omit an image, your app will support only a normal-sized tile.

It's worth noting that you shouldn't bother with a wide tile unless you're going to make it a live tile (covered in the final chapter). Otherwise, your app will occupy more space by default without adding any extra value.

Visual Studio provides placeholder images for the logo and small logo, but not the wide logo. With any of these images (including the splash screen image), you can change their names and locations, and they can be either JPEG or PNG files. Just remember to update the package manifest accordingly (and be sure the files are included in your project).

 To create an icon that fits in with the built-in apps, it should have a transparent background and the drawing inside should:

→ Be completely white
→ Be composed of simple geometric shapes
→ Use an understandable real-world metaphor

The drawing used in all two-to-three images should look the same, just scaled to different sizes.

The drawing for the 150x150 icon should generally fit in a 66x66 box centered but nudged a little higher to leave more space for any overlaid text. Typically the drawing has a 42-pixel margin on the left and right, a 37-pixel margin on top, and a 47-pixel margin on the bottom. The drawing for the 30x30 icon should generally fit in a 24x24 centered box, leaving just 3 pixels of margin so it's easier to see at the small size.

Creating white-on-transparent images requires some practice and patience. You'll want to use tools such as PAINT.NET, mentioned in this book's "Introduction" section. A few of the characters from fonts such as Wingdings, Webdings, and Segoe UI Symbol can even be used to help create a decent icon! Resources like thenounproject.com can also be helpful.

Of course, games or apps with their own strong branding usually do *not* follow these guidelines, as being consistent with their own identity outweighs being consistent with Windows.

Depending on the pixel density of the screen, Windows automatically scales all non-desktop user interfaces to prevent items from being too small to touch or too hard to read. (This applies to all Windows Store apps as well as the system UI such as the Start screen, file picker, and so on.) To prevent your images from looking unsightly by being scaled upward, you can provide multiple versions of any image: one at its normal size, one at 140% of its normal size, and one at 180% of its normal size. For a file such as Assets/Logo.png mentioned in your app manifest, you should name the files as follows:

→ Assets/Logo.**scale-100**.png (for 100% scale)

→ Assets/Logo.**scale-140**.png (for 140% scale)

→ Assets/Logo.**scale-180**.png (for 180% scale)

Windows automatically uses the correct file for the current screen and current user settings. Furthermore, the Logo, Small Logo, and Wide Logo support an additional 80 percent scale. For these, you can add one more variation to the list:

→ Assets/Logo.**scale-80**.png (for 80 percent scale)

You can use a similar technique for providing different files for high contrast mode, different cultures, and more. See Chapter 11, "Images," for more details.

You can also specify a background color for your tile. For the best results, this color (as well as the tile images) should match what you use in your splash screen. The desired effect of the splash screen is that your tile springs to life and fills the screen in a larger form.

You can also choose a "short name," which is the text that gets overlaid on the bottom of your tile. You can even specify whether you want the text to appear only on the normal-sized tile, wide tile, both, or none. Many apps turn off the text because their images already include a logo with the name.

Finally, you can decide whether you want the overlaid text to be "light" (which means white) or "dark" (which means a dark gray). Although most apps use white text, you may need to choose the dark option if you want your tile to have a light background color.

Figure 1.5 shows examples of the three image files, and Figure 1.6 shows how they look in practice, using a yellow tile background color for demonstration purposes. This was applied to a Blank App project named "BlankApp," although it was given a tile short name of "Pixelwinks," which is why both terms appear in Figure 1.6.

Notice that because Logo.png and WideLogo.png don't use transparency, you can't see the yellow background color underneath. However, in the searchable apps list and the Alt+Tab user interface, the small logo ends up being surrounded by a yellow border. Therefore, choose your background color (and determine whether you want your images to use transparency) carefully!

`SmallLogo.png`   `WideLogo.png`   `Logo.png`

FIGURE 1.5   Examples of the three logo image files.

The normal tile, using `Logo.png`   The wide tile, using `WideLogo.png`

The searchable apps list, using `SmallLogo.png`

The Alt+Tab user interface for switching between   The Task Manager, using a
desktop and Windows 8 apps, using `SmallLogo.png`   scaled-down `SmallLogo.png`

   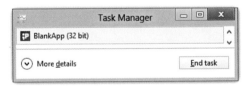

FIGURE 1.6   The three logo images in action.

Capabilities

On the Capabilities tab, you select every capability required by your app. A *capability* is a special permission for actions that users might not want certain apps to perform, whether for privacy concerns or concerns about data usage charges. In the Windows Store, prospective users are told what capabilities each app requires before they decide whether to download it. To users, they are described as *permissions*.

For the most part, user approval of all requested permissions is an implicit part of downloading an app. However, the use of privacy-related capabilities, such as location services, prompts the user the first time an app invokes a relevant API. Furthermore, some capabilities can be disabled or reenabled at any time by a user. When the Settings charm is invoked while a Windows Store app is running, it contains a "Permissions" link that displays an app's capabilities and toggle switches for any that can be turned on and off. Figure 1.7 shows what this looks like for a Blank App project after enabling most of the capabilities listed on the Capabilities tab.

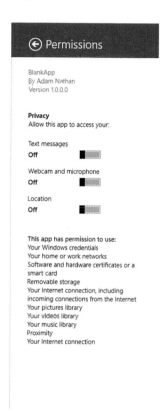

FIGURE 1.7   The "Permissions" section of the Settings charm enables turning some capabilities on or off at run-time.

The long list of available capabilities can be grouped into four different categories:

→ File capabilities

→ Device capabilities

→ Network capabilities

→ Identity capabilities

You want to restrict the set of capabilities requested by your app as much as possible, because it is a competitive advantage. For example, users might decide not to buy your fun piano app if it wants permission to use the Internet!

Most of them can be used freely, although some of them are restricted. Apps that use restricted capabilities must go through extra processes when uploaded to the Windows Store and therefore may not be permitted to use them. Fortunately, the restricted capabilities (called out in the upcoming lists) are for uncommon scenarios.

File Capabilities

As you'll read in Chapter 18, "Data," apps can read and write their own private files in an isolated spot, and those files can even participate in automatic roaming between a user's devices. Users can give apps explicit permission to read/write other "normal" files via the Windows file picker. This is all that most apps need. Beyond these two features, programmatic reading and writing of files requires special capabilities. There is one for each of the four built-in libraries (Music, Pictures, Videos, and Documents) plus another for attached storage devices:

→ **Music Library**, **Pictures Library**, and **Videos Library**—Enables enumerating and accessing all music, pictures, and videos, respectively, *without* going through the file picker.

→ **Documents Library**—Enables adding, changing, and deleting files in the Documents library on the local computer *without* going through the file picker. However, this capability is restricted to specific file type associations that must also be declared in the package manifest (on the Declarations tab). This is listed separately from the preceding three capabilities because it is a restricted capability that needs special approval from Microsoft in order to publish the app in the Windows Store. And unlike the capabilities for the Music, Pictures, and Videos libraries, this cannot be used to access Documents libraries on other computers in the same HomeGroup.

→ **Removable Storage**—Enables adding, changing, and deleting files on devices such as external hard drives or thumb drives connected to the local computer, again *without* going through the file picker. As with the preceding capability, this is restricted to file type associations that must also be declared in the package manifest.

Device Capabilities

Apps can access simple sensors such as an accelerometer without any capabilities. Accessing several types of devices does require specific capabilities, however. The list of device types will grow in the future (and can even be extended by certain third parties), but for now, there are five, listed below. For all of them except proximity, users can disable them at any time, so apps must be prepared to handle this gracefully.

→ **Location**—Reveals the computer's location, either precise coordinates from a GPS sensor (if one exists) or an estimation based on network information.

→ **Microphone**—Enables recording audio from a microphone.

→ **Webcam**—Enables recording video—or capturing still pictures—from a camera. Note that this doesn't include sound. If you want to record audio and video, you need both Webcam and Microphone capabilities.

→ **Proximity**—Enables instances of an app on multiple devices to share data just by tapping the devices together. This capability is simply about initiating the communication and is based on near field communication (NFC) technology. Once the session has been established, standard networking functionality (and capabilities) must be used.

Chapter 12, "Audio and Video," and Chapter 21, "Sensors and Other Devices," explain how to write apps that take advantage of these capabilities.

Network Capabilities

Without any network capabilities, a Windows Store app cannot do any communication over any kind of network except for the automatic roaming of application data described in Chapter 18 or the seamless opening/saving of network files enabled by the file picker. Four types of network capabilities exist:

→ **Internet (Client)**—This is the only network capability that most apps need. It provides outbound access to the Internet and public networks (going through the firewall).

→ **Internet (Client & Server)**—This is just like the preceding capability except it provides both inbound and outbound access, which is vital for peer-to-peer apps. It's a superset of "Internet (Client)" so if you request this capability in your manifest, then you don't need to request the other one.

→ **Private Networks (Client & Server)**—Provides inbound and outbound access to trusted home and work networks (going through the firewall).

→ **Enterprise Authentication**—Enables intranet access using the current Windows domain credentials. This is a restricted capability.

 Visual Studio project templates enable the "Internet (Client)" capability by default!

This is done because the Visual Studio team feared that it would be too confusing for developers if simple network-dependent calls failed in their brand new project. Therefore, be sure to remove the capability if you don't need it. Otherwise, your app's store listing will say that your app "has permission to use your Internet connection."

Identity Capabilities

This is not really a fourth category of capabilities, but rather a single outlier that doesn't fit anywhere else. The Shared User Certificates capability enables access to digital certificates that validate a user's identity. The certificate could be installed on the computer or stored on a smart card. This is mainly for enterprise environments, and it is a restricted capability.

Declarations

The Declarations tab is the one with the most options. This is where you enable your app to support one or more *contracts* or *extensions*. These are two powerful mechanisms that enable an app to communicate with the outside world in ways that you might only expect desktop apps to be able to, but still in a manner that keeps the user in control.

The defining characteristic of a contract is that it's an agreement between two or more *apps* or Windows itself. They are exposed to users through the charms bar or the file picker. An app can participate in a slick user workflow that doesn't even require it to run beforehand, thanks to the information registered via the package manifest. Extensions are a number of additional special agreements, typically between an app and a built-in Windows app such as Camera, PC Settings, or People.

Chapter 19, "Charms," and Chapter 20, "Extensions," discuss contracts and extensions in depth.

Packaging

The Packaging tab has a few items that are needed for the app's listing in the Windows Store. However, most of the values get automatically replaced when you upload the app to the store.

→ The **package name** must be unique, but you don't need to do anything with it. Visual Studio automatically fills it in with a globally-unique identifier known as a GUID. That said, for easier debugging and identification of your app's local data store, it's best to replace the GUID with a human-readable name, such as *CompanyName.AppName*.

→ The **package display name** is the name of your app in the store, but this also gets replaced when you follow the procedure to upload an app.

→ This tab requires one more image (**logo**), although this time it must be 50x50 pixels. This is displayed in the store as the logo for your app, and it should generally look the same as the image you use for your normal-sized tile. However, because no text gets overlaid, the convention is for the drawing to be perfectly centered, typically within a 40x40 square (leaving 5 pixels of margin on each side). The Blank App project provides a sample StoreLogo.png file that follows this guideline.

→ The **version**, set to 1.0.0.0 by default, is a four-part value interpreted as *Major.Minor.Build.Revision*. You can set this value however you like. The only real requirement is that each new version uploaded to the store has a higher version number than previous versions.

→ The bottom of this tab contains publisher information based on the certificate used to authenticate the package. Visual Studio configures this to work with the temporary certificate it generates, and the store upload process reconfigures it to work with your developer account.

The bottom line is that the only things you should ever need to update on this tab are the store logo and version number, and perhaps the package name for easier debugging.

The Main Page

Every app consists of one or more pages. The Blank App project is given a single page called MainPage. It defines what the user sees once your app has loaded and the splash screen has gone away. MainPage, like any page that would be used in a XAML app, is implemented across two files: MainPage.xaml contains the user interface, and MainPage.xaml.cs contains the logic, often called the *code-behind*. Listing 1.1 shows the initial contents of MainPage.xaml.

LISTING 1.1   MainPage.xaml—The Initial Markup for the Blank App's Main Page

```
<Page
  x:Class="BlankApp.MainPage"
  xmlns="http://schemas.microsoft.com/winfx/2006/xaml/presentation"
  xmlns:x="http://schemas.microsoft.com/winfx/2006/xaml"
  xmlns:local="using:BlankApp"
  xmlns:d="http://schemas.microsoft.com/expression/blend/2008"
  xmlns:mc="http://schemas.openxmlformats.org/markup-compatibility/2006"
  mc:Ignorable="d">
  <Grid Background="{StaticResource ApplicationPageBackgroundThemeBrush}">
  </Grid>
</Page>
```

At a quick glance, this file tells us:

→ This is a class called MainPage (in the BlankApp namespace) that derives from a class called Page (the root element in this file).

→ It contains an empty Grid (an element examined in Chapter 4) whose background is set to a theme-defined color. From running the app, we know this color is a very dark gray (#1D1D1D).

→ It contains a bunch of XML namespaces to make adding new elements and attributes that aren't in the default namespace more convenient. These XML namespaces are discussed in the next chapter.

Listing 1.2 shows the initial contents of MainPage.xaml.cs, the code-behind file for MainPage.xaml. Because this app does not yet do anything, it contains only a required call to InitializeComponent that constructs the page with all the visuals defined in the XAML file, and an empty OnNavigatedTo method in which initialization logic could be added. The class is marked with the partial keyword because its definition is shared with a hidden C# file that gets generated when the XAML file is compiled.

LISTING 1.2 MainPage.xaml.cs—The Initial Code-Behind for the App's Main Page

```csharp
using System;
using System.Collections.Generic;
using System.IO;
using System.Linq;
using Windows.Foundation;
using Windows.Foundation.Collections;
using Windows.UI.Xaml;
using Windows.UI.Xaml.Controls;
using Windows.UI.Xaml.Controls.Primitives;
using Windows.UI.Xaml.Data;
using Windows.UI.Xaml.Input;
using Windows.UI.Xaml.Media;
using Windows.UI.Xaml.Navigation;

// The Blank Page item template is documented at
// http://go.microsoft.com/fwlink/?LinkId=234238

namespace BlankApp
{
  /// <summary>
  /// An empty page that can be used on its own or navigated to within a Frame.
  /// </summary>
  public sealed partial class MainPage : Page
  {
    public MainPage()
    {
      this.InitializeComponent();
    }

    /// <summary>
    /// Invoked when this page is about to be displayed in a Frame.
    /// </summary>
    /// <param name="e">
    /// Event data that describes how this page was reached.
    /// The Parameter property is typically used to configure the page.
    /// </param>
    protected override void OnNavigatedTo(NavigationEventArgs e)
    {
    }
  }
}
```

Never remove the call to `InitializeComponent` **in the constructor of your code-behind class!**

`InitializeComponent` is what associates your XAML-defined content with the instance of the class at run-time.

The Application Definition

The application definition is contained in `App.xaml` and its code-behind file, `App.xaml.cs`. `App.xaml` is a special XAML file that doesn't define any visuals, but rather defines an `App` class that can handle application-level tasks. Usually the only reason to touch this XAML file is to place new application-wide resources, such as custom styles, inside its `Application.Resources` collection. Chapter 16, "Styles, Templates, and Visual States" contains many examples of this. Listing 1.3 shows the contents of `App.xaml` in the Blank App project.

LISTING 1.3   `App.xaml`—The Initial Markup for the App Class

```
<Application
  x:Class="BlankApp.App"
  xmlns="http://schemas.microsoft.com/winfx/2006/xaml/presentation"
  xmlns:x="http://schemas.microsoft.com/winfx/2006/xaml"
  xmlns:local="using:BlankApp">

  <Application.Resources>
    <ResourceDictionary>
      <ResourceDictionary.MergedDictionaries>

        <!--
            Styles that define common aspects of the platform look and feel
            Required by Visual Studio project and item templates
        -->
        <ResourceDictionary Source="Common/StandardStyles.xaml"/>
      </ResourceDictionary.MergedDictionaries>

    </ResourceDictionary>
  </Application.Resources>
</Application>
```

Note that this contains a reference to a `StandardStyles.xaml` file in a `Common` subfolder. This automatically-generated file contains styles that make it easy to achieve a look-and-feel that is consistent with other apps. Depending on what items you add to your project (or which project type you initially create), C# "helper" files are placed in the `Common` subfolder as well.

App.xaml.cs

Listing 1.4 contains the auto-generated contents of the code-behind file for App.xaml. It contains two vital pieces:

→ A constructor, which is effectively the app's main method. The plumbing that makes it the app's entry point is enabled by an "Entry point" setting in the package manifest (on the Application UI tab). When you create a project, Visual Studio automatically sets it to the namespace-qualified name of the project's App class (BlankApp.App in this example).

→ Logic inside an OnLaunched method that navigates to the app's first (and in this case only) page, and the call to Window.Current.Activate that dismisses the splash screen. If you want to add a new page and make it be the starting point of the app, or if you want to customize the initialization logic, this is where you can do it. See Chapter 7, "App Model," for more information.

LISTING 1.4   App.xaml.cs—The Initial Code-Behind for the App Class

```
using System;
using System.Collections.Generic;
using System.IO;
using System.Linq;
using Windows.ApplicationModel;
using Windows.ApplicationModel.Activation;
using Windows.Foundation;
using Windows.Foundation.Collections;
using Windows.UI.Xaml;
using Windows.UI.Xaml.Controls;
using Windows.UI.Xaml.Controls.Primitives;
using Windows.UI.Xaml.Data;
using Windows.UI.Xaml.Input;
using Windows.UI.Xaml.Media;
using Windows.UI.Xaml.Navigation;

namespace BlankApp
{
  /// <summary>
  /// Provides application-specific behavior to supplement the base class.
  /// </summary>
  sealed partial class App : Application
  {
    /// <summary>
    /// Initializes the singleton application object.  This is the first line
    /// of authored code executed; the logical equivalent of main/WinMain.
    /// </summary>
    public App()
```

LISTING 1.4   Continued

```csharp
{
  this.InitializeComponent();
  this.Suspending += OnSuspending;
}

/// <summary>
/// Invoked when the application is launched normally by the end user.
/// Other entry points are used when the application is launched to open
/// a specific file, to display search results, and so forth.
/// </summary>
/// <param name="args">Details about the launch request and process.</param>
protected override void OnLaunched(LaunchActivatedEventArgs args)
{
  Frame rootFrame = Window.Current.Content as Frame;

  // Do not repeat app initialization when the Window already has content,
  // just ensure that the window is active
  if (rootFrame == null)
  {
    // Create a Frame and navigate to the first page
    var rootFrame = new Frame();

    if (args.PreviousExecutionState == ApplicationExecutionState.Terminated)
    {
      //TODO: Load state from previously suspended application
    }

    // Place the frame in the current Window and ensure that it is active
    Window.Current.Content = rootFrame;
  }

  if (rootFrame.Content == null)
  {
    // When the navigation stack isn't restored, navigate to the first page
    if (!rootFrame.Navigate(typeof(MainPage), args.Arguments))
    {
      throw new Exception("Failed to create initial page");
    }
  }

  // Ensure the current Window is active
  Window.Current.Activate();
}
```

LISTING 1.4   Continued

```
/// <summary>
/// Invoked when application execution is being suspended.  Application state
/// is saved without knowing whether the application will be terminated or
/// resumed with the contents of memory still intact.
/// </summary>
/// <param name="sender">The source of the suspend request.</param>
/// <param name="e">Details about the suspend request.</param>
private void OnSuspending(object sender, SuspendingEventArgs e)
{
  var deferral = e.SuspendingOperation.GetDeferral();
  //TODO: Save application state and stop any background activity
  deferral.Complete();
}
}
}
```

> If you want to create a richer splash screen, perhaps with an animated progress graphic, the way to do this is by mimicking the splash screen with a custom page. Inside App.OnLaunched, you can navigate to an initial page that looks just like the real (static) splash screen but with extra UI elements and custom logic. The instance of LaunchActivatedEventArgs passed to OnLaunched even has a SplashScreen property that exposes an ImageLocation rectangle that tells you the coordinates where the real splash screen image was displayed. This makes it easy to match the splash screen's appearance no matter what the current screen's resolution is. Such a user interface is often called an "extended splash screen."

AssemblyInfo.cs

This file is not worth showing in this book. It contains a bunch of attributes where you *can* put a title, description, company name, copyright, and so on that get compiled into your assembly (the EXE or DLL). But setting these is unnecessary because all of the information used by the store is separately managed. Still, the AssemblyVersion and AssemblyFileVersion attributes, typically set to the same value, can be useful for you to keep track of distinct versions of your application:

```
[assembly: AssemblyVersion("1.0.0.0")]
[assembly: AssemblyFileVersion("1.0.0.0")]
```

By using *-syntax, such as "1.0.*", you can even let the version number auto-increment every time you rebuild your app.

Summary

You've now seen the basic structure of a Visual Studio project for a XAML-based Windows Store project. If you've previously done .NET development, much of this should look familiar. If you've previously dabbled in Windows Presentation Foundation (WPF) and/or Silverlight, the role of the XAML files and the C# files should be obvious. And if you've previously done development for Windows Phone, then all of these concepts, including things like capabilities that are a radical change for Windows PCs, shouldn't surprise you one bit. If you don't have any such experience, then you should at least be able to appreciate how easy it is to hit the ground running. Windows 8 has taken the best ideas from .NET, XAML, Windows Phone, the Web, C++, COM, and more, in order to create a compelling platform that's easy for developers to dive into. And now it's time to dive much deeper into the language of XAML.

Chapter 2

MASTERING XAML

You might be thinking, "Isn't Chapter 2 a bit early to become a *master* of XAML?" No, because this chapter focuses on the mechanics of the XAML *language*, which is a bit orthogonal to the multitude of XAML elements and APIs you'll be using when you build Windows Store apps. Learning about the XAML language is kind of like learning the features of C# before delving into .NET or the Windows Runtime. Unlike the preceding chapter, this is a fairly deep dive! However, having this background knowledge before proceeding with the rest of the book will enable you to approach the examples with confidence.

XAML is a dialect of XML that Microsoft introduced in 2006 along with the first version of Windows Presentation Foundation (WPF). XAML is a relatively simple and general-purpose declarative programming language suitable for constructing and initializing objects. XAML is just XML, but with a set of rules about its elements and attributes and their mapping to objects, their properties, and the values of those properties (among other things).

You can think of XAML as a clean, modern (albeit more verbose) reinvention of HTML and CSS. In Windows Store apps, XAML serves essentially the same purpose as HTML: It provides a declarative way to represent user interfaces. That said, XAML is actually a general-purpose language that can be used in ways that have nothing to do with UI. The preceding chapter contained a simple example of this. App.xaml does not define a user interface, but rather some characteristics of an app's entry point class. Note that almost everything that can be expressed in XAML can be naturally represented in a procedural language like C# as well.

The motivation for XAML is pretty much the same as any declarative markup language: Make it easy for programmers to work with others (perhaps graphic designers) and enable a powerful, robust tooling experience on top of it. XAML encourages a nice separation between visuals (and visual behavior such as animations) and the rest of the code, and enables powerful styling capabilities. XAML pages can be opened in Blend as well as Visual Studio (and Visual Studio has a convenient "Open in Blend…" item on its View menu), or entire XAML-based projects can be opened in Blend. This can be helpful for designing sophisticated artwork, animations, and other graphically rich touches. The idea is that a team's developers can work in Visual Studio while its designers work in Blend, and everyone can work on the same codebase. However, because XAML (and XML in general) is generally human readable, you can accomplish quite a bit with nothing more than a tool such as Notepad.

Elements and Attributes

The XAML specification defines rules that map object-oriented namespaces, types, properties, and events into XML namespaces, elements, and attributes. You can see this by examining the following simple XAML snippet that declares a `Button` control and comparing it to the equivalent C# code:

XAML:

```
<Button xmlns="http://schemas.microsoft.com/winfx/2006/xaml/presentation"
  Content="Stop"/>
```

C#:

```
Windows.UI.Xaml.Controls.Button b = new Windows.UI.Xaml.Controls.Button();
b.Content = "Stop";
```

Declaring an XML element in XAML (known as an *object element*) is equivalent to instantiating the corresponding object via a default constructor. Setting an attribute on the object element is equivalent to setting a property of the same name (called a *property attribute*) or hooking up an event handler of the same name (called an *event attribute*). For example, here's an update to the `Button` control that not only sets its `Content` property but also attaches an event handler to its `Click` event:

XAML:

```
<Button xmlns="http://schemas.microsoft.com/winfx/2006/xaml/presentation"
  Content="Stop" Click="Button_Click"/>
```

C#:

```
Windows.UI.Xaml.Controls.Button b = new Windows.UI.Xaml.Controls.Button();
b.Click += new Windows.UI.Xaml.RoutedEventHandler(Button_Click);
b.Content = "Stop";
```

This requires an appropriate method called Button_Click to be defined. The "Mixing XAML with Procedural Code" section at the end of this chapter explains how to work with XAML that requires additional code. Note that XAML, like C#, is a case-sensitive language.

Order of Property and Event Processing   •••

At runtime, event handlers are always attached *before* any properties are set for any object declared in XAML (excluding the Name property, described later in this chapter, which is set immediately after object construction). This enables appropriate events to be raised in response to properties being set without worrying about the order of attributes used in XAML.

The ordering of multiple property sets and multiple event handler attachments is usually performed in the relative order that property attributes and event attributes are specified on the object element. Fortunately, this ordering shouldn't matter in practice because design guidelines dictate that classes should allow properties to be set in any order, and the same holds true for attaching event handlers.

Namespaces

The most mysterious part about comparing the previous XAML examples with the equivalent C# examples is how the XML namespace http://schemas.microsoft.com/winfx/2006/xaml/presentation maps to the Windows Runtime namespace Windows.UI.Xaml.Controls. It turns out that the mapping to this and other namespaces is hard-coded inside the framework. (In case you're wondering, no web page exists at the schemas.microsoft.com URL—it's just an arbitrary string like any namespace.) Because many Windows Runtime namespaces are mapped to the same XML namespace, the framework designers took care not to introduce two classes with the same name, despite the fact that the classes are in separate Windows Runtime namespaces.

The root object element in a XAML file must specify at least one XML namespace that is used to qualify itself and any child elements. You can declare additional XML namespaces (on the root or on children), but each one must be given a distinct prefix to be used on any identifiers from that namespace. MainPage.xaml in the preceding chapter contains the XML namespaces listed in Table 2.1.

TABLE 2.1   The XML Namespaces in Chapter 1's `MainPage.xaml`

Namespace	Typical Prefix	Description
`http://schemas.microsoft.com/winfx/2006/xaml/presentation`	(none)	The standard UI namespace. Contains elements such `Grid`, `Button`, and `TextBlock`.
`http://schemas.microsoft.com/winfx/2006/xaml`	x	The XAML language namespace. Contains keywords such as `Class`, `Name`, and `Key`.
`using:BlankApp`	`local`	This `using:`*XXX* syntax is the way to use any custom Windows Runtime or .NET namespace in a XAML file. In this case, `BlankApp` is the .NET namespace generated for the project in Chapter 1 because the project itself was named "BlankApp."
`http://schemas.microsoft.com/expression/blend/2008`	d	A namespace for design-time information that helps tools like Blend and Visual Studio show a proper preview.
`http://schemas.openxmlformats.org/markup-compatibility/2006`	mc	A markup compatibility namespace that can be used to mark other namespaces/elements as ignorable. Normally used with the design-time namespace, whose attributes should be ignored at runtime.

The first two namespaces are almost always used in any XAML file. The second one (with the x prefix) is the *XAML language namespace*, which defines some special directives for the XAML parser. These directives often appear as attributes to XML elements, so they look like properties of the host element but actually are not. For a list of XAML keywords, see the "XAML Keywords" section later in this chapter.

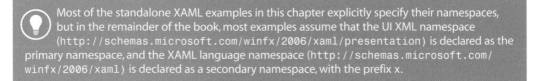

Most of the standalone XAML examples in this chapter explicitly specify their namespaces, but in the remainder of the book, most examples assume that the UI XML namespace (`http://schemas.microsoft.com/winfx/2006/xaml/presentation`) is declared as the primary namespace, and the XAML language namespace (`http://schemas.microsoft.com/winfx/2006/xaml`) is declared as a secondary namespace, with the prefix x.

Using the UI XML namespace (`http://schemas.microsoft.com/winfx/2006/xaml/presentation`) as a default namespace and the XAML language namespace (`http://schemas.microsoft.com/winfx/2006/xaml`) as a secondary namespace with the prefix x is just a convention, just like it's a convention to begin a C# file with a `using System;` directive. You could declare a `Button` in XAML as follows, and it would be equivalent to the `Button` defined previously:

```
<UiNamespace:Button
  xmlns:UiNamespace="http://schemas.microsoft.com/winfx/2006/xaml/presentation"
  Content="Stop"/>
```

Of course, for readability it makes sense for your most commonly used namespace (also known as the *primary* XML namespace) to be prefix free and to use short prefixes for any additional namespaces.

The last two namespaces in Table 2.1, which are plopped in pages generated by Visual Studio and Blend, are usually not needed.

Markup Compatibility

The markup compatibility XML namespace (`http://schemas.openxmlformats.org/markup-compatibility/2006`, typically used with an mc prefix) contains an `Ignorable` attribute that instructs XAML processors to ignore all elements/attributes in specified namespaces if they can't be resolved to their types/members. (The namespace also has a `ProcessContent` attribute that overrides `Ignorable` for specific types inside the ignored namespaces.)

Blend and Visual Studio take advantage of this feature to do things like add design-time properties to XAML content that can be ignored at runtime. `mc:Ignorable` can be given a space-delimited list of namespaces, and `mc:ProcessContent` can be given a space-delimited list of elements.

If you're frustrated by how long it takes to open XAML files in Visual Studio and you don't care about previewing the visuals, you might consider changing your default editor for XAML files by right-clicking on a XAML file in Solution Explorer then selecting **Open With…**, **XML (Text) Editor**, clicking **Set as Default**, then clicking **OK**. This has several major drawbacks, however, such as losing IntelliSense support.

Property Elements

Rich composition of controls is one of the highlights of XAML. This can be easily demonstrated with a `Button`, because you can put arbitrary content inside it; you're not limited to just text! To demonstrate this, the following code embeds a simple square to make a Stop button like what might be found in a media player:

```
Windows.UI.Xaml.Controls.Button b = new Windows.UI.Xaml.Controls.Button();
b.Width = 96;
```

```
b.Height = 38;
Windows.UI.Xaml.Shapes.Rectangle r = new Windows.UI.Xaml.Shapes.Rectangle();
r.Width = 10;
r.Height = 10;
r.Fill = new Windows.UI.Xaml.Media.SolidColorBrush(Windows.UI.Colors.White);
b.Content = r; // Make the square the content of the Button
```

Button's Content property is of type System.Object, so it can easily be set to the 10x10 Rectangle object. The result (when used with additional code that adds it to a page) is pictured in Figure 2.1.

FIGURE 2.1   Placing complex content inside a Button

That's pretty neat, but how can you do the same thing in XAML with property attribute syntax? What kind of string could you possibly set Content to that is equivalent to the preceding Rectangle declared in C#? There is no such string, but XAML fortunately provides an alternative (and more verbose) syntax for setting complex property values: *property elements*. It looks like the following:

```
<Button xmlns="http://schemas.microsoft.com/winfx/2006/xaml/presentation"
  Width="96" Height="38">
  <Button.Content>
    <Rectangle Width="10" Height="10" Fill="White"/>
  </Button.Content>
</Button>
```

The Content property is now set with an XML element instead of an XML attribute, making it equivalent to the previous C# code. The period in Button.Content is what distinguishes property elements from object elements. Property elements always take the form *TypeName.PropertyName*, they are always contained inside a *TypeName* object element, and they can never have attributes of their own (with one exception—the x:Uid attribute used for localization).

Property element syntax can be used for simple property values as well. The following Button that sets two properties with attributes (Content and Background):

```
<Button xmlns="http://schemas.microsoft.com/winfx/2006/xaml/presentation"
  Content="Stop" Background="Red"/>
```

is equivalent to this Button, which sets the same two properties with elements:

```
<Button xmlns="http://schemas.microsoft.com/winfx/2006/xaml/presentation">
  <Button.Content>
    Stop
  </Button.Content>
  <Button.Background>
    Red
```

```
  </Button.Background>
</Button>
```

Of course, using attributes when you can is a nice shortcut when hand-typing XAML.

Type Converters

Let's look at the C# code equivalent to the preceding `Button` declaration that sets both `Content` and `Background` properties:

```
Windows.UI.Xaml.Controls.Button b = new Windows.UI.Xaml.Controls.Button();
b.Content = "Stop";
b.Background = new Windows.UI.Xaml.Media.SolidColorBrush(Windows.UI.Color.Red);
```

Wait a minute. How can `"Red"` in the previous XAML file be equivalent to the `SolidColorBrush` instance used in the C# code? Indeed, this example exposes a subtlety with using strings to set properties in XAML that are a different data type than `System.String` or `System.Object`. In such cases, the XAML parser must look for a *type converter* that knows how to convert the string representation to the desired data type.

You cannot currently create your own type converters, but type converters already exist for many common data types. Unlike the XAML language, these type converters support case-insensitive strings. Without a type converter for `Brush` (the base class of `SolidColorBrush`), you would have to use property element syntax to set the `Background` in XAML as follows:

```
<Button xmlns="http://schemas.microsoft.com/winfx/2006/xaml/presentation"
  Content="Stop">
  <Button.Background>
    <SolidColorBrush Color="Red"/>
  </Button.Background>
</Button>
```

And even that is only possible because of a type converter for `Color` that can make sense of the `"Red"` string. If there wasn't a `Color` type converter, you would basically be stuck. Type converters don't just enhance the readability of XAML; they also enable values to be expressed that couldn't otherwise be expressed.

Unlike in the previous C# code, in this case, misspelling `Red` would not cause a compilation error but would cause an exception at runtime. (Although Visual Studio does provide compile-time warnings for mistakes in XAML such as this.)

Markup Extensions

Markup extensions, like type converters, extend the expressiveness of XAML. Both can evaluate a string attribute value at runtime and produce an appropriate object based on the string. As with type converters, you cannot currently create your own, but several markup extensions are built in.

Unlike type converters, markup extensions are invoked from XAML with explicit and consistent syntax. Whenever an attribute value is enclosed in curly braces ({}), the XAML parser treats it as a markup extension value rather than a literal string or something that needs to be type-converted. The following Button uses two different markup extensions as the values for two different properties:

```
<Button xmlns="http://schemas.microsoft.com/winfx/2006/xaml/presentation"
        xmlns:x="http://schemas.microsoft.com/winfx/2006/xaml"
        Height="50"
        Background="{x:Null}"   ─ Markup extension
        Content="{Binding Height, RelativeSource={RelativeSource Self}}"/>
                          │                      │
                   Positional para-          Named
                       meter               parameter
```

The first identifier in each set of curly braces is the name of the markup extension. The Null extension lives in the XAML language namespace, so the x prefix must be used. Binding (which also happens to be a class in the Windows.UI.Xaml.Data namespace), can be found in the default XML namespace. Note that the full name for Null is NullExtension, and this long form can be used as well in XAML. XAML permits dropping the Extension suffix on any markup extensions named with the suffix.

If a markup extension supports them, comma-delimited parameters can be specified. Positional parameters (such as Height in the example) are treated as string arguments for the extension class's appropriate constructor. Named parameters (RelativeSource in the example) enable you to set properties with matching names on the constructed extension object. The values for these properties can be markup extension values themselves (using nested curly braces, as done with the value for RelativeSource) or literal values that can undergo the normal type conversion process. If you're familiar with .NET custom attributes (the .NET Framework's popular extensibility mechanism), you've probably noticed that the design and usage of markup extensions closely mirrors the design and usage of custom attributes. That is intentional.

In the preceding Button declaration, x:Null enables the Background brush to be set to null. This is just done for demonstration purposes, because a null Background is not very useful. Binding, covered in depth in Chapter 17, "Data Binding," enables Content to be set to the same value as the Height property.

Escaping the Curly Braces

If you ever want a property attribute value to be set to a literal string beginning with an open curly brace ({), you must escape it so it doesn't get treated as a markup extension. This can be done by preceding it with an empty pair of curly braces, as in the following example:

```
<Button xmlns="http://schemas.microsoft.com/winfx/2006/xaml/presentation"
        Content="{}{This is not a markup extension!}"/>
```

Alternatively, you could use property element syntax without any escaping because the curly braces do not have special meaning in this context. The preceding Button could be rewritten as follows:

```
<Button xmlns="http://schemas.microsoft.com/winfx/2006/xaml/presentation">
<Button.Content>
{This is not a markup extension!}
</Button.Content>
</Button>
```

Markup extensions can also be used with property element syntax. The following Button is identical to the preceding one:

```
<Button xmlns="http://schemas.microsoft.com/winfx/2006/xaml/presentation"
        xmlns:x="http://schemas.microsoft.com/winfx/2006/xaml">
  <Button.Height>
    50
  </Button.Height>
  <Button.Background>
    <x:Null/>
  </Button.Background>
  <Button.Content>
    <Binding Path="Height">
      <Binding.RelativeSource>
        <RelativeSource Mode="Self"/>
      </Binding.RelativeSource>
    </Binding>
  </Button.Content>
</Button>
```

This transformation works because these markup extensions all have properties corresponding to their parameterized constructor arguments (the positional parameters used with property attribute syntax). For example, Binding has a Path property that has the same meaning as the argument that was previously passed to its parameterized constructor, and RelativeSource has a Mode property that corresponds to its constructor argument.

> **Markup Extensions and Procedural Code**   • • •
>
> The actual work done by a markup extension is specific to each extension. For example, the following C# code is equivalent to the XAML-based Button that uses Null and Binding:
>
> ```
> Windows.UI.Xaml.Controls.Button b = new Windows.UI.Xaml.Controls.Button();
> b.Height = 50;
> // Set Background:
> b.Background = null;
> // Set Content:
> Windows.UI.Xaml.Data.Binding binding = new Windows.UI.Xaml.Data.Binding();
> binding.Path = new Windows.UI.Xaml.PropertyPath("Height");
> binding.RelativeSource = Windows.UI.Xaml.Data.RelativeSource.Self;
> b.SetBinding(Windows.UI.Xaml.Controls.Button.ContentProperty, bi nding);
> ```

Children of Object Elements

A XAML file, like all XML files, must have a single root object element. Therefore, it should come as no surprise that object elements can support child object elements (not just property elements, which aren't children, as far as XAML is concerned). An object element can have three types of children: a value for a content property, collection items, or a value that can be type-converted to the object element.

The Content Property

Many classes designed to be used in XAML designate a property (via a custom attribute) that should be set to whatever content is inside the XML element. This property is called the *content property*, and it is just a convenient shortcut to make the XAML representation more compact.

Button's Content property is (appropriately) given this special designation, so the following Button:

```
<Button xmlns="http://schemas.microsoft.com/winfx/2006/xaml/presentation"
  Content="Stop"/>
```

could be rewritten as follows:

```
<Button xmlns="http://schemas.microsoft.com/winfx/2006/xaml/presentation">
  Stop
</Button>
```

Or, more usefully, this Button with more complex content:

```
<Button xmlns="http://schemas.microsoft.com/winfx/2006/xaml/presentation">
<Button.Content>
  <Rectangle Height="10" Width="10" Fill="White"/>
```

```
</Button.Content>
</Button>
```

could be rewritten as follows:

```
<Button xmlns="http://schemas.microsoft.com/winfx/2006/xaml/presentation">
  <Rectangle Height="10" Width="10" Fill="White"/>
</Button>
```

There is no requirement that the content property must be called `Content`; classes such as `ComboBox` and `ListBox` (also in the `Windows.UI.Xaml.Controls` namespace) use their `Items` property as the content property.

Collection Items

XAML enables you to add items to the two main types of collections that support indexing: lists and dictionaries.

Lists

A *list* is any collection that implements the `IList` interface or its generic counterpart. For example, the following XAML adds two items to a `ListBox` control whose `Items` property is an `ItemCollection` that implements `IList<object>`:

```
<ListBox xmlns="http://schemas.microsoft.com/winfx/2006/xaml/presentation">
<ListBox.Items>
  <ListBoxItem Content="Item 1"/>
  <ListBoxItem Content="Item 2"/>
</ListBox.Items>
</ListBox>
```

This is equivalent to the following C# code:

```
Windows.UI.Xaml.Controls.ListBox listbox =
  new Windows.UI.Xaml.Controls.ListBox();
Windows.UI.Xaml.Controls.ListBoxItem item1 =
  new Windows.UI.Xaml.Controls.ListBoxItem();
Windows.UI.Xaml.Controls.ListBoxItem item2 =
  new Windows.UI.Xaml.Controls.ListBoxItem();
item1.Content = "Item 1";
item2.Content = "Item 2";
listbox.Items.Add(item1);
listbox.Items.Add(item2);
```

Furthermore, because `Items` is the content property for `ListBox`, you can shorten the XAML even further, as follows:

```
<ListBox xmlns="http://schemas.microsoft.com/winfx/2006/xaml/presentation">
  <ListBoxItem Content="Item 1"/>
```

```
  <ListBoxItem Content="Item 2"/>
</ListBox>
```

In all these cases, the code works because ListBox's Items property is automatically initialized to any empty collection object. If a collection property is initially null instead (and is read/write, unlike ListBox's read-only Items property), you would need to wrap the items in an explicit element that instantiates the collection. The built-in controls do not act this way, so an imaginary OtherListBox element demonstrates what this could look like:

```
<OtherListBox>
<OtherListBox.Items>
  <ItemCollection>
    <ListBoxItem Content="Item 1"/>
    <ListBoxItem Content="Item 2"/>
  </ItemCollection>
</OtherListBox.Items>
</OtherListBox>
```

Dictionaries

A *dictionary* is any collection that implements the IDictionary interface or its generic counterpart. Windows.UI.Xaml.ResourceDictionary is a commonly used collection type that you'll see more of in later chapters. It implements IDictionary<object, object>, so it supports adding, removing, and enumerating key/value pairs in procedural code, as you would do with a typical hash table. In XAML, you can add key/value pairs to any dictionary. For example, the following XAML adds two Colors to a ResourceDictionary:

```
<ResourceDictionary
   xmlns="http://schemas.microsoft.com/winfx/2006/xaml/presentation"
   xmlns:x="http://schemas.microsoft.com/winfx/2006/xaml">
   <Color x:Key="1">White</Color>
   <Color x:Key="2">Black</Color>
</ResourceDictionary>
```

This leverages the XAML Key keyword (defined in the secondary XML namespace), which is processed specially and enables us to attach a key to each Color value. (The Color type does not define a Key property.) Therefore, the XAML is equivalent to the following C# code:

```
Windows.UI.Xaml.ResourceDictionary d = new Windows.UI.Xaml.ResourceDictionary();
Windows.UI.Color color1 = Windows.UI.Colors.White;
Windows.UI.Color color2 = Windows.UI.Colors.Black;
d.Add("1", color1);
d.Add("2", color2);
```

Note that the value specified in XAML with x:Key is treated as a string unless a markup extension is used; no type conversion is attempted otherwise.

More Type Conversion

Plain text can often be used as the child of an object element, as in the following XAML declaration of `SolidColorBrush`:

```
<SolidColorBrush>White</SolidColorBrush>
```

This is equivalent to the following:

```
<SolidColorBrush Color="White"/>
```

even though `Color` has not been designated as a content property. In this case, the first XAML snippet works because a type converter exists that can convert strings such as `"White"` (or `"white"` or `"#FFFFFF"`) into a `SolidColorBrush` object.

Although type converters play a huge role in making XAML readable, the downside is that they can make XAML appear a bit "magical," and it can be difficult to understand how it maps to instances of objects. Using what you know so far, it would be reasonable to assume that you can't declare an instance of a class in XAML if it has no default constructor. However, even though the `Windows.UI.Xaml.Media.Brush` base class for `SolidColorBrush`, `LinearGradientBrush`, and other brushes has no constructors at all, you can express the preceding XAML snippets as follows:

```
<Brush>White</Brush>
```

The type converter for `Brushes` understands that this is still `SolidColorBrush`. This might seem like an unusual feature, but it's important for supporting the ability to express primitive types in XAML, as demonstrated in "The Extensible Part of XAML."

• • •

The Extensible Part of XAML

Because XAML was designed to work with the .NET type system, you can use it with just about any object, including ones you define yourself. It doesn't matter whether these objects have anything to do with a user interface. However, the objects need to be designed in a "declarative-friendly" way. For example, if a class doesn't have a default constructor and doesn't expose useful instance properties, it's not going to be directly usable from XAML. A lot of care went into the design of the APIs in the `Windows.UI.Xaml` namespace—above and beyond the usual design guidelines—to fit XAML's declarative model.

To use an arbitrary .NET class (with a default constructor) in XAML, simply include the proper namespace with using syntax. The following XAML does this with an instance of `System.Net.Http.HttpClient` and `System.Int64`:

```
<ListBox xmlns="http://schemas.microsoft.com/winfx/2006/xaml/presentation">
  <ListBox.Items>
    <sysnet:HttpClient xmlns:sysnet="using:System.Net.Http"/>
    <sys:Int64 xmlns:sys="using:System">100</sys:Int64>
  </ListBox.Items>
</ListBox>
```

The XAML language namespace defines keywords for a few common primitives so you don't need to separately include the System namespace: x:Boolean, x:Int32, x:Double, and x:String.

XAML Processing Rules for Object Element Children

You've now seen the three types of children for object elements. To avoid ambiguity, any valid XAML parser follows these rules when encountering and interpreting child elements:

1. If the type implements IList, call IList.Add for each child.
2. Otherwise, if the type implements IDictionary, call IDictionary.Add for each child, using the x:Key attribute value for the key and the element for the value.
3. Otherwise, if the parent supports a content property (indicated by Windows.UI.Xaml.Markup.ContentPropertyAttribute) and the type of the child is compatible with that property, treat the child as its value.
4. Otherwise, if the child is plain text and a type converter exists to transform the child into the parent type (*and* no properties are set on the parent element), treat the child as the input to the type converter and use the output as the parent object instance.
5. Otherwise, treat it as unknown content and raise an error.

Rules 1 and 2 enable the behavior described in the earlier "Collection Items" section, rule 3 enables the behavior described in the section "The Content Property," and rule 4 explains the often-confusing behavior described in the "More Type Conversion" section.

Mixing XAML with Procedural Code

XAML-based Windows Store apps are a mix of XAML and procedural code. This section covers the two ways that XAML and code can be mixed together: dynamically loading and parsing XAML yourself, or leveraging the built-in support in Visual Studio projects.

Loading and Parsing XAML at Runtime

The Windows.UI.Xaml.Markup namespace contains a simple XamlReader class with a simple static Load method. Load can parse a string containing XAML, create the appropriate Windows Runtime objects, and return an instance of the root element. So, with a string containing XAML content somewhat like MainPage.xaml from the preceding chapter, the following code could be used to load and retrieve the root Page object:

```
string xamlString = …;
// Get the root element, which we know is a Page
Page p = (Page)XamlReader.Load(xamlString);
```

After Load returns, the entire hierarchy of objects in the XAML file is instantiated in memory, so the XAML itself is no longer needed. Now that an instance of the root element exists, you can retrieve child elements by making use of the appropriate content properties or collection properties. The following code assumes that the Page has a StackPanel object as its content, whose fifth child is a Stop button:

```
string xamlString = …;
// Get the root element, which we know is a Page
Page p = (Page)XamlReader.Load(xamlString);
// Grab the Stop button by walking the children (with hard-coded knowledge!)
StackPanel panel = (StackPanel)p.Content;
Button stopButton = (Button)panel.Children[4];
```

With a reference to the Button control, you can do whatever you want: Set additional properties (perhaps using logic that is hard or impossible to express in XAML), attach event handlers, or perform additional actions that you can't do from XAML, such as calling its methods.

Of course, the code that uses a hard-coded index and other assumptions about the user interface structure isn't satisfying, because simple changes to the XAML can break it. Instead, you could write code to process the elements more generically and look for a Button element whose content is a "Stop" string, but that would be a lot of work for such a simple task. In addition, if you want the Button to contain graphical content, how can you easily identify it in the presence of multiple Buttons?

Fortunately, XAML supports naming of elements so they can be found and used reliably from procedural code.

Naming XAML Elements

The XAML language namespace has a Name keyword that enables you to give any element a name. For the simple Stop button that we're imagining is embedded somewhere inside a Page, the Name keyword can be used as follows:

```
<Button x:Name="stopButton">Stop</Button>
```

With this in place, you can update the preceding C# code to use Page's FindName method that searches its children (recursively) and returns the desired instance:

```
string xamlString = …;
// Get the root element, which we know is a Page
Page p = (Page)XamlReader.Load(xamlString);
// Grab the Stop button, knowing only its name
Button stopButton = (Button)p.FindName("stopButton");
```

FindName is not unique to Page; it is defined on FrameworkElement, a base class for many important classes in the XAML UI Framework.

Naming Elements Without x:Name

The x:Name syntax can be used to name elements, but FrameworkElement also has a Name property that accomplishes the same thing. You can use either mechanism on such elements, but you can't use both simultaneously. Having two ways to set a name is a bit confusing, but it's handy for these classes to have a Name property for use by procedural code. Sometimes you want to name an element that doesn't derive from FrameworkElement (and doesn't have a Name property), so x:Name is necessary for such cases.

Visual Studio's Support for XAML and Code-Behind

Loading and parsing XAML at runtime can be interesting for some limited dynamic scenarios. Windows Store projects, however, leverage work done by MSBuild and Visual Studio to make the combination of XAML and procedural code more seamless. When you compile a project with XAML files, the XAML is included as a resource in the app being built and the plumbing that connects XAML with procedural code is generated automatically.

The automatic connection between a XAML file and a code-behind file is enabled by the Class keyword from the XAML language namespace, as seen in the preceding chapter. For example, MainPage.xaml had the following:

```
<Page x:Class="BlankApp.MainPage" …>
  …
</Page>
```

This causes the XAML content to be treated as a partial class definition for a class called MainPage (in the BlankApp namespace) derived from Page. The other pieces of the partial class definition reside in auto-generated files as well as the MainPage.xaml.cs code-behind file. Visual Studio's Solution Explorer ties these two files together by making the code-behind file a subnode of the XAML file, but that is an optional cosmetic effect enabled by the following XML inside of the .csproj project file:

```
<Compile Include="MainPage.xaml.cs">
  <DependentUpon>MainPage.xaml</DependentUpon>
</Compile>
```

You can freely add members to the class in the code-behind file. And if you reference any event handlers in XAML (via event attributes such as Click on Button), this is where they should be defined.

Whenever you add a page to a Visual Studio project (via Add New Item…), Visual Studio automatically creates a XAML file with x:Class on its root, creates the code-behind source file with the partial class definition, and links the two together so they are built properly.

The additional auto-generated files alluded to earlier contain some "glue code" that you normally never see and you should never directly edit. For a XAML file named `MainPage.xaml`, they are:

→ `MainPage.g.cs`, which contains code that attaches event handlers to events for each event attribute assigned in the XAML file.

→ `MainPage.g.i.cs`, which contains a field definition (private by default) for each named element in the XAML file, using the element name as the field name. It also contains an `InitializeComponent` method that the root class's constructor must call in the code-behind file. This file is meant to be helpful to IntelliSense, which is why it has an "i" in its name.

The "g" in both filenames stands for *generated*. Both generated source files contain a partial class definition for the same class partially defined by the XAML file and code-behind file.

If you peek at the implementation of `InitializeComponent` inside the auto-generated file, you'll see that the hookup between C# and XAML isn't so magical after all. It looks a lot like the code shown previously for manually loading XAML content and grabbing named elements from the tree of instantiated objects. Here's what the method looks like for the preceding chapter's `MainPage` if a `Button` named `stopButton` were added to it:

```
public void InitializeComponent()
{
  if (_contentLoaded)
    return;

  _contentLoaded = true;
  Application.LoadComponent(this, new System.Uri("ms-appx:///MainPage.xaml"),
    Windows.UI.Xaml.Controls.Primitives.ComponentResourceLocation.Application);

  stopButton = (Windows.UI.Xaml.Controls.Button)this.FindName("stopButton");
}
```

The `LoadComponent` method is much like `XamlReader`'s `Load` method, except it works with a reference to an app's resource file.

> 💡 To reference a resource file included with your app, simply use a URI with the format `"ms-appx:///relative path to file"`. XAML files are already treated specially, but adding a new resource file to your app is as simple as adding a new file to your project with a **Build Action** of **Content**. Chapter 11, "Images," shows how to use resources such as image files with the `Image` element.

XAML Keywords

The XAML language namespace (`http://schemas.microsoft.com/winfx/2006/xaml`) defines a handful of keywords that must be treated specially by any XAML parser. They mostly control aspects of how elements get exposed to procedural code, but several are useful independent of procedural code. You've already seen some of them (such as `Key`, `Name`, and `Class`), but Table 2.2 lists all the ones relevant for Windows Store apps. They are listed

> **Special Attributes Defined by the W3C**   •••
>
> In addition to keywords in the XAML language namespace, XAML also supports two special attributes defined for XML by the World Wide Web Consortium (W3C): `xml:space` for controlling whitespace parsing and `xml:lang` for declaring the document's language and culture. The `xml` prefix is implicitly mapped to the standard XML namespace; see `http://www.w3.org/XML/1998/namespace`.

with the conventional x prefix because that is how they usually appear in XAML and in documentation.

TABLE 2.2   Keywords in the XAML Language Namespace, Assuming the Conventional x Namespace Prefix

Keyword	Valid As	Meaning
`x:Boolean`	An element.	Represents a `System.Boolean`.
`x:Class`	Attribute on root element.	Defines a namespace-qualified class for the root element that derives from the element type.
`x:Double`	An element.	Represents a `System.Double`.
`x:FieldModifier`	Attribute on any nonroot element but must be used with `x:Name` (or equivalent).	Defines the visibility of the field to be generated for the element (which is private by default). The value must be specified in terms of the procedural language (for example, `public`, `private`, and `internal` for C#).
`x:Int32`	An element.	Represents a `System.Int32`.
`x:Key`	Attribute on an element whose parent is a dictionary.	Specifies the key for the item when added to the parent dictionary.
`x:Name`	Attribute on any nonroot element but must be used with `x:Class` on root.	Chooses a name for the field to be generated for the element, so it can be referenced from procedural code.
`x:Null`	An element or an attribute value as a markup extension. Can also appear as `x:NullExtension`.	Represents a `null` value.
`x:StaticResource`	An element or an attribute value as a markup extension. Can also appear as `x:StaticResourceExtension`.	References a XAML resource
`x:String`	An element.	Represents a `System.String`.

Keyword	Valid As	Meaning
x:Subclass	Attribute on root element and must be used with x:Class.	Specifies a subclass of the x:Class class that holds the content defined in XAML. This is needed only for languages without support for partial classes, so there's no reason to use this in a C# XAML project.
x:TemplateBinding	An element or an attribute value as a markup extension.	Binds to an element's properties from within a template, as described in Chapter 16. Can also appear as x:TemplateBindingExtension.
x:Uid	Attribute on any element	Marks an element with an identifier used for localization.

Summary

You have now seen how XAML fits in with the rest of an app's code and, most importantly, you now have the information needed to translate most XAML examples into a language such as C# and vice versa. However, because type converters and markup extensions are "black boxes," a straightforward translation is not always going to be obvious.

As you proceed further, you might find that some APIs can be a little clunky from procedural code because their design is often optimized for XAML use. For example, the XAML UI Framework exposes many small building blocks to help enable rich composition, so some scenarios can involve manually creating a lot of objects. Besides the fact the XAML excels at expressing deep hierarchies of objects concisely, Microsoft spent more time implementing features to effectively hide intermediate objects in XAML (such as type converters) rather than features to hide them from procedural code (such as constructors that create inner objects on your behalf).

Most people understand the benefit of XAML's declarative model, but some lament XML as the choice of format. The primary complaint is that it's verbose; too verbose to type. This is true: Almost nobody enjoys typing lots of XML, but that's where tools come in. Tools such as IntelliSense and visual designers can spare you from typing a single angle bracket! The transparent and well-specified nature of XML enables you to easily integrate new tools into the development process (creating a XAML exporter for your favorite tool, for example) and also enables easy hand-tweaking or troubleshooting.

In some areas (such as complicated paths and shapes), typing XAML by hand isn't even practical. In fact, the trend from when XAML was first introduced in beta form has been to remove some of the handy human-typeable shortcuts in favor of a more robust and extensible format that can be supported well by tools. But I still believe that being familiar with XAML and seeing the APIs through both procedural and declarative perspectives is the best way to learn the technology. It's like understanding how HTML works without relying on a visual tool.

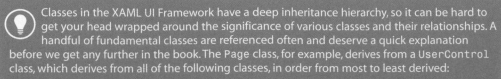

Classes in the XAML UI Framework have a deep inheritance hierarchy, so it can be hard to get your head wrapped around the significance of various classes and their relationships. A handful of fundamental classes are referenced often and deserve a quick explanation before we get any further in the book. The Page class, for example, derives from a `UserControl` class, which derives from all of the following classes, in order from most to least derived:

→ `Control`—The base class for familiar controls such as Button and ListBox. Control adds many properties to its base class, such as Foreground, Background, and FontSize, as well as the capability to be given a completely new visual template. Part III, "Understanding Controls," examines the built-in controls in depth.

→ `FrameworkElement`—The base class that adds support for styles, data binding, XAML resources, and a few common mechanisms such as tooltips and context menus.

→ `UIElement`—The base class for all visual objects with support for routed events, layout, and focus. These features are discussed in Chapter 4, "Layout," and Chapter 5, "Interactivity."

→ `DependencyObject`—The base class for any object that can support dependency properties, also discussed in Chapter 5.

→ `Object`—The base class for all .NET classes.

Throughout the book, the simple term *element* is used to refer to an object that derives from `UIElement` or `FrameworkElement`. The distinction between `UIElement` and `FrameworkElement` is not important because the framework doesn't include any other public subclasses of `UIElement`.

Chapter 3

SIZING, POSITIONING, AND TRANSFORMING ELEMENTS

When building an app, one of the first things you must do is arrange a bunch of elements on its surface. This sizing and positioning of elements is called *layout*. XAML apps are provided a feature-rich layout system that covers everything from placing elements at exact coordinates to building experiences that scale and rearrange across a wide range of screen resolutions and aspect ratios. This is essential for handling the diversity of Windows 8 devices, as well as the different view states your app can take on a single Windows 8 screen. These view states are discussed in the next chapter.

In XAML apps, layout boils down to interactions between parent elements and their child elements. Parents and their children work together to determine their final sizes and positions. Although parents ultimately tell their children where to render and how much space they get, they are more like collaborators than dictators; parents also *ask* their children how much space they would like before making their final decision.

Parent elements that support the arrangement of multiple children are known as *panels*, and they derive from a class called Panel. All the elements involved in the layout process (both parents and children) derive from UIElement.

Because layout is such an important topic, this book dedicates two chapters to it. This chapter focuses on the children, examining the common ways that you can control layout on a child-by-child basis. Several properties control these aspects, most of which are summarized in Figure 3.1 for an arbitrary element inside an arbitrary panel. Size-related properties are shown in blue, and position-related properties are shown in red. In addition, elements can have transforms applied to them (shown in green) that can affect both size and position.

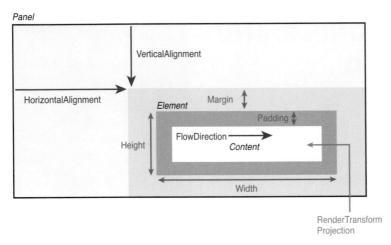

FIGURE 3.1   The main child layout properties examined in this chapter

The next chapter continues the layout story by examining the variety of built-in parent panels, each of which arranges its children in unique ways.

Controlling Size

Every time layout occurs (such as when an app is snapped or the screen is rotated), child elements tell their parent panel their desired size. Elements tend to *size to their content*, meaning that they try to be large enough to fit their content and no larger. This size can be influenced on individual instances of children via several straightforward properties.

Height **and** Width

All `FrameworkElements` have simple `Height` and `Width` properties (of type `double`), and they also have `MinHeight`, `MaxHeight`, `MinWidth`, and `MaxWidth` properties that can be used to specify a range of acceptable values. Any or all of these can be easily set on elements in C# or in XAML.

An element naturally stays as small as possible, so if you use `MinHeight` or `MinWidth`, it is rendered at that height/width unless its content forces it to grow. In addition, that growth can be limited by using MaxHeight and MaxWidth (as long as these values are larger than their Min counterparts). When using an explicit Height and Width at the same time as their Min and Max counterparts, Height and Width take precedence as long as they are in the range from Min to Max. The default value of MinHeight and MinWidth is 0, and the default value of MaxHeight and MaxWidth is Double.PositiveInfinity (which can be set in XAML as simply "Infinity").

To complicate matters, FrameworkElement also contains a few more size-related properties:

→ DesiredSize (inherited from UIElement)

→ RenderSize (inherited from UIElement)

→ ActualHeight and ActualWidth

> ## ! Avoid setting explicit sizes!
>
> Giving controls explicit sizes makes it difficult to adapt to different screen sizes and orientations, and could cause text to be cut off if you ever translate it into other languages. Therefore, you should avoid setting explicit sizes unless absolutely necessary. Fortunately, setting explicit sizes is rarely necessary, thanks to the panels described in the next chapter.

> ### • • •
> ## The Special "Auto" Length
>
> FrameworkElement's Height and Width have a default value of Double.NaN (where NaN stands for *not a number*), meaning that the element will be only as large as its content needs it to be. This setting can also be explicitly specified in XAML using "NaN" (which is case sensitive) or the preferred "Auto" (which is not case sensitive). To check if one of these properties is autosized, you can use the static Double.IsNaN method.

Unlike the other six properties that are *input* to the layout process, however, these are read-only properties representing *output* from the layout process. An element's DesiredSize is calculated during layout, based on other property values (such as the aforementioned Width, Height, MinXXX, and MaxXXX properties) and the amount of space its parent currently gives it. It is used internally by panels.

RenderSize represents the final size of an element after layout is complete, and ActualHeight and ActualWidth are exactly the same as RenderSize.Height and RenderSize.Width, respectively. That's right: Whether an element specified an explicit size, specified a range of acceptable sizes, or didn't specify anything at all, the behavior of the parent can alter an element's final size on the screen. These three properties are, therefore, useful for advanced scenarios in which you need to programmatically act on an element's size. The values of all the other size-related properties, on the other hand, aren't very interesting to base logic on. For example, when not set explicitly, the value of Height and Width are Double.NaN, regardless of the element's true size.

Be careful when writing code that uses ActualHeight **and** ActualWidth **(or** RenderSize**)!**

Every time the layout process occurs, it updates the values of each element's RenderSize (and, therefore, ActualHeight and ActualWidth as well). However, you can't rely on the values of these properties at all times. It's safe to rely on their values within an event handler for the LayoutUpdated event defined on FrameworkElement. At the same time, you must not alter layout from within a LayoutUpdated hander. If you do, an exception will be thrown pointing out that you introduced a cycle.

UIElement defines an UpdateLayout method to force any pending layout updates to finish synchronously, but you should avoid using this method. Besides the fact that frequent calls to UpdateLayout can harm performance because of the excess layout processing, there's no guarantee that the elements you're using properly handle the potential reentrancy in their layout-related methods.

Margin **and** Padding

Margin and Padding are two similar properties that are also related to an element's size. All FrameworkElements have a Margin property, and all Controls (plus many other elements) have a Padding property. Their only difference is that Margin controls how much extra space gets placed around the *outside* edges of the element, whereas Padding controls how much extra space gets placed around the *inside* edges of the element.

Both Margin and Padding are of type Thickness, an interesting class that can represent one, two, or four double values. Here is how the values are interpreted when set in XAML:

→ When set to a list of **four values**, the numbers represent the left, top, right, and bottom edges, respectively.

→ When set to a list of **two values**, the first number is used for the left and right edges and the second number is used for the top and bottom edges. So "12,24" is a shortcut way of specifying "12,24,12,24".

→ When set to a **single value**, it is used for all four sides. So "12" is a shortcut way of specifying "12,12", which is a shortcut for "12,12,12,12".

→ Negative values may be used for margins (and often are), but are not allowed for padding.

→ The commas are optional. You can use spaces instead of, or in addition to, commas. "12,24" is the same as "12 24" and "12, 24".

When creating a Thickness in C#, you can use its constructor that accepts either a single value or all four values:

```
this.TextBox.Margin = new Thickness(12);          // Margin="12" in XAML
this.TextBox.Margin = new Thickness(12,24,12,24); // Margin="12,24" in XAML
```

Note that the handy two-number syntax is a shortcut only available through XAML. Thickness does not have a two-parameter constructor.

? What unit of measurement is used by XAML?

The various length properties use units of pixels, although they do not always map directly to physical pixels on the screen. Windows automatically scales your app content to either 100%, 140%, or 180% of its natural size based on the size and resolution (and therefore dots-per-inch, or DPI) of the screen. This is why Visual Studio provides different screen size options for the same resolutions in both the simulator and the designer. The latter can be controlled via the Device tool window shown in Figure 3.2.

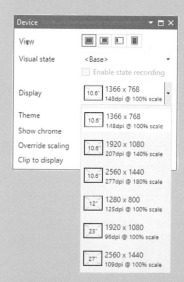

FIGURE 3.2   Size matters when it comes to the device's screen, due to the automatic scaling called out in the "Display" dropdown.

The effect of this scaling can be easily seen with the following XAML placed in a Page:

```
<StackPanel HorizontalAlignment="Left">
  <Rectangle Fill="Red" Height="100" Width="1000"/>
  <TextBlock Name="textBlock" FontSize="40"/>
</StackPanel>
```

The code-behind sets the TextBlock's Text to the Page's current dimensions as reported by the XAML UI Framework:

```
this.textBlock.Text = "Page size: " + this.ActualWidth + "x" +
this.ActualHeight
```

Figure 3.3 shows the result on two different simulator settings. In both cases, the red Rectangle is 1,000 units long as far as your code is concerned. However, it gets scaled larger on the smaller screen (and the Page's reported bounds are now smaller than the true resolution). Depending on the screen, a user can also bump up the scale from 100% to 140% or 140% to 180% by selecting the "Make everything on your screen bigger" option in the "Ease of Access" section of the PC Settings app.

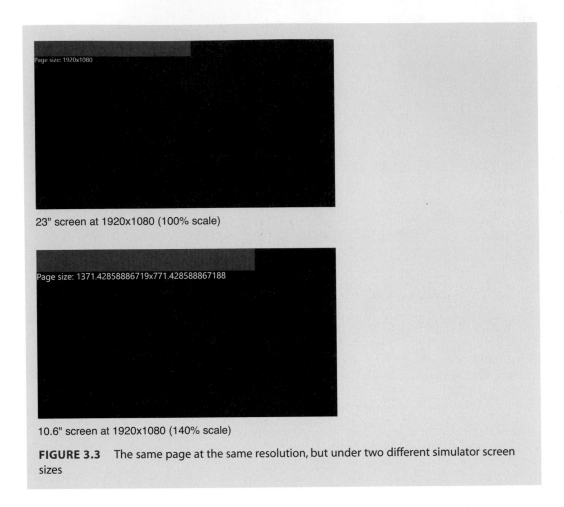

23" screen at 1920x1080 (100% scale)

10.6" screen at 1920x1080 (140% scale)

FIGURE 3.3   The same page at the same resolution, but under two different simulator screen sizes

Controlling Position

This section doesn't discuss positioning elements with (X,Y) coordinates, as you might expect. Parent panels define their own unique mechanisms for enabling children to position themselves, and those are discussed in the next chapter. A few mechanisms are common to all FrameworkElement children, however, and that's what this section examines. These mechanisms are related to alignment and a concept called *flow direction*.

Alignment

The HorizontalAlignment and VerticalAlignment properties enable an element to control what it does with any extra space that its parent panel gives it. Each property has a corresponding enumeration with the same name, giving the following options:

→ **HorizontalAlignment**—Left, Center, Right, and Stretch

→ **VerticalAlignment**—Top, Center, Bottom, and Stretch

Stretch is the default value for both properties, although various controls override the setting. The effects of HorizontalAlignment can easily be seen by placing a few Buttons in a StackPanel (described further in the next chapter) and marking them with each value from the enumeration:

```
<StackPanel>
  <Button HorizontalAlignment="Left" Content="Left" Background="Red"/>
  <Button HorizontalAlignment="Center" Content="Center" Background="Orange"/>
  <Button HorizontalAlignment="Right" Content="Right" Background="Green"/>
  <Button HorizontalAlignment="Stretch" Content="Stretch" Background="Blue"/>
</StackPanel>
```

Notice that an enumeration value such as HorizontalAlignment.Left is able to be specified in XAML as simply Left. This is thanks to a type converter that is able to handle any enumeration. The rendered result appears in Figure 3.4.

These two properties are useful only when a parent panel gives the child element more space than it needs. For example, adding VerticalAlignment values to elements in the StackPanel used in Figure 3.4 would make no difference, because each element is already given the exact amount of height it needs (no more, no less).

FIGURE 3.4   The effects of HorizontalAlignment on Buttons in a StackPanel

Content Alignment

In addition to HorizontalAlignment and VerticalAlignment properties, the Control class also has Horizontal**Content**Alignment and Vertical**Content**Alignment properties. These properties determine how a control's *content* fills the space *within* the control. (Therefore, the relationship between alignment and content alignment is somewhat like the relationship between Margin and Padding.)

• • •

Interaction Between Stretch Alignment and Explicit Element Size

When an element uses Stretch alignment (horizontally or vertically), an explicit Height or Width setting still takes precedence. MaxHeight and MaxWidth also take precedence, but only when their values are smaller than the natural stretched size. Similarly, MinHeight and MinWidth take precedence only when their values are *larger* than the natural stretched size. When Stretch is used in a context that constrains the element's size, it acts like an alignment of Center (or Left if the element is too large to be centered in its parent).

The content alignment properties are of the same enumeration types as the corresponding alignment properties, so they provide the same options. However, the default value for HorizontalContentAlignment is Left, and the default value for VerticalContentAlignment is Top. However, some elements implicitly choose different defaults. Buttons, for example, center their content in both dimensions by default.

Figure 3.5 demonstrates the effects of `HorizontalContentAlignment`, simply by taking the previous XAML snippet and changing the property name as follows:

```
<StackPanel>
  <Button HorizontalContentAlignment="Left" HorizontalAlignment="Stretch"
          Content="Left" Background="Red"/>
  <Button HorizontalContentAlignment="Center" HorizontalAlignment="Stretch"
          Content="Center" Background="Orange"/>
  <Button HorizontalContentAlignment="Right" HorizontalAlignment="Stretch"
          Content="Right" Background="Green"/>
  <Button HorizontalContentAlignment="Stretch" HorizontalAlignment="Stretch"
          Content="Stretch" Background="Blue"/>
</StackPanel>
```

Each `Button` also has its `HorizontalAlignment` set to `Stretch` rather than its default of `Left` so the differences in `HorizontalContentAlignment` are visible. Without this, each `Button` would auto-size to its content and there would be no extra space for the content to move within.

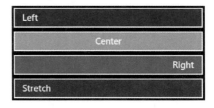

FIGURE 3.5   The effects of `HorizontalContentAlignment` on Buttons in a `StackPanel`

In Figure 3.5, the `Button` with `HorizontalContentAlignment=` `"Stretch"` might not appear as you expected. Its inner `TextBlock` is technically stretched, but it's meaningless because `TextBlock` (which is not a `Control`) doesn't have the same notion for stretching its inner text. For other types of content, `Stretch` can indeed have the intended effect.

FlowDirection

`FlowDirection` is a property on `FrameworkElement` (and several other classes) that can reverse the way an element's inner content flows. It applies to some panels and their arrangement of children, and it also applies to the way content is aligned inside child controls. The property is of type `FlowDirection`, with two values: `LeftToRight` (`FrameworkElement`'s default) and `RightToLeft`.

The idea of `FlowDirection` is that it should be set to `RightToLeft` when the current culture corresponds to a language that is read from right to left. This reverses the meaning of left and right for settings such as content alignment. The following XAML demonstrates this, with `Button`s that force their content alignment to `Top` and `Left` but then apply each of the two `FlowDirection` values:

```
<StackPanel>
  <Button FlowDirection="LeftToRight"
          HorizontalContentAlignment="Left" Width="320"
          Background="Red">LeftToRight</Button>
```

```
<Button FlowDirection="RightToLeft"
        HorizontalContentAlignment="Left" Width="320"
        Background="Orange">RightToLeft</Button>
</StackPanel>
```

The result is shown in Figure 3.6.

Notice that `FlowDirection` does not affect the flow of letters within these Buttons. English letters always flow left to right, and Arabic letters always flow right to left, for example. But

FIGURE 3.6 The effects of `FlowDirection` on Buttons with `Left` content alignment

`FlowDirection` reverses the notion of left and right for other pieces of the user interface, which typically need to match the flow direction of letters.

`FlowDirection` must be explicitly set to match the current culture (and can be done on a single, top-level element). This should be part of your localization process.

Applying 2D Transforms

The XAML framework contains a handful of built-in two-dimensional transform classes (derived from `Transform`) that enable you to change the size and position of elements independently from the previously discussed properties. Some also enable you to alter elements in more exotic ways, such as by rotating or skewing them.

All `UIElements` have a `RenderTransform` property that can be set to any `Transform` in order to change its appearance *after* the layout process has finished (immediately before the element is rendered). They also have a handy `RenderTransformOrigin` property that represents the starting point of the transform (the point that remains stationary). Figure 3.7 demonstrates the impact of setting `RenderTransformOrigin` to five different (x,y) values.

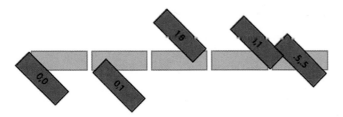

FIGURE 3.7 Five common `RenderTransformOrigins` used on Buttons rendered on top of unrotated Buttons

`RenderTransformOrigin` can be set to a `Windows.Foundation.Point`, with (0,0) being the default value. This represents the top-left corner, shown by the first button in Figure 3.7. An origin of (0,1) represents the bottom-left corner, (1,0) is the top-right corner, and (1,1) is the bottom-right corner. You can use numbers greater than 1 to set the origin to a point outside the bounds of an element, and you can use fractional values. Therefore, (.5,.5) represents the middle of the object. The reason the corner-pivoting appears slightly off in Figure 3.7 is an artifact of the default appearance of Buttons. They have an invisible three-pixel-wide region around their visible rectangle. If you imagine each button extending three pixels in each direction, the pivoting of the first four buttons would be exactly on each corner.

The value for RenderTransformOrigin can be specified in XAML with two comma-delimited numbers (and no parentheses). For example, a Button rotated around its center, such as the one at the far right of Figure 3.7, can be created as follows:

```
<Button RenderTransformOrigin=".5,.5">
  <Button.RenderTransform>
    <RotateTransform Angle="45"/>
  </Button.RenderTransform>
</Button>
```

This section looks at all the built-in 2D transforms, all in the Windows.UI.Xaml.Media namespace:

→ RotateTransform

→ ScaleTransform

→ SkewTransform

→ TranslateTransform

→ CompositeTransform

→ TransformGroup

→ MatrixTransform

RotateTransform

RotateTransform, which was just demonstrated, rotates an element according to the values of three double properties:

→ **Angle**—Angle of rotation, specified in degrees (default value = 0)

→ **CenterX**—Horizontal center of rotation (default value = 0)

→ **CenterY**—Vertical center of rotation (default value = 0)

The default (CenterX,CenterY) point of (0,0) represents the top-left corner.

> **What's the difference between using the** `CenterX` **and** `CenterY` **properties on transforms such as** `RotateTransform` **versus using the** `RenderTransformOrigin` **property on** `UIElement`**?**
>
> When a transform is applied to a `UIElement`, the `CenterX` and `CenterY` properties at first appear to be redundant with `RenderTransformOrigin`. Both mechanisms control the origin of the transform.
>
> However, `CenterX` and `CenterY` enable absolute positioning of the origin rather than the relative positioning of `RenderTransformOrigin`. Their values are specified as device-independent pixels, so the top-right corner of an element with a `Width` of 20 would be specified with `CenterX` set to 20 and `CenterY` set to 0 rather than the point (1,0). Also, when multiple `RenderTransforms` are grouped together (described later in the chapter), `CenterX` and `CenterY` on individual transforms enable more fine-grained control. Finally, the individual `double` values of `CenterX` and `CenterY` are easier to use with data binding than the `Point` value of `RenderTransformOrigin`.
>
> That said, `RenderTransformOrigin` is generally more useful than `CenterX` and `CenterY`. For the common case of transforming an element around its middle, the relative (.5,.5) `RenderTransformOrigin` is easy to specify in XAML, whereas accomplishing the same thing with `CenterX` and `CenterY` would require writing some C# code to calculate the absolute offsets.
>
> Note that you can use `RenderTransformOrigin` on an element simultaneously with using `CenterX` and `CenterY` on its transform. In this case, the two X values and two Y values are combined to calculate the final origin point.

Whereas Figure 3.7 shows rotated `Buttons`, Figure 3.8 demonstrates what happens when `RotateTransform` is applied *to the inner content* of a `Button`. To achieve this, the simple string that typically appears inside a `Button` is replaced with an explicit `TextBlock` as follows:

```
<Button Background="Orange">
  <TextBlock RenderTransformOrigin=".5,.5">
   <TextBlock.RenderTransform>
     <RotateTransform Angle="45"/>
   </TextBlock.RenderTransform>
    45°
  </TextBlock>
</Button>
```

FIGURE 3.8   Using `RotateTransform` on the content of a `Button`

ScaleTransform

`ScaleTransform` enlarges or shrinks an element horizontally, vertically, or in both directions. This transform has four straightforward `double` properties:

→ **ScaleX**—Multiplier for the element's width (default value = 1)

→ **ScaleY**—Multiplier for the element's height (default value = 1)

→ **CenterX**—Origin for horizontal scaling (default value = 0)

→ **CenterY**—Origin for vertical scaling (default value = 0)

A ScaleX value of 0.5 shrinks an element's rendered width in half, whereas a ScaleX value of 2 doubles the width. CenterX and CenterY work the same way as with RotateTransform.

Listing 3.1 applies ScaleTransform to three Buttons in a StackPanel, demonstrating the ability to stretch them independently in height or in width. Figure 3.9 shows the result.

LISTING 3.1   Applying ScaleTransform to Buttons in a StackPanel

```
<StackPanel Width="200">
  <Button Background="Red">No Scaling</Button>
  <Button Background="Orange">
  <Button.RenderTransform>
    <ScaleTransform ScaleX="2"/>
  </Button.RenderTransform>
    X</Button>
  <Button Background="Yellow">
  <Button.RenderTransform>
    <ScaleTransform ScaleX="2" ScaleY="2"/>
  </Button.RenderTransform>
    X + Y</Button>
  <Button Background="Lime">
  <Button.RenderTransform>
    <ScaleTransform ScaleY="2"/>
  </Button.RenderTransform>
    Y</Button>
</StackPanel>
```

Figure 3.10 displays the same Buttons from Listing 3.1 (and Figure 3.9) but with explicit CenterX and CenterY values set. The point represented by each pair of these values is displayed in each Button's text. Notice that the lime Button isn't moved to the left like the orange Button, despite being marked with the same CenterX of 70. That's because CenterX is relevant only when

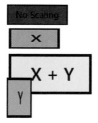

FIGURE 3.9   The scaled Buttons from Listing 3.1

ScaleX is a value other than 1, and CenterY is relevant only when ScaleY is a value other than 1.

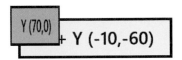

FIGURE 3.10   The Buttons from Listing 3.1 but with explicit scaling centers

(?) How do transforms such as ScaleTransform **affect** FrameworkElement's
ActualHeight **and** ActualWidth **properties or** UIElement's RenderSize **property?**

Applying a transform to FrameworkElement never changes the values of these properties.
Therefore, because of transforms, these properties can "lie" about the size of an element on the
screen. For example, all the Buttons in Figures 3.9 and 3.10 have the same ActualHeight,
ActualWidth, and RenderSize.

Such "lies" might surprise you, but they're for the best. First, it's debatable how such values should
even be expressed for some transforms. More importantly, the point of transforms is to alter an
element's appearance without the element's knowledge. Giving elements the illusion that they
are being rendered normally enables arbitrary controls to be plugged in and transformed
without special handling.

(?) How does ScaleTransform **affect** Margin **and** Padding**?**

Padding is scaled along with the rest of the content (because Padding is internal to the
element), but Margin does not get scaled. As with ActualHeight and ActualWidth, the
numeric Padding property value does not change, despite the visual scaling.

SkewTransform

SkewTransform slants an element according to the values of four double properties:

→ **AngleX**—Amount of horizontal
skew (default value = 0)

→ **AngleY**—Amount of vertical skew
(default value = 0)

→ **CenterX**—Origin for horizontal
skew (default value = 0)

→ **CenterY**—Origin for vertical
skew (default value = 0)

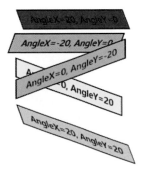

These properties behave much like the
properties of the previous transforms.

FIGURE 3.11   SkewTransform applied to
Buttons in a StackPanel

Figure 3.11 demonstrates `SkewTransform` applied as a `RenderTransform` on several `Button`s, using the default center of the top-left corner.

TranslateTransform

`TranslateTransform` simply moves an element according to two `double` properties:

→ **X**—Amount to move horizontally (default value = `0`)

→ **Y**—Amount to move vertically (default value = `0`)

`TranslateTransform` is an easy way to "nudge" elements one way or another. Most likely, you'd do this dynamically based on user actions (and perhaps in an animation). With all the panels described in the next chapter, it's unlikely that you'd need to use `TranslateTransform` to arrange a static user interface.

Combining Transforms

If you want to transform an element multiple ways simultaneously, such as rotate *and* scale it, a few different options are available:

→ `CompositeTransform`

→ `TransformGroup`

→ `MatrixTransform`

CompositeTransform

The `CompositeTransform` class is the easiest way to combine transforms. It has all the properties of the previous four transforms, although some have slightly different names: `Rotation`, `ScaleX`, `ScaleY`, `SkewX`, `SkewY`, `TranslateX`, `TranslateY`, `CenterX`, and `CenterY`.

FIGURE 3.12   A `Button` scaled, skewed, and rotated with a single `CompositeTransform`

Figure 3.12 shows several transforms being applied to a single `Button` as follows:

```
<Button Background="Orange">
  <Button.RenderTransform>
    <!-- The composite transform order is always
         scale, then skew, then rotate, then translate -->
    <CompositeTransform Rotation="45" ScaleX="5" ScaleY="1" SkewX="30"/>
  </Button.RenderTransform>
  OK
</Button>
```

TransformGroup

CompositeTransform always applies its transforms in the same order: scale, skew, rotate, and then translate. If you require a nonstandard order, you can use a TransformGroup instead then put its child transforms in any order. For example, the following XAML looks like it might have the same effect as the previous XAML, but Figure 3.13 shows that the result is much different:

```
<Button Background="Orange">
  <Button.RenderTransform>
    <TransformGroup>
      <!-- First rotate, then scale, then skew! -->
      <RotateTransform Angle="45"/>
      <ScaleTransform ScaleX="5" ScaleY="1"/>
      <SkewTransform AngleX="30"/>
    </TransformGroup>
  </Button.RenderTransform>
  OK
</Button>
```

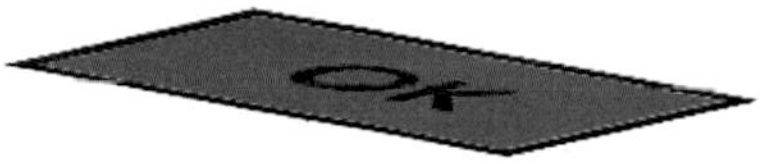

FIGURE 3.13   This time, the Button is rotated, scaled, and then skewed

TransformGroup is just another Transform-derived class, so it can be used wherever any transform is used.

For maximum performance, the system calculates a combined transform out of a TransformGroup's children and applies it as a single transform (much as if you had used CompositeTransform). Note that you can apply multiple instances of the same transform to a TransformGroup. For example, applying two separate 45° RotateTransforms would result in a 90° rotation.

MatrixTransform

MatrixTransform is a low-level mechanism that can be used to represent all combinations of rotation, scaling, skewing, and translating. MatrixTransform has a single Matrix property (of type Matrix) representing a 3x3 affine transformation matrix. (*Affine* means that straight lines remain straight.) Its Matrix property has the following subproperties representing 6 values in a 3x3 matrix:

$$\begin{bmatrix} M11 & M12 & 0 \\ M21 & M22 & 0 \\ OffsetX & OffsetY & 1 \end{bmatrix}$$

The final column's values cannot be changed.

• • •

`MatrixTransform`'s String Syntax

`MatrixTransform` is the only transform that can be specified as a simple string in XAML. For example, you can translate a `Button` 10 units to the right and 20 units down with the following syntax:

```
<Button RenderTransform="1,0,0,1,10,20"/>
```

The comma-delimited list represents the `M11`, `M12`, `M21`, `M22`, `OffsetX`, and `OffsetY` values, respectively. The values `1`, `0`, `0`, `1`, `0`, `0` give you the identity matrix (meaning no transform is done), so making `MatrixTransform` act like `TranslateTransform` is as simple as starting with the identity matrix and then using `OffsetX` and `OffsetY` as `TranslateTransform`'s X and Y values. Scaling can be done by treating the first and fourth values (the 1s in the identity matrix) as `ScaleX` and `ScaleY`, respectively. Rotation and skewing are more complicated because they involve sin, cos, and angles specified in radians.

If you're comfortable with the matrix notation, representing transforms with this concise (and less-readable) syntax can be a time saver when you're writing XAML by hand.

Applying 3D Transforms

Although you can use DirectX in a XAML app to work with a full 3D graphics engine, the XAML UI Framework does not directly expose full 3D capabilities. However, it does enable you to perform the most common 3D effects with *perspective transforms*. These transforms escape the limitations of the 2D transforms by enabling you to rotate and translate an element in any or all of the three dimensions.

Perspective transforms are normally done with a class called `PlaneProjection`, which defines `RotationX`, `RotationY`, and `RotationZ` properties. The X and Y dimensions are defined as usual, and the Z dimension extends into and out of the screen, as illustrated in Figure 3.14. X increases from left-to-right, Y increases from top-to-bottom, and Z increases from back-to-front.

Although plane projections act like transforms, they derive from a class called `Projection` rather than `Transform`. Therefore, one cannot be assigned to an element via its `RenderTransform` property, but rather a separate property called `Projection`. The following plane projections are marked on playing card images, producing the result in Figure 3.15:

```
<StackPanel Orientation="Horizontal">
  <Image Source="Images/CardHA.png" Width="150" Margin="12">
    <Image.Projection>
      <PlaneProjection RotationX="55"/>
    </Image.Projection>
  </Image>
  <Image Source="Images/CardH2.png" Width="150">
    <Image.Projection>
      <PlaneProjection RotationY="55"/>
    </Image.Projection>
  </Image>
  <Image Source="Images/CardH3.png" Width="150" Margin="36">
    <Image.Projection>
```

```
      <PlaneProjection RotationZ="55"/>
    </Image.Projection>
  </Image>
  <Image Source="Images/CardH4.png" Width="150" Margin="48">
    <Image.Projection>
      <PlaneProjection RotationX="30" RotationY="30" RotationZ="30"/>
    </Image.Projection>
  </Image>
</StackPanel>
```

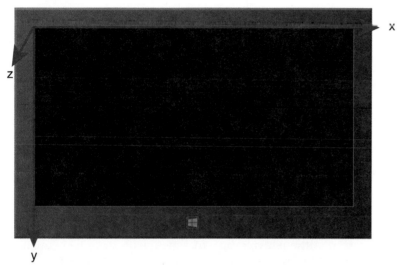

FIGURE 3.14   The three dimensions, relative to the screen.

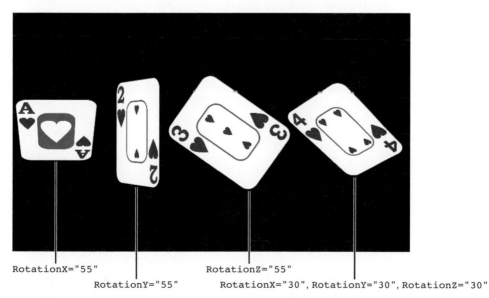

FIGURE 3.15   Using a plane projection to rotate the card around the X, Y, and Z axes, then all three axes.

Notice that rotating around only the Z axis is like using a 2D `RotateTransform`, although the direction is reversed.

Much like the 2D transform classes, `PlaneProjection` defines additional properties for changing the center of rotation: `CenterOfRotationX`, `CenterOfRotationY`, and `CenterOfRotationZ`. The first two properties are relative to the size of the element, on a scale from 0 to 1. The `CenterOfRotationZ` property is always in terms of absolute pixels, as elements never have any size in the Z dimension to enable a relative specification.

PlaneProjection defines six properties for translating an element in any or all dimensions. `GlobalOffsetX`, `GlobalOffsetY`, and `GlobalOffsetZ` apply the translation after the rotation, so the offsets are relative to the global screen coordinates. `LocalOffsetX`, `LocalOffsetY`, and `LocalOffsetZ` apply the translation before the rotation, causing the rotation to be relative to the rotated coordinate space.

> • • •
>
> ### Matrix3DProjection
>
> One other type of projection exists that can be assigned to an element's `Projection` property: `Matrix3DProjection`, which also derives from the `Projection` base class. This is a low-level construct that enables you to specify the projection as a 4x4 3D transformation matrix. This can be handy if you are already working with 3D transformation matrices, otherwise the simpler `PlaneProjection` is all you need to use.

Summary

That concludes our tour of the layout properties that child elements can use to influence the way they appear on the screen. Although you can experiment with them by manually typing XAML and observing the results, tools such as Blend and the Visual Studio designer make it even easier to get a feel for how values for complicated properties such as `RenderTransform` and `Projection` effect any element.

The most important part of layout, however, is the parent panels. This chapter repeatedly uses a simple `StackPanel` for simplicity, but the next chapter formally introduces this panel and all the other panels as well.

Chapter 4

LAYOUT

Layout is a critical component of an app's usability on a wide range of devices, but without good platform support, getting it right can be difficult. Arranging the pieces of a user interface simply with static pixel-based coordinates and static pixel-based sizes can work in limited environments, such as in Windows Phone 7.*x* apps in which all devices are guaranteed to have the same screen resolution. However, such interfaces start to crumble under the diversity enabled by Windows 8.

Windows 8 screens can range from small handheld devices to enormous HDTVs or projector screens and, more importantly, the resolution, DPI, and aspect ratios can all vary greatly. Furthermore, users expect most apps to gracefully handle different orientations and different view states, both of which can greatly change an app's ideal layout. Apps that don't take advantage of the space given to it are frustrating to use. But the space given an app isn't the only factor to consider when it comes to layout. Content that changes in unpredictable ways (such as text being translated into different languages or dynamically-downloaded content) also requires flexible layout.

The first step to mastering layout is knowing how to retrieve the characteristics of the current device and space given to your app by the current user, as well as how to know when it changes. This chapter begins by explaining how to discover the current dimensions of your app, which can be affected by all of the aforementioned conditions. It then examines the discovery of two specific features that often force you to change your layout: view states, a new Windows 8 concept, and orientations. What you do based on this information, and whether you even care to take explicit actions, is highly dependent on your user interface and your goals.

The bulk of the chapter examines an important feature in the XAML UI Framework that helps you tackle challenging layout: *panels*. In some cases, smart use of panels can make the same XAML adjust gracefully to all the different shapes and sizes your app could become, avoiding the need to do the sort of detection of dimensions, view state, and orientation covered first. More likely, panels can at least help you minimize the amount of manual UI adjustments you need to make to changing conditions.

Finally, this chapter ends with a discussion on strategies to deal with *content overflow*—in other words, what happens when parents and children can't agree on the use of available space. As with panels, the techniques discussed in this section, such as scrolling and scaling, can reduce the amount of manual work you need to do to handle the diversity of sizes and views.

Discovering the Current Dimensions

You might want to make several adjustments to your user interface depending on the exact dimensions given to your app or simply whether the screen is taller than it is wide (portrait versus landscape orientations). You can discover the size of your app at any time with the `Window.Current.Bounds` property of type `Windows.Foundation.Rect`.

Because the size of your app can change at any time (most likely due to snapping or an orientation change rather than a resolution change), it's important to be notified of any changes if you do indeed need to make adjustments. You can accomplish this by attaching an event handler to the `Window.Current.SizeChanged` event. The `WindowSizeChangedEventArgs` instance passed to the handler has a `Size` property that's equivalent to `Window.Current.Bounds`, so there are two ways to get the size of your app inside such handlers.

 Remember to detach event handlers!

Because an app's host window but might potentially have multiple pages whose code attaches a `SizeChanged` event handler, remember to detach each handler when appropriate to avoid keeping pages alive longer than desired!

Note that all `FrameworkElements` have a `LayoutUpdated` event that gets raised whenever their layout is invalidated. If you attach a `LayoutUpdated` event handler to the root element that is set as the window's content (`Window.Current.Content`), then that suffices as an alternative to a `SizeChanged` handler. Alternatively, if the window's content is a `Frame` (as it always is unless you've altered the Visual Studio-generated `App.xaml.cs`), then you could attach a handler to each `Page`'s `LayoutUpdated` event. This could be simpler to manage in a multipage app. Furthermore, inside a `LayoutUpdated` event handler, you can discover the current size of your app by inspecting the root's `ActualWidth` and `ActualHeight` properties. These properties are equivalent to `Window.Current.Bounds.Width` and `Window.Current.Bounds.Height`.

Note that `Window.Current.Bounds` is a property of type `Windows.Foundation.Rect` rather than `Windows.Foundation.Size`. This means that it exposes `Left` and `Top` properties in addition to `Width` and `Height`. All four values accurately represent the app's position on the screen, so by inspecting the `Left` value, you can tell whether you've been snapped to the left or right side of the screen, or if you're filled on the left or right side! It makes sense for certain apps to take advantage of this knowledge, such as a piano app in which the keys should always face an edge of the screen.

Discovering the Current View State

Unlike developers of desktop apps, which need to consider handling multiple resolutions (and orientations) gracefully, developers of Windows Store apps also have *view states* to worry about. View states exist to support the ability to have two such apps on the screen side-by-side. Technically, supporting this is no different than a desktop app gracefully handling its window being resized. Practically, however, this *is* a lot different, because this new mechanism gives users higher expectations for how an app behaves when it is resized. But you should embrace it. Having two apps on the screen simultaneously is a nice selling point for Windows-based tablets, and handling view states well is a great selling point for apps.

Figure 4.1 shows the four possible view states, although in many cases the snapped state is the only one that requires special attention.

The minimum widths for the two Fullscreen view states shouldn't be surprising considering the minimum resolution of 1024x768 for Windows Store apps. The reason that the filled view state is guaranteed to be at least 1024 pixels wide (potentially wider than fullscreen portrait!) is that Windows allows snapping only when the horizontal resolution is at least 1366 pixels: 320 for the snapped app, 22 for the splitter, and the rest for the filled app.

Note that the 320 number represents logical pixels. This means that the shape of a snapped app ends up being different on two screens with the same resolution but different DPI. You can see this in Visual Studio's simulator. If you snap an app on the 23" screen with 1920x1080 resolution, `Windows.Current.Bounds` reports a size of 320x1080 as you'd expect because it's a 96-DPI screen. But on the 207-DPI 10.6" screen with the same resolution, the pixels are scaled up 40% from a smaller logical resolution of 1371.429x771.4286. Therefore, if you snap an app on this higher-DPI screen with the same resolution, the app looks "fatter," and `Windows.Current.Bounds` reports a size of 320x771.4286. The constant logical width of 320 results in a wider app because the logical screen width is smaller.

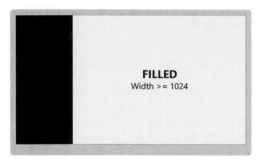

FIGURE 4.1   A Windows Store app can be viewed in one of four different view states at any time.

Although it's relatively easy to test the snapped and filled view states when running your app on your local computer or the simulator, you can quickly preview all view states—at multiple resolutions and DPI settings—in the Visual Studio XAML designer (or in Blend) by changing "View" inside the "Device" tool window. Figure 4.1, as well as other figures in this chapter, was generated this way.

Can snapping be done in a portrait orientation?

No, Windows does not currently allow this, no matter how high the resolution. This means that, at least for Windows 8, snapped and filled view states imply a landscape orientation.

To discover the current view state, you can check the static `Windows.UI.ViewManagement.ApplicationView.Value` property. This property is an `ApplicationViewState` enumeration with four values corresponding to the names in Figure 4.1. To detect when the view state changes, you can look no further than the previously discussed `Window.Current.SizeChanged` event (or `LayoutUpdated` event). Any view state change is guaranteed to change the app's size, so the size-related events are not only sufficient, but the recommended approach. Simply check the `ApplicationView.Value` value inside such event handlers. The big question is, "What should I do in response to view state changes?" You should think of these different view states the same way you would think about a user resizing a desktop app's window. A change in view state should not cause a jarring transition or loss of user state. The snapped view state, of course, often requires a significantly different layout in order to provide a good user experience. Besides shrinking, eliminating, and otherwise rearranging elements, you would likely switch to vertical scrolling in the snapped view state versus horizontal scrolling of the same content in the other view states.

> **You cannot opt out of snapping!**
>
> Whether you like it or not, users will be able to snap your app. You can choose to ignore view state changes, but the result likely won't be satisfactory. Whether your UI simply gets truncated, gets squished, or gets scrollbars depends on what elements are on your page and how your code naturally deals with being given only 320 pixels of width.

> The design guidelines state that snapping an app should not result in a loss of features. Although this is often not feasible, one thing you can do to mitigate this is to have some sort of link to the feature in your snapped view then programmatically unsnap your app when needed. This can be done with the static `Windows.UI.ViewManagement.ApplicationView.TryUnsnap` method. As the name indicates, it is not guaranteed to succeed. It returns `true` if successful, and `false` otherwise. You can see an example of this behavior by snapping the PC Settings app then selecting one of the items in its list.
>
> It should go without saying, but you should only programmatically unsnap your app for a scenario in which a user is actively trying to use a feature that requires more screen real estate. You should also not add any sort of "unsnap button" to your snapped view. Let users use the app management features built into Windows.

Why should I care about distinguishing between the fullscreen and filled view states? They're basically the same thing!

It's true that most apps don't need to treat a switch between fullscreen and filled any differently than a resolution or orientation change. There's one difference between the two view states that is potentially important, however: A filled app cannot place content on both left and right edges of the physical screen (because another app is adjacent to one of those edges). Therefore, if an app has controls along the left and right edges optimized for thumb use while holding a tablet, it might want to reposition them for the filled view state.

Discovering the Current Orientation

On the surface, it seems that checking `ApplicationView.Value` is enough to determine the current orientation because the fullscreen view states distinguish between landscape and portrait and the other view states are landscape-only. (Note that a simple check of the ratio of `Window.Current.Bounds.Height` compared to `Windows.Current.Bounds.Width` isn't good enough because an app doesn't always occupy the whole screen. A snapped app would appear to be in a portrait orientation.) Along those lines, attaching a handler to the `SizeChanged` event should be sufficient for detecting orientation changes.

For the most part, this is true. However, recall from Chapter 1, "Anatomy of a Windows Store App," that Windows can tell you whether the device is flipped, giving four possible orientations:

→ **Landscape** (horizontal)

→ **Landscape-flipped** (horizontal but upside down)

→ **Portrait** (vertical, with the hardware Start button on the left)

→ **Portrait-flipped** (vertical, with the hardware Start button on the right)

It's hard to imagine a valid reason for adjusting a user interface based on flipped versus nonflipped, other than some kind of tutorial that wants to place an arrow pointing to the hardware Start button. Nevertheless, if you care about distinguishing between the flipped and nonflipped orientations, you discover the current orientation is via the static `Windows.Graphics.Display.DisplayProperties.CurrentOrientation` property. This property is a `DisplayOrientations` enumeration with the four possible values plus `None`. The reason for the `None` value (and the plural name) is that it's also the type of a static `AutoRotationPreferences` property on the same class that reveals the app's setting for "supported rotations" in the package manifest, as described in Chapter 1. In this case, it's used like a flags enumeration in which any or all of the four valid orientations could be set. For properties such as `CurrentOrientation`, however, the value is always exactly one (non-`None`) value.

To be notified of changes to the `CurrentOrientation` property, you can attach a handler to the static `Windows.Graphics.Display.DisplayProperties.OrientationChanged` event. Because `OrientationChanged` is a static event, you should be careful to detach event handlers if your app might attach several of them. Also, because the timing between `SizeChanged` and `OrientationChanged` is unpredictable, you should not look at `Window.Current.Bounds` inside an `OrientationChanged` handler.

The static `Windows.Graphics.Display.DisplayProperties` class exposes several interesting characteristics about the current screen in addition to its current orientation: Its native orientation (the primary way it is designed to be held/viewed), the scale factor applied to all non-desktop UI (100%, 140% or 180%), its DPI, whether stereoscopic 3D is enabled, and its International Color Consortium (ICC) color profile. The latter three also have corresponding property-change events.

The scale factor, exposed by `DisplayProperties.ResolutionScale` represents the mapping between logical and physical pixels. It is a property of the enumeration type `ResolutionScale`. For example, in the earlier example of the 207-DPI 10.6" screen with 1920x1080 resolution in which the pixels are scaled up 40%, the value of `ResolutionScale` is `ResolutionScale.Scale140Percent`.

Panels

A panel (any class that derives from `Panel`) can contain children and arrange them in specific ways. The XAML UI Framework contains several panels, and you can create your own. This section examines the four main built-in panels, all in the `Windows.UI.Xaml.Controls` namespace:

→ `Canvas`

→ `StackPanel`

→ `Grid`

→ `VariableSizedWrapGrid`

Canvas

`Canvas` is the most basic panel, because it supports only the "classic" notion of positioning elements with explicit coordinates. You can position elements in a `Canvas` by using its `Left` and `Top` properties. These properties are special *attached properties* that can be *attached* to other elements. Listing 4.1 demonstrates this, introducing previously unseen XAML syntax designed specifically for attached properties.

LISTING 4.1   Buttons Arranged in a Canvas

```
<Page …>
  <Canvas x:Name="canvas">
    <Button Background="Red">Left=0, Top=0</Button>
    <Button x:Name="b" Canvas.Left="25" Canvas.Top="25"
            Background="Orange">Left=25, Top=25</Button>
  </Canvas>
</Page>
```

When the XAML parser encounters this `Canvas.Left` and `Canvas.Top` syntax, it requires that `Canvas` (sometimes called the *attached property provider*) have static methods called `SetLeft` and `SetTop` that can set the value accordingly. Therefore, the declaration of the `Button` named b in Listing 4.1 is equivalent to the following C# code:

```
Button b = new Button();
Canvas.SetLeft(b, 25);
Canvas.SetTop(b, 25);
b.Background = new SolidColorBrush(Color.Orange);
b.Content = "Left=25, Top=25";
canvas.Children.Add(b);
```

Although the XAML in Listing 4.1 nicely represents the logical attachment of `Left` and `Top` to `Canvas`, the C# code reveals that there's no real magic here— just a method call that associates an element with an otherwise unrelated property. One of the interesting things about the attached property abstraction is that no .NET property is a part of it! Note also that `Canvas`, like all `Panels`, has a `Children` collection of `UIElements`. Adding a child element in XAML is equivalent to adding it to its `Children` collection.

The `Canvas.Left` and `Canvas.Top` values serve as margins (to which the element's own `Margin` values are added). If an element doesn't use either of these attached properties (leaving them with their default value of `Double.NaN`), it is placed in the top-left corner of the `Canvas` (the equivalent of setting `Left` and `Top` to `0`). Figure 4.2 demonstrates this with the rendered result of the XAML in Listing 4.1.

Attached Properties

Although attached properties, sometimes called *attachable properties*, are a general-purpose mechanism, they were designed with the needs of layout panels in mind. Various `Panel`-derived classes define attached properties for controlling how their children are arranged. This way, each `Panel` can apply its own custom behavior to arbitrary children without requiring all possible child elements to be burdened with their own set of relevant properties. It also enables systems such as layout to be easily extensible, because anyone can write a new `Panel` with custom attached properties.

FIGURE 4.2   The `Buttons` in a `Canvas` from Listing 4.1

Table 4.1 evaluates the way that some of the child layout properties discussed in the preceding chapter apply to elements inside a `Canvas`.

TABLE 4.1   Canvas's Interaction with Child Layout Properties

Property	Usable Inside Canvas?
Margin	Partially. On the two sides used to position the element (Top and Left), the relevant two out of four margin values are added to the attached property values. Right and Bottom have no effect.
HorizontalAlignment and VerticalAlignment	No. Elements are given only the exact space they need.

The default Z order (defining which elements are "on top of" other elements) is determined by the order in which the children are added to the parent. In XAML, this is the order in which children are listed in the file. Elements added later are placed on top of elements added earlier. That is why, in Figure 4.2, the orange Button is on top of the red Button. This is relevant not just for the built-in panels that enable elements to overlap (such as Canvas) but whenever a RenderTransform causes an element to overlap another (as shown in Figures 3.9, 3.10, and 3.11 in the preceding chapter).

However, you can customize the Z order of any child element by marking it with the ZIndex attached property that is defined on Canvas. ZIndex is an integer with a default value of 0 that you can set to any number (positive or negative). Elements with larger ZIndex values are rendered on top of elements with smaller ZIndex values, so the element with the smallest value is in the back, and the element with the largest value is in the front. In the following example, ZIndex causes the red button to be on top of the orange button, despite being an earlier child of the Canvas:

```
<Canvas>
  <Button Canvas.ZIndex="1" Background="Red">On Top!</Button>
  <Button Background="Orange">On Bottom with a Default ZIndex=0</Button>
</Canvas>
```

If multiple children have the same ZIndex value, the order is determined by their order in the panel's Children collection, as in the default case.

Therefore, programmatically manipulating Z order is as simple as adjusting the ZIndex value. To cause the preceding red Button to be rendered behind the orange Button, you can set the attached property value to any number less than or equal to zero. The following line of C# does just that (assuming that the red button's name is redButton):

```
Canvas.SetZIndex(redButton, 0);
```

Note that although ZIndex is defined on Canvas, this mechanism works with all panels!

Although Canvas is too primitive a panel for creating flexible user interfaces, it is the most lightweight panel. So, you should keep it in mind for maximum performance when you need precise control over the placement of elements. Games, for example, tend to use Canvas because each element requires a precise position (perhaps calculated by a physics engine). The otherwise statically-placed content can still scale as needed simply by applying a transform to the Canvas or a parent element.

StackPanel

StackPanel is a popular panel because of its simplicity and usefulness. As its name suggests, it simply stacks its children sequentially. Examples in previous chapters use StackPanel because it doesn't require the use of any attached properties to get a reasonable-looking user interface. In fact, StackPanel is one of the few panels that doesn't define any of its own attached properties!

With no attached properties for arranging children, you just have one way to customize the behavior of StackPanel—setting its Orientation property to Horizontal or Vertical. Vertical is the default Orientation. Figure 4.3 shows simple Buttons in two StackPanels with only their Orientation set.

Orientation="Vertical" (default)   Orientation="Horizontal"

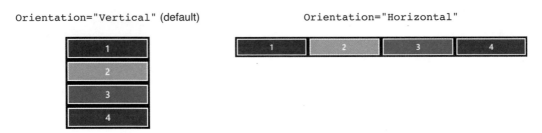

FIGURE 4.3   Buttons in a StackPanel, using both Orientations

> StackPanel **and Right-to-Left Environments**
>
> When FlowDirection is set to RightToLeft, stacking occurs right to left for a StackPanel with Horizontal Orientation, rather than the default left-to-right behavior.

Table 4.2 evaluates the way that some of the child layout properties apply to elements inside a StackPanel.

TABLE 4.2   StackPanel's Interaction with Child Layout Properties

Property	Usable Inside StackPanel?
Margin	Yes. Margin controls the space between an element and the StackPanel's edges as well as space between elements.
HorizontalAlignment and VerticalAlignment	Partially, because alignment is effectively ignored in the direction of stacking (children get the exact amount of space they need). For Orientation="Vertical", VerticalAlignment is meaningless. For Orientation="Horizontal", HorizontalAlignment is meaningless.

Grid

Grid is the most versatile panel and probably the one you'll use most often. (Visual Studio and Blend use Grid by default, even when you create a Blank App project.) It enables you to arrange its children in a multirow and multicolumn fashion, and it provides a number of features to control the rows and columns in interesting ways. Working with Grid is like working with a table or CSS grid in HTML.

Listing 4.2 uses Grid to build a user interface somewhat like the Windows Start screen. It defines a 7x8 Grid and arranges children in many of its cells.

LISTING 4.2   First Attempt at a Start Screen Clone Using a Grid

```xml
<Grid Background="#1D1D1D">

  <!-- Define seven rows: -->
  <Grid.RowDefinitions>
    <RowDefinition/> <!-- The area above the tiles -->
    <RowDefinition/> <!-- Tile row #1 -->
    <RowDefinition/> <!-- Tile row #2 -->
    <RowDefinition/> <!-- Tile row #3 -->
    <RowDefinition/> <!-- Tile row #4 -->
    <RowDefinition/> <!-- Tile row #5 -->
    <RowDefinition/> <!-- The area below the tiles -->
  </Grid.RowDefinitions>

  <!-- Define eight columns: -->
  <Grid.ColumnDefinitions>
    <ColumnDefinition/> <!-- Left margin -->
    <ColumnDefinition/> <!-- Tile column #1 -->
    <ColumnDefinition/> <!-- Tile column #2 -->
    <ColumnDefinition/> <!-- Tile column #3 -->
    <ColumnDefinition/> <!-- Tile column #4 -->
    <ColumnDefinition/> <!-- The user's name -->
    <ColumnDefinition/> <!-- The user's photo -->
    <ColumnDefinition/> <!-- Right margin -->
  </Grid.ColumnDefinitions>

  <!-- The "Start" text -->
  <TextBlock Grid.Row="0" Grid.Column="1" FontSize="54" FontFamily="Segoe UI"
             FontWeight="Light" VerticalAlignment="Center" Margin="0,0,0,26">
      Start
  </TextBlock>

  <!-- The simulated live tiles -->
  <Rectangle Grid.Row="1" Grid.Column="1" Margin="4" Fill="DodgerBlue"/>
  <Rectangle Grid.Row="1" Grid.Column="3" Margin="4" Fill="Coral"/>
```

```
<Rectangle Grid.Row="2" Grid.Column="1" Margin="4" Fill="PaleVioletRed"/>
<Rectangle Grid.Row="2" Grid.Column="3" Margin="4" Fill="LimeGreen"/>
<Rectangle Grid.Row="3" Grid.Column="1" Margin="4" Fill="White"/>
<Rectangle Grid.Row="3" Grid.Column="3" Margin="4" Fill="DodgerBlue"/>
<Rectangle Grid.Row="4" Grid.Column="1" Margin="4" Fill="LimeGreen"/>
<Rectangle Grid.Row="4" Grid.Column="3" Margin="4" Fill="Yellow"/>
<Rectangle Grid.Row="4" Grid.Column="4" Margin="4" Fill="PaleVioletRed"/>
<Rectangle Grid.Row="5" Grid.Column="1" Margin="4" Fill="Tan"/>
<Rectangle Grid.Row="5" Grid.Column="3" Margin="4" Fill="DodgerBlue"/>
<Rectangle Grid.Row="5" Grid.Column="4" Margin="4" Fill="LimeGreen"/>

<!-- The current user's name and photo -->
<TextBlock Grid.Row="0" Grid.Column="5" FontSize="28" FontFamily="Segoe UI"
           FontWeight="Light" HorizontalAlignment="Right"
           VerticalAlignment="Center" Margin="0,0,8,28">
    Adam Nathan
</TextBlock>
<Image Grid.Row="0" Grid.Column="6" Source="profile.png"
       VerticalAlignment="Center" Stretch="None" Margin="0,0,0,26"/>
</Grid>
```

For the basic usage of Grid, you define the number of rows and columns by adding that number of RowDefinition and ColumnDefinition elements to its RowDefinitions and ColumnDefinitions properties. (This is a little verbose but handy for giving individual rows and columns distinct sizes.) You can then position child elements in the Grid using its Row and Column attached properties, which are zero-based integers. When you don't explicitly specify any rows or columns, a Grid is implicitly given a single cell. And when you don't explicitly set Grid.Row or Grid.Column on child elements, the value 0 is used for each.

Grid cells can be left empty, and multiple elements can appear in the same Grid cell. In this case, elements are simply rendered on top of one another according to their Z order. As with Canvas, child elements in the same cell don't interact with each other in terms of layout; they simply overlap.

Figure 4.4 shows the result of Listing 4.2 in the Visual Studio XAML designer, because the grid lines help to put the visuals in context.

There are a few noticeable problems with Figure 4.4: The first row should have more vertical space, the user name and photo have too much horizontal space, and the spacing and shape of the pseudo-tiles (Rectangle elements) don't look right. In fact, most of the tiles are intended to appear in their wide mode. All this is caused by the fact that every row has the same height, every column has the same width, and every element is confined to a single cell. Fortunately, we can solve all of these problems with some explicit Heights and Widths on RowDefinition and ColumnDefinition, respectively, and two more attached properties defined by Grid: RowSpan and ColumnSpan. Listing 4.3 applies these changes.

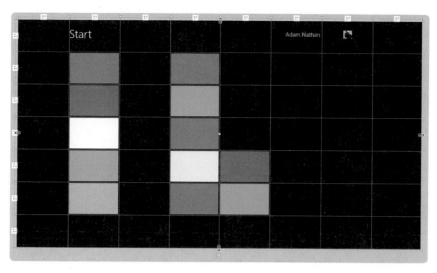

FIGURE 4.4   The first attempt at a Start screen is not satisfactory.

LISTING 4.3   An Improved Start Screen Clone

```xml
<Grid Background="#1D1D1D">

  <!-- Define seven rows: -->
  <Grid.RowDefinitions>
    <RowDefinition Height="180"/> <!-- The area above the tiles -->
    <RowDefinition Height="128"/> <!-- Tile row #1 -->
    <RowDefinition Height="128"/> <!-- Tile row #2 -->
    <RowDefinition Height="128"/> <!-- Tile row #3 -->
    <RowDefinition Height="128"/> <!-- Tile row #4 -->
    <RowDefinition Height="128"/> <!-- Tile row #5 -->
    <RowDefinition/>              <!-- The area below the tiles -->
  </Grid.RowDefinitions>

  <!-- Define eight columns: -->
  <Grid.ColumnDefinitions>
    <ColumnDefinition Width="116"/> <!-- Left margin -->
    <ColumnDefinition Width="128"/> <!-- Tile column #1 -->
    <ColumnDefinition Width="128"/> <!-- Tile column #2 -->
    <ColumnDefinition Width="128"/> <!-- Tile column #3 -->
    <ColumnDefinition Width="128"/> <!-- Tile column #4 -->
    <ColumnDefinition/>             <!-- The user's name -->
    <ColumnDefinition Width="40"/>  <!-- The user's photo -->
    <ColumnDefinition Width="46"/>  <!-- Right margin -->
  </Grid.ColumnDefinitions>
```

```
<!-- The "Start" text -->
<TextBlock Grid.Row="0" Grid.Column="1" FontSize="54" FontFamily="Segoe UI"
           FontWeight="Light" VerticalAlignment="Center" Margin="0,0,0,26">
    Start
</TextBlock>

<!-- The simulated live tiles -->
<Rectangle Grid.Row="1" Grid.Column="1" Grid.ColumnSpan="2" Margin="4"
           Fill="DodgerBlue"/>
<Rectangle Grid.Row="1" Grid.Column="3" Grid.ColumnSpan="2" Margin="4"
           Fill="Coral"/>
<Rectangle Grid.Row="2" Grid.Column="1" Grid.ColumnSpan="2" Margin="4"
           Fill="PaleVioletRed"/>
<Rectangle Grid.Row="2" Grid.Column="3" Grid.ColumnSpan="2" Margin="4"
           Fill="LimeGreen"/>
<Rectangle Grid.Row="3" Grid.Column="1" Grid.ColumnSpan="2" Margin="4"
           Fill="White"/>
<Rectangle Grid.Row="3" Grid.Column="3" Grid.ColumnSpan="2" Margin="4"
           Fill="DodgerBlue"/>
<Rectangle Grid.Row="4" Grid.Column="1" Grid.ColumnSpan="2" Margin="4"
           Fill="LimeGreen"/>
<Rectangle Grid.Row="4" Grid.Column="3" Margin="4" Fill="Yellow"/>
<Rectangle Grid.Row="4" Grid.Column="4" Margin="4" Fill="PaleVioletRed"/>
<Rectangle Grid.Row="5" Grid.Column="1" Grid.ColumnSpan="2" Margin="4"
           Fill="Tan"/>
<Rectangle Grid.Row="5" Grid.Column="3" Margin="4" Fill="DodgerBlue"/>
<Rectangle Grid.Row="5" Grid.Column="4" Margin="4" Fill="LimeGreen"/>

<!-- The current user's name and photo -->
<TextBlock Grid.Row="0" Grid.Column="5" FontSize="28" FontFamily="Segoe UI"
           FontWeight="Light" HorizontalAlignment="Right"
           VerticalAlignment="Center" Margin="0,0,8,28">
    Adam Nathan
</TextBlock>
<Image Grid.Row="0" Grid.Column="6" Source="profile.png"
       VerticalAlignment="Center" Stretch="None" Margin="0,0,0,26"/>
</Grid>
```

RowSpan and ColumnSpan have a value of 1 by default and can be set to any number greater than 1 to make an element span that many rows or columns. (If a value greater than the number of rows or columns is given, the element simply spans the maximum number that it can.) Figure 4.5 demonstrates the improved result from Listing 4.3, again in the Visual Studio XAML designer.

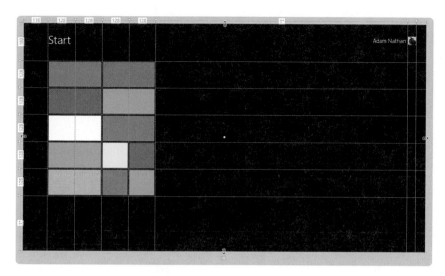

FIGURE 4.5   Using RowSpan, ColumnSpan, and some explicit row/column sizes improves the appearance of the Start screen clone.

Table 4.3 evaluates the way that some of the child layout properties apply to elements inside a Grid.

TABLE 4.3   Grid's Interaction with Child Layout Properties

Property	Usable Inside Grid?
Margin	Yes. Margin controls the space between an element and the edges of its cell.
HorizontalAlignment and VerticalAlignment	Yes. Unlike with the previous panels, both directions are completely usable unless an autosized cell causes an element to have no extra room. Therefore, by default, most elements completely stretch to fill their cells.

Sizing the Rows and Columns

The hardcoded row heights and column widths in the Start screen example work for certain resolutions, but more work would need to be done to make the UI flexible enough to handle all possible resolutions. This could be done with code-behind that checks the current screen size and adjust values accordingly, but Grid exposes sophisticated sizing options that can sometimes make such code unnecessary.

Unlike FrameworkElement's Height and Width properties, RowDefinition's and ColumnDefinition's corresponding properties do not default to Auto (or Double.NaN). And unlike almost all other Height and Width properties, theirs are of type GridLength rather than double. This way, Grid can uniquely support three different types of RowDefinition and ColumnDefinition sizing:

→ **Absolute sizing**—Setting Height or Width to a numeric value representing logical pixels (like all other Height and Width values). Unlike the other types of sizing, an absolute-sized row or column does not grow or shrink as the size of the Grid or size of the elements changes. In Figure 4.5, all but one row and one column use absolute sizing.

→ **Autosizing**—Setting Height or Width to Auto (case insensitive), which gives child elements the space they need and no more (like the default setting for other Height and Width values). For a row, this is the height of the tallest element, and for a column, this is the width of the widest element. This is a better choice than absolute sizing whenever text is involved to be sure it doesn't get cut off because of localization.

→ **Proportional sizing (sometimes called *star sizing*)**—Setting Height or Width to special syntax to divide available space into equal-sized regions or regions based on fixed ratios. A proportional-sized row or column grows and shrinks as the Grid is resized.

Absolute sizing and autosizing are straightforward, but proportional sizing needs more explanation. It is done with *star syntax* that works as follows:

→ When a row's height or column's width is set to *, it occupies all the remaining space.

→ When multiple rows or columns use *, the remaining space is divided equally between them.

→ Rows and columns can place a coefficient in front of the asterisk (like 2* or 5.5*) to take proportionately more space than other columns using the asterisk notation. A column with width 2* is always twice the width of a column with width * (which is shorthand for 1*) *in the same* Grid. A column with width 5.5* is always twice the width of a column with width 2.75* *in the same* Grid.

The "remaining space" is the height or width of the Grid minus any rows or columns that use absolute sizing or autosizing. Figure 4.6 demonstrates these different scenarios with simple columns in a Grid.

The default height and width for Grid rows and columns is *. That's why the last row and the username column in Figure 4.5 occupy all remaining space.

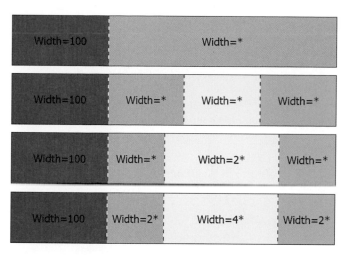

FIGURE 4.6   Proportional-sized Grid columns in action

 Why doesn't Grid provide built-in support for percentage sizing, like in HTML and CSS?

The most common use of percentage sizing—setting the width or height of an item to 100%—is handled by setting an element's HorizontalAlignment or VerticalAlignment property to Stretch inside most panels. For more complicated scenarios, Grid's proportional sizing effectively provides percentage sizing, but with a syntax that takes a little getting used to. For example, to have a column always occupy 25% of a Grid's width, you can mark it with * and ensure that the remaining columns have a total width of 3*.

Microsoft chose this syntax so developers wouldn't have to worry about keeping the sum of percentages equal to 100 as rows or columns are dynamically added or removed. In addition, the fact that proportional sizing is specified relative to the remaining space (as opposed to the entire Grid) makes its behavior more understandable than an HTML table when mixing proportional rows or columns with fixed-size rows or columns.

 How can I give Grid cells background colors, padding, and borders, as with cells of an HTML table?

There is no intrinsic mechanism to give Grid cells such properties, but you can simulate them easily, thanks to the fact that multiple elements can appear in any Grid cell. To give a cell a background color, you can simply plop in a Rectangle with the appropriate Fill (as in Figures 4.3 and 4.4) or a Border with the appropriate Background, which stretches to fill the cell by default. To give a cell padding, you can use autosizing and set the Margin on the appropriate child element. For borders, you can again use a Rectangle but give it an explicit Stroke of the appropriate color, or you can use a Border element and set its BorderBrush appropriately.

Just be sure to add such Rectangles or Borders to the Grid *before* adding any of the other children (or explicitly mark them with the ZIndex attached property), so their Z order puts them behind the main content.

···

Using `GridLength` from Procedural Code

In XAML, a type converter converts strings such as `"100"`, `"auto"`, and `"2*"` to `GridLength` structures. From C#, you can use one of two constructors to construct the appropriate `GridLength`. The key is a `GridUnitType` enumeration that identifies which of the three types of values you're creating.

For absolute sizing, you can use the constructor that takes a simple `double` value (such as `100`):

```
GridLength length = new GridLength(100);
```

Or, you can use another constructor that accepts a `GridUnitType` value:

```
GridLength length = new GridLength(100, GridUnitType.Pixel);
```

In both examples, the length is 100 device-independent pixels.

`Double.NaN` isn't a supported value for the `GridLength` constructors, so for autosizing you must use `GridUnitType.Auto`:

```
GridLength length = new GridLength(0, GridUnitType.Auto);
```

The number passed as the first parameter is ignored. However, the preferred approach is to use the static `GridLength.Auto` property, which returns an instance of `GridLength` just like the one created by the preceding line of code. For proportional sizing, you can pass a number along with `GridUnitType.Star`:

```
GridLength length = new GridLength(2, GridUnitType.Star);
```

This example is equivalent to specifying 2* in XAML. You can pass 1 with `GridUnitType.Star` to get the equivalent of *.

 In addition to `Height`, `RowDefinition` exposes `MinHeight` and `MaxHeight` properties (of type `double`, as usual) to provide more options of creating flexible layout. Similarly, `ColumnDefinition` exposes `MinWidth` and `MaxWidth` properties of type `double`.

Comparing `Grid` to Other Panels

`Grid` is the best choice for most complex layout scenarios because it can do everything done by the previous panels and more. `Grid` can also accomplish layout that would otherwise require multiple panels. To demonstrate that `Grid` is usually the best choice, it's interesting to see how to mimic the behavior of other panels with `Grid`, knowing that you can take advantage of `Grid`'s extra features at any time.

Mimicking `Canvas` with `Grid`

If you leave `Grid` with a single row and column and set the `HorizontalAlignment` and `VerticalAlignment` of all children to values other than `Stretch`, the children get added to the single cell just as they do in a `Canvas`. Setting `HorizontalAlignment` to `Left` and `VerticalAlignment` to `Top` is like setting `Canvas.Left` and `Canvas.Top` to `0`. Applying `Margin` values to each element can give you the same effect as setting `Canvas`'s attached properties to the same values. This is what the Visual Studio designer does when the user places and moves items on the design surface.

Mimicking `StackPanel` with `Grid`

A single-column `Grid` with autosized rows looks just like a vertical `StackPanel` when each element is manually placed in consecutive rows. Similarly, a single-row `Grid` with auto-sized columns looks just like a horizontal `StackPanel` when each element is manually placed in consecutive columns.

VariableSizedWrapGrid

`VariableSizedWrapGrid` is not as versatile as `Grid`, but it can do one trick that `Grid` cannot: wrap its elements when there's not enough space. Although its name ends in "Grid," `VariableSizedWrapGrid` is more like a `StackPanel` than a `Grid`. It stacks its children vertically (by default) or horizontally based on its `Orientation` property, and it doesn't define any attached properties for placing items in specific rows or columns. The stack simply wraps into new rows/columns as needed.

Figure 4.7 demonstrates how the following `VariableSizedWrapGrid` placed directly in a `Page` handles various layout conditions that can be inflicted by a user. It contains 10 buttons that differ only by `Background` and `Content`:

```
<Page …>
    <VariableSizedWrapGrid Orientation="Horizontal" Background="Brown">
        <Button FontSize="50" Width="200" Background="#0000ff">0</Button>
        …
    </VariableSizedWrapGrid>
</Page>
```

This panel is useful for displaying an indeterminate number of items with a more interesting layout than a simple list, much like the Windows file picker. Note that there's still no guarantee that every child element can be viewed, as with the last button in Figure 4.7 in the snapped view. In this example, the app should probably add scrolling behavior. Scrolling is covered later in this chapter.

> Although `Grid` looks like it can practically do it all, `StackPanel` and `VariableSizedWrapGrid` are better choices when dealing with an indeterminate number of child elements (typically as an items panel for an items control, described in Chapter 9, "Items Controls").

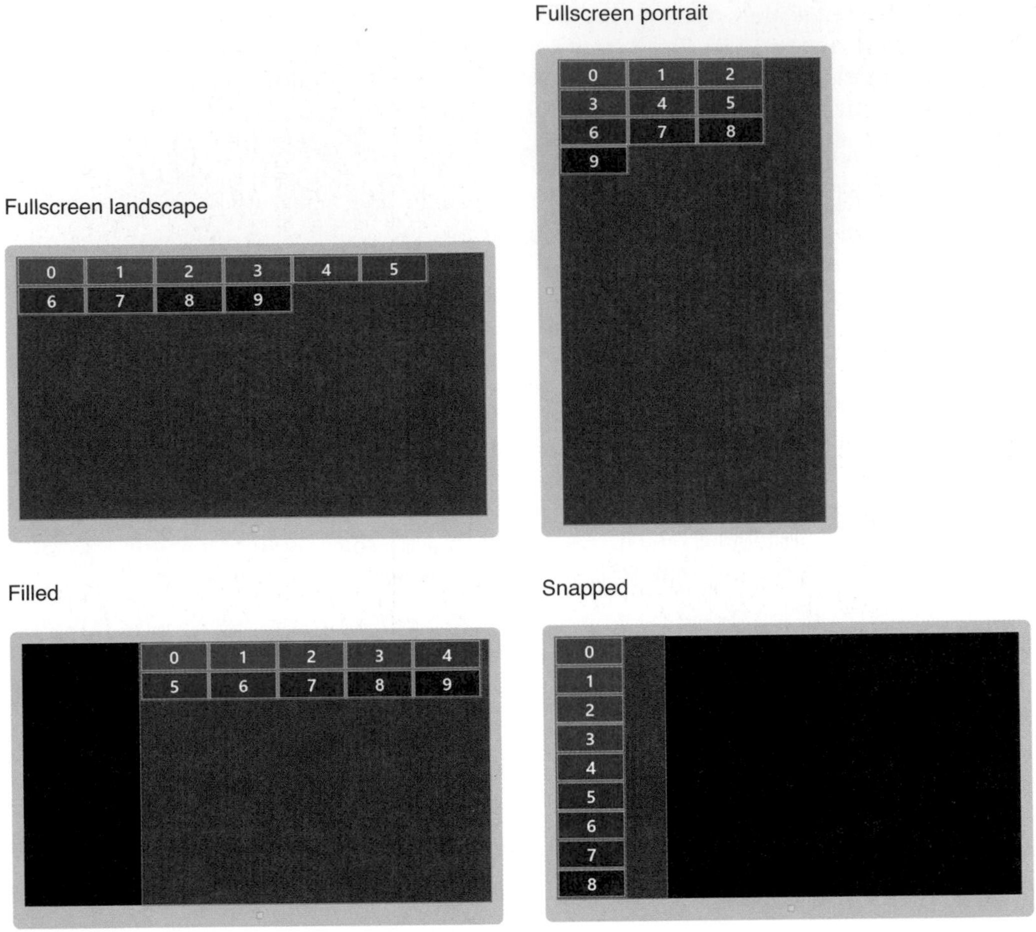
Fullscreen portrait
0
1
2
3
4
5
6
7
8
9
Fullscreen landscape
0
1
2
3
4
5
6
7
8
9
Filled
0
1
2
3
4
5
6
7
8
9
Snapped
0
1
2
3
4
5
6
7
8

FIGURE 4.7 The horizontal `VariableSizedWrapGrid` shifts the placement of its children as the available horizontal space changes.

`VariableSizedWrapGrid` defines two attached properties that can be placed on its children: `RowSpan` and `ColumnSpan`. As with `Grid`, this enables a single element to span multiple rows/columns. Figure 4.8 is an update to Figure 4.7 that demonstrates this. The `Button` labeled "2" has been marked with:

```
VariableSizedWrapGrid.RowSpan="2"
```

And the `Button` labeled "8" has been marked with:

```
VariableSizedWrapGrid.ColumnSpan="2"
```

In addition to their change to shades of green (for emphasis), the `Button` with "2" has been given a `VerticalAlignment` of `Stretch` so it can take advantage of the extra space given to it. Similarly, the `Button` with "8" has been given a `Width` of 400 rather than 200.

Fullscreen portrait

Fullscreen landscape

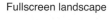

Filled

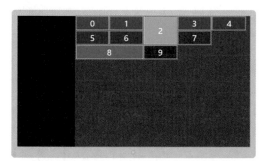

Snapped

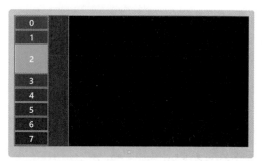

FIGURE 4.8   The use of RowSpan and ColumnSpan changes the wrapping behavior compared to FIGURE 4.7.

In addition to the two attached properties, VariableSizedWrapGrid defines six properties for controlling its behavior:

→ **Orientation**—This is just like StackPanel's property, and Vertical is the default. Vertical is the way most apps arrange their elements: stacked top to bottom and then wrapped left to right. Horizontal is the opposite, as demonstrated in Figures 4.6 and 4.7: stacked left to right and then wrapped top to bottom.

→ **ItemHeight**—A uniform height for all child elements. The way each child fills that height depends on its own VerticalAlignment, Height, and so forth. Any elements taller than ItemHeight get clipped.

→ **ItemWidth**—A uniform width for all child elements. The way each child fills that width depends on its own HorizontalAlignment, Width, and so forth. Any elements wider than ItemWidth get clipped.

→ **MaximumRowsOrColumns**—An integer that forces wrapping after a specific number of rows or columns, based on the orientation. When `Vertical`, you can think of this property as "Maximum Rows." When `Horizontal`, you can think of this property as "Maximum Columns." When left as its default value of `-1`, wrapping happens automatically based on the space given to the panel.

→ **VerticalChildrenAlignment**—Can be set to Top (the default), Center, Bottom, or Stretch. This matters only if ItemHeight or RowSpan is set in such a way to give a child more space than its natural height.

 Why does `VariableSizedWrapGrid` **have such a verbose name, rather than something simple like** `WrapGrid`**?**

It's given the lengthy name because there already is a WrapGrid panel that has all the features of VariableSizedWrapGrid except for the RowSpan and ColumnSpan attached properties (the "variable sized" feature). It also has an extra feature that VariableSizedWrapGrid does not: *virtualization* support, which is a performance optimization for large numbers of items.

The reason that WrapGrid is not covered in this chapter is because it is permitted to be used only inside an items control, which is a topic in Chapter 9.

→ **HorizontalChildrenAlignment**—Can be set to Left (the default), Center, Right, or Stretch. This matters only if ItemWidth or ColumnSpan is set in such a way to give a child more space than its natural width.

•••

`VariableSizedWrapGrid` **and Right-to-Left Environments**

When FlowDirection is set to RightToLeft, wrapping occurs right to left for a VariableSizedWrapGrid with Vertical Orientation, and stacking occurs right to left for a VariableSizedWrapGrid with Horizontal Orientation.

Table 4.4 evaluates the way that some of the child layout properties apply to elements inside a VariableSizedWrapGrid.

TABLE 4.4   VariableSizedWrapGrid's Interaction with Child Layout Properties

Property	Usable Inside VariableSizedWrapGrid?
Margin	Yes. Margins are included when VariableSizedWrapGrid calculates the size of each item for determining default stack widths or heights.
HorizontalAlignment and VerticalAlignment	Partially. Alignment can be used in the opposite direction of stacking, just like with StackPanel. But alignment can also be useful in the direction of stacking when VariableSizedWrapGrid's ItemHeight or ItemWidth gives an element extra space to align within.

Handling Content Overflow

The built-in panels make their best effort to accommodate the size needs of their children. But sometimes they are forced to give children smaller space than they would like, and sometimes children refuse to render completely within that smaller space. For example, perhaps an element is marked with an explicit width that's wider than the containing panel. Or perhaps an element contains so many children that they can't all fit on the screen. In such cases, a content overflow problem exists.

You can deal with content overflow by using several different strategies:

→ Clipping

→ Scrolling

→ Scaling

→ Wrapping

→ Trimming

The first three strategies are examined in this section. You've already seen examples of wrapping with `VariableSizedWrapGrid`. Trimming refers to a more intelligent form of clipping, and it is supported only for text by `TextBlock` and `RichTextBlock`. They have a `TextTrimming` property that can be set to `None` (the default) or `WordEllipsis`. With the latter value, text gets trimmed with ellipses (…) at word boundaries rather than being truncated at an arbitrary place.

Clipping

Clipping (that is, truncating or cropping) children is the default way that panels handle them when they are too large. Clipping can happen at the edges of a panel or within a panel (such as at the edges of a `Grid` cell). This behavior can be controlled to some degree, however.

The following 2x2 `Grid` contains two `TextBlocks`. The top one gets clipped by the right edge of its cell, but the bottom one does not. That's because a `Canvas` ignores any size constraints that its parent tries to impose. Furthermore, a `Canvas` never clips its children. Figure 4.9 shows what this XAML looks like in the Visual Studio designer:

```
<Page …>
  <Grid Width="200" Height="200"
      Background="{StaticResource ApplicationPageBackgroundBrush}">
    <Grid.RowDefinitions>
      <RowDefinition/>
      <RowDefinition/>
    </Grid.RowDefinitions>
    <Grid.ColumnDefinitions>
      <ColumnDefinition/>
      <ColumnDefinition/>
```

```
    </Grid.ColumnDefinitions>
    <!-- Top TextBlock -->
    <TextBlock Grid.Row="0">This text doesn't fit in the cell.</TextBlock>
    <!-- Bottom TextBlock -->
    <Canvas Grid.Row="1">
      <TextBlock>This text doesn't fit in the cell.</TextBlock>
    </Canvas>
  </Grid>
</Page>
```

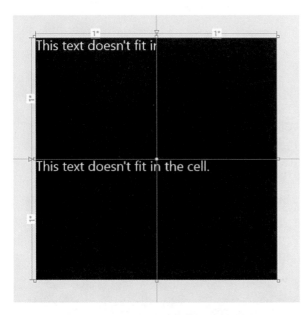

FIGURE 4.9   Placing the bottom `TextBlock` in a `Canvas` avoids the clipping done by the `Grid` cell.

 Although `Canvas` can be used as an intermediate element to prevent clipping in other panels, increasing an element's `RowSpan` and/or `ColumnSpan` is usually the best way to enable it to "bleed" into adjacent cells when trying to prevent clipping in a `Grid`.

> **! Clipping occurs before** RenderTransforms **are applied!**
>
> When enlarging an element with ScaleTransform as a RenderTransform, the element can easily surpass the bounds of the parent panel yet doesn't get clipped (unless it reaches the edge of the page). *Shrinking* an element with ScaleTransform as a RenderTransform is more subtle. If the unscaled element would have been clipped because it exceeds its parent's bounds, the scaled element is still clipped exactly the same way, even if the entire element can fit! That's because clipping is part of the layout process and already determined by the time RenderTransform is applied. Figure 4.10 demonstrates this by applying a ScaleTransform to the top TextBlock with a ScaleX value of .7.

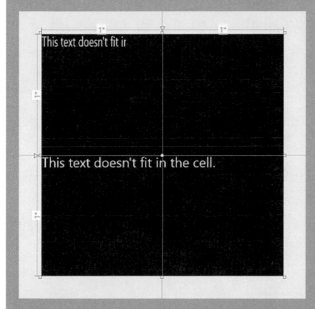

FIGURE 4.10   Even when a transform squishes the top text, it is still clipped as if no transform has been applied.

Scrolling

For most apps, the ability to scroll through content that is too large to view all at once is critical. The XAML UI Framework makes this easy because all you need to do is wrap an element in a ScrollViewer control, and the element instantly becomes scrollable. ScrollViewer makes use of ScrollBar controls and hooks them up to your content automatically.

ScrollViewer has a Content property that can be set to a single item, typically an entire panel. Because Content is ScrollViewer's content property in the XAML sense, you can place the item requiring scrolling as its child element. Here's an example:

```
<Page …>
  <ScrollViewer>
    <StackPanel>
```

```
        …
    </StackPanel>
    </ScrollViewer>
</Page>
```

Figure 4.11 shows the Page containing the simple StackPanel, with and without a ScrollViewer.

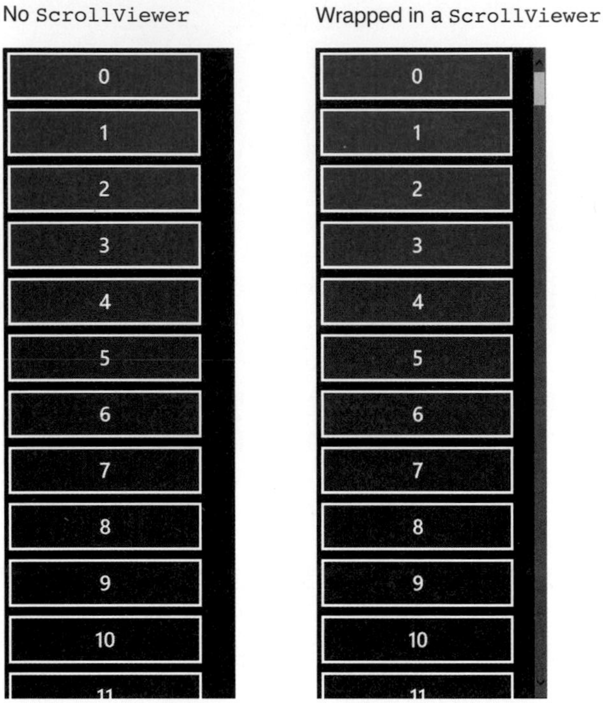

No ScrollViewer   Wrapped in a ScrollViewer

FIGURE 4.11   ScrollViewer enables scrolling of an element that is larger than the space given to it.

The ScrollBar controls act like standard scrollbars. They appear only when the app has focus and the mouse pointer moves over the app. They respond to a variety of input, such as arrow keys for fine-grained scrolling, Page Up and Page Down for coarser scrolling, and Ctrl+Home or Ctrl+End to jump to the beginning or end, respectively, when the ScrollViewer has keyboard focus. Touch manipulation also works as expected on the entire scrollable area when running on a device that supports it.

Customizing ScrollViewer

Scrolling is vertical-only by default, which is a poor choice for Windows Store apps because they typically scroll in a horizontal direction instead. If the StackPanel in Figure 4.11 were marked with a Horizontal Orientation instead, you would see only the left-most part of it, but there would still be a vertical-only scrollbar that had no effect (because all the content fits on the screen in the vertical dimension).

Fortunately, ScrollViewer exposes several properties and methods for customizing its scrolling. Its two most important properties are VerticalScrollBarVisibility and HorizontalScrollBarVisibility. Both of these properties are of type ScrollBarVisibility, an enumeration that defines four distinct states specific to its two scrollbars:

→ **Visible**—The scrollbar is always visible in the appropriate contexts (for example, when an app has focus and a mouse pointer moves over it), regardless of whether it's needed. When it's not needed, it has a disabled look and doesn't respond to input. (But this is different from the ScrollBarVisibility value called Disabled.)

→ **Auto**—The scrollbar is visible if the content is big enough to require scrolling in that dimension. Otherwise, the scrollbar is never visible.

→ **Hidden**—The scrollbar is always invisible but still logically exists, in that scrolling can still be done with touch and with arrow keys. Therefore, the content is still given all the length it wants in that dimension. This mode should be avoided because the scrollable behavior isn't obvious without the scrollbar.

→ **Disabled**—The scrollbar is not only invisible but it doesn't exist, so scrolling is not possible via any input method. In this case, the content is given only the length of its parent rather than all the length it wants.

The default value for VerticalScrollBarVisibility is Visible, and the default value for HorizontalScrollBarVisibility is Disabled.

Depending on the content inside ScrollViewer, the subtle difference between Hidden and Disabled can be not so subtle. For example, Figure 4.12 shows two different Pages containing a ScrollViewer with the same VariableSizedWrapGrid. The only difference is that in one Page the ScrollViewer has VerticalScrollBarVisibility set to Disabled, and in the other page the ScrollViewer has it set to Hidden. (In both cases, HorizontalScrollBarVisibility is set to Visible.)

In the Hidden case, the panel is given as much height as it desires (the same as if VerticalScrollBarVisibility were set to Visible or Auto), so it makes use of it and arranges all children on the same column. In this arrangement, the visible horizontal scrollbar is useless because no scrolling can be done in that direction. However, vertical scrolling can be done with touch or a keyboard, even though no vertical scrollbar is visible.

In the Disabled case, the VariableSizedWrapGrid is given only the height of the Page, so wrapping occurs as if no ScrollViewer existed. In this case, the horizontal scrollbar works as expected.

`VerticalScrollBarVisibility=Hidden, HorizontalScrollBarVisibility=Visible`

`VerticalScrollBarVisibility=Disabled, HorizontalScrollBarVisibility=Visible`

0	15	30	45	60	75	90	105	120	135	150	1
1	16	31	46	61	76	91	106	121	136	151	1
2	17	32	47	62	77	92	107	122	137	152	1
3	18	33	48	63	78	93	108	123	138	153	1
4	19	34	49	64	79	94	109	124	139	154	1
5	20	35	50	65	80	95	110	125	140	155	1
6	21	36	51	66	81	96	111	126	141	156	1
7	22	37	52	67	82	97	112	127	142	157	1
8	23	38	53	68	83	98	113	128	143	158	1
9	24	39	54	69	84	99	114	129	144	159	1
10	25	40	55	70	85	100	115	130	145	160	1
11	26	41	56	71	86	101	116	131	146	161	1
12	27	42	57	72	87	102	117	132	147	162	1
13	28	43	58	73	88	103	118	133	148	163	1
14	29	44	59	74	89	104	119	134	149	164	1

FIGURE 4.12   Although the vertical scrollbar is invisible in both cases, the different values for `VerticalScrollBarVisibility` drastically alter the layout of the `VariableSizedWrapGrid`.

(?) How can I trigger code to execute when a scrollbar appears or disappears?

Because even a "visible" scrollbar is sometimes not visible on the screen, `ScrollViewer` defines a separate pair of visibility properties—`ComputedHorizontalScrollBarVisibility` and `ComputedVerticalScrollBarVisibility`—that reveal the *actual* visibility at any point in time. The next chapter explains how you can write event handlers to detect when the values of properties such as these change.

`ScrollViewer` contains methods for programmatically scrolling to a specific horizontal or vertical offset, as well as many properties that reveal the size of *extent* (all inner content), the size of the *viewport* (the viewable region), and the size of the remaining scrollable area (the difference between the extent and the viewport). In addition, it has some properties that warrant an explanation:

→ **HorizontalScrollMode** and **VerticalScrollMode** can be set to Disabled to prevent the default *overscroll effect*: content temporarily pushed past the end when scrolling via touch. When set to Auto, scrolling is considered to be on "rails." This means that if you move your finger or mouse pointer in an *almost* horizontal or *almost* vertical motion, the scrolling snaps to one dimension as if you're moving perfectly horizontal or perfectly vertical.

→ **IsHorizontalScrollChainingEnabled** and **IsVerticalScrollChainingEnabled** are Boolean properties that enable a scrolling action to be transferred from a child element to its parent once the child scrolling has reached the end.

→ **IsScrollInertiaEnabled** can be set to false to disable the additional scrolling that happens based on the acceleration when scrolling is done via touch.

The remaining properties exist to support *snap points*.

Snap Points

Snap points are "magnetic" spots that enable items in an otherwise freely scrollable region to snap into place. This technique is commonly used on phones or tablets to enable swiping through something like a series of photos while ensuring that a single photo is entirely visible after the swipe. The Windows 8 Photos app behaves this way (after tapping on a photo to make it fill the screen), although it does this with a more sophisticated control built on top of ScrollViewer: FlipView, discussed in Chapter 9.

If you want to enable snap points with only one item visible on the screen at a time, then FlipView is a much better choice. But if you want to enable them while viewing multiple items on the screen at the same time, then you can use ScrollViewer with its HorizontalSnapPointsType and/or VerticalSnapPointsType properties set appropriately. HorizontalSnapPointsType and VerticalSnapPointsType can be independently set to one of the following values from SnapPointsType enumeration:

→ **None**—Snapping is disabled.

→ **MandatorySingle**—The ScrollViewer always snaps to the next snap point when scrolling completes, regardless of how much inertia there is.

→ **Mandatory**—The ScrollViewer always snaps to a snap point when scrolling completes, but it might scroll past several snap points depending on how much inertia there is.

→ **OptionalSingle**—Like MandatorySingle, but the user can also position the ScrollViewer at an arbitrary spot by carefully dragging it (without flicking).

→ **Optional**—Like Mandatory, but the user can also position the ScrollViewer at an arbitrary spot by carefully dragging it (without flicking). This is the default value.

The following XAML enables snapping to the `Rectangle` boundaries inside the `StackPanel`:

```
<ScrollViewer HorizontalScrollBarVisibility="Visible"
              HorizontalSnapPointsType="Mandatory">
  <StackPanel Orientation="Horizontal">
    <Rectangle Fill="Red" Height="200" Width="200"/>
    <Rectangle Fill="Red" Height="200" Width="200"/>
    …
  </StackPanel>
</ScrollViewer>
```

Support for this snapping behavior is built directly into panels such as `StackPanel`. Note that there's no requirement that the items all have the same size. By default, horizontal snapping is done with the left edge of the app and the left edge of the closest item. Vertical snapping is done with the top edge of the app and the top edge of the closest item. This can be customized, however, by setting `ScrollViewer`'s `HorizontalSnapPointsAlignment` and/or `VerticalSnapPointsAlignment` properties to one of the following values:

→ **Near**—The default behavior. Left-edge snapping for horizontal scrolling and top-edge snapping for vertical scrolling.

→ **Far**—The opposite of near. Right-edge snapping (the right edge of the app and the right edge of the closest item) for horizontal scrolling and bottom-edge snapping (the bottom edge of the app and the bottom edge of the closest item) for vertical scrolling.

→ **Center**—Snaps the center of the app with the center of the closest item.

 **Snap points affect only touch manipulation!**

When a snap-point-enabled `ScrollViewer` is scrolled via mouse or keyboard, the snap points have no effect. This limitation might be removed in a future version of Windows.

Scaling

Although scrolling is a popular and long-standing way to deal with large content, dynamically shrinking or enlarging content to "just fit" in a given space is more appropriate for several scenarios. For example, it doesn't make sense for most games to change the shape of their game surface. Whether the game board or playing field must maintain a specific aspect ratio, or you want to avoid giving widescreen players an unfair advantage by seeing more of the scrolling world ahead, the typical approach is to scale up the game surface as much as possible and use letterboxing to fill any extra space (or perhaps show extra UI elements like game stats). If your app uses vector graphics, then you can scale to your heart's content. If it uses bitmaps, as many games do, then you might have to place an upper limit on any scaling done, and/or provide multiple sizes of the bitmap assets.

The XAML UI Framework makes scaling extremely easy, in more ways than the transforms seen in the preceding chapter. An element called Viewbox can be used to automatically scale content in a few different ways. And the ScrollViewer we just examined also has support for interactive zooming.

Viewbox

ScaleTransform can scale elements *relative to their own size,* but it doesn't provide a mechanism to scale elements *relative to the available space* without writing some custom code. Fortunately, the Viewbox element provides an easy mechanism to scale arbitrary content within a given space.

Viewbox, like ScrollViewer, can have only one child element. By default, Viewbox stretches in both dimensions to fill the space given to it. But it also has Stretch property to control how its single child gets scaled within its bounds. The property is a Stretch enumeration, which has the following values:

→ **None**—No scaling is done. This is the same as not using Viewbox at all.

→ **Fill**—The child's dimensions are set to equal the Viewbox's dimensions. Therefore, the child's aspect ratio is not necessarily preserved.

→ **Uniform**—The child is scaled as large as it can be while still fitting entirely within the Viewbox and preserving its aspect ratio. Therefore, there will be extra space in one dimension if its aspect ratio doesn't match. This is the default value.

→ **UniformToFill**—The child is scaled to entirely fill the Viewbox while preserving its aspect ratio. Therefore, the content will be cropped in one dimension if its aspect ratio doesn't match.

These options are demonstrated in Figure 4.13 using some XAML-based clipart created by the amazing Daniel Cook from lostgarden.com. This is not an image, but rather many vector shapes that scale without degradation.

A second property of Viewbox controls whether you want to use it only to shrink content or enlarge content (as opposed to doing either). This property is called StretchDirection, and it is a StretchDirection enumeration with the following values:

→ **UpOnly**—Enlarges the content, if appropriate. If the content is already too big, Viewbox leaves the current content size as is.

→ **DownOnly**—Shrinks the content, if appropriate. If the content is already small enough, Viewbox leaves the current content size as is.

→ **Both**—Enlarges or shrinks the content, whichever is needed to get the stretching described earlier. This is the default value.

It's amazing how easy it is to choose between a scrolling strategy and a scaling strategy for dealing with large content. Just wrap the same content in either a `ScrollViewer` or `Viewbox`!

Stretch=None

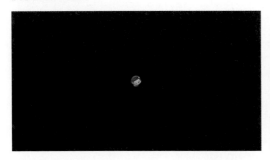

Stretch=Fill

Stretch=Uniform

Stretch=UniformToFill

FIGURE 4.13   Each of the four values for `Viewbox`'s `Stretch` property changes the girl's layout.

> ! Viewbox **removes all wrapping!**
>
> Viewbox is handy for many situations, but it's not a good choice for content you'd normally like to wrap. That's because the content is given as much space as it needs in both directions before it is potentially scaled. Figure 4.14 demonstrates this by using the VariableSizedWrapGrid with ten Buttons from Figure 4.7, but wrapping it in a Viewbox.
>
>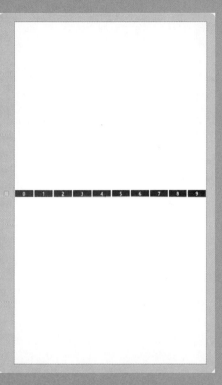

FIGURE 4.14   The VariableSizedWrapGrid used in Figure 4.7 has no need to wrap when placed in a Viewbox.

No matter the view state or orientation, the result is a single line of content that could potentially be much smaller than you would have liked. Giving Viewbox a StretchDirection of UpOnly rather than the default of Both doesn't help either. The layout of Viewbox's content happens before any potential scaling. Therefore, UpOnly prevents the Buttons from shrinking, but they are still arranged in a single line, as shown in Figure 4.15.

FIGURE 4.15   Giving the `Viewbox` from Figure 4.14 a `StretchDirection="UpOnly"` prevents the `Buttons` from shrinking but doesn't affect the inner `VariableSizedWrapGrid's` layout.

The result of this is similar to the use of `VerticalScrollBarVisibility="Hidden"` in Figure 4.12, except that there's no way to scroll to the remaining content in this case, even with the keyboard.

Interactive Zooming with `ScrollViewer`

`ScrollViewer` can do another trick besides scrolling: By default, it enables pinch-to-zoom touch gestures on its content. If you don't want this behavior, you can set its `ZoomMode` property to `Disabled` rather than its default value of `Enabled`.

If you want to customize how far the content can be zoomed in or out, then set `ScrollViewer`'s `MinZoomFactor` and `MaxZoomFactor` properties, which have default values of .1 and 10, respectively. ScrollViewer also exposes zoom-specific customizations that work just like the similarly named properties for customizing scrolling: `IsZoomChainingEnabled`, `IsZoomInertiaEnabled`, and `ZoomSnapPointsType`.

You can programmatically retrieve the current zoom factor with the read-only `ZoomFactor` property, and you can add zoom snap points to the `ZoomSnapPoints` property.

Summary

With all the features described in this chapter and the preceding chapter, you can control layout in many interesting ways. This isn't like the old days, where your only options were pretty much just choosing a size and choosing an (X,Y) point on the screen. This chapter covered all the built-in panels that you would use directly in a page, but there are some additional ones that are meant for more limited contexts. WrapGrid and CarouselPanel are described in Chapter 9.

The built-in panels—notably Grid—are a key part of enabling rapid development of apps that can be tailored to screens of all shapes and sizes. But one of the most powerful aspects of XAML layout is that parent panels can themselves be children of other panels. Although each panel was examined in isolation in this chapter, panels can be nested to provide impressive versatility. As you'll see in Chapter 9, controls such as ListBox use such panels to arrange their own items, and you can swap in arbitrary other panels to radically change their appearance without losing all their behaviors.

Chapter 5

INTERACTIVITY

Now that you know how to arrange your app's user interface, it's time to make it interactive. This chapter covers a few pieces of important plumbing in the XAML UI Framework—dependency properties, routed events, and commands. Much like the relationship between the two preceding chapters, this chapter provides the foundation for the input events discussed in the next chapter.

The topics in this chapter are some of the main culprits responsible for the framework's steep learning curve. Becoming familiar with these concepts now enables you to approach the rest of this book (or any other documentation) with confidence. Dependency properties and routed events are at the core of the entire design of the XAML UI Framework.

Dependency Properties

Classes in the XAML UI Framework expose several properties, because properties are easy to set in XAML. Many of these properties are a special kind called a *dependency property* that enable styling, automatic data binding, animation, and more. You might first meet this concept with skepticism, because it complicates the picture of types having simple fields, properties, methods, and events. But when you understand the problems that dependency properties solve, you will learn to like them.

A dependency property *depends* on multiple providers for determining its value at any point in time. These providers could be an animation continuously changing its value, a parent element whose property value propagates down to its children, and so on. Arguably the biggest feature of a dependency property is its built-in ability to provide change notification.

The motivation for adding such intelligence to properties is to enable rich functionality directly from declarative markup. Because the key to a class's declarative-friendly design is heavy use of properties, Button, for example, has 70 public instance properties (61 of which are inherited from Control and its base classes)! Properties can be easily set in XAML—directly or by using a design tool—without any procedural code. Without the extra plumbing in dependency properties, however, it would be hard for the simple action of setting properties to get the desired results without the need to write additional code.

In this section, we briefly look at the implementation of a dependency property to make this discussion more concrete, and then we dig deeper into some of the ways that dependency properties add value on top of plain properties:

→ Change notification

→ Property value inheritance

→ Support for multiple providers

Understanding most of the nuances of dependency properties is usually important only for custom control authors. However, all developers need to be aware of what dependency properties are and how they work. For example, you can only style and animate dependency properties. After working with XAML for a while, you might find yourself wishing that *all* properties would be dependency properties!

A Dependency Property Implementation

In practice, dependency properties are just normal properties hooked into some extra infrastructure. This is all accomplished via APIs in the XAML UI Framework; no programming languages (other than XAML) have an intrinsic understanding of a dependency property.

Listing 5.1 demonstrates how ButtonBase, the base class of Button, effectively implements one of its dependency properties called IsPressed.

LISTING 5.1   A Standard Dependency Property Implementation

```
public class ButtonBase : ContentControl
{
  // The dependency property
  public static readonly DependencyProperty IsPressedProperty =
    DependencyProperty.Register("IsPressed", typeof(bool), typeof(ButtonBase),
      new PropertyMetadata(false, OnIsPressedChanged));

  // A .NET property wrapper (optional)
```

```
public bool IsPressed
{
  get { return (bool)GetValue(ButtonBase.IsPressedProperty); }
  set { SetValue(ButtonBase.IsPressedProperty, value); }
}

// A property changed callback (optional)
static void OnIsPressedChanged(
  DependencyObject o, DependencyPropertyChangedEventArgs e) { … }
  …
}
```

The static `IsPressedProperty` field is the actual dependency property, represented by the `DependencyProperty` class. By convention, all `DependencyProperty` fields are public, static, and have a `Property` suffix. Several pieces of infrastructure require that you follow this convention: localization tools, XAML loading, and more. This is why the MSDN documentation for so many classes in the XAML UI Framework lists all the annoying *XXX*`Property` members with boilerplate descriptions!

Dependency properties are usually created by calling the static `DependencyProperty.Register` method, which requires a name (`IsPressed`), a property type (`bool`), and the type of the class claiming to own the property (`ButtonBase`). Optionally (via different overloads of `Register`), you can pass callbacks for handling property value changes and/or setting its initial value. `ButtonBase` calls an overload of `Register` to give the dependency property a default value of `false` and to attach a delegate for change notifications.

Finally, the traditional .NET property called `IsPressed` implements its accessors by calling `GetValue` and `SetValue` methods inherited from `DependencyObject`, the low-level base class from which all classes with dependency properties must derive. `GetValue` returns the last value passed to `SetValue` or, if `SetValue` has never been called, the default value registered with the property. The `IsPressed` .NET property (sometimes called a *property wrapper* in this context) is not strictly necessary; consumers of `ButtonBase` (or a derived class like `Button`) could directly call the `GetValue`/`SetValue` methods because they are exposed publicly. But the .NET property makes programmatic reading and writing of the property much more natural for consumers, and it enables the property to be set via XAML.

 Visual Studio has a snippet called `propdp` that automatically expands into a definition of a dependency property, which makes defining one much faster than doing all the typing yourself!

On the surface, Listing 5.1 looks like an overly verbose way of representing a simple Boolean property. However, because `GetValue` and `SetValue` internally use an efficient sparse storage system and because `IsPressedProperty` is a static field (rather than an instance field), the dependency property implementation saves per-instance memory compared to a typical property. If all the properties on XAML-based controls were wrappers around instance fields (as most properties are), they would consume a significant amount of memory because of all the local data attached to each instance. Having 70 fields for each `Button`, not to mention the fields for all the other controls, would add up quickly! Instead, almost all of `Button`'s public properties are dependency properties.

 Property wrappers are bypassed at runtime when setting dependency properties in XAML!

Although the XAML compiler depends on the property wrapper at compile time, at runtime, the underlying `GetValue` and `SetValue` methods are called directly! Therefore, to maintain parity between setting a property in XAML and in C#, it's crucial that property wrappers not contain any logic in addition to the `GetValue`/`SetValue` calls. If you want to add custom logic, that's what the registered callbacks are for. All built-in property wrappers abide by this rule, so this warning is for anyone writing a custom class with its own dependency properties.

The benefits of the dependency property implementation extend to more than just memory usage, however. The implementation centralizes and standardizes a fair amount of code and enables the three features listed earlier that we now examine one-by-one.

Change Notification

Change notification is mostly leveraged internally by the system (for features such as animation). Whenever the value of a dependency property changes, a number of actions are automatically triggered. In Listing 5.1, `OnIsPressedChanged` gets called automatically whenever anyone changes the value of `IsPressed`.

Property Value Inheritance

The term *property value inheritance* (or *property inheritance* for short) doesn't refer to traditional object-oriented class-based inheritance but rather the flowing of property values down the tree of elements. An example of this can be seen with the following XAML:

```
<Page …
    FontSize="200" FontStyle="Italic" FontWeight="Bold" Foreground="Red">
    <StackPanel>
        <TextBlock>Guess my appearance!</TextBlock>
        <TextBlock FontSize="40">Guess my appearance!</TextBlock>
        <CheckBox>Guess my appearance!</CheckBox>
        <Button>Guess my appearance!</Button>
    </StackPanel>
</Page>
```

This sets four text-related properties on the root page that are meant to be inherited by the text in the TextBlock, CheckBox, and Button descendants. For the most part, these settings flow all the way down the tree and are inherited by these elements. The second TextBlock's FontSize does not change because it is explicitly marked with a FontSize of 40, overriding the inherited value of 200. The inherited FontStyle setting of Italic, on the other hand, affects all four elements because none of them have this set explicitly.

Still, it's hard to guess the resultant appearance of all four elements in this situation. Figure 5.1 shows the result.

FIGURE 5.1 The four text-related property values set on the root Page aren't consistently inherited by its elements.

The first TextBlock successfully inherits all four property values, and the second one inherits all three that aren't locally set with a different value. However, the CheckBox inherits only Bold and Italic, and the Button inherits only Italic! What's going on? The behavior of property value inheritance can be subtle in cases like this for two reasons:

→ Not every dependency property participates in property value inheritance

→ Other higher-priority sources might set the property value, as explained in the next section.

In this case, the latter reason is to blame. A few controls, such as Button and CheckBox, internally set some of their font properties to match current system settings. The result can be especially confusing because such controls end up "swallowing" any inheritance from proceeding further down the element tree. For example, if you add a TextBlock as an explicit child of the CheckBox or Button, its FontSize and Foreground properties would be set to their default values (giving the exact same result as seen in Figure 5.1), unlike the other TextBlocks.

Support for Multiple Providers

Many powerful mechanisms independently attempt to set the value of dependency properties. Without a well-defined mechanism for handling these disparate property value providers, the system would be a bit chaotic, and property values could be unstable. Of course, as their name indicates, dependency properties were designed to depend on these providers in a consistent and orderly manner.

The following list reveals the property value providers that can set the value of most dependency properties, in order from highest to lowest precedence:

1. Active animations

2. Local value

3. Template properties

4. Style setters

5. Property value inheritance

6. Default value

You've already seen some of the property value providers, such as property value inheritance (#5). *Local value* (#2) technically means any call to `DependencyObject.SetValue`, but this is typically seen with a simple property assignment in XAML or C# (because of the way dependency properties are implemented, as shown previously with `ButtonBase.IsPressed`). *Default value* (#6) refers to the initial value registered with the dependency property, which naturally has the lowest precedence.

If one or more animations are running, they have the power to alter the current property value or completely replace it. Therefore, animations (the topic of Chapter 15, "Animation") can trump all other property value providers—even local values! This is often a stumbling block for people who are new to XAML. The other providers, which involve styles and templates, are explained further in Chapter 16, "Styles, Templates, and Visual States."

This order of precedence explains why some of `CheckBox`'s and `Button`'s property values were not impacted by property value inheritance in Figure 5.1. The setting of these two controls' font properties to match system settings is done via style setters (#4). Although this has precedence over property value inheritance (#5), you can still override these font settings using any mechanism with a higher precedence, such as setting local values on `CheckBox` and/or `Button`.

> ### Clearing a Local Value
>
> If you ever want to clear a locally set property value and let the system set the value from the relevant provider with the next highest precedence, explicitly setting the property to its default value isn't good enough. It's still a local value that overrides everything else. Instead, you must use DependencyObject's ClearValue method. This can be called on a TextBlock tb as follows in C#:
>
> ```
> tb.ClearValue(TextBlock.FontSizeProperty);
> ```
>
> (TextBlock.FontSizeProperty is the static DependencyProperty field.) After calling ClearValue, the local value is removed from the equation when the base value is recalculated.

Attached Properties

The preceding chapter introduced attached properties. Attached properties are a special form of dependency properties, so this section looks at how to implement one. It turns out that it's quite simple.

Recall that setting Canvas.Left on an element in XAML is equivalent to calling Canvas's static SetLeft method. Internally, methods such as SetLeft simply call the same DependencyObject.SetValue method that a normal dependency property accessor calls, but on the passed-in element (that derives from DependencyObject):

```
public static void SetLeft(UIElement element, double value)
{
  element.SetValue(Canvas.LeftProperty, value);
}
```

Similarly, attached properties also define a static Get*XXX* method (where *XXX* is the name of the property) that calls the familiar DependencyObject.GetValue method:

```
public static double GetLeft(UIElement element)
{
  return (double)element.GetValue(Canvas.LeftProperty);
}
```

As with property wrappers for normal dependency properties, these Get*XXX* and Set*XXX* methods must not do anything other than make a call to GetValue and SetValue.

The attached property field, Canvas. LeftProperty in this example, must be registered with DependencyProperty. Register**Attached** instead of DependencyProperty.Register.

 Just like with propdp, Visual Studio has a snippet called propa that automatically expands into a definition of an attached property.

Attached Properties as an Extensibility Mechanism   ...

Similar to previous Microsoft frameworks, `FrameworkElement` defines a `Tag` property (of type `System.Object`) that enables you to store arbitrary custom data in any element. But attached properties are a more powerful and flexible mechanism for attaching custom data to any object deriving from `DependencyObject`. It's often overlooked that attached properties even enable you to effectively add custom data to instances of sealed classes!

A further twist to the story of attached properties is that although setting them in XAML relies on the presence of the static Set*XXX* method, you can bypass this method in C# and call `DependencyObject.SetValue` directly. This means that you can use *any* dependency property as an attached property in procedural code. For example, the following code attaches `Viewbox`'s `StretchDirection` property to a `Button` and assigns it a value of UpOnly:

```
// Attach an unrelated property to a Button and set its value:
button.SetValue(Viewbox.StretchDirectionProperty, StretchDirection.UpOnly);
```

Although this seems nonsensical, and it certainly doesn't magically enable new stretching functionality on this `Button`, you have the freedom to consume this property value in a way that makes sense to your app.

There are more realistic ways to extend elements in this manner. `FrameworkElement`'s `Tag` property is a dependency property, so you can attach it to an instance of any `DependencyObject` that doesn't already have its own `Tag` property. For example, `PlaneProjection` is a sealed class without a `Tag` property (because it is not a `FrameworkElement`). Yet the following code attaches custom data to a `PlaneProjection` instance:

```
PlaneProjection projection = new PlaneProjection();
projection.SetValue(FrameworkElement.TagProperty, "my custom data");
```

This is just one of the ways to achieve extensibility without the need for traditional inheritance.

Routed Events

Just as the XAML UI Framework's dependency properties add infrastructure and features on top of the simple notion of properties, *routed events* add infrastructure and features on top of the simple notion of events. Routed events are events that are designed to work well with a tree of elements.

XAML is natural for representing a user interface because of its hierarchical nature. But regardless of whether elements in a user interface are expressed in XAML or C#, they form a tree based on their parent/child relationships.

When a routed event is raised by an element, it travels up the element tree to the root, getting raised on each element in a simple and consistent fashion, without the need for any custom code. This process is known as *event bubbling*. In fact, you can think of the term "routed event" as a fancy way of saying "bubbling event." When routed events were introduced in WPF, you could choose one of three routing strategies: bubbling, tunneling (travel downward), or direct. In Windows Store apps, there is no choice, so the "routed" name is mostly a historical artifact.

Event bubbling helps most applications remain oblivious to details of the visual tree (which is good for restyling) and is crucial to successful element composition. For example, consider the media-player-style Stop Button in Chapter 2, "Mastering XAML." A user might tap directly on the Rectangle inside the Button, but the event bubbles up to the Button, enabling it to react appropriately. (Yet if you want to detect taps directly on the Rectangle for some reason, you have the freedom to do so as well.) Without routed events, producers of the inner content or consumers of the Button would have to write code to patch everything together.

The Visual Tree

Different elements publicly expose their child(ren) in different ways, such as a Content versus Child versus Children property, but internally they all use the same protected members on UIElement to inform the system of the formal relationship. This formal element tree is also some-times referred to as the *visual tree*. It usually contains intermediate elements that aren't explicitly constructed in your XAML or C#, but are an artifact of an element's current visual template (discussed in Chapter 16).

You can see this for yourself by inspecting the visual tree with a VisualTreeHelper class that exposes static GetChildCount, GetChild, and GetParent methods. The following recursive method prints a simple representation of a visual tree to the debugger's output window:

```csharp
static void PrintVisualTree(int depth, DependencyObject obj)
{
  // Print the object with preceding spaces that represent its depth
  Debug.WriteLine(new string(' ', depth) + obj);

  // Recursive call for each child
  for (int i = 0; i < VisualTreeHelper.GetChildrenCount(obj); i++)
    PrintVisualTree(depth + 1, VisualTreeHelper.GetChild(obj, i));
}
```

Imagine that you have the following trivial MainPage.xaml:

```xml
<Page x:Class="Chapter5.MainPage" …>
  <Viewbox>
    <Button>Tap me</Button>
  </Viewbox>
</Page>
```

Calling PrintVisualTree(0, this) in MainPage's code-behind file (which must be done *after* layout has occurred at least once, such as in a handler for MainPage's Loaded event) produces the following output:

```
Chapter5.MainPage
 Windows.UI.Xaml.Controls.Viewbox
  Windows.UI.Xaml.Controls.Border
   Windows.UI.Xaml.Controls.Button
    Windows.UI.Xaml.Controls.Grid
```

```
Windows.UI.Xaml.Controls.Border
 Windows.UI.Xaml.Controls.ContentPresenter
  Windows.UI.Xaml.Controls.Grid
   Windows.UI.Xaml.Controls.TextBlock
 Windows.UI.Xaml.Shapes.Rectangle
 Windows.UI.Xaml.Shapes.Rectangle
```

Because they enable you to peer inside the deep composition of elements, visual trees can be surprisingly complex. The `Border` element wrapping the `Button` is a "visual implementation detail" of `Viewbox`, and the elements inside `Button` are its own visual implementation details. Notice that `Button` internally uses two `Grid`s to arrange its content! The deepest child, the `TextBlock`, is what renders the "Tap me" string inside the `Button`.

Fortunately, although visual trees are an essential piece of infrastructure, you often don't need to worry about them unless you're radically restyling controls. Code such as `PrintVisualTree` should be used only for experimentation, or if you're writing some sort of visual tree inspection tool. That's because depending on a specific visual tree at runtime breaks one of the framework's core tenets—the separation of look and logic. When someone restyles a control such as `Viewbox` or `Button` using the techniques described in Chapter 16, the contents of the visual tree can radically change. You should not write code that would fail in such a condition.

A Routed Event in Action

Routed events have several similarities with dependency properties. Just as dependency properties are represented as public static `DependencyProperty` fields with a conventional `Property` suffix, routed events are represented as public static `RoutedEvent` fields with a conventional `Event` suffix. A routed event is registered somewhat like a dependency property, and a corresponding normal event—or *event wrapper*—is defined to enable more familiar use from C# and adding a handler in XAML with event attribute syntax. In most cases, routed events don't look very different from normal events. As with dependency properties, no programming languages (other than XAML) have an intrinsic understanding of the *routed* designation. The extra support is based on a handful of APIs.

Routed events have one important difference from dependency properties, however. You cannot define your own. In fact, the entire XAML UI Framework defines only 23 routed events—and they all live on `UIElement`! All these events are related to user input (touch, mouse, pen, or keyboard) and are covered in depth in the next chapter. Let's briefly look at one example now.

The `PointerReleased` routed event is raised when a press of a finger, mouse button, or pen is finished. (For the finger example, it means the finger has stopped making contact with the screen.) The XAML in Listing 5.2 handles this event on the root `Page` element.

LISTING 5.2 Leveraging Event Bubbling to Handle Events on the Root Page

```
<Page x:Class="Chapter5.MainPage" PointerReleased="MainPage_PointerReleased" …>
  <Grid Background="Blue">
    <Rectangle Fill="Red" Width="100" Height="100"/>
  </Grid>
</Page>
```

The `MainPage_PointerReleased` event handler referenced in Listing 5.2 is defined in a code-behind file:

```
void MainPage_PointerReleased(object sender, PointerRoutedEventArgs e)
{
  …
}
```

Regardless of where the finger, mouse pointer, or pen is when the event occurs (as long as it's somewhere over the `Page`), the `Page`-level handler gets called thanks to event bubbling. If the handler is attached on the `Rectangle` instead, then only releases directly on top of the `Rectangle` would cause the handler to be called. If the handler is attached on the `Rectangle` *and* the `Page`, then it would get called twice when the release happens on top of the `Rectangle`.

Handlers for all routed events have a signature matching the pattern for general .NET event handlers: The first parameter is a `System.Object` typically named `sender`, and the second parameter (typically named `e`) is a class that derives from `RoutedEventArgs`. The `sender` parameter passed to a handler is always the element to which the handler was attached. The `e` parameter is (or derives from) an instance of `RoutedEventArgs`, a subclass of `EventArgs` that exposes one property called `OriginalSource`. `OriginalSource` is the element that originally raised the event. Because of bubbling, the `sender` and `OriginalSource` can easily be different elements (although the `sender` would be an ancestor of `OriginalSource`). For Listing 5.2, the `sender` passed to `MainPage_PointerReleased` would always be the `Page`, but the `OriginalSource` would either be the `Grid` or the `Rectangle`.

Halting Bubbling

None of the routed events directly pass a `RoutedEventArgs` instance to its handlers, but rather a derived type such as the `PointerRoutedEventArgs` class seen in the preceding example. These classes add event-specific properties above and beyond the `OriginalSource` property, but they all share one extra property in common: `Handled`.

`Handled` is a Boolean property that is not meant to be inspected, but rather set. A handler can set it to `true` to mark the event as "handled," which halts the bubbling. In the code-behind file for Listing 5.2, if `MainPage_PointerReleased` set `e.Handled` to `true`, then it wouldn't end up being called multiple times even if the handler were attached to all three elements.

Several controls internally handle low-level routed events (preventing their bubbling) and take some alternate action. For example, Button (via its ButtonBase base class) handles PointerPressed, PointerReleased and KeyUp routed events (the latter only when the released key is Enter or the Spacebar), and then raises its own (non-routed) Click event. This is done to provide a single event for the logical action of clicking a Button, even if the "click" was done via a keyboard shortcut.

As a result, PointerPressed and PointerReleased (and sometimes KeyUp) get swallowed when such events originate from within a Button. If you add a Button to the Page in Listing 5.2 and then tap the Button, the MainPage_PointerReleased does *not* get called upon the release. Incidentally, if the goal is to detect taps anywhere on a Page, you should attach a handler to the routed Tapped event instead of PointerReleased because the latter gets raised at the end of basically any gesture (such as a swipe). And Button doesn't prevent the bubbling of the Tapped event.

• • •

Halting a Routed Event Is an Illusion

Although setting Handled to true in a routed event handler appears to stop the bubbling, individual handlers further up the tree can opt to receive the events anyway! This can be done only from procedural code, using an AddHandler method defined on UIElement.

AddHandler, and a companion RemoveHandler method, are analogous to DependencyObject's GetValue and SetValue methods. They are an alternate way to attach/detach event handlers to an element—for its routed events only.

AddHandler has three parameters: a RoutedEvent object that identifies the event (one of the static fields on UIElement with an Event suffix), the delegate for handling the event, and a Boolean handledEventsToo value. If you pass true for handledEventsToo, then the handler gets invoked regardless of anyone's attempt to halt bubbling.

For example, imagine that the code-behind file for Listing 5.2 leveraged this trick to attach the same event handler to the Page:

```
public MainPage()
{
  InitializeComponent();
  this.AddHandler(UIElement.PointerReleasedEvent,
    new PointerEventHandler(MainPage_PointerReleased), true);
}
```

If the page also contained a Button, this handler would now be notified about PointerReleased events occurring from within the Button because its internal handling of PointerReleased is ignored.

The use of AddHandler (and RemoveHandler) is interesting only for doing this handledEventsToo trick. Otherwise, you can just use the standard += and -= C# syntax for attaching/detaching event handlers, or attach the handlers in XAML.

> **Don't be fooled by events that claim to be routed events!**
>
> You might be surprised to read that the XAML UI Framework contains only 23 routed events, because *tons* of events in the framework use a `RoutedEventHandler` or similar delegate type that passes a `RoutedEventArgs` (or derived) instance to its event handlers. This is pervasive in controls, such as `Button`'s `Click` event, any items control's `SelectionChanged` event, and `TextBox`'s `TextChanged` event, to name a few. And nothing prevents you from defining your own .NET events that use the `RoutedEventHandler` delegate type. Yet none of these events (other than the 23 on `UIElement`) are actually routed events! For compatibility with Silverlight, the XAML UI Framework misrepresents many events in this manner. Silverlight had originally done this so the tools that targeted WPF (such as Visual Studio's designer and Blend) would automatically work with Silverlight, and so WPF code could be more easily ported to Silverlight. (In WPF, all these events are routed events, and third parties can define their own.) However, the result is confusing for anyone who understands what routed events are and tries to take advantage of their unique features! Just remember that if there is no corresponding static `RoutedEvent` field, then the event is not routed.
>
> By the way, this overuse of `RoutedEventArgs` is the reason that it doesn't define a `Handled` property despite the fact that halting the bubbling is a standard feature of routed events. Instead, the property is placed on every relevant `RoutedEventArgs`-derived class that is used by *real* routed events!

Commands

Although events are widely used in Windows Store apps, it's good to be aware of built-in support for *commands*, a more abstract and loosely coupled version of events. Whereas events are tied to details about specific user actions (such as a `Button` being clicked or a `ComboBoxItem` being selected), commands represent actions independent from their user interface exposure—a logical notion like `Open` or `Refresh`. An app might want to expose such actions through many mechanisms simultaneously: `Button`s in an `AppBar`, keyboard shortcuts, and so on.

You could handle the multiple exposures of the same commands with events fairly well. For example, you could define a generic `Refresh` event handler and attach each handler to the appropriate events on the relevant elements (the `Click` event on a `Button`, a `KeyDown` event that detects a specific keyboard shortcut, and so on). In addition, you'd probably want to enable and disable the appropriate controls whenever the `Refresh` action is invalid. This two-way communication gets a bit more cumbersome, especially if you don't want to hard-code a list of controls that need to be updated.

Commands are designed to make such scenarios easy. The support reduces the amount of code you need to write (and in some cases eliminates all procedural code), and it gives you more flexibility to change your user interface without breaking the underlying logic. They are a core part of the Model-View-ViewModel (MVVM) pattern, a popular pattern for structuring code in XAML-based projects. MVVM is focused on keeping a strong separation between the user interface (view), behaviors (view model), and underlying data (model). Following an MVVM architecture means avoiding—sometimes completely eliminating—code-behind files! Commands, along with data binding (discussed in Chapter 17, "Data Binding") make this possible.

This book doesn't delve into the MVVM pattern because there are entire books dedicated to the topic, but the following are good resources for learning more:

→ http://msdn.microsoft.com/en-us/magazine/dd419663.aspx (an article based on WPF)

→ http://jesseliberty.com/2010/05/08/mvvm-its-not-kool-aid-3 (a blog post based on Silverlight)

So what exactly is a command? It's any object implementing the ICommand interface from the System.Windows.Input namespace, whose name is an artifact left over from WPF and Silverlight. ICommand defines three simple members:

→ **Execute**—The method that executes the command-specific logic

→ **CanExecute**—A method that returns true if the command is enabled or false if it is disabled

→ **CanExecuteChanged**—An event that is raised whenever the value of CanExecute changes

If you want to create a Refresh command, you could define and implement a RefreshCommand class implementing ICommand, find a place to store it (perhaps as a static field on your App class), call Execute from relevant event handlers (when CanExecute returns true), and handle the CanExecuteChanged event to toggle the IsEnabled property on the relevant pieces of user interface. This doesn't sound much better than simply using events, however, unless you're devoted to following a pattern such as MVVM.

One thing that makes this more palatable is that all buttons (via ButtonBase) have a Command property that can be set to any ICommand (plus a CommandParameter property whose value gets passed to ICommand.Execute). When any button with a non-null Command is clicked, it automatically invokes the command's Execute method (when CanExecute returns true). In addition, such buttons automatically keep their value for IsEnabled synchronized with the value of CanExecute by leveraging the CanExecuteChanged event.

Although WPF and Silverlight expose several built-in command objects for common actions (such as Cut, Copy, and Paste), no such objects are included in the XAML UI Framework for Windows Store apps.

Summary

In this chapter, you learned about all the core plumbing that enables rich interactivity and the ways in which these mechanisms are optimized for hierarchical elements in a user interface. With multiple types of properties, multiple types of events, and surprisingly complex visual trees, the landscape isn't quite as simple as you might have expected. Hopefully you can now appreciate some of the value of these mechanisms. Throughout the rest of the book, these concepts generally fade into the background as we focus on accomplishing specific development tasks.

Chapter 6

HANDLING INPUT: TOUCH, MOUSE, PEN, AND KEYBOARD

When creating a Windows Store app, one particular task might sound daunting: You must make the app work well regardless of whether the user leverages a touchscreen, a mouse, a hardware keyboard, the software keyboard, or even a stylus (referred to as a *pen* in this chapter). No other platform has the same kind of expectations for its apps to the degree that Windows 8 does.

Fortunately, a lot of care went into making this task much easier than you might imagine. The following three-part strategy deals with the wide range of input devices:

→ As much as possible, leverage the interactions already built into the framework's controls. They are designed to work well with all input types and in a manner that's consistent with user expectations.

→ For custom interactions, Microsoft's guidance is to "code for touch, because you'll get the right behavior for mouse and pen for free." This chapter shows you how that can happen.

→ Consider creating optimized experiences for specific input devices if it makes sense for your app. For example, a productivity app should provide useful keyboard shortcuts, and a drawing app should leverage extra features that only a pen can provide.

The first part is the topic of Part III of this book, but the latter two are the focus of this chapter.

Touch Input

Windows Store apps can leverage a large number of events that enable any kind of touch interaction imaginable. (Note that the term *touch* includes touching with more than one finger simultaneously, which is sometimes called *multitouch*.) This rich functionality is exposed through UIElement, so it is pervasive as well as flexible. It's worth noting that because of the rich built-in behaviors of the built-in controls, certain types of

 How do I handle input from a game controller?

Windows 8 supports Xbox 360-compatible game controllers, although this is directly exposed to developers only via XInput, a C++ DirectX API. That's not a problem, however, because the nature of the Windows Runtime makes it straightforward to expose such functionality to a C# XAML app.

The Windows SDK sample at http://code.msdn.microsoft.com/windows-apps/XInput-and-JavaScript-c72fe535 wraps XInput in a simple C++ Windows Runtime component that can be consumed from C#. (The sample happens to show it used from JavaScript.)

apps don't ever need to directly interact directly with any of these events. Controls such as ScrollViewer, as seen in the preceding chapter, handle a number of touch events on your behalf and already do what you (and users) expect them to do.

Touch events can be separated into three categories:

→ **Pointers**—The lowest-level raw events

→ **Gestures**—Higher-level events for motions calculated from the pointer events

→ **Manipulations**—The highest-level events for complex gestures

As you'll see, all three categories are relevant for more types of input than just touch. Also note that although the touch digitizer is typically integrated into the screen, it can be part of an external device as well (such as the Microsoft Touch Mouse). This section occasionally uses the terms *screen* and *digitizer* interchangeably.

Pointers

Windows 8 introduces a new concept called a *pointer*. No, this isn't a C++-style pointer, it's an abstraction for three separate kinds of input: touch, mouse, and pen. This enables an app to use a single set of APIs for the things that touch, mouse, and pen have in common, which is quite a bit.

The pointer abstraction involves four main classes: PointerDevice, Pointer, PointerPoint, and PointerPointProperties. Figure 6.1 demonstrates their meaning and relationship. A single PC can (and often does) have multiple PointerDevices, each PointerDevice can support multiple Pointers (such as five fingers for touch), and each Pointer can generate a series of PointerPoints.

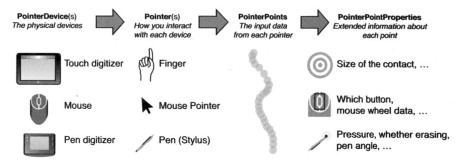

FIGURE 6.1   The four main pointer classes that consolidate interactions with touch, mouse, and pen input

PointerDevice

PointerDevice (in the Windows.Devices.Input namespace) exposes low-level properties that reveal many details about the hardware. The most interesting ones are MaxContacts for the maximum number of simultaneous pointers supported (1 for a mouse and 5 for many touch digitizers) and PointerDeviceType, which is set to either Touch, Mouse, or Pen. It also exposes two static methods: one for enumerating all current PointerDevices, and one that returns the PointerDevice responsible for a specific Pointer. For example, a Surface returns three PointerDevices (one of each type) when a Touch Cover or Type Cover (with its built-in trackpad) is connected.

The Windows.Devices.Input namespace also contains a TouchCapabilities class that is awkward to use but provides shortcuts to information you can otherwise glean by enumerating all PointerDevices. After instantiating a TouchCapabilities object, you can check whether the current PC has *any* digitizer (touch or pen) with its TouchPresent property whose value is 1 for true or 0 for false. You can also check its Contacts property, which returns the minimum MaxContacts value from all current touch and pen PointerDevices.

Pointer

The Pointer class is simple. It exposes four properties. The main one, PointerId, is a uint that uniquely identifies it. This is helpful for tracking individual fingers, for example, when multiple fingers are raising events simultaneously. Its PointerDeviceType property exposes the same information as the same-named property from PointerDevice. The remaining two properties, IsInContact and IsInRange, are duplicated on the PointerPoint and PointerPointProperties classes, and they are described in the next two sections.

PointerPoint

The PointerPoint class is much more than a simple coordinate on the screen. It exposes the following properties:

→ **Position**—The coordinates expressed as a Windows.Foundation.Point. Windows occasionally adjusts Position automatically due to a feature called *touch input prediction*. This attempts to compensate for inaccurate touches. For example, if a user taps near a hyperlink, Windows will likely adjust Position to be directly on the hyperlink.

→ **RawPosition**—The coordinates directly reported by the input device. Unlike Position, RawPosition does not get adjusted by touch input prediction.

→ **IsInContact**—Whether the pointer is currently touching the digitizer.

→ **Timestamp**—Occurrence of this input, in terms of milliseconds since boot time.

→ **FrameId**—An ID that groups multiple touches that should be treated as a unit.

→ **Properties**—A PointerPointProperties instance containing extra information.

→ **PointerId**—The numeric ID of the Pointer responsible for this PointerPoint.

→ **PointerDevice**—The PointerDevice responsible for the Pointer.

PointerPoint also exposes a static GetCurrentPoint method that enables you to get the current PointerPoint for any Pointer (identified by its ID) at any time. It also exposes a static GetIntermediatePoints method described later in this chapter.

PointerPointProperties

The PointerPointProperties instance exposed by PointerPoint is a treasure trove of information. Most of it is specific to mouse and pen devices (and, therefore, described later), but the following properties are relevant for touch:

→ **ContactRect**—The bounding rectangle of the contact area (for digitizers that support giving this information). Be careful about relying exclusively on this data, however, because some digitizers report a zero-sized rectangle. Like PointerPoint.Position, this data can be adjusted by touch input prediction.

→ **ContactRectRaw**—The raw version of ContactRect. Like PointerPoint.RawPosition, this is unaffected by touch input prediction.

→ **IsInRange**—Reports whether the finger is close to the touch digitizer but not quite touching it. (If the touch digitizer supports this kind of z-axis detection.)

→ **IsPrimary**—Reports whether this input belongs to the primary Pointer (the first one that made contact out of the ones currently in contact with the digitizer).

→ **TouchConfidence**—This is false if the contact got rejected by the PointerDevice, because it seems to be an accidental touch.

Pointer Events

With all the background out of the way, it's now time to see the primary way your code can be exposed to these pointer classes. The pointer events are all routed events and all exposed by UIElement, so every visual element on your pages can raise them, and they bubble up through the element tree. The following pointer events are relevant to touch:

→ **PointerPressed**—Raised when a Pointer first makes contact with the element.

→ **PointerMoved**—Raised continuously as a Pointer moves over the element.

→ **PointerReleased**—Raised when a previously pressed `Pointer` releases contact under normal circumstances.

→ **PointerEntered**—Raised when a `Pointer` first enters the element's bounds.

→ **PointerExited**—Raised when a `Pointer` leaves the element's bounds.

→ **PointerCanceled**—Raised when the `Pointer` is lost due to an unusual reason, such as the user rotating the device or disconnecting the relevant (external) `PointerDevice`.

> **(!) When a pointer is pressed, it is not always released!**
>
> Every `PointerPressed` event is *usually* paired with an eventual `PointerReleased` event, but not always. If a specific `PointerReleased` is never raised, then a `PointerCanceled` or `PointerCaptureLost` event would be released instead. (Although in certain scenarios, both `PointerReleased` *and* `PointerCaptureLost` can be raised.)
>
> Most of the time, it makes sense to attach the same `PointerReleased` handler to `PointerCanceled` and `PointerCaptureLost` so you consider the action "done" even if it terminates abnormally. Some apps, however, might want to commit an action only on `PointerReleased` and *undo* it on `PointerCanceled`.

→ **PointerCaptureLost**—Raised when pointer capture, explained in the next section, terminates.

When multiple `Pointers` (fingers) are in contact simultaneously, the pointer events get raised for each one independently. Handlers for all pointer events are given an instance of `PointerRoutedEventArgs`, which contains the following:

→ **GetPosition**—A method that returns the relevant `PointerPoint`.

→ **Pointer**—The `Pointer` instance that generated the event (although the `PointerPoint` already reveals its ID, which is often all you need to know).

→ **GetIntermediatePoints**—An advanced method that returns a collection of `PointerPoints` that might have accumulated between the current `PointerMoved` event and the previous one raised. That's right, the data from touch and pen digitizers can be so high-resolution that the stream of input gets coalesced into lower-resolution chunks for performance reasons. (Mice are already low-resolution so `GetIntermediatePoints` always returns an empty collection when the `PointerDevice` is a mouse.) Therefore, this enables you to get the highest-resolution data possible and is typically passed along to the `GestureRecognizer` described in the upcoming "Gestures" section.

→ **Handled**—Can be set to `true` to "halt" bubbling, as described in the preceding chapter.

→ **KeyModifiers**—Reveals if certain keyboard keys were pressed at the time of the event, described further in the "Keyboard Input" section.

GetPosition is a method rather than a simple property because it enables you to get the position in more than one way: either relative to the top-left corner of the app, or relative to the top-left corner of any rendered UIElement. To get the app-relative position, you can pass null as the single parameter to GetPosition. To get an element-relative position, you pass the desired element as the parameter. The latter approach is much more common, especially because it automatically accounts for any transforms applied to the passed-in element (or an ancestor).

Capturing Pointers

Suppose you want to support dragging and dropping of UIElements. It's easy to imagine using the PointerPressed, PointerMoved, and PointerReleased/PointerCanceled events to implement drag-and-drop. You could start a drag action by setting a Boolean variable inside an element's PointerPressed handler, move the element to remain under the pointer if the Boolean is true inside its PointerMoved handler, and then clear the Boolean inside its PointerReleased (and PointerCanceled) event to end the dragging. It turns out that this simple scheme isn't quite good enough, however, because it's easy to move your finger/mouse/pen too fast or move the dragged element under another element, causing the Pointer to separate from the element you're trying to drag and get left behind.

To solve this problem, UIElements support *capturing* and *releasing* any Pointer. When an element captures one, it receives all its pointer events, even when the Pointer is not within its bounds. Actually, even when the Pointer is outside the bounds of the app (when snapped or filled)!

When an element releases a Pointer from its capture, the event behavior returns to normal. Capture and release can be done with two simple methods defined on UIElement—CapturePointer and ReleasePointerCapture, both of which have a single Pointer argument. In addition, a parameterless ReleasePointerCaptures method releases all Pointers captured by the element, and a read-only PointerCaptures property gives you a list of its currently-captured Pointers.

Therefore, for a drag-and-drop implementation, you should capture the Pointer inside a handler for PointerPressed and release it inside a handler for PointerReleased (and the two similar events). The only thing left to figure out is the best way to actually move the element inside PointerMoved, and that depends on its parent Panel. Listing 6.1 demonstrates such an implementation in order to create a page with a draggable red square. It is the code-behind file for the following simple MainPage.xaml content:

```
<Page x:Class="Chapter6.MainPage" …>
  <Canvas Background="{StaticResource ApplicationPageBackgroundThemeBrush}">
    <Rectangle x:Name="shape" Fill="Red" Width="100" Height="100" />
  </Canvas>
</Page>
```

LISTING 6.1   `MainPage.xaml.cs:` Performing Simple Drag and Drop

```
using System;
using Windows.UI.Input;
using Windows.UI.Xaml.Controls;
using Windows.UI.Xaml.Input;

namespace Chapter6
{
  public sealed partial class MainPage : Page
  {
    public MainPage()
    {
      InitializeComponent();

      // Event for beginning drag
      shape.PointerPressed += Shape_PointerPressed;

      // Event for dragging
      shape.PointerMoved += Shape_PointerMoved;

      // All the events that should terminate the drag
      shape.PointerReleased += Shape_PointerReleased;
      shape.PointerCanceled += Shape_PointerReleased;
      shape.PointerCaptureLost += Shape_PointerReleased;
    }

    void Shape_PointerPressed(object sender, PointerRoutedEventArgs e)
    {
      shape.CapturePointer(e.Pointer);
    }

    void Shape_PointerMoved(object sender, PointerRoutedEventArgs e)
    {
      // Only move the shape if one pointer is currently pressed
      if (shape.PointerCaptures != null && shape.PointerCaptures.Count == 1)
      {
        PointerPoint point = e.GetCurrentPoint(null);

        // Center the shape under the pointer
        Canvas.SetLeft(shape, point.Position.X - (shape.ActualWidth / 2));
        Canvas.SetTop(shape, point.Position.Y - (shape.ActualHeight / 2));
      }
    }

    void Shape_PointerReleased(object sender, PointerRoutedEventArgs e)
```

LISTING 6.1   Continued

```
    {
       shape.ReleasePointerCapture(e.Pointer);
    }
  }
}
```

There are several things to note about Listing 6.1:

→ With the availability of the PointerCaptures property, we don't need to define a separate isDragging variable to be set on PointerPressed and cleared on PointerReleased. The code in the PointerMoved handler is able to conditionalize its logic on the state of capture.

→ It's important that all capture APIs are used directly on the shape field because that element is where the event handlers are attached. If Shape_PointerPressed accidentally called **this**.CapturePointer instead, then Shape_PointerMoved and Shape_PointerReleased would not be called subsequently because the Page would capture all the events!

→ In the PointerReleased handler, the call to ReleasePointerCapture causes the PointerCaptureLost event to be raised, which invokes PointerReleased again. That's okay, because ReleasePointerCapture is a no-op if the passed-in Pointer isn't captured.

→ This simplistic drag-and-drop is a bit different from "official" dragging and dropping because it doesn't reject the input if multiple Pointers are in contact simultaneously. It does, however, prevent dragging when multiple Pointers are in contact *with the shape* simultaneously (by checking for exactly one captured Pointer). Otherwise, if you touch the Rectangle with two fingers simultaneously and pull them apart, the shape's position would rapidly oscillate between each finger's position due to Shape_PointerMoved being called for each Pointer in turn.

→ If you were to try this same example with a Button instead of a Rectangle, you would need to attach Shape_Pressed and Shape_Released with the AddHandler method instead of +=, and with true passed for the handledEventsToo parameter. This is due to the halting of event bubbling described in the preceding chapter.

 UIElement.PointerCaptures **can be** null!

Before any capturing is done, an element's PointerCaptures property is null. When capture happens, it becomes a collection with a nonzero Count. After capture has been released, however, it stays non-null. It becomes an empty collection with a Count of 0. This is why the PointerMoved handler in Listing 6.1 must check for both conditions when determining whether an element is currently capturing any Pointers.

Hit Testing

Although one element's capture can prevent another element from raising pointer events that it otherwise would, there are several other conditions that can cause an element directly underneath a `Pointer` to not raise such events. An element meeting all these conditions is said to be *hit-testable*, although *hittable* would be a slightly better term.

A `UIElement` is hit-testable when the following are all true:

➜ Its `Visibility` property is set to `Visible` (which it is by default).

➜ It must render something. This means having a nonzero `ActualWidth` and `ActualHeight`, and for many elements this also means having a non-null `Background` or `Fill`. (A Transparent `Background` or `Fill` is fine.)

➜ Its `IsHitTestVisible` property is set to `true` (which it is by default).

➜ For a `Control`, its `IsEnabled` property is set to `true` (which it is by default).

The `IsHitTestVisible` property is a separate knob that enables you to have an element stay visible but not respond to any input. A `Control`'s `IsEnabled` property exists to not only make it unhittable, but visually indicate that with a disabled appearance. The hit-testability of an element is filled with subtleties, as the warnings in this section point out.

 Why does `UIElement` **define a** `Visibility` **property that's a two-value enumeration (**`Visible` **or** `Collapsed`**) rather than a simple Boolean** `IsVisible` **property?**

Code would be simpler to write if it was a Boolean property, but this decision is the unfortunate result of what I like to call *viral compatibility*. It's defined this way to be compatible with Silverlight-based Windows Phone apps, which use the same property. Easy porting of apps from Windows Phone to Windows 8 and vice versa is important to Microsoft as well as developers, so this is understandable.

But why did Silverlight for Windows Phone define it this way? To be compatible with the original Silverlight platform (for the desktop and the Web). Why did Silverlight define it this way? To be mostly compatible with WPF, which defined `Visibility` as a *three-value* enumeration: `Visible`, `Collapsed`, and `Hidden` (which means invisible but still participating in layout, much like a `Visible` element with its `Opacity` set to 0).

This is basically the same situation as the routed events confusion described in the preceding chapter. It's great that Microsoft values compatibility so much, and your Windows Store apps will benefit from this principle for years to come. This is one case, however, where I wish the chain would have been broken somewhere along the line.

> ⓘ **Transparent regions raise input events, but** `null` **regions do not!**
>
> If an element's `Background` or `Fill` is left at its default `null` value, then its background region (with no other content) never raises any input events. If you set either property to `Transparent`, however, the result looks identical but it now raises such events everywhere in its bounds. Along those lines, setting an element's `Opacity` to 0 does not affect its event-related behavior at all, unlike setting its `Visibility` to `Collapsed`.
>
> Elements with non-vector-based content—`Image` and `MediaElement`—are hit-testable on their entire bounds even if they contain transparent content (via the alpha channel). You can think of them as always having a `Background` set to `Transparent`. The same is true for `TextBlock`, which has no `Background` or `Fill` property either.

> ⓘ **Setting a** `Page`'s `Background` **has no effect!**
>
> Despite inheriting a `Background` property from `Control`, setting a `Page`'s `Background` does nothing. Its child element (almost always a `Panel`) must be given one instead. This is important not just for the visual appearance of a `Page` but its hit-testability as well. An empty page raises no input events, acting as if its Background is always set to `null`.

> ⓘ **The true bounds of a** `Canvas` **can result in confusing hit-testing behavior!**
>
> Because a `Canvas`'s children can be rendered outside its bounds, it's easy to forget that it has a default actual size of zero in situations for which it doesn't get stretched (such as being placed inside a `StackPanel`). Because pointer events for `Canvas` itself (ignoring events bubbled up from any children) get raised only within its bounds (and only then when it has a non-null `Background`), you can run into situations in which `Canvas`-level pointer events are raised only for its children.

The *hit-testable* term implies that you can in fact *test* an element for its *hittability*. Checking all its relevant properties (and keeping in mind special rules for certain elements) isn't enough, because the element could still be obscured by an element above it that blocks all its input. Fortunately, you can easily test an element's hittability with the `VisualTreeHelper.FindElementsInHostCoordinates` method, which has several overloads.

Calling `FindElementsInHostCoordinates` means asking for all hittable elements that intersect a specific `Point` or `Rect`, passed as the first parameter. The second parameter is the element to use as the root of the search, enabling you to scope the question to a specific subtree of elements. Note that the `Point` or `Rect` is relative to the passed-in root element! (This element is the "host" mentioned in the method's name.) As with the element passed to `GetCurrentPoint`, this takes relevant transforms into account.

`FindElementsInHostCoordinates` has overloads that accept a third parameter: a Boolean `includeAllElements` that, when `true`, ignores hit-testability and simply returns all elements in the subtree that intersect the coordinate or region. The collection of returned elements is ordered from top to bottom, so the topmost element that would truly be "hit" by relevant input is the 0th element.

Tracking Multiple Pointers

Listing 6.2 demonstrates responding to and tracking multiple Pointers, using the following simple MainPage.xaml:

```
<Page x:Class="Chapter6.MainPage" …>
  <Canvas x:Name="canvas" Background="BlueViolet"/>
</Page>
```

It displays the ID of each pointer currently in contact and keeps it centered under each pointer's location, as shown in Figure 6.2 on a device that supports at least five simultaneous touch points.

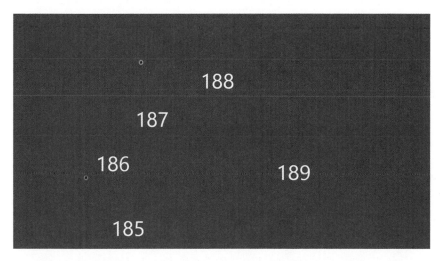

FIGURE 6.2   Pressing five fingers on the screen shows five Pointer IDs at the right locations.

LISTING 6.2   MainPage.xaml.cs: Tracking Multiple Pointers

```
using System.Collections.Generic;
using Windows.UI.Input;
using Windows.UI.Xaml.Controls;
using Windows.UI.Xaml.Input;

namespace Chapter6
{
  public sealed partial class MainPage : Page
  {
    public MainPage()
    {
```

LISTING 6.2   Continued

```csharp
  InitializeComponent();
}


// Keep track of which TextBlocks are used for which Pointers
Dictionary<uint, TextBlock> textBlocks = new Dictionary<uint, TextBlock>();

protected override void OnPointerPressed(PointerRoutedEventArgs e)
{
  canvas.CapturePointer(e.Pointer);

  // Create a new TextBlock for this new Pointer
  TextBlock textBlock = new TextBlock {
    Text = e.Pointer.PointerId.ToString(), FontSize = 80 };

  PlaceTextBlockUnderPointerPoint(textBlock, e.GetCurrentPoint(canvas));

  // Keep track of the TextBlock and add it to the canvas
  textBlocks[e.Pointer.PointerId] = textBlock;
  canvas.Children.Add(textBlock);
}

protected override void OnPointerMoved(PointerRoutedEventArgs e)
{
  // Only do this if this Pointer is currently pressed
  if (textBlocks.ContainsKey(e.Pointer.PointerId))
  {
    // Retrieve the right TextBlock
    TextBlock textBlock = textBlocks[e.Pointer.PointerId];

    PlaceTextBlockUnderPointerPoint(textBlock, e.GetCurrentPoint(canvas));
  }
}

protected override void OnPointerReleased(PointerRoutedEventArgs e)
{
  // Remove the TextBlock from the canvas and the dictionary
  if (textBlocks.ContainsKey(e.Pointer.PointerId))
  {
    canvas.Children.Remove(textBlocks[e.Pointer.PointerId]);
    textBlocks.Remove(e.Pointer.PointerId);
    canvas.ReleasePointerCapture(e.Pointer);
  }
}
```

LISTING 6.2   Continued

```
  protected override void OnPointerCanceled(PointerRoutedEventArgs e)
  {
    OnPointerReleased(e);
  }

  protected override void OnPointerCaptureLost(PointerRoutedEventArgs e)
  {
    OnPointerReleased(e);
  }

  void PlaceTextBlockUnderPointerPoint(TextBlock textBlock, PointerPoint point)
  {
    Canvas.SetLeft(textBlock, point.Position.X - (textBlock.ActualWidth / 2));
    Canvas.SetTop(textBlock, point.Position.Y - (textBlock.ActualHeight / 2));
  }
 }
}
```

Here are a few notes about Listing 6.2:

➜ The implementation is not much different from the drag-and-drop example in Listing 6.1. The main difference is that the elements being dragged (TextBlocks, in this case) are dynamically created and added to the Canvas on PointerPressed and then removed on PointerReleased. For this reason, the events being handled are at the root Page level rather than on the draggable elements.

➜ Rather than attaching event handlers to the relevant Page events, Listing 6.2 overrides the corresponding On*XXX* methods instead. Often, a class that exposes an event *XXX* also exposes an On*XXX* method that subclasses can override. Either approach can be used, and the result is the same. Note that the base implementation of each method is responsible for raising the corresponding event, so if you still want the event to be raised to any consumers of the object, you should invoke the base method inside the override.

➜ Listing 6.2 performs pointer capture, although it's not strictly necessary because of the handling done at the Page level. There is one benefit, however. It keeps the TextBlock "attached" to its finger when the app is snapped or filled and the finger travels over other app (as long as the finger stays on screen).

Gestures

From the pointer events alone, it would take quite a bit of code to reliably detect user gestures such as press-and-hold, cross-slide item selection, and double taps. Even detecting a proper tap is more complicated than you might think. Furthermore, having apps write such code would be a recipe for disastrous user experiences because of the lack of consistency that would result.

Fortunately, Windows has a *gesture recognizer* that performs calculations based on the raw pointer events and raises appropriate additional events when it recognizes standard gestures. For example, if a user briefly touches a finger on a touchscreen then releases it, we already know that this causes a `PointerPressed` event to be raised followed by a `PointerReleased` event. However, if the timeframe between the two events is short enough, *and* if the amount of finger motion between the two events is small enough (so it doesn't appear to be a swipe or slide), *and* if only one finger is in contact the whole time, then the gesture recognizer raises a `Tapped` event. This higher-level event is what most apps consume.

This mechanism not only provides consistency for gestures among all apps, but with all system UI as well, such as the Start screen. And because it operates on pointers, it applies to touch, mouse, and pen. Figure 6.3 displays the basic Windows 8 touch gestures and what they are intended to mean.

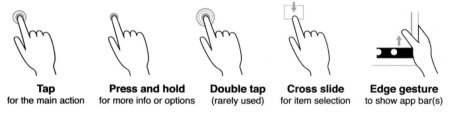

FIGURE 6.3   The basic Windows 8 gestures

You can interact with the gesture recognizer directly via the `Windows.UI.Input.GestureRecognizer` class, but you often don't need to do this because `UIElement` already does it for you. Instead, you can simply leverage gesture events exposed on all `UIElements`.

GestureRecognizer

Let's take a quick look at the Windows Runtime `GestureRecognizer` class for completeness. You might want to use it for advanced scenarios. For example, it exposes properties that enable you to tweak its settings: distance thresholds for detecting a cross slide, whether visual feedback is shown for gestures, and so on. Ignoring the more complex manipulations covered later, `GestureRecognizer` recognizes the following gestures and raises the following events relevant for touch (all single-finger only):

→ `Tapped`—Raised for a simple tap

→ `RightTapped`—Raised for a right tap (for touch, this is a released press-and-hold gesture)

→ `Holding`—Raised during the stages of press-and-hold

→ **CrossSliding**—Raised during the stages of a swipe within an area that scrolls in the perpendicular direction (used for selection and only for touch)

GestureRecognizer also recognizes double taps, but it doesn't expose an event for this. Instead, inside a Tapped event handler, you can check the TapCount property of the passed-in TappedEventArgs instance, which is set to 1 for a single tap or 2 for a double tap.

Each of the GestureRecognizer events has a unique EventArgs type passed to its handlers, but they all have two properties in common: PointerDeviceType (revealing whether the source is Touch, Mouse, or Pen) and Position (of type Point).

If you want to interact with the GestureRecognizer directly, you must instantiate one, tell it which events you're interested in, attach handlers to those events, and, most importantly, pass it PointerPoints at all the appropriate times. Listing 6.3 demonstrates this in the code-behind file for a hypothetical MainPage.

 Some of the system settings that impact gesture recognition, such as the maximum time between taps for a double tap, or the minimum pressing time for a press-and-hold, are exposed by read-only properties on the Windows.UI.ViewManagement.UISettings class.

What does the RightTapped **event mean for touch input?**

No, it doesn't mean using your right hand! For touch, RightTapped is raised after releasing a single-finger press-and-hold gesture, because logically that action should do the same thing as a right click from a mouse.

LISTING 6.3   How to Make GestureRecognizer Raise Its Events

```
using Windows.System;
using Windows.UI.Input;
using Windows.UI.Xaml.Controls;
using Windows.UI.Xaml.Input;

namespace Chapter6
{
  public sealed partial class MainPage : Page
  {
    GestureRecognizer gestureRecognizer;

    public MainPage()
    {
      this.InitializeComponent();

      // Initialize gesture recognizer
      gestureRecognizer = new GestureRecognizer();
      gestureRecognizer.GestureSettings = GestureSettings.Tap |
        GestureSettings.RightTap | GestureSettings.DoubleTap |
```

LISTING 6.3   Continued

```
      GestureSettings.HoldWithMouse | GestureSettings.CrossSlide;

  // Attach handlers for recognized gestures (not shown in this listing)
  gestureRecognizer.Tapped += GestureRecognizer_Tapped;
  gestureRecognizer.RightTapped += GestureRecognizer_RightTapped;
  gestureRecognizer.Holding += GestureRecognizer_Holding;
  gestureRecognizer.CrossSliding += GestureRecognizer_CrossSliding;
}

//
// Handlers for recognized gestures:
//
…

//
// Forward all pointer input to the gesture recognizer so it can do its job:
//

protected override void OnPointerPressed(PointerRoutedEventArgs e)
{
  CapturePointer(e.Pointer);
  gestureRecognizer.ProcessDownEvent(e.GetCurrentPoint(this));
}

protected override void OnPointerMoved(PointerRoutedEventArgs e)
{
  // Pass all intermediate potentially-coalesced points:
  gestureRecognizer.ProcessMoveEvents(e.GetIntermediatePoints(this));
}

protected override void OnPointerReleased(PointerRoutedEventArgs e)
{
  gestureRecognizer.ProcessUpEvent(e.GetCurrentPoint(this));
  ReleasePointerCapture(e.Pointer);
}

protected override void OnPointerCanceled(PointerRoutedEventArgs e)
{
  OnPointerReleased(e);
}

protected override void OnPointerCaptureLost(PointerRoutedEventArgs e)
{
  OnPointerReleased(e);
```

LISTING 6.3   Continued

```
   }

   // This is for mouse only, but here for completeness:
   protected override void OnPointerWheelChanged(PointerRoutedEventArgs e)
   {
     bool isShiftKeyDown = ((e.KeyModifiers & VirtualKeyModifiers.Shift) ==
                            VirtualKeyModifiers.Shift);
     bool isControlKeyDown = ((e.KeyModifiers & VirtualKeyModifiers.Control) ==
                            VirtualKeyModifiers.Control);

     gestureRecognizer.ProcessMouseWheelEvent(e.GetCurrentPoint(this),
       isShiftKeyDown, isControlKeyDown);
   }
 }
}
```

For performance reasons, Listing 6.3 tells the gesture recognizer to look only for the specific gestures being handled by the app. Notice the use of the oddly named GestureSettings.HoldWithMouse flag. This detects press-and-hold for a mouse as well as touch and pen. If you want only press-and-hold to be detected for touch and pen, you can use the GestureSettings.Hold flag instead. Also notice the use of GetIntermediatePoints inside OnPointerMoved. GestureRecognizer's ProcessMoveEvents method is designed for this, because it wants the highest-resolution data possible.

The Holding event acts like three events combined into one. Event handlers are given a value from a HoldingState enumeration with three possible values: Started, Completed, and Canceled. The event is raised with the Started value as soon as the sole finger has been pressing long enough in a relatively stationary position. The event is raised with the Completed event once the finger is lifted. If the finger ends up moving too much before breaking contact or a second finger makes contact, then it is raised with Canceled instead. (Interestingly, if anything unusual happens, such as the screen rotating or a pen getting close to the screen, the event is sometimes raised with Completed rather than Canceled.) If GestureRecognizer is told to detect right taps, RightTapped is raised immediately after a Completed Holding event (but for touch only, because mice and pens have a distinct way to generate a right tap).

Although the CrossSliding event is supposed to be raised for perpendicular swiping, GestureRecognizer has no idea which direction is perpendicular, or whether the swipe is done in a scrollable region. It's up to the consumer to figure this out. In reality, GestureRecognizer simply recognizes a vertical swipe gesture (because scrolling is usually done horizontally). You can change it to recognize horizontal swipes instead by setting GestureRecognizer's CrossSlideHorizontally property to true. Like Holding,

CrossSliding reports many different states to event handlers with a CrossSlidingState enumeration. The typical pattern is an event raised with a Started state, followed by many with a Dragging state, followed by one with a Completed state.

EdgeGesture

You might have noticed that one of the gestures in Figure 6.3 isn't reported by GestureRecognizer: the *edge gesture*, a

Avoid using GestureRecognizer **with built-in controls such as** Button **and** ListBox!

You can run into cases in which logic inside certain controls interferes with GestureRecognizer logic. This sometimes surfaces as an exception complaining that the pointer is already in use. GestureRecognizer is designed to be used with simple shapes (covered in Chapter 14, "Vector Graphics") or custom controls.

swipe from the top or bottom edge of the screen. This gesture is meant to toggle the visibility of a bottom (and optionally a top) app bar. (The equivalent gestures on the left and right edges are not exposed to apps, because these are reserved for app switching and the charms bar.)

The edge gesture is exposed by a dedicated EdgeGesture class in the Windows.UI.Input namespace that internally uses GestureRecognizer to recognize a vertical slide but filters it based on its position. The reason this is a separate class is that it responds to keyboard shortcuts in addition to pointer input. (Pressing either Windows+Z or the context menu key is treated as an edge gesture.)

To use EdgeGesture, you first call its static GetForCurrentView method to obtain an instance. Then you can handle its three events:

→ **Starting**—Raised when a matching gesture has started, but it's still possible the pointer will move in such a way that cancels the gesture.

→ **Completed**—Raised when the gesture has successfully completed (the finger has lifted or the key has been pressed).

→ **Canceled**—Raised after Starting if the gesture doesn't end up being an edge gesture after all. For example, if a finger swipes up from the bottom edge but turns around and swipes back down, Canceled is raised.

When you use an AppBar control, covered in Part III, it automatically detects edge gestures and shows/hides accordingly. Therefore, you normally don't need to handle this event directly.

Handlers for these events are given an EdgeGestureEventArgs instance with a single property called Kind. This is an EdgeGestureKind enumeration is basically the same as PointerDeviceType except it includes a value for Keyboard. Confusingly, its only values are Touch, Mouse, and Keyboard, so an edge gesture made by a pen is reported as Touch instead.

EdgeGesture **events cannot currently be raised by mouse input!**

This is a bug specific to XAML apps that will likely be fixed in a future version of Windows.

UIElement **Gesture Events**

Listing 6.3 contains a lot of boilerplate code for something that is so common. That's why UIElement internally interacts with GestureRecognizer and exposes its own gesture events. With these convenient events, you don't have to do anything other than attach handlers. Plus, unlike the GestureRecognizer events, the UIElement events are routed events.

The basic UIElement single-finger gesture events should look familiar:

→ **Tapped**—Raised for a simple tap

→ **RightTapped**—Raised for a right tap (for touch, this is a released press-and-hold gesture)

→ **DoubleTapped**—Raised for a double tap

→ **Holding**—Raised during the stages of press-and-hold

These map closely to the GestureRecognizer events discussed in the preceding section. Note the addition of a DoubleTapped event, which is a much simpler and consistent way to handle this gesture. However, there are no events for the cross slide or edge gesture. That's because most scenarios are covered by built-in controls that internally handle this event from GestureRecognizer, so it would have been overkill to provide the more convenient events on UIElement.

Analogous to GestureRecognizer's GestureSettings flags, UIElement exposes several properties for toggling the recognition of specific gestures: IsTapEnabled, IsRightTapEnabled, IsDoubleTapEnabled, and IsHoldingEnabled. However, unlike with GestureRecognizer, these are all enabled (true) by default.

Manipulations

A more complex class of gestures, known as *manipulations*, can also be detected and reported by the Windows gesture recognizer. These are meant to handle panning, rotating, and zooming, as shown in Figure 6.4.

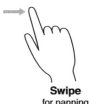
Swipe
for panning

Twist
for rotating

Pinch or Stretch
for zooming

FIGURE 6.4   The more complex Windows 8 gestures known as manipulations

The biggest difference between these gestures and the previously discussed ones is not just the use of multiple fingers, but that all of them (even the single-finger swipe) can be done while other fingers are touching the screen. Unlike a cross slide, a swipe is still a swipe even if many fingers are doing it, and you can swipe, twist, and pinch/stretch simultaneously.

Logically, these actions are straightforward to apply to elements, because their concepts map exactly to applying a `TranslateTransform`, `RotateTransform`, and/or `ScaleTransform`. Detecting *when* you should apply these transforms and with *what values* would be an entirely different story, however, if it weren't for the following manipulation events exposed by `UIElement`:

→ `ManipulationStarting` and `ManipulationStarted`

→ `ManipulationDelta`

→ `ManipulationInertiaStarting`

→ `ManipulationCompleted`

These events are also exposed by `GestureRecognizer`, although there is no `ManipulationStarting` event and `ManipulationDelta` is named `ManipulationUpdated` instead. Unlike our examination of the simpler gesture events, this section focuses on the `UIElement` events.

These events combine the information from independent fingers and package the data in an easy-to-consume form. Unlike the basic gestures, elements must opt into the manipulation events. For a `UIElement` to raise them, its `ManipulationMode` property must be set appropriately on itself or a parent. This property is a flags enumeration that can be set to a list of specific manipulations bitwise-ORed together, or `All` or `None`.

You can set a flags enumeration value in XAML by using comma-separated values, for example:

`ManipulationMode="Rotate, Scale"`

Using Manipulation Events

`ManipulationStarting` gets raised as soon as *any* input is detected, followed by `ManipulationStarted`, which gets raised the instant that the recognizer detects that a translation, rotation, or scale is underway. `ManipulationDelta` gets raised for each `PointerMoved` raised during this process, and `ManipulationCompleted` gets raised after `PointerReleased` is raised for *all* fingers.

The `ManipulationDelta` event gives you rich information about how the element is expected to be translated/rotated/scaled. You can then apply this data directly to the relevant transforms. The `ManipulationDeltaRoutedEventArgs` instance passed to handlers contains a `Delta` property of type `ManipulationDelta` that exposes the following properties:

→ **Translation**—A `Point` property with `X` and `Y` values.

→ **Scale**—A `float` property representing the distance change as a percentage. For example, doubling the distance would report a value of `1.0`.

→ **Rotation**—A `float` property that specifies the angle in degrees.

→ **Expansion**—A `float` property that is redundant with `Scale`, but it reports the difference in terms of absolute device-independent pixels instead of a relative value.

Actually, `ManipulationDeltaRoutedEventArgs` has *two* properties of type `ManipulationDelta`. `Delta` reports the changes compared to the last time the event was raised, but `Cumulative` reports the changes compared to when `ManipulationStarted` was raised. So no matter how you prefer to consume the data, there should be a way that pleases you! You can also instantly halt the manipulation by calling `ManipulationDeltaRoutedEventArgs`'s `Complete` method.

Listing 6.4 contains the code-behind file for the following `Page`, making it possible to move, rotate, and zoom the contained photo with standard swipe, rotate, and pinch gestures:

```
<Page x:Class="Chapter6.MainPage" …>
  <Canvas Background="Crimson">
    <Image Source="photo.png" RenderTransformOrigin=".5,.5"
           ManipulationMode="All"
           ManipulationStarted="Image_ManipulationStarted"
           ManipulationDelta="Image_ManipulationDelta">
      <Image.RenderTransform>
        <CompositeTransform x:Name="transform"/>
      </Image.RenderTransform>
    </Image>
  </Canvas>
</Page>
```

The result is shown in Figure 6.5.

LISTING 6.4   `MainPage.xaml.cs`: Handling Manipulation Events to Enable Panning, Rotating, and Zooming

```
using Windows.Foundation;
using Windows.UI.Xaml.Controls;
using Windows.UI.Xaml.Input;

namespace Manipulation
{
  public sealed partial class MainPage : Page
  {
    // The transform state at the beginning of the current gesture:
    Point startingTranslation;
    double startingRotation;
    double startingScale;
```

LISTING 6.4   Continued

```
public MainPage()
{
  InitializeComponent();
}

void Image_ManipulationStarted(object sender,
                               ManipulationStartedRoutedEventArgs e)
{
  // Capture the initial state so Cumulative values can be added to these:
  startingTranslation = new Point { X = transform.TranslateX,
                                    Y = transform.TranslateY };
  startingRotation = transform.Rotation;
  startingScale = transform.ScaleX; // Same as ScaleY
}

void Image_ManipulationDelta(object sender,
                             ManipulationDeltaRoutedEventArgs e)
{
  // Update the transform
  transform.TranslateX = startingTranslation.X + e.Cumulative.Translation.X;
  transform.TranslateY = startingTranslation.Y + e.Cumulative.Translation.Y;
  transform.Rotation = startingRotation + e.Cumulative.Rotation;
  transform.ScaleX = transform.ScaleY = startingScale * e.Cumulative.Scale;
}
}
}
```

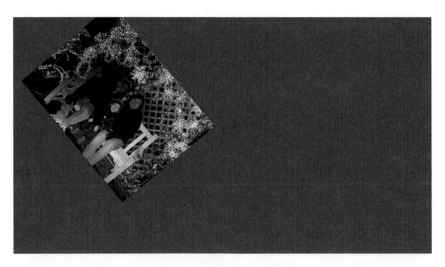

FIGURE 6.5   Enabling panning, rotating, and zooming on an Image by handling the ManipulationStarted and ManipulationDelta events

The Image conveniently has a
CompositeTransform applied as its
RenderTransform, so the code inside the
ManipulationDelta handler needs only
to update the transform's properties with
data from the
ManipulationDeltaRoutedEventArgs
instance. Note that setting them to the
Cumulative values isn't enough because
these values are only deltas from the
start of the *current* gesture, and previous
gestures might have already transformed
the element. That's why the
ManipulationStarted event is also
handled. By adding the deltas to the pre-
gesture values, each new gesture adds on
to the previous one. When you use the
manipulation events, pointer capture
occurs automatically, so you don't have
to worry about manual capture and release.

 If possible, use `ScrollViewer`**'s built-in panning and zooming functionality rather than handling manipulation events!**

ScrollViewer's panning and zooming support, described in the preceding chapter, is implemented with a second thread to produce the smoothest possible performance. In contrast, handling the manipulation events and setting corresponding transforms must be done on the UI thread. This can cause noticeable lags, depending on what else is happening on the UI thread.

Interestingly, the manipulation events still get raised when ScrollViewer panning and zooming occurs, but you can't stop the manipulation because of the use of a separate thread. You can still act upon this information, however, to keep other elements in sync.

Inertia

Manipulation events include support for giving objects inertia, so they can gradually slow to a stop when a gesture is done rather than stopping instantly. This makes the gestures feel more realistic and make it easy to support things like "flicking" an object to make it move a distance based on the speed of the flick.

Inertia is enabled based on the value of ManipulationMode. Therefore, when it is set to All, as in the XAML for Listing 6.4, it is enabled. With the Photo_ManipulationDelta implementation in Listing 6.4, everything works as expected "for free" because the passed-in values are calculated accordingly. Note that when ManipulationDelta is raised in response to inertia, the passed-in ManipulationDeltaRoutedEventArgs instance's IsInertial property is set to true.

Between the stream of ManipulationDelta events raised due to actual input and the stream of ManipulationDelta events raised due to inertia, the ManipulationInertiaStarting event is raised. This gives you an opportunity to customize the inertia. Note that ManipulationCompleted is not raised until *all* ManipulationDelta events are raised, including ones due to inertia.

If you want the photo manipulation example to work the same way but without inertia, you can change the following attribute in XAML:

```
ManipulationMode="All"
```

to:

```
ManipulationMode="TranslateX, TranslateY, Rotate, Scale"
```

This explicitly sets all the relevant `ManipulationMode` values, but without the three inertia values (`TranslateInertia`, `RotateInertia`, `ScaleInertia`).

Mouse Input

One of the biggest shocks to a WPF or Silverlight developer learning about Windows Store apps is often, "Hey, where are the mouse events?" And now you know the answer: Mouse events are, for the most part, the same pointer events and gesture events used for touch. If you look back at these events, you'll see that they map to the behavior of a mouse. Furthermore, even mouse dragging is treated as translation and holding Ctrl while scrolling the mouse wheel is treated as zooming in the manipulation events.

Of course, there are some mouse-specific APIs exposed for cases in which the common abstraction isn't rich enough, which this section discusses. Let's quickly go through the same areas covered by the "Touch Input" section but examine only the mouse-specific APIs.

`MouseDevice` and `MouseCapabilities`

In addition to the generic `PointerDevice` class, the `Windows.Devices.Input` namespace contains a `MouseDevice` class with two interesting members:

→ A static `GetForCurrentView` method that returns the current `MouseDevice` if one exists (or the primary one if there is more than one mouse)

→ A `MouseMoved` event that is just like `PointerMoved`, but raised only for pointer movement from this specific mouse

So there still is one "mouse event" in the framework—it's just a little hard to find! Note that the `MouseDevice` class has no relation to `PointerDevice` other than its similar name.

Similar to `TouchCapabilities`, an awkward `MouseCapabilities` class provides information about any connected mice. After instantiating a `MouseCapabilities` object, you can check a number of pseudo-Boolean properties whose values are 1 for `true` or 0 for `false`: `MousePresent` tells you whether a mouse is attached, `HorizontalWheelPresent` and `VerticalWheelPresent` properties tell you whether any attached mouse supports a horizontal/vertical scroll wheel, and `SwapButtons` tells you whether any attached mouse has reversed left and right buttons. In addition, its `NumberOfButtons` property is a `uint` that reveals how many buttons the mouse has (or the *maximum* number if multiple mice are present).

Revisiting Pointer Events and `PointerPointProperties`

There's one pointer event that was omitted from the discussion in the "Touch Input" section because it is specific to a mouse (or perhaps a fancy pen): `PointerWheelChanged`. Handlers for `PointerWheelChanged` are given the same `PointerRoutedEventArgs` instance as all the other pointer events, but they can retrieve the `PointerPointProperties` object (via `PointerPoint.Properties`) to get the following additional details about the event:

→ **IsHorizontalMouseWheel**—This is true if `PointerWheelChanged` is triggered by a horizontal mouse wheel, and `false` if triggered by a vertical mouse wheel.

→ **MouseWheelDelta**—Reveals how much the wheel position changed since the last time the event was raised (in terms of "notches" or some hardware-specific distance threshold).

Where is the event for handling the pressing of a mouse's middle button?

Information about the middle mouse button, if it exists, and any other buttons are exposed via `PointerPointProperties`. You can handle the `Tapped` event and determine which button was pressed by looking at the associated `PointerPoint`.

In fact, many of the properties exposed by `PointerPointProperties` are mouse (or pen)-specific, and you might want to inspect them in response to *any* pointer event. Mice can have up to five standard buttons recognized by Windows (left, middle, right, and two *extended buttons*) so it can be crucial to know which button is pressed/released beyond the basic information conveyed by `Tapped` vs. `RightTapped` events. The following `PointerPointProperties` properties enable this:

→ **IsLeftButtonPressed**, **IsMiddleButtonPressed**, **IsRightButtonPressed**, **IsXButton1Pressed**, and **IsXButton2Pressed**—These Boolean properties tell you which buttons are depressed at the time of the event.

→ **PointerUpdateKind**—An enumeration value that tells you which of the five mouse buttons was just pressed or released to trigger the current event (if applicable).

Although all the pointer events described in the "Touch Input" section also apply to mice, they can behave slightly differently. For example, don't forget that whereas `PointerMoved` (and `PointerEntered`/`PointerExited`) events get raised only between `PointerPressed` and `PointerReleased` (or equivalent) events for touch, this is not the case for a mouse pointer. If you write code that relies on the touch-specific ordering of events (for example, do some initialization in a `PointerPressed` handler required by the `PointerMoved` handler), you could easily write an app that crashes as soon as it is used with a mouse!

Revisiting `GestureRecognizer`

`GestureRecognizer` has one mouse (and pen)-specific event not covered previously: `Dragging`. Whereas a single-finger touch-based swipe gesture generates series of `CrossSliding` events depending on its direction, the same motion from a mouse with any button down (or from a pen while in contact) generates a series of `Dragging` events instead.

Like `CrossSliding`, `Dragging` reports many different states to event handlers with an enumeration—this time called `DraggingState`. The pattern is the same: an event raised with a `Started` state, followed by many with a `Continuing` state, followed by one with a `Completed` state. Unlike `CrossSliding`, `Dragging` is reported for any direction.

Revisiting `UIElement` Gesture Events

`UIElement` exposes some additional mouse (and pen)-specific gesture routed events that are all related to the lower-level `Dragging` event:

Why is the `Dragging` **event not applicable for touch?**

This decision was made to better handle the common ways in which touch is used, such as swiping anywhere on a surface to pan it without worrying about accidentally dragging-and-dropping an item inside that surface. You could, of course, still choose to implement touch-based dragging using either the raw pointer events or the translation manipulation events, because neither set of events discriminates based on the pointer device. And if you care about inertia, you'd want to use the manipulation events rather than the `Dragging` event anyway.

→ **DragOver** and **Drop**—Maps to `Dragging` events with states of `Started`/`Continuing` and `Completed`, respectively

→ **DragEnter** and **DragLeave**—Like `PointerEntered` and `PointerExited`, but raised only when dragging (meaning a mouse button is depressed)

These events work only in limited contexts, however. To see them raised on a drop target, its `AllowDrop` property (or an ancestor's) must be set to `true`. Furthermore, the drop source must be made draggable. For example, it could be an element inside a `GridView` (covered in Chapter 9, "Items Controls") with its `CanDragItems` property set to `true`.

Pen Input

Windows 8 includes fantastic support for pen (also known as a stylus) input.

`UIElement`'s `Holding` **event is never raised for mouse input!**

`UIElement` internally uses `GestureRecognizer` with the `Hold` setting rather than the `HoldWithMouse` setting. Therefore, `RightTapped` is a much better event to use than `Holding`. It covers the press-and-hold case for touch while also behaving reasonably for mouse and pen. This is a bug that could be fixed in a future version of Windows. In the meantime, if you want a mouse-enabled press-and-hold experience, you can interact with `GestureRecognizer` directly.

Although Figure 6.1 shows a pen digitizer as an external device, it can be integrated directly into the screen just like a touch digitizer. Indeed, this is how tablets such as Surface typically work. So when you read *digitizer* in this section, you can typically think *screen*.

By now, it has been drilled into your head that the pointer, gesture, and manipulation events work great for pen input. Furthermore, it should come as no surprise that from these events, you can access pen-specific information to interact with pen-specific tricks: pressure sensitivity, eraser mode, and more.

Note that when a pen is in use, touch input is ignored. This is an important part of a *palm rejection* feature, which makes it easier to write on a screen without worrying about touching the screen at the same time.

There is no `PenDevice` or `PenCapabilities` class analogous to `MouseDevice` and `MouseCapabilities`. And there are no additional events you haven't already seen from the "Touch Input" and "Mouse Input" sections. There are, however, many properties on `PointerPointProperties` that are pen-specific:

→ **IsBarrelButtonPressed**—This is `true` if the button along the side of the pen's body is depressed during the event.

→ **IsEraser**—This is `true` if the input is from the "eraser" on the rear of the pen.

→ **IsInRange**—This is `true` if the pen is close to the digitizer but not quite touching it. (Although this was already mentioned in the "Touch Input" section, I'm listing it again here because it's commonly used with pens.)

→ **IsInverted**—This is `true` if the rear of the pen is being used instead of the front. (Unlike `IsEraser`, this can be `true` even when the pen is not touching the digitizer.)

→ **Pressure**—A `float` value from `0.0` to `1.0` that indicates how hard the pen is pressed against the digitizer (or `0.5` if pressure sensitivity isn't supported).

→ **Orientation**—A `float` value that reveals the angle that the pen is held, in terms of degrees relative to the z-axis (perpendicular to the digitizer).

→ **Twist**—Another `float` value that represents an angle in degrees. This value, however, changes as the pen is spun in-place in the user's fingers (independent of the pen's `Orientation`).

→ **XTilt**—A `float` value revealing the angle (in degrees) of how much the pen is tilted to the left or right. The value is negative when tilted to the left and positive when tilted to the right.

→ **YTilt**—A `float` value revealing the angle (in degrees) of how much the pen is tilted to the top or bottom. The value is negative when tilted down (toward the user) and positive when tilted up (away from the user).

 Pens typically generate `PointerMoved` **events even when they aren't touching the digitizer!**

Because a typical pen digitizer supports the detection of pen input when the pen is *in range* but not *in contact*, pen motion acts more like a mouse than a finger. When `PointerMoved` events are raised, you cannot assume that the pen is in contact with the digitizer. You can, however, check the `IsInRange` and `IsInContact` properties to figure out exactly what is going on.

 What does the `RightTapped` **event mean for pen input?**

A pen can perform a right tap by tapping the digitizer with its barrel button depressed. Unlike touch, `RightTapped` is not raised if you attempt to do a press-and-hold gesture with a pen. (Although unlike a mouse, press-and-hold with a pen does raise `UIElement`'s `Holding` event.)

All properties exposed by `PointerPointProperties` use smart default values so they behave reasonably when not supported by the current `PointerDevice`. Even if you act on some pen-specific properties such as `Pressure`, you typically can do it unconditionally rather than having to check the `PointerDeviceType`.

Keyboard Input

In contrast to the other areas, the keyboard input APIs look traditional—and even simpler—compared to past Microsoft technologies. Although an app might be used with a software keyboard or hardware keyboard, the resulting input looks identical.

Because keyboard input is not tied into pointer events, and because gestures and manipulations are based on pointers, users cannot automatically perform standard gestures with a keyboard. The one exception is the edge gesture, discussed earlier, which is automatically invoked by Windows+Z or the context menu key. When this happens, only the `EdgeGesture.Completed` event is raised because there's no way to start then cancel the gesture in this fashion.

 How can I tell whether a hardware keyboard is present?

You can instantiate a `KeyboardCapabilities` class from the `Windows.Devices.Input` namespace and check the value of its one and only property: `KeyboardPresent`. Its value is 1 for `true` or 0 for `false`. Although it's not mentioned in its name, this refers to the *hardware* keyboard. On a device with a touchscreen, the software keyboard is always available when the hardware keyboard is not.

UIElement **Keyboard Events**

`UIElement` exposes two simple routed events for keyboard input: `KeyDown` and `KeyUp`. The `EventArgs` parameter passed to keyboard event handlers is a `KeyRoutedEventArgs` instance that contains the following properties:

→ **Key**—The key that was pressed or released. This property is of type `Windows.System.VirtualKey`, a large enumeration of every possible key.

→ **KeyStatus**—Reports extended information for certain keys.

→ **Handled**—The typical routed event property that can "halt" bubbling.

The `KeyStatus` property is a `Windows.UI.Core.CorePhysicalKeyStatus` structure. In case you didn't get all the hints from its name, this is "core" information that is needed only for advanced scenarios. It exposes the following properties:

→ **RepeatCount**—Tracks the number of times the `KeyDown` event gets repeated for a single, prolonged key press. For example, when you hold down the spacebar long enough, a flurry of `KeyDown` events are raised before `KeyUp` is raised.

→ **ScanCode**—The key's numeric scan code.

→ **IsExtendedKey**—Whether the key maps to an extended ASCII character.

→ **IsMenuKeyDown**—Whether the Alt key is depressed at the time this event is raised.

→ **IsKeyReleased** and **WasKeyDown**—Provide extra information about the key's status.

Although the software keyboard causes KeyDown and KeyUp events to be raised just like a hardware keyboard, the software keyboard does not raise these events for a few reserved combinations: Ctrl+A (select all), Ctrl+Z (undo), Ctrl+X (cut), Ctrl+C (copy), and Ctrl+V (paste).

> 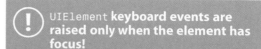 UIElement **keyboard events are raised only when the element has focus!**
>
> Sometimes an element has focus automatically, but sometimes you need to take explicit action. The upcoming "Focus" section explains more.
>
> Alternatively, you can be notified of every keystroke regardless of focus by attaching a handler to the lower-level AcceleratorKeyActivated event available from Window.Current.CoreWindow. Dispatcher. The event is named as such because keyboard shortcuts (also called accelerator keys) only make sense if they are able to work without focus requirements.

> (!) **In the keyboard APIs, the "menu" refers to the Alt key!**
>
> Members such as VirtualKey.Menu and CorePhysicalKeyStatus.IsMenuKeyDown refer to the Alt key. Although this naming seems like an odd break from .NET tradition, it is consistent with the old VK_MENU constant from Win32. Therefore, this name is an artifact of VirtualKey being a Windows Runtime API (designed by the Windows team) rather than a .NET API. The same can be said for why the enumeration is named **Virtual**Key rather than simply Key. However, you can think of the Alt key as "the key used to reveal the menu in several desktop apps" as a way to justify its Menu name.
>
> Note that the context menu key, which not all keyboards have, is exposed with another confusing name: VirtualKey.Application.

Getting Key States at Any Time

If the KeyDown, KeyUp, and AcceleratorKeyActivated events were all you had to work with, detecting key combinations (such as Alt+G) would be awkward. Each key is reported one-at-a-time, so you would need a member variable representing the state of Ctrl to set on KeyDown and clear on KeyUp. Then you could check its value when receiving another event for the letter G.

Fortunately, there are two methods for determining the state of any key at any time: GetKeyState and GetAsyncKeyState. These methods are tucked away in Window.Current.CoreWindow, a surprisingly obscure place for an important feature. This is not just useful for key combinations, but for code that isn't driven by input events, such as a game loop.

With both `GetKeyState` and `GetAsyncKeyState`, you can simply pass in a `VirtualKey` value, and you get back one or more values from a `CoreVirtualKeyStates` enumeration:

➔ **None**—The key is not pressed.

➔ **Down**—The key is pressed.

➔ **Locked**—The key is engaged in a locked state, such as Caps Lock, although this often shows up for regular keys when held down as part of a key combination.

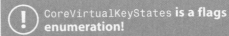 **CoreVirtualKeyStates is a flags enumeration!**

Not only is it a flags enumeration, but it is common for a combined state of Down and Locked to be reported for any key held down as part of a key combination. Therefore, to be safe, you should always test for specific values with Boolean logic rather than equality.

The following code uses a `DispatcherTimer` in a `Page`'s constructor to continuously check the state of the Alt and G keys in order to report when Alt+G is pressed:

```
public MainPage()
{
  InitializeComponent();

  // Start a timer that continuously invokes the delegate on the UI thread:
  DispatcherTimer timer = new DispatcherTimer();
  timer.Tick += delegate
  {
    CoreVirtualKeyStates menuState =
      Window.Current.CoreWindow.GetKeyState(VirtualKey.Menu);
    CoreVirtualKeyStates gState =
      Window.Current.CoreWindow.GetKeyState(VirtualKey.G);

    if ((menuState & CoreVirtualKeyStates.Down) == CoreVirtualKeyStates.Down &&
        (gState & CoreVirtualKeyStates.Down) == CoreVirtualKeyStates.Down)
    {
      // Alt+G is pressed
    }
  };
  timer.Start();
}
```

The preceding code is meant to simulate a game loop, but the following code is a variation that checks the state of the keyboard only when the `KeyDown` event is raised. It leverages the `KeyDown` event to detect when G is pressed, then checks whether the Alt key is also pressed at the same time:

```
protected override void OnKeyDown(KeyRoutedEventArgs e)
{
  if (e.Key == VirtualKey.G)
  {
    CoreVirtualKeyStates menuState =
```

```
      Window.Current.CoreWindow.GetKeyState(VirtualKey.Menu);

    if ((menuState & CoreVirtualKeyStates.Down) == CoreVirtualKeyStates.Down)
    {
        // Alt+G is pressed
    }
  }
}
```

If the Alt key is indeed pressed, then OnKeyDown would have already been raised for that key, which would have been ignored at the time. This is a much simpler approach then tracking the state of each key across multiple KeyDown and KeyUp events.

 What's the difference between CoreWindow.GetKeyState **and** CoreWindow.GetAsyncKeyState?

Their names are confusing, especially because they have identical signatures, but they are named after Win32 APIs with the same names. GetKeyState represents the state of a key at the time of a relevant input event, whereas GetAsyncKeyState represents the state of a key *right now*. Most of the time, GetKeyState is the right choice for apps.

How do I find out whether the *left* **or** *right* **Alt, Ctrl, or Shift key was pressed?**

Although the KeyDown and KeyUp events report the generic VirtualKey.Menu, VirtualKey.Control, and VirtualKey.Shift values, the VirtualKey enumeration does contain separate values for LeftMenu versus RightMenu, LeftControl versus RightControl, and LeftShift versus RightShift (as well as LeftWindows versus RightWindows). You can pass these more specific values to GetKeyState or GetAsyncKeyState to find out which one is currently pressed, or if both are pressed.

GetKeyState and GetAsyncKeyState can be used to get the state of mouse buttons on-demand as well, because the VirtualKey enumeration includes values for LeftButton, MiddleButton, RightButton, XButton1, and XButton2. However, if the left and right mouse buttons are logically swapped, these methods are not aware of it. Asking about LeftButton and RightButton always returns information about the physical left and right buttons, respectively.

Keyboard Modifiers in Pointer Events

Although the keyboard events are not pointer events, the pointer events do report some information about the current state of the keyboard via the PointerRoutedEventArgs. KeyModifiers property. The idea is that certain special keys are pressed to "modify" another gesture.

The property is of type `Windows.System.VirtualKeyModifiers`, another enumeration. It reveals whether certain keys are currently pressed: `Control`, `Shift`, `Windows`, `Menu` (the Alt key), or `None`. Naturally, this is a flags enumeration because any number of these can be pressed simultaneously. Therefore, you don't want to check for equality unless you care about the state of every modifier key. For example, the following code checks whether Alt is pressed while the pointer is moving but doesn't rule out Shift+Alt or Ctrl+Alt, and so on:

```
protected override void OnPointerMoved(PointerRoutedEventArgs e)
{
  if ((e.KeyModifiers & VirtualKeyModifiers.Menu) == VirtualKeyModifiers.Menu)
  {
    // Alt is pressed, potentially also with Ctrl, Shift, and/or Windows
  }
}
```

On the other hand, the following code checks for Alt and nothing else:

```
protected override void OnPointerMoved(PointerRoutedEventArgs e)
{
  if (e.KeyModifiers == VirtualKeyModifiers.Menu)
  {
    // Alt is the only modifier pressed
  }
}
```

Focus

As mentioned previously, a `UIElement` receives keyboard input (and raises keyboard events) only if it has focus. For that to happen, it must first be *eligible* for focus, which means it must:

→ Be enabled (`IsEnabled=true`)

→ Be visible (`Visibility=Visible`)

→ Be hit-testable (`HitTestVisible=true`)

→ Be included in tab navigation (`IsTabStop=true`)

This list of requirements usually isn't a big burden because the four properties listed are `true` by default.

Focus can be given only to `Controls` (indeed, some of the properties in this list are defined only by `Control`), so keyboard events can't originate from *any* `UIElement` despite being defined by `UIElement`. They can be handled on non-`Control` `UIElements` *containing* `Controls`, however, thanks to event bubbling.

Out of the set of focus-eligible `Controls`, the first one is given focus by default (although sometimes knowing which one is first can be tricky). The user can change which `Control` has focus by pressing the `Tab` key. This cycles through each eligible control, and also shows a system-defined *focus rectangle* (that unsightly dotted rectangle) around the control. Tapping a `Control` also gives it focus, so focus isn't *just* about the keyboard.

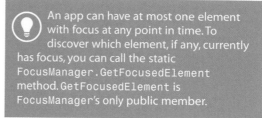

An app can have at most one element with focus at any point in time. To discover which element, if any, currently has focus, you can call the static `FocusManager.GetFocusedElement` method. `GetFocusedElement` is `FocusManager`'s only public member.

You can programmatically get and set an element's focus state with two APIs on `UIElement`: a `FocusState` property and a `Focus` method.

`FocusState` is a read-only property. It is an enumeration value that not only reveals whether an element has focus, but *how* it got focus. In addition to its `Unfocused` value, it has three possible "focused" values: `Keyboard`, `Pointer`, and `Programmatic`. The last value refers to calls to `Focus`.

Calling the `Focus` method *attempts* to set an element's focus, because it might not be eligible for focus. (It's also possible to call `Focus` too early, such as on a `Page` before its `OnNavigatedTo` method is called.) Therefore, it returns `true` if successful, and `false` otherwise. It's odd, but you must pass `Focus` a `FocusState` value. Typically, you would pass `Programmatic`, but with the other values you can mimic keyboard or pointer focus for a rare case in which code depends on the type of focus given.

`UIElement` defines `GotFocus` and `LostFocus` events that are raised when focus changes. These are its only two events that are *not* routed events (even though its handler's signatures use `RoutedEventArgs`, as explained in the preceding chapter).

Summary

Although this chapter is structured in terms that developers are used to thinking about—touch, mouse, pen, and keyboard—you've now seen the *two* primary types of input received by elements—pointer input and keyboard input. You also examined all the standard gestures—including the more complex gestures known as manipulations—that Windows automatically and consistently recognizes based on the raw pointer input. Of course, you're free to develop your own gestures based on the same pointer input that is normally fed to `GestureRecognizer`, such as an iOS-style four-finger swipe.

By finishing this chapter, you also reached a milestone in understanding XAML apps. The first four chapters in Part II (Chapters 3–6) are technically about everything that the core `UIElement` class has to offer. `UIElement` defines a ton of members, but they're all about layout and input. Now that you learned practically everything there is to learn about `UIElement`, we can move much faster through the features available to XAML apps.

Chapter 7

APP MODEL

Compared to desktop apps, Microsoft has chosen a much different approach for how and when Windows Store apps run. The result is much more like apps on a smartphone or competing tablet platforms. To the user, the experience of downloading an app from the Windows Store is obviously different than installing a desktop app. Being able to trust that you can delete an unwanted app is also a refreshing change. (When a user deletes a Windows Store app, all of its local data is removed as well. However, if the app ever saved user data, such as in the Documents, Music, Pictures, or Videos libraries, that data is kept intact.) Windows Store apps also tend to do a good job at remembering a user's *session*—coming back however the user had left it, even after rebooting or perhaps even when launching the app from a different device.

The scheme of how and when Windows Store apps run, also referred to as their *lifecycle*, enables some of this. But the most important features that are enabled by the app lifecycle are better performance and better battery life, because an offscreen app typically is not running, even though most users might not realize this.

A large portion of this chapter examines how the app lifecycle works and how you need to interact with it in order to create a well-behaved app. But there are other pieces to what is sometimes called the *app model*: how one app can launch another, how to work with the Windows Store to enable free trials and in-app purchases, and how to enable navigation between separate Pages inside your app. These topics are all covered in this chapter. The first three topics are general Windows Runtime features that apply to all apps, with APIs that live in the `Windows.ApplicationModel` namespace. The navigation topic, on the other hand, is XAML-specific.

Understanding the App Lifecycle

Whereas a desktop app can be in one of two execution states at any time, *running* or *not running*, Windows Store apps have a third possible state: *suspended*. A suspended app is basically paused; it is still in memory, but all of its threads have been suspended. (The Windows kernel ensures that an app can't be suspended in a critical section that could cause a system-wide deadlock.)

This new state is useful for preventing inactive apps from hogging additional resources. The goal is for the one or two apps in the foreground to have the luxury of as much computing power as possible, and to enable better battery life by running less. At the same time, a suspended app can switch back to the running state quickly.

Many different situations can cause an app to transition from one state to another, and the `Application` class (the base class of a project's `App` class defined in `App.xaml` and `App.xaml.cs`) exposes events or virtual methods that enable you to detect most of these transitions. Figure 7.1 displays the three execution states with all possible transitions. The four green arrows represent transitions that have corresponding notifications. Those notifications (either events or `OnXXX` virtual methods) all live on the `Application` class. The two red arrows represent transitions that happen without notifying the app.

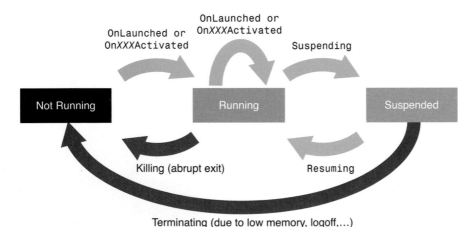

FIGURE 7.1   The three execution states, all possible transitions, and corresponding `Application` notifications

Figure 7.1 shows that there are six basic actions that can cause an app to transition among the three execution states:

→ Launching

→ Activating

→ Suspending

→ Resuming

→ Killing

→ Terminating

In the face of all this, your goal should be to provide a typical user experience with the following characteristics:

→ **After the user switches away from an app, bringing it back should return the app just how the user left it.** Although if it shows automatically updating content like a Twitter feed, it should certainly refresh it. To most users, there is no meaningful distinction between an offscreen app that is still running versus a suspended app versus a suspended app that is later terminated. (Although in the terminated case, the user needs to explicitly launch the app again to bring it back.) Either way, the app should keep track of the user's session.

→ **After the user explicitly closes an app, launching it again should give the user a "fresh" session.** The user closes an app either with a big swipe down from the top edge of the screen or by pressing Alt+F4.

To enable this pattern, an app must save any session state when suspending, and then restore it when appropriate. The rest of this section discusses when it is appropriate, because the correct approach can be subtle.

These are just guidelines, of course. For some apps, it might make sense to always maintain the same session no matter what. For other apps, it might make sense to start the app fresh if a long amount of time has passed since it was previously suspended or terminated. And for others, it might sense to give the user a choice of whether to resume where he or she left off or to start over with a fresh session. (For games, this would likely already be a choice presented to the user on a "paused screen," so it could simply present the same screen when returning in this fashion.)

Let's now examine the six actions and how to respond to them. We start with the two different ways to exit the *running* state (Killing versus Suspending), then the two ways to exit the *suspended* state (Resuming versus Terminating), and finally the two ways to exit the *not running* state (Launched versus Activated). After this, we look at a helper class called for managing session state called `SuspensionManager`.

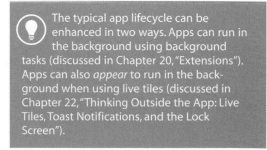

The typical app lifecycle can be enhanced in two ways. Apps can run in the background using background tasks (discussed in Chapter 20, "Extensions"). Apps can also *appear* to run in the background when using live tiles (discussed in Chapter 22, "Thinking Outside the App: Live Tiles, Toast Notifications, and the Lock Screen").

Killing

An app transitions only from *running* directly to *not running* (the red "Killing" arrow in Figure 7.1) when it is forced to do so, as with the following conditions:

→ The user logs off (which includes shutting down or restarting the computer) and the app hasn't already been suspended.

→ The user invokes "End task" in Task Manager, or an equivalent command in a command-line tool such as TaskKill.

→ The app hangs, or the code it executes in response to suspension takes longer than 5 seconds, or the code it executes in response to launch/activation (while the splash screen is showing) takes longer than 15 seconds.

→ The app is under the debugger's control and the developer ends the process in Visual Studio.

→ The app calls Application's Exit method (Application.Current. Exit).

It should not be a surprise that there's no way for an app to respond to these exceptional conditions. After this happens, any session state persisted by the app should be ignored by future launches because it could be corrupted.

 If your app "crashes" (throws an unhandled exception for an unknown reason), don't attempt to handle it and provide a message to the user. The best user experience is to let the app exit quickly. Note that Windows will send a "problem report" to Microsoft if the user consents, and you can view the details of these reports via your dashboard on the Windows Dev Center website.

Do not call Application's Exit **method!**

Apps that attempt to kill themselves are likely to not get accepted into the Windows Store, especially if they show an explicit close button in their user interface. Apps should instead let Windows manage their lifetime, and let users perform the standard "close" gestures.

Suspending

Whereas *killing* is the rude and rare way for an app to stop running, *suspending* is the gentle and common way. Immediately before suspension occurs, Application's Suspending event is raised. This is the time for an app to save any necessary session state, because it's possible the app will be terminated (without any notification) before it ever runs again. This is also the time to release any files, devices, or other exclusive resources so other apps can use them while your app is suspended. (Remember that suspending an app just pauses it, much like pausing it in a debugger, so resources don't get automatically released in this state.)

A user cannot directly suspend an app. Instead, an app is suspended by Windows for one of three different conditions:

→ Five seconds after it has been removed from the screen and replaced with another active app (the Start screen doesn't count), as long as it wasn't removed by a "close" gesture (the big swipe or Alt+F4).

→ When Windows enters a low-power mode. (This is a heuristic influenced by a number of factors.) On devices that support it, this means the *connected standby* mode in which drivers and background tasks still run.

→ Ten seconds after the user performs a "close" gesture.

For the first condition, the five-second delay and the caveats exist to optimize fast app-switching. For the last condition, the ten-second delay enables faster relaunching/reactivating of the app during that window of time (presumably when closing it was an accident), and the suspension is done to give the app a chance to do any of its typical state-saving, resource-releasing, or other bookkeeping. (After this suspension, Windows automatically closes the app.) You can see this ten-second delay by closing any app and watching its entry in Task Manager. This also explains why the Visual Studio debugger takes a long time to stop debugging (ten seconds, to be exact) when you close an app currently being debugged.

This behavior for when a user explicitly closes an app is a bit strange, because in this case the app is supposed to ignore any saved session state the next time it is launched. However, this behavior means that the app doesn't have to go out of its way to perform the same "shutdown" logic for suspending versus closing.

If the user launches or activates the app within ten seconds of closing it, then the pending suspension gets cancelled! The existing app instance's `OnLaunched` or `OnXXXActivated` method is called, and the app should pretend it is a fresh instance. Again, this is okay because the app should provide a fresh session after being explicitly closed by a user anyway.

 How do I make my game automatically pause as soon as the user closes or switches away from it?

The `Suspending` event is certainly no good for this, because the game would continue for at least five seconds! Although no `Application` event is raised as soon as the user closes or switches away from an app, there are two such events defined on the host `Window` (accessed via the static `Window.Current` property). Its `Activated` event is instantly raised whenever an app gains or loses focus, and you can tell which happened by checking the passed-in `WindowActivationState` property. Its `VisibilityChanged` event is instantly raised whenever it becomes visible or invisible, and you can tell which happened by checking the passed-in `VisibilityChangedEventArgs.Visible` property. These events provide a perfect opportunity to react immediately. `Activated` is more appropriate for pausing a game, because it also gets raised when the user switches focus from a filled game to a snapped app sharing the screen, but `VisibilityChanged` does not get raised in this scenario.

Handling the `Suspending` Event

Visual Studio-generated projects handle `Application`'s `Suspending` event in a handler called `OnSuspending` in `App.xaml.cs`. In a Blank App project, however, it's waiting for you to do something useful:

```
private void OnSuspending(object sender, SuspendingEventArgs e)
{
  var deferral = e.SuspendingOperation.GetDeferral();
```

```
//TODO: Save application state and stop any background activity
deferral.Complete();
}
```

The SuspendingEventArgs instance has a single SuspendingOperation property that exposes the GetDeferral method used in this snippet and a Deadline property that tells you how long you have to finish your logic in response to this event (currently five seconds).

As for the actual work, you should serialize any relevant data into a local file using the application data APIs covered in Chapter 18, "Data." However, the SuspensionManager class covered later in this chapter does a lot of this work on your behalf, so you can just use it instead.

Deferral

As with the preceding code snippet, the code inside a Suspending event handler is often sandwiched between a call to GetDeferral and a call to the returned object's Complete method. (The returned object is a SuspendingDeferral and Complete is its only method.) This is needed only if the code you execute is asynchronous. In this case, it tells the system to wait until you call Complete *or until the Deadline passes*. Using a deferral does *not* enable you to escape the five-second requirement!

The reason this deferral mechanism is needed is that as soon as you await, the current thread of execution returns to the system code that raised the event. Without this mechanism, the system would think you were done with your suspension logic and would instantly suspend the app without giving the asynchronous code a chance to finish.

In theory, you can omit the calls to GetDeferral and Complete if the code is completely synchronous. In practice, this usually doesn't happen, because code that persists state outside the app's own memory is usually asynchronous. The application data APIs do include synchronous *application settings* APIs, but the recommendation for persisting session state is to use a file rather than settings. Files give you more flexibility in data persistence than settings, as explained in Chapter 18.

Resuming

An app is resumed (changed from *suspended* to *running*) as soon as it is brought back on-screen. This raises Application's Resuming event. However, an app often doesn't need to handle Resuming, because there's usually nothing that needs to be done. After all, the app stayed in memory the whole time with all its variables intact, so it can just continue where it left off. Suspending is like pausing an app in a debugger, and resuming is like unpausing it.

However, if an app previously released any exclusive resources in a handler for Suspending, these likely need to be obtained again in a handler for Resuming. In addition, if an app shows auto-updating information, this would be a good time to force it to refresh.

Terminating

"Terminating" sounds bad, but it's not. Unlike killing, it's the graceful way for an app to enter the *not running* state. Whereas killing covers all the ways in which a running app suddenly stops running, termination can happen only to an app that is successfully suspended.

Windows tries to keep as many suspended apps in memory as possible, but when memory is tight (or the user is logging off), it must start terminating. There is no notification for this. After all, the terminated app isn't running at the time! That's okay, because each app should have prepared for this when it was being suspended. Because of this, you should think about termination as a "deeper" suspension, almost like putting Windows itself in hibernation mode rather than sleep mode. The next time a terminated app is launched, it is expected to continue where the user left off. That's because the user never actually closed the app.

 You can easily test the suspending, resuming, and terminating actions when debugging an app in Visual Studio! The "Debug Location" toolbar, shown in Figure 7.2, enables you to trigger these conditions, although instead of using the term *Terminate*, it uses *Suspend and shutdown*. This, of course, is an accurate description of what it means to terminate an app.

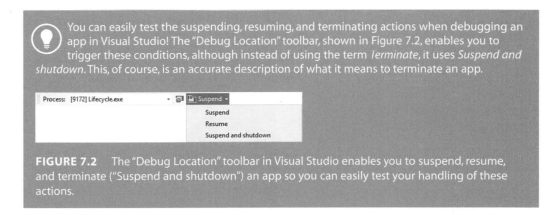

FIGURE 7.2   The "Debug Location" toolbar in Visual Studio enables you to suspend, resume, and terminate ("Suspend and shutdown") an app so you can easily test your handling of these actions.

How does Windows decide which suspended app to terminate under a low memory condition?

It is *not* a first-in, first-out algorithm. Instead, Windows targets the apps based on heuristics. Apps that use the most memory, processor cycles, power, and so on, are likely to be targeted first.

Launching

An app starts out in the *not running* state. It can transition to *running* in one of two ways:

→ **Launching**—The user clicks its primary tile, a secondary tile (if the app has any), or performs an equivalent action, such as clicking the app in the potentially filtered "All apps" list. These conditions cause `Application.OnLaunched` to be called.

→ **Activating**—The user invokes the app via a contract or extension (if it supports any), such as entry points in the Search or Share charm. This causes an `Application.On`*XXX*`Activated` method to be called instead.

As seen in Chapter 1, "Anatomy of a Windows Store App," the Visual Studio-generated `App.xaml.cs` overrides `OnLaunched` in order to initialize the app's content and navigate to the main `Page`. Nothing is done for the "activating" cases, because that is for specialized features that need to be explicitly added to a project.

Inside `OnLaunched`, you must initialize the app's content based on the previous execution state (explained in a moment), and call `Window.Current.Activate` in order to dismiss the splash screen. The call to `Activate` must be made within 15 seconds, otherwise Windows will kill your app. This is why many apps choose to show an extended splash screen that mimics the real one (typically with an added `ProgressRing`), because if initialization involves network access, you can never be sure how long that will take. Another, perhaps more satisfying approach, is to show your initial user interface in some sort of "empty" form with indicators that its content is still loading.

When you call `Window.Current.Activate`, the `Window`'s `Activate` event is raised. Note that this *window activation* concept is completely different from *app activation*. A `Window` is activated whenever it is given focus and deactivated whenever it loses focus.

 Window's Activated **event gets raised when the** Window **gets activated** *or deactivated*!

The event should have been called `ActivatedChanged`. In the `WindowActivatedEventArgs` instance passed to handlers, you can check the `WindowActivationState` property for one of three values: `PointerActivated`, `CodeActivated`, or `Deactivated`.

As a previous FAQ alluded, this event basically gets raised hand-in-hand with Window's `VisibilityChanged` event, because a Windows Store app typically becomes visible at the same time it gets focus, and becomes invisible at the same time it loses focus. App snapping is the one exception. In that case, the user can switch focus between the two visible apps, which causes `Activated` to get raised, but not `VisibilityChanged`.

LaunchActivatedEventArgs

The `LaunchActivatedEventArgs` instance passed to `OnLaunched` exposes the following properties:

→ **SplashScreen**—Exposes the location of the image inside the splash screen and a separate `Dismissed` event for when it goes away. This is helpful for providing your own extended splash screen that mimics the real one, which is highly recommended.

→ **PreviousExecutionState**—Reveals what the app was previously doing with a value from an `ApplicationExecutionState` enumeration. This is critical information needed for you to handle the launch correctly. Although this enumeration contains the three expected values of `NotRunning`, `Running`, and `Suspended`, it also includes two variations of `NotRunning`: `Terminated` and `ClosedByUser`.

→ **Arguments** and **TileId**—strings that are only non-null when an app is launched from a secondary tile. As shown in Chapter 22, an app can associate two such strings with any additional tiles that are created.

➜ **ActivationKind**—An enumeration value always set to Launch. This is an artifact of the IActivatedEventArgs interface that LaunchActivatedEventArgs implements.

Properly Reacting to PreviousExecutionState

You can see the proper pattern for handling launch by looking at the OnLaunched implementation in a Visual Studio-generated App.xaml.cs file:

```
protected override void OnLaunched(LaunchActivatedEventArgs args)
{
  Frame rootFrame = Window.Current.Content as Frame;

  // Do not repeat app initialization when the Window already has content,
  // just ensure that the window is active
  if (rootFrame == null)
  {
    // Create a Frame and navigate to the first page
    var rootFrame = new Frame();

    if (args.PreviousExecutionState == ApplicationExecutionState.Terminated)
    {
      //TODO: Load state from previously suspended application
    }

    // Place the frame in the current Window and ensure that it is active
    Window.Current.Content = rootFrame;
  }
  …
  // Ensure the current Window is active
  Window.Current.Activate();
}
```

This can be summarized as, "Just show the current Window if it has already been initialized (meaning the app is already running), restore session state if the app was previously terminated, and otherwise create a fresh session." This, of course, sounds strange, especially if you're not familiar with the app lifecycle. Common questions are:

➜ Why would the app already be running?

➜ Why do we restore state in the Terminated case and don't do anything special for the Suspended case?

The answers lie in the meaning of each PreviousExecutionState value, which can *still* be subtle even if you've read and understood everything thus far!

PreviousExecutionState is **Running** only when the launch is caused by the clicking of a secondary tile. This is the odd-looking transition from *running* to *running* in Figure 7.1. The app never stops running, but this event gives it a chance to respond to whatever clicking the secondary tile is supposed to enable. Although this code path doesn't get executed for an app that doesn't explicitly support secondary tiles, the default Visual Studio implementation simply shows the current Window. This is the correct behavior for apps with secondary tiles as well, because such apps should check for this (via args.Arguments and/or args.TileId) and update its user interface appropriately, regardless of PreviousExecutionState.

A PreviousExecutionState of **Suspended** is not normally seen inside OnLaunched because this doesn't get called by an app resuming! This occurs only when a secondary tile has been clicked and the app was suspended at the time rather than running. In this case, the Resuming event is raised immediately before OnLaunched is called.

A PreviousExecutionState of **Terminated** means that the app was previously successfully suspended and then later terminated. Therefore, as part of this launch, any session state persisted during suspension should be restored in addition to the normal initialization. This is the only time session state ever needs to be manually restored.

A PreviousExecutionState of **ClosedByUser** means just that. Note that although this means the app was eventually suspended and terminated just as in the Terminated case, ClosedByUser is reported only when the original suspension was caused by a user's "close" gesture. Therefore, even though there is likely persisted session state that *could* be restored, it should normally not be. This enables you to follow the convention that when a user closes an app, the next launch should appear like a fresh instance.

That only leaves the PreviousExecutionState of **NotRunning**. Because this doesn't include terminating and normal closing, this is reported when one of the following is true:

➜ The app was previously killed.

➜ This is the first time the user has run the app.

➜ The app was previously closed by the user *within the last ten seconds*.

Here's that odd ten-seconds-after-closing-an-app condition again. When the user quickly relaunches the app after closing it, which cancels the pending suspension and termination, the previous state is reported as NotRunning rather than ClosedByUser! This is therefore indistinguishable from your app being killed!

This quirky behavior is one reason why it's good to follow the guideline of starting with a fresh session after an app is closed by the user. As long as you never handle ClosedByUser differently than NotRunning, you'll be fine. Otherwise, a closed app would exhibit different behavior when reopened after 9 seconds versus 11 seconds!

Activating

Application provides a family of methods that you can override for different activation conditions, covering six specific cases and a catch-all for the rest:

→ OnCachedFileUpdaterActivated

→ OnFileActivated

→ OnFileOpenPickerActivated

→ OnFileSavePickerActivated

→ OnSearchActivated

→ OnShareTargetActivated

→ OnActivated

 Do not restore session state when PreviousExecutionState **is** NotRunning**!**

Even if you decide to act differently than the guidelines, you need to be careful about attempting to restore session state when PreviousExecutionState is NotRunning, because the most likely reason for this (other than the first ever launch of the app) is that the app previously crashed. And if you do a great job at restoring that session, then you might crash again! When this happens, the user might not be able to successfully launch your app again without uninstalling and reinstalling it, which would wipe out the corrupt session state.

When an app is activated for one of these six special cases, *only* the more specific method is invoked. OnActivated is reserved for any cases not covered by the first six. (These six are singled out because they are the only ones with additional context that deserve distinct EventArgs objects.) The IActivatedEventArgs instance passed to OnActivated exposes the same Kind, PreviousExecutionState, and SplashScreen properties mentioned in the preceding section. For OnActivated, however, checking Kind (of type ApplicationKind) is needed in order to understand what just happened. The ApplicationKind enumeration contains twelve choices, although only five are relevant for OnActivated because six are handled by the more specific OnXXXActivated methods, and one (Launch) is handed by OnLaunched.

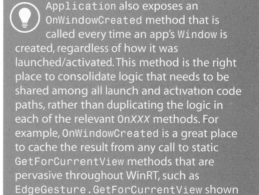 Application also exposes an OnWindowCreated method that is called every time an app's Window is created, regardless of how it was launched/activated. This method is the right place to consolidate logic that needs to be shared among all launch and activation code paths, rather than duplicating the logic in each of the relevant OnXXX methods. For example, OnWindowCreated is a great place to cache the result from any call to static GetForCurrentView methods that are pervasive throughout WinRT, such as EdgeGesture.GetForCurrentView shown in the preceding chapter.

> • • •
> ## Launch Versus Activation
>
> Although XAML apps treat launching and activating as two different concepts, the core of Windows considers launching to be *one type* of activation. Viewed this way, OnLaunched is just a seventh specialization of OnActivated (that could have been named OnLaunchActivated to match the naming of the other six On*XXX*Activated methods).
>
> This helps to explain a number of things:
>
> → Why the name of the type passed to OnLaunched is called Launch**Activated**EventArgs.
>
> → Why LaunchActivatedEventArgs exposes a useless Kind property always set to Launch. (Similarly, SearchActivatedEventArgs exposes a Kind property always set to Search, and so on.) These specialized types all derive from IActivatedEventArgs, which includes the Kind property.
>
> → Why documentation often talks about "activation" when they are referring to launching and/or activation.
>
> The other six On*XXX*Activated methods are also specific to XAML apps. This not only enables more concise implementations, but it enables the XAML UI Framework to present you with customized EventArgs objects for each one.

The various types of activations are covered in Chapters 19, "Charms," and 20, "Extensions."

Managing Session State with SuspensionManager

Session state is a set of app-specific data that captures things such as which item in a list is currently selected, which page of an article is being viewed, or the current scrollbar position. Unlike user data, such as an email message currently being composed inside your app, it's usually okay if session data somehow gets lost. It provides great value for keeping the user in context across multiple physical executions of an app. But if the user accidentally closes an app by swiping downward instead of sideways, it's usually not worth making an effort to expose the option to restore it on next launch. (The biggest exception to this is probably the user's session in a game. That tends to be highly valued data, yet isn't typically stored in a user-managed storage location.)

A Scheme for Representing Session State

Session state is typically represented as a Dictionary with string keys and arbitrary values, such as the following:

```
static Dictionary<string, object> sessionState = new Dictionary<string, object>();
```

Session state values are therefore typically set and retrieved as follows:

```
// Store a value
sessionState["CurrentIndex"] = 5;

// Retrieve a value
```

```
if (sessionState.ContainsKey("CurrentIndex"))
  index = sessionState["CurrentIndex"];
```

Because this data must be persisted somewhere, the only requirement for the values is that they are serializable. The Dictionary could be persisted as follows, using the best practice of writing it into a local file private to the app:

```
public static async Task SaveAsync()
{
  // Serialize synchronously to avoid asynchronous access to shared state
  MemoryStream memoryStream = new MemoryStream();
  DataContractSerializer serializer = new DataContractSerializer(
    typeof(Dictionary<string, object>));
  serializer.WriteObject(memoryStream, sessionState);

  // Write the data to a local app data file
  StorageFile file = await ApplicationData.Current.LocalFolder.CreateFileAsync(
    "_sessionState.xml", CreationCollisionOption.ReplaceExisting);
  using (Stream fileStream = await file.OpenStreamForWriteAsync())
  {
    memoryStream.Seek(0, SeekOrigin.Begin);
    await memoryStream.CopyToAsync(fileStream);
    await fileStream.FlushAsync();
  }
}
```

This uses the .NET DataContractSerializer, which serializes the data as XML.

Session state could then be restored as follows:

```
public static async Task RestoreAsync()
{
  sessionState = new Dictionary<string, object>();

  // Read previously-persisted data from the file
  StorageFile file = await ApplicationData.Current.LocalFolder.GetFileAsync(
    "_sessionState.xml");
  if (file != null)
  {
    using (IInputStream inputStream = await file.OpenSequentialReadAsync())
    {
      // Deserialize
      DataContractSerializer serializer =
        new DataContractSerializer(typeof(Dictionary<string, object>));
      sessionState = (Dictionary<string, object>)serializer.ReadObject(
```

```
      inputStream.AsStreamForRead());
    }
  }
}
```

Introducing SuspensionManager

A SuspensionManager class exists that can do all this saving and restoring work (and a bit more) for you. It exposes a SessionState property that is the same type of Dictionary used in the previous snippets, as well as similar SaveAsync and RestoreAsync methods.

To use this, you must call RestoreAsync inside OnLaunched for the previously terminated condition:

```
if (args.PreviousExecutionState == ApplicationExecutionState.Terminated)
{
  // Restore the saved session state only when appropriate
  await SuspensionManager.RestoreAsync();
}
```

You can set and retrieve session state values as follows:

```
// Store a value
SuspensionManager.SessionState["CurrentIndex"] = 5;

// Retrieve a value
if (SuspensionManager.SessionState.ContainsKey("CurrentIndex"))
  index = SuspensionManager.SessionState["CurrentIndex"];
SuspensionManager.SessionState["CurrentIndex"] = 5;
```

You must also call SaveAsync inside your handler for Application's Suspending event:

```
async Task OnSuspending(object sender, SuspendingEventArgs e)
{
  // The deferral is needed due to the async nature of SaveAsync
  var deferral = e.SuspendingOperation.GetDeferral();
  await SuspensionManager.SaveAsync();
  deferral.Complete();
}
```

This is all very natural. The only odd thing is how you include SuspensionManager in your app. It is *not* part of any standard libraries. Instead, you can copy the code from most of the official Windows SDK samples at http://code.msdn.microsoft.com. Or, depending on what you do in Visual Studio, Visual Studio will automatically add the code to your project. For example, if you add a new "Basic Page" to your project instead of a "Blank Page," Visual Studio will also add SuspensionManager.cs to your project's

Common folder. That's because the generated page derives from a `LayoutAwarePage` class (whose source also gets included in your project) that internally leverages `SuspensionManager`. Similarly, if you select a project template other than "Blank App" when creating a new project, `SuspensionManger.cs` will be included in the project *and* the relevant calls to it will be made inside `App.xaml.cs`.

Don't forget to add the calls to `SuspensionManager`'s `RestoreAsync` **and** `SaveAsync` **methods to** `App.xaml.cs`**!**

If you start with a Blank App project in Visual Studio, the calls to `SuspensionManager` do *not* get automatically added to `App.xaml.cs`, even if you later add an item that automatically includes `SuspensionManager.cs` in your project.

You can leverage session state as a cache. For example, if your app makes a network request when launched, consider caching the resultant data and using it instead of a live network request when appropriate. Apps using data binding can consider caching the entire data context as a single entry in one of the dictionaries. (See Chapter 17, "Data Binding.")

Programmatically Launching Apps

Apps aren't always launched by the user; one app can launch another with the `Windows.System.Launcher` class. The apps that are launched can be other Windows Store apps or even desktop apps! However, you cannot pick an arbitrary app and launch it. The target app must have registered a specific URI scheme for this to work.

Is there any way for a Windows Store app to launch a specific app with specific command-line parameters?

There is a way only if the target app has registered an appropriate URI scheme to support this.

Launching an App for a File

The following code shoes how to launch the default app for viewing PNG files using `Launcher`'s `LaunchFileAsync` method:

```
async Task LaunchOtherApp()
{
  StorageFile file = await Package.Current.InstalledLocation.GetFileAsync(
                        @"Assets\Logo.png");
  if (file != null)
  {
    // Launch the default image viewer (which could be a desktop app)
    bool success = await Launcher.LaunchFileAsync(file);
    if (!success)
    {
```

```
    …
  }
 }
}
```

This code uses a handy API accessible via `Windows.ApplicationModel.Package` that provides access to files packaged with your app.

 When launching another app, your app must already be visible!

This requirement helps to avoid user confusion. It means that even attempting to launch an app inside a `Page`'s `OnNavigatedTo` method doesn't work reliably. Instead, you should use `Launcher` only in response to some user input.

Launching an App for a URI

The following code shows how to launch the default Web browser using `Launcher`'s `LaunchUriAsync` method:

```
async Task LaunchOtherApp()
{
  // Launch the default Web browser (which could be a desktop app)
  bool success = await Launcher.LaunchUriAsync(new Uri("http://pixelwinks.com"));
  if (!success)
  {
    …
  }
}
```

When you launch an app for a URI, the file type no longer matters. For example, if you call `LaunchUriAsync` with `http://blog.adamnathan.net/images/logo.png`, it still launches the default Web browser rather than the default image viewer because the URI scheme is `http`. If the URI starts with `mailto:`, then the default mail program is used.

Custom URI schemes are supported as well as the standard ones. The Maps app has registered the `bingmaps` scheme (documented at `http://bit.ly/Qc8rC3`). If you launch `bingmaps:///`, then the app shows the map at the user's previous location, but this behavior can be customized via many query string parameters. For example, you can launch a map of donut shops in Seattle with `bingmaps:///?q=donuts&where=seattle`.

To use `LaunchUriAsync` **with an intranet URI, your app must have the "Home or Work Networking" capability!**

This fact can cause people to waste a lot of time debugging, because when you try to call `LaunchUriAsync` with an intranet URI and no such capability, it returns `false` with no extra information!

You may *not* use URIs beginning with `file:` with `LaunchUriAsync`. You must find a way to get an appropriate `StorageFile` object and call `LaunchFileAsync` instead.

How can I launch a custom app (that I also wrote)?

You should invent a custom URI scheme and register your second app to handle it. (See Chapter 20.) Your first app can then launch it with a URI beginning with that custom scheme. This works out nicely even if the user doesn't have the second app installed, because calling LaunchUriAsync with an unknown scheme presents the user interface shown in Figure 7.3. Sadly, following the "Look for an app in the Store" link does not currently help the user find the relevant app.

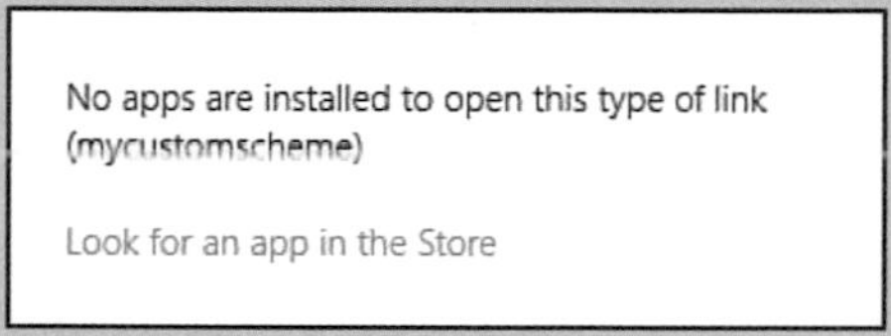

No apps are installed to open this type of link (mycustomscheme)

Look for an app in the Store

FIGURE 7.3   The result of attempting to launch a URI with an unknown scheme (mycustomscheme://...)

Customizing App Launch

Both LaunchFileAsync and LaunchUriAsync methods have an overload that accepts a LauncherOptions instance for additional customization. For example, if you set its DisplayApplicationPicker property to true, it will present the user with the typical choose-an-app user interface shown in Figure 7.4. This also gives the user the ability to tap elsewhere to cancel the opening of the file altogether.

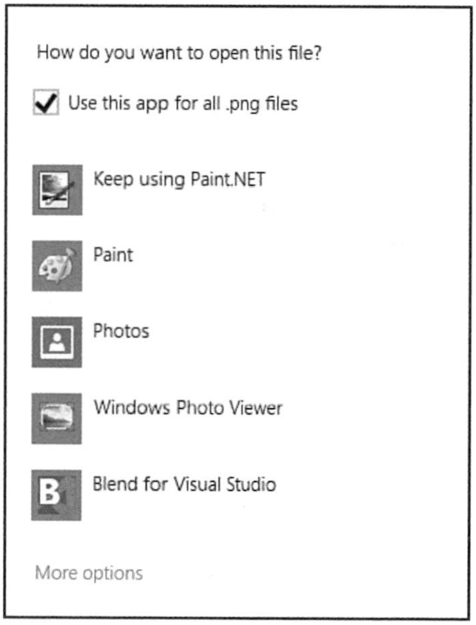

By default, the user interface in Figure 7.4 is shown in the center of the *screen* (so not even over the app's bounds if the app is snapped). However, you can control its position by setting one or more subproperties on LauncherOption's UI property. InvocationPoint can be set to a Point representing where the user performed the action that triggered the Launcher call. Or SelectionRect can be set to a similar Rect. (SelectionRect overrides InvocationPoint.) When you do this, the placement of the application picker is similar to the placement of a context menu. You can also customize the placement by setting PreferredPlacement to Above, Below, Left, or Right, which is relative to

How do you want to open this file?

✓ Use this app for all .png files

Keep using Paint.NET

Paint

Photos

Windows Photo Viewer

Blend for Visual Studio

More options

FIGURE 7.4   The user interface shown when you set LauncherOptions. DisplayApplicationPicker to true

`InvocationPoint` or `SelectionRect` and will be respected as long as there is enough room on the screen.

The following code demonstrates the use of this `LauncherOptions` object:

```
LauncherOptions options = new LauncherOptions();
options.DisplayApplicationPicker = true;
options.UI.InvocationPoint = new Point(100, 400);
options.UI.PreferredPlacement = Placement.Below;
…
bool success = await Launcher.LaunchFileAsync(file, options);
```

With `LauncherOption`'s `FallbackUri` property, you can provide an alternate URI if no app is available to launch the main URI. With its `PreferredApplicationDisplayName` and `PreferredApplicationPackageFamilyName` properties, you can help Windows suggest the right app to users.

Note that the positioning of the application picker can be relevant even if you don't set `DisplayApplicationPicker` to `true`, because it also gets shown if no appropriate app is installed.

Interacting with the Windows Store

The *app model* for Windows Store apps includes the capability to support many *business models* in the Windows Store. Besides the standard options of selling an app or providing it free (perhaps with advertisements inside), you can provide a free trial and/or in-app purchases, both with a lot of flexibility.

Enabling such features involves more than just choosing some options in your Windows Dev Center dashboard. Your app requires logic that determines what to do based on whether the user is running the trial or the full version, and what to do based on whether the user has purchased certain in-app features. You can discover all this information via the `Windows.ApplicationModel.Store.CurrentApp` static class.

> When a user moves from a "trial version" of an app to a "full version," or when a user makes an in-app purchase, the only thing he or she is buying is a *license*. The app bits don't change, so there aren't actually separate versions of an app or separate features that get downloaded (through the Windows Store, anyway). It is the responsibility of your code to properly handle the different licensing conditions and perhaps provide the illusion of separate app versions.

Supporting a Free Trial

In your Windows Dev Center dashboard, you can select whether your app currently supports a free trial, and you can optionally make it a time-based trial that expires after a certain amount of time! In your code, the mechanism for supporting a free trial is almost as easy. You check a Boolean `CurrentApp.LicenseInformation.IsTrial` property and base arbitrary logic off of that. Before using any properties of `CurrentApp.LicenseInformation`, however, you should ensure `CurrentApp.LicenseInformation.IsActive` is `true`. If it is `false`, then the license has either expired (for a time-based trial), has been revoked, or is somehow missing. In that case, you should not enable any features that are meant for paid users or for a limited time only.

The following code summarizes the necessary logic:

```
void CheckLicense()
{
  if (CurrentApp.LicenseInformation.IsActive)
  {
    if (CurrentApp.LicenseInformation.IsTrial)
    {
      // This is the free trial, so adjust the app accordingly.
    }
    else
    {
      // This is the full license, so adjust the app accordingly.
    }
  }
  else
  {
    // The license is expired, revoked, or missing. Run in the most limited mode.
  }
}
```

You would typically call a method like `CheckLicense` during your app's initialization. However, `CurrentApp.LicenseInformation` also exposes a `LicenseChanged` event. You should handle this as well, using the same `CheckLicense` method as the handler. That way, if users buy the full license while your app is running, you can reward them with an app that instantly responds with its newly purchased functionality. (You can also revoke features if the license expires while the app is running.)

If you set up a time-based trial in your Windows Dev Center dashboard, you don't need to do any date-based or time-based math in your code. The Windows Store manages this for you and simply makes the trial expire when appropriate. (When this happens, `IsActive` becomes `false`.) However, the `CurrentApp.LicenseInformation.ExpirationDate` property tells you when the expiration will happen, in case you want to show a motivating message such as, "You only have 4 days remaining before you must purchase this app!" You can easily calculate the number of remaining days as follows:

```
int numDays =
  (CurrentApp.LicenseInformation.ExpirationDate - DateTimeOffset.Now).Days;
```

Enabling the Full License to Be Purchased

It's common practice to periodically (and politely) remind users of the free trial to purchase the full license. For this to be most effective, you want to provide some sort of link or Button that makes it effortless for them to make the purchase.

One way you could do this is by calling Launcher.LaunchUriAsync with CurrentApp.LinkUri. This is the link to the appropriate page in the Web-based version of the Windows Store. Even better, you can use a URI with the ms-windows-store scheme to launch the appropriate page in the Windows Store app. This URI scheme also supports launching custom search queries in the app, as well as linking to its Updates page. You can find documentation on this scheme at http://bit.ly/T6lNPg.

You can still do better than that, though. The CurrentApp object exposes a method for launching standard a purchasing dialog directly from within your app! You can invoke it as follows:

```
async Task BuyFullLicense()
{
  try
  {
    // Show the standard purchase dialog
    await CurrentApp.RequestAppPurchaseAsync(false /* XML receipt? */);
    // The purchase succeeded! Let the LicenseChanged event handler respond.
  }
  catch
  {
    // The user cancelled the action, or there was an error
  }
}
```

If the purchase succeeds, the LicenseChanged event is raised, just as when the purchase is made in the Windows Store. If you pass true for RequestAppPurchaseAsync, it returns an XML-formatted string that is a receipt for the app purchase as well as any in-app purchases that have been made. You can retrieve this same XML string at any later time by calling CurrentApp.GetAppReceiptAsync.

The XML includes a CertificateId that you can use to verify its authenticity by fetching the public certificate at https://go.microsoft.com/fwlink/?LinkId=246509&cid=*CertificateId*. The details of the XML schema are described in MSDN documentation for this method.

> Verifying the authenticity of the receipt (leveraging your own Web service) is optional, but it is a best practice. You can also use the Windows.System.Profile. HardwareIdentification.GetPackageSpecificToken method to capture a device-specific identifier in case you want content to be restricted to a specific device or certain number of devices.

Getting Listing Details

When ~~nagging~~ politely asking users to purchase your app, you might want to remind them how inexpensive it is, or display other information from its store listing. This would be dangerous information to hard-code into your app, however. Besides the fact that you might later change your mind about the app's price and change it in the Windows Store, the price and currency varies from region to region.

Fortunately, you can retrieve the details of your app's current listing from `CurrentApp`'s `LoadListingInformationAsync` method. This asynchronously returns a `ListingInformation` object with the following properties:

→ **CurrentMarket**—A string containing a BCP-47 language identifier, such as en-us, that identifies the region (and therefore price and currency) used for Windows Store transactions.

→ **Name** and **Description**—strings for the app's name and description, specific to CurrentMarket, as this might vary.

→ **FormattedPrice**—The price of the app, specific to `CurrentMarket`. This is thankfully represented as an already formatted `string`, so all you need to do is display it as-is.

→ **AgeRating**—A uint representing the minimum appropriate age for customers of the app. Windows Store currently uses values of 3, 7, 12, or 16. This value doesn't change based on `CurrentMarket`.

→ **ProductListings**—A collection of `ProductListing` objects representing each available in-app purchase. See the next section for more details.

Supporting In-App Purchases

In your Windows Dev Center dashboard, you configure a list of features available for in-app purchasing. You can give each feature a name and a price, but you can also choose more sophisticated options like making a given feature work only for a limited time, or even limiting how many times the feature can be used before it expires! This flexibility makes it possible to provide a subscription-based experience, virtual in-app currency, and more. As with free trials, the determination of whether the user currently has a license to use a feature is completely managed for you by the Windows Store.

When you add a feature to your app's listing in your Windows Dev Center dashboard, you must give it a string ID. This is a name that your code will use to identify the feature, so it must be unique within your app. This ID is not exposed to customers, so you don't need to worry about nice formatting or localization. For example, IDs for a game could be `"HolidayTheme"` and `"20ExtraLives"`.

Determining Whether a Feature Can Be Used

The `LicenseInformation` object has one more property we haven't examined yet: `ProductLicenses`. This is what your code must use to check on the current state of each feature available for in-app purchase. In these Windows Store APIs, such features are called *products*.

ProductLicenses is a (read-only) Dictionary with string keys and ProductLicense values. The key is the ID that identifies the feature in your Windows Dev Center dashboard. Each ProductLicense exposes three simple properties: IsActive, ExpirationDate (again, for informational purposes only), and ProductId, which is the same string ID.

Therefore, the pattern for checking for a feature's valid license looks much like the pattern for checking on the status of a trial:

```
void CheckFeatureLicenses()
{
  // Check the "HolidayTheme" feature
  if (CurrentApp.LicenseInformation.ProductLicenses["HolidayTheme"].IsActive)
  {
    // The feature can be used. If this is a limited-time offer, consider
    // using CurrentApp.LicenseInformation.ProductLicenses["…"].ExpirationDate
    // to help explain that to the user.
  }
  else
  {
    // The feature cannot be used.
  }

  // Check the "20ExtraLives" feature
  …
}
```

The same LicenseChanged event applies to in-app purchases as well, so this type of CheckFeatureLicenses method should also be a handler for LicenseChanged (or called by a method like the previous CheckLicense, if your app supports a trial *and* in-app purchases). Because in-app purchases are initiated from within your app, you can already know when a new one becomes valid without handling the event, but you might not otherwise know when a limited-time one becomes invalid.

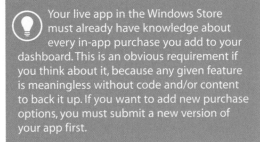

Your live app in the Windows Store must already have knowledge about every in-app purchase you add to your dashboard. This is an obvious requirement if you think about it, because any given feature is meaningless without code and/or content to back it up. If you want to add new purchase options, you must submit a new version of your app first.

Enabling a Feature to Be Purchased

There's a reason for the name *in-app purchases*; they not only *can* be bought within your app, they *must* be bought within your app! You can trigger the purchase of a feature much like triggering the purchase of the full app license. Instead of calling

RequestAppPurchaseAsync, you call RequestProductPurchaseAsync, which requires the ID for the feature being purchased:

```
async Task BuyHolidayThemeFeature()
{
  // Only do this if the user doesn't already own the feature
  if (!CurrentApp.LicenseInformation.ProductLicenses["HolidayTheme"].IsActive)
  {
    try
    {
      // Show the standard purchase dialog
      await CurrentApp.RequestProductPurchaseAsync(
        "HolidayTheme", false /* Don't return an XML receipt */);
      // The purchase succeeded! Let the LicenseChanged event handler respond.
    }
    catch
    {
      // The user cancelled the action, or there was an error
    }
  }
}
```

RequestProductPurchaseAsync can optionally return the same XML receipt that is optionally returned by RequestAppPurchaseAsync and returned by GetAppReceiptAsync.

ListingInformation object returned by CurrentApp.LoadListingInformationAsync as the data source. Recall that it has a ProductListings property that is a collection of ProductListing objects. Each ProductListing, which represents an available in-app purchase, exposes three properties: Name, FormattedPrice, and ProductId.

You should use Name whenever mentioning the feature because (a) you can dynamically change it in the Windows Store and (b) it can be customized for the current market, just like other properties on ListingInformation. You can use FormattedPrice to tell the user up-front how much each feature costs in the current market. (This property works just like the app's own FormattedPrice property on ListingInformation.) Although ProductId is not meant to be displayed to the user, you can pass it along to a generic feature-purchasing method when the user selects an item from your feature list.

Testing Windows Store Features

Testing all the functionality exposed by `CurrentApp` presents a chicken-and-egg problem. When you write a new app that uses these APIs, they will fail because the app has no listing in the Windows Store. Even if you add calls to these APIs to a new version of an already listed app, you're always one step behind the live metadata. (You certainly don't want to expose a new in-app purchase for your live app if it doesn't support it yet!) Furthermore, it can be difficult to test the various permutations of licenses with your real Microsoft account.

The `Windows.ApplicationModel.Store` namespace has a simple solution for all these problems. It contains a `CurrentApp`**Simulator** class that looks just like `CurrentApp`. Therefore, you can simply replace all references to `CurrentApp` with `CurrentApp`**Simulator** to test your app in every possible situation related to the Windows Store and user licenses.

 Don't forget to replace all references to `CurrentAppSimulator` **with** `CurrentApp` **before submitting your app to the store!**

If you forget to do so, your app will fail the certification process. And that's good news, because it would be far worse for such an app to be published to your customers!

These two classes unfortunately don't share a common interface or base class (other than `System.Object`), so you can't abstract away the difference in a single location. However, you can store common references to objects they return, such as `LicenseInformation`, and you can have most of your apps use these fields or properties. This at least reduces the number of places that directly reference `CurrentApp` or `CurrentAppSimulator`. You could also consider leveraging conditional compilation in C# to toggle between the two options with a single symbol change.

The first time your app uses `CurrentAppSimulator`, it automatically generates an XML file in your app's local data folder. This file contains fake metadata corresponding to what would normally be in the Windows Store, as well as the status of the current user's fake licenses. You can open this file directly with Notepad or your favorite text editor by pointing it to `%USERPROFILE%\AppData\Local\Packages\`*PackageFamilyName*`\LocalState\ Microsoft\Windows Store\ApiData\WindowsStoreProxy.xml`. You can see your project's value of *PackageFamilyName* on the Packaging tab in Visual Studio's package manifest designer. It is derived from your package name (from the same tab), which is set to a GUID by default. Listing 7.1 shows the contents of this auto-generated file.

LISTING 7.1   `WindowsStoreProxy.xml`: The Default Windows Store-Like Data Used by `CurrentAppSimulator`

```xml
<?xml version="1.0" encoding="utf-16" ?>
<CurrentApp>
  <ListingInformation>
    <App>
      <AppId>00000000-0000-0000-0000-000000000000</AppId>
      <LinkUri>
        http://apps.microsoft.com/webpdp/app/00000000-0000-0000-0000-000000000000
      </LinkUri>
      <CurrentMarket>en-US</CurrentMarket>
      <AgeRating>3</AgeRating>
      <MarketData xml:lang="en-us">           ┐
        <Name>AppName</Name>                  │
        <Description>AppDescription</Description>   │  Market-specific data
        <Price>1.00</Price>                   │
        <CurrencySymbol>$</CurrencySymbol>    │
      </MarketData>                           ┘
    </App>
    <Product ProductId="1" LicenseDuration="0">  ┐
      <MarketData xml:lang="en-us">              │
        <Name>Product1Name</Name>               │  One in-app purchase available
        <Price>1.00</Price>                     │  (ID="1")
        <CurrencySymbol>$</CurrencySymbol>      │
      </MarketData>                             │
    </Product>                                  ┘
  </ListingInformation>
  <LicenseInformation>
    <App>
      <IsActive>true</IsActive>
      <IsTrial>true</IsTrial>    ———— Currently a trial user
    </App>
    <Product ProductId="1">
      <IsActive>true</IsActive>  ———— Has purchased in-app feature "1"
    </Product>
  </LicenseInformation>
</CurrentApp>
```

Listing

Licenses

The XML schema maps to the APIs exposed by `CurrentApp` and `CurrentAppSimulator`. By default it acts like the current user is an active trial user who has the option to purchase the full license for $1. The app also has an in-app purchase available with an ID of 1, but the user has already purchased it.

If you use `CurrentAppSimulator` to make changes to the state of licenses at runtime (in this case, testing `RequestAppPurchaseAsync` to purchase the full license), this does not get automatically persisted to the XML file. Every time you launch the app, you have a clean slate for testing.

Of course, the power of this mechanism is that you can freely edit the XML file for your needs, and then launch the app with your customized data in place. (`CurrentAppSimulator` generates `WindowsStoreProxy.xml` only if it doesn't already exist.) You can list additional in-app purchases, change which licenses the user has or if they expire, and so on. The XML schema is documented along with `CurrentAppSimulator` on MSDN. The only big gotcha is that `ExpirationDate` must be expressed in the ISO 8601 combined date and time format: *yyyy-mm-ddThh:mm:ss.ssZ*. For example, 11:00AM on February 7, 2015 would be specified as `2015-02-07T11:00:00.00Z`.

`CurrentAppSimulator` has one method that `CurrentApp` does not have: `ReloadSimulatorAsync`. You can pass this method an XML file (represented in a `StorageFile` object) with the same schema as the default `WindowsStoreProxy.xml` file in order to reinitialize its state. This can make managing your testing much easier (and more automated). See Chapter 18 for more information about working with `StorageFile`.

Leveraging Navigation

Although simple apps might have only one `Page`, most apps have multiple `Page`s. The XAML UI Framework contains quite a bit of functionality to make it easy for an app to navigate from one page to another (and back), much like in a Web browser. Visual Studio templates also give you a lot of code to handle many small details, such as presenting a proper-looking back button, standard keyboard navigation, and automatic integration of navigation and session state.

Although a Blank App project is given a single page by default, you can add more pages by right-clicking the project in Solution Explorer then selecting Add, New Item…, and one of the many `Page` choices. The different choices are mostly distinguished by different preconfigured layouts and controls. They are quite sophisticated, and even show a custom view for when the app is snapped!

In addition, if you create a Grid App or Split App project, these are already set up as multi-`Page` apps. Figure 7.5 shows the behavior of the Split App project before any customizations are made. Selecting a group on the first `Page` (`ItemsPage`) automatically navigates to its details on the second page (`SplitPage`). When the user clicks the back button in the top left corner, the app navigates back to the first page.

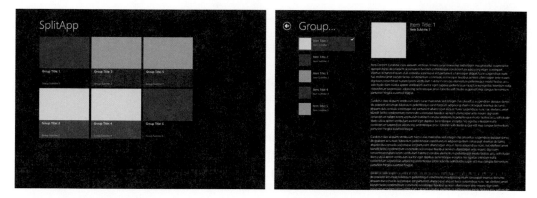

FIGURE 7.5   A Split App project contains two pages: one that shows groups, and one that shows the items inside each group.

Basic Navigation and Passing Data

Although it's natural to think of a Page as the root element of an app (especially for single-page apps), all Pages are contained in a Frame. Frame provides several members to enable Page-to-Page navigation. It is often accessed from the Frame property defined on each Page.

To navigate from one page to another, you call Frame's Navigate method with the type (*not* an instance) of the destination page. An instance of the new page is automatically created and navigated to, complete with a standard Windows 8 animation.

For example, when an item is clicked in a Split App's ItemsPage, it navigates to a new instance of SplitPage as follows:

```
void ItemView_ItemClick(object sender, ItemClickEventArgs e)
{
  // Navigate to the appropriate destination page, configuring the new page
  // by passing required information as a navigation parameter
  var groupId = ((SampleDataGroup)e.ClickedItem).UniqueId;
  this.Frame.Navigate(typeof(SplitPage), groupId);
}
```

Navigate has two overloads, one that accepts only the type of the destination page, and one that also accepts a custom System.Object that gets passed along to the destination page. In this case, this second parameter is used to tell the second page which group was just clicked. If you use SuspensionManager in your project, its automatic management of navigation state means that whatever you pass as the custom Object for Navigate must be serializable.

The target SplitPage receives this custom parameter via the NavigationEventArgs instance passed to the Page's OnNavigatedTo method. It exposes the object with its Parameter property.

A call to Navigate raises a sequence of events defined on Frame. First is Navigating, which happens before the navigation begins. It enables the handler to cancel navigation by setting the passed-in NavigatingCancelEventArgs instance's Cancel property to true. Then, if it isn't canceled, one of three events will be raised: Navigated if navigation completes successfully, NavigationFailed if it fails, or NavigationStopped if Navigate is called again before the current navigation finishes.

Page has three virtual methods that correspond to some of these events. OnNavigatingFrom enables the current page to cancel navigation. OnNavigatedFrom and OnNavigatedTo, the latter of which has already made an appearance in Chapter 1, correspond to both ends of a successful navigation. If you want to respond to a navigation failure or get details about the error, you must handle the events on Frame.

Navigating Forward and Back

Just like a Web browser, the Frame maintains a back stack and a forward stack. In addition to the Navigate method, it exposes GoBack and GoForward methods. Table 7.1 explains the behavior of these three methods and their impact on the back and forward stacks.

TABLE 7.1   Navigation Effects on the Back and Forward Stacks

Action	Result
Navigate	Pushes the current page onto the back stack, empties the forward stack, and navigates to the desired page
GoBack	Pushes the current page onto the forward stack, pops a page off the back stack, and navigates to it
GoForward	Pushes the current page onto the back stack, pops a page off the forward stack, and navigates, it exposes GoBack and GoForward to it

GoBack throws an exception when the back stack is empty (which means you're currently on the app's initial page), and GoForward throws an exception when the forward stack is empty. If a piece of code is not certain what the states of these stacks are, it can check the Boolean CanGoBack and CanGoForward properties first. Frame also exposes a BackStackDepth readonly property that reveals the number of Pages currently on the back stack.

Therefore, you could imagine implementing Page-level GoBack and GoForward methods as follows:

```
void GoBack()
{
  if (this.Frame != null && this.Frame.CanGoBack) this.Frame.GoBack();
}

void GoForward()
{
  if (this.Frame != null && this.Frame.CanGoForward) this.Frame.GoForward();
}
```

? How do I pass data from one page to another when navigating backward?

Sometimes an app uses a scheme that navigates to a new page in order to have the user select something or fill out a form, and then that data needs to be communicated *back* to the original page when the new page is dismissed. You've already seen how to pass data to the next page when calling Navigate, but there is no equivalent mechanism for passing data to the preceding page when calling GoBack. (The same is true for GoForward.)

Instead, you must find a shared place to store the data where both pages know to look. For example, this could be your own static member on one of your classes, or, it exposes GoBack and GoForward perhaps even session state might be appropriate to use for this.

• • •

Frame's Content **Property**

Instead of calling Navigate, you can place content in a Frame by setting its Content property. (This is what the Visual Studio-generated code in App.xaml.cs does.) This is much different than calling Navigate, however, because doing so clears the back and forward stacks. It also doesn't trigger the typical navigation animation.

Furthermore, the Frame control can holds arbitrary content via its Content property. This is not a normal thing to do, but using Frame in this way enables hosting the content in an isolated fashion. For example, properties that would normally be inherited down the element tree stop when they reach the Frame. In this respect, Frame acts like a frame in HTML.

Page **Caching**

By default, Page instances are *not* kept alive on the back and forward stacks; a new instance gets created when you call GoBack or GoForward! This means you must take care to remember and restore their state, although you will probably already have code to do this in order to do a good job handling suspension.

You can change this behavior on a Page-by-Page basis by setting Page's NavigationCacheMode property to one of the following values:

→ **Disabled**   The default value that causes the page to be recreated every time.

→ **Required**—Keeps the page alive and uses this cached instance every time (for GoForward and GoBack, not for Navigate).

→ **Enabled**—Keeps the page alive and uses the cached instance only if the size of the Frame's cache hasn't been exceeded. This size is controlled by Frame's CacheSize property. This property represents a number of Pages and is set to 10 by default.

Using Required or Enabled can result in excessive memory usage, and it can waste CPU cycles if an inactive Page on the stack is doing unnecessary work (such as having code running on a timer). Such pages can use the OnNavigatedFrom method to pause its processing and the OnNavigatedTo method to resume it, to help mitigate this problem.

When you navigate to a Page by calling Navigate, you get a new instance of it, regardless of NavigationCacheMode. No special relationship exists between two instances of a Page other than the fact that they happen to come from the same source code. You can leverage this by reusing the same type of Page for multiple levels of a navigation hierarchy, each one dynamically initialized to have the appropriate content. However, if you want every instance of the same page to act as if it's the same page (and "remember" its data from the previously-seen instance), then you need to manage this yourself, perhaps with static members on the relevant Page class.

LayoutAwarePage

As mentioned earlier in this chapter, if you add any Page more sophisticated than a Blank Page to your project, it derives from a LayoutAwarePage base class whose source also gets included in your project. Its primary purpose is to map the Windows view states to XAML visual states (covered in Chapter 16, "Styles, Templates, and Visual States"), but it also adds a lot of functionality related to navigation.

For convenience, LayoutAwarePage defines virtual GoBack and GoForward methods just like the ones implemented earlier. It also defines a handy GoHome method that keeps navigating backward until it reaches the first Page:

```
protected virtual void GoHome(object sender, RoutedEventArgs e)
{
  // Use the navigation frame to return to the topmost page
  if (this.Frame != null)
  {
    while (this.Frame.CanGoBack) this.Frame.GoBack();
  }
}
```

Note that all three of these helper methods avoid throwing exceptions. They exit silently if it's not possible to go back or forward.

LayoutAwarePage also adds standard keyboard and mouse shortcuts for navigation. It enables navigating back when the user presses Alt+Left and navigating forward when the user presses Alt+Right. For a mouse, it enables navigating back if XButton1 is pressed and forward if XButton2 is pressed. These two buttons are the browser-style previous and next buttons that appear on some mice.

LayoutAwarePage also hooks into some extra functionality exposed by SuspensionManager in order to automatically maintain navigation history as part of session state. All you need to do is call one more method inside OnLaunched (or OnWindowCreated) to make SuspensionManager aware of the Frame:

```
var rootFrame = new Frame();
SuspensionManager.RegisterFrame(rootFrame, "AppFrame");
```

When you create a Grid App or Split App project, this call is inserted automatically. Internally, this works in part thanks to a pair of methods exposed by Frame—GetNavigationState and SetNavigationState—that conveniently provide and accept a serialized string representation of navigation history.

LayoutAwarePage also defines virtual LoadState and SaveState methods that you could choose to override instead of OnNavigatedTo and OnNavigatedFrom, but it's a matter of personal preference. LoadState is passed the "navigation parameter" object (the second parameter passed to the call to Navigate, otherwise null) as well as the session state Dictionary. SaveState is passed only the session state Dictionary.

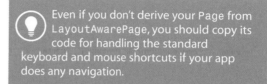

Even if you don't derive your Page from LayoutAwarePage, you should copy its code for handling the standard keyboard and mouse shortcuts if your app does any navigation.

The Back Button

You might have noticed that the SplitPage in Figure 7.5 has a nice, standard looking back button that doesn't look like a normal Button control. It actually *is* a normal Button, but it is given a special style defined in StandardStyles.xaml. You can do the same thing with your own custom Button on a custom Page.

For example, the following Buttons are shown on the left of Figure 7.6:

```
<StackPanel Orientation="Horizontal">
  <Button>Back</Button>
  <Button>Back</Button>
  <Button>Back</Button>
</StackPanel>
```

The results of adding the following Style attributes are shown on the right of Figure 7.6:

```
<StackPanel Orientation="Horizontal">
  <Button Style="{StaticResource BackButtonStyle}">Back</Button>
  <Button Style="{StaticResource PortraitBackButtonStyle}">Back</Button>
  <Button Style="{StaticResource SnappedBackButtonStyle}">Back</Button>
</StackPanel>
```

Elements inside SplitPage.xaml dynamically switch its BackButtonStyle to either PortraitBackButtonStyle or SnappedBackButtonStyle based on the current view state. (The difference between BackButtonStyle and PortraitBackButtonStyle is only in its Margin.)

Before   After

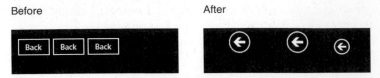

FIGURE 7.6   The effect of applying special back button styles to Buttons

Other Ways to Use Frame

Not every app needs to follow the pattern of a Window hosting a Frame that hosts Page(s).
A Window's content doesn't have to be a Frame, and you can embed Frames anywhere
UIElements can go. We can demonstrate this by modifying a Split App project to set the
Window's Content to a custom Grid subclass that we create. Imagine this is called
RootGrid, and it must be constructed with a Frame that it wants to dynamically add to its
Children collection. It would be used in App.xaml.cs as follows:

```
// Instead of Window.Current.Content = rootFrame:
Window.Current.Content = new RootGrid(rootFrame);
```

RootGrid can be added to the project as a pair of XAML and code-behind, shown in
Listings 7.2 and 7.3.

LISTING 7.2   RootGrid.xaml: A Simple Grid Expecting to Contain a Frame

```xml
<Grid x:Class="Chapter7.RootGrid" Background="Blue"
  xmlns="http://schemas.microsoft.com/winfx/2006/xaml/presentation"
  xmlns:x="http://schemas.microsoft.com/winfx/2006/xaml">
  <!-- A 3x3 Grid -->
  <Grid.RowDefinitions>
    <RowDefinition/>
    <RowDefinition/>
    <RowDefinition/>
  </Grid.RowDefinitions>
  <Grid.ColumnDefinitions>
    <ColumnDefinition/>
    <ColumnDefinition/>
    <ColumnDefinition/>
  </Grid.ColumnDefinitions>
  <!-- Two Buttons to interact with a Frame -->
  <Button Name="BackButton" Grid.Row="1" HorizontalAlignment="Center"
    Click="BackButton_Click">Back</Button>
  <Button Name="ForwardButton" Grid.Row="1" Grid.Column="2"
    HorizontalAlignment="Center" Click="ForwardButton_Click">Forward</Button>
</Grid>
```

LISTING 7.3   `RootGrid.xaml.cs`: The Code-Behind that Places the Frame and Interacts with It

```
using Windows.UI.Xaml;
using Windows.UI.Xaml.Controls;
using Windows.UI.Xaml.Navigation;

namespace Chapter7
{
  public sealed partial class RootGrid : Grid
  {
    Frame frame;

    public RootGrid(Frame f)
    {
      InitializeComponent();
      this.frame = f;

      // Add the Frame to the middle cell of the Grid
      Grid.SetRow(this.frame, 1);
      Grid.SetColumn(this.frame, 1);
      this.Children.Add(this.frame);

      this.frame.Navigated += Frame_Navigated;
    }

    void Frame_Navigated(object sender, NavigationEventArgs e)
    {
      if (this.frame != null)
      {
        // Keep the enabled/disabled state of the buttons relevant
        this.BackButton.IsEnabled = this.frame.CanGoBack;
        this.ForwardButton.IsEnabled = this.frame.CanGoForward;
      }
    }

    void BackButton_Click(object sender, RoutedEventArgs e)
    {
      if (this.frame != null && this.frame.CanGoBack)
        this.frame.GoBack();
    }

    void ForwardButton_Click(object sender, RoutedEventArgs e)
    {
      if (this.frame != null && this.frame.CanGoForward)
        this.frame.GoForward();
    }
  }
}
```

By placing the Frame in its middle cell, RootGrid is effectively applying a thick blue border to the Frame that persists even as navigation happens within the Frame. (When used this way, Frame seems more like an iframe in HTML.) The simple back and forward Buttons in RootGrid are able to control the navigation (and enable/disable when appropriate) thanks to the APIs exposed on Frame. This unconventional app is shown in Figure 7.7, after navigating to the second page.

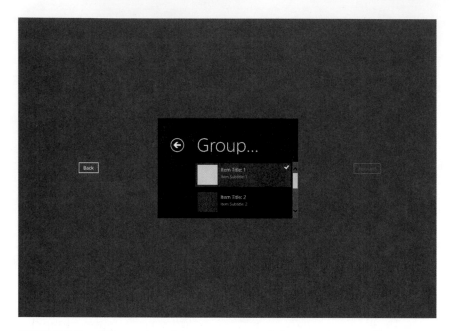

FIGURE 7.7   A Frame doesn't have to occupy all the space in an app's Window.

Although this specific use of Frame doesn't seem practical, you can do some neat things with a similar approach. One example would be to have a Page that always stays on screen containing a fullscreen Frame that navigates to various Pages. The reason this is compelling is that the outer Page can have AppBars that are accessible regardless of what the current inner Page is. (AppBars are discussed in the next chapter.)

If you decide you want your Page to truly be the root content in your app's Window, you can change the code in App.xaml.cs to eliminate the hosting Frame. This can work fine, but with no Frame, you don't get the navigation features.

Summary

This chapter thoroughly examined the application lifecycle, but here is a concise summary of how to deal with the various execution states and transition actions:

→ When **launched**:

   → Check whether the app is already running. If so, simply show the currently-hidden Window (with its Activate method).

> → If the app was previously terminated, restore the user's session state (quickly!).

> → Initialize (quickly!) and show your own custom "extended splash screen" if you need more than 15 seconds.

> → React to specifics of the tile if a secondary tile was clicked.

→ When **activated**, follow the rules for launching, but also respond to the specific request regardless of the previous execution state.

→ While **running**, save user data incrementally.

→ When **suspended**:

> → Assume you'll be terminated, so save session state (quickly!)

> → Release any exclusive resources

> → Consider updating your app's tile with current information (see Chapter 22)

→ When **resumed**, do nothing (unless some state was destroyed upon suspension that needs to be restored, such as the release of exclusive resources).

An important distinction made in these guidelines is the difference between:

→ **User data**—User-configurable settings, user-generated files, or other data that should be remembered indefinitely

→ **Session state**—Transient state, like a partially filled form for creating a new item that has not yet been saved

The management of user data should be done completely independently from an app's lifecycle and the Suspending event.

If you're familiar with the lifecycle of Windows Phone apps, the lifecycle of Windows Store apps looks deceivingly similar. The biggest difference is that suspending just pauses an in-memory app, whereas Windows Phone's *tombstoning* actually removes the app from memory, wiping out anything that wasn't explicitly persisted.

With the flexible support for trials and in-app purchases (also reminiscent of the support for Windows Phone apps), you can come up with all sorts of payment schemes with little effort. For example, instead of a typical time-based trial or a feature-limited trial, you could support a hybrid that offers full functionality for a limited time, followed by reduced functionality after the trial has expired. With an in-app purchase that can be used only once per purchase, you could sell a pack of 500 virtual coins that have special meaning inside your app.

The navigation features enabled by Frame and Page, although specific to XAML, are similar in spirit to the type of navigation features supported for HTML-based Windows Store apps. Unlike traditional Windows desktop apps, it is quite common for Windows Store apps to expose a user interface centered around navigating to different pages. For example, all the Bing apps except Maps (ironically, the one that is XAML-based) uses multiple pages.

Chapter 8

CONTENT CONTROLS

XAML would not be nearly as enjoyable to use for writing Windows Store apps without a standard set of controls, so the XAML UI Framework has plenty of standard controls included "in the box." Such controls enable you to quickly assemble common types of user interfaces that can match Windows 8 and other Windows Store apps in both appearance and behavior. These controls are optimized for touch but handle mouse, pen, and keyboard exactly how you'd expect. You've seen a few of them in previous chapters, but this part of the book takes you on a tour of the rest.

The figures in this book typically show controls under the default "dark" theme, which makes them render mostly white. (*Dark* refers to the color of the background they are meant to be placed upon.) However, the built-in controls also support a "light" theme so they can be easily used on top of white or light backgrounds instead. For example, Figure 8.1 displays the default appearance of a Button under both app themes, as well as under the four standard color variations of the high-contrast user theme (typically used only by users who need extra help seeing content on the screen). Note that when high contrast is enabled, the app theme (dark versus light) is ignored.

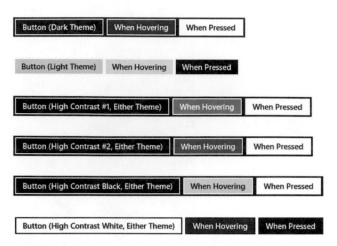

FIGURE 8.1   `Button`'s default appearances under the two app themes and four standard variations of the high-contrast user theme

In most cases, the difference in appearance is subtle. Of course, you can give controls a radically different look (based on the current theme or theme-independent) by using custom control templates, as discussed in Chapter 16, "Styles, Templates, and Visual States."

How do the dark, light, and high contrast themes work?

The first thing to understand is that there are two types of themes: those controlled by the app developer (*app themes*) and those controlled by the user (*user themes*). There are only two app themes—*dark* and *light*—and the way to control which one is used by your app is to set the `RequestedTheme` property on your `Application`-derived class to either `Dark` (the default value) or `Light` (the only other valid value). This is typically done in App.xaml as follows:

```xml
<Application x:Class="MyApp.App"
  xmlns="http://schemas.microsoft.com/winfx/2006/xaml/presentation"
  xmlns:x="http://schemas.microsoft.com/winfx/2006/xaml"
  xmlns:local="using:MyApp"
  RequestedTheme="Light">
  …
</Application>
```

You can set it in code-behind (the property is an `ApplicationTheme` enumeration) in case you want to change it based on your own user-exposed setting. However, it must be set only during initialization (before any `Window` is created), otherwise an exception is thrown. Note that the app theme you choose does not make any difference if your app has all custom visuals with custom colors. But when your app uses standard controls with their default templates, or when your app uses theme brushes (such as the `ApplicationPageBackgroundThemeBrush` background used inside Visual Studio-generated Pages), this choice affects the colors in your app. Note also that this scheme differs from Windows Phone, which gives the *user* the power to switch between a dark and light theme that affects all apps that don't hard-code all their colors.

The user can, however, change Windows to a high-contrast *user* theme instead of the default *user* theme. This can be done in the PC Settings app under "Ease of Access," which exposes a simple "High Contrast" on/off toggle switch, or it can be done in the Control Panel, which exposes the four color variations seen in Figure 8.1. From the Control Panel (Personalization, Window Color and Appearance), users can customize each relevant color individually. Therefore, even though the Control Panel displays four different high contrast "themes," it's best to think of there being only two user themes (default versus high-contrast). The choices in the Control Panel are simply shortcuts to preconfigured color choices.

When high contrast is used, its color settings override the typical theme colors, making the dark versus light app theme choice irrelevant. This is why Application's property is called `Requested`Theme rather than simply Theme. To put it another way, the two app themes have app-chosen sets of colors for the default user theme, but the high contrast theme has only user-chosen colors.

As with the app themes, a user's high contrast settings affect an app only to the degree it uses standard controls with standard templates, or theme brushes rather than hardcoded colors. You can quickly preview your app under any app or user theme in Visual Studio's XAML designer by changing the value of the Theme drop-down in the Device tool window.

The built-in controls can be grouped roughly into the following categories, which coincide somewhat with their inheritance hierarchy:

→ Content controls (this chapter)

→ Items controls (Chapter 9)

→ Text (Chapter 10)

→ Images (Chapter 11)

→ Audio and video (Chapter 12)

→ All other controls (Chapter 13)

Content controls are controls that are constrained to contain a single item. Content controls all derive from ContentControl, which has a Content property of type Object that contains the single item (first shown with Button in Chapter 2, "Mastering XAML").

Because a content control's single item can be any arbitrary object, the control can contain a potentially large tree of objects. There just can be only one *direct*

• • •

Content and Arbitrary Objects

Given that a content control's Content can be set to any object, it's natural to wonder what happens if you set the content to a non-visual object, such as an instance of BitArray or TimeZoneInfo. The way it works is fairly simple. All UIElements know how to draw themselves, so if the content derives from UIElement, it gets rendered as expected via an internal mechanism. Otherwise, if a data template is applied to the item (as described in Chapter 17, "Data Binding"), that template can provide the rendering behavior on behalf of the object. Otherwise, the content's ToString method is called, and the returned text is rendered inside a TextBlock control.

child. ScrollViewer and Frame, already examined in previous chapters, are both content controls. ScrollViewer's Content is usually set to a Panel such as Grid, so it can contain an arbitrarily complex user interface, and Frame's Content is usually set to a Page, which usually contains a Panel for the same reason.

Most content controls are buttons—classes deriving from `ButtonBase`. The following sections examine each of them:

→ `Button`

→ `HyperlinkButton`

→ `RepeatButton`

→ `ToggleButton`

→ `CheckBox`

→ `RadioButton`

We also look at two important non-button content controls: `ToolTip` and `AppBar`.

Button

Buttons are probably the most familiar and essential user interface elements. The `Button` control, pictured in Figure 8.1, has already made several appearances in this book.

Although everyone intuitively knows what a button is, its precise definition (at least for XAML apps) might not be obvious. A button is a content control that can be *clicked*. Note that this is a different concept from being *tapped*. All classes deriving from `UIElement` have a `Tapped` event, but only classes deriving from `ButtonBase` have a `Click` event.

So what's the difference between `Tapped` and `Click` (besides past versus present tense, which is a historical artifact)? `Tapped` is raised only for a simple finger press, mouse button click, or pen tap, but `Click` can be raised from keyboard input as well. As has always been the case with Windows buttons, you can click from the keyboard using the Enter or spacebar keys, if the button has focus. Note that the conditions for `Click` aren't a superset of the conditions for `Tapped` because of the way mouse input is treated. *Any* mouse button click raises a `Tapped` event (which often surprises people), whereas only a mouse *left* button click raises a `Click` event.

The `Button` class exposes no additional APIs on top of what it inherits from `ButtonBase`. In addition to its `Click` event, `ButtonBase` exposes `IsPointerOver` and `IsPressed` Boolean properties, which are mainly useful for automatically triggering visual changes when you restyle it (explained in Chapter 16). `IsPressed` covers keyboard input as well as pointer input, such as holding down the spacebar.

The most interesting feature of `ButtonBase`, however, is its `ClickMode` property. This can be set to a value of a `ClickMode` enumeration to control exactly when the `Click` event gets raised. Its values are `Release` (the default), `Press`, and `Hover`. Although changing the `ClickMode` setting on standard buttons would likely confuse users, this capability can be handy for buttons that have been restyled to look like something completely different.

Why does Click **correspond to** *lifting* **a pointer from the screen or keyboard key (by default) rather than** *pressing* **it?**

Although it might sound strange at first, this is standard behavior seen in just about every platform. A benefit of this behavior is that it gives the user a chance to change his or her mind (if he or she presses the wrong button, for example) by dragging a finger, pen, or mouse away from the button instead of simply releasing it.

How can I programmatically click a Button**?**

Button, like the other controls, has a peer class in the Windows.UI.Xaml.Automation.Peers namespace to support UI Automation: ButtonAutomationPeer. It can be used as follows with a Button called myButton:

```
ButtonAutomationPeer peer = new ButtonAutomationPeer(myButton);

peer.Invoke(); // This clicks the Button
```

HyperlinkButton

HyperlinkButton acts much like a hyperlink in HTML. It is similar to Button, but with a different default appearance and one more property: NavigateUri. This is the analog to the AREA (A) element's href attribute in HTML. You can set it to a URL, and when a user clicks the button, it automatically launches the appropriate app to act upon the content. This is equivalent to calling Launcher.LaunchUriAsync. For example, if the URL begins with http://, the default Web browser opens and shows the page. If it begins with a custom protocol, and an app is installed that can handle it, then that app gets launched appropriately (after prompting the user with a "Did you mean to switch apps?" message). If no such app is installed, then Windows informs the user. Recall that the protocol-handling app can be a desktop app as well as a Windows Store app. That's a pretty neat trick! Although HyperlinkButton has a Click event (inherited from ButtonBase), there's no need to handle it thanks to its built-in behavior. If you want to perform a custom action, however, you could certainly leave NavigateUri's value as null and perform that action inside a Click handler.

Figure 8.2 shows how the following three HyperlinkButtons render under the dark theme:

```
<StackPanel>
  <HyperlinkButton NavigateUri="http://pixelwinks.com">
    This is a HyperlinkButton.
  </HyperlinkButton>
  <HyperlinkButton BorderBrush="AliceBlue" NavigateUri="http://adamnathan.net">
    This is a HyperlinkButton with a border.
  </HyperlinkButton>
  <HyperlinkButton Foreground="Red" NavigateUri="bingmaps:///?q=pizza">
    Any questions?
  </HyperlinkButton>
</StackPanel>
```

Its default appearance differs from `Button` in that its border is invisible and its text (*if* its content is text, of course) is rendered in a shade of purple. This is to distinguish the hyperlink text from regular text, just like blue-colored text in a Web browser.

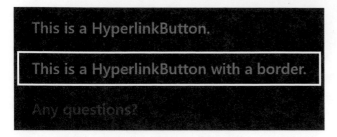

FIGURE 8.2   Examples of `HyperlinkButton`

> **(?) Why do the built-in controls use shades of purple as an accent color, and how do I leverage the user's chosen theme colors instead?**
>
> As you go through this part of the book, you'll see some controls use purple to accent their otherwise colorless appearance. I can't tell you why *purple* was chosen, but *some* color had to be chosen because the user's theme colors—the foreground and background "Start screen" colors chosen in the PC Settings app—aren't exposed to third-party apps. Unlike on Windows Phone, there is no API to retrieve the user-specified accent color. This is an explicit choice by Microsoft rather than a temporary limitation, however. These colors are reserved for system UI, such as the Start screen, charms bar, and PC Settings app. Apps should use colors consistent with their own branding. For example, the background color used by an app's tile (and presumably its splash screen) is often a great choice to use as an accent color.
>
> You can see the default colors, defined separately for dark versus light versus high-contrast, in `%ProgramFiles(x86)%\Windows Kits\8.0\Include\WinRT\XAML\design\ThemeResources.xaml`. For example, the following entries are all specific to `HyperlinkButton`:
>
> ```
> <SolidColorBrush x:Key="HyperlinkButtonBackgroundThemeBrush"
>                  Color="Transparent"/>
> <SolidColorBrush x:Key="HyperlinkButtonBorderThemeBrush" Color="Transparent"/>
> <SolidColorBrush x:Key="HyperlinkDisabledThemeBrush" Color="#66FFFFFF"/>
> <SolidColorBrush x:Key="HyperlinkForegroundThemeBrush" Color="#FF9C72FF"/>
> <SolidColorBrush x:Key="HyperlinkPointerOverForegroundThemeBrush"
>                  Color="#CC9C72FF"/>
> <SolidColorBrush x:Key="HyperlinkPressedForegroundThemeBrush"
>                  Color="#999C72FF"/>
> ```
>
> Although the dark and light theme colors are hard-coded, the high-contrast colors use system-defined properties that get updated based on the user's color choices.
>
> Some of these colors can be overridden by setting appropriate properties on the control (such as `Background`, `BorderBrush`, and `Foreground` on `HyperlinkButton`), but others must overridden by defining new XAML resources with matching key names. Chapter 16 explains how.

RepeatButton

RepeatButton acts like Button except that it continually raises the Click event as long as the button is pressed. The frequency of the raised Click events depends on the values of RepeatButton's Delay and Interval properties, whose default values are both 250 milliseconds. The default look of a RepeatButton is the same as that of Button.

The behavior of RepeatButton might sound strange at first, but it is useful (and standard) for buttons that increment or decrement a value each time they are pressed. For example, the buttons at the ends of a scrollbar exhibit the repeat-press behavior when you press and hold them. Or, if you were to build a numeric "up-down" control, you would likely want to use two RepeatButtons to control the numeric value. RepeatButton is in the Windows.UI.Xaml.Controls.**Primitives** namespace because it is likely that you would use this control only as part of a more sophisticated control rather than use it directly.

ToggleButton

ToggleButton is a "sticky" button that holds its state when it is clicked. Clicking it the first time sets its IsChecked property to true, and clicking it again sets IsChecked to false. The default appearance of ToggleButton is the same as that of Button and RepeatButton, and when IsChecked is true it retains its pressed appearance. It can be used for enabling and disabling features, such as bold/italic/underline buttons on a text editor's toolbar, and is great when space is limited. Otherwise, it's often more appropriate to use a ToggleSwitch control (covered in Chapter 13, "Other Controls") instead.

ToggleButton also has an IsThreeState property that, if set to true, gives IsChecked three possible values: true, false, or null. In fact, IsChecked is of type Nullable<Boolean> (bool? in C#). In the three-state case, the first click sets IsChecked to true, the second click sets it to null, the third click sets it to false, and so on. To vary the order of these state changes, you could create your own subclass and override ToggleButton's OnToggle method to perform your custom logic. Of course, the meaning of this third state is app-specific. Often it is used to represent a mixed state when multiple items are selected, some with the relevant feature on, and some with it off.

In addition to the IsChecked property, ToggleButton defines a separate event for each value of IsChecked: Checked for true, Unchecked for false, and Indeterminate for null. It might seem odd that ToggleButton doesn't have a single IsCheckedChanged event, but the three separate events are handy for declarative scenarios.

ToggleButton is also in the Windows.UI.Xaml.Controls.Primitives namespace because it is often isn't used directly. (Its default three-state appearance isn't satisfactory, because the indeterminate state looks no different from the unchecked state.) Instead, its primary role is to be the base class of the next two controls.

CheckBox

CheckBox, shown in Figure 8.3, is a familiar control. But wait a minute…aren't we in the middle of talking about buttons? Yes, but consider the characteristics of a CheckBox:

→ It has a single piece of *externally supplied* content (so the standard check box doesn't count).

→ It has a notion of being clicked by pointer or keyboard.

→ It retains a state of being checked or unchecked when clicked.

→ It supports a three-state mode, where the state toggles from checked to indeterminate to unchecked.

Does this sound familiar? It should, because a CheckBox is nothing more than a ToggleButton with a different appearance! CheckBox is a simple class deriving from ToggleButton that does little more than override its default style to the visuals shown in Figure 8.3. As with ToggleButton, you should consider using ToggleSwitch instead if you have the space for it and you don't require a three-state mode.

FIGURE 8.3   The CheckBox control, with all three IsChecked states shown

---

CheckBox **Keyboard Support**   •••

CheckBox supports one additional behavior that ToggleButton does not, for parity with a little-known but long-time feature of Windows check boxes. When a CheckBox has focus, pressing the plus (+) key on the number pad checks the control and pressing the minus (–) key on the number pad unchecks the control! Note that this works only if IsThreeState hasn't been set to true.

RadioButton

RadioButton is another control that derives from ToggleButton, but it is unique because it has built-in support for mutual exclusion. When multiple RadioButton controls are grouped together, only one can be checked at a time. Checking one RadioButton—even programmatically—automatically unchecks all others in the same group. In fact, users can't directly uncheck a RadioButton by clicking it; unchecking can be done only programmatically. Therefore, RadioButton is designed for multiple-choice questions. Figure 8.4 shows the default appearance of a RadioButton.

FIGURE 8.4   The RadioButton, with all three IsChecked states shown

The rarely used indeterminate state of a RadioButton (IsThreeState=true and IsChecked=null) is similar to the unchecked state in that a user cannot enable this state by clicking on it; it must be set programmatically. If the RadioButton is clicked, it changes to the checked state. But if another RadioButton in the same group becomes checked, any indeterminate RadioButtons remain in the indeterminate state. As with its base ToggleButton class, the indeterminate state looks no different than the unchecked state, so it's an especially confusing option to use in practice.

Placing several RadioButtons in the same group is straightforward. By default, any RadioButtons that share the same direct parent are automatically grouped together. For example, only one of the following RadioButtons can be checked at any point in time:

```
<StackPanel>
  <RadioButton>Option 1</RadioButton>
  <RadioButton>Option 2</RadioButton>
  <RadioButton>Option 3</RadioButton>
</StackPanel>
```

If you need to group RadioButtons in a custom manner, however, you can use the GroupName property, which is a simple string. Any RadioButtons with the same GroupName value get grouped together (as long as they have the same root element). Therefore, you can group them across different parents, as shown here:

```
<StackPanel>
  <StackPanel>
    <RadioButton GroupName="A">Option 1</RadioButton>    Different
    <RadioButton GroupName="A">Option 2</RadioButton>    parents
  </StackPanel>
  <StackPanel>
    <RadioButton GroupName="A">Option 3</RadioButton>
  </StackPanel>
</StackPanel>
```

Or you can even create subgroups inside the same parent:

```
<StackPanel>
  <RadioButton GroupName="A">Option 1</RadioButton>
  <RadioButton GroupName="A">Option 2</RadioButton>                    Different
  <RadioButton GroupName="B">A Different Option 1</RadioButton>        groups
  <RadioButton GroupName="B">A Different Option 2</RadioButton>
</StackPanel>
```

Of course, the last example here would be a confusing piece of user interface without an extra visual element separating the two subgroups!

ToolTip

Logically, a tooltip is floating content that appears when you hover over an associated element and disappears when you move the pointer away. The ToolTip control doesn't perform any of this magic, however. It's a simple content control that places its content in a white box with a grey border (in the dark theme). The magic is done by a ToolTipService class and its three attached properties. The main one is ToolTipService.ToolTip, which enables a ToolTip to be attached to any UIElement and automatically appear/disappear when appropriate. Figure 8.5 shows a typical ToolTip in action, created from the following XAML:

```
<Button>
  +
  <ToolTipService.ToolTip>
    <ToolTip>
      Add New Item
    </ToolTip>
  </ToolTipService.ToolTip>
</Button>
```

FIGURE 8.5   The ToolTip attached to a Button

Although ToolTips might not seem worthwhile when designing a "touch first" app because typical touch digitizers don't support hovering, they are indeed an important part of a well-designed user interface. In fact, each of the pointer types is able to reveal an attached ToolTip. A mouse pointer can hover over an element, of course, and so can a pen (when it is in range but not in contact). But all three pointer types can do a press-and-hold gesture as well to reveal the ToolTip. Note that when a ToolTip is attached to a Control, it never appears when the Control is disabled (IsEnabled=false).

In Figure 8.5, the attached ToolTip is *not* a child of the Button. Its Parent is null, making it the root of a visual tree completely separate from the Page's visual tree that contains the Button. This subtle fact can be significant because property values and transforms aren't inherited by the ToolTip. For example, if the entire Page (or the Button) is marked with a ScaleTransform that magnifies its contents, the ToolTip would still appear at its normal size. To magnify the ToolTip, you could manually apply a matching transform by setting ToolTip's RenderTransform property.

You don't need to use the ToolTip class when setting ToolTipService.ToolTip on an element! The property is of type Object, and if you set it to any non-ToolTip object, the property's implementation automatically creates a ToolTip and uses the property value as the ToolTip's content. Therefore, the XAML for Figure 8.5 could be simplified to the following and give the same result:

```
<Button>
  +
  <ToolTipService.ToolTip>
      Add New Item
  </ToolTipService.ToolTip>
</Button>
```

or it could be simplified further, as follows:

```
<Button Content="+" ToolTipService.ToolTip="Add New Item"/>
```

Of course, if you want to set properties directly on the ToolTip instance (such as its RenderTransform), you'll want to use an explicit element.

Because of the flexibility of content controls, a ToolTip can hold anything you want. Listing 8.1 shows how you might construct a richer one inspired by the kind you find in Microsoft Office apps. The result is shown in Figure 8.6.

LISTING 8.1   A Complex ToolTip

```
<CheckBox>
  CheckBox
  <ToolTipService.ToolTip>
    <StackPanel>
      <TextBlock FontWeight="Bold" Foreground="Blue">
        The CheckBox
      </TextBlock>
      <TextBlock TextWrapping="Wrap" Width="200">
        CheckBox is a familiar control. But it's not much
        more than a ToggleButton styled differently!
      </TextBlock>
      <StackPanel Orientation="Horizontal" Margin="-10,10,-10,-7"
                  Background="Blue">
        <Image Margin="4" Source="Assets/help.png"/>
        <TextBlock VerticalAlignment="Center" Foreground="White"
                   FontWeight="Bold">Press F1 for more help.</TextBlock>
      </StackPanel>
    </StackPanel>
  </ToolTipService.ToolTip>
</CheckBox>
```

Although a ToolTip can contain interactive controls such as Buttons, those controls never get focus, and you can't click or otherwise interact with them. (The default inverted background color of a ToolTip makes most controls appear invisible anyway. For example, in the dark theme, most controls in a ToolTip are rendered as white-on-white unless you change some colors manually.)

FIGURE 8.6   A rich tooltip is easy to create thanks to the flexibility of content controls.

The beginning of this section mentioned that `ToolTipService` defines three attached properties. Besides `ToolTip`, the other two are `Placement` and `PlacementTarget`. `Placement` customizes the `ToolTip`'s desired placement relative to the pointer: `Left`, `Right`, `Top`, `Bottom`, or `Mouse` (the default value). The last value, which really should be called `Pointer` instead, means *the location of the hovering pointer*. The other values are relative to the *element* rather than the pointer. Note that if there's not enough room to display the entire tooltip at the desired location, it will be shown in a different spot. `PlacementTarget` can be set to an instance of an element if you want the `Placement` value to be relative to a *different* element than the one under the pointer.

The `ToolTip` class itself defines `Opened` and `Closed` events (and an `IsOpen` property) in case you want to act on its appearance and disappearance. It also defines several properties for tweaking its placement: `HorizontalOffset`, `VerticalOffset`, plus the same

Placement and PlacementTarget properties defined on `ToolTipService`. If both
`ToolTip` and `ToolTipService` have an
explicit value for these, the value on
`ToolTipService` has precedence.

How can I forcibly close a `ToolTip`
that is currently showing?

`IsOpen` is a read-write property, so set its
`IsOpen` property to `false`.

AppBar

The `AppBar` is an essential control for just about every Windows Store app, because it is the place users expect to find commands that aren't worth showing by default. Similar to `ToolTip`, it's important to not only understand the control itself, but how it's expected to be used.

Visually, `AppBar` adds nothing to its inner content other than enforcing a minimum height and adding some horizontal padding. It does add automatic behavior for showing and hiding it, however (unlike `ToolTip` which relies on `ToolTipService` to show/hide it). An `AppBar` is invisible by default but automatically animates in and out when an edge gesture is performed (an appropriate swipe, right mouse button click, pressing Windows+Z, or pressing the context menu key).

If you place an AppBar directly among other elements, you'll see that it occupies space even when it is hidden. This is demonstrated with the following XAML and the result shown in Figure 8.7:

```
<Page …>
  <StackPanel Background="OrangeRed">
    <Button>One</Button>
    <AppBar Background="Green">
      <Button>Two</Button>
    </AppBar>
    <Button>Three</Button>
    <Button>Four</Button>
  </StackPanel>
</Page>
```

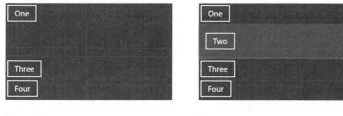

Closed   Open

FIGURE 8.7   An AppBar always occupies space in its parent element.

Attaching to a Page

The XAML demonstrated in Figure 8.7 does not show the way an AppBar is meant to be used. Instead, it is meant to be attached to a Page via Page's TopAppBar or BottomAppBar property. When you attach an AppBar to one of these, it docks to the top or bottom edge, it overlays any content underneath (as expected), and a few of its visual defaults automatically change. (When attached to a Page, its default BorderBrush becomes a translucent black instead of Transparent, and its default animation becomes a slide instead of a fade.)

The following updated XAML attaches the same AppBar as the Page's TopAppBar, which changes the result as shown in in Figure 8.8:

```
<Page …>
  <Page.TopAppBar>
    <AppBar Background="Green">
      <Button>Two</Button>
    </AppBar>
  </Page.TopAppBar>
  <StackPanel Background="OrangeRed">
    <Button>One</Button>
    <Button>Three</Button>
```

```
    <Button>Four</Button>
  </StackPanel>
</Page>
```

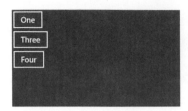
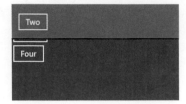

Closed   Open

FIGURE 8.8   When properly attached to a Page, an AppBar's parent element is null, and it over-lays the Page's content.

As with attaching a ToolTip to an element with ToolTipService, attaching an AppBar to a Page in this manner makes it the root of its own visual tree. Therefore, Page-level trans-forms and other property values do not impact the AppBar. Unlike with ToolTip, you must always set TopAppBar or BottomAppBar to an explicit AppBar element. (The proper-ties are of type AppBar rather than the generic Object.)

Besides Opened and Closed events and a read-write IsOpen property (just like on ToolTip), AppBar defines a Boolean IsSticky property that is false by default. When set to true, the AppBar, once open, stays open unless the user does an edge gesture to close it or the app programmatically sets IsOpen to false. When false, the AppBar has "light dismiss" behavior that causes it to automatically close when it loses focus. Note that both IsSticky values work as advertised only when an AppBar is properly attached to a Page via TopAppBar or BottomAppBar.

Design Guidelines

If you need only one AppBar, you should usually attach it on the bottom. A bottom AppBar typically has simple buttons that trigger a context-specific command, although it can often have a group of buttons that act like RadioButtons for changing the view of the current page (such as the Day, Week, and Month buttons in the Calendar app). The top AppBar is much less standardized, although it often focuses on switching to a different page altogether, as with the tab selection user interface in the Internet Explorer app. These are, of course, only guidelines. For example, the main page of the Windows Store app uses only a top AppBar.

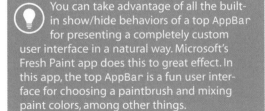

You can take advantage of all the built-in show/hide behaviors of a top AppBar for presenting a completely custom user interface in a natural way. Microsoft's Fresh Paint app does this to great effect. In this app, the top AppBar is a fun user inter-face for choosing a paintbrush and mixing paint colors, among other things.

AppBar is a bit unusual because, unlike the other controls, you need to do a bit of work to make it match design guidelines. In fact, it even works against you because the translucent black border is nonstandard. Figure 8.9 shows bottom AppBars from several Microsoft apps. From this, we see:

→ The Buttons have a distinct style that is different than Button's default style.

→ The Buttons are docked to each edge, favoring the right edge. (This is done not only to scale naturally to different resolutions, but to be in a good position for the user's thumbs when holding a tablet.)

→ The AppBar's background often matches the app's signature color (the color used as its tile background).

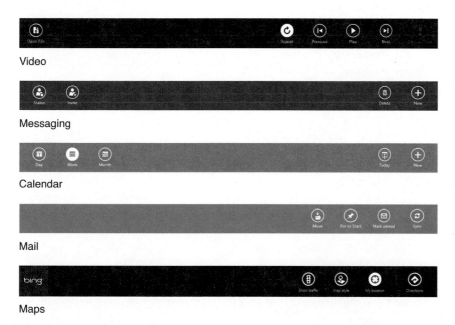

Video

Messaging

Calendar

Mail

Maps

FIGURE 8.9 The bottom AppBars from five Microsoft apps generally follow the same pattern.

Although the AppBar previously shown in Figures 8.7 and 8.8 has a single Button as its content, an AppBar's content should obviously be set to a Panel in most cases. If you need Buttons on one side only, presumably the right side, then a simple StackPanel with Orientation=Horizontal and HorizontalAlignment=Right can do the trick. For docking Buttons to both edges, you could use a single-row Grid with auto-sized columns except for one star-sized column in the middle.

You can find detailed design guidelines at http://design.windows.com. Included in these guidelines are detailed recommendations on placing Buttons in an AppBar, including conventions for choosing the left side versus right side.

The following XAML shows a more realistic `AppBar`, with multiple `Button`s docked to each side. It uses two `StackPanel`s (one left-docked, one right-docked) in a single-cell `Grid` because the XAML is much more compact compared to a `Grid` with 10 columns:

```
<Page …>
  <Page.BottomAppBar>
    <AppBar Background="DarkOrchid">
      <Grid>
        <StackPanel Orientation="Horizontal">
          <Button>Edit</Button>
          <Button>Undo</Button>
          <Button>Redo</Button>
          <Button>Save</Button>
          <Button>Delete</Button>
        </StackPanel>
        <StackPanel Orientation="Horizontal" HorizontalAlignment="Right">
          <Button>Play</Button>
          <Button>Pin to Start</Button>
          <Button>Like</Button>
          <Button>More</Button>
        </StackPanel>
      </Grid>
    </AppBar>
  </Page.BottomAppBar>
</Page>
```

Figure 8.10 displays this `AppBar`.

FIGURE 8.10   An AppBar using multiple `Panel`s to dock its `Button`s on the thumb-friendly left and right edges

> **(?) How can I use the same** AppBar **across multiple pages?**
>
> You would have to detach it from the current page and attach it to the next page when navigating from one to the other. (Because an AppBar is always attached to a Page, it would be more appropriate to call it a *page* bar.) Of course, if the Page with the AppBar(s) contains a Frame that does its own navigation (like an iframe in an HTML page), then you get to keep the single AppBar without ever detaching/reattaching it.

Styling `Button`s for `AppBar`

I'm sure you noticed that Figure 8.10 looks almost nothing like the `AppBar`s in Figure 8.9 because of the appearance of its `Button`s. Fortunately, Visual Studio-generated projects can help you get the proper look for these. The `StandardStyles.xaml` file mentioned in Chapter 1, "Anatomy of a Windows Store App," contains a style called `AppBarButtonStyle` that can be applied to any `ButtonBase`-derived control (although it is meant for `Button`s inside an `AppBar`). Figure 8.11 shows the result of applying this style to each of the `Button`s in the `AppBar` from Figure 8.10 as follows:

```
<Button Style="{StaticResource AppBarButtonStyle}">Edit</Button>
```

FIGURE 8.11   The result of naively marking all AppBar Buttons with AppBarButtonStyle

Clearly more work needs to be done, but this is a start. Although most of the text is now cut off, the buttons at least now have the correct shape, size, and margins.

Exploiting AppBarButtonStyle

Figure 8.11 makes it clear that the `Content` of each `Button` in an `AppBar` should be set to its icon (perhaps an `Image` element) so `AppBarButtonStyle` can do its job. But if its `Content` is no longer text, how can we get the standard text label below each `Button`?

It turns out that the style is designed to look for the value of `AutomationProperties.Name`, an attached property typically reserved for UI automation scenarios. (You can see this for yourself inside `StandardStyles.xaml`.) It uses the value of this `string` property as the `Text` value for a `TextBlock` below each circle. This works out nicely because screen readers leverage `AutomationProperties.Name` to read a control appropriately.

Therefore, you could use XAML such as the following to get a good-looking `AppBar` `Button` (assuming you have an appropriate image file included in your project):

```
<Button Style="{StaticResource AppBarButtonStyle}"
        AutomationProperties.Name="Edit">
  <Image Source="Assets/Edit.png"/>
</Button>
```

Figure 8.12 shows the result for just the first "edit" `Button`.

Pre-Built AppBarButtonStyles

If you snoop around `StandardStyles.xaml`, you'll find another pleasant surprise. It contains over 150 variations of `AppBarButtonStyle` for common

FIGURE 8.12   When a Button's Content is an icon and its AutomationProperties.Name is set to appropriate text, AppBarButtonStyle works nicely.

Buttons, complete with an appropriate icon and text label! They are commented out by default, so you need to uncomment any you want to use. Here are some examples:

→ PreviousAppBarButtonStyle

→ NextAppBarButtonStyle

→ PlayAppBarButtonStyle

→ PauseAppBarButtonStyle

→ SkipBackAppBarButtonStyle

→ SkipAheadAppBarButtonStyle

→ EditAppBarButtonStyle

→ SaveAppBarButtonStyle

→ DeleteAppBarButtonStyle

→ DiscardAppBarButtonStyle

→ UndoAppBarButtonStyle

→ RedoAppBarButtonStyle

→ HomeAppBarButtonStyle

→ AddAppBarButtonStyle

→ RemoveAppBarButtonStyle

→ RefreshAppBarButtonStyle

→ YesAppBarButtonStyle

→ NoAppBarButtonStyle

→ FavoriteAppBarButtonStyle

→ PhotoAppBarButtonStyle

→ VideoAppBarButtonStyle

→ MailAppBarButtonStyle

→ DownloadAppBarButtonStyle

→ UploadAppBarButtonStyle

→ PinAppBarButtonStyle

→ UnpinAppBarButtonStyle

→ MoreAppBarButtonStyle

→ SearchAppBarButtonStyle

→ SettingsAppBarButtonStyle

→ HelpAppBarButtonStyle

These styles perform a clever hack for rendering each icon. Rather than using image files (potentially two for each scale: normal color and hover color), each one uses simple text content that scales perfectly. But the text is a single character rendered with the Segoe UI Symbol font! Segoe UI Symbol is like a modern version of the Wingdings font. This font contains a lot of interesting symbols, so you can easily create your own icons not already covered by StandardStyles.xaml. You can browse the font's symbols and get the Unicode value for each one with the Character Map desktop app that ships with Windows, as shown in Figure 8.13.

You can copy and paste characters from Character Map directly into your XAML, or you could use the XML escape sequence &#x*HexValue*;, where *HexValue* is the Unicode code point shown at the bottom of Character Map for any selected character.

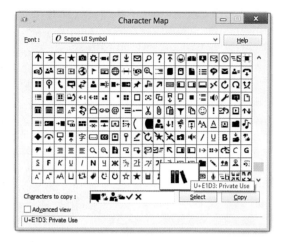

FIGURE 8.13   Browsing potential icons in the Segoe UI Symbol font is easy with Character Map.

The following XAML leverages this new information to fix the AppBar from Figures 8.10 and 8.11:

```
<Page …>
  <Page.BottomAppBar>
    <AppBar Background="DarkOrchid">
      <Grid>
        <StackPanel Orientation="Horizontal">
          <Button Style="{StaticResource EditAppBarButtonStyle}"/>
          <Button Style="{StaticResource UndoAppBarButtonStyle}"/>
          <Button Style="{StaticResource RedoAppBarButtonStyle}"/>
          <Button Style="{StaticResource SaveAppBarButtonStyle}"/>
          <Button Style="{StaticResource DeleteAppBarButtonStyle}"/>
        </StackPanel>
        <StackPanel Orientation="Horizontal" HorizontalAlignment="Right">
          <Button Style="{StaticResource PlayAppBarButtonStyle}"/>
          <Button Style="{StaticResource PinAppBarButtonStyle}"
                  AutomationProperties.Name="Pin to Start"/>
          <Button Style="{StaticResource AppBarButtonStyle}"
                  AutomationProperties.Name="Like">&#xE209;</Button>
          <Button Style="{StaticResource MoreAppBarButtonStyle}"/>
        </StackPanel>
      </Grid>
    </AppBar>
  </Page.BottomAppBar>
</Page>
```

This assumes that all the referenced styles are uncommented inside StandardStyles.xaml. All but one of the Buttons is using a specific built-in style. Those Buttons can apply the appropriate style and not need anything else. Notice that the Button with PinAppBarButtonStyle sets AutomationProperties.Name anyway. This is done to override the style's default text, which is "Pin" instead of the desired "Pin to Start."

The next Button—a Facebook-style "Like" Button—is also covered by the built-in styles, but let's pretend it is not so the example can include a custom Button. You can see how easy it is to create a custom "Like" Button thanks to the appearance of Unicode character E209 in the Segoe UI Symbol font. (AppBarButtonStyle already sets FontFamily to Segoe UI Symbol, so it doesn't have to be explicitly set on this Button.) Figure 8.14 reveals this AppBar, which finally looks as it should.

FIGURE 8.14   At last, we can produce an AppBar that looks just as good as the ones from Figure 8.9.

Use the built-in styles to easily get standard AppBar Buttons. However, you should avoid using the last three listed previously (Search, Settings, and Help), because searching should be handled by the Search charm on the charms bar, and settings/help should be handled by the Settings charm. Chapter 19, "Charms," explains how to do this.

Also note that even with the built-in ones, the automatic text labels are hard-coded strings inside your project's StandardStyles.xaml file. Therefore, you'll still have work to do if you want to translate these labels into different languages.

AppBarButtonStyle doesn't work well for all types of buttons!

When you apply the style to a ToggleButton, its sticky pressed state works exactly as you'd expect. You can also apply it to a HyperlinkButton to leverage its convenient behavior while having it render just like any other AppBar Button. It would be useful to leverage RadioButtons as well (for scenarios such as the Day/Week/Month choice in the Calendar app), but the checked state of a RadioButton doesn't render correctly with these styles without further tweaks.

When designing the contents of an AppBar, don't forget to consider your app's snapped view! You'll often need to hide Buttons to accommodate having only 320 pixels of width. In addition, many apps remove the text labels on an AppBar's Buttons and reduce their horizontal margins when snapped. AppBarButtonStyle and the related styles do have support for this, but you need to explicitly transition in an out of its Snapped view when appropriate (see Chapter 16).

A Button's Pressed Appearance

Part of the genius of using text for a Button's icon is that the default color inversion done for Button's pressed state applies to the icon just as it would for "normal" text. Figure 8.15 demonstrates this for the "Pin to Start" Button from Figure 8.14.

Normal   Hovering   Pressed

FIGURE 8.15   Because the pushpin icon is text rather than an image, it can automatically turn black when the Button is pressed.

The problem with using a real Image (as in Figure 8.12) is that the Button would look like a solid white circle when pressed. Yet, unless you use vector graphics or produce your own custom font with the needed glyphs, you'll probably need to use an Image in this way at some point. To address this problem, a Button can temporarily swap its Content to a different (black) Image when PointerPressed is raised and revert it when PointerReleased (or PointerCanceled or PointerCaptureLost) is raised. More likely, it would leverage visual states, which are described in Chapter 16.

Summary

Never before has a button been so flexible! In the XAML UI Framework, Button and all the other content controls can contain absolutely anything—but they can directly contain only one item. This chapter highlighted what makes each type of Button unique, and examined the two non-Button content controls that haven't been covered earlier in this book. Out of all these controls, the AppBar is the only one that is new compared to WPF and Silverlight. It's also the one that you'll likely spend the most time with in order to get things looking just right.

Viewbox, introduced in Chapter 4, "Layout," and a handy element called Border (which supports customizable rounded corners with its CornerRadius property) can often be mistaken for content controls—because they directly contain only one item—but they are not. They derive directly from FrameworkElement, and therefore, they lack many features given to Control. Instead of a Content property, they have a Child property.

Although XAML apps and HTML apps both have common controls that look and act the same way, they are completely separate implementations with much different exposure to developers. The HTML controls are based on the HTML5 standard and heavily use CSS and JavaScript, whereas the XAML controls expose an object and styling model familiar to WPF and Silverlight developers. In both cases, they take advantage of hardware acceleration for great performance.

Now, with the tour of content controls complete, it's time to move on to controls that can directly contain more than one item—*items controls*.

Chapter 9

ITEMS CONTROLS

Besides content controls, the other large category of XAML controls is *items controls*, which can contain an unbounded collection of items rather than just a single piece of content. All items controls derive from the abstract ItemsControl class, which, like ContentControl, is a direct subclass of Control.

Although the ItemsControl class doesn't have any notion of selected item(s), all the built-in items controls happen to derive from Selector, a subclass of ItemsControl. Selector adds the following three read/write properties to enable the concept of selection:

→ **SelectedIndex**—A zero-based integer that indicates what item is selected or -1 if nothing is selected. Items are numbered in the order in which they are added to the collection.

→ **SelectedItem**—The actual item instance that is currently selected.

→ **SelectedValue**—The value of the currently selected item. By default this value is the item itself, making SelectedValue identical to SelectedItem. You can set a separate SelectedValuePath property, however, to choose an arbitrary property or expression that should represent each item's value. This expression is known as a *property path*, and is covered in Chapter 15, "Animation."

These properties are automatically kept in sync, so if you set `SelectedIndex` to `-1`, `SelectedItem` becomes `null` (and vice versa).

`Selector` also defines an event—`SelectionChanged`—that makes it easy to detect changes to the current selection, whether it happened via pointer input, keyboard input, or programmatically. There are many ways selection can happen (even with pointer input, it can be a tap or a cross slide), so it's important to use this event for reliable detection rather than input events.

The XAML UI Framework contains five `Selectors`, and each one is described in this chapter:

- → `ComboBox`
- → `ListBox`
- → `ListView`
- → `GridView`
- → `FlipView`

`ComboBox` and `ListBox` are classic controls that have been updated for Windows Store apps, but the latter three are new to Windows 8.

This chapter also introduces the `SemanticZoom` control. It is not a `Selector`, or even an items control. However, it is designed to be used with `ListView` and/or `GridView`, so this is a good place to learn about it. Before examining each control, however, let's look at two important aspects of all items controls: the items themselves and an interesting feature known as *items panels*.

Items in the Control

`ItemsControl` stores its content in an `Items` property (of type `ItemCollection`). Each item can be an arbitrary object (`System.Object`) that by default gets rendered just as it would inside a content control. In other words, any `UIElement` is rendered as expected, and (ignoring data templates) any other type is rendered as a `TextBlock` containing the `string` returned by its `ToString` method.

The simple `ListBox` control shown in Chapter 2, "Mastering XAML," is an items control. Chapter 2 shows an example of adding `ListBoxItems` to the `Items` collection, whereas the following example adds arbitrary objects to `Items` instead (all done in XAML for convenience):

```
<ListBox xmlns:sys="using:System">
  <Button>Button</Button>
  <x:Double>1.23</x:Double>
  <sys:EventArgs/>
  <sys:UriBuilder/>
</ListBox>
```

The child elements are implicitly added to the `Items` collection because `Items` is a content property. This `ListBox`, after selecting the first item, is shown in Figure 9.1. The

`UIElement` (`Button`) is rendered normally and is fully interactive. Note that if the first item were not selected, the `Button` would look invisible because it would be rendered as white-on-white. The other three objects render according to their `ToString` methods. (Notice that `UriBuilder`'s `ToString` reports its URI, `http://localhost/` by default, rather than simply returning its type name.)

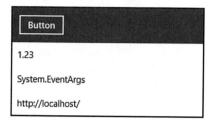

FIGURE 9.1   A `ListBox` containing arbitrary objects

Item Containers   •••

When elements other than `ListBoxItem` are placed in a `ListBox`, each one gets implicitly wrapped in a `ListBoxItem`. (You can see this from code if you traverse up the visual tree from any of the items.) This is done to preserve some common behaviors and visuals, such as the purple selection highlight seen in Figure 9.1.

`ListBoxItem` derives from `SelectorItem` (which derives from `ContentControl`). Each of the five `Selectors` has a corresponding *`SelectorName`*`Item` class that always wraps each of its items (implicitly if not already done explicitly). `ListBox` has `ListBoxItem`, `ComboBox` has `ComboBoxItem`, and so on. These classes are called *item containers*. `ItemsControl` exposes a few advanced properties related to its item containers, enabling customization of their visual style and transition animations.

Although all `Selectors` already define properties that reveal the currently selected item, `SelectorItem` also exposes a read/write `IsSelected` property that can often be a more handy way to discover or change a selection.

As mentioned in Chapter 2, the `Items` property is read-only. This means that you can add objects to the initially empty collection or remove objects, but you can't point `Items` to an entirely different collection. `ItemsControl` has a separate property—`ItemsSource`—that supports filling its items with an existing arbitrary collection. The use of `ItemsSource` is examined further in Chapter 17, "Data Binding."

To keep things simple in this chapter and to focus on the controls themselves, the examples in this chapter fill items controls with visual elements. This is a bit unrealistic, however, especially for large collections of items. The preferred approach is to give items controls nonvisual items (for example, custom business objects) and use data templates to define how each item gets rendered. Furthermore, using data binding (with the `ItemsSource` property) automatically enables richer items controls features automatically, such as item grouping. Chapter 17 discusses data templates, data binding, and features such as grouping.

Items Panels

Like all other XAML controls, the essence of items controls is not their visual appearance but rather their storage of multiple items and, for Selectors, the ways in which their items are logically selected. Although all XAML controls can be visually altered by applying a new control template, items controls have a shortcut for replacing just the piece of the control template responsible for arranging its items. This mini-template, called an *items panel*, enables you to swap out the panel used to arrange items while leaving everything else about the control intact. You can apply an items panel to any items control by setting its ItemsPanel property.

Conveniently, the panels used to arrange items within an items control are the same kind of panels used everywhere else (classes that derive from Panel). For example, a ListBox stacks its items vertically. Its default items panel is not quite a StackPanel, but rather a panel called **Virtualizing**StackPanel that adds support for UI virtualization. Therefore, the following XAML leverages the ItemsPanel property to replace the default arrangement with an explicit VirtualizingStackPanel that is told to stack its items horizontally instead:

```
<ListBox>
  <ListBox.ItemsPanel>
    <ItemsPanelTemplate>
      <VirtualizingStackPanel Orientation="Horizontal"/>
    </ItemsPanelTemplate>
  </ListBox.ItemsPanel>
  <ListBoxItem>one</ListBoxItem>
  <ListBoxItem>two</ListBoxItem>
  <ListBoxItem>three</ListBoxItem>
</ListBox>
```

You could use a simple StackPanel instead, but you would lose the UI virtualization support. For the most part, you can use all the panels discussed in Chapter 4, "Layout" (or any Panel-derived custom panel) as an items panel—except for one. VariableSizedWrapGrid contains logic that disallows its use as an items panel. That's because a closely related WrapGrid is meant to be used as an items panel instead.

• • •

UI Virtualization

UI virtualization refers to the behavior of some panels that optimizes performance when filling an items control with a large number of data objects—not item containers such as ListBoxItem. Such panels wrap each item in an item container only when it is on-screen or almost on-screen. When the item moves far enough off-screen, the item container is recycled (able to be used by another item).

The XAML UI Framework ships three virtualizing panels (which all derive from VirtualizingPanel): VirtualizingStackPanel, WrapGrid, and CarouselPanel. None of these panels work for anything other than an items panel, and the latter two even restrict which controls are allowed to use them.

> **How can I get** WrapGrid **or** CarouselPanel **to work?**
>
> These two panels often entice developers to give them a try, but they are misleading because they work only in limited situations. WrapGrid, which is just like VariableSizedWrapGrid but with the and ColumnSpan features removed (and with UI virtualization support added), can be used as the items panel for controls deriving from ListViewBase only. Out of the built-in controls, that means ListView and GridView only.
>
> CarouselPanel, which supports wrap-around for an infinite scrolling effect, can currently be used as the items panel for ComboBox only. It also happens to be ComboBox's default items panel. It enables the list of items to wrap around and provide an infinite scrolling experience, but only when there are enough items and only when touch is used.

Figure 9.2 demonstrates the effect of the preceding XAML that changes the ListBox's item arrangement from vertical to horizontal, as well as a silly variation that uses Grid as the items panel.

`<VirtualizingStackPanel/>` (default)

`<VirtualizingStackPanel Orientation="Horizontal"/>`

<Grid/>

FIGURE 9.2   The effect of various items panels on a simple ListBox whose second item is selected

Using <Grid/> as the items panel looks ridiculous because by default it has a single cell, and every item is placed inside it. (It gives the same result as using a Canvas, although you'd need to give the Canvas an explicit height for the inside of the ListBox to even be visible.)

You could, of course, configure the Grid with multiple rows and/or columns. If any items in the ListBox are marked with relevant attached properties, they get respected by the items panel. The following (only slightly less silly) update to the ListBox demonstrates this:

```
<ListBox>
  <ListBox.ItemsPanel>
    <ItemsPanelTemplate>
      <!-- Define a three-row, two-column Grid -->
      <Grid>
        <Grid.RowDefinitions>
          <RowDefinition/>
          <RowDefinition/>
          <RowDefinition/>
        </Grid.RowDefinitions>
        <Grid.ColumnDefinitions>
          <ColumnDefinition/>
          <ColumnDefinition/>
        </Grid.ColumnDefinitions>
      </Grid>
    </ItemsPanelTemplate>
  </ListBox.ItemsPanel>
  <ListBoxItem Grid.Row="2">one</ListBoxItem>
  <ListBoxItem Grid.Row="1" Grid.Column="1">two</ListBoxItem>
  <ListBoxItem>three</ListBoxItem>
</ListBox>
```

The result of applying this unusual items panel is shown in Figure 9.3.

It's worth pointing out that the theoretical elegance of mixing arbitrary Panels with arbitrary items controls does not get fully realized in practice. On the one side, the implementations of some Panels purposely restrict their uses at run-time (such as VariableSizedWrapGrid, WrapGrid, and CarouselPanel). On the other side, the

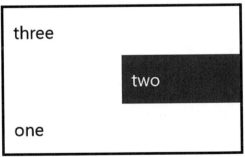

FIGURE 9.3   You can get creative with items panels.

implementations of many items controls make assumptions based on their default items panel that don't always play nicely with other Panels. The simple ListBox control is the shining example of flexibility. It works perfectly with any Panel (even custom ones) as long as the Panel itself doesn't purposely restrict its use. That's because ListBox's implementation makes no assumptions about the arrangement of its items. Every other built-in items control, however, acts strangely if you customize its items panel in certain ways. That's because they provide much richer modes of interaction that exploit characteristics of their default items panels.

ComboBox

Now let's look at each items control, one by one. The ComboBox control, shown in Figure 9.4 from the following XAML, enables users to select one item from a list:

```
<ComboBox>
  <ComboBoxItem>Small</ComboBoxItem>
  <ComboBoxItem>Medium</ComboBoxItem>
  <ComboBoxItem>Large</ComboBoxItem>
</ComboBox>
```

ComboBox is a popular control because it doesn't occupy much space. It displays only the current selection in a *selection box*, with the rest of the list shown on demand in a *drop-down* (often called a *flyout*). The drop-down can be opened and closed by tapping the control or by pressing Alt+up arrow, Alt+down arrow, or F4 when it has focus. Even when closed, the user can use the up and down arrow keys to change the current selection. When manipulated with touch, the list of items wraps around if there are more than nine, thanks to the use of CarouselPanel.

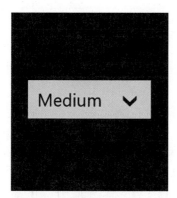
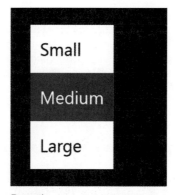

Drop-down closed   Drop-down open

FIGURE 9.4   The ComboBox fits the selection of an item into a small space.

The *drop-down*'s name (much like the downward pointing arrow) is a historical artifact, because it doesn't always drop *downward*. Space permitting, ComboBox attempts to position the list of items such that the selected item stays in the same spot. In Figure 9.4, it would expand upward if "Large" was already selected, or downward if "Small" was selected. (This logic is unfortunately specific to the default items panel's appearance, so changing it can make the drop-down's position look strange.) The drop-down gets only so tall before resorting to scrolling, and this is controllable via the MaxDropDownHeight property.

ComboBox defines two events—DropDownOpened and DropDownClosed—and a property—IsDropDownOpen—that enable you to act on the drop-down being opened or closed. For example, you can delay the filling of ComboBox items until the drop-down is opened by handling the DropDownOpened event. Note that IsDropDownOpen is a read/write property, so you can set it directly to change the state of the drop-down.

> **(?) How do I make** ComboBox *editable,* **so the user can type a new value into it?**
>
> You can't. ComboBox defines an IsEditable property for some amount of compatibility with WPF and Silverlight, but it is read-only and always returns false. You could construct a custom control that provides such an experience by using a TextBox and an associated Popup. Or, you could rely on a third-party control like Telerik's ComboBox (http://telerik.com) that acts more like the classic editable variety.

> **(?) How do I make** ComboBox **respond to keystrokes so the user can type to jump to a specific item?**
>
> This functionality is not provided automatically. You need to handle keystrokes yourself and adjust the current selection accordingly (or, rely on a third-party control). Keep in mind that ComboBox can contain non-textual items, so your logic might need to account for that.

> **(?) When the** SelectionChanged **event gets raised, how do I get the new selection?**
>
> The SelectionChanged event is designed to handle controls that allow multiple selections, so it can be a little confusing for a single-selection selector such as ComboBox. The SelectionChangedEventArgs type passed to event handlers has two properties of type IList<object>: AddedItems and RemovedItems. AddedItems contains the new selection, and RemovedItems contains the previous selection. You can retrieve a new single selection as follows:
>
> ```
> void ComboBox_SelectionChanged(object sender, SelectionChangedEventArgs e)
> {
>   object newSelection = (e.AddedItems.Count > 0) ? e.AddedItems[0] : null;
>   …
> }
> ```
>
> And, like this code, you should never assume that there's a selected item. Although a user has no way to clear a ComboBox's selection, it can be cleared programmatically.

ListBox

The familiar ListBox control, shown in Figure 9.1, is similar to ComboBox except that all items are displayed directly within the control's bounds (or you can scroll to view additional items if they don't all fit). The most important feature of ListBox is that it can support multiple simultaneous selections. This is controllable via the SelectionMode property, which accepts three values (from a SelectionMode enumeration):

→ **Single**—Only one item can be selected at a time, just like with ComboBox. This is the default value.

→ **Multiple**—Any number of items can be selected simultaneously. Tapping an unselected item adds it to `ListBox`'s `SelectedItems` collection, and tapping a selected item removes it from the collection. This behavior can be annoying if single-selection is the norm, because changing the selection is a two-step process.

→ **Extended**—Any number of items can be selected simultaneously, but the behavior is optimized for the single selection case. To select multiple items in this mode, you must hold down `Shift` (for contiguous items) or `Ctrl` (for noncontiguous items) while tapping. Note that there is no provision for multiselect in this mode without a keyboard.

Other than the `SelectionMode` property, `ListBox` defines a `SelectedItems` property to support multiselect, a `SelectAll` method, and a handy `ScrollIntoView` method that ensures that the passed-in item from its `Items` collection is visible.

The default visual tree for `ListBox` contains a `ScrollViewer`, which means you can set some `ScrollViewer` attached properties on `ListBox` to impact its behavior. For example, you can enable pinch-and-stretch zooming of its inner content as follows:

```
<ListBox ScrollViewer.ZoomMode="Enabled">
  …
</ListBox>
```

• • •

ListBox **Properties and Multiple Selection**

Although `ListBox` has a `SelectedItems` property that can be used no matter which `SelectionMode` is used, it still inherits the `SelectedIndex`, `SelectedItem`, and `SelectedValue` properties from `Selector` that don't fit in with the multiselect model.

When multiple items are selected, `SelectedItem` points to the first item in the `SelectedItems` collection (which is the item selected the earliest by the user), and `SelectedIndex` and `SelectedValue` give the index and value for that item. But it's best not to use these properties on a control that supports multiple selections. Note that `ListBox` does *not* define a `SelectedIndices` or `SelectedValues` property, however.

 How do I get the items in my items control to have automation IDs, as seen in UI Automation tools?

The easiest way to give any `FrameworkElement` an automation ID is to set its `Name` property, because that is used by default for automation purposes. However, if you want to give an element an ID that is different from its name, set the `AutomationProperties.AutomationId` attached property to the desired `string`. When non-`null`, this value is used for the automation ID. Otherwise, if `AutomationProperties.Name` is non-`null`, then that value is used. Otherwise, `Name` is used.

? **When should I use a** ListBox**?**

`ListBox` is best used for simple, perhaps text-only items. It's also best for single selection scenarios, because the two multiselect modes force you to choose between something that's annoying for single selection or something that can do multiselect with a keyboard only. If you find yourself wanting to expose items in a unique arrangement that automatically supports selection, however, as in Figure 9.3, `ListBox`'s flexibility is helpful.

ListView

You can think of `ListView` as a "fancy `ListBox`" optimized for touch and the style of Windows Store apps. Probably the most important difference is the addition of cross slide gesture support for selection—although you can turn that off by setting `IsSwipeEnabled` is `false`. (`IsSwipeEnabled` should have been called `IsCrossSlideEnabled` for consistency with the gesture recognizer.)

Several visual differences are also noticeable compared to `ListBox`. In a `ListView`, items animate in initially, items have a shrink-on-press effect, the margins are different, the selection highlight includes a checkmark, and so on. Figure 9.5 demonstrates these differences using the same `Rectangle` elements as items. Note that the background of `ListView` is `Transparent` by default, so the dark color in Figure 9.5 is the `Page` background.

 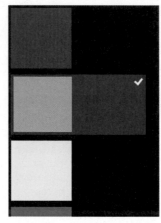

ListBox   ListView

FIGURE 9.5   `ListView` has a number of visual differences compared to `ListBox`.

The odd margin to the right of the `ListView` selection highlight is there for the scrollbar that appears under the right conditions. Unlike in `ListBox`, the selection highlight doesn't extend underneath the scrollbar so the checkmark remains unobscured.

The selection highlight includes a border that overlaps a small amount of the selected item. You can't see its shape in Figure 9.5 because the squares aren't as wide as the `ListView`, but Figure 9.6 shows its style. It looks exactly like the selection highlight used in the Start screen, file picker, and other Windows shell UI. As Figure 9.5 reveals, its size is based on the size of the item in the stacking dimension and the size of the `ListView` in the perpendicular direction.

FIGURE 9.6   The `ListView` selection highlight is consistent with signature Windows 8 user interfaces, such as the Start screen.

As with `ListBox`, `ListView` exposes `SelectionMode` and `SelectedItems` properties (the latter to handle multiselect), as well as `SelectAll` and `ScrollIntoView` methods. It has many additional features, however, some big and some small. Two small ones are richer `ScrollIntoView` functionality and support for a header. Three big ones are its selection behavior, item reordering, and data virtualization.

Richer `ScrollIntoView`

`ListView` has two overloads of `ScrollIntoView`: the one-parameter version that matches `ListBox`'s version, and one that accepts an extra `ScrollIntoViewAlignment` enumeration parameter. This provides two options:

→ **Default**—The control scrolls the minimal distance necessary to put the item entirely on the screen. Therefore, if the item is already on the screen, the control won't scroll at all. This provides the same behavior as the simpler overload and the same behavior as ListBox.

→ **Leading**—The control scrolls as much as necessary to make the item the **first** one visible (or as close as possible if there aren't enough items following it). That means the top edge when scrolling vertically, or the left edge when scrolling horizontally (via a custom items panel).

Header

`ListView` has a `Header` property that enables you to place custom UI on top of the list, such as a title. The property is of type `Object`, and it can be used just like the `Content` property of a content control. This should either be set to a `UIElement`, or used in conjunction with a `HeaderTemplate` property (see Chapter 16, "Styles, Templates, and Visual States"), because the default `TextBlock` rendering of non-`UIElement`s such as strings is small and ugly.

Selection

The big advantage of cross-slide selection support has been mentioned, but here are a few more details about the selection differences. In addition to supporting cross-slide selection (when `IsSwipeEnabled` is left at its default value of `true`), which applies only to touch input, `ListView` also supports selection via right tap. Recall that a right tap can not only be done by a mouse or pen, but by a press-and-hold touch gesture.

`ListView`'s `SelectionMode` property is a bit different from `ListBox`'s. The `ListView` property is of type **ListView**SelectionMode, which adds a `None` value to the typical `Single`, `Multiple`, and `Extended` options. The default `SelectionMode` is `Single`, as with `ListBox`.

When the `SelectionMode` is `None`, no item ever gets selected by user input, although the items can still get focus, as shown in Figure 9.7.

Although items can be selected programmatically on a `ListView` with a `SelectionMode=None`, such items never get rendered with the selection highlight, so the value of doing such a thing is dubious.

The behavior of the `Multiple` versus `Extended` `SelectionMode` is more subtle for `ListView` than it is for `ListBox`, but the result is more useful. The behavior is the same as `ListBox` for the selection gestures shared by both: simple taps and keyboard navigation. However, the `ListView`-specific selection gestures act

FIGURE 9.7   Although no items get selected in a `ListView` with `SelectionMode=None`, the second item has focus (and the corresponding focus rectangle).

in a `Multiple` fashion even when `Extended` is used. Although tapping and using arrow keys when `SelectionMode=Extended` acts in a single-select fashion unless the Shift or Ctrl key is held down, right taps and cross slides toggle the selection state of the relevant item. This means that the use of `SelectionMode=Extended` gives a traditional multiselect experience (optimized for single selection) when traditional gestures are used, but gives a modern multiselect experience (optimized for multiple selections) when newer gestures are used.

In addition to the normal selection concept enabled by the `SelectionChanged` event, `ListView` supports `Button`-style clicking of its items via a pointer tap or the Enter key (but no spacebar). You must opt into this mode by setting `IsItemClickEnabled` to `true`. (Unlike `IsSwipeEnabled`, it is `false` by default.) If you do so, pointer taps and Enter key presses no longer affect the current selection. Instead of raising `SelectionChanged`, they raise an `ItemClick` event. All the other selection gestures (including pressing the spacebar) still affect selection according to the current `SelectionMode`.

So why would you enable this "item clicking" concept in addition to selection? As weird as it might sound at first, this basically describes the behavior of the Start screen. Normal clicking of a tile doesn't *select* it; it launches the app! Selection of the items, used for tasks such as unpinning or uninstalling an app, is a relatively rare user action reserved for the extended gestures.

 Because `ListView` **handles right taps, one with focus prevents those right taps from toggling any** `AppBars`**!**

However, because it is customary to show a bottom `AppBar` (with context-specific `Buttons`) whenever an item is selected, this will not be a problem if you explicitly toggle the state of the `AppBar` in the `SelectionChanged` event handler. Regardless of how the selection change happens, you should show it if there are any selected items and hide it otherwise.

Reordering Items

Seemingly by magic, `ListView` contains automatic support for drag-and-drop reordering of items, much like on the Start screen. As you drag an item around, the other items even move around to get out of the way! This is pictured in Figure 9.8. Just like with the Start screen, dragging starts instantly for mouse or pen, but for touch the drag must start perpendicular to the panning direction to avoid confusion with the typical panning gesture. This can work end-to-end without any of your own C# code, although `ListView` does have a `DragItemStarting` event in case you want to add custom behavior.

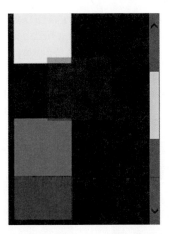

FIGURE 9.8   Dragging the red square to a new spot in the `ListView` works automatically, but you must explicitly enable this mode.

There's a trick for getting this to work, however. You must set all of the following three properties to `true`:

```
<ListView CanDragItems="True" CanReorderItems="True" AllowDrop="True">
```

With `AllowDrop` set to `true`, you can even drag and drop one of the items from the `ListView` to a different element.

> **When should I use a `ListView`?**
>
> You should use `ListView` for full-featured lists in which space is constrained, such as a side pane or for the main content when your app is snapped. Otherwise, `GridView` provides the best use of screen real estate.

Data Virtualization

`ListView` also contains support for *data virtualization*, but that requires data binding, so it is discussed in Chapter 17. Unlike UI virtualization, which is the process of constructing the item containers on demand, data virtualization is the practice of constructing the underlying items on-demand as well. This can not only be vital for large collections, but modest-sized ones that are slow to retrieve (typically because the source data is online).

GridView

If you are familiar with `ListView`, then you're already familiar with `GridView`, because it's effectively just a `ListView` with a layout that wraps its items. `ListView` and `GridView` both derive from a class called `ListViewBase`, and every API discussed in the preceding section belongs to `ListViewBase`! Both `ListView` and `GridView` add zero public APIs to their base class besides a default constructor! Therefore, you can think of `ListView` as nothing more than a `ListViewBase` with a `VirtualizingStackPanel` items panel, and you can think of

GridView as nothing more than a `ListViewBase` with a `WrapGrid` items panel. The reality is a bit more complicated, however, because the two classes have different implementation details that rely on their own default items panels.

Because all the behaviors of `GridView` are covered by the preceding section, this section highlights `GridView`'s visuals. Figure 9.9 compares `GridView` to `ListView` using the same `Rectangles` from Figure 9.5 that compared `ListView` to `ListBox`.

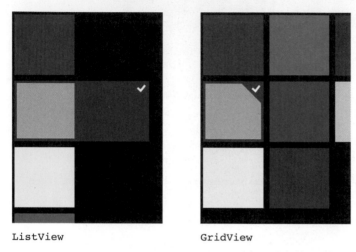

```
ListView              GridView
```

FIGURE 9.9   `ListView` and `GridView` differ only by the arrangement of their items.

GridView items are stacked vertically, just like in `ListView`. However, due to the wrapping, the default scrolling/panning direction is horizontal rather than vertical. If the items are not all the same size, the space of the largest item is given to every item. This is demonstrated in Figure 9.10, which contains a red `Rectangle` that is taller than the rest.

The automatic item reordering (when you set `CanDragItems`, `CanReorderItems`, and `AllowDrop` to `true`) works just as well for `GridView`, as shown in Figure 9.11.

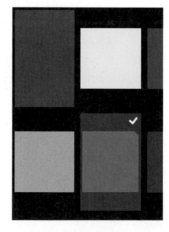

FIGURE 9.10   Every item is given the same amount of space—the size of the largest one.

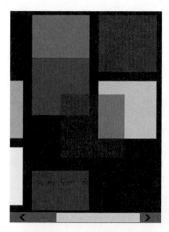

FIGURE 9.11   Drag-and-drop item reordering works seamlessly.

 As with any item arrangement done horizontally, setting `FlowDirection` to `RightToLeft` reverses the default behavior. This causes `GridView`'s items to start on the right and wrap toward the left.

FlipView

Despite the similar-sounding name and its status as a new-to-Windows-8 control, `FlipView` has nothing to do with `ListView` or `GridView`. It is designed to show only one item at a time, enabling the user to "flip" through items just like flipping pages in a book. Its items are automatically arranged with appropriate margins and snap points to make this work. This control is ideal for any kind of "help" documentation in your app, where each item in the control is a page of text.

`FlipView` derives directly from `Selector` and adds no public APIs other than its constructor. This means that, unlike the previous three controls, this doesn't enable multiselect. The single selection is the item that is currently visible inside the control.

`FlipView` automatically supports a number of gestures for navigating its items:

→ With touch, you can swipe back and forth. If you tap (or press and hold) the control, back and/or forward buttons appear that you can tap instead.

→ With a mouse or pen, you can tap the forward and back buttons that appear on hover or when the control has focus.

→ With a keyboard, you can use the left and right arrow keys (or the up and down arrow keys) to navigate back and forward, respectively.

Figures 9.12 and 9.13 illustrate the sequence of flipping from the first item to the second item using two different input techniques. These figures use the same `Rectangle` items used by previous examples. The animated transition from one item to another only occurs when swiping is used. Otherwise, the item change is instantaneous.

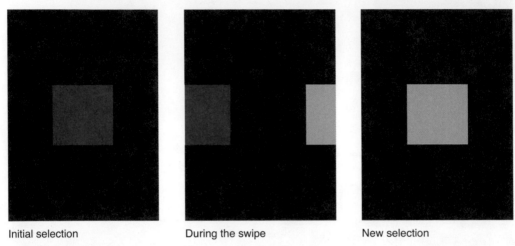

Initial selection   During the swipe   New selection

FIGURE 9.12   Flipping from the red to orange square with a swipe

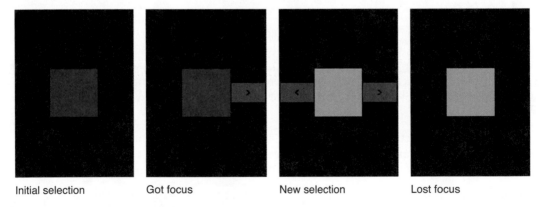

Initial selection   Got focus   New selection   Lost focus

FIGURE 9.13   Flipping from the red to orange square with the forward button

> You can make a `FlipView` flip vertically rather than horizontally by applying a `StackPanel` or `VirtualizingStackPanel` with its default `Vertical` Orientation. The back and forward buttons even render appropriately for this configuration, as shown in Figure 9.14. Furthermore, because the up and down arrow keys already are treated the same way as the left and right arrow keys, keyboard input works naturally as well.

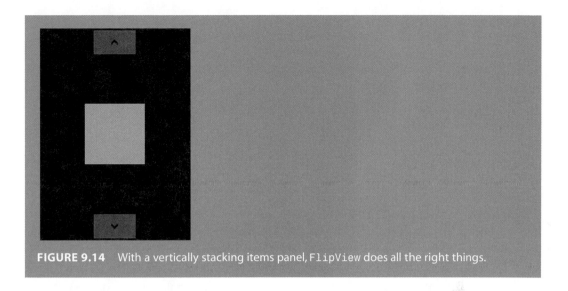

FIGURE 9.14   With a vertically stacking items panel, `FlipView` does all the right things.

SemanticZoom

Whenever this book talks about *zooming*, it's referring to basic optical zooming. *Semantic zooming*, on the other hand, refers to a type of zooming that doesn't necessarily preserve the appearance of the content. Instead, zooming out involves switching to a higher-level view of the content that's more useful for navigating it "at a distance."

The Windows shell exposes semantic zooming in several important places, such as the Start screen, the file picker, the contact picker, and search results. Many apps, such as the Photos app, also expose it. In all cases, there are two distinct views to zoom between. Figure 9.15 shows the two views for the file picker. The zoomed-in view is the default view that shows every file and subfolder in the current folder. The zoomed-out view shows only groupings (one per letter plus a few more). Zooming is done with the same pinch or stretch touch gesture used for optical zooming, although it can also be done with either the mouse wheel or +/- keys while holding down the Ctrl key.

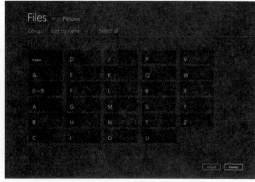

Zoomed-in view   Zoomed-out view

FIGURE 9.15   The Windows file picker uses semantic zoom to great effect.

In contrast, the Start screen's semantic zooming looks similar to an optical zoom, but in the zoomed-out view the tiles are rendered more simply, group names aren't scaled proportionally (so they can still be read easily), and the functionality changes. Instead of being able to manage individual tiles and launch apps, the zoomed-out view enables rearranging and renaming groups of tiles.

In both examples, the target action (such as selecting a file or launching an app) cannot be done from the zoomed-out view. Its primary purpose is to provide a quick way to jump to a spot in the zoomed-in view without requiring a lot of panning or scrolling.

For XAML apps, the SemanticZoom control provides the infrastructure to expose the same two-level semantic zooming functionality automatically. It has two properties—ZoomedInView and ZoomedOutView—representing the two different views. SemanticZoom is not an items control, but each view must be an object implementing an interface called ISemanticZoomInformation. And there's only one class in the XAML UI Framework that implements this interface: ListViewBase. Therefore, the only built-in controls you can use with it are ListView and GridView.

The following XAML is a simple example of how you could populate the two views of SemanticZoom:

```
<SemanticZoom ViewChangeStarted="SemanticZoom_ViewChangeStarted">
  <!-- The default zoomed-in view -->
  <SemanticZoom.ZoomedInView>
    <GridView x:Name="Nums">
      <GridViewItem>1</GridViewItem>
      <GridViewItem>2</GridViewItem>
      <GridViewItem>3</GridViewItem>
      <GridViewItem>4</GridViewItem>
      <GridViewItem>5</GridViewItem>

      …
      <GridViewItem>300</GridViewItem>
    </GridView>
  </SemanticZoom.ZoomedInView>

  <!-- The zoomed-out view -->
  <SemanticZoom.ZoomedOutView>
    <ListView>
      <ListViewItem x:Name="Group1">1-100</ListViewItem>
      <ListViewItem x:Name="Group2">101-200</ListViewItem>
      <ListViewItem x:Name="Group3">201-300</ListViewItem>
    </ListView>
  </SemanticZoom.ZoomedOutView>
</SemanticZoom>
```

The zoomed-in view contains the numbers 1-300, and the zoomed-out view merges the items into groups of 100. Both GridView and ListView are used for demonstration purposes. GridView is almost always the most appropriate for the large number of zoomed-in items, and in this case the number of zoomed-out items is small enough to make the choice irrelevant.

This simple XAML is almost all we need. The views animate in and out appropriately based on the standard gestures, and selecting an item in the zoomed-out view automatically transitions back to the zoomed-in view. The one thing that's missing is the ability to keep the two views in sync. For example, when the user selects "101-200" in the zoomed-out view, it should cause the zoomed-in view to scroll to the 101st item. With this XAML alone, however, the zoomed-in view doesn't scroll unless the user scrolls it. That's because the SemanticZoom control doesn't understand the *semantics* of the zoomed-out ListViewItems.

This can be remedied by writing some code to manually keep the views in sync. SemanticZoom exposes both ViewChangeStarted and ViewChangeCompleted events, so the following ViewChangeStarted event handler (already attached in the preceding XAML) updates the zoomed-in view immediately before each transition from zoomed-out to zoomed-in:

```
void SemanticZoom_ViewChangeStarted(object sender,
                                    SemanticZoomViewChangedEventArgs e)
{
  if (e.IsSourceZoomedInView)
  {
    // Do nothing special when zooming out
  }
  else
  {
    // Potentially scroll the zoomed-in view before zooming in
    ListViewItem item = e.SourceItem.Item as ListViewItem;
    if (item == Group1)
    {
      Nums.ScrollIntoView(Nums.Items[0], ScrollIntoViewAlignment.Leading);
    }
    else if (item == Group2)
    {
      Nums.ScrollIntoView(Nums.Items[100], ScrollIntoViewAlignment.Leading);
    }
    else
    {
      Nums.ScrollIntoView(Nums.Items[200], ScrollIntoViewAlignment.Leading);
    }
  }
}
```

Notice that the overload of ScrollIntoView is used to enable the Leading alignment option (described previously in the "ListView" section). This is the appropriate choice for semantic zooming because it matches user expectations of what it means to jump to a specific spot in the list. Notice also that the selected item that triggered the view change is buried in an `Item` subproperty of `SemanticZoomViewChangedEventArgs.SourceItem`. The `SourceItem` property (of type `SemanticZoomLocation`) also includes a `Bounds` property (of type `Rect`), which can be helpful for advanced customizations of the transition or the resultant view.

In the zoomed-in view, `SemanticZoom` automatically shows a little minus `Button` that acts much like the one at the end of the scrollbar when the Windows Shell uses semantic zoom. However, unlike in the Windows shell, it is placed above the scrollbar and visible even when the scrollbar is not. If you want to replace this `Button` with your own custom user interface, you can disable it by setting `SemanticZoom`'s `IsZoomOutButtonEnabled` property to `false`. You should be sure to have something equivalent if you do this. The `Button` not only serves as a handy zoom-out shortcut, but it's a powerful cue that informs the user that zooming is possible for the current content.

 Don't wrap `SemanticZoom` **in a** `ScrollViewer` **(with the same scrolling direction)!**

As always, make sure that a control that is meant to contain scrollable content is itself properly constrained in size. Otherwise, its own content might never scroll. This can impact programmatic scrolling with `ScrollIntoView` in a subtle and confusing way, and `SemanticZoom` is often the motivation for using `ScrollIntoView`.

If `SemanticZoom` is placed in a `ScrollViewer` that scrolls in the same orientation as `SemanticZoom`'s two views, then `SemanticZoom` is given infinite space in the direction scrolling and its views never scroll. This makes all `ScrollIntoView` calls no-ops. However, *user-driven* scrolling still appears to work just fine because the *parent* `ScrollViewer` translates the entire `SemanticZoom` control!

Summary

Items controls are vital to understand for just about any XAML app. It's hard to imagine a nontrivial XAML app that doesn't use both content controls and items controls. Unlike content controls, however, there's a lot to learn about items controls! A recurring theme throughout this chapter is the importance of data binding if you're working with a sizable or dynamic list of items. Therefore, items controls will be revisited when it's time to examine data binding in depth.

Chapter 10

TEXT

You've seen TextBlock a number of times in this book, but it's not the only text control available. It also is a much richer control than most people expect. This chapter covers the two "blocks"—TextBlock and RichTextBlock— designed for displaying text, and the analogous two "boxes"—TextBox and RichEditBox—designed for display- ing *and editing* text. It also examines the special-purpose PasswordBox that should be used if you ever need to ask the user for a password.

TextBlock

TextBlock contains a number of simple properties for modifying its font: FontFamily, FontSize, FontStyle, FontWeight, and FontStretch. The behaviors of several of these are dependent on characteristics of the font family in use. For example, FontStretch can be set to one of ten enumeration values ranging from UltraCondensed (50% of Normal) to UltraExpanded (200% of Normal) but unless such variations are installed as part of the font family, setting these has no effect. Similarly, the type of the FontWeight property is a funny FontWeight structure with a single double field, but most fonts support only two weights (normal or bold). To simplify the use of FontWeight, the Windows Runtime exposes a FontWeights class with public static fields of appropriately initialized FontWeight instances. There are eleven possible choices, such as Normal, SemiBold, Bold, ExtraBold, Light, SemiLight, and so on.

Independent of the font, `TextBlock` enables a number of modifications to the way it renders text. The obvious one is the `Foreground` property that represents the text color, but here are the others:

If you include a custom font file as content in your app's package, you can reference it with a `FontFamily` URI, such as `RelativePath/FontFile.ttf#FontName`.

→ **TextAlignment**—Can be set to `Left` (the default), `Center`, `Right`, or `Justify`.

→ **TextWrapping**—Controls whether text can wrap onto additional lines. Can be set to `NoWrap` (the default) or `Wrap`.

→ **TextTrimming**—What should happen to text that doesn't fit within the `TextBlock`'s bounds (on the last line if wrapping is enabled). Can be set to `None` (the default), which truncates the text, or `WordEllipsis`, which places an ellipsis at the end. The ellipsis is placed only at the end of whole words, meaning a word is never partially rendered when `WordEllipsis` is used, with the exception of the first word. If the `TextBlock` isn't big enough to fit the first whole word, then it will render as many letters as it can in order to make the letters plus the ellipses fit. (And if there's no room for even a single letter plus the ellipsis, it will still render them and allow them to be truncated.)

→ **CharacterSpacing**—The amount of extra space between characters (`0` by default) measured in thousandths of an em. (One *em* equals the current `FontSize`, so em measurements are always relative.) This can be set to a negative value to push letters closer together.

→ **LineHeight**—The height of each line, measured in device-independent pixels. This is relevant only when `TextWrapping` is set to `Wrap` and a separate `LineStackingStrategy` property is set to `BlockLineHeight` (which means, "respect the `LineHeight` property value"). At `LineHeight`'s default value of `0`, the setting is ignored.

Figure 10.1 demonstrates various `CharacterSpacing` values with the following XAML:

```
<StackPanel>
  <TextBlock … CharacterSpacing="-100">SPACING=-100</TextBlock>
  <TextBlock … SPACING=DEFAULT</TextBlock>
  <TextBlock … CharacterSpacing="100">SPACING=100</TextBlock>
  <TextBlock … CharacterSpacing="500">SPACING=500</TextBlock>
</StackPanel>
```

Figure 10.2 demonstrates a custom `LineHeight` with the following TextBlock:

```
<TextBlock FontSize="100" Width="900" FontWeight="Bold" Foreground="Purple"
  TextWrapping="Wrap" LineStackingStrategy="BlockLineHeight" LineHeight="60">
  THE FONT SIZE IS 100 BUT THE LINE HEIGHT IS 60!
</TextBlock>
```

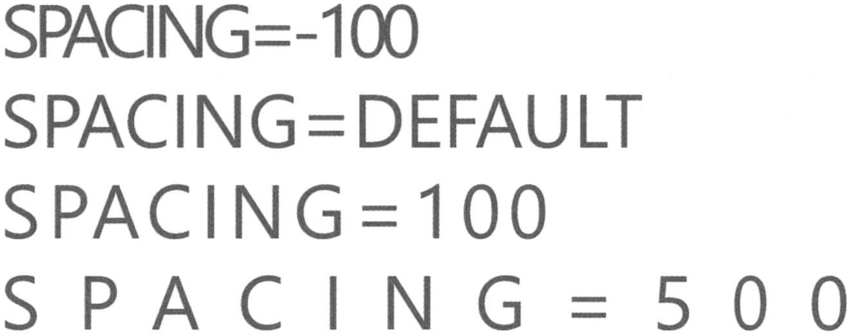

SPACING=-100

SPACING=DEFAULT

SPACING=100

S PA C I N G = 5 0 0

FIGURE 10.1   Using CharacterSpacing to adjust the horizontal spacing of text

THE FONT SIZE IS
100 BUT THE LINE
HEIGHT IS 60!

FIGURE 10.2   Using LineHeight to adjust the vertical spacing of text

Because CharacterSpacing and LineHeight are dependency properties, you can even animate their values using the techniques from Chapter 15, "Animation."

Text Content

The big secret of TextBlock is that its Text property (of type string) is *not* its content property. Instead, it is a property called Inlines that is a collection of Inline objects. Although the following TextBlock gives the same result as setting the Text property, you're really setting Inlines instead:

```
<!-- TextBlock.Inlines is being set here: -->
<TextBlock>Text in a TextBlock</TextBlock>
```

A type converter makes the value resemble a simple string, but it's actually a collection with one Inline-derived element called Run. Therefore, the preceding XAML is equivalent to the following:

```
<TextBlock><Run Text="Text in a TextBlock"/></TextBlock>
```

which is also equivalent to the following XAML because Text is Run's content property:

```
<TextBlock><Run>Text in a TextBlock</Run></TextBlock>
```

A Run is a chunk of text with identical formatting. Using a single explicit Run doesn't add value, but things can start to get interesting when you use multiple Runs in the same TextBlock. For example, the preceding TextBlock can be expressed as follows:

```
<TextBlock>
  <Run>Text</Run>
  <Run> in</Run>
  <Run> a</Run>
  <Run> TextBlock</Run>
</TextBlock>
```

This doesn't change the rendering behavior compared to the previous XAML. Run, however, has several formatting properties that can override the corresponding properties on the parent TextBlock: FontFamily, FontSize, FontStretch, FontStyle, FontWeight, Foreground, and even CharacterSpacing. The following XAML, shown in Figure 10.3, takes advantage of these:

```
<TextBlock Foreground="Brown" FontSize="30">
  <Run FontStyle="Italic" FontFamily="Georgia" Foreground="Blue">Rich</Run>
  <Run FontFamily="Comic Sans MS" CharacterSpacing="-200"> Text </Run>
  <Run FontFamily="Arial Black" Foreground="Orange" FontSize="100">in</Run>
  <Run FontFamily="Verdana" FontWeight="Bold" Foreground="Green"> a </Run>
  <Run FontFamily="Courier New" FontWeight="Bold" CharacterSpacing="200">
    TextBlock</Run>
</TextBlock>
```

FIGURE 10.3   Several uniquely formatted Runs inside a single TextBlock

Although this is a silly example, the same technique can be used for something useful like italicizing or underlining a single word in a paragraph. This is much easier than trying to use multiple TextBlocks and worrying about positioning each one correctly. And by using a single TextBlock, you get one consistent behavior for clipping, wrapping, and even text selection across the heterogeneous text.

> **(?) How can I underline text in a** TextBlock**?**
>
> There is no property on TextBlock for this. Instead, you must use another Inline-derived element called Underline within a TextBlock's content. For example:
>
> ```
> <TextBlock><Underline>Underlined text</Underline></TextBlock>
> ```

When you add content to a `TextBlock`'s `Inlines` property, the (unformatted) content is appended to its `Text` property. Therefore, it is still valid to programmatically retrieve the value of the `Text` property when only `Inlines` is explicitly set. For example, the value of `Text` is the expected "Rich Text in a TextBlock" string for the `TextBlock` in Figure 10.3.

`TextBlock` **and Whitespace**

When a `TextBlock`'s content is set via the `Text` property, any whitespace in the string is preserved. When its content is set via `Inlines` in XAML, however, whitespace is not preserved. Instead, leading and trailing whitespace is ignored, and any contiguous whitespace is coalesced into a single whitespace character (as in HTML).

Explicit Versus Implicit Runs

Although the following `TextBlock`:

```
<TextBlock>Text in a TextBlock</TextBlock>
```

is equivalent to this:

```
<TextBlock><Run>Text in a TextBlock</Run></TextBlock>
```

the behavior of the type converter is not always straightforward. For example, the following use of another `Inline` called `LineBreak` is valid:

```
<TextBlock>Text in<LineBreak/>a TextBlock</TextBlock>
```

whereas the following is not:

```
<TextBlock><Run>Text in<LineBreak/>a TextBlock</Run></TextBlock>
```

The last variation is not valid because Run's content property (`Text`) is a simple string, and you can't embed a LineBreak element inside a string. The content property of `TextBlock` (`Inlines`) is converted to one or more Runs via a type converter that specifically handles LineBreak, which is why the first use of LineBreak works. This type converter makes the following XAML:

```
<TextBlock>Text in<LineBreak/>a TextBlock</TextBlock>
```

equivalent to the following `TextBlock` containing two Runs, one on each side of the LineBreak:

```
<TextBlock><Run>Text in</Run><LineBreak/><Run>a TextBlock</Run></TextBlock>
```

Text Elements

The Inline class derives from TextElement, a class representing all kinds of text content. Note that TextElements are not UIElements; they do not individually participate in the standard UIElement mechanisms such as layout, input events, and focus. They are specifically for text controls and text-specific layout rules are applied to them.

Two types of TextElements exist—Inlines and Blocks. A Block is a rectangular region that occupies a rectangular region, whereas an Inline is a region that flows more freely with text, potentially occupying a nonrectangular space (flowing from the end of one line to the beginning of the next). There are several more types of Inline objects besides the previously seen Run, LineBreak, and Underline. All the relevant classes and their inheritance relationships are shown in Figure 10.4.

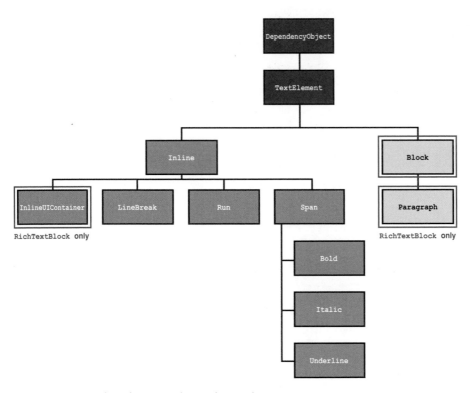

FIGURE 10.4   The inheritance hierarchy involving TextElement

If this seems like an excessive amount of structure, that's because it is! These classes were originally introduced in WPF, and in WPF, there are many types of Blocks (and more types of Inlines as well). Some of these classes can be used only by RichTextBlock, so they are discussed in the upcoming "RichTextBlock" section. In addition to Run and the simple LineBreak, the only other type of Inline that you can use inside a TextBlock is Span and its descendants.

Span itself can be used to group text with the same formatting, just like Run. (The previously mentioned formatting properties on Run are defined on TextElement, so they are common to all.) Figure 10.3 would look identical if all of its Run elements were replaced with Span. The difference between Run and Span is that Span supports nested Inlines. It has an Inlines content property, just like TextBlock, whereas Run has only a simple string Text content property.

The following XAML demonstrates the nested nature of Spans, rendered in Figure 10.5:

```
<TextBlock FontStyle="Italic">
  <Span Foreground="Brown">
    1
    <Span FontSize="20">
      2
      <Span FontWeight="Bold">3</Span>
      2
    </Span>
    1
  </Span>
</TextBlock>
```

FIGURE 10.5   The innermost Span inherits formatting from the two outer Spans as well as formatting on the containing TextBlock.

The Bold element is a shortcut for <Span FontWeight="Bold"/> and the Italic element is a shortcut for <Span FontStyle="Italic"/>. The Underline element, however, is the only way to get underlined text. The following TextBlock, shown in Figure 10.6, demonstrates these Span-derived elements:

```
<TextBlock Foreground="BlueViolet">
  <Italic>Then I said</Italic> "<Bold>stop <Underline>now</Underline></Bold>!"
</TextBlock>
```

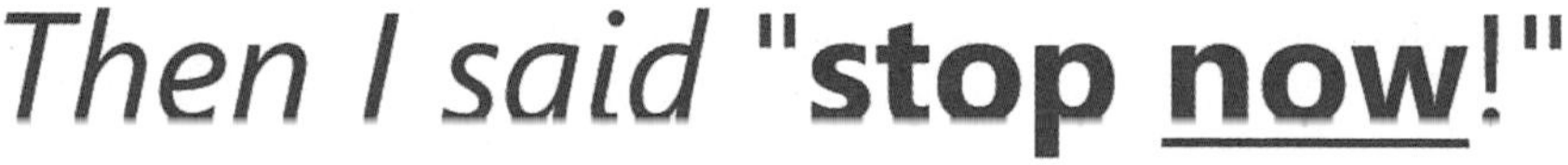

FIGURE 10.6   Using Italic, Bold, and Underline in a single TextBlock

Text Selection

As mentioned previously, TextBlock optionally supports text selection. To enable it, you must set its IsTextSelectionEnabled property to true. When you do this, people using touch input can tap any word to highlight it, and then drag two circle adornments to change the range of the selection. With a mouse or pen, a caret is rendered instead of the typical mouse pointer, and users can do the typical selection gestures of dragging to define the selection range or double tapping to select an entire word. A right tap gesture on the TextBlock (which is press-and-hold for touch input) brings up a context menu with the choices of Copy (only if any text is selected) and Select All, shown in Figure 10.7. The standard keyboard shortcuts of Ctrl+C for Copy and Ctrl+A for Select All work as well. Copying is done to the Windows clipboard, so the text can be pasted into desktop apps as well as Windows Store apps.

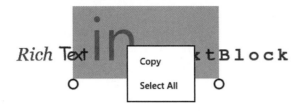

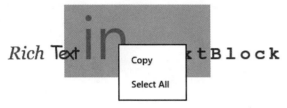

FIGURE 10.7   With `IsTextSelectionEnabled=true`, text can be selected and copied via several standard gestures.

TextBlock exposes many members related to text selection, all based around a `TextPointer` class that represents a position within its text. In addition to a parameterless `SelectAll` method, a `Select` method enables you to programmatically select a specific range of text based on two passed-in `TextPointers`. TextBlock's readonly `ContentStart` and `ContentEnd` properties point to the beginning and end of the entire text content, and from these you can call `TextPointer`'s `GetPositionAtOffset` method to retrieve a `TextPointer` pointing to any character you'd like.

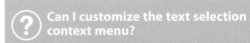

? Can I customize the text selection context menu?

No, but TextBlock raises a `ContextMenuOpening` event so you can perform custom actions whenever it gets shown.

Whenever the text selection changes, whether programmatically or from user input, TextBlock's `SelectionChanged` event is raised. You can retrieve the current text selection in two ways. TextBlock's readonly `SelectedText` property gives you the content as a string, whereas its readonly `SelectionStart` and `SelectionEnd` properties give you `TextPointers` for the beginning and end of the selection.

> **TextPointer** •••
>
> The TextPointer class is basically a character offset, but it uses heuristics to remain in the "same" spot in the face of text additions and deletions. Heuristics are needed because the correct behavior can be ambiguous. For example, after text is inserted at the same position as a TextPointer, you could consider the TextPointer to now point immediately before the new text or immediately after. To resolve such ambiguity, TextPointer has a concept of *logical direction*, exposed by a LogicalDirection enumeration with Backward and Forward values. Every TextPointer has a logical direction assigned to it, based either on how the user performed a selection, or how the TextPointer was programmatically obtained. TextPointer also exposes a GetCharacterRect method that returns the bounding Rect for any character, which is helpful for overlaying elements on top of text.
>
> The irony is that none of the editable controls currently expose TextPointer, so its primary purpose does not get exercised.

 The Windows.UI.Xaml.Documents.Typography class exposes several attached properties that can be placed on text controls to configure advanced OpenType properties on fonts that support them. For example, if you use the Gabriola font and set Typography.StandardLigatures="True" on a TextBlock, you can see a difference in how "ft" is rendered. As in the Microsoft logo, a single line connects the two letters when ligatures are used.

RichTextBlock

A typical first reaction to discovering the RichTextBlock element is, "Isn't TextBlock already rich?" TextBlock can do a lot when it comes to formatting text, but RichTextBlock adds two big new tricks:

→ Embedding arbitrary UIElements among text

→ Letting text overflow into separate elements, which enables multi-column text or other custom text layouts

Except for these two features, TextBlock and RichTextBlock are almost identical. They expose the same methods, properties, and events, although RichTextBlock happens to have an extra GetPositionFromPoint method that returns a TextPointer for the passed-in Point. RichTextBlock also has some different defaults: IsTextSelectionEnabled is true by default, and TextWrapping is Wrap by default.

One other difference is that RichTextBlock's content property is called Blocks rather than Inlines, and it naturally holds a collection of Blocks rather than Inlines. From Figure 10.4, you can see that this is a convoluted way of saying that RichTextBlock must contain a set of Paragraphs.

Paragraph's purpose is to hold a collection of `Inlines`, so it's basically the same as a `Span` with an automatically inserted `LineBreak` at the end. Although unlike `Span`, `Paragraph` inherits some extra formatting capabilities from its `Block` base class: `TextAlignment`, `LineHeight`, and `LineStackingStrategy` properties just like the ones defined on `TextBlock` and `RichTextBlock`. Figure 10.8 shows the following two-`Paragraph` `RichTextBlock` that demonstrates two `TextAlignment` settings:

```
<RichTextBlock Foreground="Chocolate">
  <Paragraph TextAlignment="Right">
    This is paragraph #1, which is <Bold>right-aligned</Bold>.
  </Paragraph>
  <Paragraph TextAlignment="Justify">
    This is paragraph #2. It is <Bold>justified</Bold>, which impacts all but the
    last line (and any lines with a LineBreak).
  </Paragraph>
</RichTextBlock>
```

Embedding `UIElement`s

The fact that `RichTextBlock` can contain embedded `UIElement`s is not obvious from looking at its APIs. This capability comes from the `InlineUIContainer` element, which is an `Inline`. It has a simple `Child` content property of type `UIElement` that it is able to host directly among the text content.

Although `InlineUIContainer` *should* be able to be added to the plain old `TextBlock`'s `Inlines` collection, doing so fails at runtime. It turns out that `InlineUIContainers` must be placed within a `Block`, and this is the reason that this feature is supported only by `RichTextBlock`.

> ## This is paragraph #1, which is **right-aligned**. This is paragraph #2. It is **justified**, which impacts all but the last line (and any lines with a LineBreak).

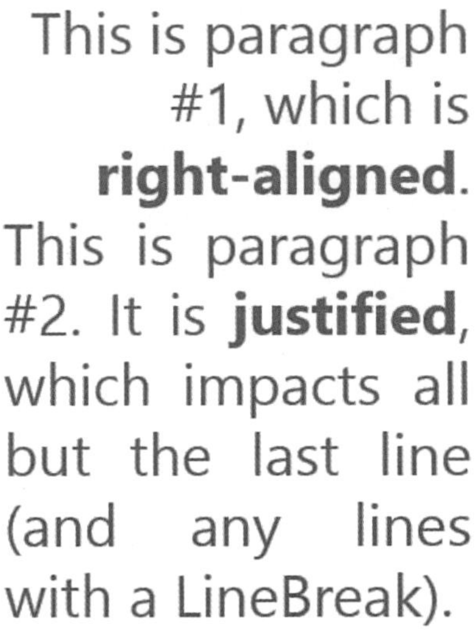

FIGURE 10.8   Each Paragraph in a RichTextBlock can be given different TextAlignments (in addition to other formatting settings).

The capability to embed a `UIElement` among text means you can insert just about anything: an image, a video, a `Panel` containing a large tree of elements, and so on. Such elements are fully interactive and can get focus, despite feeling like part of the text.

The following XAML demonstrates `InlineUIContainer` with something a bit unusual. It embeds a `StackPanel` along with its three `RadioButtons`, as shown in Figure 10.9:

```
<RichTextBlock Foreground="OrangeRed" FontSize="20">
  <Paragraph>
    I would like a
    <InlineUIContainer>
```

```
        <StackPanel>
          <RadioButton>small</RadioButton>
          <RadioButton>medium</RadioButton>
          <RadioButton>large</RadioButton>
        </StackPanel>
      </InlineUIContainer> drink, please.
    </Paragraph>
</RichTextBlock>
```

UIElements don't get rendered any differently than normal when used in this fashion. In Figure 10.9, the app is using the light theme, which is why the RadioButtons look different than they do in Chapter 8, "Content Controls."

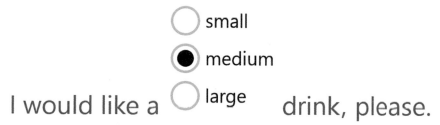

FIGURE 10.9   With InlineUIContainer, you can jam just about anything inside a RichTextBlock.

> ⚠ **InlineUIContainer isn't as helpful as it could be!**
>
> One might think that a great application for InlineUIContainer would be to embed a HyperlinkButton within text. There are two problems with this:
>
> → The default style of HyperlinkButton doesn't blend well with the default text formatting. The default FontSize is not the same, nor does the hyperlink text line up with surrounding text due to padding.
>
> → Embedded UIElements act differently than regular text when it comes to text selection. Each InlineUIContainer can be selected only as an entire unit, and its content is never included on the clipboard when copying a selection; it is simply skipped. This behavior is entirely reasonable and looks right for embedded elements such as Images. For UIElements that just look like text, however, the behavior can be surprising to users.
>
> The bottom line is that this doesn't give you the same experience as on a Web page, in which a hyperlink (or a subset of the hyperlink) can be selected and copied.

Text Overflow

If you place more text in a RichTextBlock (or TextBlock) than what fits in its bounds, you could wrap it in a ScrollViewer to make it all readable. RichTextBlock, however, supports a nifty trick that enables text that doesn't fit to spill into a special element called RichTextBlock**Overflow** that you can place anywhere. If the remaining content doesn't all fit in the `RichTextBlockOverflow`, it can spill into another `RichTextBlockOverflow`, and so on.

To enable this feature, all you need to do is set `RichTextBlock`'s `OverflowContentTarget` property to the desired `RichTextBlockOverflow` instance. `RichTextBlockOverflow` has its own `OverflowContentTarget` property so you can keep chaining `RichTextBlockOverflows` to each other. You could use this to create multicolumn text, which is a popular way for Windows Store apps to display articles, instructions, or other lengthy chunks of text. The following XAML shows how, with the result shown in Figure 10.10:

```
<Grid Background="White">
  <!-- Define a three-column grid -->
  <Grid.ColumnDefinitions>
    <ColumnDefinition/>
    <ColumnDefinition/>
    <ColumnDefinition/>
  </Grid.ColumnDefinitions>

  <!-- The single "real" RichTextBlock contains all content and formatting -->
  <RichTextBlock Foreground="Black" FontSize="20" FontFamily="Cambria"
               Margin="12" OverflowContentTarget="{Binding ElementName=o1}">
    <Paragraph>
      Lorem ipsum dolor sit amet, …
    </Paragraph>

    …
  </RichTextBlock>

  <!-- The 1st overflow element transfers its own overflow -->
  <RichTextBlockOverflow Name="o1" Grid.Column="1" Margin="12"
                       OverflowContentTarget="{Binding ElementName=o2}" />

  <!-- The 2nd overflow element renders as much as it can,
       then truncates its own overflow -->
  <RichTextBlockOverflow Name="o2" Grid.Column="2" Margin="12" />
</Grid>
```

Notice that text selection works seamlessly across the three disjoint elements as if they are a single `RichTextBlock`. The one true `RichTextBlock` is the master; it holds all the text content and formatting settings. Although a `RichTextBlockOverflow` can choose its own independent settings for standard visual properties like `Padding`, `Margin`, or `RenderTransform`, it can't override any font settings.

If the `RichTextBlock` was wrapped in a `ScrollViewer`, it would have no overflow content and the `RichTextBlockOverflows` would remain empty. Although the `OverflowContentTarget` property can be easily set to a `RichTextBlockOverflow` instance in code-behind, the preceding XAML uses a simple data binding feature (covered in Chapter 17, "Data Binding") to assign it to an element by its name.

FIGURE 10.10   Three-column text, partially selected, displayed with `RichTextBlock` and two linked `RichTextBlockOverflows`

Because each `RichTextBlock` and `RichTextBlockOverflow` is a separate element, you can get creative with layout. Figure 10.11 updates the preceding `Grid` by adding an extra row, moving the first `RichTextBlockOverflow` to the new row, and interspersing colored `Rectangles` among the text content. You could use a similar technique to wrap text around an image in a way that adjusts to changing text size or app size. This is more flexible than embedding a `UIElement` within the text, because its position would be fixed.

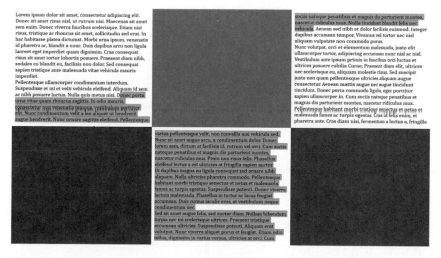

FIGURE 10.11   Text overflow and selection are still seamless no matter where `RichTextBlock` and its linked `RichTextBlockOverflows` are placed.

Figure 10.12 shows an extreme use of `RichTextBlockOverflows` to tightly wrap text around an image. Each line is rendered with one or two separate (and carefully placed!) elements in order to achieve this effect, which is obvious in the part of the figure that shows the content as viewed in the Visual Studio XAML designer. Although the star is nonrectangular, the `Image` element rendering it is indeed rectangular, so the position of each `RichTextBlockOverflow` is hard-coded for this specific content. Although the `RichTextBlock` appears to be in single-line mode (`TextWrapping=NoWrap`), the overflow feature works only if `TextWrapping` is left at its default value of `Wrap`. Therefore, the `RichTextBlock` in Figure 10.12, as well as each `RichTextBlockOverflow`, constrains its `Height` to make only one line of text fit.

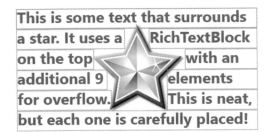

As viewed in Visual Studio's designer   The final result, with some text selected

FIGURE 10.12   Using fine-grained text overflow to carefully avoid content that appears nonrectangular

`RichTextBlock`'s readonly Boolean `HasOverflowContent` property reveals whether any of its content can overflow, regardless of whether a `RichTextBlockOverflow` is attached to receive the overflowing content.

TextBox

The `TextBox` control, pictured in Figure 10.13, enables users to type one or more lines of text. The software keyboard is automatically shown when a `TextBox` gets focus via touch and hidden when a `TextBox` loses focus. (This is true even if a hardware keyboard is present.)

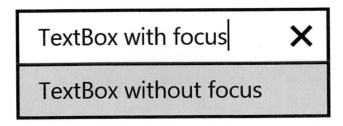

FIGURE 10.13   Two `TextBox`es, one with focus and one without

Unlike most other XAML controls, the content of TextBox is not stored as a generic System.Object. Instead, TextBox stores it in a simple string property called Text and raises a TextChanged event whenever the string changes. Because its text is stored as a simple string, TextBox doesn't support formatted text. It does inherit the standard five Font*XXX* properties from Control, which apply to all of its text uniformly. Other than that, however, TextAlignment is the only text-specific formatting you can adjust.

When a TextBox has content, has focus, and is in its default single-line mode with no wrapping, it contains an "X" button that can be tapped to quickly clear the content, which is especially handy on devices without a hardware keyboard. You can enable TextBox's multiline mode by setting AcceptsReturn for true.

> **AcceptsReturn Versus TextWrapping**   •••
>
> Setting AcceptsReturn to true not only enables typing and pasting newlines, but displaying them as well. In this mode, setting TextWrapping to Wrap affects any lines that are too long to display within the width of the TextBox.
>
> With AcceptsReturn left as false and TextWrapping left as NoWrap, a TextBox never displays more than one line. If you attempt to set Text to a string with a newline, it displays only the first line of text. However, if you set TextWrapping to Wrap while AcceptsReturn is false, the TextBox is in a weird mode in which it can *display* text with newlines, but the user can't press the Enter key to insert one. The only way it can receive newlines is programmatically or by pasting in text with newlines. Needless to say, this is a combination of property values to avoid!

You can limit the length of text that can be typed into a TextBox with its MaxLength property. Its default value is 0, which means infinite. Note that you can always programmatically set Text to a string longer than MaxLength and the TextBox will still display it.

Spelling and Text Prediction

TextBox supports two nifty features that are available by setting a corresponding Boolean property to true:

→ **IsSpellCheckEnabled**—Places red squiggles under misspelled words and provides a context menu with suggestions and other options. It also autocorrects common mistakes.

→ **IsTextPredictionEnabled**—Suggests a word while you type. This is true by default, but it is activated only when input is coming from the software keyboard. (The theory is that it would be more of a distraction than help when typing on a hardware keyboard.)

The spell check functionality, along with autocorrect, provides a similar experience to what you get in Microsoft Word. If you do a touch-based tap or a mouse- or pen-based right tap on a red-underlined word, you get a context menu like the one in Figure 10.14. If you make a common mistake (such as typing "wierd" instead of "weird"), the correction is made automatically, but performing the same gesture gives the user the option to undo the autocorrection and stop doing that specific one in the future.

After detecting a misspelled word

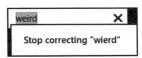
After autocorrecting a misspelled word

FIGURE 10.14   Spell check manifests itself in two different ways.

Red squiggles are triggered for more than just spelling errors. For example, if you repeat a word, the second one gets a squiggle with the context menu option of "Delete repeated word."

When you select "Ignore," it applies only to that specific TextBox instance (for the lifetime of the object). The dictionary is provided by Windows, and any words added or ignored apply to all Windows Store apps that use this feature.

Although spell check looks full-featured, it unfortunately isn't quite good enough for serious use due to some annoying behaviors. The spell check for a word isn't done until a character is typed *after* the word (such as punctuation or a space). That means if there's only one word, or if the content ends in a word with no punctuation, its spelling doesn't get checked. Also, when you add a word to the dictionary, it removes the red squiggle from that instance of the word, but it sometimes misses other occurrences, even within the same TextBox! The missed instances have to be perturbed (such as adding a space after each one) in order for their obsolete squiggles to go away. And of course, with no way for the user to view the custom words that were added to the dictionary and remove any that were added by accident, the feature isn't complete.

The text prediction functionality (on by default when using the software keyboard), is demonstrated in Figure 10.15. Tapping the suggestion replaces the word currently being typed with the suggested word.

FIGURE 10.15   With text prediction enabled, the most likely suggestion is presented in a tappable tooltip as you type a word.

> **?** **Can I supply a custom context-specific dictionary to use with text prediction?**
>
> No. Instead, you can mimic the feature with your own processing of what's being typed in a TextBox, and turn off the built-in text prediction (with IsTextPredictionEnabled=false) so it doesn't interfere with your custom user interface.

Text Selection

TextBox exposes straightforward and familiar members for text selection—SelectAll, Select, SelectedText, SelectionStart, SelectionLength, and GetRectFromCharacterIndex.

However, unlike TextBlock and RichTextBlock, these are all based on simple int character indices rather than TextPointer objects.

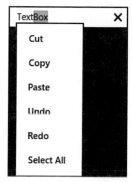

In addition to the Select All and Copy commands supported by TextBlock and RichTextBlock, TextBox's editable nature enables it to provide automatic support for Cut, Paste, Undo, and Redo as well. The availability of every command except Select All depends on context, but Figure 10.16 shows the built-in context menu when every command is available.

FIGURE 10.16 TextBox supports all the standard text commands via a context menu as well as their standard keyboard shortcuts.

You can remove the editable part of TextBox by setting its IsReadOnly property to true. When you do this, it looks identical, except the content can't be changed by the user and the "X" button never appears. Text selection can still be performed, as well as the Select All and Copy commands, just like with a TextBlock.

InputScope and the Software Keyboard

The software keyboard enables text entry on devices without an active hardware keyboard. It is sometimes referred to as the *on-screen keyboard*, the *touch keyboard*, the *soft keyboard*, the *software input panel*, or even the *input pane*. When any of the editable text controls get focus (TextBox, RichEditBox, or PasswordBox), the software keyboard automatically appears on top of the app. Although it obscures a significant portion of the screen, Windows automatically shifts the contents of a Windows Store app so the control with focus remains visible on the screen.

There are almost no APIs for interacting with the software keyboard. There's just the KeyboardCapabilities.KeyboardPresent property mentioned in Chapter 6, "Handling Input: Touch, Mouse, Pen, and Keyboard," for determining whether a hardware keyboard is being used, and an InputPane class, described in a later "Digging Deeper" sidebar, for customizing how your app responds to it being shown or hidden. Other than these two APIs, the software keyboard is designed such that apps don't need to know or care which type of keyboard is used to enter text, or if a special mode of the software keyboard is used.

 Can I force the software keyboard to disappear without requiring the user to tap on something else?

Yes, by programmatically giving focus to a control other than the text-entry control. This is commonly done in response to the user tapping the Enter key, because this key otherwise does nothing except for multiline TextBoxes, which can be frustrating for users.

It's certainly harder for a user to type on the software keyboard compared to a hardware keyboard, but the software keyboard does have its advantages. The user can switch it to a "thumbs mode," which pushes the keys to the edges for easier typing while holding a tablet with two hands. The user can also switch it into "handwriting-recognition mode" so she can write with a pen or finger and have it automatically converted into text. (I'm sure it's also only a matter of time until it has a mode that does speech recognition.) Furthermore, an app can make the keyboard change its display depending on the context. For example, it can show a ".com" button when a TextBox wants a URL, or initially show numbers and symbols when a TextBox wants a number. (That said, my family's first computer, the IBM PCjr, had similar technology that worked on the hardware keyboard: a piece of cardboard that you placed on top in order to relabel keys. That was the best way to play King's Quest.)

You can change the keyboard's display by marking a TextBox with an appropriate *input scope*. An input scope is basically a pre-defined label that can be assigned to a text box's InputScope property. Some examples are Default, Url, and Number. The Number input scope can be assigned in XAML as follows:

```
<TextBox>
  <TextBox.InputScope>
    <InputScope>
      <InputScope.Names>
        <InputScopeName NameValue="Number"/>
      </InputScope.Names>
    </InputScope>
  </TextBox.InputScope>
</TextBox>
```

Or, thankfully, the much less verbose:

```
<TextBox InputScope="Number"/>
```

The list of allowed input scopes is provided by the InputScopeNameValue enumeration. There are 18 possible choices, although most of them are specific to Asian languages. Figure 10.17 shows all the variations that are relevant for American English, with differences from the Default layout highlighted in red.

In Search and Url layouts, the "Search" and "Go" keys are just the Enter key with a different label (much like the old-fashioned cardboard keyboard overlay).

Some input scope values map to the same layout even though you could imagine them having slightly different layouts, such as Number versus TelephoneNumber. Perhaps a future release of Windows could show a distinct display for TelephoneNumber with some smarts regarding the geographic meaning of area codes, but in the meantime the distinct value at least serves as a bit of documentation for other developers or designers working on the app.

Default

Search

EmailSmtpAddress

Url

Number and TelephoneNumber

FIGURE 10.17   Different keyboard layouts are controlled by InputScope.

The various input scopes impact the keyboard's thumbs mode in a similar fashion as in Figure 10.17, although there are subtle differences (like the Enter key showing a magnifying glass icon rather than the "Search" text when the Search input scope is used). As you might expect, input scopes have no impact on the keyboard's handwriting recognition mode.

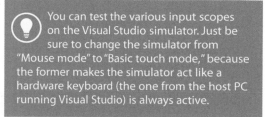

You can test the various input scopes on the Visual Studio simulator. Just be sure to change the simulator from "Mouse mode" to "Basic touch mode," because the former makes the simulator act like a hardware keyboard (the one from the host PC running Visual Studio) is always active.

? **How do I restrict what gets typed into a text box (such as allowing only digits)?**

You must write code that manually filters out unwanted characters. Input scopes do not help in this regard, because the user can still find a way to type every possible character regardless of whether the software keyboard or hardware keyboard is used. Input scopes are about providing convenience to the user; they are not about restricting or validating input.

The following KeyDown event handler does a reasonable job of allowing only digits to be entered into a TextBox, handling both the regular number keys as well as the number pad, and not getting fooled by the Shift key. However, it still doesn't protect against pasting in arbitrary text. The only reliable approach would be to validate the content *after* it is entered, using a .

```
void TextBox_KeyDown(object sender, KeyRoutedEventArgs e)
{
  switch (e.Key)
  {
    case VirtualKey.Number0: case VirtualKey.Number1: case VirtualKey.Number2:
    case VirtualKey.Number3: case VirtualKey.Number4: case VirtualKey.Number5:
    case VirtualKey.Number6: case VirtualKey.Number7: case VirtualKey.Number8:
    case VirtualKey.Number9:
    case VirtualKey.NumberPad0: case VirtualKey.NumberPad1:
    case VirtualKey.NumberPad2: case VirtualKey.NumberPad3:
    case VirtualKey.NumberPad4: case VirtualKey.NumberPad5:
    case VirtualKey.NumberPad6: case VirtualKey.NumberPad7:
    case VirtualKey.NumberPad8: case VirtualKey.NumberPad9:
      if (Window.Current.CoreWindow.GetAsyncKeyState(VirtualKey.Shift)
          != CoreVirtualKeyStates.None)
      {
        // Shift is being pressed! That means we just caught a !, @, #, $, %,
        ^,
        // &, *, (, or ) pretending to be a digit!
        // This is not allowed. Swallow the keystroke!
        e.Handled = true;
      }
      else
      {
        // This is allowed. There's nothing more to do!
      }
      break;
    default:
      // This is not allowed. Swallow the keystroke!
      e.Handled = true;
      break;
  }
}
```

The software keyboard has several nice behaviors that you might not be aware of. For example, you can double tap the shift key to turn on Caps Lock and tap it later to turn it off. You can also hold down many keys to get alternatives related to that key. Figure 10.18 shows a few examples of this.

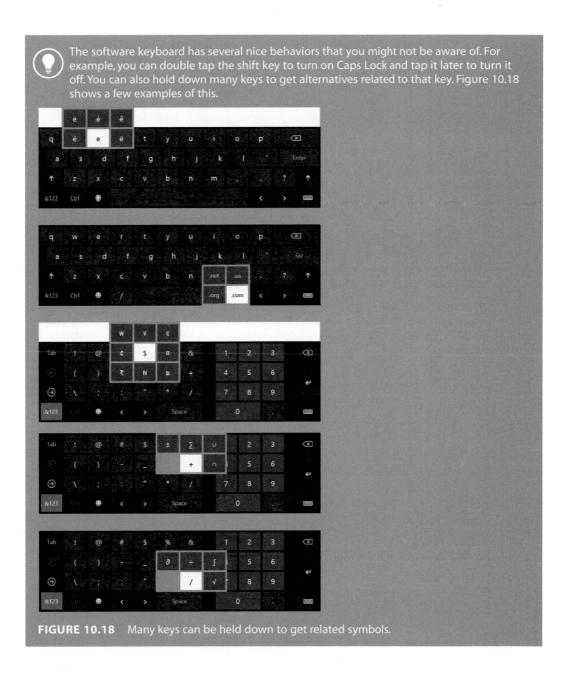

FIGURE 10.18   Many keys can be held down to get related symbols.

Responding to Showing and Hiding the Software Keyboard   • • •

For advanced scenarios, Windows.UI.ViewManagement.InputPane exposes two events that are raised immediately before the software keyboard is shown or hidden: Showing and Hiding. It also exposes an OccludedRect property that reveals the exact region of your app that is covered by the software keyboard. To get an instance of InputPane, you call the static InputPane.GetForCurrentView method.

If you want to disable the automatic shifting of your app's content done by Windows to keep the focused TextBox in view, you can handle the Showing event and set the passed-in InputPaneVisibilityEventArgs instance's EnsuredFocusedElementInView property to true. This tells Windows, "Don't bother doing anything because I'm making sure that the right things are remaining in view."

Invoking the Software Keyboard from Custom Controls   • • •

It's possible for you to write a custom control that, just like TextBox, RichEditBox, and PasswordBox, automatically invokes the software keyboard when it gets touch-based focus. To do this, your control must have a certain type of UI Automation peer class that you instantiate and return in the control's overridden OnCreateAutomationPeer method. The peer class, which should derive from FrameworkElementAutomationPeer, must implement two interfaces: ITextProvider and IValueProvider. The Windows SDK has an example of this at http://code.msdn.microsoft.com/windowsapps/Touch-keyboard-sample-43532fda.

RichEditBox

RichEditBox is a version of TextBox that enables the display and editing of rich-formatted text. The reason it's called Rich**Edit**Box rather than the more obvious Rich**Text**Box is that it's a thin wrapper over rich text formatting exposed by the Windows Runtime, which is a whole different set of APIs than the XAML-specific rich text formatting APIs. (Perhaps a future version of the XAML UI Framework will contain a RichTextBox control that supports XAML-specific TextElement-based rich formatting, similar to RichTextBlock.) The "rich edit" term also has a long history in Win32.

The implication of this is that interacting with RichEditBox feels a lot less like interacting with a typical XAML control and instead has an API style that betrays its Windows Runtime roots. RichEditBox has a Document property of type ITextDocument rather than BlockCollection. The property is readonly, and there's no public class that implements ITextDocument, so you modify the existing one rather than setting it to a new instance. ITextDocument is one of several Windows Runtime interfaces exposed in the Windows.UI.Text namespace:

→ **ITextDocument**—The top-level interface for all the text content, from which you can modify text, select text, get ranges of text, apply text formatting, control undo behavior, and more. You can even load the content from a stream and save it to a stream, optionally in Rich Text Format (RTF).

→ **ITextSelection**—Represents currently selected text; the Windows Runtime analog to TextPointer.

➜ **ITextRange**—Represents a chunk of continuous text, independent from any selection. It enables a number of powerful modifications to the range of text.

➜ **ITextParagraphFormat**—Formatting options for one or more paragraphs, such as spacing and indentation, treatment of bulleted and numbered lists, and even control of widows and orphans (see http://wikipedia.org/wiki/Widows_and_orphans).

➜ **ITextCharacterFormat**—Formatting options for one or more characters. This includes the same type of formatting seen with `TextElements`, such as bold, italic, and underline, but includes many more options, such as superscript, subscript, strikethrough, small caps, first-class embedded links, readonly regions, and so on.

`RichEditBox` isn't designed to be XAML-friendly, so you can place simple text in an instance of the control named `richEditBox` with C# code such as the following:

```
richEditBox.Document.SetText(TextSetOptions.None, "Initial text");
```

The following initializes the control with RTF-formatted text instead, producing the result in Figure 10.19:

```
richEditBox.Document.SetText(TextSetOptions.FormatRtf,
  @"{\rtf1\pard Initial text with {\b bold} or {\i italic} formatting!}");
```

Initial text with **bold** or *italic* formatting!

FIGURE 10.19   Showing content from an RTF-formatted `string` in `RichEditBox`

The following code programmatically changes the format of all the text in the control to "small caps" (small uppercase letters):

```
// Grab the default character format:
ITextCharacterFormat format = richEditBox.Document.GetDefaultCharacterFormat();
// Modify it:
format.SmallCaps = FormatEffect.On;
// Set the modified format as the new default character format:
richEditBox.Document.SetDefaultCharacterFormat(format);
richEditBox.Document.SetText(TextSetOptions.FormatRtf,
  @"{\rtf1\pard Initial text with {\b bold} or {\i italic} formatting!}");
```

Calling `SetDefaultCharacterFormat` removes existing formatting (such as bold and italic), so `SetText` is called afterward to preserve that formatting on top of the "small caps" choice.

The `ITextDocument` family of APIs in the `Windows.UI.Text` namespace is powerful. Although the API style might take some getting used to, it makes the rich formatting of `TextBlock` and `RichTextBlock` look like a toy. Its richness is not just in formatting options, but it extends to user interaction as well. For example, it not only supports double tapping with a mouse or pen to select a whole word, but triple tapping with a mouse or pen to select an entire paragraph. This matches the behavior of most text editors, such as Microsoft Word and WordPad.

`RichEditBox` can't do the two `RichTextBlock` tricks of embedding `UIElements` or overflowing into multiple controls, but that shouldn't be a surprise because `ITextDocument` is a Windows Runtime interface and therefore UI-technology-agnostic. Although embedding *interactive* controls (as in Figure 10.9) is not normally needed, the inability to embed images within text is a notable loss.

Because `RichEditBox` natively handles RTF, a user can paste RTF content from the clipboard and have it render perfectly. A user can even paste a lot of content from Microsoft Word and have it look pretty decent. Figure 10.20 shows an example of content from Microsoft Word pasted into a `RichEditBox`.

DOCUMENT TITLE
Document Subtitle

HEADING 1

On the Insert tab, the galleries include items that are designed to coordinate with the overall look of your document. You can use these galleries to insert tables, headers, footers, lists, cover pages, and other document building blocks. When you create pictures, charts, or diagrams, they also coordinate with your current document look.

Heading 2

You can easily change the formatting of selected text in the document text by choosing a look for the selected text from the Quick Styles gallery on the Home tab. You can also format text directly by using

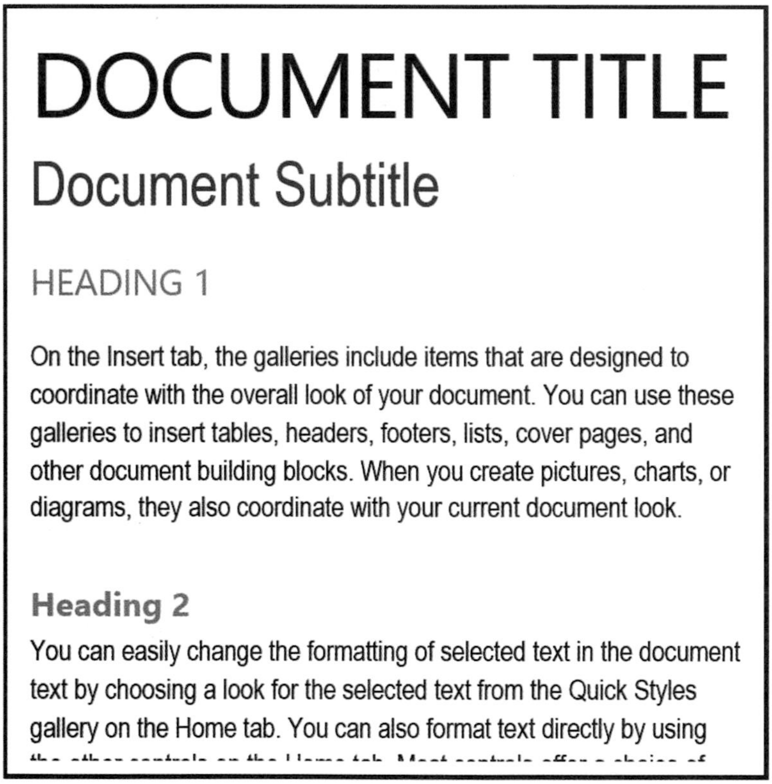

FIGURE 10.20   Sample content from Microsoft Word pasted into a `RichEditBox`

`RichEditBox` doesn't look *completely* out of place in the XAML world, however. It does, after all, derive from `Control`, so it has a long list of familiar properties and behaviors. It also defines several of the same properties as `TextBox`: `AcceptsReturn`, `TextAlignment`, `TextWrapping`, and `IsReadOnly` for more familiar control over this small amount of these basic formatting and editing capabilities, `InputScope` for the same customizations of the software keyboard, the same `IsSpellCheckEnabled` and `IsTextPredictionEnabled` features with their quirks, and a `ContextMenuOpening` event. It also exposes the same `SelectionChanged` event, although all information about the current selection must be retrieved through the `Document` (`ITextDocument`) property.

PasswordBox

PasswordBox is a simple TextBox-style control designed for the entry of a password. Rather than display the text typed in, it displays little circles. Although it doesn't have one by default, you can give it a Windows-8-style *password reveal button* if you set IsPasswordRevealButtonEnabled to true. This reveals the password while it is pressed, as demonstrated in Figure 10.21.

Password reveal button enabled   Password reveal button pressed

FIGURE 10.21   The PasswordBox with IsPasswordRevealButtonEnabled=true

Unfortunately, the password reveal button doesn't work exactly the same way as it does in the Windows shell. Rather than remaining present when the control contains text, it disappears once the control loses focus, and doesn't come back unless the password is cleared and a new one is typed.

Although it would be a strange thing to do, you can customize the symbol used to mask the password by setting PasswordChar to any character. The default circle is the bullet character (Unicode character 2022). As with the revealed password, it gets displayed in whatever font family is used by the control.

PasswordBox's behavior is intentionally limited. It doesn't support Cut, Copy, Undo, and Redo actions, although it does support Paste. Not surprisingly, it doesn't support spell check or text prediction either! It has no InputScope, so the software keyboard presented to the user is always the same. The keyboard is presented in a special password layout, however. It's like the default one, except with a "Hide keypress" button in place of the left and right arrows, the alternatives for keys (such as the ones shown in Figure 10.18) disabled, and the emoticons mode disabled. The "Hide keypress" button turns off the highlight effect when pressing on-screen keys, which is especially important if you're giving a presentation!

PasswordBox's API is also limited, because an app shouldn't do anything with a password other than pass it along to the service that needs it. Its text is stored in a string property called Password, and a simple PasswordChanged event (with no information about the old or new text) is raised when appropriate. The only other things you can do programmatically are call SelectAll, set MaxLength, or respond to the ContextMenuOpening event. You do not get notified about selection changes, nor is any information about selection exposed, because you should have no reason to care about it.

Asking the user to enter a password is a burden and requires the user to trust that your app will handle it responsibly. If you want password protection for your own custom service, you should consider leveraging the user's existing Microsoft account credentials so you don't ever need to ask for a password. Although not every user has his or her local account linked to a Microsoft account, requiring that is probably more palatable to most users compared to creating a custom account for your service.

If you must ask for a password to pass along to a third-party service, however, then you can use the from the `Windows.Security.Credentials` namespace to provide the best possible experience. This securely stores username/password pairs and roams them to trusted devices connected to the user's Microsoft account so the user needs to enter only his or her username and password once.

Even better, if the service supports the OAuth or OpenID protocols, then you can leverage the `WebAuthenticationBroker` class from the `Windows.Security.Credentials.`**Web** namespace to handle login automatically.

Credentials stored in the `PasswordVault` can be seen (without the password) and managed by users in the "Credential Manager" section of the Control Panel, which gives users much more confidence and control over the whole process.

Summary

Altogether, the collection of "blocks" and "boxes" covered in this chapter is a bit of an inconsistent mishmash. The distinction between `TextBlock` and `RichTextBlock` is logical, although the degree of richness already in `TextBlock` makes it seem odd that there even needs to be two separate controls. (Even if you were previously familiar with `TextBlock`, you probably didn't realize just how rich it was before reading this chapter!)

Although `TextBox` is essentially the editable version of `TextBlock`, the fact that it operates only on a `string` makes it a much simpler control than `TextBlock` in many ways. This is, of course, entirely reasonable, considering how `TextBoxes` are almost always used. The absence of a `RichTextBox` control leaves a small gap in the overall picture, although it is filled quite capably with `RichEditBox`, which is the richest control of them all in many ways, despite lacking a few features that `RichTextBlock` exposes.

Another oddity is that although the three "boxes" derive from `Control`, the two "blocks" derive directly from `FrameworkElement`. This means that despite living in the `Windows.UI.Xaml.Controls` namespace, `TextBlock` and `RichTextBlock` are technically not controls. (The same is true for `RichTextBlockOverflow`.) This doesn't mean much, because these elements end up replicating many of the properties on `Control`. However, they don't have some properties you might expect them to have, such as `Background`, `BorderBrush`, and `BorderThickness`. They also don't participate in focus, they can't be enabled or disabled, and they can't be given a new control template.

Chapter 11

IMAGES

This chapter is quite a bit different than the other chapters in this part of the book, because it covers only one XAML element: `Image`. Is `Image` really so complex that it deserves its own chapter? Maybe not. But this chapter also covers two large Windows Runtime topics that are relevant when using an `Image` element:

→ Automatic support for selecting different versions of files (such as image files) packaged with your app, so you can seamlessly support different scales, user themes, locales, and more.

→ Rich support for decoding, editing, and encoding images in any format (if a relevant codec is installed) that lives in the `Windows.Graphics.Imaging` namespace. This includes an image's pixels as well as its metadata.

So this chapter is not just about the `Image` element but all the things you can do with the underlying media. This is also the first of two chapters dedicated to non-vector-based content (images, audio, and video).

The `Image` Element

`Image` enables images of multiple formats to be rendered: BMP, PNG, GIF, JPEG, JPEG-XR, TIFF, and even ICO files. It has a `Source` property of type `ImageSource`, but thanks to a type converter, you can set the property to a simple string in XAML, as in this example:

```
<Image Source="Assets/Logo.png"/>
```

Source can point to an image file packaged with your app (a *resource*), a file stored in application state (see Chapter 18, "Data"), or an image from the Web. The content is fetched and processed asynchronously, so a slow network connection doesn't impact your app's responsiveness. When Source is set, it results in either an `ImageOpened` event being raised on success, or an `ImageFailed` event being raised on failure. In the latter case, the Image element is left blank (there's no failure "X" as in Internet Explorer) and the EventArgs object passed to any handlers contains an `Exception` object with failure details.

Image has the same `Stretch` property seen with `Viewbox` in Chapter 4, "Layout," for controlling how its content scales. Its default value is `Uniform`, so the content scales to fill Image's bounds as much as possible while still preserving its aspect ratio.

Like a `TextBlock`, Image is commonly used in a simple fashion, but a lot of power is lurking within. (It also doesn't derive from `Control`, so you can't give it a background or focus.) This section examines the following features in depth:

→ Referencing files with URIs

→ Custom stretching with nine-grid

→ Generating dynamic Images with `WriteableBitmap`

Referencing Files with URIs

The mapping of an Image element in XAML to the equivalent C# code is not always obvious. The preceding example:

```
<Image Source="Assets/Logo.png"/>
```

is equivalent to the following C# code placed in a Page's code-behind:

```
Image image = new Image();
image.Source = new BitmapImage(new Uri(this.BaseUri, "Assets/Logo.png"));
```

There are two things going on here. One is that a type converter hides the complexity involving `ImageSource`, the type of the Source property. An `ImageSource` cannot be directly instantiated, nor can its `BitmapSource` subclass, but `BitmapSource` has two subclasses that can be instantiated: `BitmapImage`, the one typically used, and `WriteableBitmap`, covered later in this section.

> BitmapImage, just like the Image element, has ImageOpened and ImageFailed events. However, BitmapImage also has a DownloadProgress event revealing a progress value from 0 to 100 that can easily be fed into a ProgressBar control (see Chapter 13, "Other Controls"). Once ImageOpened is raised (immediately before it gets rendered), you can check BitmapImage's PixelWidth and PixelHeight properties. You can also point BitmapImage to a new URI post-construction by settings its UriSource property.
>
> BitmapImage also defines DecodePixelWidth and DecodePixelHeight properties that, when set appropriately, can provide a huge performance benefit to apps that display many large images. These properties are meant to convey the dimensions in which the image is expected to be displayed. When specified, Images get automatically decoded to that size rather than the original size.

Second, BitmapImage must be constructed with a System.Uri. In WPF or Silverlight, you could have constructed a relative Uri, the kind seen in XAML, as follows:

```
image.Source = new BitmapImage(new Uri("Assets/Logo.png", UriKind.Relative));
```

However, this fails with an exception that explains, "The given System.Uri cannot be converted into a Windows.Foundation.Uri." BitmapImage's constructor actually requires a Windows.Foundation.Uri, the Windows Runtime class that gets automatically projected to System.Uri for .NET consumers. And Windows.Foundation.Uri doesn't allow relative paths! This is why the C# code constructs the System.Uri with a root path coming from the Page's BaseUri property.

Page's BaseUri property is set to a value such as ms-appx:/MainPage.xaml. ms-appx is the scheme for an app's resources—any files packaged with your app because they are included in your project with a Build Action of Content. Therefore, the C# code could use the absolute URI more explicitly as follows:

```
Image image = new Image();
image.Source = new BitmapImage(new Uri("ms-appx:/Assets/Logo.png"));
```

Or, more commonly, with three slashes instead of just one:

```
Image image = new Image();
image.Source = new BitmapImage(new Uri("ms-appx:///Assets/Logo.png"));
```

And the absolute URI could be used in XAML as well:

```
<Image Source="ms-appx:///Assets/Logo.png"/>
```

The path in the URI matches the folder structure in your project. If you place an image.jpg file in the root of your project, its URI is ms-appx:///image.jpg.

Why do ms-appx **URIs use three slashes instead of two?**

The form of the URI is *scheme://domainName/path*. The *domainName* is the app's package full name (specified in your package manifest and set to a GUID by default), but it can fortunately be omitted to imply the current app's package full name. This means that you can reference files in other packages, but this works only for *dependent packages*.

Because relative URIs in XAML always map to ms-appx (app resources), referencing a file in application state or on the Web must be done with absolute URIs. Referencing a file on the Web can be done as you would expect:

```
<Image Source="http://blog.adamnathan.net/images/logo.png"/>
```

or:

```
Image image = new Image();
image.Source = new BitmapImage(
  new Uri("http://blog.adamnathan.net/images/logo.png"));
```

Referencing a file in application state can be done with an ms-appdata scheme as follows:

```
<Image Source="ms-appdata:///savedFile.jpg"/>
```

or:

```
Image image = new Image();
image.Source = new BitmapImage(new Uri("ms-appdata:///savedFile.jpg"));
```

! **Make sure resource files in your project are marked with a Build Action of Content!**

Otherwise, they won't get packaged with your app. Other Build Action choices such as Embedded Resource or PRIResource do not work for this purpose.

? **How can I make** Image **render image data from an** IRandomAccessStream?

This is an important question, because the Windows Runtime uses IRandomAccessStream throughout its APIs. And the answer is simple: BitmapImage's base class (BitmapSource) exposes a SetSource method that accepts an IRandomAccessStream.

The following code demonstrates this by first obtaining an IRandomAccessStream from a file chosen by the user via the Windows file picker, then by constructing an appropriate BitmapImage that uses the IRandomAccessStream, and finally assigning the BitmapImage to the Image:

```
async Task ShowUserSelectedFile()
{
  // Get a JPEG from the user
```

```
FileOpenPicker picker = new FileOpenPicker();
picker.FileTypeFilter.Add(".jpg");
picker.FileTypeFilter.Add(".jpeg");
StorageFile file = await picker.PickSingleFileAsync();
if (file != null)
{
  // Get the image data
  using (IRandomAccessStream ras = await file.OpenAsync(FileAccessMode.Read))
  {
    // Load the data into a BitmapImage
    BitmapImage source = new BitmapImage();
    source.SetSource(ras);

    // Assign the BitmapImage to the Image element on the page
    image.Source = source;
  }
}
}
```

The .NET projection of `IRandomAccessStream` implements `IDisposable`, so a using block properly disposes of the stream once the `Image` has been updated.

This code is assumed to belong to a code-behind file for a `Page` with an `Image` named `image` on it, such as the following:

```
<Image Name="image"/>
```

Custom Stretching with Nine-Grid

Image has a nifty built-in *nine-grid* feature that enables you to use a single image as a flexible border by customizing how it stretches. (It's also hardware accelerated for great performance.) Without this support, you'd need to use up to nine separate images to create the same effect.

Figure 11.1 demonstrates the regular image-stretching behavior using the following `Grid` that contains the same image unstretched on the left versus stretched (and therefore pixelated) on the right:

```
<Page …>
  <Grid Background="{StaticResource ApplicationPageBackgroundThemeBrush}">
    <Grid.ColumnDefinitions>
      <ColumnDefinition Width="Auto"/>
      <ColumnDefinition/>
    </Grid.ColumnDefinitions>
    <!-- The unscaled image: -->
    <Image Source="image.png" Stretch="None"/>
    <!-- The scaled image: -->
```

```
    <Image Grid.Column="1" Source="image.png" Stretch="Fill"/>
  </Grid>
</Page>
```

FIGURE 11.1   Typical Image stretching, with `Stretch="None"` on the left and `Stretch="Fill"` on the right

With nine-grid rendering, you can logically segment the source content into a nine-cell grid. When you do this, the four corners never stretch, the middle-top and middle-bottom edges stretch only horizontally, the middle-left and middle-right edges stretch only vertically, and the middle cell stretches in both directions as normal. For this behavior to make sense, the content must be designed to be stretched in this manner. The `image.png` file in Figure 11.1 clearly is designed this way, so the grid arrangement depicted in Figure 11.2 would prevent stretching of the four corners while stretching the four middle edges in a way that avoids visible pixelation:

If this behavior were represented as a nine-cell `Grid` control (containing a

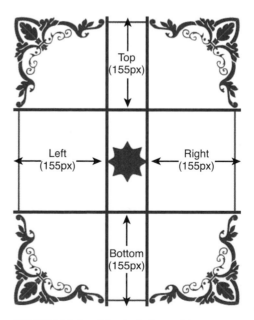

FIGURE 11.2   A logical nine-grid arrangement that avoids stretching the 155x155 pixel corners

separate chopped-up `Image` segment in each cell), it would be equivalent to the following row and column definitions:

```
<Grid.RowDefinitions>
  <RowDefinition Height="155"/>
  <RowDefinition/>
  <RowDefinition Height="155"/>
</Grid.RowDefinitions>
<Grid.ColumnDefinitions>
  <ColumnDefinition Width="155"/>
  <ColumnDefinition/>
  <ColumnDefinition Width="155"/>
</Grid.ColumnDefinitions>
```

However, using the nine-grid support is much simpler than this. You set `Image`'s `NineGrid` property to a `Thickness` value representing the Left, Top, Right, and Bottom values depicted in Figure 11.2. Recall from Chapter 3, "Sizing, Positioning, and Transforming Elements," that `Thickness` can be specified in XAML using one, two, or four values. Because this example requires a uniform value of 155 for all four measurements, `NineGrid` can be set to the simple value of 155, as shown in this update to the original `Page`:

```
<Page …>
  <Grid Background="{StaticResource ApplicationPageBackgroundThemeBrush}">
    <Grid.ColumnDefinitions>
      <ColumnDefinition/>
      <ColumnDefinition/>
    </Grid.ColumnDefinitions>
    <!-- The unscaled image: -->
    <Image Source="image.png" Stretch="None" />
    <!-- The scaled image with NineGrid support: -->
    <Image Grid.Column="1" Source="image.png" Stretch="Fill" NineGrid="155" />
  </Grid>
</Page>
```

The result of setting the `NineGrid` property is shown in Figure 11.3. Of course, this would typically done with a blank (or solid color) image middle to avoid any pixelation. The shape in the middle of this image is there for demonstration purposes only.

Note that `NineGrid` works only when an `Image` is stretched larger than its natural size. (If it is applied to an `Image` stretched to a smaller region, it stops rendering altogether.) Also, `NineGrid` applies only to stretching done with a `Stretch` value of `Fill`, `Uniform`, or `UniformToFill`. It has no effect when scaling an `Image` with a transform such as `ScaleTransform`.

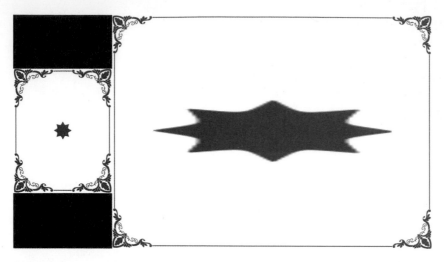

FIGURE 11.3   With `NineGrid` set, the corners and edges of the single `Image` stretch in a way that avoids the ugly pixelation seen in the middle.

Generating Dynamic `Images` with `WriteableBitmap`

`WriteableBitmap`, the other `BitmapSource` subclass, is designed for displaying dynamic pixel content. You construct an instance with a specific width and height, modify its pixels exposed via a `PixelBuffer` property, and set it as the `Source` of an `Image` element.

One common point of confusion is that `PixelBuffer` is a useless-looking Windows Runtime interface called `IBuffer`. `IBuffer` exposes only two properties: `Capacity` (the maximum number of bytes it can hold) and `Length` (the number of bytes currently in use). There's no API for reading or writing its contents!

C++ code can query the object for the `IBufferByteAccess` COM interface to read/write its data, but this is not an option for an app's C# code. Instead, you must leverage an `AsStream` extension method that wraps the object as a familiar .NET `System.IO.Stream`. (Internally, the `Stream` object leverages `IBufferByteAccess` to enable this to work.)

Therefore, suppose you have the following simple `Page` with an empty `Image`:

```
<Page …>
  <Canvas>
    <Image Name="image"/>
  </Canvas>
</Page>
```

The following code-behind creates a new 1024x768 in-memory image, fills its pixels, and uses it as the Image's Source:

```
// Needed for AsStream extension method on IBuffer:
using System.Runtime.InteropServices.WindowsRuntime;
...
public MainPage()
{
  InitializeComponent();

  // Create a blank bitmap
  WriteableBitmap bitmap = new WriteableBitmap(1024, 768);

  // Get a .NET Stream for the bitmap's bytes
  using (Stream stream = bitmap.PixelBuffer.AsStream())
  {
    // Write each pixel (4-byte BGRA format, alpha channel ignored)
    int numPixels = bitmap.PixelWidth * bitmap.PixelHeight;
    for (int i = 0; i < numPixels; i++)
    {
      stream.WriteByte((byte)(i % 255));          // B
      stream.WriteByte(0);                        // G
      stream.WriteByte((byte)(255 - (i % 255)));  // R
      stream.WriteByte(0);                        // A (ignored)
    }
  }

  // Use this as the ImageSource for an Image element
  image.Source = bitmap;
}
```

The System.Runtime.InteropServices.WindowsRuntime namespace is included so the AsStream extension method can be called. This namespace contains a number of extension methods that convert among IBuffers, arrays, and .NET Streams.

WriteableBitmap uses a pixel format known as BGRA8 (B8G8R8A8), which means that each of the four color channels is 8 bits (making each pixel 32 bits) and the order is B, G, R, then A. The loop that writes these pixel values into the Stream varies the value of the blue byte based on the pixel index, and inversely varies the value of the red byte. This results in a repeated red-blue gradient, as shown in Figure 11.4.

You can make updates to a WriteableBitmap's PixelBuffer at any time, but you must call its Invalidate method to force it to render again.

WriteableBitmap

Because Writeabl...
contents from an I...
However, this caus...
PixelBuffer prop...
that gets rendered...

Multiple Fil...

Unlike vector grap...
anything other tha...
avoid scaling Imag...
cally scales all cont...
scale factors to mal...
pieces of the Wind...

→ **180%** (80% l...
resolution (2...

→ **140%** (40% l...
and at least 1...

→ **100%** (no sca...

Scaling is also bum...
the "Make everythi...
PC Settings app. Th...
use the Visual Stud...

This automatic scal...
computer screens a...
phones and tablets...
can cause noticeab...

Loading File Va...

Fortunately, Windo...
matic scaling for a...
variations, one for...
the Image element...

For example, if you...
three variations of...

→ Assets/photo...

→ Assets/photo...

→ Assets/photo...

You don't even need a file matching the original name used in your C# or XAML! For conditions when the app is scaled 180%, Windows will first look for the scale-180 version. If that isn't present, it will look for the next best thing: the scale-140 version. If that isn't present, it will look for the scale-100 version. And if that isn't present, it will look for the exact photo.jpg file specified in your app (and fail if this vanilla version isn't present). These additions to the original filename are called *resource qualifiers*.

Note that there's no support for an 80% scale version, unlike with the Logo, Small Logo, and Wide Logo image files that you can use in your package manifest. Unlike your Start screen tile, Windows never scales an app to be smaller than 100%.

If you prefer to organize your three sets of assets into three separate folders, you can use the following naming pattern instead, which moves the resource qualifiers from the filename to a folder name:

→ Assets/**scale-100**/photo.jpg

→ Assets/**scale-140**/photo.jpg

→ Assets/**scale-180**/photo.jpg

This works the same way as the other naming scheme. You must choose one or the other, at least for a single file, because otherwise the MakePri tool that's invoked by Visual Studio when building your app will fail.

Just like with images referenced in your package manifest, this automatic image selection also includes support for high contrast! Therefore, if you're hardcore, you can supply *twelve* variations of every image asset by combining the three scale resource qualifiers with four possible contrast resource qualifiers:

→ Assets/photo.**scale-100_contrast-standard**.jpg

→ Assets/photo.**scale-100_contrast-white**.jpg

→ Assets/photo.**scale-100_contrast-black**.jpg

→ Assets/photo.**scale-100_contrast-high**.jpg

→ Assets/photo.**scale-140_contrast-standard**.jpg

→ Assets/photo.**scale-140_contrast-white**.jpg

→ Assets/photo.**scale-140_contrast-black**.jpg

→ Assets/photo.**scale-140_contrast-high**.jpg

→ Assets/photo.**scale-180_contrast-standard**.jpg

→ Assets/photo.**scale-180_contrast-white**.jpg

→ Assets/photo.**scale-180_contrast-black**.jpg

→ Assets/photo.**scale-180_contrast-high**.jpg

FIGURE 11.4   The I

Beware of t
transitions!

Every call from man
between managed-
the Windows names
careful to avoid beir
looking property ac

Notice that the code
bitmap.PixelWidt
loop would make tw
the property getter
enough images. Eve
and a half unnecess

Although the just-in
condition (as it knov
access, regardless of

Because PixelBuffe
unless you first copy
the Stream. Anothei
IBufferByteAccess
component can be (

contrast-standard, which means normal contrast, is the default choice. Therefore, that qualifier could have been omitted, just like scale-100 could be omitted from the first four filenames. The contrast-high qualifier matches any high contrast theme, whereas contrast-white matches the High Contrast White theme, and contrast-black matches the High Contrast Black, High Contrast #1, and High Contrast #2 themes. When combining these two resource qualifiers, one or both can be specified in the path rather than the filename, similar to the simpler example where only scale was specified.

The automatic resource qualifier support applies only when the file is fetched!

An important thing to keep in mind when you test different images for different scales or contrasts is that Images don't automatically get refreshed when the user changes the screen's resolution, DPI, or theme. Therefore, if you change the "Make everything on your screen bigger" setting while running your app (or changing the simulator's pixel density), you will see your app's content get scaled but you will **not** see Images refresh with the appropriate content unless you close and reopen the app. Although you could write code that manually refreshes content in response to the DisplayProperties.LogicalDpiChanged and AccessibilitySettings. HighContrastChanged events, this is typically not enough of a problem to worry about in practice.

When you use Image elements with files that have multiple variations, you should explicitly specify their Width and/or Height. Although this goes against the typical advice of letting things size themselves, you don't want the elements to change their (pre-scaled) size when a different variation is fetched!

If you decide to forgo providing multiple sizes of your image assets, then at least consider making the files 180% of the specified size in XAML so the content only gets scaled down rather than scaled up. This can still look bad at 100% scale, however, especially for non-photographic content.

• • •

Resource Qualifiers

The scale and contrast resource qualifiers are not the only ones handled automatically by Windows! There are many that can be mixed and matched to customize which image files (or other resource files packaged in your app) get loaded in a staggering number of different environments. In addition to scale and contrast, there are:

→ **language-XXX** or **lang-XXX**, where *XXX* is any BCP-47 language tag such as en-us. This represents the current preferred language for the app to use.

→ **homeregion-XXX**, where *XXX* is any BCP-47 *region* tag, which can be a two-letter region code such as us or a three-digit geographic code such as 702 for Singapore. Unlike language, this represents where the user lives. (Just because a user speaks Japanese doesn't mean he or she lives in Japan.)

> → **layoutdir-*XXX***, where *XXX* is either RTL (right-to-left), LTR (left-to-right), TTBRTL (top-to-bottom, right-to-left), or TTBLTR (top-to-bottom, left-to-right). Image already reverses its content when its FlowDirection property is RightToLeft, but this enables you to do something completely custom for cultures with a different reading directionality.
>
> → **config-*XXX***, where *XXX* is the value of the MS_CONFIGURATION_ATTRIBUTE_VALUE environment variable. This is for advanced testing purposes and not appropriate to use outside tightly controlled environments.
>
> → **targetsize-*XXX***, where *XXX* is a number that represents both the width and height of a square image. Note that this qualifier is not automatically leveraged within apps; it is used by Windows Explorer when showing file-type-association or protocol icons.
>
> → **altform-*XXX***, which can be used for your own custom purposes if you're using Windows Runtime resources APIs directly (in the Windows.ApplicationModel.Resources.Core namespace). So it also is not relevant for Image.
>
> These resource qualifiers always have the *name-value* form, and can be chained together with an underscore, as seen previously with scale and contrast. They can be used in the resource's filename or path, and when used in the path, each one can be delimited with a path separator rather than an underscore. The language qualifier has a special shortcut that enables just its value to be used when using the folder syntax.
>
> For example, an app requesting photo.jpg could end up fetching it from en-US/homeregion-us/contrast-high/photo.scale-140_layoutdir-RTL.jpg.
>
> Remember that this applies only to resource files (ms-appx URIs).

Loading File Variations Manually

If your app loads external files (such as from your own Web server), then you cannot take advantage of automatic resource qualifier support. However, you can certainly mimic in C# it by inspecting the aspects of the current environment you care about. The following code demonstrates how you might fetch different files based on the current automatic scaling and contrast mode:

```csharp
void LoadImage(Image image, string filename)
{
  // Either "Scale100Percent", "Scale140Percent", or "Scale180Percent":
  string scale = DisplayProperties.ResolutionScale.ToString();

  // Getting the current user theme is a bit more onerous:
  AccessibilitySettings settings = new AccessibilitySettings();
  string contrast = "Standard";
  if (settings.HighContrast)
  {
    // Either "High Contrast White", "High Contrast Black",
    //        "High Contrast #1", or "High Contrast #2:"
    contrast = settings.HighContrastScheme;
  }
```

```
  // Pass along this info in a way that the Web server is prepared to handle:
  image.Source = new BitmapImage(new Uri("http://pixelwinks.com/" + filename +
    "?scale=" + scale + "&contrast=" + WebUtility.UrlEncode(contrast)));
}
```

Of course, the Web server has to play along, and not only understand your custom resource qualifier scheme, but have the appropriate files to serve!

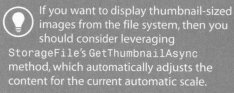

If you want to display thumbnail-sized images from the file system, then you should consider leveraging `StorageFile`'s `GetThumbnailAsync` method, which automatically adjusts the content for the current automatic scale.

 You should strive to arrange elements on pixel boundaries divisible by 5. This ensures that the elements do not experience pixel shifting when automatically scaled.

Decoding Images

With the `BitmapDecoder` class in the `Windows.Graphics.Imaging` namespace, you get access to the decoding process that occurs automatically when displaying image content in an `Image` element. This enables you to do interesting things, such as getting the pixel data for an image file, or retrieving any metadata stored inside, such as tagged people.

To demonstrate `BitmapDecoder` throughout this section, we'll start with a method almost identical to the `ShowUserSelectedFile` example from a previous FAQ sidebar:

```
async Task DecodeUserSelectedFile()
{
  // Get a JPEG from the user
  FileOpenPicker picker = new FileOpenPicker();
  picker.FileTypeFilter.Add(".jpg");
  picker.FileTypeFilter.Add(".jpeg");
  StorageFile file = await picker.PickSingleFileAsync();
  if (file != null)
  {
    // Get the image data
    using (IRandomAccessStream ras = await file.OpenAsync(FileAccessMode.Read))
    {
      // Create the decoder
      BitmapDecoder decoder = await BitmapDecoder.CreateAsync(ras);
      // Use the decoder
      UseDecoder(decoder);
    }
  }
}
```

This code obtains an `IRandomAccessStream` from a file chosen by the user via the Windows file picker, because it is necessary in order to create a `BitmapDecoder`. After creating a `BitmapDecoder` based on this stream, it calls a `UseDecoder` method. This is a placeholder method that we'll implement a few different ways in this section, so the surrounding boilerplate code doesn't need to be repeated.

Some image formats permit multiple frames, such as an animated GIF, a multipage TIFF file, or an icon file that includes multiple sizes. `BitmapDecoder` exposes this situation with its `FrameCount` property. It also defines a `GetFrameAsync` method for retrieving a `BitmapFrame` object. `BitmapFrame` exposes much of the same functionality as `BitmapDecoder`, but specific to the chosen frame.

> ### Choosing a Specific Decoder
>
> An advanced overload of `BitmapDecoder.CreateAsync` enables you to pass a `Guid` that identifies the specific installed decoder you want to use. To make this easier, `BitmapDecoder` exposes a static `Guid` property for each of the built-in decoders: BMP, PNG, GIF, JPEG, JPEG-XR, TIFF, and ICO. In addition, you can enumerate all installed decoders with the static `BitmapDecoder.GetDecoderInformationE numerator` method.

Getting Pixel Data

`BitmapDecoder` exposes a `GetPixelDataAsync` method that ultimately gives you a raw byte array with the image's pixel data flattened into one dimension. However, this is done via an intermediate `PixelDataProvider` class as follows:

```
async Task UseDecoder(BitmapDecoder decoder)
{
  PixelDataProvider provider = await decoder.GetPixelDataAsync();
  byte[] pixels = provider.DetachPixelData();

  …
}
```

`DetachPixelData` can be called only once per `PixelDataProvider` instance, because it does not hold onto a copy of the bytes. (`PixelDataProvider` exists solely because of a limitation with the projection mechanism for Windows Runtime APIs: asynchronous methods cannot return arrays!)

`BitmapDecoder` has `PixelWidth` and `PixelHeight` properties that reveal the image's dimensions, but without knowing the pixel format and alpha mode of the image, you can't know how to interpret the returned byte array. You must check `BitmapDecoder`'s `BitmapPixelFormat` and `BitmapAlphaMode` properties to discover this information. `GetPixelDataAsync` automatically converts any custom color spaces to the standard RGB color space, and automatically rotates the pixel data if orientation metadata exists and is set to a nondefault value. (Incidentally, so does the `Image` element.) To get the correct dimensions in the face of potential rotation, you should use `BitmapDecoder`'s **Oriented**`PixelWidth` and **Oriented**`PixelHeight` properties instead of `PixelWidth` and `PixelHeight`.

To simplify your code, you can force the returned `byte` array to use a specific pixel format and alpha mode with an overload of `GetPixelDataAsync`. This overload also lets you apply a `BitmapTransform`, decide whether to respect orientation metadata, and decide whether to convert non-RGB color spaces. The following code leverages this overload to force each pixel to be four bytes long in RGBA order. It then applies a simple color inversion effect before writing these modified pixels to a `WriteableBitmap` in order to display it:

```
async Task UseDecoder(BitmapDecoder decoder)
{
  // Force each pixel to be 4 bytes (B, G, R, then A)
  PixelDataProvider provider = await decoder.GetPixelDataAsync(
    BitmapPixelFormat.Bgra8, BitmapAlphaMode.Straight, new BitmapTransform(),
    ExifOrientationMode.RespectExifOrientation,
    ColorManagementMode.ColorManageToSRgb);
  byte[] pixels = provider.DetachPixelData();

  // Invert the colors by subtracting each B, G, and R from 255 (byte.MaxValue)
  for (int i = 0; i < pixels.Length; i += 4)
  {
    pixels[i]     = (byte)(byte.MaxValue - pixels[i]);    // B
    pixels[i + 1] = (byte)(byte.MaxValue - pixels[i+1]);  // G
    pixels[i + 2] = (byte)(byte.MaxValue - pixels[i+2]);  // R
                                                          // Leave A alone
  }

  // Create a new WriteableBitmap to contain the edited pixels
  WriteableBitmap bitmap = new WriteableBitmap((int)decoder.OrientedPixelWidth,
                                               (int)decoder.OrientedPixelHeight);

  // Get a .NET Stream for the bitmap's bytes
  using (Stream stream = bitmap.PixelBuffer.AsStream())
  {
    // Write all pixels using the existing BGRA array
    await stream.WriteAsync(pixels, 0, pixels.Length);
  }

  // Assign the BitmapImage to the Image element on the page
  image.Source = bitmap;
}
```

This assumes a `Page` such as the following with an `Image` named `image`:

```
<Page …>
  <Viewbox>
    <Image Name="image"/>
  </Viewbox>
</Page>
```

The result of applying this inversion to the copy of a photo's pixels and feeding them to the `WriteableBitmap` is shown in Figure 11.5.

Original pixels   Inverted pixels

FIGURE 11.5   `BitmapDecoder`'s access to an image file's pixels enables the creation of much more interesting `WriteableBitmaps`.

`BitmapFrame` exposes the same properties discussed in this section (`BitmapAlphaMode`, `BitmapPixelFormat`, `PixelWidth`, `PixelHeight`, `OrientedPixelWidth`, and `OrientedPixelHeight`) as well as the two `GetPixelDataAsync` methods. You can therefore retrieve, interpret, and modify pixels for a specific frame in an image with the same techniques.

•••

BitmapTransform

The `BitmapTransform` class that can be passed to `GetPixelDataAsync` is a simple Windows Runtime class that has no formal relationship with the XAML-specific `Transform` family of classes. It is similar in spirit, however. It exposes several properties that enable you to describe how you want to transform an image's pixels. You can specify a scale factor for the width and height independently, you can specify a rotation (but only 0°, 90°, 180°, or 270°), you can specify a horizontal or vertical flip, and you can specify a rectangular region for cropping the image. `BitmapTransform` enables you to choose one of four standard interpolation algorithms to be used when scaling pixels: `Linear`, `Cubic`, `Fant`, and `NearestNeighbor` (the default).

If you don't want `GetPixelDataAsync` to do any transform, you must still pass a valid instance of `BitmapTransform` rather than `null`. This is why the code that produces Figure 11.5 constructs an instance.

The following is an update to that code that rotates the pixels 90° clockwise rather than inverting the colors:

```
async Task UseDecoder(BitmapDecoder decoder)
{
  // Force each pixel to be 4 bytes (B, G, R, then A) and rotate the content
    PixelDataProvider provider = await decoder.GetPixelDataAsync(
      BitmapPixelFormat.Bgra8, BitmapAlphaMode.Straight,
```

```
        new BitmapTransform { Rotation = BitmapRotation.Clockwise90Degrees },
        ExifOrientationMode.RespectExifOrientation,
        ColorManagementMode.ColorManageToSRgb);
    byte[] pixels = provider.DetachPixelData();

    // Create a new WriteableBitmap to contain the edited pixels,
    // with flipped width & height to account for the BitmapTransform rotation
    WriteableBitmap bitmap = new WriteableBitmap((int)decoder.OrientedPixelHeight,
                                                 (int)decoder.OrientedPixelWidth

    // Get a .NET Stream for the bitmap's bytes
    using (Stream stream = bitmap.PixelBuffer.AsStream())
    {
      // Write all pixels using the existing BGRA array
      await stream.WriteAsync(pixels, 0, pixels.Length);
    }

    // Assign the BitmapImage to the Image element on the page
    image.Source = bitmap;
}
```

Notice that the rotation does *not* affect `OrientedPixelWidth` and `OrientedPixelHeight` (only orientation metadata inside the image file does), so `WriteableBitmap` must be constructed with those two values reversed for the result to come out as expected.

> `BitmapDecoder` and `BitmapFrame` expose a `GetThumbnailAsync` method that enables you to operate on a thumbnail-sized version of the original image file. This is different from `StorageFile`'s method of the same name, because this one fetches a thumbnail embedded in the image file—if it exists. Some image formats, such as JPEG, support thumbnails. If the current image (or frame) has no thumbnail, `GetThumbnailAsync` throws an exception.
>
> `BitmapDecoder` also exposes a `GetPreviewAsync` method, which is a higher resolution thumbnail supported by JPEG-XR files. (RAW files also support this, but there is no built-in RAW decoder.)

Reading Metadata

Some image formats support embedded metadata that reveals all kinds of things about when and where a photo was taken; what camera, flash, and lens was used; people in the photo; and so on. There are three different ways to read this metadata, each one more powerful than the previous one:

→ Reading `ImageProperties` from a file

→ Reading common `BitmapProperties` from a decoder

→ Reading raw metadata with a metadata query language

Reading (and Writing) `ImageProperties` **from a File**

The first way to access basic image metadata doesn't actually require a `BitmapDecoder` (or even opening the file yourself). The `StorageFile` object returned from APIs such as the file picker exposes many collections of metadata values represented by the following classes and their properties:

- → **BasicProperties** (DateModified, ItemDate, and Size)

- → **ImageProperties** (Width, Height, CameraManufacturer, CameraModel, DateTaken, Keywords, Latitude, Longitude, Orientation, PeopleNames, Rating, and Title)

- → **DocumentProperties** (Author, Comment, Keywords, and Title)

- → **MusicProperties** (Album, AlbumArtist, Artist, Bitrate, Composers, Conductors, Duration, Genre, Producers, Publisher, Rating, Subtitle, Title, TrackNumber, Writers, and Year)

- → **VideoProperties** (Width, Height, Bitrate, Directors, Duration, Keywords, Latitude, Longitude, Orientation, Producers, Publisher, Rating, Subtitle, Title, Writers, and Year)

You can get `BasicProperties` with a call to `GetBasicPropertiesAsync`, and you can get the rest with a similar call on `StorageFile`'s `Properties` property. For example, the following code retrieves the orientation and date taken for a user-selected photo from the file picker:

```
// Get a JPEG from the user
FileOpenPicker picker = new FileOpenPicker();
picker.FileTypeFilter.Add(".jpg");
picker.FileTypeFilter.Add(".jpeg");
StorageFile file = await picker.PickSingleFileAsync();

if (file != null)
{
  // Get image properties directly from the file
  ImageProperties properties = await file.Properties.GetImagePropertiesAsync();
  DateTimeOffset dateTaken = properties.DateTaken;
  PhotoOrientation orientation = properties.Orientation;

  …
}
```

Some of the properties—Width, Height, Latitude, Longitude, Orientation, and PeopleNames— are readonly. (Latitude and Longitude are readonly because they are each calculated from *four* separate pieces of metadata. To update these values, you need to use an approach described later in this chapter.) For the ones that are writeable, you can change the property values and call `SavePropertiesAsync` to commit the change to the physical file:

```
// Get image properties directly from the file
ImageProperties properties = await file.Properties.GetImagePropertiesAsync();
// Overwrite DateTaken with a lie
properties.DateTaken = DateTimeOffset.Now;
// Save the change to the file
await properties.SavePropertiesAsync();
```

Note that an app needs no special capability to overwrite this metadata; the user opened the door to such modifications by using the file picker to send this file to the app!

What's the difference between the `DateTime` **data type and** `DateTimeOffset`**?**

`DateTime` refers to a logical point in time that is independent of any time zone, whereas `DateTimeOffset`, the type of the `ImageProperties.DateTaken` property, is a real point in time with an offset relative to the UTC time zone. `DateTimeOffset` is the most appropriate choice for something like the date a photo was taken, because that point in time should never be reinterpreted even if you are now in a different time zone. An Alarm Clock app, however, should use `DateTime` for the alarm time. If you had set your alarm for 8:00 AM while travelling, you probably expect it to go off at 8:00 AM no matter what time zone you happen to be in at the time.

For most scenarios, using `DateTimeOffset` is preferable to `DateTime`. However, it was introduced into the .NET Framework years after `DateTime`, so the better name was already taken. (Designers of the class rejected calling it `DateTime2` or `DateTimeEx`.) Fortunately, consumers of these data types can use them interchangeably for the most part.

It's important to note that the Windows Runtime fixed this design mistake. Its single `DateTime` type—`Windows.Foundation.DateTime`—acts like `DateTimeOffset`. Even better, `Windows.Foundation.DateTime` gets automatically projected to `DateTimeOffset` in .NET. (You never see `Windows.Foundation.DateTime` in C# code, just like you never see `Windows.Foundation.Uri`.) This is precisely why `ImageProperties.DateTaken` appears to be a `DateTimeOffset` property.

Reading Common `BitmapProperties` from a Decoder

The second way to access image metadata is much richer than the first, and a bit more complicated. It requires a `BitmapDecoder`, which exposes a `BitmapProperties` property. (`BitmapFrame` exposes the same property.) The following code demonstrates how to get the same two orientation and date-taken properties for a user-selected photo by filling in a new implementation for the `UseDecoder` method referenced previously:

```
async Task UseDecoder(BitmapDecoder decoder)
{
  try
  {
    // GetPropertiesAsync throws when codec doesn't support all passed-in values!
```

```
  BitmapPropertySet props = await decoder.BitmapProperties.GetPropertiesAsync(
    new string[] { "System.Photo.Orientation", "System.Photo.DateTaken" });
  BitmapTypedValue value;
  if (props.TryGetValue("System.Photo.Orientation", out value))
  {
    ushort orientation = (ushort)value.Value;
  }
  if (props.TryGetValue("System.Photo.DateTaken", out value))
  {
    DateTimeOffset dateTaken = (DateTimeOffset)value.Value;
  }
}
catch
{
  // GetPropertiesAsync throws when codec doesn't support all passed-in values!
}
}
```

Notice the many differences between this approach and the simpler `ImageProperties` approach:

→ Each piece of metadata is represented by a `string` name rather than a strongly typed property. The .NET projection of `BitmapPropertySet` implements `IDictionary<string, BitmapTypedValue>`, so the values are retrieved based on their keys in typical .NET fashion. The `BitmapTypedValue` representing each piece of metadata has a `Value` property of type `System.Object` and a `Type` property of type `PropertyType` (an enumeration covering every possible data type).

→ The `GetPropertiesAsync` method is hostile in the face of unsupported properties (it throws an exception), so you must guard against that. Not all formats support every piece of metadata. BMP files, for example, don't support *any* metadata!

→ The data types for the same metadata values can be a bit more "raw." It turns out that the `ushort` value returned for the photo's orientation uses the same values in the `PhotoOrientation` enumeration seen previously, so it can be cast to `PhotoOrientation` for more readable code.

Unlike the much more limited `ImageProperties`, `BitmapProperties` exposes most of the metadata stored within an image file. There's a long list of common properties you can request by name, grouped into four categories based on their namespace-like prefix:

→ **System.XXX**, where *XXX* can be `ApplicationName`, `Author`, `Comment`, `Copyright`, `DateAcquired`, `Keywords`, `Rating`, `SimpleRating`, `Subject`, or `Title`.

→ **System.Photo.XXX**, where *XXX* can be `Aperture`, `Brightness`, `CameraManufacturer`, `CameraModel`, `CameraSerialNumber`, `Contrast`, `DateTaken`, `DigitalZoom`, `EXIFVersion`, `ExposureBias`, `ExposureTime`, `Flash`, `FlashEnergy`, `FlashManufacturer`, `FlashModel`, `FNumber`, `FocalLength`, `FocalLengthInFilm`, `ISOSpeed`, `LensManufacturer`, `LensModel`,

LightSource, MakerNote, MaxAperture, MeteringMode, Orientation, PeopleNames, PhotometricInterpretation, ProgramMode, RelatedSoundFile, Saturation, Sharpness, ShutterSpeed, SubjectDistance, TranscodedForSync, or WhiteBalance.

→ **System.Image.XXX**, where *XXX* can be ColorSpace, CompressedBitsPerPixel, Compression, HorizontalResolution, ImageID, ResolutionUnit, or VerticalResolution.

→ **System.GPS.XXX**, where *XXX* can be Altitude, Latitude, Longitude, or many more values (an astonishing 30 in total).

Note that all metadata retrieved from a BitmapDecoder is readonly. (The type of BitmapDecoder's BitmapProperties property is BitmapProperties**View**, which doesn't expose a mechanism for saving new values.) To change metadata via BitmapProperties, you must use a Bitmap**Encoder** instead.

Reading Raw Metadata with a Metadata Query Language

The third and final approach for reading metadata uses the same BitmapProperties code as the second approach, but with different strings to represent each property. Instead of using a predefined System... string, you can use a custom query with the Windows Imaging Component (WIC) metadata query language.

This low-level approach gives direct access to any and all metadata in the file (more than what is provided by the two other approaches). Metadata can be stored in different formats, such as Exchangeable image file format (Exif) or Extensible Metadata Platform (XMP), and in different ways within the same format (such as ASCII versus Unicode strings). Whereas BitmapProperties consolidates many possibilities into a consistent logical view, raw metadata queries provide no such luxury.

The following code updates the UseDecoder method to get the same two orientation and date-taken metadata values from the user-selected JPEG file—*if* they happen to be stored in one specific Exif format:

```
async Task UseDecoder(BitmapDecoder decoder)
{
  try
  {
    // GetPropertiesAsync throws when codec doesn't support all passed-in values!
    BitmapPropertySet props = await decoder.BitmapProperties.GetPropertiesAsync(
      new string[] { "/app1/ifd/{ushort=274}", "/app1/ifd/exif/{ushort=36867}" });
    BitmapTypedValue value;
    if (props.TryGetValue("/app1/ifd/{ushort=274}", out value))
    {
      ushort orientation = (ushort)value.Value;
    }
    if (props.TryGetValue("/app1/ifd/exif/{ushort=36867}", out value))
    {
      string dateTaken = (string)value.Value;
```

```
    }
  }
  catch
  {
    // GetPropertiesAsync throws when codec doesn't support all passed-in values!
  }
}
```

Notice that the retrieved date taken is a raw string, and not even in a format that
`DateTimeOffset` can automatically parse (for example, `2013:04:01 22:43:37`).

Further examination of image metadata formats and WIC's metadata query language is
beyond the scope of this book.

Encoding Images

The opposite of `BitmapDecoder` is a `BitmapEncoder` class from the same namespace. With
it, you can create and modify images, and then save them to multiple formats. You can
also write metadata values, if the target format supports it.

`BitmapEncoder` exposes an API that's similar to `BitmapDecoder`, or at least as similar as
possible considering the different requirements of the task. `BitmapEncoder`'s `CreateAsync`
method forces you to choose which encoder (and therefore which codec) to use by
passing in a `Guid` identifying it in addition to the `IRandomAccessStream`. As with
`BitmapDecoder`, `BitmapEncoder` exposes several public static `Guid` properties for the built-
in BMP, GIF, JPEG, JPEG-XR, PNG, TIFF encoders. (There is no built-in ICO encoder,
despite there being a built-in ICO decoder.) You can enumerate all supported encoders
with the static `BitmapEncoder.GetEncoderInformationEnumerator` method.

To demonstrate `BitmapEncoder`, we'll start with an **Encode**UserSelectedFile method
similar to the preceding section's `DecodeUserSelectedFile` method:

```
async Task EncodeUserSelectedFile()
{
  // Get a target JPEG file from the user
  FileSavePicker picker = new FileSavePicker();
  picker.FileTypeChoices.Add("JPEG file", new string[] { ".jpg", ".jpeg" });
  StorageFile file = await picker.PickSaveFileAsync();
  if (file != null)
  {
    // Get the image data
    using (IRandomAccessStream ras =
          await file.OpenAsync(FileAccessMode.ReadWrite))
    {
      // Create the JPEG encoder
      BitmapEncoder encoder =
        await BitmapEncoder.CreateAsync(BitmapEncoder.JpegEncoderId, ras);
```

```
        // Use the encoder
        await UseEncoder(encoder);

        // WARNING: This throws an exception when encoding fails:
        await encoder.FlushAsync();
      }
    }
}
```

This time, the file picker is used in its "save mode" to get a stream we can write into. Whether the user chooses an existing file to overwrite or types in a new filename, our code works the same way.

The file is opened in ReadWrite mode rather than just Read, because BitmapEncoder needs to write the encoded image into the returned stream. That stream is passed to BitmapEncoder.CreateAsync, which is used to create the built-in JPEG encoder. We'll implement UseEncoder in a moment.

EncodeUserSelectFile awaits the completion of the asynchronous UseEncoder method to ensure that FlushAsync isn't called too early, and that the stream isn't disposed too early. FlushAsync must be called once you're finished encoding. This is also the point where most exceptions might be raised.

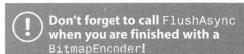

Don't forget to call FlushAsync **when you are finished with a** BitmapEncoder!

However, you should call it only once you're done with it. After FlushAsync is called, you must create a new BitmapEncoder instance for further encoding work.

• • •

Choosing Encoding Options

Some encoders expose options that enable you to customize the encoded result. For example, the built-in JPEG encoder has a configurable quality setting and subsampling mode (used for image compression), the built-in PNG encoder has a configurable filter mode, and the built-in TIFF encoder has a configurable compression mode.

To pass such options to an encoder, you construct one with an overload of CreateAsync that accepts a collection of options as its third parameter. Each option is represented as a BitmapTypedValue, the same data type used for image metadata, so the easiest way to call this method is to create a BitmapPropertySet instance, fill it with appropriate values, and then pass it along.

The Windows.Graphics.Imaging namespace contains enumerations for some of these options (JpegSubsamplingMode, PngFilterMode, and TiffCompressionMode).

Writing Pixel Data

BitmapEncoder exposes a SetPixelData method that is analogous to the more complex overload of BitmapDecoder's GetPixelDataAsync method. In addition to passing a flattened byte array (with pixels in row-major order), you must specify everything needed for the encoder to interpret the array: the pixel format, alpha mode, width, and height. You must also provide DPI values for both dimensions (or 0 to omit that metadata). The following implementation of UseEncoder creates a red-blue gradient image exactly like the one created with WriteableBitmap in Figure 11.4:

```
async Task UseEncoder(BitmapEncoder encoder)
{
  const int PixelWidth = 1024;
  const int PixelHeight = 728;
  const int BytesPerPixel = 4;
  const double DPI = 96.0; // Arbitrary value

  // Allocate bytes for the new image
  byte[] pixels = new byte[PixelWidth * PixelHeight * BytesPerPixel];

  // Write each pixel (4-byte BGRA format, alpha channel ignored)
  for (int i = 0; i < pixels.Length; i += BytesPerPixel)
  {
    int pixelIndex = i / 4;
    pixels[i] = (byte)(pixelIndex % 255);              // B
    pixels[i + 1] = 0;                                 // G
    pixels[i + 2] = (byte)(255 - (pixelIndex % 255));  // R
    pixels[i + 3] = 0;                                 // A (ignored)
  }

  encoder.SetPixelData(BitmapPixelFormat.Bgra8, BitmapAlphaMode.Ignore,
    PixelWidth, PixelHeight, /*horizontal*/ DPI, /*vertical*/ DPI, pixels);
}
```

SetPixelData is a synchronous method because the data is not committed until FlushAsync is called (by the EncodeUserSelectedFile caller in this example).

Although the underlying image-generation algorithm is the same as the WriteableBitmap example, the use of BitmapEncoder enables saving the dynamic content as a regular image file. Figure 11.6 shows the resulting file after executing EncodeUserSelectedFile.

BitmapEncoder supports writing multiple-frame images as well. SetPixelData writes the pixel data for the *current* frame. This is the first and only frame by default, but you can call BitmapEncoder's parameterless GoToNextFrameAsync method to do the following three things:

1. Commit the pixel data for the current frame (the same thing that FlushAsync does, but leaving the encoder in a useable state)
2. Append a new empty frame to image being encoded
3. Set the new frame as the current frame

Therefore, encoding a multiple-frame image involves a repeating pattern of `SetPixelData` then `GoToNextFrameAsync` pairs, although the final call to `SetPixelData` must be followed by a call to `FlushAsync` instead.

An overload of `GoToNextFrameAsync` enables you to pass a collection of encoding options, just like what you can pass to the overload of `CreateAsync`. It turns out that the encoding options passed to `CreateAsync` apply only to the *first* frame! You must explicitly pass them to `GoToNextFrameAsync` in order to apply them to subsequent frames.

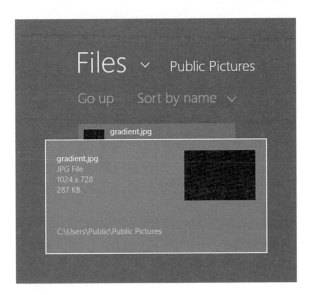

FIGURE 11.6   After the user picks a new `gradient.jpg` filename, the dynamic content gets encoded and saved into the new file.

Writing Metadata

The same three approaches for reading metadata apply to writing metadata as well. The file-based `ImageProperties` approach already supports reading *and* writing most of its properties, and that was shown in the "Decoding Images" section. The two `BitmapProperties` approaches can be used with `BitmapEncoder`'s `BitmapProperties` property. This property is of type `BitmapProperties` rather than `BitmapPropertiesView`, so it enables writing properties with its `SetPropertiesAsync` method as well as reading them with its `GetPropertiesAsync` method.

The following code can be added to the end of the `UseEncoder` method to write two pieces of metadata into the red-blue gradient file:

```
BitmapPropertySet properties = new BitmapPropertySet();

// Set the same two properties used earlier in this chapter
properties.Add("System.Photo.Orientation",
```

```
  new BitmapTypedValue((ushort)PhotoOrientation.Normal, PropertyType.UInt16));
properties.Add("System.Photo.DateTaken",
  new BitmapTypedValue(DateTimeOffset.Parse("1/1/2014"), PropertyType.DateTime));

// Set two additional properties
properties.Add("System.Subject",
  new BitmapTypedValue("Lots of red, lots of blue", PropertyType.String));
properties.Add("System.Rating", new BitmapTypedValue(75, PropertyType.UInt32));

// Perform the update
await encoder.BitmapProperties.SetPropertiesAsync(properties);
```

MSDN contains documentation for each property, including its type and possible values. For example, `System.Rating` is a numeric value in which 1–12 is treated as one star, 13–37 as two stars, 38–62 as three stars, 63–87 as four stars, and any higher as five stars. (A value of zero is treated as no rating.)

After adding this code to set the four metadata values, the results can be seen in Windows Explorer, as shown in Figure 11.7. (The orientation value isn't shown; it's used to determine how Windows should display the contents.)

As with reading metadata, you can use WIC metadata query language for each property name rather than the simpler `System.XXX` values, if you have advanced scenarios that require it.

FIGURE 11.7   Viewing metadata for the image file generated by `BitmapEncoder`

Transcoding

Transcoding refers to the conversion of data from one encoding to another. So far, the encoding examples have created a new image (the silly gradient-filled image), but you can transcode an existing image by obtaining its current data via `BitmapDecoder`, feeding it into `BitmapEncoder`, and then changing it however you see fit.

You could do this by manually copying all pixel data and metadata obtained from the decoder over to the encoder, but `BitmapEncoder` has a nice shortcut for this scenario. Rather than creating a `BitmapEncoder` with its `CreateAsync` method, you can create one with its `Create`**ForTranscoding**`Async` method. You simply give it the instance of the `IRandomAccessStream` that was given to a `BitmapDecoder`, and the `BitmapDecoder` instance as well.

Listing 11.1 contains a new version of the `InvertUserSelectedFile` originally used with `WriteableBitmap`. It performs the same simple inversion shown with the swimming pool photo in Figure 11.5. This time, however, the code can edit the user-selected file in-place, saving the inverted result back to the source.

LISTING 11.1   Modifying a User-Selected File In-Place by Inverting Its Pixels and Changing Metadata

```
async Task InvertUserSelectedFile()
{
  // Get a JPEG from the user
  FileOpenPicker picker = new FileOpenPicker();
  picker.FileTypeFilter.Add(".jpg");
  picker.FileTypeFilter.Add(".jpeg");
  StorageFile file = await picker.PickSingleFileAsync();
  if (file != null)
  {
    // Get the image data
    using (IRandomAccessStream ras =
            await file.OpenAsync(FileAccessMode.ReadWrite))
    {
      // Create the decoder
      BitmapDecoder decoder = await BitmapDecoder.CreateAsync(ras);

      // Create the encoder for transcoding
      BitmapEncoder encoder =
        await BitmapEncoder.CreateForTranscodingAsync(ras, decoder);

      // Get the current pixels, forcing each to be 4 bytes (B, G, R, then A)
      PixelDataProvider provider = await decoder.GetPixelDataAsync(
        BitmapPixelFormat.Bgra8, BitmapAlphaMode.Straight, new BitmapTransform(),
        ExifOrientationMode.RespectExifOrientation,
        ColorManagementMode.ColorManageToSRgb);
      byte[] pixels = provider.DetachPixelData();

      // Invert the colors by subtracting each channel from 255 (byte.MaxValue)
      for (int i = 0; i < pixels.Length; i += 4)
      {
        pixels[i]     = (byte)(byte.MaxValue - pixels[i]);     // B
        pixels[i + 1] = (byte)(byte.MaxValue - pixels[i + 1]); // G
        pixels[i + 2] = (byte)(byte.MaxValue - pixels[i + 2]); // R
                                                               // Leave A alone
      }

      // Use the new pixels
      encoder.SetPixelData(BitmapPixelFormat.Bgra8, BitmapAlphaMode.Straight,
```

LISTING 11.1   Continued

```
      decoder.OrientedPixelWidth, decoder.OrientedPixelHeight,
      decoder.DpiX, decoder.DpiY, pixels);

    // Update a property (leaving the rest at their current values)
    BitmapPropertySet properties = new BitmapPropertySet();
    properties.Add("System.ApplicationName",
      new BitmapTypedValue("Photo Inverter", PropertyType.String));

    // Perform the update
    await encoder.BitmapProperties.SetPropertiesAsync(properties);

    // Save the updates to the original file
    // WARNING: This throws an exception when encoding fails:
    await encoder.FlushAsync();
    }
  }
}
```

This listing combines most of what we've learned about decoding *and* encoding. Notice that the stream passed to `BitmapDecoder` must be opened with `ReadWrite` access because it is the same stream passed to `BitmapEncoder`. You don't need to (or get to) pick the encoder when using this shortcut; it is based on the type of decoder. This means that you can't transcode an ICO file because there's no encoder to match the decoder. If you attempt to do so, `CreateForTranscodingAsync` throws an exception that explains, "The component cannot be found."

Listing 11.1 is an end-to-end "photo inverter." Of course, with `BitmapTransform`, it's easy to build a photo flipper, photo rotator, photo resizer, or photo cropper. For a horizontal photo flipper, the middle part of Listing 11.1 (between the creation of the encoder and the updating of metadata) could be replaced with the following:

```
// Get the current pixels, forcing each to be 4 bytes (B, G, R, then A)
PixelDataProvider provider = await decoder.GetPixelDataAsync(
  BitmapPixelFormat.Bgra8, BitmapAlphaMode.Straight,
  new BitmapTransform { Flip = BitmapFlip.Horizontal },
  ExifOrientationMode.RespectExifOrientation,
  ColorManagementMode.ColorManageToSRgb);
byte[] pixels = provider.DetachPixelData();

// No other pixel modification necessary

// Use the new pixels
encoder.SetPixelData(BitmapPixelFormat.Bgra8, BitmapAlphaMode.Straight,
  decoder.OrientedPixelWidth, decoder.OrientedPixelHeight,
  decoder.DpiX, decoder.DpiY, pixels);
```

For a photo cropper, you could replace it with the following code instead, where chosenX, chosenY, chosenWidth, and chosenHeight are uint variables presumably set via a user interface:

```
// Get the current pixels, forcing each to be 4 bytes (B, G, R, then A)
PixelDataProvider provider = await decoder.GetPixelDataAsync(
  BitmapPixelFormat.Bgra8, BitmapAlphaMode.Straight, new BitmapTransform {
    Bounds = new BitmapBounds {
      X = chosenX, Y = chosenY, Width = chosenWidth, Height = chosenHeight
    }
  },
  FxifOrientationMode.RespectExifOrientation,
  ColorManagementMode.ColorManageToSRgb);
byte[] pixels = provider.DetachPixelData();


// No other pixel modification necessary


// Use the new pixels
encoder.SetPixelData(BitmapPixelFormat.Bgra8, BitmapAlphaMode.Straight,
  chosenWidth, chosenHeight, decoder.DpiX, decoder.DpiY, pixels);
```

Notice that the cropped width and height values need to be passed along to SetPixelData, because the decoder's (Oriented)PixelWidth and (Oriented)PixelHeight properties have no relation to the cropped pixels array obtained from GetPixelDataAsync.

Even if you perform no transformation on the transcoded image, perhaps because you want to edit only its metadata, there is no guarantee that the image data will be identical after the update. This can happen if the original decoded image was encoded with a different encoder with options that aren't supported by the built-in encoder.

If the only "transcoding" you want to do is editing an image's metadata, BitmapEncoder has a separate shortcut for this. You can call its static CreateForInPlacePropertyEncodingAsync method that accepts only a BitmapDecoder parameter. (No stream needs to be directly passed to it, although the stream passed to the BitmapDecoder must be opened with ReadWrite access.)

CreateForInPlacePropertyEncodingAsync allows you to call only GetPropertiesAsync and SetPropertiesAsync (via its BitmapProperties property) and FlushAsync on the returned BitmapEncoder instance. Every other call will throw an exception.

This shortcut exists for two reasons. One is that, if successful, it is guaranteed to preserve the original image data. The other is performance. When used in this way, the encoder attempts to write any new property values without reencoding the pixel data. However, this type of fast metadata encoding doesn't work for all metadata formats (but it does for the common ones such as Exif and XMP). It also doesn't work if the existing metadata block in the image file doesn't contain enough padding to store all the new values.

If the encoder returned by CreateForInPlacePropertyEncodingAsync is unable to perform fast metadata encoding, it throws an exception. Therefore, you should be prepared to handle this and fall back on creating the encoder with CreateForTranscodingAsync instead.

Summary

You've seen how the simple-sounding Image element packs a lot of power with seamless fetching and rendering of content from a number of sources, local or remote, stretching support that includes nine-grid rendering in addition to the typical XAML stretching options, and the ability to display dynamic in-memory images when using a WriteableBitmap as its source.

You've also seen how sophisticated the resource qualifier support is. Although this support applies to *any* resource file, it is most commonly leveraged for image files. The flexibility of resource qualifiers along with the power of the Image element makes it possible to create highly adaptive and scalable user interfaces even when you choose not to use vector graphics.

With the decoding and encoding support in the Windows Runtime, basic image transformations become trivial. You can focus your efforts on the specific pixel-based algorithms and not worry about the rest of the details. And because the Windows file picker enables apps to plug in seamless support for arbitrary storage locations, you can automatically transform photos that come from services such as Facebook or SkyDrive without any extra work!

One thing that's relevant to the Image element that was not covered in this chapter is its built-in support for Play To, enabling users to stream its content to a device on the home network (such as a certified Play To television). This is covered in Chapter 19, "Charms."

Chapter 12

AUDIO AND VIDEO

Some of the most popular tablet apps—on any platform—are media-playing apps. Granted, this is mostly due to the popularity of the services behind them (Netflix, YouTube, Hulu, Vimeo, and so on), but audio and video is a big part of what most people do on a computer. All varieties of apps, and especially games, have the need for integrated audio and video playback in ways that are seamlessly blended with the rest of their content. Therefore, it shouldn't surprise you that Windows Store apps are given a powerful set of high-performance media features to leverage. Best of all, you don't need to be an expert in order to use these features!

This chapter is similar to the preceding one, because the focus isn't so much on the handful of media controls, but rather what you can do with a variety of media content. All the support is based on Windows Media technology, which exposes many Windows Runtime APIs in the `Windows.Media` namespace. This chapter is organized around three primary activities: playback, capture, and transcoding.

Windows Media supports deeper extensibility than what you can accomplish with C#, Visual Basic, or JavaScript in a Windows Store app. You can extend the set of supported formats, codecs, effects, and even content protection systems by creating and using *media extensions* (sometimes called Media Foundation components). These are COM-based C++ components that must be packaged with your app in order to be used. And unlike traditional COM components, they are always completely local to your app. If multiple apps want to use the same extension, they must each contain a copy of it. Although writing such C++ extensions is beyond the scope of this book, you can check out the informative "Media extensions sample" available in the Windows SDK at `http://code.msdn.microsoft.com/ Media-extensions-sample-7b466096`.

Playback

Of course, the most common thing to do with audio and video is to play it. The XAML UI Framework contains one element for doing this, and it's appropriately called `MediaElement`. However, Microsoft has released an open-source element that introduces a lot of functionality on top of `MediaElement`. It is called `MediaPlayer`. This section takes a look at both of these elements.

MediaElement

`MediaElement` is a `UIElement` that displays a video (and plays its audio) much like `Image` displays image content. It plays audio-only files, too, so `MediaElement` is the XAML analog to HTML's audio and video tags rolled into one.

You can set `MediaElement`'s source to a `Uri` that points an audio or video file, for example:

```
<MediaElement Source="Assets/video.mp4"/>
```

When you set `MediaElement`'s `Source`, the content is fetched asynchronously, and then either a `MediaOpened` or `MediaFailed` event gets raised.

All the `Uri` options discussed in the preceding chapter for `Image` apply to `MediaElement` as well, so you can point to a file packaged with your app, a file on the Web, or a file in app local storage. And you can use all the same resource qualifier support in order to use different variations of the file for different environments.

> **(?)   What audio/video formats are supported by** `MediaElement`**?**
>
> `MediaElement` can play anything that the built-in `Video` app can play. That means MP4 and WMV for video (H.264 and VC-1) including ASF for streaming; and MP3, AAC (also known as M4A), and WMA for audio. These are the only system-wide formats, and they are fully hardware-accelerated for great performance and reliability on the entire range of devices running Windows 8.
>
> You can support additional formats if you have an appropriate media extension DLL packaged with your app. Microsoft is intentionally restricting the ability to install system-wide support for additional formats and codecs because that could make poorly written extension negatively impact *every* app (as it has in the past).
>
> The Windows SDK sample referenced in this chapter's introduction includes the C++ source code for an MPEG-1 decoder that is built and packaged with a C# app that consumes it. You can also support adaptive streaming via this mechanism by installing the Smooth Streaming Client SDK available at http://visualstudiogallery.msdn.microsoft.com and referencing it in your app. This packages the necessary prebuilt media extension DLL with your app.

If you place a `MediaElement` in a `Grid`, it will stretch to fill its cell. (Its inner content stretches in a uniform-to-fill fashion, so it will be letterboxed if necessary. `MediaElement` has no `Stretch` property for controlling this.) If you place it in a `Canvas`, it will render at its natural dimensions. As with all `UIElements` (except for `WebView`, covered in the next chapter), you can blend `MediaElements` with other UI. However, there are currently limitations on applying custom `Opacity` values and applying projections to a `MediaElement`.

`MediaElement` has a `SetSource` method just like `BitmapSource`'s method seen in the preceding chapter, so you can easily initialize it with an `IRandomAccessStream` that comes from a variety of sources, such as a file that a user retrieves from the file picker or files that you programmatically retrieve from the user's Videos library. However, `MediaElement`'s `SetSource` method also requires you to pass the relevant MIME type (as a `string`) in order to determine the format of the media file. For a video stream, this would be a `string` such as `video/mp4`, `video/x-ms-asf`, or `video/x-ms-wmv`. For an audio stream, this would be a `string` such as `audio/mp3` or `audio/x-ms-wma`. Fortunately, every `StorageFile` exposes its MIME type via its `ContentType` property. (This is not to be confused with its `FileType` property, which is the file extension.)

> `MediaElement` supports *content protection*, also known as *digital rights management* or DRM. This includes PlayReady, but the support is extensible using the same media extension mechanism. To integrate with PlayReady using a prebuilt media extension, install the Microsoft PlayReady Client SDK available at http://visualstudiogallery.msdn.microsoft.com.

> `MediaElement` even supports stereoscopic 3D video (video you view with 3D glasses), if both the current device and current video file support it. You can check whether the device supports it with the static `DisplayProperties.StereoEnabled` Boolean property, and you can check whether the current video file supports it with `MediaElement`'s `IsStereo3DVideo` Boolean property. This support works only with 3D metadata that is encoded in the H.264 SEI format.
>
> `MediaElement` won't automatically play 3D video in 3D, however, because the user might not currently be wearing 3D glasses! When both `StereoEnabled` and `IsStereo3DVideo` are `true`, you can then enable the 3D playback by setting `MediaElement`'s `Stereo3DVideoRenderMode` property to `Stereo` instead of `Mono`. If `MediaElement` is unable to detect the video's *packing mode* (whether the two images in each frame creating the 3D illusion are placed side-by-side or top-to-bottom), you can set its `Stereo3DVideoPackingMode` property appropriately.

 If you're wondering whether `MediaElement` can play content with a particular MIME type, you can pass the MIME type `string` to its `CanPlayType` method. However, `CanPlayType` must be the most noncommittal API ever created; it returns either `Probably`, `Maybe`, or `NotSupported`!

The reason that these are the only choices is that a MIME type alone doesn't give `MediaElement` enough information to know for sure. For the `video/mp4` example, it still doesn't know the codec or bitrate, and this can be the difference between success and failure. Therefore, the only surefire way to know whether playback is possible is to set it as a `MediaElement`'s source and see whether you get a `MediaOpened` event or a `MediaFailed` event.

MediaElement exposes a number of readonly properties that enable you to discover characteristics of the opened media: NaturalVideoWidth and NaturalVideoHeight, AspectRatioWidth and AspectRatioHeight (which is a bit redundant because you already know the dimensions), NaturalDuration, and AudioStreamCount. For video files with multiple audio streams, you can control which one plays by setting AudioStreamIndex. You can also get the language of any stream (as a BCP-47 language identifier) by calling GetAudioStreamLanguage with the appropriate index.

Using MediaElement to play an audio-only file seems a little strange because you must attach the element somewhere in the current visual tree in order for it to work, despite the fact that there's nothing to visually show. Fortunately, MediaElement is invisible and unhittable when it plays audio, as if it has a size of zero regardless of its Width, Height, or how it is stretched by its parent. Therefore, it doesn't matter where you place it on your Page.

When MediaElement is playing an audio file, its IsAudioOnly property reports true. Whether the audio is playing from an audio-only file or a video file, you can enable extra features by appropriately categorizing the type of audio. Setting AudioCategory to a value other than its default of Other enables it to be used for background audio, covered in Chapter 20, "Extensions." Setting AudioDeviceType to Console or Communications instead of its default value of Multimedia can change how Windows plays it, based on the user's Control Panel settings. (If you set AudioCategory, then AudioDeviceType is automatically updated to match.) For example, Windows gives preferential treatment to communications sounds, reducing the volume of other concurrent audio by default. You can also set Balance (a double whose default value is 0) to any number from -1 to 1. This controls the volume ratio for stereo speakers, so -1 means 100% on the left speaker, 0 means evenly split, and 1 means 100% on the right speaker.

Customizing Playback

Once MediaElement's source is set and MediaOpened is raised, the media starts playing automatically. If you don't want it to, then set AutoPlay to false. When the user switches away from your app, any playing MediaElement automatically pauses. It then automatically resumes once your app comes back to the foreground. The only way to change this behavior is with background audio support covered in Chapter 20.

You can use MediaElement's Play, Stop, and Pause methods (the latter only if CanPause is true) to control playback. If CanSeek is true, you can seek to a specific position by setting its Position property to a TimeSpan value. When Position is externally set, a SeekCompleted event is raised as soon as the target location is ready for playback. Note that the CanPause and CanSeek properties are readonly; their value depends on the media being played, because not all media supports these actions.

You can make the media loop by setting IsLooping to true or mute it by setting IsMuted to true. You can also set Volume to any double value from 0 to 1 (the default is 0.5). When Volume is changed, a VolumeChanged event is raised.

You can speed up or slow down playback with DefaultPlaybackRate (a double set to 1.0 by default). The neat thing is that although the audio stays in sync, this setting doesn't affect its pitch! This is just like the popular "Play speed" option in Windows Media Player that is perfect for watching otherwise-slow-paced lectures. Whenever the value of `DefaultPlaybackRate` (or `PlaybackRate`) changes, the `RateChanged` event is raised.

The relationship between `DefaultPlaybackRate` and `PlaybackRate` is confusing. `PlaybackRate` is the actual rate while the content is playing, but it gets automatically set to the value of `DefaultPlaybackRate` whenever playback begins. Therefore, changing `PlaybackRate` only has an impact if it is set while content is already playing, and its impact only lasts for the current session. Normally, the best thing to do is to only set `DefaultPlaybackRate` and ensure you call `Play` *after* setting it.

If you're using `MediaElement` for real-time communications, you should not only set `AudioCategory` to `Communications`, but you should set `RealTimePlayback` to true. This raises the priority of refreshing the video content. In this mode, playback can occur only at its default `1.0` rate.

? How can I get metadata associated with audio or video, such as artist or genre?

You can use the same technique used to get `ImageProperties` in the previous chapter, except you can get `MusicProperties` or `VideoProperties` instead. For example:

```
// Get an MP4 file from the user
FileOpenPicker picker = new FileOpenPicker();
picker.FileTypeFilter.Add(".mp4");
StorageFile file = await picker.PickSingleFileAsync();
if (file != null)
{
    // Get music properties from the file
    MusicProperties properties = await file.Properties.GetMusicPropertiesAsync();
    string artist = properties.Artist;
    IList<string> genres = properties.Genre;

    …
}
```

States and Events

At any time, `MediaElement` can be in one of the following states, revealed by its readonly `CurrentState` property: `Closed`, `Opening`, `Buffering`, `Playing`, `Paused`, or `Stopped`. `Closed` is the initial state. It transitions to `Opening` after the source is set, but before `MediaOpened` or `MediaFailed` is raised. During this state, any calls to `Play`, `Pause`, or `Stop` are queued until the media is opened. A `CurrentStateChanged` event is raised for every state transition. A `MediaEnded` event is raised once the content reaches the end and stops playback. This doesn't get raised due to programmatic `Stop` calls, and it never gets raised if the content is looping.

Whenever content is buffering or downloading (in the case of content from a remote server), `BufferingProgressChanged` and `DownloadProgressChanged` events are raised. In handlers for these events, you can check MediaElement's BufferingProgress and DownloadProgress properties, but be aware that these are double values with a range from 0–1 rather than the typical range of 0–100. When applicable, download requests are done in byte ranges. In such cases, a separate DownloadProgressOffset property indicates the starting position of the current range being downloaded, expressed as a percentage of the total download size. The DownloadProgress property then indicates the end point of the current range.

Markers

Some media files can have embedded *markers* at specific points in time. There are a few different types of markers, and each one can have associated text. For example, many media players recognize markers of type "caption" and automatically overlay their text at the appropriate times. Some video files use *index markers* to mark chapters or have other bookmarks that aid in user navigation, much like with a DVD. Markers also enable the host to perform custom actions in sync with specific events in the media.

MediaElement exposes these markers with its Markers property. This is a collection of TimelineMarker objects that expose three simple properties: Text (a string), Type (a string), and Time (a TimeSpan). You can inspect the collection once MediaOpened is raised. When media content with embedded markers plays, a MarkerReached event is raised at the Time of each marker. This enables you to perform any desired action at the right time.

You can modify the Markers collection at runtime! This means that even if you're going to play a media file without any, you can programmatically add whatever markers you'd like. For example:

```
mediaElement.Markers.Add(
  new TimelineMarker {
    Text = "1", Time = TimeSpan.FromSeconds(5), Type = "custom"
  }
);
```

You can set these at any time—even while the media is playing—and the MarkerReached event will be raised for each one when appropriate, just as if the original media defined them! Note that you cannot encode and persist these changes into the media.

The Markers collection might not include all markers!

The Markers collection contains only markers from the media's header; not any encoded as a separate stream. That's because such streams might not be available yet at the time MediaOpened is raised. If a file contains both header-embedded script commands and separate-stream script commands, this collection contains only those embedded in the file header. This is because MediaOpened is raised after reading the headers and metadata, but the full source might still be buffering and thus any separate stream markers are not available yet. Separate-stream script commands do trigger the MarkerReached event when encountered during media playback. However these markers are not accessible ahead of time using the Markers property.

Adding Effects

MediaElement enables you to add both audio and video effects with its AddVideoEffect and AddAudioEffect methods. (You can later remove them by calling RemoveAllEffects.) You pass a string ID, a Boolean that states whether the effect is optional, and extra configuration that can be null if it doesn't apply.

The Windows Runtime currently includes just one built-in effect: video stabilization. Its ID is "Windows.Media.VideoStabilizationEffect" but you can just use the static VideoEffects.VideoStabilization string property instead. You therefore add it to a MediaElement (named mediaElement) as follows:

```
// Apply the video stabilization effect
mediaElement.AddVideoEffect(
    VideoEffects.VideoStabilization, true /*it's optional*/, null);
```

By making an effect optional, it means that playback will still occur even if there's some reason the effect can't be used.

Just like with custom formats, media extensions can be used to enable powerful custom effects. The same Windows SDK sample referenced in this chapter's introduction includes C++ source code for several video effects: grayscale, invert, fisheye, pinch, and warp. (The last three are enabled by passing custom parameters to the same PolarEffect used to implement them all.)

> **! Added effects apply to the *next* source!**
>
> You must apply any effects *before* setting MediaElement's source to the content that is meant to receive the effects.

> If you play full-screen background video to enhance the appearance of your app, you might want to disable the video when your app is viewed over Remote Desktop, to avoid creating significant performance problems. You can customize your app however you'd like when running under Remote Desktop by checking the static InteractiveSession.IsRemote property. This is the sole class (and member) in the Windows.System.RemoteDesktop namespace.

MediaPlayer

The main scenario for using MediaElement directly is audio and *noninteractive* video. For example, you could use a looping video clip as an animated background, incorporate video in a fancy extended splash screen, or insert a video interlude between levels of a game. Oh perhaps you want to use it in a video-based storybook with limited or highly customized interactivity.

Although MediaElement certainly exposes enough programmatic capabilities to build a great interactive media player, it's a lot of work. Not only that, but there's already an excellent one you can use that wraps MediaElement for you!

This pre-built media player is not part of any framework that ships with Windows. Rather, it is a free open-source control provided by Microsoft and available at http://player-framework.codeplex.com. (There are versions of the control for many other platforms as well.) This is an evolution of the same video player codebase that Microsoft used for the

Beijing and Vancouver Olympics, the 2012 Super Bowl, Wimbledon, and a number of other massive live events. Because of this, it supports a number of advanced features: many forms of advertising integration, closed captioning, feature-rich playback controls, and adaptive streaming (via the Smooth Streaming Client SDK mentioned at the beginning of this chapter). The control isn't (yet) perfect, but you can easily tweak its source code for your needs.

Once you install the `.vsix` extension for Visual Studio, you can add "Microsoft Media Platform: Player Framework" to your project references. When you bring up the Reference Manager dialog in Visual Studio, you can find it under Windows, Extensions. After this, you can place the `Microsoft.PlayerFramework.MediaPlayer` control on your `Page` and set its `Source` to a `Uri`, just like with `MediaElement`:

```xml
<Page … xmlns:p="using:Microsoft.PlayerFramework">
  <Canvas Background="{StaticResource ApplicationPageBackgroundThemeBrush}">
    <p:MediaPlayer
      Source="http://smf.blob.core.windows.net/samples/videos/bigbuck.mp4"/>
  </Canvas>
</Page>
```

The result of doing this is shown in Figure 12.1.

FIGURE 12.1   `MediaPlayer` includes many built-in playback features.

Without writing any code or setting extra properties, `MediaPlayer` has a lot of functional elements: a play/pause `Button`, a volume `Slider` and mute `Button`, a `Slider` for seeking that also indicates download progress, time-elapsed and time-remaining labels, plus the ability to jump back or forward 30 seconds by tapping on these two labels.

With a few additional properties set as follows, `MediaPlayer` gains functional replay and fast-forward `Button`s, a closed captions `Button` (functional if the video contains them), and a signal strength indicator (relevant only for adaptive streaming):

```
<p:MediaPlayer IsReplayVisible="True" IsFastForwardVisible="True"
               IsCaptionsVisible="True" IsSignalStrengthVisible="True"
  Source="http://smf.blob.core.windows.net/samples/videos/bigbuck.mp4"/>
```

The result of adding these properties is shown in Figure 12.2.

FIGURE 12.2   More `MediaPlayer` features are just a few property sets away.

`MediaPlayer` not only wraps `MediaElement`, but it exposes a superset of its APIs. Therefore, everything discussed about `MediaElement` applies to `MediaPlayer` as well. `MediaPlayer` adds a *lot* of properties and events to support enabling/disabling and showing/hiding of all its extra UI elements. If you're serious about providing a first-class interactive video player, then be sure to check out `MediaPlayer`.

> With the simple `Playlist` class included in the Windows Runtime, you can integrate standard playlist files with `MediaPlayer` or your own custom use of `MediaElement`. You can load a playlist file by calling `LoadAsync`, access and edit its collection of files (represented by a `Files` property that's a collection of `StorageFiles`), and then save it with either `SaveAsync` or `SaveAsAsync` methods. `Playlist` supports three file formats: M3U (`.m3u`), Windows Media (`.wpl`), and Zune (`.zpl`).

If your app is meant for prolonged video watching, then you should attempt to prevent the screen from turning off—or a screen saver from turning on—due to perceived user inactivity. You can do this by instantiating a `DisplayRequest` object (the only class in the `Windows.System.Display` namespace) and calling `RequestActive`. When you're ready for the screen behavior to go back to normal, call `RequestRelease`. Be careful, though, because all three methods (including the constructor) might throw an exception. If `RequestActive` returns without throwing an exception, then the screen is guaranteed to stay on for the life of your request. If your app gets suspended, the request is automatically reactivated when the app returns to the running state.

Capture

Just as there are two options for media playback, there are two options for media capture. `CameraCaptureUI` makes it easy to perform basic capture by leveraging built-in Windows UI. In contrast, `CaptureElement` enables you to provide a completely custom user experience for capture, and to perform types of capture that aren't available via `CameraCaptureUI`. This section looks at both approaches.

> **The capture features require the Microphone and/or Webcam capabilities!**
>
> This stands to reason, because audio capture is performed with a microphone, and video capture is performed with a camera. Although most Windows 8 tablets and laptops have a built-in microphone and one or two built-in cameras, these features (and capabilities) work with external devices as well, such as a classic Webcam.

CameraCaptureUI

The `CameraCaptureUI` class enables you to launch the built-in Camera app experience (in a more limited mode and directly inside your app) in order to easily capture a photo or video. The experience is just like choosing the Camera app inside the Windows file picker, except it's full-screen and there's a back button on the top-left instead of a cancel button on the bottom-right.

Capturing a Photo

Assuming you have an `Image` named `image` on your `Page`:

```
<Image Name="image"/>
```

the following code-behind launches the camera UI in photo-taking mode:

```
async Task CapturePhoto()
{
  CameraCaptureUI camera = new CameraCaptureUI();
  try
  {
    // Get a JPEG image from the camera
    StorageFile file = await camera.CaptureFileAsync(CameraCaptureUIMode.Photo);
    if (file != null)
```

```
      {
        using (IRandomAccessStream ras = await file.OpenAsync(FileAccessMode.Read))
        {
          // Load the data into a BitmapImage
          BitmapImage source = new BitmapImage();
          source.SetSource(ras);

          // Assign the BitmapImage to the Image element on the page
          this.image.Source = source;
        }
      }
    }
  catch
  {
    // CaptureFileAsync throws if the app is snapped!
    …
  }
}
```

As with other code interacting with UI, the call to CaptureFileAsync must be made on the main thread (also called the *UI thread*).

If you use CameraCaptureUI with only CameraCaptureUIMode.Photo, then you don't need the Microphone capability, just the Webcam one. The first time this code executes, the user is prompted to give his or her consent. After that, the camera UI in Figure 12.3 is shown. The user can switch between available cameras, customize each camera's options (which might vary) and even use a timer. The "Video Mode" button is disabled in Figure 12.3 because CameraCaptureUIMode.Photo was chosen.

If a front-facing camera is used, the preview video feed is automatically mirrored horizontally. This is standard practice for video conferencing apps like Skype, although in this case the effect is jarring because as soon as you take the photo, you see the result without mirroring.

After tapping on the screen to take the photo, the user is given a choice to accept it, retake it, or crop it. The cropping UI is also shown in Figure 12.3. Once the user accepts the photo, the file is saved (in JPEG format) to the app's local temporary data folder. The camera UI then disappears and the StorageFile referencing the temporary file is returned to your app.

If you forget to enable the Webcam capability in your package manifest, the call to CaptureFileAsync doesn't fail, but the resultant camera UI looks like Figure 12.4. When the user dismisses it, it returns a null file, just as when the user cancels photo-taking.

Viewing some camera options before taking the photo   Cropping the photo after taking it

FIGURE 12.3   The built-in camera UI provides a lot of options to the user, just like the Camera app.

FIGURE 12.4   The built-in camera UI explains when a necessary capability is missing.

Before calling `CaptureFileAsync`, you can set several subproperties on `CameraCaptureUI`'s `PhotoSettings` property to make a number of customizations:

> → **AllowCropping**—Set this to `false` to remove the cropping feature.

> → **CroppedAspectRatio**—Set this to a `Size` to lock the aspect ratio of the cropped region. When you do this, cropping becomes mandatory.

> **CaptureFileAsync throws an exception if it is called while the app is snapped!**
>
> You can guard against this by always programmatically unsnapping your app right before invoking the camera UI (which should be done only in response to an explicit user action). If the user happens to snap your app while the camera UI is showing, it quietly dismisses and `CaptureFileAsync` returns `null`.

> → **CroppedSizeInPixels**—Set this to a `Size` to force the exact dimensions of the cropped region instead. This also makes cropping mandatory.

> → **Format**—Choose between `Jpeg` (the default), `JpegXR`, and `Png`.

→ **MaxResolution**—Limit the highest resolution that the user can select from a number of predefined options in the CameraCaptureUIMaxPhotoResolution enumeration. The default value is HighestAvailable.

Capturing a Video

Assuming you have a MediaElement (or MediaPlayer) named video on your Page:

```
<MediaElement Name="video"/>
```

the following code-behind launches the camera UI in video-capture mode:

```
IRandomAccessStream stream;
…
async Task CaptureVideo()
{
  CameraCaptureUI camera = new CameraCaptureUI();
  try
  {
    // Get an MP4 video from the camera
    StorageFile file = await camera.CaptureFileAsync(CameraCaptureUIMode.Video);
    if (file != null)
    {
      this.stream = await file.OpenAsync(FileAccessMode.Read);

      // Load the data into the MediaElement
      this.video.SetSource(stream, file.ContentType);

      // Don't dispose the stream until MediaOpened is raised!
    }
  }
  catch
  {
    // CaptureFileAsync throws if the app is snapped!
    …
  }
}
```

As far as the use of CameraCaptureUI goes, this is a one-word change from Photo to Video. (CameraCaptureUIMode also has a PhotoOrVideo option if you want to allow either.) This time, however, the stream is passed to the MediaElement's SetSource method along with the MIME type (video/mp4). Unlike in the Image case, the stream cannot be disposed until MediaElement's MediaOpened event is raised, so the stream is stored as a member variable that can be disposed in a MediaOpened handler:

```
void Video_MediaOpened(object sender, RoutedEventArgs e)
{
```

```
    this.stream.Dispose();
}
```

This mode, as well as the `PhotoOrVideo` mode, requires both Microphone and Webcam capabilities because audio gets captured as well. If you have only Webcam but not Microphone, the camera UI shows the same message as in Figure 12.4, which can be quite confusing!

Before capturing video, the user has even more options available to customize, such as which audio device to use and whether to enable any built-in effects like video stabilization. After the user captures video (with one tap to start recording and other to stop), he is presented with a trimming option rather than a cropping option.

Before calling `CaptureFileAsync`, you can set a few subproperties on `CameraCaptureUI`'s **Video**Settings property to make a number of customizations:

→ **AllowTrimming**—Set this to `false` to remove the trimming feature.

→ **MaxDurationInSeconds**—Set this to a `float` to limit the length of the video clip. When you do this, trimming becomes mandatory. (The user can record a much longer clip and then decide which portion to use.)

→ **Format**—Choose between `Mp4` (the default) and `Wmv`.

→ **MaxResolution**—Limit the highest resolution that the user can select. Your choices are `HighestAvailable` (the default), `LowDefinition`, `StandardDefinition`, or `HighDefinition`.

CaptureElement

`CaptureElement` is basically the capture equivalent of `MediaElement`. `MediaElement` contains all the plumbing necessary for playback with no built-in adornments, and the same could be said about `CaptureElement` for capture. It is a `UIElement` with only two properties (excluding ones inherited from its `FrameworkElement` base class): `Source` and `Stretch`. That's right, unlike `MediaElement`, `CaptureElement` *does* support the same types of stretching supported by `Image` and `Viewbox`: `None`, `Fill`, `Uniform`, and `UniformToFill` (the default value).

`CaptureElement`'s `Source` property is of type `MediaCapture`, a Windows Runtime class that does all the hard work. It enables you to capture videos, photos, as well as two options lacking from `CameraCaptureUI`: video-only recordings (with no audio) and audio-only recordings.

Showing a Preview

The first step in allowing a user to capture a photo or video is showing her a live video feed so she can frame her shot. If you define a `CaptureElement` named `captureElement` on your `Page`:

```
<CaptureElement Name="captureElement"/>
```

Then the following code-behind can fill it with live content from the device's default camera:

```
MediaCapture capture = new MediaCapture();
…
async Task ShowPreview()
{
  try
  {
    // Requires Microphone and Webcam capabilities!
    await this.capture.InitializeAsync();

    // Source can only be set after the MediaCapture is initialized
    this.captureElement.Source = capture;

    // Show the live content
    await this.capture.StartPreviewAsync();
  }
  catch (UnauthorizedAccessException)
  {
    // The app wasn't granted the necessary capabilities
    …
  }
}
```

The call to `InitializeAsync` requires both Microphone and Webcam capabilities, otherwise it throws an `UnauthorizedAccessException`. If the user revokes these capabilities while your app is using a `MediaCapture` object (via the Settings charm), it ceases to work and raises a `Failed` event.

If you don't care about audio, you can avoid the need for the Microphone capability by calling an `InitializeAsync` overload that accepts custom settings. With this, you can set the `StreamingCaptureMode` to `Video` rather than the default value of `AudioAndVideo` as follows:

```
await this.capture.InitializeAsync(new MediaCaptureInitializationSettings {
StreamingCaptureMode = StreamingCaptureMode.Video });
```

In this case, any captured video will be audio-free.

The `MediaCaptureInitializationSettings` instance that can be passed to the overload of `InitializeAsync` exposes two `string` properties—`AudioDeviceId` and `VideoDeviceId`—that enable you to switch audio capture to a specific microphone and video capture to a specific camera.

StartPreviewAsync starts rendering the live video feed inside the CaptureElement. You can later call StopPreviewAsync to end the feed. To mimic the video mirroring done by CameraCaptureUI, you can call MediaCapture's SetPreviewMirroring(true) method or apply a ScaleTransform to the CaptureElement with a ScaleX of -1. MediaCapture exposes a similar SetPreviewRotation method that allows only 90° increments, but again you could accomplish the same thing (and more) with a RotateTransform.

MediaCapture's Failed event is raised in a number of situations. For example, if the Camera app is already snapped on the screen when the user triggers ShowCameraFeed in this app, Failed is raised because the camera is an exclusive resource that must be used only by one app at a time. The code for showing the live video feed is simple, but there are a lot of issues to be aware of, explained in the following warning sidebars.

> (!) **The first call to** InitializeAsync **must be done on the main thread!**
>
> Although CameraCaptureUI.CaptureFileAsync has the same limitation, this requirement for MediaCapture.InitializeAsync might not be as obvious because it normally doesn't show any UI. The reason for this requirement is that the *first* time the user triggers this functionality in your app, he or she is presented with a dialog asking for consent, as shown in Figure 12.5. Subsequent use does not ask for consent, although the user can allow or block access at any time via the Settings charm. This main thread requirement is true for all the "sensitive" capabilities, because all relevant APIs prompt in the same fashion.
>
>
>
> **FIGURE 12.5**   The consent dialog shown during the first call to MediaCapture.InitializeAsync must be triggered from the main thread.
>
> Because of this "in your face" behavior, you should avoid automatically initializing a MediaCapture when your app is launched unless it is vital to the operation of your app.

> (!) **Switching away from an app instantly terminates** MediaCapture!
>
> This is done automatically, which is nice because it means you don't need to worry about releasing this exclusive resource upon suspension (or if another app tries to use it while your app is still running). This does leave the MediaCapture instance in an unusable state, however. Therefore, upon your app's return to the screen (in a VisibilityChanged handler for your Window), you must recreate and reinitialize a new MediaCapture, and then set it as a new source for the CaptureElement.

> ⚠ **MediaCapture events are raised on a different thread!**
>
> Every class deriving from `DependencyObject`, which is most classes in the XAML UI Framework, must be created and accessed on the main thread. However, `MediaCapture`'s events, as with some other events in Windows Runtime APIs, are raised on a different thread. This means that attempting to access a `UIElement` in such an event handler fails:
>
> ```
> // A handler for MediaCapture's Failed event
> void Capture_Failed(MediaCapture sender, MediaCaptureFailedEventArgs e)
> {
>   // This throws an exception:
>   this.textBlock.Text = "Failure capturing video.";
> }
> ```
>
> The exception thrown explains, "The application called an interface that was marshalled for a different thread. (Exception from HRESULT: 0x8001010E (RPC_E_WRONG_THREAD))."
>
> With `DependencyObject`'s `Dispatcher` property of type `CoreDispatcher`, however, you can marshal a call back to the main thread. It can be used as follows:
>
> ```
> // A handler for MediaCapture's Failed event
> async Task Capture_Failed(MediaCapture sender, MediaCaptureFailedEventArgs e)
> {
>   await this.Dispatcher.RunAsync(CoreDispatcherPriority.Normal, () =>
>   {
>     // This now works, because it's running on the main thread:
>     this.textBlock.Text = "Failure capturing video.";
>   });
> }
> ```
>
> Here, an anonymous method is used for `RunAsync`'s second parameter (which must be a parameterless `DispatchedHandler` delegate) to keep the code as concise as possible.

Capturing a Photo

With a `MediaCapture` instance initialized as in the previous section, the live video preview optionally showing, and an `Image` named `image` on your `Page`, you can capture a photo as follows:

```
MediaCapture capture = new MediaCapture();
…
async Task CapturePhoto()
{
  // Capture a JPEG into a new stream
  ImageEncodingProperties properties = ImageEncodingProperties.CreateJpeg();
  using (IRandomAccessStream ras = new InMemoryRandomAccessStream())
  {
    await this.capture.CapturePhotoToStreamAsync(properties, ras);
    await ras.FlushAsync();
```

```
    // Load the data into a BitmapImage
    ras.Seek(0);
    BitmapImage source = new BitmapImage();
    source.SetSource(ras);

    // Assign the BitmapImage to the Image element on the page
    this.image.Source = source;
  }
}
```

You can construct your own custom
`ImageEncodingProperties` instance for
advanced scenarios, but for most cases,
you should retrieve one from its static
`CreateJpeg`, `CreateJpegXR`, or `CreatePng`
methods.

MediaCapture enables capturing a photo
directly to a file instead of a stream. Its
`CapturePhotoToStorageFileAsync`
method accepts an `IStorageFile` as its second
parameter instead of an `IRandomAccessStream`.

Adjusting Camera Settings

`MediaCapture` has a `VideoDeviceController` property (of type `VideoDeviceController`)
that enables you to programmatically adjust whatever settings it exposes. This can include
things such as brightness, contrast, exposure, white balance, hue, and backlight compen-
sation. For more advanced cameras, you can control focus, zoom, pan, roll, and tilt! The
value of every setting is represented as a `double`. The following code shows how to set
Brightness to 8 via a `MediaCapture` named `capture`:

```
// Try to disable automatic adjustment of the setting
if (capture.VideoDeviceController.Brightness.TrySetAuto(false))
{
  // Try to set it to 8
  if (capture.VideoDeviceController.Brightness.TrySetValue(8))
  {
    // Success!
  }
}
```

Each property on `VideoDeviceController` is a `MediaDeviceControl` object that exposes
the two `TrySetXXX` methods used in this snippet and corresponding `TryGetXXX` methods.
It also has a `Capabilities` property that reveals whether the setting is supported by the
current camera, whether automatic adjustment is supported, its
default/minimum/maximum values, and the step size. The preceding code didn't bother
checking whether `Brightness` is supported, because all the `TryXXX` methods on
`VideoDeviceController` return `false` for unsupported settings.

These are all global settings, although each physical camera has its own set. For example,
if the user changes his or her front-facing camera's brightness from within your app, then
that change will persist and be seen the next time the front-facing camera is used in any
app (including the built-in Camera app).

Although you're mostly on your own when it comes to replicating features from `CameraCaptureUI` in code based on `CaptureElement`, there is one helpful piece of built-in UI you can take advantage of. If you call the static `CameraUIOptions.Show` method with an instance of an initialized `MediaCapture`, Windows automatically displays the dialog shown in Figure 12.6 over the bottom-right corner of your app. This is the same dialog used in the Camera app and `CameraCaptureUI`, and it enables modifying the settings exposed by the relevant `VideoDeviceController`. You don't have to write any code to make this happen other than the single call to show the dialog!

Note, however, that this is only the "More options" dialog that normally appears only after selecting "More" in the typical "Camera options" dialog seen in Figure 12.3. Therefore, if you want to enable the user to configure the resolution, audio device, or effects, you're still on your own.

FIGURE 12.6   The dialog that appears when you call `CameraUIOptions.Show` is conveniently narrow enough to fit inside a snapped app.

Capturing a Video

Capturing video with `MediaCapture` looks similar to capturing a photo, although the logic must be split into separate starting and stopping actions. The following code-behind assumes you have a `MediaElement` or `MediaPlayer` named `video` on your `Page`:

```
MediaCapture capture = new MediaCapture();
IRandomAccessStream ras = new InMemoryRandomAccessStream();
…
async Task StartCapturingVideo()
{
  // Capture WMV video into the stream
  MediaEncodingProfile profile =
    MediaEncodingProfile.CreateWmv(VideoEncodingQuality.Auto);
  await this.capture.StartRecordToStreamAsync(profile, this.ras);
}

async Task StopCapturingVideo()
{
  await this.capture.StopRecordAsync();
```

```
  await this.ras.FlushAsync();

  // Load the data into the MediaElement
  this.ras.Seek(0);
  this.video.SetSource(this.ras, "video/x-ms-wmv");

  // Don't dispose this.ras until MediaOpened is raised!
}
```

Instead of an ImageEncodingProperties instance, StartRecordToStreamAsync requires a MediaEncodingProfile to encode the resulting video stream. You can create one from the static CreateWmv or CreateMp4 methods, or you can also create a profile based on an existing media file with CreateFromFileAsync or CreateFromStreamAsync. Note that MediaCapture supports only one-pass constant bitrate encoding.

In addition to MediaCapture's Failed event, which you should always handle, MediaCapture has a RecordLimitation Exceeded event that you should handle whenever you're recording audio/video. When it is raised, it will not record any more content, so you should call StopRecordAsync and perform your normal logic for processing the recording.

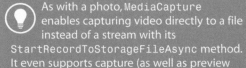 As with a photo, MediaCapture enables capturing video directly to a file instead of a stream with its StartRecordToStorageFileAsync method. It even supports capture (as well as preview playback) to a *custom sink*, which is another type of media extension.

Capturing Audio Only

Capturing audio with MediaCapture is like capturing video. You just need to create a different MediaEncodingProfile. Three preconfigured options are provided by the static CreateMp3, CreateM4a, and CreateWma methods. Capturing just audio enables us to simplify some things, however. We can stop showing the video preview. And if we initialize MediaCapture for audio-only usage, then we no longer require the Webcam capability! The following code shows this updated initialization along with the methods to start/stop capturing audio. This assumes that the MediaElement on the Page is now called audio:

```
MediaCapture capture = new MediaCapture();
IRandomAccessStream ras = new InMemoryRandomAccessStream();
…
async Task Initialize()
{
  try
  {
    // Initialize this way so we only require the Microphone capability
    await this.capture.InitializeAsync(new MediaCaptureInitializationSettings {
      StreamingCaptureMode = StreamingCaptureMode.Audio });
  }
```

```
  catch (UnauthorizedAccessException)
  {
    // Could not use the microphone!
  }
}

async Task StartCapturingAudio()
{
  // Capture MP3 audio into the stream
  MediaEncodingProfile profile =
    MediaEncodingProfile.CreateMp3(AudioEncodingQuality.Auto);
  await this.capture.StartRecordToStreamAsync(profile, this.ras);
}

async Task StopCapturingAudio()
{
  await this.capture.StopRecordAsync();
  await this.ras.FlushAsync();

  // Load the data into the MediaElement
  this.ras.Seek(0);
  this.audio.SetSource(this.ras, "audio/mp3");

  // Don't dispose this.ras until MediaOpened is raised!
}
```

Just like `VideoDeviceController`, `MediaCapture` has an `AudioDeviceController` property that enables you to adjust microphone settings, such as its volume and mute status.

Transcoding

Similar to the transcoding done with `BitmapDecoder` and `BitmapEncoder` in the preceding chapter, the Windows Media APIs enables some simple transcoding options for audio/video files. This is exposed via a single `MediaTranscoder` class. With it, you can do four basic tasks:

→ Change the encoding quality

→ Change the media format

→ Trim the media

→ Add effects

Changing the Quality

Leveraging the same `MediaEncodingProfile` class used to encode video from `MediaCapture`, you can transcode any supported media format to any other supported media format. Although you can save the output in a higher-quality encoding than the input, you obviously can't *improve* the quality. The main scenario here is reducing the size of a media file by reducing its quality.

Using `MediaTranscoder` is a two-step process. First you *prepare* it with the source media, target media, and a profile, which gives you an instance of `PrepareTranscodeResult`. If this result object tells you it can perform the transcoding (via its `CanTranscode` property), then you can call its `TranscodeAsync` method to do the work. Otherwise, you can check its `FailureReason` property to understand why `CanTranscode` is `false`.

`MediaTranscoder` supports a source and target of type `IRandomAccessStream` with its `PrepareStreamTranscodeAsync` method, so code that calls this would look similar to code from the preceding chapter. However, the following code uses a separate `Prepare**File**TranscodeAsync` method to directly read and write from one `StorageFile` to another. This is a nice shortcut when you're already working with two files, as with this example that uses the Windows file picker to get both the source and target files:

```
async Task ShrinkUserSelectedFile()
{
  // Get a source MP4 file from the user
  FileOpenPicker openPicker = new FileOpenPicker();
  openPicker.FileTypeFilter.Add(".mp4");
  StorageFile sourceFile = await openPicker.PickSingleFileAsync();
  if (sourceFile != null)
  {
    // Get a target MP4 file from the user
    FileSavePicker savePicker = new FileSavePicker();
    savePicker.FileTypeChoices.Add("MP4 file", new string[] { ".mp4" });
    StorageFile targetFile = await savePicker.PickSaveFileAsync();
    if (targetFile != null)
    {
      // Specify the output format (QVGA: 320x240)
      MediaEncodingProfile profile =
        MediaEncodingProfile.CreateMp4(VideoEncodingQuality.Qvga);


      // Transcode!
      MediaTranscoder transcoder = new MediaTranscoder();
      PrepareTranscodeResult result = await transcoder.PrepareFileTranscodeAsync(
                                      sourceFile, targetFile, profile);
      if (result.CanTranscode)
      {
        await result.TranscodeAsync();
      }
```

```
      else
      {
          // Check result.FailureReason: InvalidProfile, CodecNotFound, or Unknown
      }
    }
  }
}
```

The VideoEncodingQuality options (besides Auto) are summarized in Table 12.1.

TABLE 12.1   Values in the VideoEncodingQuality Enumeration

Value	Resolution (in Pixels)	Aspect Ratio
Qvga	320×240	4:3
Ntsc	486×440	4:3
Pal	576×520	4:3
Vga	640×480	4:3
Wvga	800×480	5:3
HD720p	1280×720	16:9
HD1080p	1920×1080	16:9

Whenever calling an asynchronous method, you can choose to not await but rather directly receive the returned IAsyncOperation. With this, you could do something more advanced like support cancellation. IAsyncOperation has a simple Cancel method that you can call while the operation is still running. (You can also leverage the AsTask extension method if you're used to working with the .NET Task APIs.) For user-friendly apps, cancellation of potentially long-running activities, such as transcoding a large media file, is a must.

In the case of the TranscodeAsync method, however, you can do something even more slick. It returns an IAsyncActionWithProgress<double>, which means that you can get incremental progress updates (a double value from 0 to 100) that can be fed to a ProgressBar or similar control. To apply this to the transcoding example, you can replace this block of code:

```
if (result.CanTranscode)
{
  await result.TranscodeAsync();
}
```

with this:

```
if (result.CanTranscode)
{
  this.progressBar.Visibility = Visibility.Visible;

  IAsyncActionWithProgress<double> action = result.TranscodeAsync();

  // Handler for progress updates
```

```
    action.Progress = async (self, value) =>
    {
      // Called on a different thread
      await this.Dispatcher.RunAsync(CoreDispatcherPriority.Normal, () =>
      {
        // Update a ProgressBar control on the main thread
        this.progressBar.Value = value; // value is 0-100
      });
    };

    // Handler for completion
    action.Completed = async (self, status) =>
    {
      // Called on a different thread
      await this.Dispatcher.RunAsync(CoreDispatcherPriority.Normal, () =>
      {
        // Hide the ProgressBar because transcoding is done
        this.progressBar.Visibility = Visibility.Collapsed;
      });
    };
}
```

> The biggest complication is that both the Progress callbacks and Completed callback
> occur on a different thread, so the Page's Dispatcher must be used to marshal back to
> the main thread in order to update the UI. The two anonymous methods are marked async
> so they can use the await keyword with the calls to RunAsync.

Changing the Format

Changing a media file's format is done the same way as changing its quality. It comes
down to your choice of MediaEncodingProfile (and in this example, what file extensions
you force in the file picker):

```
async Task ConvertUserSelectedMp4ToWmv()
{
  // Get a source MP4 file from the user
  FileOpenPicker openPicker = new FileOpenPicker();
  openPicker.FileTypeFilter.Add(".mp4");
  StorageFile sourceFile = await openPicker.PickSingleFileAsync();
  if (sourceFile != null)
  {
    // Get a target WMV file from the user
    FileSavePicker savePicker = new FileSavePicker();
```

```csharp
        savePicker.FileTypeChoices.Add("WMV file", new string[] { ".wmv" });
        StorageFile targetFile = await savePicker.PickSaveFileAsync();
        if (targetFile != null)
        {
          // Specify the output format
          MediaEncodingProfile profile =
            MediaEncodingProfile.CreateWmv(VideoEncodingQuality.Auto);

          // Transcode!
          MediaTranscoder transcoder = new MediaTranscoder();
          PrepareTranscodeResult result = await transcoder.PrepareFileTranscodeAsync(
                                          sourceFile, targetFile, profile);
          if (result.CanTranscode)
          {
            await result.TranscodeAsync();
          }
          else
          {
            // Check result.FailureReason: InvalidProfile, CodecNotFound, or Unknown
          }
        }
      }
    }
}
```

Trimming

To trim a file, you use `TrimStartTime` and `TrimStopTime` properties exposed by `MediaTranscoder`. The following code demonstrates:

```csharp
async Task TrimUserSelectedFile()
{
  // Get a source MP4 file from the user
  FileOpenPicker openPicker = new FileOpenPicker();
  openPicker.FileTypeFilter.Add(".mp4");
  StorageFile sourceFile = await openPicker.PickSingleFileAsync();
  if (sourceFile != null)
  {
    // Get a target MP4 file from the user
    FileSavePicker savePicker = new FileSavePicker();
    savePicker.FileTypeChoices.Add("MP4 file", new string[] { ".mp4" });
    StorageFile targetFile = await savePicker.PickSaveFileAsync();
    if (targetFile != null)
    {
      // Just use the source format
      MediaEncodingProfile profile =
        await MediaEncodingProfile.CreateFromFileAsync(sourceFile);
```

```
      MediaTranscoder transcoder = new MediaTranscoder();

      // Trim
      transcoder.TrimStartTime = TimeSpan.FromSeconds(1.5);
      transcoder.TrimStopTime = TimeSpan.FromSeconds(4);

      // Transcode!
      PrepareTranscodeResult result = await transcoder.PrepareFileTranscodeAsync(
                                        sourceFile, targetFile, profile);
      if (result.CanTranscode)
      {
        await result.TranscodeAsync();
      }
      else
      {
        // Check result.FailureReason: InvalidProfile, CodecNotFound, or Unknown
      }
    }
  }
}
```

By using a target MediaEncodingProfile that matches the source profile, the transcoding is able to be done without reencoding the content, which avoids any potential quality degradation. If you want to force the encoding for some reason, you can set MediaTranscoder's AlwaysReencode property to true. Along the lines of things that are strange to do, MediaTranscoder enables you to disable its hardware acceleration by setting HardwareAccelerationEnabled to false.

Adding Effects

MediaTranscoder exposes AddVideoEffect and AddAudioEffect methods just like MediaElement. (Although for some reason it has a method named ClearEffects rather than RemoveAllEffects. Both do the same thing.) It exposes simpler overloads that require only the string ID of the effect, if you want the effect to be required and you don't need to pass any settings. Therefore, you can replace the preceding example's two lines of trimming code with the following line of code to add video stabilization to the source video file:

```
// Apply the video stabilization effect
transcoder.AddVideoEffect(VideoEffects.VideoStabilization);
```

The ability to insert effects makes the transcoding process completely extensible for anyone who writes a media extension.

Summary

The Windows Runtime includes a lot of options for audio/video playback, capture, and transcoding. `MediaPlayer` and `CameraCaptureUI` give you a complete user experience so you can enable many tasks just like the built-in Video and Camera apps. More importantly, XAML elements such as `MediaElement` and `CaptureElement`, it's easy to seamlessly integrate any of this functionality into your apps that aren't trying to simply be a media player or camera.

I'm particularly struck by how few lines of code it is to perform transcoding. No more searching for buggy shareware programs the next time I want to convert an MP4 file to WMV! Combined with the power of the Windows file picker's extensibility, you can easily imagine scenarios such as trimming and applying video stabilization to a video you've stored on Facebook.

With `CaptureElement`, you can support a long list of scenarios that aren't supported by `CameraCaptureUI`: enabling the user to do rapid-fire capturing of successive photos, programmatically capturing photos at certain points in time, streaming the video in real-time, video-only or audio-only capture, or even simply being able to capture from the snapped state. That said, if all you need is standard photo and/or video capture for which the `CameraCaptureUI` workflow is acceptable, then by all means, use it! Users will appreciate its familiarity as well as all its standard bells and whistles.

Three topics related to audio and video are saved for later chapters: working with the user's Music and Videos library (Chapter 18, "Data"), enabling users to stream content to a device on the home network with Play To (Chapter 19, "Charms"), and enabling your app's audio to continue playing in the background (Chapter 20, "Extensions").

Chapter 13

OTHER CONTROLS

Just because the controls in this chapter mostly defy categorization, don't think that they aren't important! It's rare to find an app that doesn't at least use a `ProgressBar`, `ProgressRing`, or `ToggleSwitch` somewhere. And one control in particular—`WebView`—opens the door to a number of interesting options for constructing an app. This chapter groups the remaining controls as follows:

→ Range controls

→ Popup controls

→ A few leftovers

Range Controls

Range controls do not render arbitrary content like all the previously examined controls. Instead, a range control stores and displays a numeric value that falls within a specified range.

The core functionality of range controls comes from a `RangeBase` base class. This class defines properties of type `double` that store the current value and the endpoints of the range: `Value`, `Minimum`, and `Maximum`. It also defines a simple `ValueChanged` event.

This section examines the two major built-in range controls—`ProgressBar` and `Slider`. A `ScrollBar` control also derives from `RangeBase`, but you're unlikely to want to use it directly. Instead, you would use a `ScrollViewer`, which internally manages its `ScrollBars`.

ProgressBar

In an ideal world, you would never need to use a ProgressBar in your app. But when faced with long-running operations, showing users a ProgressBar helps them realize that progress is indeed being made. Therefore, using a ProgressBar in the right places can dramatically improve usability. (Of course, it doesn't improve usability as much as making the slow operation fast enough in the first place!) Figure 13.1 displays the default look of a ProgressBar with its Value set to 40.

FIGURE 13.1   A ProgressBar showing 40% progress

ProgressBar has a default Minimum of 0 and a default Maximum of 100. It adds only three public properties to what RangeBase already provides:

→ **IsIndeterminate**—When this is set to true, ProgressBar shows a standard horizontal "five dancing dots" animation shown in Figure 13.2 (so the values of Minimum, Maximum, and Value don't matter). This is a great feature when you have no clue how long something will take, such as waiting for something from the network. This animation is typically shown at the top of whatever region is waiting for the update.

→ **ShowError**—Displays an error state when set to true. (Oddly, this makes the control blank instead of communicating an error clearly.)

→ **ShowPaused**—Displays a paused state when set to true (which is also subtle).

FIGURE 13.2   Three snapshots of the animation performed by an indeterminate ProgressBar

 Set ProgressBar's IsIndeterminate **property back to** false **when it is not visible!**

When you use a ProgressBar, it is typically always on the relevant Page but hidden most of the time. However, even a hidden ProgressBar is still actively animating if IsIndeterminate is true, which can cause a noticeable degradation in performance! Therefore, you should always set IsIndeterminate to false when the ProgressBar is not in use.

Slider

Slider is a bit more complicated than ProgressBar because it enables users to change the current value by moving its *thumb* through the range, with any number of optional *ticks*. The default appearance of Slider (with no ticks) is shown in Figure 13.3. The ToolTip shown while dragging or hovering can be disabled by setting IsThumbToolTipEnabled to false.

Set at 40 out of 100

A `ToolTip` shows the exact value while dragging or hovering

FIGURE 13.3 Slider looks like a ProgressBar, but it has a draggable thumb (a white square under the dark theme).

Users can also tap on the slider to make the thumb jump to the tapped location, or use the up or right arrow keys to increase the value and the down or left arrow keys to decrease the value. Each KeyDown event increments or decrements the value by the amount of the SmallChange property, which is 1 by default. (Slider also has a LargeChange property inherited from RangeBase, but it is unused.)

Slider has the same default range of 0 to 100. Unlike ProgressBar, however, it defines an Orientation property (Horizontal by default). If you change the Orientation to Vertical, it looks just like the touch-optimized version of the Windows volume control slider. If you want the value to *decrease* when moving the thumb from left-to-right or bottom-to-top, you can set IsDirectionReversed to true.

Slider contains several properties for adjusting the placement and frequency of ticks. If you change TickPlacement from its default value of None, the spacing of the ticks is based on the value of TickFrequency. Figure 13.4 shows the other values of TickPlacement with a TickFrequency of 25 (using the default 0-100 range).

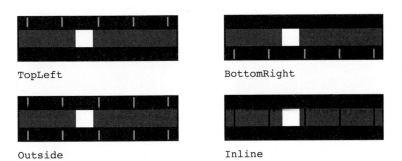

TopLeft

BottomRight

Outside

Inline

FIGURE 13.4 The values of TickPlacement (other than None), and their appearance on a horizontal Slider

The TopLeft and BottomRight values are named this way because they mean *top* and *bottom* when the Slider is horizontal, or *left* and *right* when the Slider is vertical.

By default, a Slider value changes in whole number increments. If you want to allow only coarser values, such as multiples of 5, you can set StepFrequency to a value other than its default of 1. (You could also set it to a smaller, fractional value if increments of 1 are too big.) And if you want the values to snap to ticks rather than steps, change the SnapsTo property from its default value of StepValues to Ticks.

Customizing the Current Value Display   •••

You can customize the content displayed in Slider's ToolTip by setting Slider's ThumbToolTipValueConverter to an instance of a class implementing an interface called IValueConverter (covered in Chapter 17, "Data Binding"). You must implement this yourself, but it is easy. The following simple implementation appends a " points" suffix to the number that would otherwise be displayed on its own:

```
class ToolTipValueConverter : IValueConverter
{
  public object Convert(object value, Type target, object param,
         string language)
  {
    return value + " points";
  }

  public object ConvertBack(object value, Type target, object param,
                            string language)
  {
    throw new NotImplementedException();
  }
}
```

Although the underlying ToolTip control can contain UIElements, the customization here only allows strings. If you attempt to return a UIElement from Convert, the result of its ToString method is rendered instead.

Popup Controls

The popup controls discussed in this section expose a variety of ways to float content over all the other content, giving a (mostly) "always on top" experience. There are two dialogs, a context menu, and two custom floating regions. And all but the last one are core Windows Runtime classes rather than XAML elements. Because of this, and because the one XAML element has no visuals of its own, they all look identical no matter whether the light or dark theme is used.

CoreWindowDialog

CoreWindowDialog is a title-only message box. It's what would traditionally be called a *modal dialog box* because it blocks interaction with the rest of the app until the dialog box is dismissed. Of course, this modal dialog box is more stylish and user-friendly than a desktop one, in part because it dims the rest of the app to make the situation obvious. Figure 13.5 shows what a `CoreWindowDialog` looks like when it is shown on top of an app (the multi-column `RichTextBlock` example from Chapter 10, "Text").

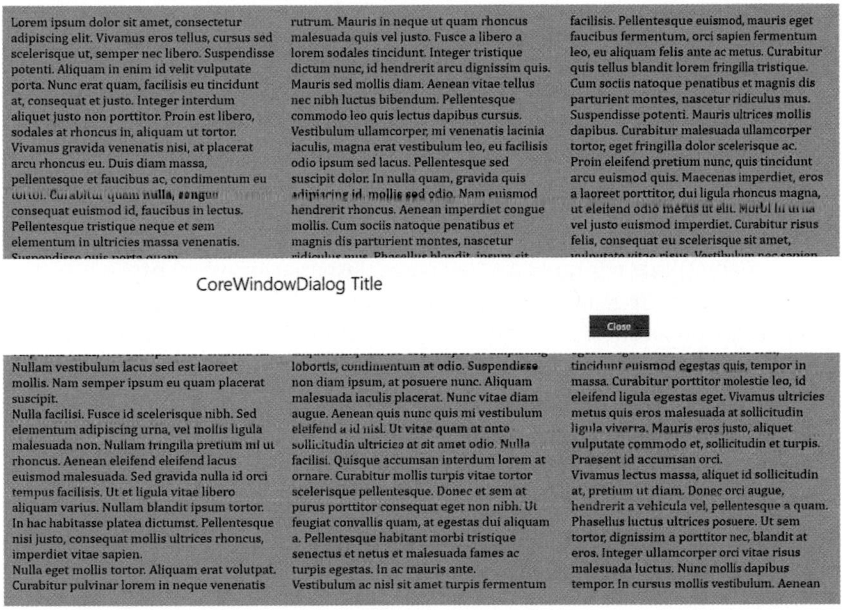

FIGURE 13.5   A `CoreWindowDialog` appears on top of the rest of the app's content.

This simple `CoreWindowDialog` was created and shown with the following helper method:

```
async Task ShowDialog()
{
  CoreWindowDialog dialog = new CoreWindowDialog("CoreWindowDialog Title");
  await dialog.ShowAsync();
}
```

Notice that the method to show the dialog (`ShowAsync`) is asynchronous. There is no synchronous version of this method, which is typical for Windows Runtime APIs. That doesn't complicate its use at all, however, thanks to the C# async and await keywords. The `ShowDialog` helper method is also made asynchronous with the async keyword, and this method `await`s the completion of `ShowAsync`, which doesn't occur until the user closes the dialog. Of course, this simple method has nothing more to do after it has been closed.

The title passed to `CoreWindowDialog`'s constructor (or later set via its `Title` property) gets trimmed with an ellipsis if needed; it never wraps. Note that the dialog does *not* have light dismiss behavior (as hinted by the dimmed area surrounding it). The user must click the `Close` button that gets included by default. `CoreWindowDialog` exposes a `Showing` event in case other parts of code want to react; however, it has no `Closing`/`Hiding` event.

CoreWindowDialog exposes a concept of custom *commands* that enable you to replace the default Close button with one to three buttons with custom labels. (If CoreWindowDialog were a XAML control, it would likely have an easy way to plug in a custom tree of UIElements. Because this is a UI-technology-agnostic Windows Runtime class, however, it needs a more formal approach for extensibility.)

To add custom commands to CoreWindowDialog, you add objects implementing the IUICommand interface to its Commands collection. IUICommand is a simple interface with three properties: a string label for the button, a delegate that is called when the button is clicked, and a generic ID that you can use to help identify commands by something other than their label (which may be localized). Note that IUICommand has no relation to the .NET-specific ICommand interface, but it is similar in spirit.

The Windows.UI.Popups namespace contains a UICommand class that implements IUICommand so you don't have to. It also contains convenience constructors that enable you to set some or all of its <properties. The following code adds three custom commands (and therefore custom buttons) to a CoreWindowDialog, with the result shown in Figure 13.6:

```
async Task ShowDialog()
{
  CoreWindowDialog dialog = new CoreWindowDialog("Do you want to save changes?");
  dialog.Commands.Add(new UICommand("Yes", OnCommand, 0));
  dialog.Commands.Add(new UICommand("No", OnCommand, 1));
  dialog.Commands.Add(new UICommand("Cancel", OnCommand, 2));
  dialog.CancelCommandIndex = 2;
  await dialog.ShowAsync();
}


void OnCommand(IUICommand command)
{
  // Handle the command here, perhaps identifying it by command.Id
}
```

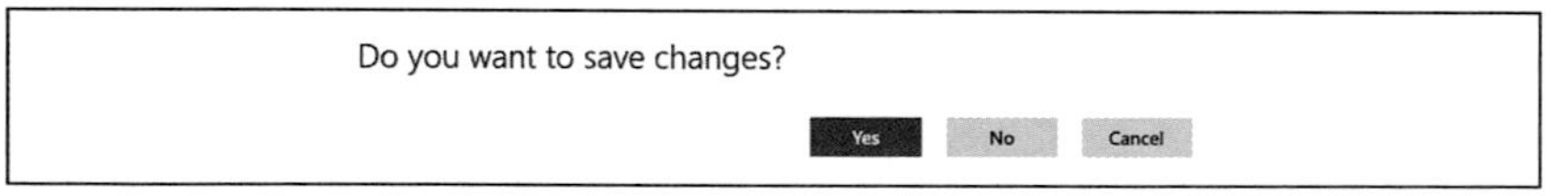

FIGURE 13.6   A common question for a CoreWindowDialog to ask, with three custom buttons enabled by three UICommands

Notice that the default Close button is nowhere to be found in Figure 13.6. It appears only when the Commands collection is empty.

This example uses 0, 1, and 2 as the IDs for the UICommands, but you can choose anything or leave them null if your code has no use for them. For example, if each UICommand uses a separate delegate, then that is already enough to distinguish which one got invoked.

When the user clicks a button, the corresponding UICommand's delegate gets invoked, and then the CoreWindowDialog automatically closes. ShowAsync returns the invoked IUICommand (actually, it returns an IAsyncOperation<IUICommand>, but the await keyword takes care of the IAsyncOperation part). Therefore, you could structure the logic without the use of any delegates:

```
async Task ShowDialog()
{
  CoreWindowDialog dialog = new CoreWindowDialog("Do you want to save changes?");
  dialog.Commands.Add(new UICommand { Label = "Yes", Id = 0 });
  dialog.Commands.Add(new UICommand { Label = "No", Id = 1 });
  dialog.Commands.Add(new UICommand { Label = "Cancel", Id = 2 });
  dialog.CancelCommandIndex = 2;
  IUICommand command = await dialog.ShowAsync();
  // Handle the command here, perhaps identifying it by command.Id
}
```

If one of your UICommands logically represents cancellation, as in Figure 13.6, you can set CoreWindowDialog's CancelCommandIndex property to the zero-based index of this UICommand. This makes the Escape key an automatic shortcut for clicking the cancel button. CoreWindowDialog also exposes a DefaultCommandIndex property (0 by default) that determines which one gets focus by default, as well as the special coloring.

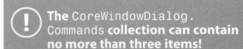 **The** CoreWindowDialog. Commands **collection can contain no more than three items!**

There is no compile-time enforcement of this, but adding any additional commands causes an exception to be thrown.

CoreWindowDialog contains special support for a *back button command* that gets rendered differently from the normal buttons. (It also doesn't count against the limit of three commands.) To enable it, you set CoreWindowDialog's BackButtonCommand property to a delegate that gets invoked when the special back button is clicked. The back button automatically appears when this property is nonnull, as shown in Figure 13.7.

FIGURE 13.7 When BackButtonCommand is set, a back button automatically appears.

Note that when the back button is clicked and the corresponding delegate is invoked, the dialog does *not* get automatically dismissed.

CoreWindowFlyout

CoreWindowFlyout is almost the same as CoreWindowDialog. Its claim to fame is

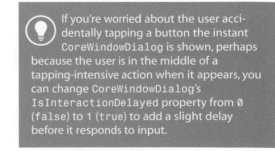 If you're worried about the user accidentally tapping a button the instant CoreWindowDialog is shown, perhaps because the user is in the middle of a tapping-intensive action when it appears, you can change CoreWindowDialog's IsInteractionDelayed property from 0 (false) to 1 (true) to add a slight delay before it responds to input.

its light dismiss behavior and its ability to be placed at a custom position. With light dismiss, the user can tap elsewhere (or press the Escape key) to close the CoreWindowFlyout, regardless of its content.

CoreWindowFlyout's API is identical to CoreWindowDialog except its constructor accepts a Point for its app-relative position and there's no CancelCommandIndex (because the user can *always* press Escape to close it). Unlike Title, there is no property to change the position after construction. There's also no settable size; it is determined by its content. Here's an example using the same options as Figure 13.7, but with the Cancel command removed:

```
async Task ShowFlyout()
{
  CoreWindowFlyout flyout = new CoreWindowFlyout(new Point(10, 10),
                                          "Do you want to save changes?");
  flyout.BackButtonCommand = OnBackButton;
  dialog.Commands.Add(new UICommand { Label = "Yes", Id = 0 });
  dialog.Commands.Add(new UICommand { Label = "No", Id = 1 });
  IUICommand command = await flyout.ShowAsync();
  …
}
```

Cancel is removed for two reasons:

1. With light dismiss, an explicit Cancel button is redundant.

2. Unlike CoreWindowDialog, CoreWindowFlyout is limited to two custom commands!

The result is shown in Figure 13.8, in context with the app content it partially covers. If the CoreWindowFlyout is dismissed without the user clicking a button, ShowAsync returns null.

The formatting of CoreWindowFlyout is a bit different from CoreWindowDialog: It doesn't dim the rest of the app but rather surrounds itself with a simple border, and its default button is rendered with the user's chosen Start screen foreground color (a tip-off that this is system-provided UI rather than XAML-based UI). Also, if its Commands collection is left empty, it renders a title with no buttons. (Again, no explicit Close button is needed due to its light dismiss behavior.)

 The CoreWindowFlyout. Commands **collection can contain no more than** *two* **items!**

Although CoreWindowDialog supports up to three buttons, CoreWindowFlyout supports only up to *two*! Again, adding any additional commands causes an exception to be thrown.

 You cannot show a CoreWindowFlyout **while another one is currently showing!**

If you attempt to do so, the call to ShowAsync throws an exception. This is true for all the classes examined in this section besides the XAML-specific Popup element, but this behavior is usually more surprising for CoreWindowFlyout (or the upcoming PopupMenu) because of its minimal screen real estate.

FIGURE 13.8   A CoreWindowFlyout appears on top of the rest of the app's content at a custom position, and it does not dim anything.

MessageDialog

MessageDialog is the Windows Runtime version of the classic message box. The only substantial difference between MessageDialog and CoreWindowDialog is that MessageDialog supports a second Content string in addition to the Title. The following code shows the MessageDialog in Figure 13.9:

```
async Task ShowDialog()
{
  MessageDialog dialog = new MessageDialog("MessageDialog Content",
                                           "MessageDialog Title");
  await dialog.ShowAsync();
}
```

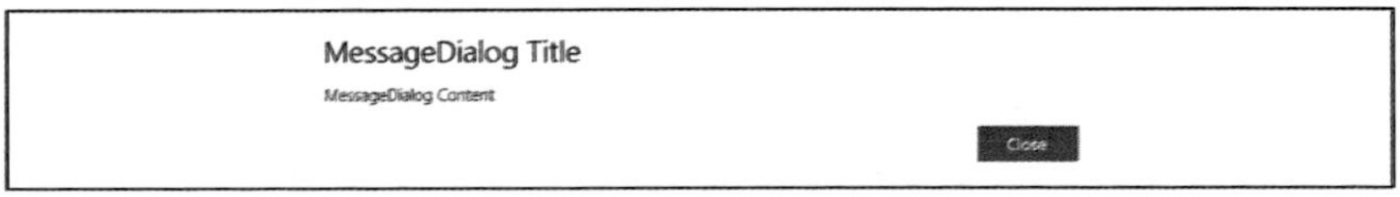

MessageDialog Title

MessageDialog Content

Close

FIGURE 13.9   MessageDialog can show text content between its title and button(s).

MessageDialog's Content property (set via its constructor in the preceding code) cannot be null. However, if you set it to an empty string, the result looks like a CoreWindowDialog. Unlike Title, which gets trimmed on a single line with an ellipsis, Content wraps. Furthermore, MessageDialog expands vertically, if needed, to fit additional lines from Content.

Just like with CoreWindowDialog, you can specify up to three custom buttons by using custom UICommands. The only remaining differences between MessageDialog and CoreWindowDialog are arbitrary:

→ MessageDialog has no BackButtonCommand property.

→ MessageDialog has no Showing event.

→ Instead of setting IsInteractionDelayed to 1, you accomplish the same thing with MessageDialog by setting its Options property to MessageDialogOptions. AcceptUserInputAfterDelay.

The MessageDialog.Commands **collection can contain no more than three items!**

This is another thing that is the same between MessageDialog and CoreWindowDialog.

PopupMenu

PopupMenu is the Windows Runtime version of a context menu. In fact, it is the same control used internally by the text controls to show commands such as Copy and Select All.

Creating a PopupMenu is simple. You construct one with its default constructor and add some UICommands to it (up to six this time). When you call ShowAsync, you give it an app-relative position. The following code demonstrates this, producing the result in Figure 13.10:

```
async Task ShowMenu()
{
  PopupMenu menu = new PopupMenu();
  menu.Commands.Add(new UICommand { Label = "[spelling suggestion #1]", Id = 0});
  menu.Commands.Add(new UICommand { Label = "[spelling suggestion #2]", Id = 1});
  menu.Commands.Add(new UICommandSeparator());
  menu.Commands.Add(new UICommand { Label = "Add to dictionary", Id = 2 });
  menu.Commands.Add(new UICommand { Label = "Ignore", Id = 3 });
  IUICommand selection = await menu.ShowAsync(new Point(10, 10));

  …
}
```

Rather than using a regular UICommand, the third item is a special UICommandSeparator object that renders as an untappable line. These are commonly used to separate commands into more understandable groups.

[spelling suggestion #1]

[spelling suggestion #2]

Add to dictionary

Ignore

net, consectetur eros tellus, cursus sed ec libero. Suspendisse id velit vulputate acilisis eu tincidunt teger interdum or. Proin est libero, quam ut tortor. Vivamus gravida venenatis nisi, at placerat arcu rhoncus eu. Duis diam massa, pellentesque et faucibus ac, condimentum eu tortor. Curabitur quam nulla, congue consequat euismod id, faucibus in lectus. Pellentesque tristique neque et sem elementum in ultricies massa venenatis. Suspendisse quis porta quam. Pellentesque fringilla placerat luctus. Sed dictum faucibus massa, vitae aliquet urna porta at. Pellentesque id nisl nec dui iaculis euismod quis id ligula. Duis hendrerit tortor vel turpis ornare hendrerit. Proin varius vulputate risus, nec suscipit dolor eleifend id. Nullam vestibulum lacus sed est laoreet mollis. Nam semper ipsum eu quam placerat suscipit. Nulla facilisi. Fusce id scelerisque nibh. Sed elementum adipiscing urna, vel mollis ligula malesuada non. Nullam fringilla pretium mi ut rhoncus. Aenean eleifend eleifend lacus euismod malesuada. Sed gravida nulla id orci tempus facilisis. Ut et ligula vitae libero aliquam varius. Nullam blandit ipsum tortor. In hac habitasse platea dictumst. Pellentesque nisi justo, consequat mollis ultrices rhoncus, imperdiet vitae sapien. Nulla eget mollis tortor. Aliquam erat volutpat. Curabitur pulvinar lorem in neque venenatis

rutrum. Mauris in neque ut quam rhoncus malesuada quis vel justo. Fusce a libero a lorem sodales tincidunt. Integer tristique dictum nunc, id hendrerit arcu dignissim quis. Mauris sed mollis diam. Aenean vitae tellus nec nibh luctus bibendum. Pellentesque commodo leo quis lectus dapibus cursus. Vestibulum ullamcorper, mi venenatis lacinia iaculis, magna erat vestibulum leo, eu facilisis odio ipsum sed lacus. Pellentesque sed suscipit dolor. In nulla quam, gravida quis adipiscing id, mollis sed odio. Nam euismod hendrerit rhoncus. Aenean imperdiet congue mollis. Cum sociis natoque penatibus et magnis dis parturient montes, nascetur ridiculus mus. Phasellus blandit, ipsum sit amet interdum posuere, est enim elementum metus, vel malesuada nunc nunc sed est. Maecenas odio ligula, blandit a tempor ut, porta vitae dolor. Praesent rhoncus luctus risus. Aliquam scelerisque porta magna vel aliquet. Aliquam leo est, tempor ac adipiscing lobortis, condimentum at odio. Suspendisse non diam ipsum, at posuere nunc. Aliquam malesuada iaculis placerat. Nunc vitae diam augue. Aenean quis nunc quis mi vestibulum eleifend a id nisl. Ut vitae quam at ante sollicitudin ultricies at sit amet odio. Nulla facilisi. Quisque accumsan interdum lorem at ornare. Curabitur mollis turpis vitae tortor scelerisque pellentesque. Donec et sem at purus porttitor consequat eget non nibh. Ut feugiat convallis quam, at egestas dui aliquam a. Pellentesque habitant morbi tristique senectus et netus et malesuada fames ac turpis egestas. In ac mauris ante. Vestibulum ac nisl sit amet turpis fermentum

facilisis. Pellentesque euismod, mauris eget faucibus fermentum, orci sapien fermentum leo, eu aliquam felis ante ac metus. Curabitur quis tellus blandit lorem fringilla tristique. Cum sociis natoque penatibus et magnis dis parturient montes, nascetur ridiculus mus. Suspendisse potenti. Mauris ultrices mollis dapibus. Curabitur malesuada ullamcorper tortor, eget fringilla dolor scelerisque ac. Proin eleifend pretium nunc, quis tincidunt arcu euismod quis. Maecenas imperdiet, eros a laoreet porttitor, dui ligula rhoncus magna, ut eleifend odio metus ut elit. Morbi in urna vel justo euismod imperdiet. Curabitur risus felis, consequat eu scelerisque sit amet, vulputate vitae risus. Vestibulum nec sapien lacus, vel sodales orci. Mauris malesuada dolor non nunc tristique sed ornare justo accumsan. Donec ante leo, euismod vel volutpat venenatis, vehicula et nibh. Donec arcu tortor, adipiscing sit amet hendrerit ac, egestas eget nunc. Praesent felis erat tincidunt euismod egestas quis, tempor in massa. Curabitur porttitor molestie leo, id eleifend ligula egestas eget. Vivamus ultricies metus quis eros malesuada at sollicitudin ligula viverra. Mauris eros justo, aliquet vulputate commodo et, sollicitudin et turpis. Praesent id accumsan erat. Vivamus lectus massa, aliquet id sollicitudin at, pretium ut diam. Donec orci augue, hendrerit a vehicula vel, pellentesque a quam. Phasellus luctus ultrices posuere. Ut sem tortor, dignissim a porttitor nec, blandit at eros. Integer ullamcorper orci vitae risus malesuada luctus. Nunc mollis dapibus tempor. In cursus mollis vestibulum. Aenean

FIGURE 13.10   A PopupMenu appears on top of the rest of the app's content at a custom position, and it does not dim anything.

PopupMenu doesn't dim the rest of the app's content, and it has light dismiss behavior (with `ShowAsync` returning `null` in that situation). It also auto-dismisses whenever a selection is made. Therefore, PopupMenu is like `CoreWindowFlyout`, but with no `Title` and with a different treatment for its commands (in style, layout, and number). This makes it considerably simpler, because `Commands` is its only property.

In addition to `ShowAsync`, PopupMenu has two overloads of a Show**ForSelection**Async method that enable you to pass a `Rect` representing an area you want the PopupMenu to appear adjacent to (but not covering). In other words, this enables the ideal placement of a context menu, where the passed-in `Rect` represents the selection that was right-tapped. The simpler overload centers the PopupMenu horizontally relative to the selection and places it directly above it (space permitting). The other overload enables you to specify a preferred placement (`Above`, `Below`, `Left`, or `Right`).

 The `PopupMenu.Commands` **collection can contain no more than six items!**

This is an odd limitation, because the items could have easily become scrollable, but it is a limitation nonetheless.

Popup

A `Popup` is a regular `UIElement` that can float on top of other elements. It doesn't have any visual appearance by itself, but it can contain any `System.Object` as the value of its `Child` property, much like a content control. Besides there being no restrictions on a Popup's content, there is no restriction on the number of Popups you can show simultaneously (just as with other UIElements). This makes it the most flexible out of all the popup controls. Popups are internally leveraged to make properly attached ToolTips and AppBars overlay the rest of a Page's content.

Figure 13.11 demonstrates the behavior of the Popup in the following Page:

```
<Page …>
  <Grid Width="420" Height="420">
    <!-- Inner Grid with a Button-in-Popup and a separate Button -->
    <Grid Background="Red" Margin="100">
      <Popup IsOpen="True">
        <Button Content="Button in Popup in Grid" Background="Blue"/>
      </Popup>
      <Button Content="Button in Grid" Height="200" Canvas.ZIndex="100"/>
    </Grid>
    <!-- A Rectangle that overlaps the inner Grid underneath it -->
    <Rectangle Width="200" Height="200" Fill="Lime"
               HorizontalAlignment="Left" VerticalAlignment="Top"/>
  </Grid>
</Page>
```

There are four interesting things to note about Figure 13.11:

→ A Popup is visible only when its IsOpen property is set to true. (It is false by default.) It raises separate Opened and Closed events when the value of IsOpen changes.

→ A Popup renders in the top-left corner of its parent by default (the red Grid in this example). You can move it by giving it a Margin and/or setting its HorizontalOffset and VerticalOffset properties.

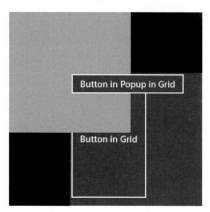

FIGURE 13.11 The Popup's content is placed in the top-left corner of its parent, but renders on top of all other elements.

→ The layout inside a Popup is like the layout inside a Canvas; a child element is given only the exact amount of space it needs.

→ Popups have a unique power: Despite being a regular UIElement, it can render on top of all other elements on the Page. Although the sibling Button in Figure 13.11 has a larger ZIndex, and although the lime Rectangle is a sibling to the Popup's *parent* (making it the Popup's *uncle*?), it appears on top of both of them!

Only three types of things can render on top of a `Popup`:

→ Another `Popup`. This includes properly attached `ToolTips` and `AppBars`, because `Popups` are used as an implementation detail. Multiple `Popups` are rendered based solely on where they are placed in the tree (with later ones on top of earlier ones); marking them with `Canvas.ZIndex` has no effect.

→ A `WebView` control (described at the end of this chapter).

→ Shell-provided UI that can overlap your page: the charms bar, app switcher, the software keyboard, notifications, and the Windows Runtime popup classes (`CoreWindowDialog`, `CoreWindowFlyout`, `MessageDialog`, and `PopupMenu`).

By default, a `Popup` opens only when `IsOpen` is explicitly set to `true` and closes only when `IsOpen` is explicitly set to `false`. However, you can set its `IsLightDismissEnabled` property to `true` to make it automatically close the next time focus changes to a different element. (Note that the `Popup` doesn't need to have focus in the first place. Any focus change can trigger dismissal as long as focus isn't given to the `Popup`.)

In contrast, the Windows Runtime popup classes are able to render on top of *any* XAML content (even `Popups`, `ToolTips`, `AppBars`, and `WebViews`).

One interesting characteristic of `Popup` is that you can create and show one without ever attaching it to a parent element. Every other `UIElement` requires being explicitly attached in some fashion, but `Popup` has internal logic to attach to the root `Frame` if it doesn't already have a parent. The following code in a `Page`'s constructor demonstrates this:

```
public MainPage()
{
  InitializeComponent();

  Popup popup = new Popup();
  popup.Child = new Button { … };
  popup.IsOpen = true; // Show without explicitly attaching it to anything
}
```

As a result of this code, the `Button` inside the `Popup` is rendered on top of the app's top-left corner. Note that such `Frame`-rooted popups do not move with the rest of the `Page` whenever the software keyboard automatically pushes the `Page` upward.

A Few More Controls

To conclude this chapter, we'll look at three more controls that share no common theme:

→ `ProgressRing`

→ `ToggleSwitch`

→ `WebView`

ProgressRing

Conceptually, ProgressRing is a version of ProgressBar that is always indeterminate and has a different default style. It uses the same five dancing dots as ProgressBar with IsIndeterminate=true, but they chase each other in a circle rather than moving in a horizontal line. ProgressRing doesn't render anything by default, so to make it animate, you must set IsActive to true. (This is the analog to ProgressBar's IsIndeterminate property.)

Figure 13.12 captures a single point in the animation, which doesn't look much like a ring. When they are in motion, however, the ring is clear.

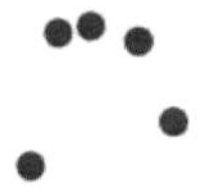

FIGURE 13.12   ProgressRing animates its five dots in a circular pattern.

Unlike ProgressBar, ProgressRing isn't a range control because its indeterminate nature has no need for a range.

You can use either ProgressRing or an indeterminate ProgressBar for the same situations. A ProgressRing is typically used for the initial *loading* of content, when there's not much on the screen to interfere with. For example, a ProgressRing is often used when simulating an extended splash screen during an application's launch. An indeterminate ProgressBar is usually preferable when *refreshing* content already on the screen, because its compact form doesn't get in the way.

> (!) **Set ProgressRing's IsActive property to false when it is not visible!**
>
> Just like with an indeterminate ProgressBar, a hidden ProgressRing is still actively animating if IsActive is true, which can cause a noticeable degradation in performance.

ToggleSwitch

Logically, ToggleSwitch is like a ToggleButton or its more well-known derived CheckBox control, just with a different default appearance that makes it look like a light switch, and with support for only two states (no indeterminate state). Figure 13.13 shows a simple ToggleSwitch with no properties set. The user can turn a ToggleSwitch on and off by tapping it or dragging the thumb.

Off by default

On, after user interaction

FIGURE 13.13   The ToggleSwitch is like a light switch that can be on or off.

ToggleSwitch exposes a Boolean `IsOn` property and raises a simple `Toggled` event when the value of `IsOn` changes.

Because a `ToggleSwitch` usually needs some sort of label that explains what is being turned on or off, it exposes a `Header` property that is formatted consistently with toggle switches used by the Windows shell. You can even customize the "On" and "Off" labels by setting the `OnContent` and/or `OffContent` properties. For example, the following `ToggleSwitch` is shown in Figure 13.14:

```
<ToggleSwitch Header="Show high scores" OnContent="Yes" OffContent="No"/>
```

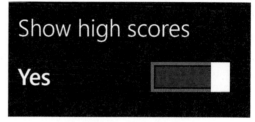

FIGURE 13.14   ToggleSwitch can have a custom header and custom on/off labels.

The `Header`, `OnContent`, and `OffContent` properties are all of type `System.Object`, so they each support the same content-rendering scheme as content controls. You could set them to custom `UIElements` instead of simple text. Or, you could set them to nonvisual data objects and use separate `HeaderTemplate`, `OnContentTemplate`, and `OffContentTemplate` properties to style them using the techniques of Chapter 16, "Styles, Templates, and Visual States."

`ToggleSwitches` are the preferred control to use for Boolean app settings rather than `CheckBoxes`. You can see them used throughout the Windows shell, such as the "Airplane mode" switch in the Networks pane, or in just about every section of the PC Settings app.

WebView

The `WebView` control is what is traditionally called a *web browser control*. It hosts HTML content, either from a URL or a string containing HTML, using the same rendering engine and JavaScript engine used by Internet Explorer. Figure 13.15 shows the following `Page` filled with a `WebView` whose `Source` (of type `System.Uri`) is set to `http://bing.com`:

```
<Page …>
  <WebView Name="webView" Source="http://bing.com"/>
</Page>
```

FIGURE 13.15   WebView with a URL Source (bing.com)

Figure 13.16 shows the same Page, but with the following code in its constructor that navigates to a literal HTML string, somewhat like the RTF string example in Chapter 10:

```
public MainPage()
{
  InitializeComponent();

  webView.NavigateToString(
    "<span style='font-size:195px;background:yellow'>" +
    "This is <i>much</i> <b>simpler</b> than RTF!");
}
```

The HTML is intentionally malformed to show that the control is as resilient as Internet Explorer (because it basically is Internet Explorer). The reason for the WebView name rather than WebBrowser is that the control doesn't have any of the basic features that any Web browser would have, such as a URL box, a progress indicator, or Back/Stop/Refresh buttons. It also doesn't show URL tooltips when hovering over a link. You could, of course, build a nice browser that leverages WebView to do all the hard work.

WebView also has a Navigate method that takes a Uri. Calling it is identical to setting the Source property. Every navigation either results in a LoadCompleted event being raised when successful or a NavigationFailed event being raised upon failure.

When a user taps normal links (http and https), the WebView navigates to the page like a Web browser. When the user taps a link with a different protocol (such as mailto, ftp, or a custom protocol registered by another app), the correct user-prompt and then app-launch behavior occurs.

> 💡 You can load HTML files packaged with your app by using a Uri with the ms-appx-web scheme. Although you can't give WebView a Uri pointing to a file in your application data folder, you can manually fetch the file, obtain its content as a string, and then call WebView's NavigateToString method. See Chapter 18, "Data," for information about working with files.

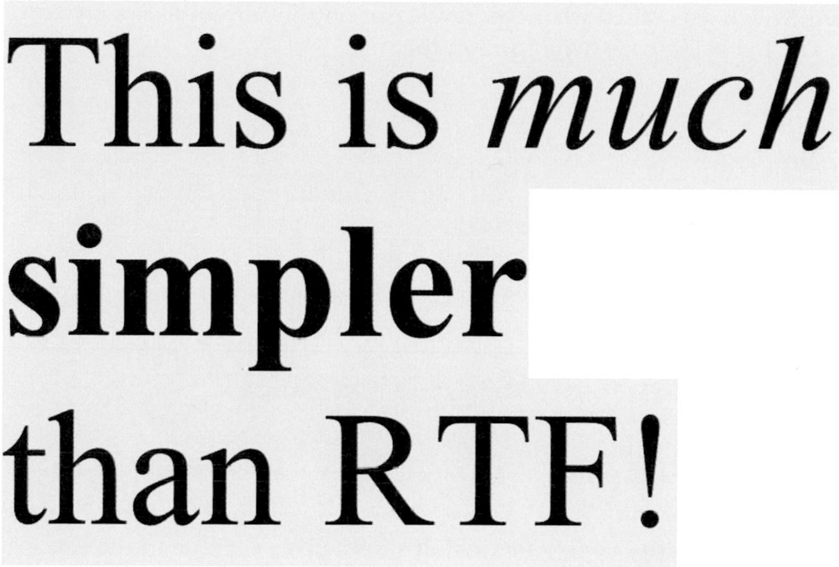

This is *much* simpler than RTF!

FIGURE 13.16   `WebView` navigated to a custom HTML `string`

`WebView` has a big limitation that is important to be aware of. Because its rendering isn't native to XAML, it can't have transforms (other than translation) or projections applied, nor does it blend with other `UIElements`. It always renders on top of all other elements, including all `Popups`, `ToolTips`, and `AppBars`! The only thing that can render on top is the list of shell-provided UI mentioned previously: the charms bar, app switcher, the software keyboard, notifications, and the Windows Runtime popup classes.

`WebView` makes it possible to build a "hybrid" app that uses HTML and CSS for its user interface and C# (plus small amounts of JavaScript) for its logic. You can easily fill the `WebView` with custom HTML, but to react to user input within the HTML content, you must write some JavaScript that can communicate back to the XAML `Page` hosting the `WebView`. You can do this by handling `WebView`'s

If you want to give the *appearance* of rendering `UIElements` on top of a `WebView`, there is a workaround. You can temporarily swap the `WebView` with an element filled with a `WebView`**Brush**. Such an element would not be interactive, nor would it automatically update if the HTML content changes, but it can suffice for many scenarios. `WebViewBrush` is covered in the next chapter.

Navigating to Web pages can cause JavaScript runtime exceptions to be thrown!

Because there are some differences in the environment presented to the JavaScript engine compared to Internet Explorer (for example, there is no `alert` function defined by default when browsing with `WebView`), you can easily encounter such exceptions while debugging your app. Although this can be annoying during debugging, it doesn't impact your app (unless the failing script is important for the behavior of the Web page).

ScriptNotify event, which gets raised whenever JavaScript on the current page calls external.notify. The following code demonstrates this:

```
public MainPage()
{
  InitializeComponent();

  webView.ScriptNotify += WebView_ScriptNotify;

  webView.NavigateToString("<script>external.notify('gotcha!')</script>");
}

void WebView_ScriptNotify(object sender, Noti fyEventArgs e)
{
  // When this gets called, e.Value == "gotcha!"
}
```

If a value is passed to the JavaScript notify method, it shows up as e.Value in the C# event handler.

 You must explicitly allow Web pages accessed via URL to raise the ScriptNotify **event!**

The simple ScriptNotify example works as-is because the HTML content is local to the app. If the current page comes from a URL, however, you must give it permission to raise the event by adding the URL to WebView's AllowedScriptNotifyUris property of type IList<Uri>. If your app uses multiple WebViews, you can give it permission for *any* instance of WebView by adding it to its static AnyScriptNotifyUri property instead. Note that despite the lack of an "s" at the end of its name, AnyScriptNotifyUri is also an IList<Uri>.

This requirement applies to any URL, even from the intranet. The entry in AllowedScriptNotifyUris (or AnyScriptNotifyUri) doesn't need to be an exact match; its domain (scheme, host, and port) are compared with the current content. These properties also support wildcard syntax, so you can trust all pages if necessary.

Summary

You've now seen all the major built-in controls that can be used for creating a wide variety of user interfaces. Although you can radically change the *look* of these controls by using the techniques discussed in Chapter 16, the core *behavior* described in this part of the book remains the same.

The suite of built-in controls will continue to be enhanced by additional toolkits that ship independently, some free and some not. For example, Microsoft's Tim Heuer has created a toolkit called Callisto (http://github.com/timheuer/callisto) that includes XAML controls for many noticeable omissions from the XAML UI Framework: `Rating`, `DatePicker`, `TimePicker`, a XAML-based `Flyout`, and much more. Telerik (http://telerik.com) sells a suite of controls (with separate but matching implementations for XAML and HTML) that includes `Chart`, `Gauge`, `NumericBox`, and `AutoCompleteBox`.

Chapter 14

VECTOR GRAPHICS

Vector graphics have been a focal point of XAML since its inception. Life becomes so much easier when your app's assets scale perfectly to any size. If you create an app that solely uses vector graphics rather than images and videos, you can avoid creating and packaging all those file variations discussed in Chapter 11, "Images," for everything except your tile and splash screen images. In addition, the automatic ability for vector graphics to be dynamic means you can trivially modify them for special situations or user customizations (such as changing colors).

Other than the media controls from Chapter 11, the built-in controls all leverage vector graphics for their own visuals. There are many ways you can leverage vector graphics for your own custom controls or artwork within your app. A number of XAML elements provide powerful options, and tools such as Blend make it easy to create sophisticated content.

This chapter focuses on the three important data types for vector graphics: Shape, Geometry, and Brush. Brushes are a vital part of all the topics in this chapter, and they have been used throughout the book for mundane tasks such as setting a control's Foreground and Background. There are many different feature-rich Brushes, which is why they deserve a dedicated section.

Shapes

A Shape is a 2D vector-based drawing that can be placed anywhere that any other element can be placed. For example, Chapter 2, "Mastering XAML," shows how easy it is to embed a square in a Button by using Rectangle (which derives from Shape):

```
<Button>
  <Rectangle Height="10" Width="10" Fill="White"/>
</Button>
```

Six classes derive from Shape:

- → Rectangle
- → Ellipse
- → Line
- → Polyline
- → Polygon
- → Path

Although Shape itself can't be used in XAML, it defines many properties for controlling the appearance of its subclasses. The two most important ones are Fill and Stroke, both of type Brush. It also defines a Stretch property that acts just like Viewbox's and Image's Stretch properties, so you can customize how it reacts if it is given more space than it would naturally have. Although Shape is a UIElement and therefore supports RenderTransform, it also defines its own GeometryTransform property that enables applying the same Transform(s) to its internal geometry instead of (or an addition to) Transform(s) to the element itself. Unlike RenderTransform, GeometryTransform impacts the layout size of the element. The rest of Shape's properties are all related to customizing its Stroke, and are covered later in the "Getting Fancy with Strokes" section.

Rectangle

Rectangle doesn't define a special Size or Bounds property; it leverages the familiar XAML layout system for controlling its size and position. For example, you could set the size of a Rectangle with its Width and Height properties (among others) inherited from FrameworkElement, and set its location using Canvas.Left and Canvas.Top if it's inside a Canvas.

Rectangle, however, defines its own RadiusX and RadiusY properties of type double that enable you to give it rounded corners. Figure 14.1 shows the following Rectangles in a StackPanel with various values of RadiusX and RadiusY:

```
<StackPanel>
  <Rectangle Width="200" Height="100"
    Fill="Orange" Stroke="Black" StrokeThickness="10" Margin="4"/>
  <Rectangle Width="200" Height="100" RadiusX="10" RadiusY="30"
    Fill="Orange" Stroke="Black" StrokeThickness="10" Margin="4"/>
  <Rectangle Width="200" Height="100" RadiusX="30" RadiusY="10"
    Fill="Orange" Stroke="Black" StrokeThickness="10" Margin="4"/>
  <Rectangle Width="200" Height="100" RadiusX="100" RadiusY="50"
    Fill="Orange" Stroke="Black" StrokeThickness="10" Margin="4"/>
</StackPanel>
```

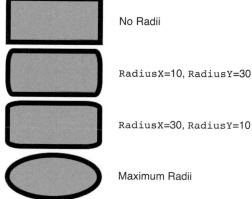

No Radii

RadiusX=10, RadiusY=30

RadiusX=30, RadiusY=10

Maximum Radii

FIGURE 14.1   Four Rectangles with different values for RadiusX and RadiusY

RadiusX can be at most half the Width of the Rectangle, and RadiusY can be at most half the Height. Setting them any higher makes no difference.

 You must explicitly set Stroke **or** Fill **for a** Shape **to be seen!**

Both Stroke and Fill are both set to null by default, which makes the Shape invisible (and unhittable by pointer input).

Ellipse

After discovering the flexibility of Rectangle and realizing that it can be made to look like an ellipse (or circle), you'd think that a separate Ellipse class would be redundant. And you'd be right! All Ellipse does is make it easier to get an elliptical shape. It defines no settable properties above and beyond what Shape and its base classes provide. Ellipse simply fills its rectangular region with the largest possible elliptical shape.

The following Ellipse could replace the last Rectangle in the previous XAML snippet, and Figure 14.1 would look identical:

```
<Ellipse Width="200" Height="100"
  Fill="Orange" Stroke="Black" StrokeThickness="10" Margin="4"/>
```

The only change is replacing the element name and removing the references to RadiusX and RadiusY.

Line

Line defines four double properties to represent a line segment connecting points (*x1*,*y1*) and (*x2*,*y2*). These properties are called X1, Y1, X2, and Y2. These are defined as four sepa-rate properties rather than two Point properties for ease of use in data-binding scenarios.

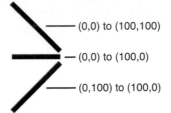

(0,0) to (100,100)

(0,0) to (100,0)

(0,100) to (100,0)

The values of Line's properties are not absolute coordinates. They are relative to the space given to the Line element by the layout system. For example, the following StackPanel contains three Lines, rendered in Figure 14.2:

FIGURE 14.2   Three Lines in a StackPanel, demonstrating that their coordinates are relative

```
<StackPanel>
    <Line X1="0" Y1="0"    X2="100" Y2="100" Stroke="Black" StrokeThickness="10"
      Margin="4"/>
    <Line X1="0" Y1="0"    X2="100" Y2="0"   Stroke="Black" StrokeThickness="10"
      Margin="4"/>
    <Line X1="0" Y1="100" X2="100" Y2="0"   Stroke="Black" StrokeThickness="10"
      Margin="4"/>
</StackPanel>
```

Notice that each Line is given the space needed by its bounding box, so the horizontal line gets only 10 pixels (for the thickness of its Stroke) plus the speci-fied Margin. Line inherits Shape's Fill property, but it is meaningless because there is never any area to fill.

Polyline

Polyline represents a sequence of lines, expressed in its Points property (a collection of Point objects). The follow-ing four Polylines are rendered in Figure 14.3:

FIGURE 14.3   Four Polylines, ranging from 2 to 5 points

```
<StackPanel>
    <Polyline Points="0,0 100,100" Stroke="Black" StrokeThickness="10" Margin="4"/>
    <Polyline Points="0,0 100,100 200,0" Stroke="Black" StrokeThickness="10"
      Margin="4"/>
```

```
<Polyline Points="0,0 100,100 200,0 300,100" Stroke="Black" StrokeThickness="10"
    Margin="4"/>
<Polyline Points="0,0 100,100 200,0 300,100 100,100" Stroke="Black"
    StrokeThickness="10" Margin="4"/>
</StackPanel>
```

In XAML, `Points` can be specified as a simple list of alternating *x* and *y* values. The commas can help with readability but are optional. You can place commas between any two values or use no commas at all.

Figure 14.4 demonstrates that setting `Polyline`'s `Fill` fills it as if a line segment connects the first `Point` with the last `Point`. Figure 14.4 was created by taking the `Polyline`s from Figure 14.3 and marking them with `Fill="Orange"`.

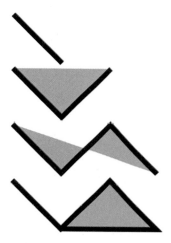

FIGURE 14.4 The same `Polyline`s from Figure 14.3, but with an explicit `Fill`

Polygon

Just as `Rectangle` makes `Ellipse` redundant, `Polyline` makes `Polygon` redundant. The only difference between `Polyline` and `Polygon` is that `Polygon` automatically adds a visible line segment connecting the first `Point` and last `Point` if one doesn't already exist.

If you take each `Polyline` from Figure 14.4 and change each element name to `Polygon`, you get the result shown in Figure 14.5. Notice that the initial line segment in the first and last `Polygon`s is noticeably longer than in Figure 14.4. This is due to `Miter` corners joining the initial line segment with the final line segment (which happens to share the same coordinates), which would extend infinitely if not for a `StrokeMiterLimit` property limiting it to 10 pixels. `Miter` and `StrokeMiterLimit` are examined in the upcoming "Getting Fancy with Strokes" section.

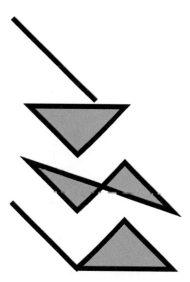

FIGURE 14.5 `Polygon`s are just like `Polyline`s, except that they always form a closed shape.

Path

All the preceding shapes are just special cases of a powerful shape called `Path`. `Path` adds only a single `Data` property to `Shape`, which can be set to an instance of any geometry, for example:

```
<Path StrokeThickness="10" Fill="Red">
  <Path.Data>
    <RectangleGeometry Rect="0,0,100,100"/>
  </Path.Data>
</Path>
```

Geometries are covered in the next section. First, let's look at a number of ways to alter the appearance of any shape's strokes.

Getting Fancy with Strokes

We've already seen examples of setting the `Stroke` property on shapes, but the `Shape` class defines a number of other stroke-related properties. One simple one is `StrokeThickness` of type `double` (with a default value of 1). But that's not all:

→ **StrokeStartLineCap** and **StrokeEndLineCap**—Customize any open segment endpoints with a value from the `PenLineCap` enumeration: `Flat` (the default), `Square`, `Round`, or `Triangle`. For any endpoints that join two segments, you can customize their appearance with `StrokeLineJoin` instead.

→ **StrokeLineJoin**—Affects corners with a value from the `PenLineJoin` enumeration: `Miter` (the default), `Round`, or `Bevel`. A separate **StrokeMiterLimit** property (with a default value of `10`) can be used to limit how far a `Miter` join extends, which can otherwise be very large for small angles. For example, the angle between the two segments back in Figure 14.5 is 0°, which is why `StrokeMiterLimit` kicks in.

→ **StrokeDashArray**—Can make the stroke a nonsolid line. It can be set to a pattern of numbers that represents the widths of dashes and the spaces between them. The odd values represent the widths (relative to `StrokeThickness`) of dashes, and the even values represent the relative widths of spaces. Whatever pattern you choose is then repeated indefinitely. A separate `double` **StrokeDashOffset** property controls where the pattern begins.

→ **StrokeDashCap**—Customizes both endpoints of each dash. This works just like `StrokeStartLineCap` and `StrokeEndLineCap`, with the same default value of `Flat`.

 What's the difference between `PenLineCap`'s `Flat` **and** `Square` **values?**

A `Flat` line cap ends exactly on the endpoint, whereas a `Square` line cap extends beyond the endpoint. Much like the `Round` line cap, you can imagine a square with the same dimensions as the `StrokeThickness` centered on the endpoint. Therefore, the line ends up extending *half* the length of the `StrokeThickness`.

Figure 14.6 shows each of the PenLineCap values applied to a Line's StrokeStartLineCap and StrokeEndLineCap. Figure 14.7 demonstrates each of the LineJoin values on the corners of a triangle.

Flat

Square

Round

Triangle

FIGURE 14.6   Each type of PenLineCap on both ends of a Line

Miter   Round   Bevel

FIGURE 14.7   Each type of LineJoin applied to a triangle

Figure 14.8 shows a few different StrokeDashArray values combined with some StrokeDashCap values.

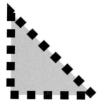 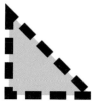 

StrokeDashArray="1,1"   StrokeDashArray="2,1"   StrokeDashArray="5,1,1,1"

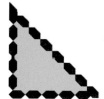 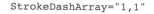 

StrokeDashArray="1,1"   StrokeDashArray="0,1"
StrokeDashCap="Triangle"   StrokeDashCap="Triangle"

FIGURE 14.8   The effects of StrokeDashArray

The values of StrokeDashArray can be confusing when StrokeDashCap is set to anything other than its default Flat value. That's because it makes each dash is naturally wider when given the same numeric value as a space. Giving a dash a width of 0, as done in the rightmost triangle in Figure 14.8, is a common practice to make each dash consist solely of its starting and ending cap. This is especially confusing if you use a StrokeDashCap of

Square, because you need different values to get results that look the same when using
Flat. For example, marking a Shape with:

StrokeDashArray="0,2" StrokeDashCap="Square"

gives almost identical results as:

StrokeDashArray="1,1" StrokeDashCap="Flat"

which is what is used by the leftmost triangle in Figure 14.8.

> **! Overuse of Shapes can lead to performance problems!**
> It's tempting to use Shapes as the building blocks for any 2D drawings. However, when you
> have Shape-based artwork, *every* Shape individually supports styles, data binding, resources,
> layout, input and focus, routed events, and so on. This is typically unnecessary overhead. Ask your-
> self whether you really need vector graphics if you find yourself using a large number of Shapes,
> or if you could get away with a single Image instead.

Geometries

A Geometry is not a visual element like Shape, but rather the simplest possible abstract
representation of a shape or path.

Geometry has a number of subclasses:

→ **RectangleGeometry**—Has a Rect property for defining its dimensions.

→ **EllipseGeometry**—Has RadiusX and RadiusY properties, plus a Center property.

→ **LineGeometry**—Has StartPoint and EndPoint properties to define a line segment.

→ **PathGeometry**—Contains a collection of PathFigure objects in its Figures content
property; a general-purpose Geometry.

→ **GeometryGroup**—Contains a collection of geometries.

These should look familiar, because they mirror the Shape classes. So what's the point of
having these separate Geometry classes? You can build up and combine arbitrary geometries to form a complex shape and set it as the content of a single Path element, which
has less overhead than using multiple Shapes. Furthermore, there are other scenarios for
which the abstract representation of a shape comes in handy. All UIElements have a Clip
property that can be set to an instance of a RectangleGeometry to describe the visual clipping. (Granted, this property could have been a simple Rect instead, but other XAML-
based frameworks enable clipping by arbitrary geometries.) Also, these geometry classes
are used internally by the various Shape classes. (Polyline and Polygon are simple abstrac-
tions over a PathGeometry.)

Because Geometry is not a UIElement, it does not inherit a RenderTransform property. Instead, it exposes its own Transform property. (This is the same as the GeometryTransform property exposed by Shape for its internal Geometry.)

Just as all basic Shapes can be represented as a Path, the first three geometries are just special cases of PathGeometry provided for convenience. You can express any rectangle, ellipse, or line segment in terms of a PathGeometry. So, let's dig a little more into the components of the powerful PathGeometry class.

PathFigures and PathSegments

Each PathFigure in a PathGeometry contains one or more connected PathSegments in its Segments content property. A PathSegment is a straight or curvy line segment, represented by one of seven derived classes:

→ **LineSegment**—A line segment (of course!)

→ **PolyLineSegment**—A shortcut for a connected sequence of LineSegments

→ **ArcSegment**—A segment that curves along the circumference of an imaginary ellipse

→ **BezierSegment**—A cubic Bézier curve

→ **PolyBezierSegment**—A shortcut for a connected sequence of BezierSegments

→ **QuadraticBezierSegment**—A quadratic Bézier curve

→ **PolyQuadraticBezierSegment**—A shortcut for a connected sequence of QuadraticBezierSegments

Bézier Curves

Bézier curves (named after engineer Pierre Bézier) are commonly used in computer graphics for representing smooth curves. Bézier curves are even used by fonts to mathematically describe curves in their glyphs.

The basic idea is that in addition to two endpoints, a Bézier curve has one or more *control points* that give the line segment its curve. These control points are not visible (and not necessarily on the curve itself) but rather are used as input to a formula that dictates where each point on the curve exists. Intuitively, each control point acts like a center of gravity, so the line segment appears to be "pulled" toward these points.

Despite the scarier-sounding name, QuadraticBezierSegment is simpler than BezierSegment and computationally cheaper. A quadratic Bézier curve has only one control point, whereas a cubic Bézier curve has two. Therefore, a quadratic Bézier curve can form only a *U*-like shape (or a straight line), but a cubic Bézier curve can also take the form of an *S*-like shape.

The following `Path` contains a `PathGeometry` with two simple `LineSegments` that create the *L* shape in Figure 14.9:

```
<Path Stroke="Black" StrokeThickness="10">
  <Path.Data>
    <PathGeometry>
      <PathFigure>
        <LineSegment Point="0,100"/>
        <LineSegment Point="100,100"/>
      </PathFigure>
    </PathGeometry>
  </Path.Data>
</Path>
```

Notice that the definition for each LineSegment includes only a single

FIGURE 14.9   A Path that contains a pair of LineSegments

Point. That's because it implicitly connects the previous point to the current one. The first `LineSegment` connects the default starting point of (0,0) to (0,100), and the second `LineSegment` connects (0,100) to (100,100). (The other six `PathSegments` act the same way.) If you want to provide a custom starting point, you can set `PathFigure`'s `StartPoint` property to a `Point` other than (0,0).

You might expect that applying a `Fill` to this `Path` is meaningless, but Figure 14.10 shows that it fills the same way as a `Polyline`, pretending that a line segment exists to connect the last point back to the starting point. Figure 14.10 was created by adding the following `Fill` to the preceding XAML:

```
<Path Fill="Orange" Stroke="Black" StrokeThickness="10">
  …
</Path>
```

To turn the imaginary line segment into a real one, you can add a third LineSegment to the PathFigure explic-itly, or you can set PathFigure's

FIGURE 14.10   The Path from Figure 14.9 with an orange Fill

`IsClosed` property to `true`. The result of doing either is shown in Figure 14.11.

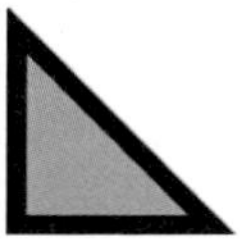

The two different values of IsClosed produce results resembling either a Polyline or Polygon. And there's a good reason for this. Internally, Polyline is using a PathGeometry with IsClosed=false on its PathFigures, and Polygon is using a PathGeometry with IsClosed=true on its PathFigures.

FIGURE 14.11   The Path from Figure 14.10, but with IsClosed="True" on the PathFigure

Because all PathSegments within a PathFigure must be connected, you can place multiple PathFigures in a PathGeometry if you want disjoint shapes or paths in the same Geometry. You could also overlap PathFigures to create results that would be complicated to replicate in a single PathFigure. For example, the following XAML overlaps the triangle from Figure 14.11 with a triangle that is given a different StartPoint but is otherwise identical:

```
<Path Fill="Orange" Stroke="Black" StrokeThickness="10">
  <Path.Data>
    <PathGeometry>
      <!-- Triangle #1 -->
      <PathFigure IsClosed="True">
        <LineSegment Point="0,100"/>
        <LineSegment Point="100,100"/>
      </PathFigure>
      <!-- Triangle #2 -->
      <PathFigure StartPoint="70,0" IsClosed="True">
        <LineSegment Point="0,100"/>
        <LineSegment Point="100,100"/>
      </PathFigure>
    </PathGeometry>
  </Path.Data>
</Path>
```

This dual-PathFigure Path is displayed in Figure 14.12.

FIGURE 14.12   Overlapping triangles created by using two PathFigures

FillRule

The behavior of the orange fill in Figure 14.12 might not be what you expected to see. PathGeometry enables you to control this fill behavior with its FillRule property. Whenever you have a Geometry with intersecting points, whether via multiple overlapping PathFigures or overlapping PathSegments in a single PathFigure, there can be multiple interpretations of which area is *inside* a shape (and can, therefore, be filled) and which area is *outside* a shape. FillRule gives you two choices on how filling is done:

→ **EvenOdd**—Fills a region only if you would cross an odd number of segments to travel from that region to the area outside the entire shape. This is the default.

→ **Nonzero**—Is a more complicated algorithm that takes into consideration the direction of the segments you would have to cross to get outside the entire shape. For many shapes, it is likely to fill all enclosed areas.

The difference between EvenOdd and Nonzero is illustrated in Figure 14.13 with the same overlapping triangles from Figure 14.12.

EvenOdd   NonZero

Polyline, Polygon, and GeometryGroup also expose a FillRule property.

FIGURE 14.13   Overlapping triangles with different values for FillRule

GeometryGroup

GeometryGroup composes one or more Geometry instances together. Like TransformGroup's relationship to Transform, GeometryGroup derives from Geometry, so it can be used anywhere that a simpler Geometry can be used. For example, the previously shown XAML for the overlapping triangles in Figure 14.12 could be rewritten to use two geometries (each with a single PathFigure) rather than one:

```
<Path Fill="Orange" Stroke="Black" StrokeThickness="10">
  <Path.Data>
    <GeometryGroup>
      <!-- Triangle #1 -->
      <PathGeometry>
        <PathFigure IsClosed="True">
          <LineSegment Point="0,100"/>
          <LineSegment Point="100,100"/>
        </PathFigure>
      </PathGeometry>
      <!-- Triangle #2 -->
      <PathGeometry>
        <PathFigure StartPoint="70,0" IsClosed="True">
          <LineSegment Point="0,100"/>
          <LineSegment Point="100,100"/>
        </PathFigure>
      </PathGeometry>
    </GeometryGroup>
  </Path.Data>
</Path>
```

GeometryGroup, like PathGeometry, has a FillRule property that is set to EvenOdd by default. It takes precedence over any FillRule settings of its children.

This, of course, begs the question, "Why would I create a GeometryGroup when I can just as easily create a single PathGeometry with multiple PathFigures?" One minor advantage of doing this is that GeometryGroup enables you to aggregate other geometries such as RectangleGeometry and EllipseGeometry, which can be easier to use. But the major advantage of using GeometryGroup is that you can set various Geometry properties independently on each child.

For example, the following `GeometryGroup` composes two identical triangles but sets the `Transform` on one of them to rotate it 25°:

```
<Path Fill="Orange" Stroke="Black" StrokeThickness="10" StrokeLineJoin="Round">
  <Path.Data>
    <GeometryGroup>
      <!-- Triangle #1 -->
      <PathGeometry>
        <PathFigure IsClosed="True">
          <LineSegment Point="0,100"/>
          <LineSegment Point="100,100"/>
        </PathFigure>
      </PathGeometry>
      <!-- Triangle #2 -->
      <PathGeometry>
        <PathGeometry.Transform>
          <RotateTransform Angle="25"/>
        </PathGeometry.Transform>
        <PathFigure IsClosed="True">
          <LineSegment Point="0,100"/>
          <LineSegment Point="100,100"/>
        </PathFigure>
      </PathGeometry>
    </GeometryGroup>
  </Path.Data>
</Path>
```

The result of this is shown in Figure 14.14. Creating this result with a single `PathGeometry` and a single `PathFigure` would be difficult. Creating it with a single `PathGeometry` containing two `PathFigures` would be easier but would still require manually doing the math to perform the rotation. With `GeometryGroup`, however, creating it is straightforward.

FIGURE 14.14   A `GeometryGroup` with two identical triangles, except that one is rotated

 Because `Fill` and all the `Stroke` properties are specified on a `Shape` rather than a `Geometry`, `GeometryGroup` doesn't enable you to combine shapes with different fills or outlines. To achieve this, you must use multiple `Shape` elements.

Representing Geometries as `Strings`

Representing each segment in a `Geometry` with a separate element is fine for simple shapes and paths, but for complicated artwork, it can get verbose. Although most people use a design tool to emit XAML-based geometries anyway rather than craft them by hand, it makes sense to keep the resultant file size as small as reasonably possible.

Therefore, XAML supports a flexible syntax for representing just about any `PathGeometry` as a `string`. The `PathGeometry` representing the simple triangle displayed in Figure 14.11:

```
<Path Fill="Orange" Stroke="Black" StrokeThickness="10">
  <Path.Data>
    <PathGeometry>
      <PathFigure IsClosed="True">
        <LineSegment Point="0,100"/>
        <LineSegment Point="100,100"/>
      </PathFigure>
    </PathGeometry>
  </Path.Data>
</Path>
```

can be represented with the following compact syntax:

```
<Path Fill="Orange" Stroke="Black" StrokeThickness="10"
 Data="M 0,0 L 0,100 L 100,100 Z"/>
```

Representing the overlapping triangles from Figure 14.12 requires a slightly longer string:

```
<Path Fill="Orange" Stroke="Black" StrokeThickness="10"
 Data="M 0,0 L 0,100 L 100,100 Z M 70,0 L 0,100 L 100,100 Z"/>
```

These `strings` contain a series of commands that control properties of `PathGeometry` and its `PathFigures`, plus commands that fill one or more `PathFigures` with `PathSegments`. The syntax is simple but powerful. Table 14.1 describes all the available commands.

TABLE 14.1   Geometry String Commands

Command	Meaning
`PathGeometry` **and** `PathFigure` **Properties**	
F *n*	Set `FillRule`, where 0 means `EvenOdd` and 1 means `Nonzero`. If you use this, it must be at the beginning of the `string`.
M *x,y*	Start a new `PathFigure` and set `StartPoint` to (*x,y*). This must be specified before using any other commands (excluding F). The M stands for *move*.
Z	End the `PathFigure` and set `IsClosed` to `true`. You can begin another disjoint `PathFigure` after this with an M command or use a different command to start a new `PathFigure` originating from the current point. If you don't want the `PathFigure` to be closed, you can omit the Z command entirely.

Command	Meaning
PathSegments	
L x,y	Create a LineSegment to (x,y).
A rx,ry d f1 f2 x,y	Create an ArcSegment to (x,y), based on an ellipse with radii rx and yx, rotated d degrees. The f1 and f2 flags can be set to 0 (false) or 1 (true) to control two of ArcSegment's properties: IsLargeArc and Clockwise, respectively.
C x1,y1 x2,y2 x,y	Create a BezierSegment to (x,y), using control points (x1,y1) and (x2,y2). The C stands for *cubic* Bézier curve.
Q x1,y1 x,y	Create a QuadraticBezierSegment to (x,y), using control point (x1,y1).
Additional Shortcuts	
H x	Create a LineSegment to (x,y), where y is taken from the current point. The H stands for *horizontal line*.
V y	Create a LineSegment to (x,y), where x is taken from the current point. The V stands for *vertical line*.
S x2,y2 x,y	Create a BezierSegment to (x,y), using control points (x1,y1) and (x2,y2), where x1 and y1 are automatically calculated to guarantee smoothness. (This point is either the second control point of the previous segment or the current point if the previous segment is not a BezierSegment.) The S stands for *smooth* cubic Bézier curve.
Lowercase commands	Any command can be specified in lowercase to cause its relevant parameters to be interpreted as *relative* to the current point rather than absolute coordinates. This doesn't change the meaning of the F, M, and Z commands, but they can also be specified in lowercase.

There are many places where you can find reusable SVG assets, such as thenounproject.com, which is filled with excellent icons that fit the style of Windows 8. There are not so many places where you can find reusable XAML-based graphics.

However, a number of SVG-to-XAML converters exist. A free (and open source) one I've used is part of the XamlTune project (http://xamltune.codeplex.com). It is not currently maintained, and resultant XAML needs manual adjustments for Windows Store apps, but it is still useful nonetheless.

For example, XamlTune produces Paths such as the following:

```
<Path Fill="#FF000000">
    <Path.Data>
        <PathGeometry FillRule="Nonzero" Figures="M63.979,55.183C79.937,…"/>
    </Path.Data>
</Path>
```

But the XAML parser for Windows Store apps doesn't support a type converter for setting PathGeometry.Figures to a geometry string. Therefore it must be converted to the following simpler Path:

```
<Path Fill="#FF000000" Data="M63.979,55.183C79.937,…"/>
```

> ● ● ●
> **Spaces and Commas in Geometry** `Strings`
>
> The spaces between commands and parameters are optional, and all commas are optional. But you must have at least one space or comma between parameters. Therefore, `M 0,0 L 0,100 L 100,100 Z` is equivalent to the more compact but much more confusing `M0 0L0 100L100 100Z`.

Brushes

It's usually not obvious, but XAML elements almost never interact directly with colors. Instead, most uses of color are wrapped inside objects known as `Brushes`. This is an extremely powerful indirection because many different brushes can be swapped in.

`Brush` itself exposes three properties: `Opacity`, `Transform`, and `RelativeTransform`. Unlike `Transform`, `RelativeTransform` is relative to the size of the area being covered with the `Brush`.

`Brush` has four subclasses, representing two *color brushes* and two *tile brushes*. Although this section mostly demonstrates `Brushes` on a `Path`, keep in mind that these `Brushes` can be used as the background, foreground, or outline of just about anything you can put on the screen—even the foreground for text!

Color Brushes

The two color brushes are `SolidColorBrush` and `LinearGradientBrush`. These `Brushes` are more flexible than most people realize.

SolidColorBrush

`SolidColorBrush`, used implicitly throughout this book, fills the target area with a single color. It has a simple `Color` property of type `Windows.UI.Color`. `Color` exposes four `Byte` properties (one per channel): `A` for alpha, `R` for red, `G` for green, and `B` for blue. Because of the syntax that treats strings such as "Blue" or "#FFFFFF" as `SolidColorBrushes`, they are indistinguishable from their underlying `Color` in XAML. In fact, color strings can take one of three different forms in XAML:

→ A name, like `Red`, `Khaki`, or `DodgerBlue`, matching one of the static properties on the `Windows.UI.Colors` class.

→ The standard RGB color space (sRGB) representation #argb, where a, r, g, and b are hexadecimal values for the `A`, `R`, `G`, and `B` properties. For example, opaque `Red` is #FFFF0000, or more simply #FF0000 (because `A` is assumed to be the maximum 255 by default).

→ The enhanced RGB color space (scRGB) representation sc#a r g b, where a, r, g, and b are floating-point values. Red, green, and blue values of 0.0 represent black, whereas three values of 1.0 represent white. In this representation, opaque `Red` is sc#1.0 1.0 0.0 0.0, or more simply sc#1.0 0.0 0.0. Commas are also allowed between each value.

If the hexadecimal representation for A, R, G, and B all repeat the same digit, you can leverage shortcut syntax in which you specify each digit only once. For example, you can shorten #AABBCCDD to #ABCD, or #CCDDEE (with an implicit FF alpha value) to #CDE (with an implicit F alpha value).

 It is usually more efficient to use colors with translucency coming from their alpha channels than to use UIElement's Opacity property to apply translucency to an otherwise-opaque solid color.

If you need to create a SolidColorBrush in C#, you can create one from a predefined Colors property as follows:

```
SolidColorBrush b = new SolidColorBrush(Colors.MintCream);
```

or from custom A, R, G, B values as follows:

```
SolidColorBrush b = new SolidColorBrush(Color.FromArgb(255, 173, 255, 47));
```

LinearGradientBrush

LinearGradientBrush fills an area with a gradient defined by colors at specific points along an imaginary line segment, with linear interpolation between those points. It contains a collection of GradientStop objects in its GradientStops content property, each of which contains a Color and an Offset. The offset is a double value relative to the bounding box of the area being filled, where 0 is the beginning and 1 is the end.

The following XAML applies a yellow-to-green gradient to a Canvas Background and a blue-to-red gradient to a trophy-shaped Path inside it:

```
<Canvas Width="100" Height="100">
  <Canvas.Background>
    <LinearGradientBrush>
      <GradientStop Offset="0" Color="Yellow"/>
      <GradientStop Offset="1" Color="Green"/>
    </LinearGradientBrush>
  </Canvas.Background>
  <!-- The trophy -->
  <Path Data="M63.979,55.183C79.937,53.135,92.441,…">
    <Path.Fill>
      <LinearGradientBrush>
        <GradientStop Offset="0" Color="Blue"/>
        <GradientStop Offset="1" Color="Red"/>
      </LinearGradientBrush>
    </Path.Fill>
  </Path>
</Canvas>
```

The result is shown in Figure 14.15. The Path data is the "Trophy" symbol by Matthew R. Miller, from thenoun-project.com collection. (The symbol is available as SVG, but I used XamlTune to convert it.)

The default interpolation of colors is done using the sRGB color space, but you can set LinearGradientBrush's ColorInterpolationMode property to ScRgbLinearInterpolation to use the scRGB color space instead. The result is a smoother gradient, as shown in Figure 14.16 when applied to both gradients from Figure 14.15.

By default, the gradient starts at the top-left corner of the area's bounding box and ends at the bottom-right corner. This is why not much blue and even less red is visible inside the trophy. The true bounding box for the trophy isn't obvious from looking at the Path in XAML, but the Visual Studio designer reveals it, as shown in Figure 14.17. The extra space is an artifact of the specified coordinates in the geometry string.

As you would expect, you can customize the gradient's starting and ending points so it doesn't always interpolate from the top-left corner to the bottom-right corner. This can be done with LinearGradientBrush's StartPoint and EndPoint properties. The values of these points are relative to the bounding box, just like the Offset in each GradientStop. Therefore, the default values for StartPoint and EndPoint are (0,0) and (1,1), respectively.

If you want to use absolute units instead of relative ones, you can set MappingMode to Absolute (rather than the default RelativeToBoundingBox).

FIGURE 14.15 A two simple LinearGradientBrushes applied to a square Canvas and the trophy inside

ScRgbLinearInterpolation

FIGURE 14.16 ColorInterpolationMode affects the appearance of both gradients.

FIGURE 14.17 The trophy's bounding box extends further to the top and left, due to the coordinates chosen in its geometry.

Note that this applies only to `StartPoint` and `EndPoint`; the `Offset` values in each `GradientStop` are always relative.

Figure 14.18 shows a few different settings of `StartPoint` and `EndPoint` on the two `LinearGradientBrushes` used in Figure 14.15 (with the default relative `MappingMode` and default interpolation). Notice that the relative values are not limited to a range of 0 to 1. You can specify smaller or larger numbers to make the gradient logically extend *past* the bounding box. (This applies to `GradientStop` `Offset` values as well.)

StartPoint = (0,0),
EndPoint = (0,1)

StartPoint = (0,1),
EndPoint = (0,0)

StartPoint = (0,0),
EndPoint = (1,0)

StartPoint = (0,5,0),
EndPoint = (1,0)

StartPoint = (-2,-2),
EndPoint = (2,2)

FIGURE 14.18   Various settings of `StartPoint` and `EndPoint` applied to both gradients

The final property for controlling `LinearGradientBrush` is `SpreadMethod`, which determines how any leftover area not covered by the gradient should be filled. This makes sense only when the `LinearGradientBrush` is explicitly set to *not* cover the entire bounding box. The default value (from the `GradientSpreadMethod` enumeration) is `Pad`, meaning that the remaining space should be filled with the color at the endpoint. You could alternatively set it to `Repeat` or `Reflect`. Both of these values repeat the gradient in a never-ending pattern, but `Reflect` reverses every other gradient to maintain a smooth transition. Figure 14.19 demonstrates each of these `SpreadMethod` values on the same two `LinearGradientBrush`es, but with the following `StartPoint` and `EndPoint` values that force the gradient to cover only the middle 10% of the bounding box:

```
<LinearGradientBrush StartPoint=".45,.45" EndPoint=".55,.55" SpreadMethod="XXX">
  …
</LinearGradientBrush>
```

Pad   Repeat   Reflect

FIGURE 14.19   Different values of `SpreadMethod` can create vastly different effects.

And don't forget, because a `Shape`'s `Stroke`, like its `Fill`, is a `Brush` rather than a simple `Color`, `Shape`s and many other elements can be outlined with complicated `Brush`es. Figure 14.20 shows the following version of the trophy that adds a thick rainbow-gradient stroke:

```
<Canvas Width="100" Height="100" Background="White">
  <!-- The trophy -->
  <Path StrokeThickness="4" Data="M63.979,55.183C79.937,53.135,92.441,…">
    <Path.Stroke>
      <LinearGradientBrush>
        <GradientStop Offset="0" Color="Red"/>
        <GradientStop Offset="0.2" Color="Orange"/>
        <GradientStop Offset="0.4" Color="Yellow"/>
        <GradientStop Offset="0.6" Color="Green"/>
        <GradientStop Offset="0.8" Color="Blue"/>
        <GradientStop Offset="1" Color="Purple"/>
      </LinearGradientBrush>
    </Path.Stroke>
    <Path.Fill>
      <LinearGradientBrush>
        <GradientStop Offset="0" Color="Blue"/>
        <GradientStop Offset="1" Color="Red"/>
      </LinearGradientBrush>
    </Path.Fill>
  </Path>
</Canvas>
```

FIGURE 14.20   Outlining the trophy with a `LinearGradientBrush`

Notice that the `Stroke`'s `LinearGradientBrush` uses six `GradientStops` spaced equally along the gradient path, rather than just two.

> To get crisp lines inside a gradient brush, you can add two `GradientStops` at the same `Offset` with different `Colors`. The following `LinearGradientBrush` does this at `Offsets` 0.2 *and* 0.6 to get two distinct lines defining the `DarkBlue` region:

```
<LinearGradientBrush EndPoint="0,1">
  <GradientStop Offset="0" Color="Aqua"/>
  <GradientStop Offset="0.2" Color="Blue"/>
  <GradientStop Offset="0.2" Color="DarkBlue"/>
  <GradientStop Offset="0.6" Color="DarkBlue"/>
  <GradientStop Offset="0.6" Color="Blue"/>
  <GradientStop Offset="1" Color="Aqua"/>
</LinearGradientBrush>
```

Figure 14.21 shows this applied as the trophy's `Fill` (and with its `Stroke` from Figure 14.20 removed).

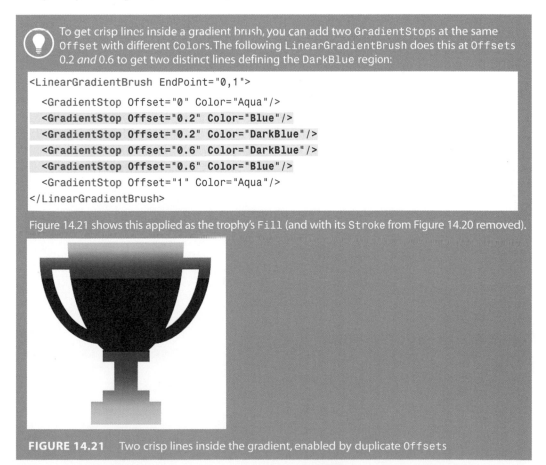

FIGURE 14.21   Two crisp lines inside the gradient, enabled by duplicate `Offsets`

Because all `Colors` have an alpha channel, you can incorporate transparency and translucency into any gradient by changing the alpha channel on any `GradientStop`'s `Color`. The following `LinearGradientBrush` varies the alpha channel to go from a translucent red to transparent, and then back to translucent:

```
<LinearGradientBrush>
  <GradientStop Offset="0" Color="#CCFF0000"/>
  <GradientStop Offset="0.5" Color="#00FF0000"/>
  <GradientStop Offset="1" Color="#CCFF0000"/>
</LinearGradientBrush>
```

Figure 14.22 shows the result of applying this `LinearGradientBrush` to the trophy, on top of a photographic background so the transparency is apparent.

FIGURE 14.22   A trophy with translucency, accomplished by using colors with non-opaque alpha channels

> **⚠ When it comes to gradients, not all transparent colors are equal!**
>
> Notice that the second `GradientStop` for Figure 14.21 uses a "transparent red" color rather than simply specifying `Transparent` as the color. That's because `Transparent` is defined as white with a 0 alpha channel (`#00FFFFFF`). Although both colors are completely invisible, the interpolation to each color does not behave the same way. If `Transparent` were used for the second `GradientStop` for Figure 14.21, you would not only see the alpha value gradually change from `0xCC` to `0`, you would also see the blue and green values gradually change from `0` to `0xFF`, giving the brush more of a gray look.

> **How can I create a radial gradient?**
>
> You can't, at least with vector graphics. WPF and Silverlight include a
> RadialGradientBrush class, but Windows Store apps do not currently have this feature.
> RadialGradientBrush was always a performance pitfall due to lack of hardware acceleration.
> For those rare instances where you want a radial gradient, Microsoft would prefer you use an
> image asset.

Tile Brushes

The two remaining brushes are *tile brushes*, because they both derive from a TileBrush
base class. However, this is one of those cases where the naming doesn't make much
sense because of compatibility with WPF and Silverlight. In WPF, you can specify the
brush's content as infinitely repeating *tiles* and configure the tiling pattern in a number of
different ways. In the XAML UI Framework for Windows Store apps, none of these
options exist. Instead, the way to think about a tile brush is a brush that contains bitmap-
based content. That content can never repeat (it can only stretch), so there's only ever
one "tile."

That said, the two built-in tile brushes are useful even without true tiling abilities. The
two types of tile brushes are ImageBrush, which enables you to fill vector graphics with
image content, and WebViewBrush, which enables you to fill vector graphics with HTML
content.

ImageBrush

ImageBrush's exposed API is similar to Image. It has a property of type ImageSource,
although it's called ImageSource rather than just Source, and it exposes the same
ImageOpened and ImageFailed events, one of which gets raised after ImageSource gets set.

Figure 14.23 shows the content of a metal.jpg file that the following XAML applies to
three different elements with an ImageBrush:

```xml
<StackPanel Background="{StaticResource ApplicationPageBackgroundThemeBrush}">
  <!-- The trophy, with a metal fill -->
  <Path Margin="5,0,0,0" Data="M63.979,55.183C79.937,53.135,92.441,…">
    <Path.Fill>
      <ImageBrush ImageSource="Assets/metal.jpg"/>
    </Path.Fill>
  </Path>
  <!-- A TextBlock, with a metal foreground -->
  <TextBlock HorizontalAlignment="Center" FontWeight="Bold">
    <TextBlock.Foreground>
      <ImageBrush ImageSource="Assets/metal.jpg"/>
    </TextBlock.Foreground>
    CONGRATULATIONS!
  </TextBlock>
```

```
<!-- A Button, with a metal background -->
<Button>
  <Button.Background>
    <ImageBrush ImageSource="Assets/metal.jpg"/>
  </Button.Background>
  Play Again
</Button>
</StackPanel>
```

The content of metal.jpg is applied as the Fill for the familiar trophy, the Foreground for a TextBlock, and the Background for a Button. Figure 14.24 shows the result. Note that the imaging system caches images for this type of repetitive use, so you don't incur multiple copies by referencing the file multiple times.

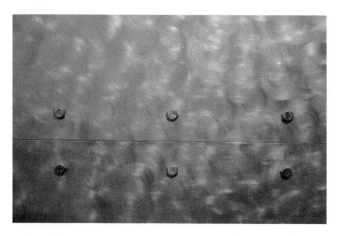

FIGURE 14.23   The metal.jpg file used in Figure 14.24

By default, the image content is stretched to fill the element's bounding box. In Figure 14.24, the horizontal image-stretching on the TextBlock and Button is obvious and perhaps undesirable. Fortunately, this behavior can be customized with three properties on the TileBrush base class. One is Stretch, which works the same way as on Image, Shape, Viewbox, and many other elements. However, TileBrush provides more customization when Stretch is set anything other than its default value of Fill. In this case, its AlignmentX property can be set to Left, Right, or Center (the default), and its AlignmentY property can be set to Top, Bottom, or Center (the default) to control how the image gets positioned within the bounding box. Figure 14.25 demonstrates the use of a Stretch of None with two different alignments.

FIGURE 14.24   An ImageBrush in action, showing off its versatility

```
Stretch="None" AlignmentX="Center"      Stretch="None" AlignmentX="Left"
AlignmentY="Center"                     AlignmentY="Top"
```

FIGURE 14.25   Applying different stretching and alignment to an ImageBrush

WebViewBrush

As mentioned in the previous chapter, the WebView control for rendering HTML has a
serious limitation in that it monopolizes all pixels and input inside its area. By filling a
Rectangle with a WebViewBrush instead, you can transform, blend, and do all the normal
UIElement tricks with HTML content.

WebViewBrush requires a WebView instance in order to work. You can think of
WebViewBrush as nothing more than an ImageBrush that is able to take a screenshot of the
WebView control. The content in a WebViewBrush doesn't automatically update, nor is it
interactive. (If WebView exposed a way to get an ImageSource of its contents, then using
that with an ImageBrush would have been a more straightforward way to support the
same functionality.)

To demonstrate, the following Page places a WebView side-by-side with a WebViewBrush-
filled Rectangle:

```
<Page …>
  <Grid Background="{StaticResource ApplicationPageBackgroundThemeBrush}">
    <Grid.ColumnDefinitions>
      <ColumnDefinition/>
      <ColumnDefinition/>
    </Grid.ColumnDefinitions>

    <!-- WebView on the left -->
    <WebView Name="webView" Margin="200,50" Source="http://xbox.com"/>

    <!-- WebViewBrush on the right -->
    <Rectangle Grid.Column="1">
      <Rectangle.Fill>
        <WebViewBrush x:Name="webViewBrush"/>
      </Rectangle.Fill>
    </Rectangle>

    <Button Grid.Column="1" Background="DarkGreen" Margin="300,15"
            VerticalAlignment="Top" Click="Button_Click">
      <Button.RenderTransform>
        <ScaleTransform ScaleX="2" ScaleY="2"/>
      </Button.RenderTransform>
      Refresh WebViewBrush
    </Button>
  </Grid>
</Page>
```

When the `Button` is clicked, the following handler associates the `WebViewBrush` with the `WebView` as follows:

```
void Button_Click(object sender, RoutedEventArgs e)
{
  webViewBrush.SetSource(webView);
}
```

By the way, the `WebViewBrush` instance is named with `x:Name` because it doesn't have a `Name` property of its own. Brushes are not `FrameworkElements`; they derive directly from `DependencyObject`.

The call to `SetSource` is needed to take a snapshot of the `WebView` contents and display it inside the `WebViewBrush`. Each time `SetSource` is called, it updates the `WebViewBrush` with the current content. `WebViewBrush` also exposes a `SourceName` property designed to be set in XAML to the name of the relevant `WebView`. `WebViewBrush`'s parameterless `Redraw` method enables you to refresh the snapshot without setting the source every time. Calling `Redraw` at least once is necessary to see anything when `SourceName` is set in XAML, because that assignment is done too early for any content to be rendered in the `WebViewBrush`.

Figure 14.26 displays the result of the preceding XAML after the Web page has been loaded and the `Button` has been clicked.

FIGURE 14.26   Applying a `WebViewBrush` to the `Rectangle` on the right with content from the `WebView` on the left

When I said "snapshot," I wasn't kidding! Even the scrollbars are included in the `WebViewBrush`'s content if they are visible at the time `SetSource` is called! Notice also that the content matches what is rendered within the bounds of the `WebView`. If the size doesn't match the bounding box of the target, the content is stretched by default. (The `WebView` in Figure 14.26 is given a `Margin` solely to demonstrate this fact.) Just as with `ImageBrush`, you can control the stretching with the `Stretch`, `AlignmentX`, and `AlignmentY` properties from the `TileBrush` base class.

The fact that the "Refresh WebViewBrush" `Button` is able to appear on top of the `WebViewBrush`-filled `Rectangle` proves the ability to blend HTML and XAML content in this way, but Figure 14.27 goes one step further by applying a 3D projection to the `Rectangle` as follows:

```
<!-- WebViewBrush on the right -->
<Rectangle Grid.Column="1">
  <Rectangle.Fill>
    <WebViewBrush x:Name="webViewBrush"/>
  </Rectangle.Fill>
  <Rectangle.Projection>
    <PlaneProjection RotationY="30"/>
  </Rectangle.Projection>
</Rectangle>
```

The figure also shows an overlaid `AppBar`, which is conspicuously unable to overlay the `WebView` on the left.

FIGURE 14.27   `WebViewBrush` enables (static) HTML content to perform any tricks that regular XAML content can perform.

This support is perfect for temporarily overlaying content on top of an otherwise-visible `WebView`, for providing the illusion of a `WebView` animating in and out, or even for a rich preview of a Web page, exactly like the Internet Explorer app's tabs in its top `AppBar`. Figure 14.28 shows yet another possible application: providing a reflection for an active `WebView`.

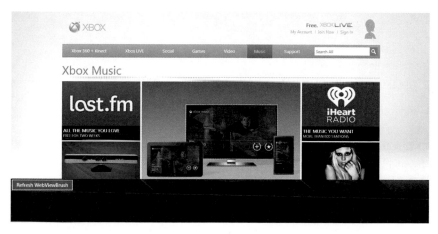

FIGURE 14.28   `WebViewBrush` can contribute to a simple reflection effect.

The following XAML creates this type of reflection:

```
<Page …>
  <Grid Background="Black">
    <Grid.RowDefinitions>
      <RowDefinition Height="500"/>
      <RowDefinition/>
    </Grid.RowDefinitions>

    <!-- WebView on the top -->
    <WebView Name="webView" Source="http://xbox.com"/>

    <!-- Flipped, compressed, and skewed WebViewBrush on the bottom -->
    <Rectangle Grid.Row="1">
      <Rectangle.Fill>
        <WebViewBrush x:Name="webViewBrush">
          <WebViewBrush.Transform>
            <TransformGroup>
              <!-- Flip and compress the brush before skewing it -->
              <ScaleTransform CenterY="65" ScaleX="1" ScaleY="-.2"/>
              <SkewTransform AngleX="50"/>
            </TransformGroup>
          </WebViewBrush.Transform>
        </WebViewBrush>
```

```
      </Rectangle.Fill>
    </Rectangle>

    <!-- A translucent Rectangle on top of the other one, for a fade effect -->
    <Rectangle Grid.Row="1">
      <Rectangle.Fill>
        <LinearGradientBrush StartPoint="0,0" EndPoint="0,1">
          <GradientStop Offset="-.5" Color="#0000"/>
          <GradientStop Offset=".2" Color="Black"/>
        </LinearGradientBrush>
      </Rectangle.Fill>
    </Rectangle>

    <Button Grid.Row="1" Background="DarkGreen" VerticalAlignment="Top"
            Click="Button_Click">
      Refresh WebViewBrush
    </Button>
  </Grid>
</Page>
```

This effect leverages the Transform property defined on all Brushes. The WebViewBrush
reflection is flipped upside down by using a ScaleTransform. But rather than setting
ScaleY to -1, the value of -.2 is used to give the reflection a little bit of perspective.
TransformGroup is used rather than CompositeTransform so the skewing is applied *after*
the other transforms.

To make the effect more subtle, a second Rectangle on top of the WebViewBrush-filled
Rectangle uses a LinearGradientBrush to fade from a "transparent black" (*not*
Transparent, which would add a lot of gray due to the transition from white) to black.

To complete our look at WebViewBrush, Figure 14.29 fills the familiar trophy using one,
using the following XAML:

```
<Page …>
  <Grid Background="{StaticResource ApplicationPageBackgroundThemeBrush}">
    <Grid.ColumnDefinitions>
      <ColumnDefinition/>
      <ColumnDefinition/>
    </Grid.ColumnDefinitions>
    <WebView Name="webView" Source="http://xbox.com"/>
    <Viewbox Grid.Column="1">
      <!-- The trophy -->
      <Path Data="M63.979,55.183C79.937,53.135,92.441,…">
        <Path.Fill>
          <WebViewBrush x:Name="webViewBrush"/>
        </Path.Fill>
      </Path>
```

```
    </Viewbox>
    <Button Grid.Column="1" Background="DarkGreen" VerticalAlignment="Top"
            Click="Button_Click">
      Refresh WebViewBrush
    </Button>
  </Grid>
</Page>
```

FIGURE 14.29   Filling the nonrectangular trophy with a `WebViewBrush`

Summary

The seamless support for vector graphics is just one of the many examples of the richness of XAML. As with many other XAML features, a big part of the power of vector graphics comes from the tight integration with the rest of the framework. The drawing primitives used to create lines, shapes, and trophies are the same ones used to create `Buttons`, `Sliders`, and `ListViews`.

Even when you "draw" vector graphics on the screen, you're still working with a completely *retained-mode* graphics system rather than an *immediate-mode* graphics system. In an immediate-mode system (such as DirectX), you must maintain the state of all visuals. In other words, it's your responsibility to draw the correct pixels when a region of the screen is invalidated. This invalidation can be caused by user actions, such as snapping an app, or by application-specific actions that require updated visuals.

In a retained-mode system, you describe higher-level concepts such as "place a 10x10 blue square at (0,0)," and the system remembers and maintains the state for you. So, what you're really saying is, "place a 10x10 blue square at (0,0) *and keep it there*." You don't need to worry about invalidation and repainting, the same way you don't worry about any of this when placing those `Buttons`, `Sliders`, and `ListViews` in your user interface.

Vector graphics have a lot of advantages over bitmap-based graphics, but with those advantages come inherent scalability issues. Not *visual* scalability issues, but rather *performance* scalability issues. Complex vector graphics can be expensive for the system to redraw. In scenarios where there might be a rapid succession of redrawing, as with a zooming animation, the cost of rendering can significantly impact the resulting user experience.

UIElement provides an interesting trick that helps in this regard, known as *cached composition*. To enable this, you set UIElement's CacheMode property to an instance of BitmapCache. For example:

```xml
<Grid …>
  <Grid.CacheMode>
    <BitmapCache/>
  </Grid.CacheMode>
  …
</Grid>
```

This caches the visuals as a bitmap in video memory and enables hardware rendering. When the cached element (including any of its children) is updated, this feature automatically and intelligently updates only the dirty region. Updates to any parents do not invalidate the cache, nor do updates to the element's transforms or opacity! Furthermore, the system automatically leverages the live element when needed in order to preserve its interactivity.

Setting CacheMode is most appropriate for static content that wouldn't already be hardware accelerated, such as a complex Path. (Solid color rectangles, images, text, and video are already hardware accelerated.) This avoids creating a bottleneck in the rendering pipeline due to the CPU-bound work of repeated tessellation and rasterization on every frame. There is a tradeoff, however. The more you cache, the bigger the memory consumption will be on the GPU.

BitmapCache falls back to software rendering when hardware acceleration is not possible. However, when rendered in software, the maximum size allowed for the cached bitmap is 2048x2048 pixels.

Chapter 15

ANIMATION

When most people think about animation, they think of a cartoon-like mechanism, where movement is simulated by displaying images in rapid succession. In XAML, animation has a more specific definition: varying the value of a dependency property over time. This could be related to motion, such as making an element gradually grow, shrink, rotate, skew, or move by animating properties on its RenderTransform or making it spin in 3D by animating properties on its Projection. Or it could be something like varying the value of a Color inside a Brush used as a Background or Fill.

XAML has always had strong support for integrating animations into your content. When exposed via design tools such as Blend, using the animation support can feel like you're using Adobe Flash. But because it's a core part of the platform, with APIs that are fairly simple, you can easily create a wide range of animations without the help of a tool. Indeed, this chapter demonstrates several different animation techniques with nothing more than short snippets of XAML and C#.

The animation support provided to Windows Store apps is even better than what has been available to XAML-based apps in the past. A number of standard animations are a core part of the Windows 8 user experience. Some of these are automatically leveraged by your app because the built-in controls already use them. For example, AppBar and ToggleSwitch use animated transitions, and ListView and

`GridView` use animations liberally: when cross-slide selecting items, dragging and dropping items, and so on. In addition, Windows 8's *animation library* makes it easy to use the standard animations for your own purposes. This animation library is exposed to XAML via two features: *theme transitions* and *theme animations*.

This chapter begins by looking at the theme transitions and theme animations that are new to Windows 8. It then looks at the standard XAML features for custom animations. Most of these custom animation features have been around since the inception of XAML, although there are some new twists for Windows 8.

Theme Transitions

Using *theme transitions* is the best way to perform animations. They match the standard animations used by the built-in apps and Windows itself. This is a boon for developers who have no business designing animated effects. It's amazing how making a wrong choice when animating a user interface (for example, the effect is too slow, too garish, or doesn't quite match user expectations) can negatively impact an app's perceived quality.

Theme transitions bring more to the table than just consistency, however. They are guaranteed to perform well. They use animations that are all hardware-accelerated, which means they leverage the graphics processing unit (GPU) rather than solely using the central processing unit (CPU). This usually produces noticeably better results because the CPU load doesn't affect currently running transitions, and the transitions don't interfere with the "real work" being done on the CPU. Hardware-accelerated animations are also called *independent animations* because they run *independently* from the UI thread. Otherwise, they are called *dependent animations*. We'll see these terms popping up again later.

Finally, a third reason to use theme transitions is that they are incredibly easy to use. I would say they are the simplest, most magical features available to Windows Store apps. Each one is presented as an abstract concept (for example, "the transition for when an element appears on the screen," or "the transition for when an element is repositioned among other elements"). Often, all you need to do is apply one or more transitions to the desired elements. All the details, such as what events trigger them, what property values on the elements need to change, how their values change (timings, easings, and so on), are handled automatically.

Applying Theme Transitions to Elements

So how do you apply a theme transition to an element? Every `UIElement` has a `Transitions` property that can be set to a collection of `Transition` objects (the base class for all theme transitions). Using one of the theme transitions called `EntranceThemeTransition` as an example, the following XAML applies one to a `Button` on a `Page`:

```
<Page …>
  <Grid Background="{StaticResource ApplicationPageBackgroundThemeBrush}">
    <Button Content="A Button with a Theme Transition">
```

```
    <Button.Transitions>
      <TransitionCollection>
        <EntranceThemeTransition/>
      </TransitionCollection>
    </Button.Transitions>
  </Button>
 </Grid>
</Page>
```

When this Page becomes visible for the first time (right after the splash screen dismisses for a single-Page app), the Button automatically animates to its position with a subtle fade-in and glide from a bit to the right. This is the standard Windows animation for an element "entering" the scene.

There are more places that TransitionCollections can be applied to elements, however:

You must use an explicit TransitionCollection **element when setting** Transitions **in XAML!**

Unlike many other collection properties, Transitions is null by default. Therefore, you must wrap your list of theme transition elements in an explicit TransitionCollection element when setting it in XAML (even if it's a list of just one). If you forget to do this, you'll get a XamlParseException that explains, "Collection property '__implicit_items' is null."

Similarly, in C#, you must instantiate a TransitionCollection and assign it as the property value, rather than just adding items to the default (null) property value. This adds a bit of verbosity, but the choice was made for performance reasons.

→ Content controls have a **ContentTransitions** property that applies to its inner content. (So does ContentPresenter, an element described in the next chapter.)

→ Items controls have an **ItemContainerTransitions** property that applies to its visual children (the item containers that wrap each item, such as ComboBoxItem and ListViewItem). (So does ItemsPresenter, an element described in the next chapter.)

→ Panels have a **ChildrenTransitions** property that applies to their children.

→ ListViewBase (and therefore ListView and GridView) have a **HeaderTransitions** property that applies to the content in its Header property.

→ Border and Popup, which aren't content controls, have a **ChildTransitions** property that applies to the content in their Child property.

With the exception of three theme transitions that add special features when applied in bulk (called out in their upcoming sections), applying a theme transition via ItemContainerTransitions or ChildrenTransitions is a shortcut for applying it on every child element. Note that all these properties of type TransitionCollection are null by default, so the explicit collection requirement applies to them all.

The Eight Theme Transitions

Windows 8 contains, appropriately enough, eight theme transitions. Let's look at them all.

EntranceThemeTransition

Timing	When an element appears for the first time
Visual Result	Glides slightly from the right with a quick fade in
Intended For	Pages or other large containers; has special staggering feature for ItemContainerTransitions and ChildrenTransitions
Properties	FromHorizontalOffset (default = 40)
	FromVerticalOffset (default = 0)
	IsStaggeringEnabled (default = true)

Instead of placing EntranceThemeTransition on a Button, the following XAML applies it to all Buttons in a StackPanel using StackPanel's ChildrenTransitions property:

```
<Page …>
  <Grid Background="{StaticResource ApplicationPageBackgroundThemeBrush}">
    <StackPanel>
      <StackPanel.ChildrenTransitions>
        <TransitionCollection>
          <EntranceThemeTransition/>
        </TransitionCollection>
      </StackPanel.ChildrenTransitions>
      <Button Background="Red" Width="100" Height="40"/>
      <Button Background="Orange" Width="100" Height="40"/>
      <Button Background="Yellow" Width="100" Height="40"/>
      <Button Background="Green" Width="100" Height="40"/>
      <Button Background="Blue" Width="100" Height="40"/>
      <Button Background="Purple" Width="100" Height="40"/>
    </StackPanel>
  </Grid>
</Page>
```

As Figure 15.1 demonstrates, EntranceThemeTransition includes special behavior when it is applied to children in a Panel or item containers in an items control. The animation is staggered, so elements earlier in the collection animate sooner than elements items later in the collection. The order is done based on the index in the collection, which, in the case of StackPanel, matches the order on the screen.

You can disable this staggering feature by setting EntranceThemeTransition's IsStaggeringEnabled property to false. In that case, the effect is no different than applying a default EntranceThemeTransition to the StackPanel using the Transitions property instead of ChildrenTransitions.

With the FromHorizontalOffset and FromVerticalOffset properties, you can make the animation less subtle by telling elements to travel a farther distance to get to their final locations. You can also make them come from different directions. Positive offsets make them travel from the right and/or bottom, and negative offsets make them travel from the left and/or top.

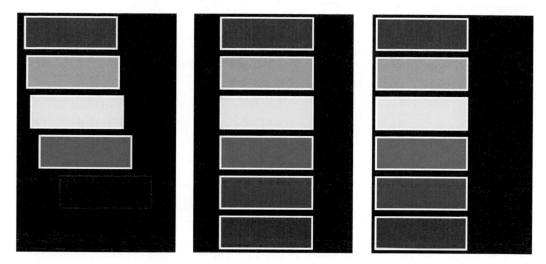

IsStaggeringEnabled=true   IsStaggeringEnabled=false   The final positions

FIGURE 15.1   The effect of `IsStaggeringEnabled` when `EntranceThemeTransition` is applied to a `ChildrenTransitions` property

Changing an element's `Visibility` to `Collapsed` and then `Visible` again doesn't trigger the animation again; the element has already made its "entrance" onto the scene. However, if you *remove* an element from the tree (the `StackPanel`'s `Children` collection in this example) and then add it back, the animation *will* kick in.

It's worth pointing out that the timing of an `EntranceThemeTransition` is smarter than you might think. All `FrameworkElements` have a `Loaded` event that is raised when it has been added to the current element tree and is about to be rendered. However, triggering this transition based on this event isn't good enough for an app's initial UI, which might still be obscured by the splash screen. Therefore, the built-in triggering of `EntranceThemeTransition` takes the dismissal of the splash screen into account. It also waits to trigger it on elements that are initially `Collapsed`. Once such elements become visible (the *first* time), the animation begins.

PopupThemeTransition

Timing	When an element appears for the first time, and also when it is removed
Visual Result	When it appears: glides from the bottom with a quick fade in
	When it is removed: quickly fades out
Intended For	Popups (context menus and other flyouts)
Properties	FromHorizontalOffset (default = 0)
	FromVerticalOffset (default = 40)

For an element's first appearance, `PopupThemeTransition` is just like an `EntranceThemeTransition` that animates vertically by default and has no staggering feature. However, it also adds a fade-out animation for when the element is removed from the visual tree. The important difference is what this theme transition is *intended for*, which is the entrance of temporary overlays such as `Popups`.

This means that Popups must be removed from the visual tree after being dismissed and then added back before being shown again so they get animated every time. That's because PopupThemeTransition is triggered only upon the element's entrance and exit from the scene. Toggling its Visibility doesn't count. For this theme transition to work on a Popup, it must be applied to Popup's ChildTransitions property.

Although ToolTip is rendered with a Popup, applying PopupThemeTransition to a ToolTip is inconsistent with standard Windows 8 behavior. You should leave ToolTips with their default fade-in and fade-out effect.

ContentThemeTransition

Timing	When an element appears for the first time, and also when it is removed
Visual Result	When it appears: glides slightly from the right with a quick fade in
	When it is removed: quickly fades out
Intended For	Large controls with changing content, such as a Frame, and applied via ContentTransitions or ChildTransitions
Properties	HorizontalOffset (default = 40)
	VerticalOffset (default = 0)

This theme transition sounds like PopupThemeTransition, except the direction of the entrance-gliding matches EntranceThemeTransition. It basically is, which works out nicely when swapping an element's content. For example, when you apply ContentThemeTransition to a content control via ContentTransitions, the initial content will glide in like an EntranceThemeTransition. However, when you change the control's content, the old element fades out while the new one glides in to replace it.

Although you could produce the same visual effect with PopupThemeTransition (if you reverse the values of PopupThemeTransition to match ContentThemeTransition), you should not get hung up on the visual result. In theory, a future version of Windows could change the animation details for each theme transition. As long as you use them in a way consistent with their intent, you should be fine.

EdgeUIThemeTransition

Timing	When an element appears for the first time, and also when it is removed
Visual Result	When it appears: slides in from above
	When it is removed: slides out in the reverse direction
Intended For	An element docked to the edge of the app that acts like AppBar
Properties	Edge (default = Top)

Despite the name, EdgeUIThemeTransition is not triggered by performing an edge gesture. It gets triggered by the typical element entrance and removal conditions.

EdgeUIThemeTransition provides a visual result that matches the sliding-in and sliding-out done by AppBar. And just like an AppBar animation, there's no fading in and out.

The Edge property represents the edge of the screen on which the gesture is supposed to happen, which determines the direction of the animation. If you choose Right, for example, the element slides from right-to-left upon entrance, and left-to-right upon removal.

Of course, because a properly attached AppBar already does the correct animations, you normally have no need to use this theme transition.

PaneThemeTransition

Timing	When an element appears for the first time, and also when it is removed
Visual Result	When it appears: slides in from the right
	When it is removed: slides out in the reverse direction
Intended For	An element docked to the edge of the app, such as a custom settings pane docked to the right.
Properties	Edge (default = Right)

PaneThemeTransition is similar to EdgeUIThemeTransition but with a different default value for its Edge property and a slightly different animation speed. Again, the important difference is the intent. PaneThemeTransition is perfect for a custom pane triggered by the Settings charm, discussed in Chapter 19, "Charms."

Besides speed, there is one subtle visual difference between the two theme transitions. With PaneThemeTransition, the animated content is clipped by the bounds of the element's resting spot. With EdgeUIThemeTransition, no clipping is done. This difference is demonstrated in Figure 15.2 with the following XAML:

```
<Page …>
  <Grid Background="{StaticResource ApplicationPageBackgroundThemeBrush}">
    <StackPanel>
      <Button Background="Red" Width="100" Height="40">
        <Button.Transitions>
          <TransitionCollection>
            <PaneThemeTransition/>
          </TransitionCollection>
        </Button.Transitions>
      </Button>
      <Button Background="Orange" Width="100" Height="40"/>
    </StackPanel>
  </Grid>
</Page>
```

`<PaneThemeTransition/>`   `<EdgeUIThemeTransition Edge="Right"/>`

FIGURE 15.2   PaneThemeTransition clips the red Button sliding in from the right, unlike EdgeUIThemeTransition.

This difference, of course, doesn't matter for an element docked to the appropriate edge.

AddDeleteThemeTransition

Timing	When an element appears for the first time, when it is removed, and when it is repositioned by a layout change
Visual Result	When it appears: fades in and grows after a short delay
	When it is removed: fades out and shrinks after a short delay
	When it is repositioned: glides to the new position
Intended For	A collection of elements
Properties	None

AddDeleteThemeTransition's claim to fame is not what it does to the element entering or exiting, but what it does to its sibling elements when applied to the parent via ItemContainerTransitions or ChildrenTransitions. The sibling elements glide to their new positions! This is pictured in Figure 15.3 for the following XAML:

```
<Page …>
  <Grid Background="{StaticResource ApplicationPageBackgroundThemeBrush}">
    <StackPanel Name="stackPanel">
      <StackPanel.ChildrenTransitions>
        <TransitionCollection>
          <AddDeleteThemeTransition/>
        </TransitionCollection>
      </StackPanel.ChildrenTransitions>
      <Button Background="Red" Width="100" Height="40"/>
      <Button Background="Orange" Width="100" Height="40"/>
      <!-- The Button that will be removed: -->
      <Button Name="yellow" Background="Yellow" Width="100" Height="40"/>
      <Button Background="Green" Width="100" Height="40"/>
      <Button Background="Blue" Width="100" Height="40"/>
      <Button Background="Purple" Width="100" Height="40"/>
    </StackPanel>
  </Grid>
</Page>
```

This demonstrates the condition of the yellow Button being removed with code such as the following:

```
this.stackPanel.Children.Remove(this.yellow);
```

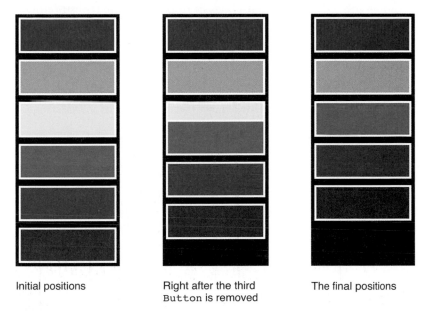

Initial positions   Right after the third   The final positions
                           Button is removed

FIGURE 15.3   The effect of AddDeleteThemeTransition when one of the elements in the StackPanel is removed

Although the yellow Button is still visible in the middle stage of Figure 15.3, it has been removed from the collection already. There's a delay applied to the shrink-and-fade-out animation that leaves time for any sibling gliding to occur first.

There's no magic here when it comes to giving those bottom three Buttons new positions. The position change is a normal part of StackPanel's layout; if you remove an element, the remaining ones are restacked such that no "hole" is left behind. All that AddDeleteThemeTransition is doing is animating these elements to their new positions that they would instantly snap to otherwise. If these Buttons were explicitly placed in a Canvas instead, no siblings would ever move.

This fact leads to some interesting behavior. As with the other transitions, if the yellow Button's Visibility is set to Collapsed instead of being removed from the StackPanel's Children collection, it does not animate out. However, the *siblings* in the Children collection still animate to their new positions! In fact, *any* layout changes cause them to animate, even if it has nothing to do with adding/removing or showing/hiding an element. For example, if the yellow Button's Height is changed, the three Buttons below it animate to their new positions forced by that change.

If you apply AddDeleteThemeTransition directly to an arbitrary element (via its Transitions property), it will do the typical animations whenever it enters and exits the scene, and it will also animate in response to any layout changes that push it around. For example, you could apply it to the orange Button in Figure 15.3 instead of the StackPanel, and it would be the only Button that glides in response to the repositioning done when adding/removing the yellow Button.

RepositionThemeTransition

Timing	When an element is repositioned by a layout change
Visual Result	Glides to the new position
Intended For	Any element that can be moved by a layout change; has special stagger-ing feature for ItemContainerTransitions and ChildrenTransitions
Properties	None

RepositionThemeTransition enables the generic "animate any layout changes" behavior from AddDeleteThemeTransition, but without the animations on entrance and exit, which can be undesirable due to the delayed fade-in when elements first enter. It also staggers the animations when applied to ItemContainerTransitions and ChildrenTransitions. Unlike with EntranceThemeTransition, this staggering cannot be turned off.

If you change the AddDeleteThemeTransition from Figure 15.3 to RepositionThemeTransition, the result would look *almost* the same. This time, the yellow Button would disappear instantly rather than waiting to animate out after the gliding occurs. Also, the three Buttons below it would move up in a staggered fashion, although it is barely noticeable with just three elements moving.

For that yellow Button in the StackPanel from Figure 15.3, let's add some code-behind that toggles its position in the Children collection every time the Page is tapped:

```
protected override void OnTapped(TappedRoutedEventArgs e)
{
  if (this.stackPanel.Children[0] == this.yellow)
  {
    // Move from index 0 to 2
    this.stackPanel.Children.Remove(this.yellow);
    this.stackPanel.Children.Insert(2, this.yellow);
  }
  else
  {
    // Move from index 2 to 0
    this.stackPanel.Children.Remove(this.yellow);
    this.stackPanel.Children.Insert(0, this.yellow);
  }
}
```

This two-step process counts as a "move" because the pair of Remove and Insert calls are made synchronously and therefore don't give the Button a chance to disappear before the Insert happens.

Figure 15.4 shows the result of invoking this code if the AddDeleteTheme Transition element. Note that this effect appears *exactly* the same regardless of whether AddDeleteThemeTransition or ReorderThemeTransition is applied to StackPanel.ChildrenTransitions, because no element visibly enters or exits.

Such animations occur only when an element moves in response to layout changes (the condition that causes LayoutUpdated to be raised) from code internal to a parent Panel. For example, increasing an element's Margin doesn't animate it, although depending on the

FIGURE 15.4   The yellow Button is animating down to its new position while the red and orange Buttons animate up to their new positions.

parent Panel it could cause other elements to animate if the theme transition is applied to them.

The effect of RepositionThemeTransition (and AddDeleteThemeTransition) applies to external factors that trigger layout changes, however, such as the user snapping and unsnapping the app. Figure 15.5 demonstrates this if we replace the previously used StackPanel with a VariableSizedWrapGrid and paste in many more copies of the six colorful Buttons.

ReorderThemeTransition

Timing	When an element appears for the first time, when it is removed, when it is repositioned by a layout change, and when dragging and dropping
Visual Result	When it appears: fades in and grows
	When it is removed, fades out and shrinks
	When it is repositioned, glides to the new position
	When it is dragged, becomes translucent and sibling elements move out of the way
Intended For	A collection of elements that support drag-and-drop reordering (therefore, elements in a ListView or GridView); designed for ItemContainerTransitions
Properties	None

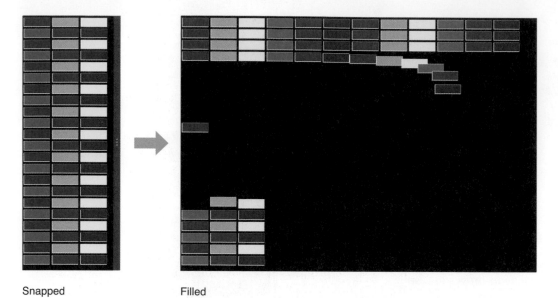

Snapped   Filled

FIGURE 15.5   With RepositionThemeTransition applied to a VariableSizedWrapGrid via ChildrenTransitions, elements automatically animate to their new positions when wrapping occurs.

ReorderThemeTransition does everything that AddDeleteThemeTransition does, but it adds sophisticated effects for drag-and-drop. This is what's used by ListView and GridView to enable the automatic drag-and-drop item reordering effect already seen in Chapter 9, "Items Controls," (Figures 9.8 and 9.11). If you apply it to the content in Figure 15.5, the result would look the same as AddDeleteThemeTransition because there's no drag-and-drop support in this case. The Buttons would all grow and fade in initially, and then layout changes would cause an unstaggered variation of the same repositioning animation.

Theme Animations

Unlike theme transitions, which are for specific animations for specific actions, theme animations are specific animations for custom actions. Although their visual details are predetermined, you get to decide when to trigger them. There are 14 of them, but before describing them, we need to look at the *storyboard* mechanism that enables them to run.

Using a Storyboard

One of the theme animations is called FadeOutThemeAnimation, and it knows how to make any element fade out. Let's see how to apply that to a simple Button on a Page. This must be done with an object called a Storyboard. Storyboards can contain one or more animations and associate them with specific elements. Here's a Page with the Button we

want to animate and the `Storyboard` that provides context to the
FadeOutThemeAnimation:

```
<Page …>
  <Page.Resources>
    <Storyboard x:Name="storyboard" TargetName="b">
      <FadeOutThemeAnimation/>
    </Storyboard>
  </Page.Resources>
  <Canvas Background="{StaticResource ApplicationPageBackgroundThemeBrush}">
    <Button Name="b">Animating Button</Button>
  </Canvas>
</Page>
```

Unlike with theme transitions, `UIElements` have no `Storyboards` property that can be
used to attach `Storyboards`. And `Storyboard` is not a `UIElement`, so it can't be placed
within the `Page` like other elements. Instead, this `Page` stores it in its `Resources` collection. The `Resources` property, defined on all `FrameworkElements`, is a dictionary that can
contain arbitrary objects given either an `x:Name` or `x:Key`, as seen in Chapter 2,
"Mastering XAML." Such objects are typically meant to be shared by multiple child
elements, although that's not the case here. The next chapter demonstrates this kind of
sharing.

With `Storyboard`'s `TargetName` property assigned appropriately, we're ready to animate.
All we need to do is call the `Storyboard`'s `Begin` method when we want it to start:

```
void StartInitialAnimations()
{
  // Start the animation
  this.storyboard.Begin();
}
```

`Storyboard` defines a number of methods that enable you to treat an animation like a
video clip—Begin, Pause, Resume, Seek, and Stop—although normally `Begin` is all that
gets called.

Let's say we want to call `StartInitialAnimations` when the `Page` appears, like the timing
of many theme transitions. As mentioned previously, handling the `Button` or `Page`'s
`Loaded` isn't good enough. If we start an animation too early, we run the risk of it not
getting seen in its entirety if it takes the splash screen awhile to be dismissed. Therefore,
the following complete code-behind for the `Page` leverages the host `Window`'s `Activated`
event for triggering the animation. It must check to trigger it only on the *first* `Activated`
event raised, however, because it gets raised every time the `Window` gets focus:

```
using Windows.UI.Core;
using Windows.UI.Xaml;
using Windows.UI.Xaml.Controls;
```

```csharp
namespace Animation
{
  public sealed partial class MainPage : Page
  {
    bool firstActivation = true;

    public MainPage()
    {
      InitializeComponent();
      Window.Current.Activated += Window_Activated;
    }

    void Window_Activated(object sender, WindowActivatedEventArgs e)
    {
      // Code that only runs for the first activation:
      if (this.firstActivation)
      {
        StartInitialAnimations();
        this.firstActivation = false;
      }
    }

    void StartInitialAnimations()
    {
      // Start the animation
      this.storyboard.Begin();
    }
  }
}
```

Running this code results in the Button quickly and smoothly fading out as soon as the splash screen is dismissed. Of course, this animation-triggering logic still doesn't match the general-purpose logic within theme transitions (which waits if the element is initially Collapsed), but it's good enough for this simple example.

> **? How can I trigger an animation without writing any C# code?**
>
> The best way to do this is to place a Storyboard inside a VisualState. VisualStates are a styling feature explained in the next chapter. There is one other way, however. It's limited and just there for compatibility with WPF and Silverlight, but it's worth knowing about nonetheless.
>
> Although elements have no Storyboards property, they do have a property called Triggers (defined on FrameworkElement), which is sort of the same thing. It enables you to attach one or more Storyboards to an element, although they have to be wrapped in two intermediate

elements. The following XAML applies the same FadeOutThemeAnimation to the same Button used previously but with no code-behind needed:

```
<Button Name="b">Animating Button
  <Button.Triggers>
    <EventTrigger RoutedEvent="FrameworkElement.Loaded">
      <EventTrigger.Actions>
        <BeginStoryboard>
          <Storyboard TargetName="b">
            <FadeOutThemeAnimation/>
          </Storyboard>
        </BeginStoryboard>
      </EventTrigger.Actions>
    </EventTrigger>
  </Button.Triggers>
</Button>
```

In this case, the Storyboard doesn't need a name because there's no code-behind referencing it, although it does still need TargetName to be set despite already being "attached" to the Button.

The BeginStoryboard element takes the place of the call to Storyboard's Begin method; it's the declarative equivalent. The EventTrigger takes the place of attaching an event handler in C#; it handles *when* to trigger the animation. But this is the part that makes it so limited. For Windows Store apps, the RoutedEvent property, which specifies the triggering event, can be set only to FrameworkElement.Loaded. (Recall from Chapter 5, "Interactivity," that the Loaded event isn't even a routed event, but that doesn't prevent it from working here!)

Of course, as we've already discussed, triggering animations based on the Loaded event isn't a good idea, at least for elements that get loaded during initialization of the first Page (under the splash screen). For elements that are added dynamically, however, or for elements whose animation repeats indefinitely, this mechanism could potentially come in handy.

The 14 Theme Animations

Windows 8 includes 14 theme animations. We're not going to examine each of these with the same depth as the theme transitions, but here they are:

→ **FadeOutThemeAnimation**—Animate an element's Opacity to 0.

→ **FadeInThemeAnimation**—Animate an element's Opacity back to 1. The default styles of many controls use the pair of FadeOutThemeAnimation and FadeInThemeAnimation, such as ScrollBar. This has no effect if FadeOutThemeAnimation or a similar custom animation didn't previously act upon the element.

→ **PopInThemeAnimation**—Makes the element glide in slightly from the right. (Oddly, this matches the motion of EntranceThemeTransition rather than PopupThemeTransition.) You can customize the motion with its FromHorizontalOffset and FromVerticalOffset properties, with default values of 40 and 0, respectively.

→ **PopOutThemeAnimation**—Animate an element's Opacity to 0, like when an element with PopupThemeTransition is removed.

→ **PointerDownThemeAnimation**—Creates a "pressed-in" effect by making an element shrink slightly. The default styles of ListViewItem and GridViewItem use this when they are pressed.

→ **PointerUpThemeAnimation**—Undoes the PointerDownThemeAnimation by restoring the element to its previous scale. This has no effect if PointerDownThemeAnimation or a similar custom animation didn't previously act upon the element.

→ **RepositionThemeAnimation**—This does nothing by default, but if you set its FromHorizontalOffset and FromVerticalOffset properties to values other than their default of 0, this makes the element glide into place, as with RepositionThemeAnimation. The default style of ToggleSwitch uses this to animate its "knob" between the on and off position.

→ **SwipeHintThemeAnimation**—This is the same animation that happens when the user presses and holds an item in a ListView or GridView, and it's meant to be used as a hint to the user that the cross slide selection gesture is now possible. This animation is used by the default styles of ListViewItem and GridViewItem for exactly that. This pushes the element slightly downward and then makes it quickly return to its original position. You can customize the direction and distance of the push by setting its ToHorizontalOffset and ToVerticalOffset properties to values other than their defaults of 0 and 10, respectively.

→ **SwipeBackThemeAnimation**—This is just like SwipeHintThemeAnimation and exposes the same two properties with the same default values. The only visual difference is that the initial push happens quickly and the return to its original position happens more slowly. It's the animation that happens when you deselect an item in a ListView or GridView with a cross slide gesture.

→ **DragItemThemeAnimation**—Makes the element quickly grow to its current size and then keeps it in a translucent state, just like when dragging an item in a ListView or GridView. Indeed, the default styles of ListViewItem and GridViewItem use this when dragging begins. This animation is meant to be stopped when you are done with it, rather than reversed with a different animation.

→ **DragOverThemeAnimation**—This is the animation applied to the siblings of the element being dragged for a reordering action. It makes them move out of the way. By default, this does nothing, but you can set its ToOffset property to a value other than its default of 0, and Direction property to Top (the default), Left, Bottom, or Right. For example, if Direction is Top and ToOffset is 100, the element gets pushed 100 pixels upward. The default styles for ListViewItem and GridViewItem use this, as we saw in Chapter 9.

→ **DropTargetItemThemeAnimation**—This also applies to the siblings of the element being dragged for reordering, and it is also used by the default styles of

ListViewItem and GridViewItem. It makes the element quickly shrink. This animation is meant to be stopped when you are done with it, rather than reversed with a different animation.

→ **SplitOpenThemeAnimation** and **SplitCloseThemeAnimation**—These are highly specialized animations used by ComboBox when opening and closing its dropdown. The animated element gradually gets revealed from its middle with a motion that moves outward in both vertical directions. The animation requires several properties to be set and is unlikely to be directly useful unless you're writing your own ComboBox control.

 Why can't I get FadeInThemeAnimation **to work?**

Just like with PointerUpThemeAnimation and PointerDownThemeAnimation, FadeInThemeAnimation produces a visual change only if it's applied to an element that has previously been animated with FadeOutThemeAnimation or an equivalent custom animation. These two animations change an element's opacity from 100% (for fading in) or 0% (for fading out). In the case of FadeInThemeAnimation, an element that is already opaque remains opaque.

Because these animations appear to work by altering an element's Opacity property, you might think that you could successfully apply FadeInThemeAnimation to an element whose Opacity is initially set to 0. However, this isn't the case. FadeInThemeAnimation and FadeOutThemeAnimation unfortunately operate on an element's internal member in order to change its opacity, so it doesn't cooperate with other mechanisms that touch the public Opacity property.

Tweaking Theme Animations

In addition to the already described properties that some of the theme animations expose, all animations expose a number of properties from their base class called Timeline. They also expose a simple Completed event. Every animation, even custom ones, must derive from Timeline. (The only reason this class isn't given the name Animation is that Storyboard also derives from it.)

These properties enable a variety of interesting changes, such as delaying the animation, changing its speed, making it the animation automatically play backwards once it completes, and so on. For example, the following FadeOutThemeAnimation makes an element repetitively fade out and then back in indefinitely:

```
<FadeOutThemeAnimation AutoReverse="True" RepeatBehavior="Forever"/>
```

It's the XAML equivalent of the old HTML blink tag, and just as obnoxious!

Because the point of using theme animations is to match the visual behavior of Windows and other apps, these Timeline properties are best suited for custom animations. Therefore, we'll look at them more closely later in this chapter.

Don't set the Duration **property of theme animations!**

One of the properties inherited by all animations is Duration, but setting it on a theme animation doesn't work properly. If you want to speed up or slow down a theme animation, you can set its SpeedRatio property instead to a value other than its default of 1.

Custom Animations

In addition to the 14 theme animations, the XAML UI Framework contains seven animation classes that enable you to describe your own custom animations and apply them the same way that the theme animations are applied.

The seven custom animation classes cover four possible data types that can be animated: double, Point, Color, and object. If you want to vary the value of a double property over time (such as Width, Height, Opacity, Canvas.Left, and so on), you can use an instance of DoubleAnimation. If you instead want to vary the value of a Point property over time (such as a LinearGradientBrush's StartPoint or EndPoint property), you can use an instance of PointAnimation. DoubleAnimation is by far the most commonly used custom animation class due to large the number of useful double properties on many elements.

Using a double dependency property as an example, let's see how to animate a Button's Opacity from 0 to 1 with a DoubleAnimation to make it smoothly fade in (something that FadeInThemeAnimation is unable to accomplish without a corresponding FadeOutThemeAnimation). The following is an update to the same Page we've been using for previous examples:

```
<Page …>
  <Page.Resources>
    <Storyboard x:Name="storyboard" TargetName="b" TargetProperty="Opacity">
      <DoubleAnimation From="0" To="1"/>
    </Storyboard>
  </Page.Resources>
  <Canvas Background="{StaticResource ApplicationPageBackgroundThemeBrush}">
    <Button Name="b" Opacity="0">Animating Button</Button>
  </Canvas>
</Page>
```

With From and To, the DoubleAnimation specifies the initial and end values for a double property—*any* double property. Unlike theme animations, custom animations are not preconfigured to work on a specific property. Therefore, the Storyboard must associate it with not only the specific Button, but its Opacity property that we want to animate.

With the same code-behind used previously that calls the Storyboard's Begin method the first time the Window's Activated event is raised, this animation successfully fades the Button in over the course of one second. The explicit Opacity="0" marked on the Button isn't needed to make the animation work, but it *is* needed to prevent a flash of it being visible immediately before the animation begins.

It's important to note that classes such as DoubleAnimation take care of smoothly changing the double value over time via *linear interpolation*. In other words, for this one-second animation, the value of Opacity is .05 when .1 seconds have elapsed (5% progress in both the value and time elapsed), .5 when .5 seconds have elapsed (50% progress in both the value and time elapsed), and so on. This is different than the interpolation used by the theme transitions and theme animations, but there are ways for custom animations to get their more "springy" behavior as well, described later.

 Animation classes can vary the value of a _dependency_ property only!

This is one reason why the proliferation of dependency properties on elements in the XAML UI Framework is so handy.

Figuring out how to apply an animation to get the desired results can take a little practice. For example, you can't make an element fade in or out by animating its Visibility property. That's because there's no middle ground between Visible and Hidden. For another example, animating the Width of a Grid's column is not straightforward because ColumnDefinition.Width is defined as a GridLength structure, which has no corresponding animation class built in. Instead, you could animate ColumnDefinition's MinWidth and/or MaxWidth properties, both of type double, or you could set ColumnDefinition's Width to Auto and then insert an element in that column whose Width you animate.

Independent versus Dependent Animations

Speaking of animating an element's Width, it would be natural to try to repurpose the previous DoubleAnimation to animate the Button's Width instead of its Opacity. After all, Width is a dependency property, and it's of type double. So this should work, right? Well, yes, but not by default.

Animations that operate on an element's Opacity, RenderTransform, or Projection can run on the GPU (in other words, are hardware accelerated) because the underlying visual surface being manipulated doesn't need to change. So can animations on the Canvas.Left and Canvas.Top attached properties, which is effectively the same as animating a TranslateTransform. These are examples of independent animations.

Other animations, such as directly changing an element's Width and Height, are dependent animations. For the Button example, every time its Width changes, a sequence of events occurs (for example, layout updates and changes to its inner contents that can be arbitrarily complex) that ultimately result in its visual surface needing to be re-rendered. These are examples of dependent animations.

In previous XAML technologies, it was easy to introduce poor-performing animations if you weren't careful (and didn't know the rules about which animations are hardware accelerated). In Windows 8, there's one small safeguard meant to help prevent this situation: By default, _dependent animations (any animations that can't be hardware-accelerated) don't run at all_!

To make an animation work despite its lack of hardware acceleration, you must set its EnableDependentAnimation property to true. Therefore, the following update to the preceding `Page` successfully animates the `Width` of the now-always-opaque `Button`, performance be damned:

```
<Page …>
  <Page.Resources>
    <Storyboard x:Name="storyboard" TargetName="b" TargetProperty="Width">
      <DoubleAnimation From="0" To="500" EnableDependentAnimation="True"/>
    </Storyboard>
  </Page.Resources>
  <Canvas Background="{StaticResource ApplicationPageBackgroundThemeBrush}">
    <Button Name="b" Width="0">Animating Button</Button>
  </Canvas>
</Page>
```

"But Adam," you might say, "I work with some careless developers who could easily let such animations creep into our codebase with `EnableDependentAnimation` set to `true`!" That is true, but at least this property gives you, the knowledgeable developer who is reading this book, a red flag to search for if your app has performance issues. Or, you can one-up your coworkers and set the static `Timeline.AllowDependentAnimations` property to `false` somewhere in your C# code. (Note the slightly different property name.) Once set, this disables *all* dependent animations in your app, regardless of their settings! (You cannot set it to `true` to achieve the reverse.) "Take that, coworkers," you might now exclaim. "They'll be left scratching their heads when their dependent animations don't work regardless of their `EnableDependentAnimation` values!"

All joking aside, dependent animations aren't *that* big of a deal if used judiciously. Sometimes you can't achieve the effect you want with an independent animation, so you might be able to enable dependent animations with a clear conscience.

The best way to animate the size and location of an element is to attach a ScaleTransform and/or TranslateTransform and animate its properties instead. Such animations are independent animations, unlike animating `Width` and `Height`. Animating ScaleTransform's ScaleX and ScaleY is generally more useful than animating `Width` and `Height` anyway because it enables you to keep the transform centered, and also change the size by a percentage rather than a fixed number of units. Animating TranslateTransform is also better than animating something like Canvas.Left and Canvas.Top because it works regardless of what Panel contains the element.

Controlling Duration

Both `DoubleAnimations` used thus far have the default duration of one second, but you can change this by setting its `Duration` property inherited from `Timeline`:

```
<DoubleAnimation From="0" To="1" Duration="0:0:5"/>
```

This changes the duration to five seconds. The syntax for specifying the length of time in XAML is the same as what `TimeSpan.Parse` accepts: *days*.*hours*:*minutes*:*seconds*.*fraction*.

> **⚠ Be careful when specifying a TimeSpan or `Duration` as a string!**
>
> TimeSpan.Parse, which is also used automatically by a type converter for TimeSpan and Duration for the benefit of XAML, accepts shortcuts in its syntax so you don't need to specify every piece of *days.hours:minutes:seconds.fraction*. However, the behavior is not what you might expect. The string "2" means 2 *days*, not 2 seconds! Given that most animations are no more than a few seconds long, the typical syntax used is *hours:minutes:seconds* or *hours:minutes:seconds.fraction*. So, 2 seconds can be expressed as "0:0:2", and half a second can be expressed as "0:0:0.5" or "0:0:.5".

> •••
>
> **The Difference Between Duration and TimeSpan**
>
> The Duration property is of type Duration rather than TimeSpan (although there is an implicit conversion). The reason for this is that Duration has two special values that can't be expressed by TimeSpan: Duration.Automatic and Duration.Forever (or just `"Automatic"` and `"Forever"` in XAML).
>
> Automatic is the default value for every animation class's Duration property, which is equivalent to a one-second TimeSpan. Forever is nonsensical for a simple animation such as DoubleAnimation because such a Duration would make it stay at its initial value indefinitely. The class can't interpolate values between now and the end of time!

Flexibility with `From` and `To`

The following Page adds a ScaleTransform to the Button and applies two Storyboards to animate it: one triggered by PointerEntered, and one triggered by the PointerExited family of events:

```xml
<Page …>
  <Page.Resources>
    <!-- Two Storyboards, one for growing and one for shrinking -->
    <Storyboard x:Name="growStoryboard" TargetName="t" TargetProperty="ScaleX">
      <DoubleAnimation From="1" To="1.4"/>
    </Storyboard>
    <Storyboard x:Name="shrinkStoryboard" TargetName="t" TargetProperty="ScaleX">
      <DoubleAnimation From="1.4" To="1"/>
    </Storyboard>
  </Page.Resources>
  <Canvas Background="{StaticResource ApplicationPageBackgroundThemeBrush}">
    <Button Content="Animating Button" Margin="50" RenderTransformOrigin=".5,.5"
            PointerEntered="Button_Entered" PointerExited="Button_Exited"
            PointerCanceled="Button_Exited" PointerCaptureLost="Button_Exited">
      <Button.RenderTransform>
        <ScaleTransform x:Name="t"/>
      </Button.RenderTransform>
    </Button>
  </Canvas>
</Page>
```

The code-behind starts the right Storyboard based on the event, and produces the result in Figure 15.6:

```csharp
using Windows.UI.Xaml.Controls;
using Windows.UI.Xaml.Input;

namespace Chapter15
{
  public sealed partial class MainPage : Page
  {
    public MainPage()
    {
      InitializeComponent();
    }

    void Button_Entered(object sender, PointerRoutedEventArgs e)
    {
      this.growStoryboard.Begin();
    }

    void Button_Exited(object sender, PointerRoutedEventArgs e)
    {
      this.shrinkStoryboard.Begin();
    }
  }
}
```

Initial appearance

While the mouse pointer hovers

FIGURE 15.6   A custom animation increases the Button's horizontal scale on PointerEntered.

This works pretty well. However, if the pointer exits while the growStoryboard animation is still running, there's a jarring jump from the current animated scale up to 1.4 before it starts to shrink, and vice versa.

To fix this jarring "jump" effect, you can omit the From setting on both animations! When you omit From, the animation begins with the current value of the target property, whatever that might be. Therefore, the previous two animations should be updated as follows:

```
<!-- Two Storyboards, one for growing and one for shrinking -->
<Storyboard x:Name="growStoryboard" TargetName="t" TargetProperty="ScaleX">
    <DoubleAnimation To="1.4"/>
</Storyboard>
<Storyboard x:Name="shrinkStoryboard" TargetName="t" TargetProperty="ScaleX">
    <DoubleAnimation To="1"/>
</Storyboard>
```

Note that if the ScaleTransform named t was explicitly given a ScaleX of 2 rather than its default value of 1, the initial run of growStoryboard would *shrink* the scale rather than grow it!

In fact, the To setting is also optional if you've specified From. An animation with a From but no To means, "animate from the From value to the current value."

Instead of To, you can alternatively set a By property. This uses From + By for the final value, or *currentValue* + By if From is not specified. The following means "animate the current value *by* .4":

```
<DoubleAnimation By=".4"/>
```

You can also use negative values.

Note that the preceding DoubleAnimation is *not* the same thing as the one inside growStoryboard. If you were to use that instead (and leave shrinkStoryboard without a From value), then fast-enough entering and exiting of the pointer would cause the target Button to grow bigger and bigger! That's because .4 would be added to the current animated value of ScaleX each time!

The three basic custom animation classes—DoubleAnimation, ColorAnimation, and PointAnimation—all expose From, To, and By properties.

> **(?) Why doesn't my custom animation do anything?**
>
> There are two common reasons for this. The first is related to the interpolation that must be done with a property value if you omit From or To from the animation. Unlike properties such as Opacity and ScaleX whose default value is 1, recall from Chapter 3, "Sizing, Positioning, and Transforming Elements," that the default value of properties such as Width and Height is Double.NaN. If you attempt to animate a property whose value is Double.NaN and don't specify both From and To (or By), the animation system has no way to interpolate values and silently fails. In this case, you need to add an explicit value somewhere. Either give the target element an explicit initial value, or add the missing From/To/By on the animation.
>
> Even if you do that, you are likely to run into the most common reason for an animation silently failing, and that's having a dependent animation that doesn't have EnableDependentAnimation set to true, as described previously. If that *still* doesn't work, check to see whether your coworker has snuck in a line of code somewhere in your app that sets Timeline.AllowDependentAnimations to false to globally disable them all!

Tweaking Animations with `Timeline` Properties

Now is a good time to look at the `Timeline` properties that are useful for every animation, whether it's a custom animation or a theme animation.

BeginTime

If you don't want an animation to begin immediately when you call its storyboard's `Begin` method (or trigger it via XAML), you can insert a delay by setting `BeginTime` to an instance of a `TimeSpan`:

```
<DoubleAnimation To="100" BeginTime="0:0:2"/>
```

This delays the animation by two seconds.

Besides being potentially useful in isolation, `BeginTime` can be useful for specifying a sequence of animations that start one after the other. You can even set `BeginTime` to a negative value:

```
<!-- Start the animation half-way through: -->
<DoubleAnimation From="50" To="100" Duration="0:0:5" BeginTime="-0:0:2.5"/>
```

This starts the animation immediately, but at 2.5 seconds into the timeline (as if the animation really started 2.5 seconds previously). Therefore, the preceding animation is equivalent to one with `From` set to 75, `To` set to 100, and `Duration` set to 2.5 seconds.

Note that `BeginTime` is of type `Nullable<TimeSpan>` rather than `Duration` because the extra expressiveness of `Duration` is not needed. (It would be nonsensical to set a `BeginTime` of `Forever`!)

SpeedRatio

The `SpeedRatio` property is a multiplier applied to `Duration`. It's set to 1 by default, but you can set it to any `double` value greater than 0:

```
<!-- Make the animation twice as slow: -->
<DoubleAnimation From="50" To="100" Duration="0:0:5" BeginTime="0:0:5"
                 SpeedRatio="2"/>
```

A value less than 1 slows down the animation, and a value greater than 1 speeds it up. `SpeedRatio` does not affect `BeginTime`; the preceding animation still has a 5-second delay, but the transition from 50 to 100 takes only 2.5 seconds rather than 5.

AutoReverse

If `AutoReverse` is set to `true`, the animation "plays backward" as soon as it completes. The reversal takes the same amount of time as the forward progress. For example, the following animation makes the value go from 50 to 100 in the first 5 seconds, and then from 100 back to 50 over the course of 5 more seconds:

```
<DoubleAnimation From="50" To="100" Duration="0:0:5" AutoReverse="True"/>
```

SpeedRatio affects the speed of *both* the forward animation and backward animation. Therefore, giving the preceding animation a SpeedRatio of 2 would make the entire animation run for 5 seconds and giving it a SpeedRatio of 0.5 would make it run for 20 seconds. Note that any delay specified via BeginTime does *not* delay the reversal; it always happens immediately after the normal part of the animation completes.

RepeatBehavior

By setting RepeatBehavior, you can accomplish one of four different behaviors:

→ Making the animation repeat itself a certain number of times, regardless of its duration

→ Making the animation repeat itself until a certain amount of time has elapsed

→ Cutting off the animation early

→ Making it repeat forever

To repeat an animation a certain number of times, you can set RepeatBehavior to a number followed by "x":

```
<!-- Perform the animation twice in a row: -->
<DoubleAnimation From="50" To="100" Duration="0:0:5" AutoReverse="True"
                RepeatBehavior="2x"/>
```

When AutoReverse is true, the reversal is repeated as well. So, the preceding animation goes from 50 to 100 to 50 to 100 to 50 over the course of 20 seconds. If BeginTime is set to introduce a delay, that delay is *not* repeated. RepeatBehavior accepts a double, so you can repeat by a fractional amount.

To repeat the animation until a certain amount of time has elapsed, you set RepeatBehavior to a TimeSpan instead. The following animation is equivalent to the preceding one:

```
<!-- Perform the animation twice in a row: -->
<DoubleAnimation From="50" To="100" Duration="0:0:5" AutoReverse="True"
                RepeatBehavior="0:0:20"/>
```

Twenty seconds is needed to make the animation complete two full cycles because AutoReverse is set to true. Note that the TimeSpan-based RepeatBehavior is not scaled by SpeedRatio; if you set SpeedRatio to 2 in the preceding animation, it performs the full cycle four times rather than two.

To use RepeatBehavior as a way to cut off an animation early, you use a TimeSpan value shorter than the natural duration. The following animation makes the value go from 50 to 75 over the course of 2.5 seconds:

```
<!-- Stop the animation halfway through: -->
<DoubleAnimation From="50" To="100" Duration="0:0:5" RepeatBehavior="0:0:2.5"/>
```

Finally, you can make an animation repeat indefinitely by setting `RepeatBehavior` to `Forever`, as shown previously with the blinking `FadeOutThemeAnimation` example.

The Total Timeline Length of an Animation   • • •

With all the different adjustments that can be made to an animation by using properties such as BeginTime, SpeedRatio, AutoReverse, and RepeatBehavior, it can be hard to keep track of how long it will take an animation to finish after it is initiated. Its Duration value certainly isn't adequate for describing the true length of time! Instead, the following formula describes an animation's true duration:

$$\text{Total Timeline Length} = \texttt{BeginTime} + \left(\frac{\texttt{Duration} * (\texttt{AutoReverse ? 2:1})}{\texttt{SpeedRatio}} * \texttt{RepeatBehavior} \right)$$

This applies if RepeatBehavior is specified as multiplier (or left as its default value of 1x). If RepeatBehavior is specified as a TimeSpan, the total timeline length is simply the value of RepeatBehavior plus the value of BeginTime.

FillBehavior

By default, when an animation completes, the target property remains at the final animated value unless some other animation later changes the value. This is typically the desired behavior, but if you want the property to jump back to its pre-animated value after the animation completes, you can set `FillBehavior` to `Stop` (rather than its default value of `HoldEnd`).

Storyboards with Multiple Animations

As mentioned when `Storyboards` were introduced, they can contain one *or more* animations. Here's an update to the `Button`-scaling XAML that scales it in both direction simultaneously (and omits the `From` values to avoid the "jump" effect):

```
<Page …>
  <Page.Resources>
    <!-- Two Storyboards, one for growing and one for shrinking -->
    <Storyboard x:Name="growStoryboard" TargetName="t">
      <DoubleAnimation To="1.4" Storyboard.TargetProperty="ScaleX"/>
      <DoubleAnimation To="1.4" Storyboard.TargetProperty="ScaleY"/>
    </Storyboard>
    <Storyboard x:Name="shrinkStoryboard" TargetName="t">
      <DoubleAnimation To="1" Storyboard.TargetProperty="ScaleX"/>
      <DoubleAnimation To="1" Storyboard.TargetProperty="ScaleY"/>
    </Storyboard>
  </Page.Resources>
  <Canvas Background="{StaticResource ApplicationPageBackgroundThemeBrush}">
    <Button Content="Animating Button" Margin="50" RenderTransformOrigin=".5,.5"
            PointerEntered="Button_Entered" PointerExited="Button_Exited"
            PointerCanceled="Button_Exited" PointerCaptureLost="Button_Exited">
```

```
      <Button.RenderTransform>
        <ScaleTransform x:Name="t"/>
      </Button.RenderTransform>
    </Button>
  </Canvas>
</Page>
```

The code-behind doesn't need to change, because there's still just one Storyboard to begin in Button_Entered and one to begin in Button_Exited.

Each Storyboard contains two animations, with each one targeting a different property on the same target. Both animations start simultaneously, but if you want a Storyboard to contain animations that begin at different times, you can give each animation a different BeginTime value.

What makes this possible is that Storyboard's TargetProperty (and TargetName) properties can be applied to individual animations as attached properties. If these are still specified on the Storyboard, any individual markings on animations override them.

The only limitation is that two animations in the same Storyboard can't use the same TargetProperty on the same TargetName. Multiple theme animations can be used in the same Storyboard, and you can mix and match both theme animations and custom animations. However, this can sometimes be tricky because it's not always clear which properties are animated by a theme animation.

Property Paths

Rather than showing only DoubleAnimation, the following example uses ColorAnimation to repeatedly animate the middle Color of a three-stop gradient from white to black and back again:

```
<Page …>
  <Page.Resources>
    <Storyboard x:Name="gradientStoryboard" TargetName="stop"
                TargetProperty="Color">
      <ColorAnimation From="White" To="Black" Duration="0:0:2"
                      AutoReverse="True" RepeatBehavior="Forever"
                      EnableDependentAnimation="True"/>
    </Storyboard>
  </Page.Resources>
  <Canvas Background="{StaticResource ApplicationPageBackgroundThemeBrush}">
    <Rectangle Width="200" Height="200">
      <Rectangle.Fill>
        <LinearGradientBrush>
          <GradientStop Color="Blue" Offset="0"/>
          <GradientStop x:Name="stop" Color="White" Offset="0.5"/>
          <GradientStop Color="Blue" Offset="1"/>
        </LinearGradientBrush>
```

```
      </Rectangle.Fill>
    </Rectangle>
  </Canvas>
</Page>
```

The idea of animating a Color might sound strange, but it has a numeric representation comprised of its A, R, G, and B properties, so ColorAnimation can interpolate those values much as DoubleAnimation does for its single value. Because the animation never ends, the Storyboard can be started in the Page's constructor:

```
this.gradientStoryboard.Begin();
```

The result is shown in Figure 15.7.

Starting at white   Halfway through   Ending at black

FIGURE 15.7   A color inside a gradient can be animated with a ColorAnimation.

The syntax for TargetProperty doesn't have to be a simple property name. It can be a *property path*, which is a more complicated expression representing a chain of properties to follow starting at TargetName. Although you never need to use this syntax because you can always directly name the target, the following update to the preceding Page shows how it can be used:

```
<Page …>
  <Page.Resources>
    <Storyboard x:Name="gradientStoryboard" TargetName="r"
              TargetProperty="(Fill).GradientStops[1].Color">
      <ColorAnimation From="White" To="Black" Duration="0:0:2"
                    AutoReverse="True" RepeatBehavior="Forever"
                    EnableDependentAnimation="True"/>
    </Storyboard>
  </Page.Resources>
  <Canvas Background="{StaticResource ApplicationPageBackgroundThemeBrush}">
    <Rectangle Name="r" Width="200" Height="200">
      <Rectangle.Fill>
        <LinearGradientBrush>
          <GradientStop Color="Blue" Offset="0"/>
```

```
        <GradientStop Color="White" Offset="0.5"/>
        <GradientStop Color="Blue" Offset="1"/>
      </LinearGradientBrush>
    </Rectangle.Fill>
  </Rectangle>
 </Canvas>
</Page>
```

The syntax for `TargetProperty` mimics what you would have to type to access the property in C#, although without casting. This `Storyboard` assumes that the `Rectangle`'s `Fill` is set to some object with a `GradientStops` property that can be indexed, assumes that it has at least two items, and assumes that the second item has a `Color` property of type `Color`. If any of these assumptions is incorrect, the animation silently fails. Of course, in this case these are all correct assumptions, so the `Rectangle` successfully animates, the same way as shown in Figure 15.7.

The "Fill" part of the property path must be placed in parentheses because it is otherwise ambiguous with a property path's support for specifying type names along with each property name, for example, (*TypeName*.*PropertyName*).(*TypeName*.*PropertyName*).…. This support exists for attached properties, which need that extra context. Therefore, here are just a few of the valid property paths that could have been used in the preceding example, from shortest to longest:

```
(Fill).GradientStops[1].Color
Shape.Fill.GradientStops[1].Color
Rectangle.Fill.GradientStops[1].Color
(Rectangle.Fill).GradientStops[1].Color
Rectangle.Fill.LinearGradientBrush.GradientStops[1].Color
(Rectangle.Fill).(LinearGradientBrush.GradientStops)[1].Color
Rectangle.Fill.LinearGradientBrush.GradientStops[1].GradientStop.Color
(Rectangle.Fill).(LinearGradientBrush.GradientStops)[1].(GradientStop.Color)
```

Tweaking `Storyboards` with `Timeline` Properties

A `Storyboard` is more than just a simple container that associates animations with target objects and their properties. Because `Storyboard` derives from `Timeline`, it has many of the same properties discussed previously: `Duration`, `BeginTime`, `SpeedRatio`, `AutoReverse`, `RepeatBehavior`, and `FillBehavior` (and the `Completed` event).

The following `Storyboard` fades one `TextBlock` in and out at a time, for an effect somewhat like that of a movie trailer. The `Storyboard` itself is marked with a `RepeatBehavior` to make the entire sequence of animation repeat indefinitely. Figure 15.8 shows how this is rendered at three different spots of the sequence:

```
<Page …>
  <Page.Resources>
    <Storyboard x:Name="storyboard" TargetProperty="Opacity"
                RepeatBehavior="Forever">
```

```xml
        <DoubleAnimation Storyboard.TargetName="title1" BeginTime="0:0:2"
          From="0" To="1" Duration="0:0:2" AutoReverse="True"/>
        <DoubleAnimation Storyboard.TargetName="title2" BeginTime="0:0:6"
          From="0" To="1" Duration="0:0:2" AutoReverse="True"/>
        <DoubleAnimation Storyboard.TargetName="title3" BeginTime="0:0:10"
          From="0" To="1" Duration="0:0:2" AutoReverse="True"/>
        <DoubleAnimation Storyboard.TargetName="title4" BeginTime="0:0:14"
          From="0" To="1" Duration="0:0:2" AutoReverse="True"/>
        <DoubleAnimation Storyboard.TargetName="title5" BeginTime="0:0:18"
          From="0" To="1" Duration="0:0:2" AutoReverse="True"/>
      </Storyboard>
    </Page.Resources>
    <Grid Background="{StaticResource ApplicationPageBackgroundThemeBrush}">
      <TextBlock HorizontalAlignment="Center" VerticalAlignment="Center"
        Opacity="0" FontSize="50" Name="title1">In a world</TextBlock>
      <TextBlock HorizontalAlignment="Center" VerticalAlignment="Center"
        Opacity="0" FontSize="50" Name="title2">where apps need to be built
      </TextBlock>
      <TextBlock HorizontalAlignment="Center" VerticalAlignment="Center"
        Opacity="0" FontSize="50" Name="title3">one book</TextBlock>
      <TextBlock HorizontalAlignment="Center" VerticalAlignment="Center"
        Opacity="0" FontSize="50" Name="title4">will explain it all.</TextBlock>
      <TextBlock HorizontalAlignment="Center" VerticalAlignment="Center"
        Opacity="0" FontSize="50" Name="title5">
        Windows 8 Apps with XAML and C# Unleashed</TextBlock>
    </Grid>
</Page>
```

FIGURE 15.8 Snapshots of the movie-trailer-like title sequence

Setting the `Timeline`-inherited properties on `Storyboard` affects the entire set of child animations, although in a slightly different way than setting the same property individually on all children. For example, setting `RepeatBehavior="Forever"` on every child animation rather than on this `Storyboard` itself would wreak havoc. The first title would fade in and out as expected, but then at 6 seconds *both* `title1` and `title2` would fade in and out together. At 10 seconds `title1`, `title2`, and `title3` would fade in and out simultaneously, and so on.

Similarly, setting `SpeedRatio="2"` on each `DoubleAnimation` would make each fade take 1 second rather than 2, but the final animation would still start 18 seconds after the animation starts. On the other hand, setting `SpeedRatio="2"` on the `Storyboard` would speed up the entire animation, including each `BeginTime`, by a factor of two. Therefore, the final animation would start 9 seconds after the animation starts. Setting `Duration` to a time shorter than the natural duration can cut off the entire sequence of animations early.

Custom Keyframe Animations

So far, all the information about custom animations applies to three basic classes: `DoubleAnimation`, `ColorAnimation`, and `PointAnimation`. But there are seven custom animation classes. The remaining four all enable *keyframes*, which provide specific values at specific times. You certainly can't miss this distinction from their names. They are called `DoubleAnimationUsingKeyFrames`, `ColorAnimationUsingKeyFrames`, `PointAnimationUsingKeyFrames`, and `ObjectAnimationUsingKeyFrames`.

The keyframe animation classes have the same members as their counterparts, except for the `From`, `To`, and `By` properties. Instead, they have a `KeyFrames` collection that can hold keyframe instances specific to the type being animated. There are four types of keyframes, which this section examines.

Linear Keyframes

Listing 15.1 uses `DoubleAnimationUsingKeyFrames` to help move a circle (`Ellipse`) in a zigzag pattern, as illustrated in Figure 15.9. The blue lines are there to show the path that the circle travelled to get to its final spot. Because the `Image` is inside a `Canvas`, the motion is accomplished by animating the `Canvas.Left` and `Canvas.Top` attached properties rather than using the more versatile `TranslateTransform`. These are still independent animations, however!

LISTING 15.1   The Zigzag Animation for Figure 15.9

```
<Page ...>
  <Page.Resources>
    <Storyboard x:Name="storyboard" TargetName="circle">
      <DoubleAnimation Storyboard.TargetProperty="(Canvas.Left)"
          From="0" To="500" Duration="0:0:3"/>
      <DoubleAnimationUsingKeyFrames Storyboard.TargetProperty="(Canvas.Top)"
          Duration="0:0:3">
        <LinearDoubleKeyFrame Value="0" KeyTime="0:0:0"/>
        <LinearDoubleKeyFrame Value="200" KeyTime="0:0:1"/>
        <LinearDoubleKeyFrame Value="0" KeyTime="0:0:2"/>
        <LinearDoubleKeyFrame Value="200" KeyTime="0:0:3"/>
      </DoubleAnimationUsingKeyFrames>
    </Storyboard>
  </Page.Resources>
```

LISTING 15.1   Continued

```
<Canvas Background="{StaticResource ApplicationPageBackgroundThemeBrush}">
  <Ellipse Name="circle" Width="50" Height="50" Fill="Orange"/>
</Canvas>
</Page>
```

FIGURE 15.9   Zigzag motion is easy to create with a keyframe animation.

The circle's motion consists of two animations that begin in parallel when the image loads. One is a simple `DoubleAnimation` that increases its horizontal position linearly from `0` to `500`. The other is the keyframe-enabled animation, which oscillates the vertical position from `0` to `200` then back to `0` then back to `200`.

Each keyframe instance (`LinearDoubleKeyFrame`) in Listing 15.1 gives a specific value and a time for that value to be applied. Although the exact vertical position of the circle is specified

 An attached property must be wrapped in parentheses when specified as a TargetProperty!

Notice that in Listing 15.1, both `Canvas.Left` and `Canvas.Top` are referenced inside parentheses when used as the value for `Storyboard`'s `TargetProperty` property. This is a requirement for any attached properties used in a property path. Without the parentheses, the animation would look for a property on `Ellipse` called `Canvas` (expecting it to return an object with `Left` and `Top` properties) and fail because it doesn't exist.

for 0, 1, 2, and 3 seconds, the animation still needs to calculate intermediate values between these "key times." Because each keyframe is represented with an instance of `LinearDoubleKeyFrame`, the intermediate values are derived from simple linear interpolation. For example, at 0.5, 1.5, and 2.5 seconds, the calculated value is 100.

But `DoubleAnimationUsingKeyFrames`'s `KeyFrames` property is a collection of base `DoubleKeyFrame` objects, so it can be filled with other types of keyframe objects. In addition to `LinearDoubleKeyFrame`, `DoubleKeyFrame` has three other subclasses: `SplineDoubleKeyFrame`, `DiscreteDoubleKeyFrame`, and `EasingDoubleKeyFrame`.

Spline Keyframes

All three `LinearXXXKeyFrame` classes have a corresponding `SplineXXXKeyFrame` class. It can be used just like its linear counterpart, so updating `DoubleAnimationUsingKeyFrames` from Listing 15.1 as follows produces the same result:

```
<DoubleAnimationUsingKeyFrames Storyboard.TargetProperty="(Canvas.Top)"
  Duration="0:0:3">
  <SplineDoubleKeyFrame Value="0" KeyTime="0:0:0"/>
  <SplineDoubleKeyFrame Value="200" KeyTime="0:0:1"/>
  <SplineDoubleKeyFrame Value="0" KeyTime="0:0:2"/>
  <SplineDoubleKeyFrame Value="200" KeyTime="0:0:3"/>
</DoubleAnimationUsingKeyFrames>
```

The spline keyframe classes have an additional `KeySpline` property that differentiates them from the linear classes. `KeySpline` can be set to an instance of a `KeySpline` object, which describes the desired motion as a cubic Bézier curve. `KeySpline` has two properties of type `Point` that represent the curve's control points. (The start point of the curve is always `0`, and the end point is always `1`.) A type converter enables you to specify a `KeySpline` in XAML as a simple list of two points. For example, the following update changes the circle's motion from the simple zigzag in Figure 15.9 to the more complicated motion in Figure 15.10:

```
<DoubleAnimationUsingKeyFrames Storyboard.TargetProperty="(Canvas.Top)"
  Duration="0:0:3">
  <SplineDoubleKeyFrame KeySpline="0,1 1,0" Value="0" KeyTime="0:0:0"/>
  <SplineDoubleKeyFrame KeySpline="0,1 1,0" Value="200" KeyTime="0:0:1"/>
  <SplineDoubleKeyFrame KeySpline="0,1 1,0" Value="0" KeyTime="0:0:2"/>
  <SplineDoubleKeyFrame KeySpline="0,1 1,0" Value="200" KeyTime="0:0:3"/>
</DoubleAnimationUsingKeyFrames>
```

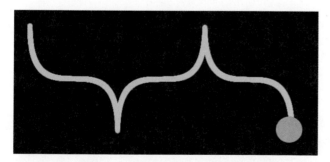

FIGURE 15.10   With KeySpline specified, the interpolation between keyframes is now based on cubic Bézier curves.

Finding the right value for `KeySpline` that gives the desired effect can be tricky and almost certainly requires the use of a design tool such as Blend. But several free tools can be found online that help you visualize Bézier curves based on the specified control points.

Discrete Keyframes

A *discrete keyframe* indicates that no interpolation should be done from the previous keyframe. Updating `DoubleAnimationUsingKeyFrames` from Listing 15.1 as follows produces the motion illustrated in Figure 15.11:

```
<DoubleAnimationUsingKeyFrames Storyboard.TargetProperty="(Canvas.Top)"
  Duration="0:0:3">
  <DiscreteDoubleKeyFrame Value="0" KeyTime="0:0:0"/>
  <DiscreteDoubleKeyFrame Value="200" KeyTime="0:0:1"/>
  <DiscreteDoubleKeyFrame Value="0" KeyTime="0:0:2"/>
  <DiscreteDoubleKeyFrame Value="200" KeyTime="0:0:3"/>
</DoubleAnimationUsingKeyFrames>
```

FIGURE 15.11   Discrete keyframes makes the circle's vertical position jump from one key value to the next, with no interpolation.

Of course, different types of keyframes can be mixed into the same animation. The following mixture makes the circle follow the path shown in Figure 15.12:

```
<DoubleAnimationUsingKeyFrames Storyboard.TargetProperty="(Canvas.Top)"
  Duration="0:0:3">
  <DiscreteDoubleKeyFrame Value="0" KeyTime="0:0:0"/>
  <LinearDoubleKeyFrame Value="200" KeyTime="0:0:1"/>
  <DiscreteDoubleKeyFrame Value="0" KeyTime="0:0:2"/>
  <SplineDoubleKeyFrame KeySpline="0,1,1,0" Value="200" KeyTime="0:0:3"/>
</DoubleAnimationUsingKeyFrames>
```

Because the first keyframe's time is at the beginning, its type is irrelevant. That's because each frame indicates only how interpolation is done *before* that frame.

As with `SplineXXXKeyFrame`, every `LinearXXXKeyFrame` class has a corresponding `DiscreteXXXKeyFrame`. But there's one discrete keyframe class that has no linear or spline counterpart: `DiscreteObjectKeyFrame`. This works with `System.Object`, so it simply changes the value of *any* property to the specified `Value` at the specified `KeyTime`. For example, the following `Storyboard` "animates" the text in a `TextBlock` from lowercase to uppercase:

```
<Storyboard x:Name="storyboard" TargetName="textBlock" TargetProperty="Text">
  <ObjectAnimationUsingKeyFrames>
    <DiscreteObjectKeyFrame Value="play" KeyTime="0:0:0"/>
    <DiscreteObjectKeyFrame Value="Play" KeyTime="0:0:1"/>
    <DiscreteObjectKeyFrame Value="PLay" KeyTime="0:0:2"/>
    <DiscreteObjectKeyFrame Value="PLAy" KeyTime="0:0:3"/>
    <DiscreteObjectKeyFrame Value="PLAY" KeyTime="0:0:4"/>
  </ObjectAnimationUsingKeyFrames>
</Storyboard>
```

FIGURE 15.12   Mixing three types of keyframes into a single animation

Only discrete keyframe animations can be used with System.Object because interpolation is impossible.

Easing Keyframes

Every LinearXXXKeyFrame and SplineXXXKeyFrame class also has a corresponding EasingXXXKeyFrame class. The easing keyframe classes have an EasingFunction property gives a lot of flexibility in how the interpolation is done. Easing functions deserve their own separate section, and we'll examine them now.

Animations that use only DiscreteObjectKeyFrames—or animations with a Duration of 0—don't need their EnableDependentAnimation property set to true because no "real" animation (interpolation) can take place.

Note that this exemption doesn't apply to an animation that uses only discrete keyframes of other types. This is a strange policy because you could represent any discrete double keyframe animation as a discrete Object keyframe animation and get the same results (as in Figure 15.11). But if the animation is dependent (for example, animates the circle's Width instead of Canvas.Top), the one form requires EnableDependentAnimation (and can be disabled with Timeline.Allow DependentAnimations) whereas the other is exempt!

Easing Functions

You've seen examples of the linear interpolation used with the three main custom animation classes, and the possible spline interpolation that can be used with three of the custom keyframe animation classes. All of the custom animation classes except the discrete-only ObjectAnimationUsingKeyFrames class enable an easing function to be plugged in to customize the interpolation. DoubleAnimation, ColorAnimation, and PointAnimation directly define an EasingFunction property, and the others can work with Easing*XXX*KeyFrame objects that define the same property.

EasingFunction can be set to a class deriving from EasingFunctionBase that controls the rate of acceleration and deceleration in arbitrarily complex ways. The XAML UI Framework ships with 11 such objects. Each of them supports three different modes with a property called EasingMode. It can be set to EaseIn, EaseOut (the default value), or EaseInOut. Here's how you can apply an easing function object—QuadraticEase—to a basic DoubleAnimation:

```
<DoubleAnimation Storyboard.TargetProperty="(Canvas.Top)" From="200" To="0"
  Duration="0:0:3">
<DoubleAnimation.EasingFunction>
  <QuadraticEase/>
</DoubleAnimation.EasingFunction>
</DoubleAnimation>
```

And here is how you change EasingMode to something other than EaseOut:

```
<DoubleAnimation Storyboard.TargetProperty="(Canvas.Top)" From="200" To="0"
  Duration="0:0:3">
<DoubleAnimation.EasingFunction>
  <QuadraticEase EasingMode="EaseIn"/>
</DoubleAnimation.EasingFunction>
</DoubleAnimation>
```

EaseIn inverts the interpolation done with EaseOut, and EaseInOut produces the EaseIn behavior for the first half of the animation and the EaseOut behavior for the second half.

Power Easing Functions

Table 15.1 demonstrates how five of the easing functions work in all three modes by showing the path an object takes if its horizontal position animates linearly but its vertical position animates from bottom to top, with each easing function and mode applied.

TABLE 15.1   Five Power Easing Functions

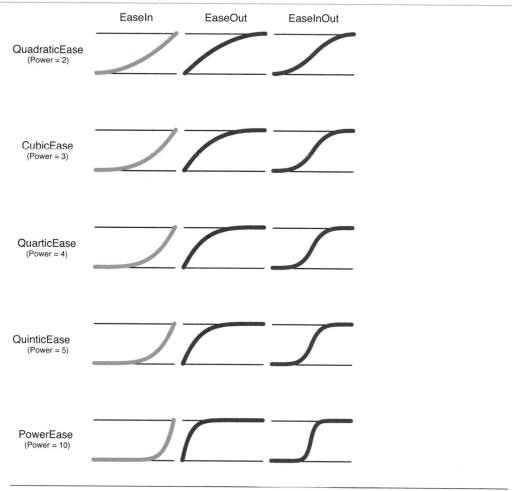

All five functions do interpolation based on a simple power function. With the default linear interpolation, when time has elapsed 50% (.5), the value has changed by 50% (.5). But with quadratic interpolation, the value has changed by 25% (.5 * .5 = .25) when time has elapsed 50%. With cubic interpolation, the value has changed by 12.5% (.5 * .5 * .5 = .125) when time has elapsed 50%, and so on. Although there are four distinct classes for powers 2 through 5, all you need is the general-purpose `PowerEase` class that performs the interpolation with the value of its `Power` property. The default value of `Power` is 2 (making it the same as `QuadraticEase`) but Table 15.1 demonstrates it with `Power` set to `10`, just to show how the transition keeps getting sharper as `Power` increases. Applying `PowerEase` with `Power` set to `10` can look as follows:

```
<DoubleAnimation Storyboard.TargetProperty="(Canvas.Top)" From="200" To="0"
  Duration="0:0:3">
```

```
<DoubleAnimation.EasingFunction>
  <PowerEase Power="10"/>
</DoubleAnimation.EasingFunction>
</DoubleAnimation>
```

Other Easing Functions

Table 15.2 demonstrates the remaining six easing functions in all three modes.

TABLE 15.2   The Other Six Built-In Easing Functions

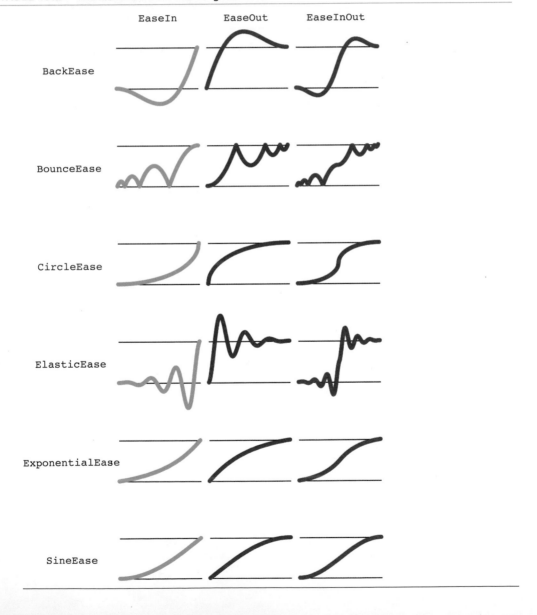

Each of these six functions has unique (and sometimes configurable) behavior:

→ **BackEase**—Moves the animated value slightly back (away from the target value) before progressing. BackEase has an Amplitude property (default=1) that controls how far back the value goes.

→ **BounceEase**—Creates what looks like a bouncing pattern (at least when used to animate position). BounceEase has two properties for controlling its behavior. Bounces (default=3) controls how many bounces occur during the animation, and Bounciness (default=2) controls how much the amplitude of each bounce changes from the previous bounce. For EaseIn, Bounciness=2 doubles the height of each bounce. For EaseOut, Bounciness=2 halves the height of each bounce. So for the more natural EaseOut case, a higher Bounciness actually makes the element appear *less* bouncy!

→ **CircleEase**—Accelerates (for EaseIn) or decelerates (for EaseOut) the value with a circular function.

→ **ElasticEase**—Creates what looks like an oscillating spring pattern (at least when used to animate position). Like BounceEase, it has two properties for controlling its behavior. Oscillations (default=3) controls how many oscillations occur during the animation, and Springiness (default=3) controls the amplitude of oscillations. The behavior of Springiness is subtle: Larger values give smaller oscillations (as if the spring is thicker and more difficult to stretch), and smaller values give larger oscillations (which, in my opinion, seems to make the motion *more* springy rather than *less*).

→ **ExponentialEase**—Interpolates that value with an exponential function, using the value of its Exponent property (default=2).

→ **SineEase**—Interpolates the value with a function based on the sine formula.

 BackEase and ElasticEase can produce unexpected negative values!

Because BackEase and ElasticEase make changes to the value outside the range of From to To, any animation starting at zero (for EaseIn or EaseInOut) or ending at zero (for EaseOut or EaseInOut) will likely veer into negative territory. If such an animation is applied to a value that cannot be negative, such as an element's Width or Height, an exception will be thrown.

What EaseOut and EaseInOut Actually Mean

•••

EaseIn is easy to understand because it corresponds exactly to how most people think about an animated value progressing as a function of time. To understand what the EaseOut and EaseInOut modes actually do, imagine that QuadraticEase is implemented with following method to perform its interpolation:

```
double DoQuadraticInterpolation(double normalizedTime)
{
    return normalizedTime * normalizedTime;
}
```

For EaseIn, DoQuadraticInterpolation would be called repeatedly with values starting at 0 and ending at 1. For EaseOut, DoQuadraticInterpolation would be called repeatedly with values starting at 1 and ending at 0. (The normalizedTime would be 1 - normalizedTime.) The value returned by DoQuadraticInterpolation would then need to be inverted in this case; in other words 1 - *returnedValue*.

For the EaseInOut case, the behavior is different between the first half of the animation (normalizedTime values from 0 up to but not including 0.5) and the second half (normalizedTime values from 0.5 to 1). For the first half, the normalizedTime value passed to DoQuadraticInterpolation would be doubled (spanning the full range of 0 to 1 in half the time), but the value returned would be halved. For the second half, the normalizedTime value passed to DoQuadraticInterpolation would be doubled *and* inverted (spanning the full range of 1 to 0 in half the time). The value returned from DoQuadraticInterpolation would then be halved and inverted, and finally .5 would be added to the value (because this is the second half of progress toward the final value). This is why every deterministic EaseInOut animation is symmetrical and hits 50% progress when 50% of the time has elapsed.

Manual Animations

Of course, even with all the fancy animation support discussed in this chapter, nothing prevents you from animating the old fashioned way. The classic way to implement animations such as the ones in this chapter is to set up a timer and a callback function that is periodically called based on the frequency of the timer. Inside the callback function, you can manually update the target property (doing a little math to determine the current value based on the elapsed time) until it reaches the final value. At that point, you can stop the timer and/or remove the event handler.

Thanks to the retained-mode graphics model, this approach doesn't take much work. The XAML UI Framework even has its own DispatcherTimer class that can be used for implementing such a scheme. You get to choose DispatcherTimer's frequency by setting its Interval property, you can attach an event handler to its Tick event, and then you can call its Start and Stop methods.

The Difference Between DispatcherTimer and ThreadPoolTimer

The key difference between DispatcherTimer and the other timer class available to C# (System.Threading.ThreadPoolTimer) is that handlers for DispatcherTimer are always invoked on the main thread. This is convenient because you don't need to use CoreDispatcher to explicitly marshal back to the main thread, as shown in Chapter 12, "Audio and Video."

Although this approach might be familiar, performing animation with a timer is not recommended. The timers are not in sync with the monitor's vertical refresh rate, nor are they in sync with the rendering engine, nor do they take advantage of hardware acceleration.

Instead of implementing custom timer-based animation, you could perform custom frame-based animation by attaching an event handler to the static `Rendering` event on a class called `CompositionTarget`. Rather than being raised at a customizable interval, this event is raised post-layout and pre-render *once per frame*.

Using the frame-based `Rendering` event is not only preferred over a timer-based approach, it can even preferred over the animation classes that are the focus of this chapter when dealing with hundreds of objects that require high-fidelity animations. For example, collision detection or other physics-based animations should be done using this approach. The `Rendering` event generally gives the best performance and the most customizations (because you can write arbitrary code in the event handler), although there are tradeoffs. In normal conditions, frames are rendered only when part of the user interface is invalidated. But as long as any event handler is attached to `Rendering`, frames get rendered continuously. Therefore, using `Rendering` is best for short-lived animations.

The blue "paths" in Figures 15.9–15.12 were generated with the help of the `Rendering` event. While the `Storyboard` was running and moving the orange circle, the following handler for `CompositionTarget.Rendering` placed a smaller blue circle (dot) in the orange circle's current location on every frame:

```
void CompositionTarget_Rendering(object sender, object e)
{
  // A new small blue circle
  Ellipse dot = new Ellipse { Fill = new SolidColorBrush(Colors.Aqua),
                              Width = 10, Height = 10 };

  // Center it in the current location of the orange circle
  Canvas.SetLeft(dot, Canvas.GetLeft(this.circle) + this.circle.Width / 2);
  Canvas.SetTop(dot, Canvas.GetTop(this.circle) + this.circle.Height / 2);

  // Insert it in the beginning so it's underneath the orange circle:
  this.canvas.Children.Insert(0, dot);
}
```

This requires the `Canvas` to be given the name canvas. The orange circle (already named circle) could have been given an explicit `ZIndex` so the new blue circles could have been *added* to the `Children` collection rather than *inserted* at the beginning, but either way works. Note that for tracing the spline animation in Figures 15.10 and 15.12, the `Storyboard` needed to be slowed down considerably (with a `SpeedRatio` of `.01`) to produce solid lines, because the circle moved too quickly otherwise. Figure 15.13 shows what the animation from Figure 15.10 looks like when it runs at normal speed and the position is traced via the `CompositionTarget_Rendering` handler.

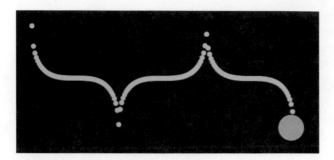

FIGURE 15.13   Tracing the animation from Figure 15.10 at its normal speed

Summary

Here is a concise way to describe the four main types of animations available to you:

→ **Theme transitions:** Specific animations for specific actions

→ **Theme animations:** Specific animations for custom actions

→ **Custom animations:** Custom animations for custom actions

→ **Manual animations:** Custom code that doesn't leverage any animation features, other than perhaps the `Rendering` event

The theme transitions are a huge timesaver when it comes to adding high-quality, high-performance, and consistent animations to your app. Try to recreate a transition with custom animations, and you'll appreciate just how much they do for you!

With all the animation choices, you can do something as simple as a subtle rollover effect or as complex as an animated cartoon. `Storyboards`, which are a necessary part of performing animations, help to orchestrate complex series of animations.

An important aspect of all these animations (except manual ones) is that they are "time resolution independent." Similar in spirit to the automatic scaling done for graphics based on DPI, transitions and animations do not speed up as hardware gets faster; they simply get smoother! The frame rate is varied based on a variety of conditions, and you as the animation developer don't need to care.

Going overboard with animation can harm the usability and performance of your app. A good way to diagnose performance problems related to rendering is to enable a special frame rate counter as follows:

```
Application.Current.DebugSettings.EnableFrameRateCounter = true;
```

This overlays six numbers in the top left corner of your app, shown in Figure 15.14.

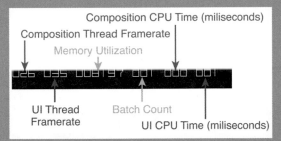

FIGURE 15.14   The information shown when setting `EnableFrameRateCounter` to `true`

The *composition thread* is used by independent animations. You should strive to keep this frame rate at 30 (frames per second) or higher. The UI thread is used for dependent animations. You should strive to keep this frame rate at 15 or higher.

A higher *batch count* increases the likelihood that animations will experience glitches. This refers to the fact that commands sent to the GPU are batched. The more batches needed to draw a frame, the more expensive the CPU cost of issuing those commands to the GPU.

Composition CPU time isn't very actionable for developers outside of Microsoft, but it should stay below 15 milliseconds. *UI CPU time* can get arbitrarily high, but if you see high values in a steady state (such as 100 milliseconds), you should try to pinpoint the code responsible for this.

You can also enable an "overdraw heat map" by setting the following property to `true`:

```
Application.Current.DebugSettings.IsOverdrawHeatMapEnabled = true;
```

This points out areas where the same pixels are drawn more than once by coloring them in various shades of red.

You can enable the frame rate counter (although not the overdraw heat map) across all your apps without modifying their code. To do so, you must create and set the following registry key:

For 64-bit: `HKEY_LOCAL_MACHINE\SOFTWARE\Wow6432Node\Microsoft\Xaml\EnableFrameRateCounter` = 1 (a DWORD)

For 32-bit: HKEY_LOCAL_MACHINE\SOFTWARE\Microsoft\Xaml\EnableFrameRateCounter = 1 (a DWORD)

Chapter 16

STYLES, TEMPLATES, AND VISUAL STATES

Arguably the most celebrated feature in XAML-based UI is the ability to give any control a radically different look without having to give up all of the built-in functionality that it provides. Even with Cascading Style Sheets (CSS), HTML lacks this much power, which is the reason most websites and HTML-based apps use images to represent buttons rather than "real buttons." Of course, it's easy to simulate a button's behavior with an image in HTML, but what if you want to give a completely different look to a SELECT element (HTML's version of ComboBox)? It's a lot of work if you want to do more than change simple properties such as its foreground and background colors.

This chapter explains the three main components of XAML control restyling support:

→ **Styles**—A simple mechanism for separating property values from user interface elements (similar to the relationship between CSS and HTML). Styles are also the foundation for applying the other mechanisms in this chapter.

→ **Templates**—Powerful objects that most people are referring to when they talk about "restyling" XAML controls.

→ **Visual States**—An important part of templates, which enable them to adjust their visuals based on the current states of the templated controls.

As you'll see, an important enabler of the restyling support is the semantics of resources.

 Why are developers allowed to completely customize the look of XAML controls? They were designed for consistency with Windows!

The point is to enable apps to infuse their own branding into the entire user experience. Despite the lack of consistency (or even *because of* lack of consistency), apps with unique user experiences can do very well. XAML's philosophy is to make an application's experience limited only by the skill of its designers rather than by the underlying platform. It's hard to disagree with that stance.

Styles

A *style*, represented by the `Windows.UI.Xaml.Style` class, is a simple entity. It groups together property values that could otherwise be set individually. The intent is to then share this group of values among multiple elements. There have been examples in this book in which property values were duplicated on multiple elements. Using a `Style` to avoid the duplication is a much cleaner solution.

Take, for example, the three customized `Buttons` in Figure 16.1. This look is achieved by setting seven properties. Without a `Style`, you would need to duplicate these identical assignments on all three `Buttons` as follows:

```
<Page …>
  <Grid Background="{StaticResource ApplicationPageBackgroundThemeBrush}">
    <StackPanel Margin="20" Orientation="Horizontal">
      <Button FontSize="22" Background="Purple" Foreground="White"
        Height="60" Width="60" RenderTransformOrigin=".5,.5" Content="1">
        <Button.RenderTransform>
          <RotateTransform Angle="10"/>
        </Button.RenderTransform>
      </Button>
      <Button FontSize="22" Background="Purple" Foreground="White"
        Height="60" Width="60" RenderTransformOrigin=".5,.5" Content="2">
        <Button.RenderTransform>
          <RotateTransform Angle="10"/>
        </Button.RenderTransform>
      </Button>
      <Button FontSize="22" Background="Purple" Foreground="White"
        Height="60" Width="60" RenderTransformOrigin=".5,.5" Content="3">
        <Button.RenderTransform>
          <RotateTransform Angle="10"/>
        </Button.RenderTransform>
      </Button>
    </StackPanel>
  </Grid>
</Page>
```

FIGURE 16.1   Three `Buttons` whose looks have been customized

With a `Style`, you can add a level of indirection—setting the properties in one place and pointing each `Button` to this new element:

```
<Page …>
  <Grid Background="{StaticResource ApplicationPageBackgroundThemeBrush}">
    <StackPanel Margin="20" Orientation="Horizontal">
      <StackPanel.Resources>
        <Style x:Key="PurpleTiltStyle" TargetType="Button">
          <Setter Property="FontSize" Value="22"/>
          <Setter Property="Background" Value="Purple"/>
          <Setter Property="Foreground" Value="White"/>
          <Setter Property="Height" Value="60"/>
          <Setter Property="Width" Value="60"/>
          <Setter Property="RenderTransformOrigin" Value=".5,.5"/>
          <Setter Property="RenderTransform">
            <Setter.Value>
              <RotateTransform Angle="10"/>
            </Setter.Value>
          </Setter>
        </Style>
      </StackPanel.Resources>
      <Button Style="{StaticResource PurpleTiltStyle}" Content="1"/>
      <Button Style="{StaticResource PurpleTiltStyle}" Content="2"/>
      <Button Style="{StaticResource PurpleTiltStyle}" Content="3"/>
    </StackPanel>
  </Grid>
</Page>
```

Style definition

Applying the Style

The same `Style` instance is set as the value for each `Button`'s property called `Style`. The `Style` property is defined on `FrameworkElement`, so it can be used with non-`Controls` such as `Rectangles` and `Ellipses` as well.

`Style` uses a collection of `Setters` to set the target properties. Creating a `Setter` is a matter of specifying the name of a dependency property and a desired value for it. The `Style` is placed in a `Resources` collection so elements can assign it as the value of their `Style` property with `{StaticResource resourceName}` syntax. This works regardless of whether the `Style` in the `Resources` collection is named with `x:Key` or `x:Name`, although in the latter case the generated field can be handy for code-behind.

Notice that the `Style` is added to `StackPanel`'s `Resources` collection. It could alternatively be added to the parent `Grid`'s `Resources` collection, or the `Page`'s `Resources` collection. The only requirement is that references to the `Style` resource must be contained within the same scope. `Application` even defines a `Resources` collection (seen in `App.xaml`) that can be used to define `Styles` that apply across the entire app.

Note that despite its name, there's nothing inherently visual about a `Style`. But it's typically used for setting properties that affect visuals. Indeed, `Style` enables the setting of dependency properties only, which tend to be visual in nature.

Any individual element can override aspects of its Style by directly setting a property to a local value. For example, the first Button in Figure 16.1 could do the following to retain the rotation, size, and so on, from controlStyle yet have a red Background rather than a purple one:

```
<Button Style="{StaticResource PurpleTiltStyle}" Background="Red" Content="1"/>
```

This works because of the order of precedence for dependency property values presented in Chapter 5, "Interactivity." The local value trumps anything set from a Style.

Style Selectors

`FrameworkElement`'s `Style` property isn't the only property of type `Style` in the XAML UI Framework. `ItemsControl` has an `ItemContainerStyle` property that applies to each item container such as `ListViewItem` or `ComboBoxItem`, and `GroupStyle` (described in the next chapter) has a similar `ContainerStyle` property.

These classes also have an `ItemContainerStyleSelector` and `GroupStyleSelector` property, respectively, that can be set to a custom class deriving from `StyleSelector`. This class defines a `SelectStyle` method that gets invoked whenever an item container or group is about to be rendered, enabling you to use custom logic to apply a potentially different `Style` to every item.

Using a Base `TargetType`

Although the `Style` in Figure 16.1 is shared among three `Buttons`, it can be shared by any kind of `Control` if you mark it with `TargetType="Control"` instead:

```
<Page …>
…
        <Style x:Key="PurpleTiltStyle" TargetType="Control">
…

        <Button Style="{StaticResource PurpleTiltStyle}" Content="1"/>
        <ToggleSwitch Style="{StaticResource PurpleTiltStyle}"/>
        <ProgressRing IsActive="True" Style="{StaticResource PurpleTiltStyle}"/>
…
</Page>
```

The result is shown in Figure 16.2. Note that `ToggleSwitch`'s default appearance enforces a minimum width, so it ignores the `Style`'s `Width` setting.

FIGURE 16.2   Heterogeneous controls given the same `Style`

StandardStyles.xaml

`StandardStyles.xaml`, which gets automatically included in Visual Studio-generated projects, has many good examples of `Style`s, as well as some hidden gems you might want to use in your apps. The following `Style` called `BasicTextStyle` sets several properties that make a `TextBlock` match the typical style of labels in Windows 8 apps better:

```xml
<Style x:Key="BasicTextStyle" TargetType="TextBlock">
  <Setter Property="Foreground"
          Value="{StaticResource ApplicationForegroundThemeBrush}"/>
  <Setter Property="FontSize"
          Value="{StaticResource ControlContentThemeFontSize}"/>
  <Setter Property="FontFamily"
          Value="{StaticResource ContentControlThemeFontFamily}"/>
  <Setter Property="TextTrimming" Value="WordEllipsis"/>
  <Setter Property="TextWrapping" Value="Wrap"/>
  <Setter Property="Typography.StylisticSet20" Value="True"/>
  <Setter Property="Typography.DiscretionaryLigatures" Value="True"/>
  <Setter Property="Typography.CaseSensitiveForms" Value="True"/>
</Style>
```

This `Style` is leveraged by more `Style`s in `StandardStyles.xaml`, because they can inherit from one another! The following two `Style`s add an additional property to `BaselineTextStyle` by using the `BasedOn` property:

```xml
<!-- BasicTextStyle + FontWeight=SemiBold: -->
<Style x:Key="TitleTextStyle" TargetType="TextBlock"
       BasedOn="{StaticResource BaselineTextStyle}">
  <Setter Property="FontWeight" Value="SemiBold"/>
</Style>

<!-- BasicTextStyle + FontWeight=SemiLight: -->
<Style x:Key="BodyTextStyle" TargetType="TextBlock"
       BasedOn="{StaticResource BaselineTextStyle}">
```

```
  <Setter Property="FontWeight" Value="SemiLight"/>
</Style>
```

And this `Style` overrides two of the base properties:

```
<!-- BasicTextStyle with different FontSize and Foreground: -->
<Style x:Key="CaptionTextStyle" TargetType="TextBlock"
       BasedOn="{StaticResource BaselineTextStyle}">
  <Setter Property="FontSize" Value="12"/>
  <Setter Property="Foreground"
          Value="{StaticResource ApplicationSecondaryForegroundThemeBrush}"/>
</Style>
```

Recall `BackButtonStyle` in Chapter 7, "App Model." That `Style` is complex (it uses a custom control template, explained later in this chapter), but the derived `PortraitBackButtonStyle` simply sets a different `Margin`:

```
<Style x:Key="PortraitBackButtonStyle" TargetType="Button"
       BasedOn="{StaticResource BackButtonStyle}">
  <Setter Property="Margin" Value="26,0,26,36"/>
</Style>
```

The same is true for the long list of `AppBarButtonStyles` introduced in Chapter 8, "Content Controls." The base `AppBarButtonStyle` is complex, but each derived one, such as `PinAppBarButtonStyle`, has only three simple properties to set:

```
<Style x:Key="PinAppBarButtonStyle" TargetType="ButtonBase"
       BasedOn="{StaticResource AppBarButtonStyle}">
  <Setter Property="AutomationProperties.AutomationId" Value="PinAppBarButton"/>
  <Setter Property="AutomationProperties.Name" Value="Pin"/>
  <Setter Property="Content" Value="&#xE141;"/>
</Style>
```

 Instead of keeping the following Background setting on root Grids in Visual Studio-generated Pages:

```
<Grid Background="{StaticResource ApplicationPageBackgroundThemeBrush}">
```

you could instead use a `Style` defined in `StandardStyles.xaml`:

```
<Grid Style="{StaticResource LayoutRootStyle}">
```

This not only applies the same Background, but it applies the staggered `EntranceThemeTransition` to its children:

```
<Style x:Key="LayoutRootStyle" TargetType="Panel">
  <Setter Property="Background"
          Value="{StaticResource ApplicationPageBackgroundThemeBrush}"/>
```

```
    <Setter Property="ChildrenTransitions">
      <Setter.Value>
        <TransitionCollection>
          <EntranceThemeTransition/>
        </TransitionCollection>
      </Setter.Value>
    </Setter>
</Style>
```

Implicit Styles

Unlike other objects placed in a `Resources` collection, you can omit the `x:Key` *and* `x:Name` from a `Style`! If you do this, the target type of the `Style` (for example, `typeof(Button)`) is used as the key in the `ResourceDictionary`. This is handy, because it causes the `Style` to be implicitly applied to all elements of that target type within the same scope. This is typically called a *typed style* or *implicit style* as opposed to a *named style*.

The scope of a typed `Style` is determined by the location of the `Style` resource. For example, it would implicitly apply to all relevant elements in a `Page` if it's added to the `Page`'s `Resources` collection or all relevant elements in the app if it's added to `Application`'s `Resources` collection. For example, the following could be added inside `Application.Resources` in `App.xaml` to make the `Foreground` of every `Button` red instead of white:

```
<!-- Implicit style. Apply this to all Buttons. -->
<Style TargetType="Button">
  <Setter Property="Foreground" Value="Red"/>
</Style>
```

Each individual `Button` can still override its appearance by explicitly setting a different `Style` or explicitly setting individual properties. Any `Button` can restore its default `Style` by setting its `Style` property to `null`.

 **TargetType must match exactly for an implicit style to be applied!**

With a named style, it's okay for the target element to be a subclass of the TargetType, but this is not the case for implicit styles. This is done to prevent surprises. For example, maybe you've created a Style for all ToggleButtons in your application but you don't want it applied to any CheckBoxes. (CheckBox is a subclass of ToggleButton.) For controls, this behavior is determined by its DefaultStyleKey property. Built-in controls always set this to typeof(*XXX*), where *XXX* is the control, but custom controls could potentially do something different.

Theme Dictionaries

To handle the light versus dark app themes and high contrast user theme, `ResourceDictionary` has a `ThemeDictionaries` property that can contain separate `ResourceDictionarys`, one for each possible theme. The correct one automatically gets merged into the host `ResourceDictionary` based on the current theme.

These theme dictionaries can contain any resource, such as complete Styles, but it's more common for them to contain specific Brushes referenced by a single theme-independent Style. The following XAML demonstrates:

```xml
<Page …>
  <Grid Background="{StaticResource ApplicationPageBackgroundThemeBrush}">
    <StackPanel Margin="20" Orientation="Horizontal">
      <StackPanel.Resources>
        <ResourceDictionary>
          <ResourceDictionary.ThemeDictionaries>
            <ResourceDictionary x:Key="Default">
              <!-- Dark theme resources -->
              <SolidColorBrush x:Key="CustomBackgroundBrush" Color="Purple"/>
              <SolidColorBrush x:Key="CustomForegroundBrush" Color="White"/>
            </ResourceDictionary>
            <ResourceDictionary x:Key="Light">
              <!-- Light theme resources -->
              <SolidColorBrush x:Key="CustomBackgroundBrush" Color="Tan"/>
              <SolidColorBrush x:Key="CustomForegroundBrush" Color="Black"/>
            </ResourceDictionary>
            <ResourceDictionary x:Key="HighContrast">
              <!-- High Contrast theme resources -->
              <SolidColorBrush x:Key="CustomBackgroundBrush"
                Color="{StaticResource SystemColorButtonFaceColor}"/>
              <SolidColorBrush x:Key="CustomForegroundBrush"
                Color="{StaticResource SystemColorButtonTextColor}"/>
            </ResourceDictionary>
          </ResourceDictionary.ThemeDictionaries>
          <Style x:Key="TiltStyle" TargetType="Button">
            <Setter Property="FontSize" Value="22"/>
            <Setter Property="Background"
                    Value="{StaticResource CustomBackgroundBrush}"/>
            <Setter Property="Foreground"
                    Value="{StaticResource CustomForegroundBrush}"/>
            <Setter Property="Height" Value="60"/>
            <Setter Property="RenderTransformOrigin" Value=".5,.5"/>
            <Setter Property="RenderTransform">
              <Setter.Value>
                <RotateTransform Angle="10"/>
              </Setter.Value>
            </Setter>
          </Style>
        </ResourceDictionary>
      </StackPanel.Resources>
      <Button Style="{StaticResource TiltStyle}" Content="Button"/>
    </StackPanel>
```

```
    </Grid>
</Page>
```

Note that in order to set the
ResourceDictionary's
ThemeDictionaries property, you must
assign the Resources property to an
explicit ResourceDictionary instance
rather than using the existing instance.
The three valid keys to use in the
ThemeDictionaries collection are
Default (or Dark), Light, and
HighContrast. The result of applying
this new theme to a Button is shown in Figure 16.3.

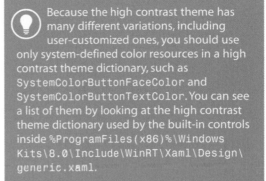

Because the high contrast theme has
many different variations, including
user-customized ones, you should use
only system-defined color resources in a high
contrast theme dictionary, such as
SystemColorButtonFaceColor and
SystemColorButtonTextColor. You can see
a list of them by looking at the high contrast
theme dictionary used by the built-in controls
inside %ProgramFiles(x86)%\Windows
Kits\8.0\Include\WinRT\Xaml\Design\
generic.xaml.

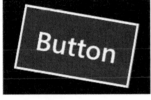

Dark   Light   High contrast

FIGURE 16.3   The same Button viewed under the three different themes

More About Resource Lookup

The StaticResource markup extension accepts a single parameter representing the key or
name of the item in a Resources collection. But, as described previously, that item
doesn't have to be inside the current element's collection. It could be in any ancestor's
collection, or even in the Application-level collection. This is how StandardStyles.xaml
is able to work. Recall from Chapter 1, "Anatomy of a Windows Store App," that
App.xaml imports the content of StandardStyles.xaml into the Application-derived
class's Resources collection:

```
<Application …>
  <Application.Resources>
    <ResourceDictionary>
      <ResourceDictionary.MergedDictionaries>

        <!--
            Styles that define common aspects of the platform look and feel
            Required by Visual Studio project and item templates
        -->
```

```
      <ResourceDictionary Source="Common/StandardStyles.xaml"/>
    </ResourceDictionary.MergedDictionaries>

  </ResourceDictionary>
 </Application.Resources>
</Application>
```

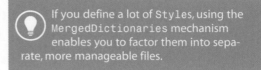

If you define a lot of `Styles`, using the `MergedDictionaries` mechanism enables you to factor them into separate, more manageable files.

`StaticResource` walks the element tree to find the item. It first checks the current element's `Resources` collection. If the item is not found, it checks the parent element, its parent, and so on, until it reaches the root element. At that point, it checks the `Resources` collection on the `Application` object. (And at each level, any theme dictionaries are merged in as appropriate.)

Because of this behavior, resources are typically stored in the root element's resource dictionary or in the `Application`-level dictionary for maximum sharing potential. Note that although each individual resource dictionary requires unique keys, the same key can be used in multiple collections. The one "closest" to the element accessing the resource will win because of the way the tree gets walked. This enables you to define one version of a `Style` or other resource for the entire app, but then override it with a different one at arbitrary spots.

Templates

`Controls` have many properties you can use to customize their look: `Button` has configurable `Background` and `Foreground` `Brushes` (which can even be fancy gradients), `Slider`'s ticks can be relocated by setting the `TickPlacement` property, and so on. But you can do only so much with such properties.

A template, on the other hand, allows you to completely replace an element's visual tree with anything you can dream up, while keeping all of its functionality intact. And templates aren't just some add-on mechanism for third parties; the default visuals for every `Control` are defined in templates (and customized for light versus dark versus high contrast themes). The source code for every control is completely separated from its default visual tree representations (or "visual source code").

Templates and the desire to separate visuals from logic are also the reasons that XAML controls don't expose more simple properties for tweaking their look. For example, you might want to extend the length of the actual "switch" part of a `ToggleSwitch`, or change the switch color. These relatively simple changes can be accomplished only by defining a new template for `ToggleSwitch`, however. `ToggleSwitch` has no `SwitchBrush` or `SwitchColor` property because a `ToggleSwitch` with a custom template might not even have that graphical representation!

There are a few different kinds of templates. What has been described so far is the focus of this section: *control templates*. Control templates are represented by the `ControlTemplate` class that derives from the `FrameworkTemplate` base class. The other

FrameworkTemplate-derived classes are DataTemplate (described in the next chapter) and ItemsPanelTemplate (described in Chapter 9, "Items Controls").

Introducing Control Templates

ControlTemplate can contain a custom tree of elements that defines a new appearance for any Control. You can attach it to any Control by setting it as a value for its Template property. The following XAML adds a ControlTemplate to one of two regular Buttons, producing the results shown in Figure 16.4:

```xaml
<StackPanel Orientation="Horizontal">
  <!-- A simple Button -->
  <Button Content="Without Custom Template"/>

  <!-- A Button with a custom ControlTemplate -->
  <Button Content="With Custom Template">
    <Button.Template>
      <ControlTemplate>
        <Grid>
          <Ellipse Width="100" Height="100">
            <Ellipse.Fill>
              <LinearGradientBrush StartPoint="0,0" EndPoint="0,1">
                <GradientStop Offset="0" Color="Blue"/>
                <GradientStop Offset="1" Color="Red"/>
              </LinearGradientBrush>
            </Ellipse.Fill>
          </Ellipse>
          <Ellipse Width="80" Height="80">
            <Ellipse.Fill>
              <LinearGradientBrush StartPoint="0,0" EndPoint="0,1">
                <GradientStop Offset="0" Color="White"/>
                <GradientStop Offset="1" Color="Transparent"/>
              </LinearGradientBrush>
            </Ellipse.Fill>
          </Ellipse>
        </Grid>
      </ControlTemplate>
    </Button.Template>
  </Button>
</StackPanel>
```

To get this look, the template's visual tree uses two circles (created with Ellipse elements) placed inside a single-cell Grid. Despite the custom look, the resultant Button still has a Click event and all the other programmatic behavior you'd expect. After all, it is still an instance of the Button class!

FIGURE 16.4   Two Buttons, one with a fancy round custom `ControlTemplate`

Of course, directly setting a control's template inline isn't common. You could define one as a resource and then reference it when setting the `Template` property on multiple controls. However, even more common is to set the `Template` property inside a `Style`. This is what makes `Styles` such as `BackButtonStyle` so powerful; they don't just set simple properties, but `Template` as well.

Respecting the Target Control's Properties

There's a bit of a problem with custom template in Figure 16.4. Any `Button` it is applied to will look the same, no matter what the values of its properties are. Most notably, the right `Button` in Figure 16.4 has `"With Custom Template"` as its content, but it never gets displayed. If you're creating a control template that's meant to be broadly reusable, you need to do some work to respect various properties of the target control (sometimes called the *templated parent*).

Respecting `ContentControl`'s `Content` Property

The key to inserting property values from the target element inside a control template is a specialized form of data binding. Although data binding is covered in the next chapter, its use in control templates is simple. You can set a property to the markup extension value:

```
{TemplateBinding XXX}
```

where *XXX* is the name of a dependency property on the target control. (That's right, like so many features, this one works only with properties that are dependency properties.) This not only fetches the correct value, but keeps it up-to-date if the value changes.

Note that `TemplateBinding` is a shortcut for the following more complicated data-binding expression that explicitly says to fetch the property value from the templated parent:

```
{Binding RelativeSource={RelativeSource TemplatedParent}, Path=XXX}
```

The difference here is that *XXX* can be a property *path* (the same kind introduced in the preceding chapter) rather than a simple property name.

Given this, somewhere in our custom `Button` template, we could add a `TextBlock` whose `Text` gets set to the target `Button`'s `Content` as follows:

```
<TextBlock Text="{TemplateBinding Button.Content}"/>
```

ControlTemplate, like Style, has a TargetType property that restricts what it can be applied to. If we mark the ControlTemplate with TargetType="Button" then the setting of the Text property can be simplified further:

```
<TextBlock Text="{TemplateBinding Content}"/>
```

Of course, a Button can contain nontext Content, so using a TextBlock to display it creates an artificial limitation. To ensure that all types of Content get displayed properly in the template, you can use a generic ContentControl instead of a TextBlock. The following update does just that. The ContentControl is given a Margin and wrapped in a Viewbox so it's displayed at a reasonable size relative to the rest of the Button:

```
<StackPanel Orientation="Horizontal">
  <!-- A simple Button -->
  <Button Content="Without Custom Template"/>

  <!-- A Button with a custom ControlTemplate -->
  <Button Content="With Custom Template">
    <Button.Template>
      <ControlTemplate TargetType="Button">
        <Grid>
          <Ellipse Width="100" Height="100">
            <Ellipse.Fill>
              <LinearGradientBrush StartPoint="0,0" EndPoint="0,1">
                <GradientStop Offset="0" Color="Blue"/>
                <GradientStop Offset="1" Color="Red"/>
              </LinearGradientBrush>
            </Ellipse.Fill>
          </Ellipse>
          <Ellipse Width="80" Height="80">
            <Ellipse.Fill>
              <LinearGradientBrush StartPoint="0,0" EndPoint="0,1">
                <GradientStop Offset="0" Color="White"/>
                <GradientStop Offset="1" Color="Transparent"/>
              </LinearGradientBrush>
            </Ellipse.Fill>
          </Ellipse>
          <Viewbox Width="100" Height="100">
            <ContentControl Margin="20" Content="{TemplateBinding Content}"/>
          </Viewbox>
        </Grid>
      </ControlTemplate>
    </Button.Template>
  </Button>
</StackPanel>
```

Figure 16.5 shows the updated result. Figure 16.6 shows the same Button on the right if its Content is replaced with an Image. In both cases, the content is reflected in the new visuals as expected, thanks to the use of ContentControl.

FIGURE 16.5   The same two Buttons from Figure 16.4, but with an updated ControlTemplate for the Button on the right

FIGURE 16.6   If the Button with the updated custom ControlTemplate contains complex content, it still works as expected.

Rather than use a ContentControl inside a control template, you should use the lighter-weight ContentPresenter element. ContentPresenter displays content just like ContentControl, but it was designed specifically for use in control templates. ContentPresenter is a primitive building block, whereas ContentControl is a full-blown control with its own control template (that contains a ContentPresenter)!

For Figures 16.5 and 16.6, you can replace this:

```
<ContentControl Margin="20" Content="{TemplateBinding Content}"/>
```

with this:

```
<ContentPresenter Margin="20" Content="{TemplateBinding Content}"/>
```

and get the same result. ContentPresenter even has a built-in shortcut; if you omit setting its Content to {TemplateBinding Content}, it implicitly assumes that's what you want. So, you can replace the preceding line of code with the following:

```
<ContentPresenter Margin="20"/>
```

This works only when the control template is given an explicit TargetType of ContentControl or a ContentControl-derived class (such as Button).

The remaining templates in this chapter use ContentPresenter instead of ContentControl, because that's what real-world templates use. Note that ItemsControl has a simpler companion element called ItemsPresenter.

Respecting Other Properties

No matter what type of control you're creating a control template for, there are undoubt-edly other properties that should be honored if you want the template to be reusable: Height and Width, perhaps Background, Padding, and so on. Some properties (such as Foreground, FontSize, FontWeight, and so on) might automatically inherit their desired values thanks to property value inheritance in the visual tree, but other properties need explicit attention.

Listing 16.1 takes the most recent version of our custom template, morphs it to respect the Background, Padding, and Content properties of the target Button, and packages it up in a default Style for all Buttons on the Page. This new version of the template also implicitly respects the size of the target element by *removing* the explicit Height and Width settings and letting the layout system do its job. Listing 16.1 uses a ContentPresenter rather than a ContentControl, although both produce the same result.

LISTING 16.1   Updates to the ControlTemplate for Button That Make It More Reusable

```
<Page …>
  <Page.Resources>
    <Style TargetType="Button">
      <Setter Property="Template">
        <Setter.Value>
          <!-- The new custom template -->
          <ControlTemplate TargetType="Button">
            <Grid>
              <Ellipse>
                <Ellipse.Fill>
                  <LinearGradientBrush StartPoint="0,0" EndPoint="0,1">
                    <GradientStop Offset="0" Color=
                      "{Binding RelativeSource={RelativeSource TemplatedParent},
                                Path=Background.Color}"/>
                    <GradientStop Offset="1" Color="Red"/>
                  </LinearGradientBrush>
                </Ellipse.Fill>
              </Ellipse>
              <Ellipse RenderTransformOrigin=".5,.5">
                <Ellipse.RenderTransform>
                  <ScaleTransform ScaleX=".8" ScaleY=".8"/>
                </Ellipse.RenderTransform>
                <Ellipse.Fill>
                  <LinearGradientBrush StartPoint="0,0" EndPoint="0,1">
                    <GradientStop Offset="0" Color="White"/>
                    <GradientStop Offset="1" Color="Transparent"/>
                  </LinearGradientBrush>
                </Ellipse.Fill>
              </Ellipse>
```

LISTING 16.1   Continued

```
          <Viewbox Width="100" Height="100">
            <ContentPresenter Margin="{TemplateBinding Padding}"/>
          </Viewbox>
        </Grid>
      </ControlTemplate>
    </Setter.Value>
  </Setter>
  </Style>
</Page.Resources>
<Grid Background="{StaticResource ApplicationPageBackgroundThemeBrush}">
  <StackPanel Orientation="Horizontal" VerticalAlignment="Top" >
    <!-- Three buttons that use the custom template via the default style -->
    <Button Height="100" Width="100" FontSize="80"
            Padding="20" Margin="5">1</Button>
    <Button Height="150" Width="250" FontSize="90" Background="Yellow"
            Padding="20" Margin="5">2</Button>
    <Button Height="200" Width="200" FontSize="100" Background="Purple"
            Padding="20" Margin="5" Foreground="Black" FontStyle="Italic">
            3</Button>
  </StackPanel>
</Grid>
</Page>
```

The target Button's Padding is now used as the ContentPresenter's Margin. It's common to use the element's Padding in a template as the Margin of an inner element. After all, that's basically the definition of Padding!

In addition, a few nonintuitive changes have been made to the template's visual tree to accommodate an externally specified size and Background. We could have used {TemplateBinding Background} as the Fill for the outer Ellipse, giving each Button the flexibility to specify a solid color, a gradient, and so on. But perhaps the "red glow" at the bottom is a characteristic that we'd like to keep consistent wherever the template is used. In other words, we want to replace only the blue part of the gradient with the externally specified Background. However, GradientStop.Color can't be directly set to {TemplateBinding Background} because Color is of type Color, whereas Background is of type Brush! Therefore, the listing uses the more complex Binding syntax instead, which supports referencing the Color subproperty via a property path. (Note that this Binding works only when Background is set to a SolidColorBrush because other Brushes don't have a Color property!)

Both Ellipses (or the parent Grid) could have been given an explicit Height and Width matching those of the target Button by binding to its ActualHeight and ActualWidth properties. Instead, these values are omitted altogether because the root element is implicitly given the templated parent's size anyway. This means that an individual target Button now has the power to make itself look like an ellipse by specifying different values for Width and Height. If we want to preserve the perfect circular look, we can wrap the entire visual tree in a Viewbox.

The final trick used by Listing 16.1 is the ScaleTransform on the inner circle to make it 80% of the size of the outer circle. In previous versions, this transform is unnecessary because both the outer and inner circles have a hard-coded size. But with a dynamic size, ScaleTransform enables us to effectively perform a little math on the size. (If we want a fixed-size difference between the circles, a simple Margin would do the trick.)

Figure 16.7 shows the rendered result of this Page. Each Button has local has values for Padding and Content that are explicitly used by the control template. The second two buttons also have explicit Background values used by the top of their gradients, whereas the first Button's gradient picks up the default Transparent Background in its gradient.

The Buttons' values for Width and Height are implicitly respected by the template, and properties such as FontSize, Foreground, and FontStyle are implicitly picked up by the template's ContentPresenter thanks to property value inheritance. This is why the "3" shows up as black and italic automatically. Note that the size of the font isn't actually reflected in the rendered output because the template wraps the ContentPresenter inside a Viewbox to keep it within the bounds of the outer circle. The Margin specified on each Button is not used by the template, but it still affects the StackPanel layout as usual, giving a little bit of space between each Button.

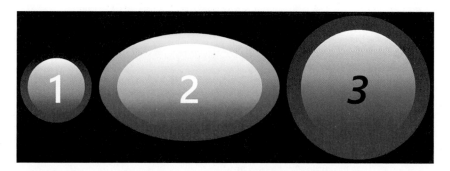

FIGURE 16.7   Buttons from Listing 16.1 that tweak the look of their custom template with local property values

Although XAML controls are supposed to be lookless by nature and have an implementation independent of their actual visuals, many controls "cheat" a little and expose a TemplateSettings property with subproperties meant for the templates in their default Styles. These are calculated values that help these templates provide the desired results because they can't do the same type of calculations in XAML. These properties can also be useful for custom templates you create.

Hijacking Existing Properties for New Purposes

Sometimes, you might want to parameterize some aspect of a control template, despite there being no corresponding property on the target control. For example, the template in Listing 16.1 still has a hard-coded red `Brush`. If you want to keep the gradient standardized and therefore kept inside the template, what can you do to allow individual `Button`s to customize both colors? There's no corresponding property already on `Button` to be set!

One option is to define a custom control. It wouldn't be too much work to write a new class that derives from `Button` and adds a single `BottomColor` or `BottomBrush` property. But that's a bit heavyweight for such a simple task. Another option would be to define several control templates that each uses a different color. But that would be reasonable only if the set of desired colors were small and known. Yet another option would be to define an appropriate attached property somewhere, perhaps on a utility class that already exists.

Instead, what many people resort to is a devious little hack known as *hijacking* a dependency property. This involves looking at the target control for any dependency properties of the desired type to see whether you can leverage them in an unintended way. For example, all `Control`s have three properties of type `Brush`: `Background`, `Foreground`, and `BorderBrush`. Because `Background` and `Foreground` already play important roles in Listing 16.1, neither one would be appropriate to use for the bottom color. (There would be no way to set it independently of the other two.) But `BorderBrush` is a different story. It's completely unused by the template in Listing 16.1, so why not use that?

There is no reason not to use it, other than the fact that it makes the usage of the template confusing and less readable. Nevertheless, here's how you could update the outer `Ellipse`'s `LinearGradientBrush` to hijack `BorderBrush`:

```
<LinearGradientBrush StartPoint="0,0" EndPoint="0,1">
  <GradientStop Offset="0" Color=
                "{Binding RelativeSource={RelativeSource TemplatedParent},
                          Path=Background.Color}"/>
  <GradientStop Offset="1" Color=
                "{Binding RelativeSource={RelativeSource TemplatedParent},
                          Path=BorderBrush.Color}"/>
</LinearGradientBrush>
```

If the target control doesn't have an appropriate property, you might even be able to hijack an attached property from an unrelated element! If this hack leaves a bad taste in your mouth, then by all means use an alternative approach. One could argue that this is what the family of `AppBarButton` styles do in `StandardStyles.xaml`, which stretch the meaning of the `AutomationProperties.Name` attached property in order to work with two customizable properties, one for inside the circular button and one for the extra text underneath it:

```
<Style x:Key="PinAppBarButtonStyle" TargetType="ButtonBase"
       BasedOn="{StaticResource AppBarButtonStyle}">
  <Setter Property="AutomationProperties.AutomationId" Value="PinAppBarButton"/>
  <Setter Property="AutomationProperties.Name" Value="Pin"/>
  <Setter Property="Content" Value="&#xE141;"/>
</Style>
```

Setting `Template` Inside a `Style`

It's worth emphasizing why setting the `Template` property inside a `Style` is so powerful. It has two important advantages:

→ It gives you the effect of default templates when combined with an explicit `Style`, as leveraged in Listing 16.1. Independent of this, there is no such thing as a default control template.

→ It enables you to provide default yet overridable property values that control the look of the template. In other words, it enables you to respect the templated parent's properties but still provide your own default values.

The final point is important. When Listing 16.1 changed the custom template's top gradient color from a hard-coded `Blue` to pick up the `Button`'s `Background.Color`, the default value became `Transparent`, as seen with the first `Button` in Figure 16.7. If we want the default color to still be `Blue`, but still enable individual `Button`s to change it, then we can accomplish this in the `Style` as follows:

```
<Style TargetType="Button">
  <Setter Property="Background" Value="Blue"/>
  <Setter Property="Template">
    <Setter.Value>
      <ControlTemplate TargetType="Button">
        … The same template from Listing 16.1 …
      </ControlTemplate>
    </Setter.Value>
  </Setter>
</Style>
```

The same could be done if we made the change to bind the bottom gradient color to `BorderBrush` but keep the default color as red:

```
<Setter Property="BorderBrush" Value="Red"/>
```

The `AppBarButton` styles do the same thing. Because `AutomationProperties.Name` is set to `"Pin"` in a `PinAppBarButtonStyle` `Setter`, the code in Chapter 8 was able to override it with the locally set `"Pin to Start"` value.

How do I make small tweaks to an existing control template rather than create a brand-new one from scratch?

There is no mechanism for tweaking existing templates (like Style's BasedOn). Instead, you must retrieve a XAML representation for any existing Style or template, modify it, and then apply it as a brand-new Style or template. In fact, even if you want to create a completely different look, the best way to become familiar with how to design robust control templates is to look at the built-in control templates used by default Styles.

To obtain the "visual source code" in XAML for a built-in control template, you can do one of the following:

→ With the Windows SDK installed, you can look inside %ProgramFiles(x86)%\Windows Kits\8.0\Include\WinRT\Xaml\Design\generic.xaml.

→ Create the appropriate control in Blend or the Visual Studio XAML designer, right click and then choose Edit Template, Edit a Copy… to get a copy of its style pasted into your XAML.

You can learn some neat techniques or find fascinating implementation details. For example, here is how the control template inside Button's default style represents the dotted focus rectangle that appears when giving one focus with the Tab key:

```
<Grid>
  ...
  <Rectangle x:Name="FocusVisualWhite" IsHitTestVisible="False" Opacity="0"
    StrokeDashOffset="1.5" StrokeEndLineCap="Square" StrokeDashArray="1,1"
    Stroke="{StaticResource FocusVisualWhiteStrokeThemeBrush}"/>
  <Rectangle x:Name="FocusVisualBlack" IsHitTestVisible="False" Opacity="0"
    StrokeDashOffset="0.5" StrokeEndLineCap="Square" StrokeDashArray="1,1"
    Stroke="{StaticResource FocusVisualBlackStrokeThemeBrush}"/>
</Grid>
```

It's simply two overlaid dotted Rectangle elements!

In generic.xaml, you can also see the long list of theme-specific resources in the three theme dictionaries.

Visual States

You might have noticed that something is still missing from all versions of the custom Button template used in the preceding section. None of them have any visual reaction to being pressed, hovered over, or disabled. This might not be *that* big of a deal, depending on their usage, but imagine applying the same template to CheckBox or ToggleButton. (This can be done by changing the TargetType to ButtonBase or a more specific type.) Because the template doesn't show different visuals for the Checked versus Unchecked versus Indeterminate states, it's a pretty lousy template for these controls!

Therefore, a good control template must consider all possible visual states relevant for the target control and handle them appropriately. There are two questions we need to answer:

→ How do I find out all the visual states that need to be respected? Each control has a large number of properties, and it might not always be clear which ones are visually important.

→ How do I make a control template respond to such state changes?

It turns out that controls have a formal notion of visual states, represented by a `VisualState` class. A control can specify any number of these states, and then control templates can leverage these. Blend even provides special support for managing them when authoring a template via its "States" tool window.

Therefore, the answer to the first question is to look at the relevant template inside `%ProgramFiles(x86)%\Windows Kits\8.0\Include\WinRT\Xaml\Design\generic.xaml` (for built-in controls), or use Blend or Visual Studio to create a copy of the template, or use Blend's States tool window. The answer to the second question is the topic of the rest of this section.

Responding to Visual State Changes

The states defined by each control are grouped into mutually exclusive *state groups*. For example, `Button` has four states in a group called `CommonStates`—Normal, PointerOver, Pressed, and Disabled—and three states in a group called `FocusStates`—Unfocused, Focused, and PointerFocused. At any time, `Button` is in one state from every group, so it is `Normal` and `Unfocused` by default. This grouping mechanism exists to avoid a long list of states meant to cover every combination of independent properties (such as `NormalUnfocused`, `NormalFocused`, `PointerOverUnfocused`, `PointerOverFocused`, and so on).

A template for `Button` can express modifications to make to its elements when transitioning to each state. This is done by assigning a `VisualStateManager.VisualStateGroups` attached property to the root element inside the control template. This property must be set to a collection of `VisualStateGroup` objects, each with a collection of `VisualStates`. These `VisualStateGroups` and `VisualStates` must have names that match what the target control supports. Only the control author can make up new groups and states; the control *template* author can react only to what's there.

The contents of each `VisualState` describes what happens to the visuals when the control transitions to that state. Quite appropriately, the way this is done is with none other than the familiar `Storyboards` from the preceding chapter! The best way to get a grasp on how visual states work is to see an example. Listing 16.2 contains the real control template from `Button`'s default `Style`, annotated with a few comments. The core part of the template is quite simple: a `Grid` containing a `Border` containing a `ContentPresenter`, with two overlaid `Rectangles` to create the dotted focus rectangle. Most of the template manages the transitions between each of the four `CommonStates` and each of the three `FocusStates`.

LISTING 16.2   Button's Control Template from its Default `Style`

```
<ControlTemplate TargetType="Button">
  <Grid>
    <!-- Attached to the root element, as required: -->
    <VisualStateManager.VisualStateGroups>
      <!-- Group #1 -->
      <VisualStateGroup x:Name="CommonStates">
        <!-- Nothing to do when transitioning to Normal: -->
        <VisualState x:Name="Normal"/>
        <VisualState x:Name="PointerOver">
          <!-- Instantly change the Background and Foreground: -->
          <Storyboard>
            <ObjectAnimationUsingKeyFrames Storyboard.TargetProperty="Background"
                                        Storyboard.TargetName="Border">
              <DiscreteObjectKeyFrame KeyTime="0"
                Value="{StaticResource ButtonPointerOverBackgroundThemeBrush}"/>
            </ObjectAnimationUsingKeyFrames>
            <ObjectAnimationUsingKeyFrames Storyboard.TargetProperty="Foreground"
                Storyboard.TargetName="ContentPresenter">
              <DiscreteObjectKeyFrame KeyTime="0"
                Value="{StaticResource ButtonPointerOverForegroundThemeBrush}"/>
            </ObjectAnimationUsingKeyFrames>
          </Storyboard>
        </VisualState>
        <VisualState x:Name="Pressed">
          <!-- Instantly change the Background and Foreground: -->
          <Storyboard>
            <ObjectAnimationUsingKeyFrames Storyboard.TargetProperty="Background"
                                        Storyboard.TargetName="Border">
              <DiscreteObjectKeyFrame KeyTime="0"
                Value="{StaticResource ButtonPressedBackgroundThemeBrush}"/>
            </ObjectAnimationUsingKeyFrames>
            <ObjectAnimationUsingKeyFrames Storyboard.TargetProperty="Foreground"
                Storyboard.TargetName="ContentPresenter">
              <DiscreteObjectKeyFrame KeyTime="0"
                Value="{StaticResource ButtonPressedForegroundThemeBrush}"/>
            </ObjectAnimationUsingKeyFrames>
          </Storyboard>
        </VisualState>
        <VisualState x:Name="Disabled">
          <!-- Instantly change the Background, Border, and Foreground: -->
          <Storyboard>
            <ObjectAnimationUsingKeyFrames Storyboard.TargetProperty="Background"
                                        Storyboard.TargetName="Border">
              <DiscreteObjectKeyFrame KeyTime="0"
```

LISTING 16.2   Continued

```
                    Value="{StaticResource ButtonDisabledBackgroundThemeBrush}"/>
            </ObjectAnimationUsingKeyFrames>
            <ObjectAnimationUsingKeyFrames Storyboard.TargetProperty="BorderBrush"
                                        Storyboard.TargetName="Border">
              <DiscreteObjectKeyFrame KeyTime="0"
                Value="{StaticResource ButtonDisabledBorderThemeBrush}"/>
            </ObjectAnimationUsingKeyFrames>
            <ObjectAnimationUsingKeyFrames Storyboard.TargetProperty="Foreground"
                  Storyboard.TargetName="ContentPresenter">
              <DiscreteObjectKeyFrame KeyTime="0"
                Value="{StaticResource ButtonDisabledForegroundThemeBrush}"/>
            </ObjectAnimationUsingKeyFrames>
          </Storyboard>
        </VisualState>
      </VisualStateGroup>

      <!-- Group #2 -->
      <VisualStateGroup x:Name="FocusStates">
        <!-- Nothing to do when transitioning to Unfocused: -->
        <VisualState x:Name="Unfocused"/>
        <VisualState x:Name="Focused">
          <!-- Instantly show the two focus Rectangles: -->
          <Storyboard>
            <DoubleAnimation Duration="0" To="1" Storyboard.TargetProperty="Opac-
ity" Storyboard.TargetName="FocusVisualWhite"/>
            <DoubleAnimation Duration="0" To="1" Storyboard.TargetProperty="Opac-
ity" Storyboard.TargetName="FocusVisualBlack"/>
          </Storyboard>
        </VisualState>
        <!-- Nothing to do when transitioning to PointerFocused: -->
        <VisualState x:Name="PointerFocused"/>
      </VisualStateGroup>
    </VisualStateManager.VisualStateGroups>

    <!-- The actual elements in the root Grid -->
    <Border x:Name="Border" BorderBrush="{TemplateBinding BorderBrush}"
            BorderThickness="{TemplateBinding BorderThickness}"
            Background="{TemplateBinding Background}" Margin="3">
      <!-- Respect a LOT of properties in the ContentPresenter: -->
      <ContentPresenter x:Name="ContentPresenter"
        ContentTemplate="{TemplateBinding ContentTemplate}"
        ContentTransitions="{TemplateBinding ContentTransitions}"
        Content="{TemplateBinding Content}"
        HorizontalAlignment="{TemplateBinding HorizontalContentAlignment}"
```

LISTING 16.2   Continued

```
            Margin="{TemplateBinding Padding}"
            VerticalAlignment="{TemplateBinding VerticalContentAlignment}"/>
      </Border>
      <Rectangle x:Name="FocusVisualWhite" IsHitTestVisible="False" Opacity="0"
        StrokeDashOffset="1.5" StrokeEndLineCap="Square" StrokeDashArray="1,1"
        Stroke="{StaticResource FocusVisualWhiteStrokeThemeBrush}"/>
      <Rectangle x:Name="FocusVisualBlack" IsHitTestVisible="False" Opacity="0"
        StrokeDashOffset="0.5" StrokeEndLineCap="Square" StrokeDashArray="1,1"
        Stroke="{StaticResource FocusVisualBlackStrokeThemeBrush}"/>
    </Grid>
</ControlTemplate>
```

Controls such as `Button` have internal logic to transition to the named states that they define by calling a static `VisualStateManager.GoToState` method. This triggers that transition that starts any relevant `Storyboards` in the control template.

There are two big takeaways from this listing. One is that although you can perform animated transitions from one state to another, `Button`'s default template chooses to do instantaneous transitions. It accomplishes this with single-keyframe `ObjectAnimationUsingKeyFrames` "animations" and `DoubleAnimations` with `Durations` of `0`. These are both ways to effectively shoehorn simple property sets into the `Storyboard` model.

The other takeaway is that you don't need to bother "undoing" your animations when transitioning to a different state. The relevant `Storyboards` are automatically stopped, which instantly removes the result of the previous animations. For example, although the transition to `Button`'s `Focused` state changes the `Opacity` of the two `Rectangles` to 1, no animations are needed in the other two states to animate it back to `0`.

> Part of the power of the `LayoutAwarePage` base class (used by most of the types of `Pages` you can create in Visual Studio) is that it contains logic to handle visual states corresponding to the values of the `ApplicationViewState` enumeration: `FullScreenLandscape`, `FullScreenPortrait`, `Snapped`, and `Filled`. This enables control templates to specify a distinct appearance for each view state and have the right one applied automatically when used within a `LayoutAwarePage`.

Visual Transitions

Let's say you start with `Button`'s default template but morph it such that the two focus `Rectangles` fade in gradually when the control transitions to the `Focused` state. In this case, the harsh stopping of these animations when transitioning out of `Focused` probably won't be satisfactory. Because `Unfocused` and `PointerFocused` are left empty, the result is an instant jump to the default visual behavior. This could be solved by adding `Storyboards` with explicit animations to the default values, but one would have to be added for every property animated by any other state in the group, to account for all possible transitions.

Fortunately, VisualStateGroup has a much better solution for this. It defines a Transitions property that can be set to one or more VisualTransition objects that can automatically generate appropriate animations to smooth the transition between any states. VisualTransition has To and From string properties that can be set to the names of the source and target states. You can omit both properties to make it apply to all transitions, specify only a To to make it apply to all transitions to that state, and so on. When transitioning from one state to another, the Visual State Manager chooses the most specific VisualTransition that matches the transition. The order of precedence is as follows:

1. A VisualTransition with matching To and From

2. A VisualTransition with a matching To and no explicit From

3. A VisualTransition with a matching From and no explicit To

4. The default VisualTransition, with no To or From specified

If VisualStateGroup's Transitions property isn't set, the default transition between any states is a zero-duration animation.

To specify the characteristics of a VisualTransition, you can set its GeneratedDuration property to control the duration of the generated linear animation. You can also set its GeneratedEasingFunction property to get a nonlinear animation between states. For the most customization, you can even set its Storyboard property to a Storyboard with arbitrary custom animations.

Listing 16.3 updates our custom Button template from Listing 16.1 in order to take advantage of visual states. The red part of the gradient now turns yellow when the pointer hovers over it, pressing the Button makes it shrink, disabling it turns the red or yellow to gray, and giving it focus makes it bounce continuously.

 Visual transitions and VisualStateGroup's Transitions property are unrelated to the theme transitions (and corresponding Transitions properties) discussed in the preceding chapter. They share unfortunately similar names.

Animations generated by VisualTransitions are independent only!

This means that if you change a Color in one VisualState then apply a VisualTransition with a GeneratedDuration longer than zero, it will have no effect on the Color change. It will still happen instantaneously. The way to make this work is to give the relevant state transitions an explicit VisualTransition whose Storyboard property is set to a Storyboard containing an explicitly dependent animation. Listing 16.3 contains an example of this.

LISTING 16.3   The ControlTemplate for `Button` from Listing 16.1, Enhanced with Visual States

```xml
<Page …>
  <Page.Resources>
    <Style TargetType="Button">
      <Setter Property="Template">
        <Setter.Value>
          <!-- The custom template -->
          <ControlTemplate TargetType="Button">
            <Grid RenderTransformOrigin=".5,.5">

              <VisualStateManager.VisualStateGroups>
                <!-- Group #1: -->
                <VisualStateGroup x:Name="CommonStates">
                  <!-- Transitions for Group #1: -->
                  <VisualStateGroup.Transitions>
                    <!-- Manually handle the transition to/from PointerOver
                         because an explicit dependent animation is needed: -->
                    <VisualTransition From="PointerOver">
                      <VisualTransition.Storyboard>
                        <Storyboard TargetName="glow" TargetProperty="Color">
                          <ColorAnimation From="Yellow" Duration="0:0:.4"
                                          EnableDependentAnimation="True"/>
                        </Storyboard>
                      </VisualTransition.Storyboard>
                    </VisualTransition>
                    <VisualTransition To="PointerOver">
                      <VisualTransition.Storyboard>
                        <Storyboard TargetName="glow" TargetProperty="Color">
                          <ColorAnimation To="Yellow" Duration="0:0:.4"
                                          EnableDependentAnimation="True"/>
                        </Storyboard>
                      </VisualTransition.Storyboard>
                    </VisualTransition>
                    <!-- Make transitions to/from Pressed instantaneous: -->
                    <VisualTransition To="Pressed" GeneratedDuration="0"/>
                    <VisualTransition From="Pressed" To="PointerOver"
                                      GeneratedDuration="0"/>
                  </VisualStateGroup.Transitions>

                  <!-- States for Group #1: -->
                  <VisualState x:Name="Normal"/>
                  <VisualState x:Name="PointerOver">
                    <!-- Still needed to make sure the yellow "sticks" after
                         the explicit transition: -->
                    <Storyboard TargetName="glow" TargetProperty="Color">
```

LISTING 16.3   Continued

```xml
                    <ColorAnimation To="Yellow" Duration="0"/>
                </Storyboard>
            </VisualState>
            <VisualState x:Name="Pressed">
                <!-- "Push in" the visuals: -->
                <Storyboard TargetName="rootTransform">
                    <DoubleAnimation To=".9" Storyboard.TargetProperty="ScaleX"
                                     Duration="0"/>
                    <DoubleAnimation Storyboard.TargetProperty="ScaleY" To=".9"
                                     Duration="0"/>
                </Storyboard>
            </VisualState>
            <VisualState x:Name="Disabled">
                <!-- Just a simple change to gray: -->
                <Storyboard TargetName="glow" TargetProperty="Color">
                    <ColorAnimation To="Gray" Duration="0"/>
                </Storyboard>
            </VisualState>
        </VisualStateGroup>

        <!-- Group #2 -->
        <VisualStateGroup x:Name="FocusStates">

            <!-- Transitions for Group #2: -->
            <VisualStateGroup.Transitions>
                <VisualTransition From="Focused">
                    <VisualTransition.Storyboard>
                        <!-- Gracefully undo the Focused animation: -->
                        <Storyboard TargetName="rootTransform"
                                    TargetProperty="TranslateY">
                            <DoubleAnimation To="0" Duration="0:0:.4">
                                <DoubleAnimation.EasingFunction>
                                    <QuadraticEase/>
                                </DoubleAnimation.EasingFunction>
                            </DoubleAnimation>
                        </Storyboard>
                    </VisualTransition.Storyboard>
                </VisualTransition>
            </VisualStateGroup.Transitions>

            <!-- States for Group #2: -->
            <VisualState x:Name="Unfocused"/>
            <VisualState x:Name="Focused">
                <!-- A continuous animation: -->
                <Storyboard TargetName="rootTransform"
```

LISTING 16.3   Continued

```xml
                          TargetProperty="TranslateY">
              <DoubleAnimation To="-20" RepeatBehavior="Forever"
                               AutoReverse="True" Duration="0:0:.4">
                <DoubleAnimation.EasingFunction>
                  <QuadraticEase/>
                </DoubleAnimation.EasingFunction>
              </DoubleAnimation>
            </Storyboard>
          </VisualState>
          <VisualState x:Name="PointerFocused"/>
        </VisualStateGroup>
      </VisualStateManager.VisualStateGroups>

      <!-- Used for Pressed and Focused animations: -->
      <Grid.RenderTransform>
        <CompositeTransform x:Name="rootTransform"/>
      </Grid.RenderTransform>

      <Ellipse>
        <Ellipse.Fill>
          <LinearGradientBrush StartPoint="0,0" EndPoint="0,1">
            <GradientStop Offset="0" Color=
              "{Binding RelativeSource={RelativeSource TemplatedParent},
                        Path=Background.Color}"/>
            <GradientStop x:Name="glow" Offset="1" Color="Red"/>
          </LinearGradientBrush>
        </Ellipse.Fill>
      </Ellipse>
      <Ellipse RenderTransformOrigin=".5,.5">
        <Ellipse.RenderTransform>
          <ScaleTransform ScaleX=".8" ScaleY=".8"/>
        </Ellipse.RenderTransform>
        <Ellipse.Fill>
          <LinearGradientBrush StartPoint="0,0" EndPoint="0,1">
            <GradientStop Offset="0" Color="White"/>
            <GradientStop Offset="1" Color="Transparent"/>
          </LinearGradientBrush>
        </Ellipse.Fill>
      </Ellipse>
      <Viewbox Width="100" Height="100">
        <ContentPresenter Margin="{TemplateBinding Padding}"/>
      </Viewbox>
    </Grid>
  </ControlTemplate>
```

LISTING 16.3   Continued

```
          </Setter.Value>
        </Setter>
      </Style>
    </Page.Resources>
    ...
</Page>
```

The Grid is now marked with a centered RenderTransformOrigin and is given a CompositeTransform so the animations can act appropriately. The red part of the gradient is also given a name (glow) so animations can reference it.

To smoothly animate the red to/from glow with a dependent animation, the transitions to/from the PointerOver state are given explicit Storyboards. Note that the PointerOver state still needs its own Storyboard for "steady state" of remaining yellow while hovering, but that animation can have a Duration of 0 (and therefore doesn't need to be marked with EnableDependentAnimation).

Figure 16.8 shows the effect of some of these animations on various visual states.

> The easiest way to manage VisualStates and the transitions between them is to give the animations inside each VisualState a Duration of 0—making the animations more like Setters than real animations—and specify the desired animations between states (with non-zero Durations) via VisualStateGroup's VisualTransitions property. An exception to this would be states with continual animations, such as the bouncing done in the Focused state in Listing 16.3.

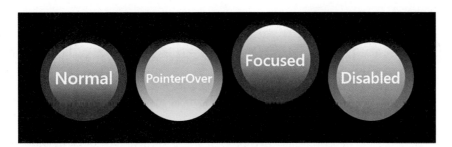

FIGURE 16.8   Four distinct visual effects from Listing 16.3

> • • •
>
> **Named Elements in Templates**
>
> Outside a template, naming an element with x:Name generates a field for programmatic access. This is not the case when using x:Name inside a template, however, as with glow in Listing 16.3. This is because a template can be applied to multiple elements in the same scope. The main purpose of naming elements in a template is for referencing them from animations. But if you want programmatic access to a named element inside a template, you can use the template's FindName method after the template has been applied to a target.

Summary

The combination of Styles, templates, and visual states is powerful and often confusing to someone learning about XAML. Adding to the confusion is the fact that Styles can (and often do) contain templates, elements in templates all have their own Styles (whether marked explicitly or inherited implicitly).

These mechanisms are so powerful, in fact, that often you can restyle an existing control as an alternative to writing your own custom control. This is great news, because restyling an existing control is usually significantly easier than writing a new control, and it can perhaps be done entirely by a graphic designer rather than a programmer.

Chapter 17

DATA BINDING

No matter where data originally comes from (and the options for this are described in the next chapter), you can attach its in-memory representation to various controls by leveraging data binding. Instead of iterating through a data source and manually adding a ListViewItem to a ListView for each one, for example, it would be nice to just say, "Hey, ListView! Get your items from over here. And keep them up to date, please. Oh yeah, and format them to look like this." Data binding enables this and much more.

Introducing Binding

The key to data binding is a Binding markup extension that "glues" two properties together and keeps a channel of communication open between them. You can set up a Binding once and then have it do all the synchronization work for the remainder of the application's lifetime.

Imagine that you have a TextBlock with text that you want to automatically update as the user types in a TextBox, such as the following:

```
<StackPanel Orientation="Horizontal">
  <!-- The user should type a username here -->
  <TextBox Name="textBox"
TextChanged="TextBox_TextChanged"/>
  <!-- This displays, "Hi, username!" -->
  <TextBlock>
    <Run>Hi, </Run>
    <Run x:Name="run"/>
```

```
    <Run>!</Run>
  </TextBlock>
</StackPanel>
```

This can be accomplished by updating the named Run's text manually whenever the TextBox's TextChanged event is raised:

```
void TextBox_TextChanged(object sender, TextChangedEventArgs e)
{
  this.run.Text = this.textBox.Text;
}
```

By using a Binding object instead, you can remove this event handler and replace it with the following one-time initialization:

```
<StackPanel Orientation="Horizontal">
  <!-- The user should type a username here -->
  <TextBox Name="textBox"/>
  <!-- This displays, "Hi, username!" -->
  <TextBlock>
    <Run>Hi, </Run>
    <Run Text="{Binding ElementName=textBox, Path=Text}"/>
    <Run>!</Run>
  </TextBlock>
</StackPanel>
```

Binding has the notion of a *source* property and a *target* property. The source property (textBox.Text, in this case) is specified in two pieces with ElementName and Path (which is a property path). The target property is the Run's Text property, because that is the property assigned to a Binding.

With this change, the Run's Text property updates automatically as the TextBox's Text property changes. Note that the Run no longer needs an x:Name because nobody needs to reference it anymore.

 The Binding markup extension supports specifying Path as a positional parameter, so you can shorten the preceding Binding as follows:

```
<Run Text="{Binding Text, ElementName=textBox}"/>
```

•••

Binding's RelativeSource

Besides ElementName, another way to specify the source object is to use Binding's RelativeSource property. The property is of type RelativeSource, which also happens to be a markup extension. Here are the two ways RelativeSource can be used:

To make the source element equal the target element:

```
{Binding RelativeSource={RelativeSource Self}, Path=…}
```

To make the source element equal the target element's templated parent (as shown in the preceding chapter):

```
{Binding RelativeSource={RelativeSource TemplatedParent}, Path=…}
```

Using RelativeSource with the mode Self is handy for binding one property of an element to another without having to give the element a name. An interesting example is the following ProgressBar, whose ToolTip is bound to its own value:

```
<ProgressBar ToolTipService.ToolTip=
  "{Binding RelativeSource={RelativeSource Self}, Path=Value}"/>
```

Using Binding in C#

The following translates the use of the Binding markup extension to C#, assuming the relevant Run is given the name run:

```
Binding binding = new Binding();
// Set source object
binding.Source = this.textBox;
// Set source property
binding.Path = new PropertyPath("Text");
// Attach to target property
this.run.SetBinding(Run.TextProperty, binding);
```

In C#, you can't set run's Text property to a Binding instance, because Text is of type string! The magic that is abstracted away by the markup extension in XAML is simply a call to run's SetBinding method (inherited from FrameworkElement) that identifies which property to associate with the binding using the relevant static DependencyProperty property. This makes it clear that for a property to be a target of data binding, it must be a dependency property.

Notice that this uses Binding's Source property to set the source object rather than ElementName. Both are valid in either context, but it's most natural to use ElementName in XAML and Source in C#.

 There are two ways to set Binding in C#. One is to call the SetBinding instance method on the relevant FrameworkElement. The other is to call the SetBinding static method on a class called BindingOperations. You pass this method the same objects you would pass to the instance method, but it has an additional first parameter that represents the target object. The benefit of the static method is that the first parameter is defined as a DependencyObject, so it enables data binding on objects that don't derive from FrameworkElement.

Binding to Plain Properties

Although the target property must be a dependency property, the source property can be any (public) property. This can be demonstrated with a slight twist to the previous example. In this case, the TextBlock next to the TextBox displays the number of characters in its text by binding to the simple Length property on the string Text property:

```
<StackPanel Orientation="Horizontal">
  <!-- The user can type anything here -->
  <TextBox Name="textBox"/>
  <!-- This displays the # of characters -->
  <TextBlock>
    <Run>Characters used: </Run>
    <Run Text="{Binding ElementName=textBox, Path=Text.Length}"/>
  </TextBlock>
</StackPanel>
```

In this case, the character count automatically stays up-to-date, but that's only because the parent Text property is a dependency property, and its value changes whenever Length changes. In general, the target is *not* notified to changes in the source when the source property is a plain property. As discussed in Chapter 5, "Interactivity," dependency properties have plumbing for change notification built in. This facility is the key to the ability to keep the target property and source property in sync.

If you want to bind to an arbitrary plain property that does not have the same kind of relationship with a dependency property, you should do one of two things if you want automatic updates:

→ Redefine it as a dependency property.

→ Make the source object implement the System.ComponentModel.INotifyPropertyChanged interface, which has a single PropertyChanged event.

Customizing the Data Flow

In the examples so far, data updates flow from the source to the target. But, in some cases, the target property can be directly changed by users, and it would be useful to support the flowing of such changes back to the source. Indeed, Binding supports this (and more) via its Mode property, which can be set to one of the following values of the BindingMode enumeration:

→ **OneWay**—The target is updated whenever the source changes.

→ **TwoWay**—A change to either the target or source updates the other.

→ **OneTime**—This works just like OneWay, except changes to the source are not reflected at the target. The target retains a snapshot of the source at the time the Binding is initiated.

TwoWay binding is appropriate for editable forms in which you might have TextBoxes that get filled with data that the user is allowed to change. In fact, whereas most dependency properties default to OneWay binding, dependency properties such as TextBox.Text default to TwoWay binding. This can be demonstrated with the following trivial XAML:

```
<StackPanel>
  <TextBox Name="textBox1" Text="{Binding ElementName=textBox2, Path=Text}"/>
  <TextBox Name="textBox2" Text="{Binding ElementName=textBox1, Path=Text}"/>
</StackPanel>
```

The text in these two TextBoxes always remains in sync. You can type/paste in the first one and watch the second one change, or vice versa.

Sharing the Source with DataContext

It's common for many elements in the same user interface to bind to the same source object (different source *properties*, but the same source *object*). For this reason, Binding supports an implicit data source rather than explicitly marking every one with a Source, RelativeSource, or ElementName. This implicit data source is also known as a *data context*.

To designate a source object such as the photos collection as a data context, you find a common parent element and set its DataContext property to the source object. (All FrameworkElements have this DataContext property of type Object.) When the system encounters a Binding without an explicit source object, it traverses up the element tree until it finds a non-null DataContext.

Therefore, you can use DataContext as follows to make both of the following TextBlocks bind to the same string:

```
<StackPanel DataContext="A DataContext string">
  <TextBlock>
    <Run># of characters: </Run>
    <!-- Bind to string's Length property -->
    <Run Text="{Binding Length}"/>
  </TextBlock>
  <TextBlock>
    <Run>The string is: </Run>
    <!-- Bind to the string itself -->
    <Run Text="{Binding}"/>
  </TextBlock>
</StackPanel>
```

This also takes advantage of dropping the "Path=" and specifying the path as a position parameter in the markup extension. Note the odd-looking "empty" {Binding}. When no Path is specified, the binding is done to the entire source object. Chapter 10, "Text," has an example of this with RichTextBlock, whose OverflowContentTarget property needs to be set to another UIElement, not just the *name* of a UIElement:

```
<RichTextBlock Foreground="Black" FontSize="20" FontFamily="Cambria"
               Margin="12" OverflowContentTarget="{Binding ElementName=o1}">
  …
</RichTextBlock>
```

For the current two-TextBlocks in a StackPanel example, the result is:

```
# of characters: 20
The string is: A DataContext string
```

Because DataContext is a simple property, it's easy to set from C#. This is the way it is usually set, rather than in XAML, because it's the most convenient for complex or dynamic objects. Often DataContext is set on a Page, and all Bindings within the Page share that source object unless DataContext is overridden lower in the tree (or any Bindings explicitly specify a source).

Binding to a Collection

One of the most common uses of data binding is to bind the items of an items control to a collection. You might try to assign a Binding to an items control's Items property, but, alas, Items is not a dependency property. All items controls expose a separate Items**Source** dependency property that exists specifically for data binding. Therefore, if you have a Page as follows:

```
<Page …>
  <Grid Background="{StaticResource ApplicationPageBackgroundThemeBrush}">
    <GridView ItemsSource="{Binding}"/>
  </Grid>
</Page>
```

with the following simple code-behind that sets the data context to a simple array:

```
using Windows.UI.Xaml.Controls;

namespace Chapter17
{
  public sealed partial class MainPage : Page
  {
    public MainPage()
    {
      InitializeComponent();
      this.DataContext = new string[] { "one", "two", "three" };
    }
  }
}
```

Then you get the three-item `GridView` pictured in Figure 17.1.

Figure 17.2 shows what happens if you change the data context to the set of files in the user's Pictures Library (which requires the Pictures Library capability):

FIGURE 17.1   A `GridView` whose data source is a simple three-element array

```csharp
using System;
using System.Threading.Tasks;
using Windows.Storage;
using Windows.UI.Xaml.Controls;

namespace Chapter17
{
  public sealed partial class MainPage : Page
  {
    public MainPage()
    {
      InitializeComponent();
      SetDataContext();
    }

    async Task SetDataContext()
    {
      // This requires the Pictures Library capability
      StorageFolder pictures = KnownFolders.PicturesLibrary;
      this.DataContext = await pictures.GetFilesAsync();
    }
  }
}
```

Improving the Display

Clearly, the default display of the files from the Pictures Library in Figure 17.2—a `ToString` rendering—is not acceptable. One simple way to improve this is to leverage a `DisplayMemberPath` property present on all items controls. This property works hand in hand with `ItemsSource`. If you set it to an appropriate property path, the corresponding property value gets rendered for each item.

For the target property to automatically stay updated with changes to the source collection (that is, the addition and removal of elements), the source collection must implement an interface called `INotifyCollectionChanged`. Fortunately, the .NET Framework has a built-in class that does this for you. It's called `ObservableCollection`. It implements both `INotifyCollectionChanged` and `INotifyPropertyChanged`, so it enables all change notification features.

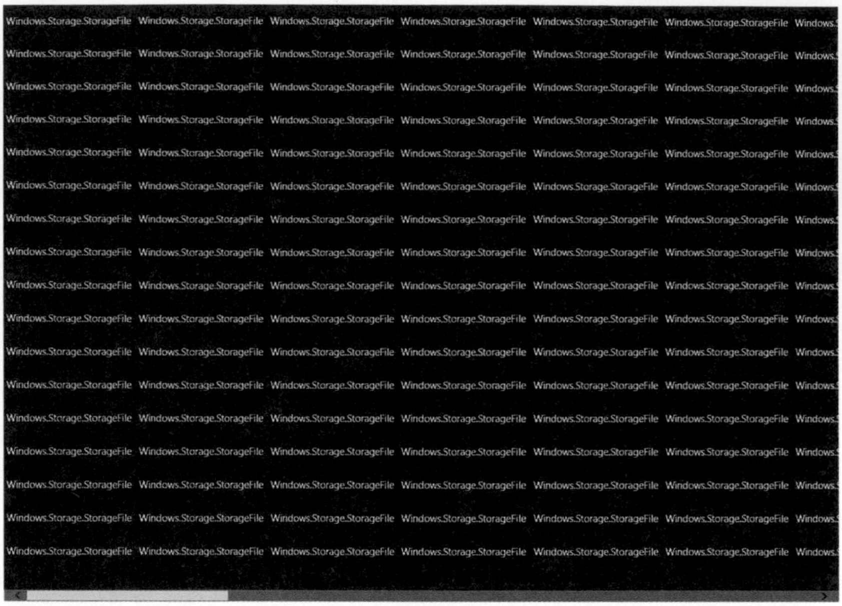

FIGURE 17.2   The `GridView` with an updated data source set to the collection of files in the Pictures Library

Each of the `StorageFile` objects in Figure 17.2 has a `Name` property, so adding the following to the `Page`'s XAML produces the result in Figure 17.3:

```
<Page …>
  <Grid Background="{StaticResource ApplicationPageBackgroundThemeBrush}">
    <GridView ItemsSource="{Binding}" DisplayMemberPath="Name"/>
  </Grid>
</Page>
```

This is a slight improvement, but not much. One way (not specific to data binding) is to use a data template, and another way is to use a value converter. These are the subjects of the next section.

> **(!)   `ItemsControl`'s `Items` and `ItemsSource` properties can't be modified simultaneously!**
>
> You must decide whether you want to populate an items control manually via `Items` or with data binding via `ItemsSource`, and you must not mix these techniques. `ItemsSource` can be set only when the `Items` collection is empty, and `Items` can be modified only when `ItemsSource` is `null`. Therefore, if you want to add or remove items to/from a data-bound `GridView`, you must do this to the underlying collection (`ItemsSource`) rather than at the user interface level (`Items`). Note that regardless of which method is used to *set* items in an items control, you can always *retrieve* items via the `Items` collection.

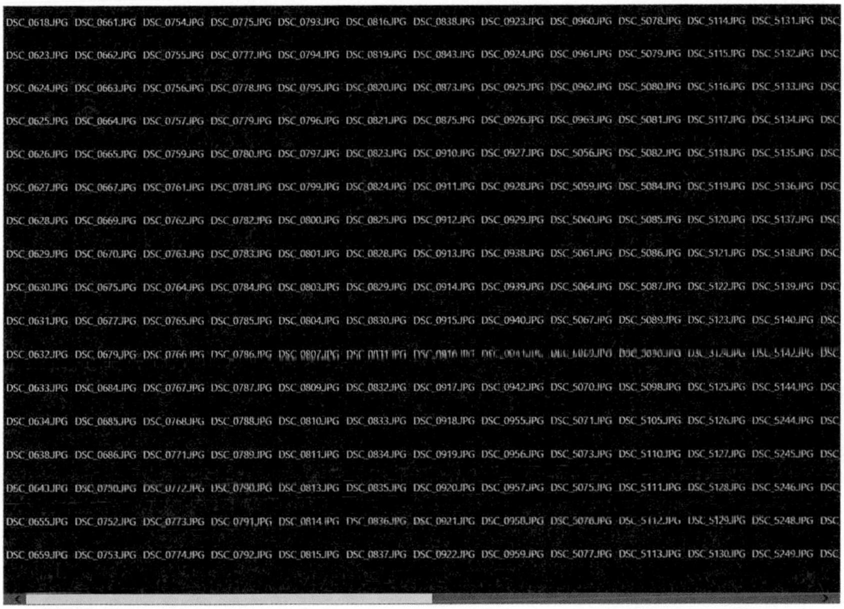

FIGURE 17.3 `DisplayMemberPath` is a simple mechanism for customizing the display of items in a data-bound collection.

Controlling Rendering

Data binding is simple when the source and target properties are compatible data types and the default rendering of the source is all you need to display. But often a bit of customization is required. The need for this in the previous section is obvious, because you want to display `Images`, not raw `strings`, in the `GridView`.

These types of customizations would be easy *without* data binding because you're writing all the code to retrieve the data on your own. But with the two mechanisms discussed in this section, you don't need to give up the benefits of data binding to get the desired results in more customized scenarios

Using Data Templates

A *data template* is a piece of user interface that you'd like to apply to an arbitrary object when it is rendered. Many controls have properties (of type `DataTemplate`) for attaching a data template appropriately. For example, `ContentControl` has a `ContentTemplate` property for controlling the rendering of its `Content` object, and `ItemsControl` has an `ItemTemplate` that applies to each of its items. In addition, `ComboBox` has a `SelectionBoxItemTemplate` property, `ListViewBase` has a `HeaderTemplate` property, and `ToggleSwitch` has three such properties: `HeaderTemplate`, `OnContentTemplate`, and `OffContentTemplate`

By setting one of these properties to an instance of a `DataTemplate`, you can swap in a completely new visual tree. The following update applies a `DataTemplate` to produce the result in Figure 17.4:

```
<Page …>
  <Grid Background="{StaticResource ApplicationPageBackgroundThemeBrush}">
    <GridView ItemsSource="{Binding}">
      <GridView.ItemTemplate>
        <DataTemplate>
          <Grid>
            <Rectangle Fill="Blue" Width="100" Height="100"/>
            <TextBlock Text="{Binding Name}"/>
          </Grid>
        </DataTemplate>
      </GridView.ItemTemplate>
    </GridView>
  </Grid>
</Page>
```

Notice that the way to adapt the single data template to each item is to use data binding! When you apply a data template, it is implicitly given an appropriate data context. When applied as an `ItemTemplate`, the data context is implicitly the current item in `ItemsSource`. Note that `Binding` must be used in this case, not `TemplateBinding` as in control templates.

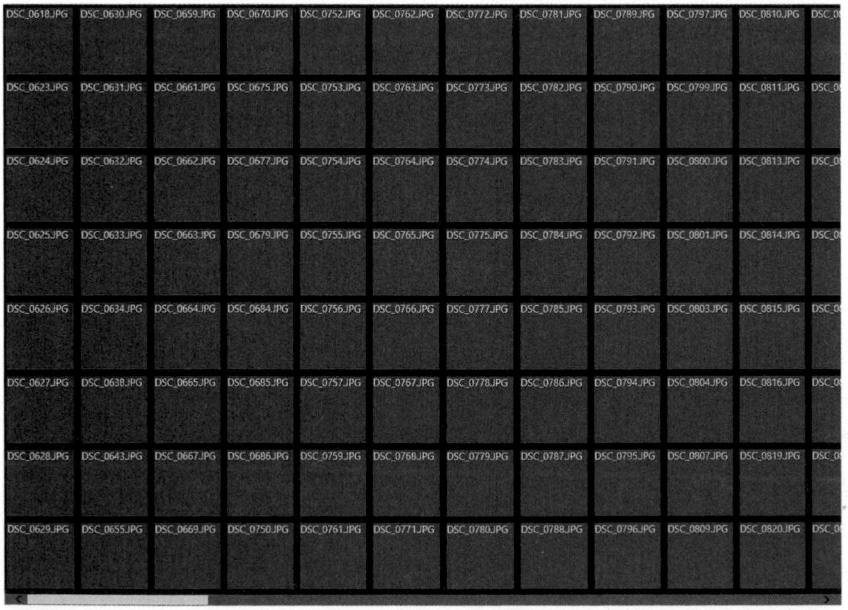

> Although data templates can be used on non-data-bound objects (such as a `GridView` with a manually constructed set of items), you'll almost always want to use data binding *inside* the template to customize the appearance of the visual tree based on the underlying object(s).

FIGURE 17.4   A simple data template makes each item in the `GridView` appear as a blue square with text.

The result of Figure 17.4 is still not satisfactory. We know that these files are images, so it makes sense to display thumbnails. However, `StorageFile` doesn't expose a suitable `Uri` or `ImageSource` property for a thumbnail (or even the full picture, for that matter) that we could use with an `Image`-based data template.

Therefore, we can define a data-binding-friendly (and simpler) version of the `StorageFile` class as follows:

```
class Photo
{
  public ImageSource Thumbnail { get; set; }
  // More properties can be added as needed
}
```

This is commonly referred to as part of a *view model*: a representation that sits in-between the view (the `GridView`) and the model (the file system objects). With this class defined, we can make the data context be an `ObservableCollection` of `Photo` objects (observable so the UI receives updates) and populate that collection by changing the `Page`'s code-behind as follows:

```
using System;
using System.Collections.ObjectModel;
using System.Threading.Tasks;
using Windows.Storage;
using Windows.Storage.FileProperties;
using Windows.UI.Xaml.Controls;
using Windows.UI.Xaml.Media.Imaging;

namespace Chapter17
{
  public sealed partial class MainPage : Page
  {
    // The new data source
    ObservableCollection<Photo> photos = new ObservableCollection<Photo>();

    public MainPage()
    {
      InitializeComponent();
      SetDataContext();
    }

    async Task SetDataContext()
    {
      // Can set this now because updates will be propagated
      this.DataContext = this.photos;
```

```
// This requires the Pictures Library capability
StorageFolder pictures = KnownFolders.PicturesLibrary;

foreach (StorageFile file in await pictures.GetFilesAsync())
{
    // Retreive the thumbnail
    StorageItemThumbnail thumbnail =
        await file.GetThumbnailAsync(ThumbnailMode.PicturesView);

    if (thumbnail != null)
    {
        using (thumbnail)
        {
            // Create an ImageSource from the thumbnail stream
            BitmapImage source = new BitmapImage();
            source.SetSource(thumbnail);

            // Create a new Photo object and add it to the collection
            this.photos.Add(new Photo { Thumbnail = source });
        }
    }
}
```

Finally, we must update the data template to leverage this new Thumbnail property on the new Photo object:

```
<Page …>
  <Grid Background="{StaticResource ApplicationPageBackgroundThemeBrush}">
    <GridView ItemsSource="{Binding}">
      <GridView.ItemTemplate>
        <DataTemplate>
          <Image Width="200" Source="{Binding Thumbnail}"/>
        </DataTemplate>
      </GridView.ItemTemplate>
    </GridView>
  </Grid>
</Page>
```

With these changes, we get the result in Figure 17.5, which is finally a satisfactory representation of the user's photos from the Pictures Library. The key to making this work is the synchronous property for getting each thumbnail, rather than an asynchronous method.

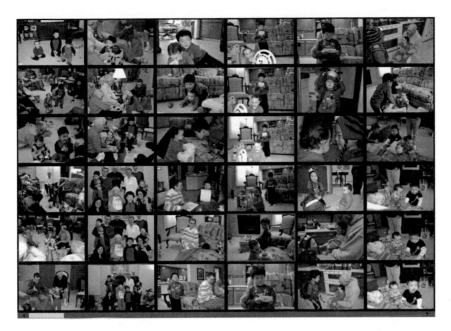

FIGURE 17.5   The `GridView` binds to an `ObservableCollection` of custom `Photo` objects that expose the thumbnail in a data-binding-friendly manner.

• • •

Template Selectors

Sometimes it can be desirable to heavily customize a data template based on the input data. Although a lot can be done inside a single data template, you can use a *template selector* to select a custom template at runtime when it is time for the data to be rendered. This works much like `Style` selectors. To do this, you create a class that derives from `DataTemplateSelector` and override its virtual `SelectTemplate` method. You can then associate an instance with the appropriate element by setting that element's *XXX*`TemplateSelector` property. Every class that defines an *XXX*`Template` property also has a corresponding *XXX*`TemplateSelector` property.

Using Value Converters

Whereas data templates can customize the way data is rendered, value converters can morph each piece of data before it reaches the target. They enable you to plug in custom logic without giving up the benefits of data binding.

Value converters are sometimes used to reconcile a source and target that are different data types. For example, you could change the background or foreground color of an element based on the value of some non-`Brush` data source, à la conditional formatting in Microsoft Excel. Or you could use it to enhance the information displayed, without the need for separate elements.

Imagine that we want to set the Header of the photo-filled GridView so it displays the number of photos. We could bind the Header property to the collection's Count property from the same implicit data context and set HeaderTemplate to a DataTemplate that improves its display:

```
<Page …>
  <Grid Background="{StaticResource ApplicationPageBackgroundThemeBrush}">
    <GridView ItemsSource="{Binding}" Header="{Binding Count}">
      <GridView.HeaderTemplate>
        <DataTemplate>
          <TextBlock Style="{StaticResource HeaderTextStyle}" Text="{Binding}"/>
        </DataTemplate>
      </GridView.HeaderTemplate>
      <GridView.ItemTemplate>
        <DataTemplate>
          <Image Width="200" Source="{Binding Thumbnail}"/>
        </DataTemplate>
      </GridView.ItemTemplate>
    </GridView>
  </Grid>
</Page>
```

The TextBlock in the new DataTemplate leverages the standard HeaderTextStyle style from StandardStyles.xaml. This produces the result in Figure 17.6.

FIGURE 17.6   The GridView's Header displays the raw Count from the collection of photos.

This is okay, but the number could use a little context. And with a value converter, we can do better than a static " photo(s)" suffix. (I don't know about you, but when I see a user interface report something like "1 item(s)," it just looks lazy to me.) We can customize the text based on the value, so we can display "1 photo" (singular) versus "2 photos" (plural) versus a special message for zero.

A value converter is any class that implements IValueConverter, so the following class can perform the aforementioned custom logic:

```
namespace Chapter17
{
  public class RawCountToDescriptionConverter : IValueConverter
  {
    public object Convert(object value, Type targetType, object parameter,
                          string language)
    {
      // Let Parse throw an exception if the input is bad
      int num = int.Parse(value.ToString());
      if (num == 0)
      {
        return "There are no photos yet. Add some!";
      }
      else
      {
        return num.ToString("N0") + (num == 1 ? " photo" : " photos");
      }
    }

    public object ConvertBack(object value, Type targetType, object parameter,
                              string language)
    {
      return DependencyProperty.UnsetValue;
    }
  }
}
```

This interface has two simple methods—Convert, which is passed the source instance that must be converted to the target instance, and ConvertBack, which does the opposite. ConvertBack is called only when TwoWay data binding is done, so this value converter returns a standard dummy value for this case. The implementation of Convert not only customizes the message, but it provides a thousands separator with the N0 formatting. Note that this uses hard-coded English strings, whereas a production-quality converter uses a localizable resource (or makes use of the passed-in language parameter).

This converter can be applied to the Page as follows:

```
<Page … xmlns:local="using:Chapter17">
  <Page.Resources>
    <!-- Create an instance of the converter that can be referenced -->
    <local:RawCountToDescriptionConverter x:Key="myConverter"/>
  </Page.Resources>
  <Grid Background="{StaticResource ApplicationPageBackgroundThemeBrush}">
    <GridView ItemsSource="{Binding}"
              Header="{Binding Count, Converter={StaticResource myConverter}}">
      <GridView.HeaderTemplate>
        <DataTemplate>
          <TextBlock Style="{StaticResource HeaderTextStyle}" Text="{Binding}"/>
        </DataTemplate>
      </GridView.HeaderTemplate>
      <GridView.ItemTemplate>
        <DataTemplate>
          <Image Width="200" Source="{Binding Thumbnail}"/>
        </DataTemplate>
      </GridView.ItemTemplate>
    </GridView>
  </Grid>
</Page>
```

This produces the result in Figure 17.7. Binding has a Converter property that can be set to any value converter, which is often defined as a resource so it can be referenced in XAML. It also has ConverterParameter and ConverterLanguage properties that can be set to custom values. These values get passed to the converter as the parameter and language parameters seen previously.

 How do I use a value converter to perform a conversion on each item when binding to a collection?

You can apply a data template to the ItemsControl's ItemTemplate property and then apply value converters to any Bindings done *inside* the data template. If you apply the value converter to the ItemsControl's Binding instead, an update to the source collection would prompt the Convert method to be called once for the entire collection (not on a per-item basis). You can implement such a converter that accepts a collection and returns a morphed collection, but that would not be an efficient approach.

FIGURE 17.7   The GridView's Header displays custom text courtesy of a value converter.

Customizing the View of a Collection

Instead of binding directly to a collection, you can insert a *view* between the source and target objects that adds support for grouping and navigating items. This view is an object implementing the ICollectionView interface, and you can create one by creating an object known as CollectionViewSource.

Grouping

For the example of displaying a user's photos, it's natural to want to group them based on the day (or month or year) they were taken. To enable this, let's first add an appropriate property to the Photo class:

```
class Photo
{
  public ImageSource Thumbnail { get; set; }
  public DateTimeOffset DateTaken { get; set; }
  // More properties can be added as needed
}
```

Then, the following code updates the `SetDataContext` method shown previously with support for grouping the photos based on the day they were taken:

```
async Task SetDataContext()
{
  // This requires the Pictures Library capability
  StorageFolder pictures = KnownFolders.PicturesLibrary;

  foreach (StorageFile file in await pictures.GetFilesAsync())
  {
    // Retreive the thumbnail
    StorageItemThumbnail thumbnail =
      await file.GetThumbnailAsync(ThumbnailMode.PicturesView);
    if (thumbnail != null)
    {
      using (thumbnail)
      {
        // Create an ImageSource from the thumbnail stream
        BitmapImage source = new BitmapImage();
        source.SetSource(thumbnail);

        // Create a new Photo object and add it to the collection
        this.photos.Add(new Photo { Thumbnail = source, DateTaken =
          (await file.Properties.GetImagePropertiesAsync()).DateTaken });
      }
    }
  }

  // Create a view to use as the data context
  CollectionViewSource viewSource = new CollectionViewSource();
  viewSource.IsSourceGrouped = true;
  this.DataContext = viewSource;

  // Here's where the underlying collection gets associated with the view.
  // Use LINQ (requires "using System.Linq") to group the photos appropriately.
  viewSource.Source = from photo in this.photos
                      group photo by photo.DateTaken.Date into g
                      orderby g.Key
                      select g;
}
```

With this change alone, the `GridView`'s items don't get grouped. For that to happen, you also need to add a `GroupStyle` object to the `GroupStyle` property defined by all items controls. GroupStyle enables you to specify a template for each group's header, a Panel for each group's items, and more. The following update to the Page's XAML produces the result in Figure 17.8. Note that the GridView has been changed to a ListView because each group is already wrapping its items in a grid-like fashion:

```xml
<Page …>
  <Page.Resources>
    <local:DateConverter x:Key="myConverter"/>
  </Page.Resources>
  <Grid Background="{StaticResource ApplicationPageBackgroundThemeBrush}">
    <ListView ItemsSource="{Binding}">
      <ListView.ItemTemplate>
        <DataTemplate>
          <Image Width="200" Source="{Binding Thumbnail}"/>
        </DataTemplate>
      </ListView.ItemTemplate>

      <!-- A style for each group -->
      <ListView.GroupStyle>
        <GroupStyle>
          <!-- The group header shows the date -->
          <GroupStyle.HeaderTemplate>
            <DataTemplate>
              <TextBlock Style="{StaticResource SubheaderTextStyle}"
                Margin="5" FontWeight="Bold"
                Text="{Binding Key, Converter={StaticResource myConverter}}"/>
            </DataTemplate>
          </GroupStyle.HeaderTemplate>

          <!-- The panel for arranging the items in the group -->
          <GroupStyle.Panel>
            <ItemsPanelTemplate>
              <VariableSizedWrapGrid Orientation="Horizontal"/>
            </ItemsPanelTemplate>
          </GroupStyle.Panel>
        </GroupStyle>
      </ListView.GroupStyle>
    </ListView>
  </Grid>
</Page>
```

FIGURE 17.8   The familiar page now displays the photos in a ListView with grouping support enabled.

The data-bound text in each group header is the Key property created by the grouping done in the LINQ query. Although this has the time stripped out (thanks to the grouping by photo.DateTaken.**Date**), the default display would show a time of 12:00:00 AM with each date without further customization. The Binding inside the HeaderTemplate leverages a new DateConverter value converter to customize each label, which is implemented as follows:

```
public class DateConverter : IValueConverter
{
  DateTimeFormatter formatter =
    new DateTimeFormatter("dayofweek month day year");

  public object Convert(object value, Type targetType, object parameter,
                        string language)
  {
    return this.formatter.Format((DateTime)value);
  }

  public object ConvertBack(object value, Type targetType, object parameter,
                            string language)
  {
    return DependencyProperty.UnsetValue;
  }
}
```

You can imagine supporting much fancier groupings with this mechanism, such as calculating date ranges and returning strings such as "Last Week", "Last Month", and so on.

There is quite a bit going on behind-the-scenes to make this work. When a CollectionViewSource is a data binding source, either explicitly or implicitly via DataContext or, a separate view object is what *actually* gets used as the source. This object is exposed via CollectionViewSource's readonly View property and is the object implementing ICollectionView.

ICollectionView has a CurrentItem property, so because the Page's data context is this view object, you could make the ListView's Header show the date from the current selection as follows:

```
<ListView ItemsSource="{Binding}" Header="{Binding CurrentItem.DateTaken}">
```

Navigating

In this context, *navigating* a view refers to managing the current item—not the kind of navigation discussed in Chapter 7, "App Model." ICollectionView not only has a CurrentItem property (and a corresponding CurrentPosition property that exposes the current item's zero-based index), but it also has a handful of methods for programmatically changing the current item: MoveCurrentToNext, MoveCurrentToPrevious, MoveCurrentToPosition, and so on.

Although a bit wordy, these navigation methods are straightforward to use. They enable not only updating the selected item in an items control without explicitly referencing it, but any additional elements that want to display information about the current item can be automatically updated as well, as long as they bind to the same source. If you paste a second, identical ListView from Figure 17.8 onto the Page (perhaps side-by-side in a two-column Grid), you'll see that selection changes made to one affects the other simultaneously!

Summary

Data binding is a powerful feature, although its use is also optional. After all, it's not hard to write code that ties two objects together. But writing such code can be tedious, error prone, and a maintenance hassle, especially when managing multiple data sources that might need to be synchronized as items are added, removed, and changed. Such code also tends to tightly couple business logic with the user interface, which makes apps more brittle.

But there's more to data binding than cutting down on the amount of code you need to write. Much of the appeal of data binding comes from the fact that the majority of it can be done declaratively. This has some important implications. Design tools such as Visual Studio and Blend can (and do) surface data-binding functionality, so nonprogrammers can add sophisticated functionality to a user interface. This support also enables designers to specify easily removable dummy data for testing data-bound user interfaces.

Chapter 18

DATA

The preceding chapter discusses binding to in-memory data. Excluding hard-coded data in your source code, from where might such data come? Windows 8 apps have three primary options:

→ App Data

→ User Data

→ Networking

This chapter, the first of this part of the book that solely covers Windows Runtime features that aren't specific to XAML apps, examines these three choices.

App Data

App data refers to any persistent data that an app reads and writes "privately." An app's settings or a game's high scores are an example of this type of data. App data normally does not get directly exposed to users, and one app cannot view such data from another app. Most importantly, when an app is uninstalled, all of its app data automatically gets deleted as well.

There are two types of app data: *app settings* and *app files*. Access to both of these mechanisms is available via the `Windows.Storage.ApplicationData` class.

App Settings

App settings are small, primitive values that are easy to store and retrieve. Using them looks much like using session state with SuspensionManager. However, these are typically used for settings that persist regardless of how the app exited. Furthermore, you have two options: *local settings* and *roaming settings*.

Local Settings

The following code shows how to do the three basic actions of reading/writing/deleting a local setting:

```
ApplicationDataContainer settings = ApplicationData.Current.LocalSettings;

// (1) Store a setting
settings.Values["CurrentIndex"] = 5;

// (2) Retrieve a setting
object value = settings.Values["CurrentIndex"];
if (value != null)
{
  // The setting exists
  int currentIndex = (int)value;
}

// (3) Delete a setting (this silently returns if the setting doesn't exist)
settings.Values.Remove("CurrentIndex");
```

Although this code checks for a null value to determine whether the specific setting exists, another approach is to call the settings.Values.ContainsKey method.

ApplicationDataContainer, the type of the LocalSettings property, enables you to create and name subcontainers for organizing your settings into different buckets or "folders." This is managed with its CreateContainer and DeleteContainer methods. You can nest them, but only up to 32 levels deep.

> **Only a few primitive data types can be used as a value for an app setting!**
>
> App settings always have a string key and a value that's either a bool, byte, int, uint, long, ulong, float, double, or string. (You can combine multiple primitive values into an ApplicationDataCompositeValue instance, however, as described in the "Roaming Settings" section.) There is no built-in support for binary data. For this, you should use an app file instead.

> You can version app data (settings or files) by calling the ApplicationData.SetVersionAsync method with a custom version number. Before reading any app data, you can check the version of the stored data with the ApplicationData.Version property and take appropriate action. This enables you to make breaking changes to your schema and upgrade old data whenever it is encountered.

> **! Using too many settings can slow your app's launch!**
>
> App settings are simpler to use than app files, but you have less control over them. All settings are automatically read from disk when your app is launched. With app files, on the other hand, you control when each file is opened and read.

Roaming Settings

Traditionally, to roam a user's settings to any device, you set up a Web service, deal with user accounts, security, synchronization, and so on. Or find a service that can do this for you in a satisfactory way. For most apps, it's not worth the hassle or cost.

However, Windows 8 apps can roam settings simply by changing the word `Local` to `Roaming` in the preceding code, as follows:

```
ApplicationDataContainer settings = ApplicationData.Current.RoamingSettings;
```

That's it! If the user has a Microsoft account linked to the logged-in account, then Windows automatically replicates settings to Microsoft's cloud when they are updated, and it synchronizes the data to wherever the user logs in (if the same version of the same app is installed on the device). In the case of a conflict, the last writer wins.

If the user isn't leveraging a Microsoft account, then roaming settings don't act differently from local settings. Local settings and roaming settings are two completely independent containers that are both stored locally; the only difference is the synchronization policy associated with the roaming ones. An app can use both types of settings for separate reasons. If your session state is small enough, you can enable roaming "session state" with `RoamingSettings` and not even bother with `SuspensionManager`.

In the off-chance that an app is used on multiple devices by the same user simultaneously, an update to the roaming settings in one place eventually causes `ApplicationData`'s `DataChanged` event to be raised in the other instance(s). By attaching a handler to this event, you can choose to refresh your app with the synchronized update.

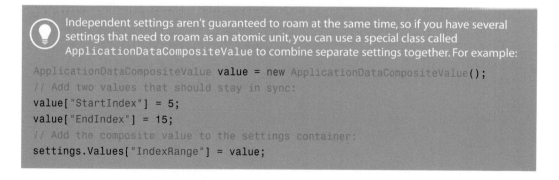

> Independent settings aren't guaranteed to roam at the same time, so if you have several settings that need to roam as an atomic unit, you can use a special class called `ApplicationDataCompositeValue` to combine separate settings together. For example:
>
> ```
> ApplicationDataCompositeValue value = new ApplicationDataCompositeValue();
> // Add two values that should stay in sync:
> value["StartIndex"] = 5;
> value["EndIndex"] = 15;
> // Add the composite value to the settings container:
> settings.Values["IndexRange"] = value;
> ```

> ! **Roaming works only if the total amount of data remains small!**
>
> Each app receives a quota for roaming data, which is 100 kilobytes at the time of this writing. This applies to the combination of roaming settings *and* roaming files. If you exceed this limit, roaming will silently stop happening until the size of the data goes back under the threshold.
>
> You can programmatically discover your app's quota by checking `ApplicationData`'s `RoamingStorageQuota` property, which returns the number of kilobytes. However, it's unfortunately up to you to figure out the total number of bytes currently being used!

> ! **Don't rely on roaming to happen instantaneously!**
>
> In many circumstances, roaming data should propagate quickly, but that is not always the case. If the network connection has high latency, Windows will delay roaming. Of course, delays also happen if changes are made while the user is offline, or if the user disables roaming on a particular network to avoid charges.

App Files

App files are regular files on the local file system, but in a private location specific to your app. Therefore, as with app settings, you can interact with app files without needing any capabilities. You can create any number of files and subfolders without worrying about quotas (except for roaming files), although there is still the limitation of supporting subfolders up to only 32 levels deep.

This section examines the three types of app files: *local files*, *roaming files*, and *temporary files*. It also includes files packaged with your app ("packaged files" or "resources") for completeness. Although such files are not part of the app data mechanism, shipping read-only data files with your app can be a great option to keep in mind.

> **How can I save files to arbitrary spots on the local file system?**
>
> You can't automatically, and good riddance to that ability! Other than your app's own isolated location, or a few special locations such as the user's libraries (which require capabilities), the only way this can happen is by the user explicitly picking the location and filename via the file picker. In all these cases, you save *user data* instead of app data.

Packaged Files

Although you can't add or edit the files packaged with your app, you can retrieve one as follows:

```
StorageFolder folder = Package.Current.InstalledLocation;
StorageFile file = await localFolder.GetFileAsync("Assets\\Logo.png");
```

This file location corresponds to the URI `ms-appx:///Assets/Logo.png`.

Local Files

The following code demonstrates creating a local file called `MyFile.txt` in a `MyFolder` subfolder and writing `"data"` into it:

```
StorageFolder folder = ApplicationData.Current.LocalFolder;
StorageFile file = await folder.CreateFileAsync("MyFolder\\MyFile.txt",
  CreationCollisionOption.ReplaceExisting);
if (file != null)
{
  await FileIO.WriteTextAsync(file, "data");
}
```

The file gets saved as **%USERPROFILE%\AppData\Local\Packages*PackageFamilyName*\ LocalState**\MyFolder\MyFile.txt. You can never access it via this full path in your code. You can, however, access it with the URI `ms-appdata:///`**local**`/MyFolder/MyFile.txt`. For example, you can make an `Image` element display content from a local file as follows:

```
<Image Source="ms-appdata:///local/image.png"/>
```

 The `CreationCollisionOption` enumeration value that can be passed to `StorageFolder`'s `CreateFileAsync` method enables several different behaviors for what to do when the file already exists: replacing it, failing, opening it, or even automatically choosing a new filename (by appending a number) for the new file.

 You can read, write, and append content to a `StorageFile` with handy APIs exposed by the static `Windows.Storage.FileIO` class. These methods work directly on the file; no streams are involved. There are methods for working with `string`s, collections of `string`s (one per line), byte arrays, or buffers represented by `IBuffer`.

 You can get Windows to automatically index local data from your app for fast searches. To do this, simply create a top-level local folder called `Indexed` and place everything there! (Further subfolders are okay.) Both the file contents and file metadata get indexed.

Roaming Files

As with local settings versus roaming settings, you can switch from local files to roaming files by changing a single `Local` to a `Roaming`:

```
StorageFolder folder = ApplicationData.Current.RoamingFolder;
StorageFile file = await folder.CreateFileAsync("MyFolder\\MyFile.txt",
  CreationCollisionOption.ReplaceExisting);
if (file != null)
{
  await FileIO.WriteTextAsync(file, "data");
}
```

The file gets saved locally as %USERPROFILE%\AppData\Local\Packages\ *PackageFamilyName***Roaming**State\MyFolder\MyFile.txt, and has all the same synchronization behavior discussed previously for roaming settings. You can access it with the URI ms-appdata:///**roaming**/MyFolder/MyFile.txt. For the image example, that looks as follows:

```
<Image Source="ms-appdata:///roaming/image.png"/>
```

Remember to handle ApplicationData's DataChanged event to refresh your app in response to external changes to a file, because this applies equally to roaming settings and files. Note that any changes made locally to a file don't get roamed until your code closes the file.

> ! **Roaming doesn't work with files whose names begin with white-space!**
>
> This is a limitation of the underlying synchronization engine.

Temporary Files

This should be no surprise at this point, but working with temporary files is just a matter of changing the folder:

```
StorageFolder folder = ApplicationData.Current.TemporaryFolder;
StorageFile file = await folder.CreateFileAsync("MyFolder\\MyFile.txt",
  CreationCollisionOption.ReplaceExisting);
if (file != null)
{
  await FileIO.WriteTextAsync(file, "data");
}
```

This file is saved as %USERPROFILE%\AppData\Local\Packages*PackageFamilyName*\ **Temp**State\MyFolder\MyFile.txt, and you can access it with the URI ms-appdata:/// **temp**/MyFolder/MyFile.txt.

Placing files in the temporary folder is just like placing them in the local folder. The only difference is the intent of the files, and that Windows provides a mechanism for helping users automatically delete temporary files. You should assume that temporary files only exist for the current app session.

> If you're interested in using a local database within your app, check out SQLite (http://www.sqlite.org) and the sqlite-net project (http://github.com/ praeclarum/sqlite-net) that exposes the functionality to .NET languages. Even better, you can install SQLite as a Visual Studio extension. Under Tools, Extensions and Updates, Online, you can search for "SQLite." After installing it, you can add it to any project via Add Reference, Windows, Extensions, SQLite.

User Data

User data refers to files that are visible to the user and likely to be managed outside of your app. For example, a painting app would likely enable the user to save a creation as a regular image file. (Before the user saves it, however, it is likely to be stored as an app file so the work-in-progress doesn't get lost.) User files do *not* get deleted when an app is uninstalled.

An app cannot create, change, or delete user files without special permission. That permission either comes implicitly from the use of the Windows file picker, or explicitly from a relevant capability.

File Picker

The file picker is a powerful component. If a user selects an existing file or folder, or uses it to name a new file or folder, he or she is giving your app permission to work with that file or folder. And this file/folder can come from anywhere, even SkyDrive or arbitrary Web services thanks to the file picker's extensibility.

The file picker has three modes, exposed as three different classes in the `Windows.Storage.Pickers` namespace: `FileOpenPicker`, `FileSavePicker`, and `FolderPicker`. You see the `FileOpenPicker` used in Chapter 11, "Images," as follows:

```
// Get a JPEG from the user
FileOpenPicker picker = new FileOpenPicker();
picker.FileTypeFilter.Add(".jpg");
picker.FileTypeFilter.Add(".jpeg");
StorageFile file = await picker.PickSingleFileAsync();
```

In addition to `PickSingleFileAsync`, you can call `PickMultipleFilesAsync`, which returns a collection of `StorageFiles`. You can customize the text on the "Open" button by setting `CommitButtonText` to a custom `string`, customize the view by setting `ViewMode` to `List` or `Thumbnail`, and change `SuggestedStartLocation` to one of many values in the `PickerLocationId` enumeration: `Desktop`, `Downloads`, `DocumentsLibrary`, `PicturesLibrary`, `HomeGroup`, and so on.

In Chapter 11, you also see the `FileSavePicker` used as follows:

```
// Get a target JPEG file from the user
FileSavePicker picker = new FileSavePicker();
picker.FileTypeChoices.Add("JPEG file", new string[] { ".jpg", ".jpeg" });
StorageFile file = await picker.PickSaveFileAsync();
```

`FileSavePicker` has the same `CommitButtonText` property, which you can set if you want to change the "Save" button's text, and the same `SuggestedStartLocation` property. In addition, you can set `SuggestedFileName` or `SuggestedSaveFile` to pre-fill the text box shown to the user. Or you can set `DefaultFileExtension` if you don't want to suggest a specific filename.

The `FolderPicker` works similarly to the other two classes:

```
// Get an entire folder from the user
FolderPicker picker = new FolderPicker();
StorageFolder folder = await picker.PickSingleFolderAsync();
```

FolderPicker supports the same SuggestedStartLocation and ViewMode properties supported by FileOpenPicker. After you receive a StorageFolder from the FolderPicker, you have read/write access to the entire folder, including subfolders. Note that only appropriate folders are exposed via the file picker, so the user can never select the Program Files or Windows folders, for example.

 The file picker can't be shown from a snapped app!

If you attempt to show any forms of the file picker while your app is snapped, nothing happens and the relevant call returns null. If you enable users to launch the file picker from your snapped view, you should programmatically unsnap your app (with ApplicationView.TryUnsnap) before launching the file picker.

Libraries and Other Special Folders

With the right capability granted to your app, you can access the user's Music, Pictures, or Videos libraries without any prompt or file picker. (The Documents Library capability is more restrictive, because it works only for file type associations registered by the app, discussed in Chapter 20, "Extensions.") The same is true for a few more special folders: the HomeGroup folder, the removable devices folder, and the DLNA devices folder.

Doing this is trivial. As with the different types of app files, all you need to do is start off with the right StorageFolder. For example:

```
// This requires the Music Library capability:
StorageFolder music = KnownFolders.MusicLibrary;
// This requires the Pictures Library capability:
StorageFolder pictures = KnownFolders.PicturesLibrary;
// This requires the Videos Library capability:
StorageFolder videos = KnownFolders.VideosLibrary;
```

After you have the StorageFolder, you can use all the regular file APIs to enumerate, read, write, create, and delete files. Recall that with each StorageFile, you can get relevant metadata. This can be retrieved with calls to methods such as GetMusicPropertiesAsync, GetImagePropertiesAsync, and GetVideoPropertiesAsync. This makes it easy to provide a nice browser-style experience for each collection of specific file types.

The other folders exposed by KnownFolders are DocumentsLibrary, HomeGroup, MediaServerDevices (DLNA devices), and RemovableDevices.

StorageFolder exposes a GetFoldersAsync method that enables you to specify a CommonFolderQuery enumeration value (as well as an overload that enables you to retrieve the files in chunks) for grouping the results by common media properties. For example, you can specify GroupByAlbum, GroupByArtist, GroupByGenre, GroupByRating, or many more. This is valid only for library folders or subfolders, and the HomeGroup folder.

Networking

If the data you need to access isn't app data or user data, then you must need to directly fetch it over the network. Windows 8 apps have the following options for networking:

→ Performing direct HTTP Requests

→ Performing background download/upload

→ Using sockets (or WebSockets)

→ Working with syndicated feeds (RSS or Atom)

HTTP Requests

With the `HttpClient` class in the `System.Net.Http` namespace, you can send and receive HTTP requests: GET, PUT, POST, DELETE, or others. The following code uses this class to perform a search via the Bing API:

```
HttpClient client = new HttpClient();

// Make the client look like Internet Explorer 10
client.DefaultRequestHeaders.Add("user-agent",
  "Mozilla/5.0 (compatible; MSIE 10.0; Windows NT 6.2; WOW64; Trident/6.0)");

// Perform an HTTP GET
HttpResponseMessage response = await client.GetAsync(
  "http://api.bing.net/xml.aspx?Appid=<AppID>&query=windows&sources=web");

// Throws an exception if response.IsSuccessStatusCode is false
response.EnsureSuccessStatusCode();

string content = await response.Content.ReadAsStringAsync();
```

Some Web servers require a user-agent header with each request, so this code uses a user-agent header that matches Internet Explorer 10. Depending on your request, you can get different results by mimicking different browsers.

The HTTP GET is performed with the (asynchronous, of course) `GetAsync` method. `HttpClient` also exposes `PutAsync`, `PostAsync`, and `DeleteAsync` methods, as well as a `SendAsync` method for custom requests. The call to `EnsureSuccessStatusCode` is simply a way to convert failed requests into exceptions. This is completely optional. Although the returned `HttpResponseMessage` contains a lot of information, the call to `ReadAsStringAsync` retrieves the content as a `string`. In this example, the content is an XML string.

The Bing API requires an AppID belonging to a registered developer, which should replace the "<AppId>" in the URL passed to GetAsync. You can get one at the Bing Developer Center (http://www.bing.com/developers). Here's the XML returned by ReadAsStringAsync if you leave the AppID as the bogus string:

```xml
<?xml version="1.0" encoding="UTF-8"?>
<?pageview_candidate ?>
<SearchResponse Version="2.2"
  xmlns="http://schemas.microsoft.com/LiveSearch/2008/04/XML/element">
  <Query>
    <SearchTerms>windows</SearchTerms>
  </Query>
  <Errors>
    <Error>
      <Code>1002</Code>
      <Message>Parameter has invalid value.</Message>
      <Parameter>SearchRequest.AppId</Parameter>
      <Value>&lt;AppID&gt;</Value>
      <HelpUrl>http://msdn.microsoft.com/en-us/library/dd251042.aspx</HelpUrl>
    </Error>
  </Errors>
</SearchResponse>
```

The returned XML is not pretty-printed, however.

> 💡 The common pattern of calling GetAsync, EnsureSuccessStatusCode, and ReadAsStringAsync has a shortcut. HttpClient's GetStringAsync method does all three actions and asynchronously returns the string (or throws an exception). The following code uses this shortcut to invoke the Bing API the same way as previously done:
>
> ```csharp
> HttpClient client = new HttpClient();
>
> // Make the client look like Internet Explorer 10
> client.DefaultRequestHeaders.Add("user-agent",
>   "Mozilla/5.0 (compatible; MSIE 10.0; Windows NT 6.2; WOW64; Trident/6.0)");
>
> // Perform an HTTP GET and get the response as a string
> string content = await client.GetStringAsync(
>   "http://api.bing.net/xml.aspx?Appid=<AppID>&query=windows&sources=web");
> ```
>
> HttpClient defines a similar GetStreamAsync method that returns a Stream instead.

If you're interested in working with APIs exposed by SkyDrive (perhaps because the built-in roaming quota is too small for your needs), Hotmail, or Messenger, visit the Live Connect Developer Center at http://go.microsoft.com/fwlink/?LinkId=203291 for more information.

Background Transfer

If you download a large file that can take a significant amount of time, you should use the `BackgroundDownloader` class instead of `HttpClient`. `BackgroundDownloader` helps your app behave appropriately in the face of suspension or changing network conditions.

You can instantiate a `BackgroundDownloader`, and then call its `CreateDownload` method, which accepts a source `Uri` and a destination `StorageFile`. This returns a `DownloadOperation` object that enables starting, pausing, resuming, and progress reporting. If your app (and therefore a download) is terminated, you can enumerate pending downloads the next time your app runs with the static `BackgroundDownloader.GetCurrentDownloadsAsync` method and resume them.

A similar `Background**Uploader**` class exists, with a `CreateUpload` method that returns a `BackgroundUploader` object.

Sockets

The `Windows.Networking.Sockets` namespace contains classes that enable you to send and receive data via TCP sockets (reliable bidirectional streams), UDP sockets (unreliable datagrams), or WebSockets (both styles, but over HTTP):

→ `DatagramSocket` is a UDP socket.

→ `StreamSocket` is a TCP socket.

→ `MessageWebSocket` is basically a UDP-like WebSocket.

→ `StreamWebSocket` is basically a TCP-like WebSocket.

Syndication

The `Windows.Web.Syndication` namespace contains functionality for accessing RSS and Atom feeds. The RSS support covers standards 0.91 to 2.0, and the Atom support covers standards 0.3 to 1.0.

The following complete code-behind is for an RSS Reader page that shows the latest items from Engadget's RSS feed:

```
using System;
using System.Threading.Tasks;
using Windows.UI.Xaml.Controls;
using Windows.Web.Syndication;
```

```
namespace RssReader
{
  public sealed partial class MainPage : Page
  {
    public MainPage()
    {
      InitializeComponent();
      FillContentAsync();
    }

    async Task FillContentAsync()
    {
      SyndicationClient client = new SyndicationClient();
      try
      {
        SyndicationFeed feed = await client.RetrieveFeedAsync(
          new Uri("http://engadget.com/rss.xml"));

        this.DataContext = feed;
      }
      catch
      {
        // Handle any errors, such as a 404 from an unavailable site
        …
      }
    }

    void ListView_SelectionChanged(object sender, SelectionChangedEventArgs e)
    {
      if (e.AddedItems.Count == 0)
        return;

      // Show the selected item's content in the WebView because it is HTML
      this.webView.NavigateToString(
        (e.AddedItems[0] as SyndicationItem).Summary.Text);
    }
  }
}
```

The SyndicationFeed object returned by RetrieveFeedAsync exposes information about
the feed itself (such as a title) and a collection of SyndicationItem objects that reveals all
the information about each entry in the feed. Rather than extract such info in C#, this

code sets the returned feed as the `Page`'s data context so the XAML can data bind to it. Here is the corresponding XAML:

```xml
<Page …>
  <Grid Background="{StaticResource ApplicationPageBackgroundThemeBrush}">
    <Grid.ColumnDefinitions>
      <ColumnDefinition/>
      <ColumnDefinition/>
    </Grid.ColumnDefinitions>

    <!-- A ListView on the left shows the title of each item -->
    <ListView Header="{Binding Title.Text}" ItemsSource="{Binding Items}"
              SelectionChanged="ListView_SelectionChanged">

      <!-- Display the feed title in a larger-than-default TextBlock -->
      <ListView.HeaderTemplate>
        <DataTemplate>
          <TextBlock Style="{StaticResource HeaderTextStyle}" Text="{Binding}"/>
        </DataTemplate>
      </ListView.HeaderTemplate>

      <!-- Display only the title for each item in a subheader style -->
      <ListView.ItemTemplate>
        <DataTemplate>
          <TextBlock Style="{StaticResource SubheaderTextStyle}" Margin="10"
                     Text="{Binding Title.Text}"/>
        </DataTemplate>
      </ListView.ItemTemplate>
    </ListView>

    <!-- A WebView on the right renders the selected item's content -->
    <WebView Name="webView" Grid.Column="1"/>
  </Grid>
</Page>
```

This `Page` has a `ListView` on the left and a `WebView` on the right. The `ListView`'s `Header` is bound to the feed title (`Title.Text` on the `SyndicationFeed` object) and its `ItemsSource` is bound to the feed's `Items` collection. Each item's title is shown by binding to `Title.Text`. When a selection is made, `ListView_SelectionChanged` is invoked to make the `WebView` render the content from the selected item. (This is done because the content in each item is HTML.) The result is shown in Figure 18.1.

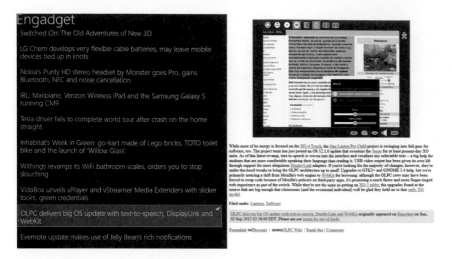

FIGURE 18.1   A simple RSS reader is easy to create with `SyndicationClient` to fetch and parse the feed and `WebView` to display the HTML content.

You can perform Atom feed *publication* with the `AtomPubClient` class in the `Windows.Web.AtomPub` namespace.

Feed items often contain custom elements or attributes. To retrieve these, you can access the XML representation via `SyndicationFeed`'s and `SyndicationItem`'s `GetXmlDocument` method or `ElementExtensions` property.

Connection Info

Through the static `NetworkInformation` class, you can discover details about all current network connections. You can also be notified of any changes via its `NetworkStatusChanged` property. For example, `NetworkInformation`'s `GetConnectionProfiles` method returns a collection of `ConnectionProfiles`, which have methods that expose the cost of the connection (including whether the user is roaming or over the data limit) and how much of the connection is used. You can use information like this to warn a user who is about to download a large file through your app while on a costly network.

Summary

The options for working with data are powerful yet straightforward. They balance the needs of app developers with the important need for users to be able to trust what their apps are doing.

To me, what is most striking about the features in this chapter is how easy Microsoft made it to index your app's data and to roam it. With automatic roaming, it's trivial to keep a consistent experience across devices. You don't need to directly interact with a Web service or understand anything about Microsoft accounts.

Chapter 19

CHARMS

The charms bar, shown in Figure 19.1, provides a consistent mechanism for users to accomplish a few tasks with any apps that support them. Each "charm," except for Start, brings up a corresponding pane on the right edge of the screen. And each of these panes can be exploited by apps to varying degrees. This chapter explains how you can take advantage of each one.

Search

If your app supports searching its content, you should expose this functionality via the Search charm. You do this by supporting the search contract. If invoked while your app is open, this makes the Search charm default to searching your app. However, supporting this contract also makes your app searchable even when your app isn't running.

FIGURE 19.1
The charms bar with its five charms

The easiest way to support the search contract is to right-click your project in Visual Studio, select **Add, New Item…**, and then choose **Search Contract** from the list. Unless you change its name, this adds a `Page` called `SearchResultsPage1.xaml` to your app. It also adds "Search" to the list of supported declarations to your package manifest, which registers the app as a search provider. The generated `Page` is used to display search results, and this is enabled by the following code that gets automatically added to `App.xaml.cs`:

```
/// <summary>
/// Invoked when the application is activated to display search results.
/// </summary>
/// <param name="args">Details about the activation request.</param>
protected override void OnSearchActivated(SearchActivatedEventArgs args)
{
  Chapter19.SearchResultsPage1.Activate(args.QueryText,
                                        args.PreviousExecutionState);

}
```

If you run your app after following these steps and then invoke the Search charm, you see the result in Figure 19.2. Your app is automatically added to the list of searchable apps, and it is selected by default when your app is running.

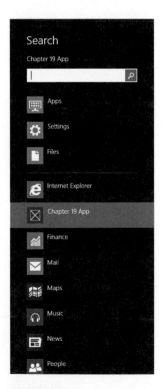

FIGURE 19.2   Your app appears in the Search pane once you support the search contract.

If you search for something, `SearchResultsPage1` is displayed, which is shown in Figure 19.3. The auto-generated page has a number of built-in features. It has a standard display with a functional back button that navigates to the previous page (if your app was running when Search was invoked) and a customized snapped view. The only thing missing is the logic to produce results!

 What determines the order of the list of searchable apps in the Search pane?

Windows adjusts the order based on how often the user performs a search with each one. The same technique is used in other panes as well.

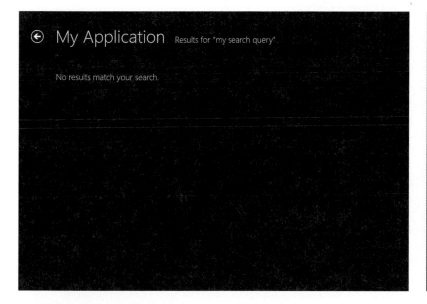

Fullscreen and filled view   Snapped view

FIGURE 19.3   The auto-generated search results page does a good job of handling search queries, although it needs your help to produce actual results.

Reporting Search Results

You can respond to `OnSearchActivated` however you'd like, but if you leverage the auto-generated search results `Page`, then it is designed for a specific pattern. It expects you to define a class to represent each search result with properties called `Image`, `Title`, `Subtitle`, and `Description`. The XAML uses data templates defined in `StandardStyles.xaml` that bind to these properties. Therefore, you can define the following class:

```
sealed class SearchResult
{
  public Uri Image { get; set; }
```

```
  public string Title { get; set; }
  public string Subtitle { get; set; }
  public string Description { get; set; }
}
```

Then, you need to report the appropriate search results for the current query inside SearchResultsPage1's Filter_SelectionChanged method. The following addition to the auto-generated method demonstrates adding hardcoded search results:

```
void Filter_SelectionChanged(object sender, SelectionChangedEventArgs e)
{
  // Determine what filter was selected
  var selectedFilter = e.AddedItems.FirstOrDefault() as Filter;
  if (selectedFilter != null)
  {
    // Mirror the results into the corresponding Filter object to allow the
    // RadioButton representation used when not snapped to reflect the change
    selectedFilter.Active = true;

    // TODO: Respond to the change in active filter by setting
    // this.DefaultViewModel["Results"] to a collection of items with bindable
    // Image, Title, Subtitle, and Description properties
    SearchResult[] list = new SearchResult[] {
      new SearchResult { Title = "One", Subtitle = "Item #1", Description =
        "The first item.", Image = new Uri("ms-appx:///Assets/SmallLogo.png") },
      new SearchResult { Title = "Two", Subtitle = "Item #2", Description =
        "The second item.", Image = new Uri("ms-appx:///Assets/SmallLogo.png") },
      new SearchResult { Title = "Three", Subtitle = "Item #3", Description =
        "The third item.", Image = new Uri("ms-appx:///Assets/SmallLogo.png") },
      new SearchResult { Title = "Four", Subtitle = "Item #4", Description =
        "The fourth item.", Image = new Uri("ms-appx:///Assets/SmallLogo.png") },
      new SearchResult { Title = "Five", Subtitle = "Item #5", Description =
        "The fifth item.", Image = new Uri("ms-appx:///Assets/SmallLogo.png") }
    };

    this.DefaultViewModel["Results"] = list;

    // Ensure results are found
    object results;
    ICollection resultsCollection;
    if (this.DefaultViewModel.TryGetValue("Results", out results) &&
        (resultsCollection = results as ICollection) != null &&
        resultsCollection.Count != 0)
    {
      VisualStateManager.GoToState(this, "ResultsFound", true);
      return;
```

```
    }
  }

  // Display informational text when there are no search results.
  VisualStateManager.GoToState(this, "NoResultsFound", true);
}
```

With this addition, any search produces the five results shown in Figure 19.4.

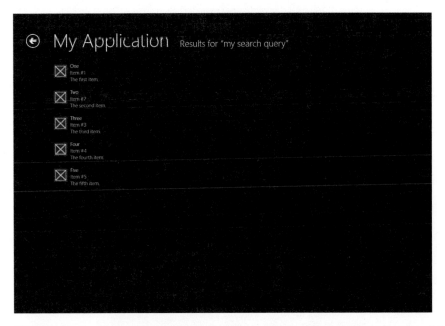

FIGURE 19.4   Five hardcoded search results are displayed when the collection of them is set as `DefaultViewModel["Results"]`.

You can support filters on your search results by adding some to the `filterList` variable in `SearchResultsPage`'s `LoadState` method:

```
protected override void LoadState(object navigationParameter,
                                Dictionary<string, object> pageState)
{
  var queryText = navigationParameter as String;

  // TODO: Application-specific searching logic.  The search process is
  //       responsible for creating a list of user-selectable result categories:
  //
  //       filterList.Add(new Filter("<filter name>", <result count>));
  //
  //       Only the first filter, typically "All", should pass true as a 3rd
```

```
//      argument in order to start in an active state.  Results for the active
//      filter are provided in Filter_SelectionChanged.

var filterList = new List<Filter>();
filterList.Add(new Filter("All", 5, true));
filterList.Add(new Filter("First Category", 2, false));
filterList.Add(new Filter("Second Category", 3, false));

// Communicate results through the view model
this.DefaultViewModel["QueryText"] = '\u201c' + queryText + '\u201d';
this.DefaultViewModel["Filters"] = filterList;
this.DefaultViewModel["ShowFilters"] = filterList.Count > 1;
}
```

This produces the result in Figure 19.5. Of course, you must report the proper
number of items in each filter, and you must filter the list appropriately inside
Filter_SelectionChanged based on the selectedFilter variable.

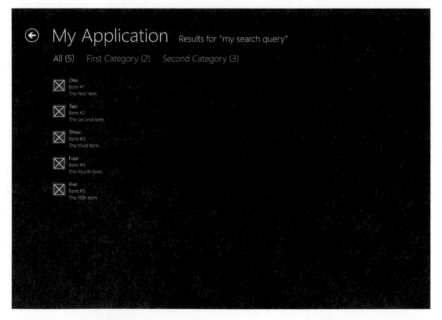

FIGURE 19.5   You can easily support filtered search results by adding a little bit of code to
LoadState and Filter_SelectionChanged.

The auto-generated search results page doesn't handle empty queries in a satisfactory way!

Empty search strings get passed along to SearchResultsPage1 just like any other query, but it's better to initialize the app as if it's launched normally in this case. That's because if the user invokes the Search charm then selects your app before typing the search query, your app gets invoked with an empty query. If you show the search results page (presumably with no results), this can seem odd to the user because from her perspective, she hasn't initiated the search yet.

Providing Custom Suggestions

Your app can provide search suggestions that are shown inside the Search pane as the user types. To do this, you must retrieve an instance of the Windows.ApplicationModel. Search.SearchPane class and handle its OnSuggestionsRequested event:

```
SearchPane searchPane = SearchPane.GetForCurrentView();
searchPane.SuggestionsRequested += OnSuggestionsRequested;
```

This is best done in App.xaml.cs from OnWindowCreated so you won't miss the event even if the app wasn't originally activated via the Search charm.

The following implementation of the OnSuggestionsRequested handler reports hardcoded suggestions if the user types a matching string (in a case-insensitive fashion):

```
// Sample static custom suggestions
static readonly string[] suggestions = { "Suggestion #1",
  "Suggestion #2", "Suggestion #3", "Suggestion #4", "Suggestion #5" };

void OnSuggestionsRequested(SearchPane sender,
                            SearchPaneSuggestionsRequestedEventArgs e)
{
  if (!string.IsNullOrEmpty(e.QueryText))
  {
    foreach (string suggestion in suggestions)
    {
      if (suggestion.StartsWith(e.QueryText,
                          StringComparison.CurrentCultureIgnoreCase))
      {
        // Add the suggestion to the Search pane (Note: no more than 5 are shown)
        e.Request.SearchSuggestionCollection.AppendQuerySuggestion(suggestion);
```

```
        }
      }
    }
}
```

The result is shown in Figure 19.6. Note that no more than five suggestions are ever shown, so the `foreach` in `OnSuggestionsRequested` can exit early in cases where the list of potential suggestions is long.

When the user selects a suggestion, SearchPane's `ResultSuggestionChosen` event is raised with details about the choice. The Search pane automatically remembers the user's previous searches and provides them as suggestions as well—at a higher priority than suggestions you provide! You can turn this off by setting SearchPane's `SearchHistoryEnabled` property to `false`.

In addition to `AppendQuerySuggestion`, `SearchSuggestionCollection` exposes `AppendSearchSeparator` and `AppendResultSuggestion` methods. `AppendSearchSeparator` is used to categorize the suggestions, although note that each separator counts against the limit of five items.

`AppendResultSuggestion` enables you to produce a richer-looking suggestion that has an image and description in addition to the main title. The following code uses all three methods to produce the result in Figure 19.7:

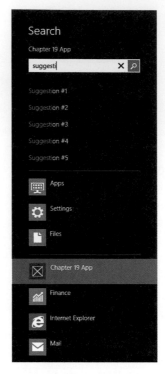

FIGURE 19.6 App-provided search suggestions in the Search pane

> SearchPane exposes a number of handy features. For example, you can ask whether it's currently visible or get the current query. You can set a placeholder `string` for the search box by setting its `PlaceholderText` property. You can programmatically show it with its `Show` method. You can also handle several informative events, such as `QueryChanged`, `QuerySubmitted`, and `VisibilityChanged`.

```
e.Request.SearchSuggestionCollection.AppendQuerySuggestion("Suggestion #1");
e.Request.SearchSuggestionCollection.AppendQuerySuggestion("Suggestion #2");
e.Request.SearchSuggestionCollection.AppendQuerySuggestion("Suggestion #3");
e.Request.SearchSuggestionCollection.AppendSearchSeparator("Recommendations");
e.Request.SearchSuggestionCollection.AppendResultSuggestion("Suggestion #4",
  "Details about this suggestion.", "tag", storageFile, "Alt image text");
```

The result suggestion's tag ("tag" in this example) is not displayed, but is passed along to the ResultSuggestionChosen event.

Providing Suggestions from Indexed Files

In some cases, such as an app that provides a browsing experience for one of the user's libraries, you might want to provide suggestions based on local files. The Search pane provides a special feature for precisely this scenario, if the local files are indexed. You can call SearchPane's SetLocalContent SuggestionSettings with an instance of a LocalContentSuggestionSettings object that specifies what files to include. The following code enables this for all libraries for which the app has the relevant capability:

FIGURE 19.7   Leveraging a separator and a richer suggestion in the suggestions list

```
SearchPane searchPane =
SearchPane.GetForCurrentView();
var lcss = new LocalContentSuggestionSettings { Enabled = true };
searchPane.SetLocalContentSuggestionSettings(lcss);
```

As with the code that handles the SuggestionsRequested event, this should be done inside OnWindowCreated. Note that you must explicitly set the Enabled property to true, because it is false by default. If you don't have any of the relevant folder-access capabilities, the call to SetLocalContentSuggestionSettings throws an exception. If you have at least one, then it silently uses whichever ones you have access to.

If you prefer to be more explicit about which folders to include, you can specify them. For example, the following update forces the suggestions to only come from the Pictures library (and therefore require the Pictures Library capability):

```
SearchPane searchPane = SearchPane.GetForCurrentView();
var lcss = new LocalContentSuggestionSettings { Enabled = true };
lcss.Locations.Add(KnownFolders.PicturesLibrary);
searchPane.SetLocalContentSuggestionSettings(lcss);
```

By default, all file metadata is considered in the search, but you can restrict which properties to include by adding property names to LocalContentSuggestionSettings's PropertiesToMatch collection. You can even use an Advanced Query Syntax (AQS) string to restrict the file set. For example, the following update limits the suggestions to PNG files in the Pictures library:

```
SearchPane searchPane = SearchPane.GetForCurrentView();
var lcss = new LocalContentSuggestionSettings { Enabled = true };
lcss.Locations.Add(KnownFolders.PicturesLibrary);
lcss.AqsFilter = "ext:=.png";
searchPane.SetLocalContentSuggestionSettings(lcss);
```

You can learn about AQS at
http://bit.ly/R5ZyxB.

Although this feature is easy to use, the
results might not always suit your needs.
For one example, the suggested filenames don't include their extension,
which might not be ideal for your
scenario. Also, due to a limitation of the
Windows indexer, files with underscores
in their name do not get included.

> As with the Start screen, you should
> consider automatically treating text
> input as input for the Search pane.
> Although you can do this by handling
> KeyDown and programmatically showing the
> Search pane (while populating the search box
> with the character corresponding to the key
> just typed), SearchPane provides a much
> easier mechanism to enable this common
> interaction. Simply set SearchPane's
> ShowOnKeyboardInput property to true. Just
> be careful, because as long as this property is
> true, all keystrokes are sent to the Search
> pane.

Share

The Share charm is a richer version of
the Windows clipboard, enabling one app to send another anything that they both claim
to support: plain text, rich text, images, specific document types, or completely custom
binary data. It also enables an app to automatically decide what information is currently
worth sharing, unlike the explicit selection and copying done with clipboard operations.
With this sharing scheme, an app can play the part of the sender (source), receiver
(target), or both, for any number of formats.

Being a Share Source

If your app contains data that is potentially worth sharing (above and beyond text that
can be copied and pasted via normal gestures), it should be a share source. Most apps fall
into this category. For example, games should enable the user to share a high score, news
apps should enable the user to share an article, drawing apps should enable the user to
share each creation, and so on.

You can be a share source without any supporting a contract or anything special in the
package manifest. You must provide a *data package* to the *data package manager* when
requested. This involves handling a DataRequested event as follows:

```
DataTransferManager dtm = DataTransferManager.GetForCurrentView();
dtm.DataRequested += OnDataRequested;
```

This event gets raised whenever the user invokes the Share charm.

The following implementation of `OnDataRequested` stuffs the data package with data:

```
void OnDataRequested(DataTransferManager sender, DataRequestedEventArgs e)
{
  // These are shown in the Share pane, and may also be used by the target
  e.Request.Data.Properties.Title = "DataPackage Title";
  e.Request.Data.Properties.Description = "Description for the share pane";

  // Data in various formats
  e.Request.Data.SetText("Text to share");
  e.Request.Data.SetHtmlFormat(
    HtmlFormatHelper.CreateHtmlFormat("<b>Richer</b> content to share"));
  e.Request.Data.SetUri(new Uri("http://bing.com"));
}
```

How the data gets used ultimately depends on the share target. However, the two properties being set—`Title` and `Description`—are shown in the Share pane that gets displayed when the user invokes the Share charm. The main data can be specified in many formats—plain text, HTML, URI, RTF, `IStorageItem` (the interface implemented by `StorageFile` and `StorageFolder`), image, or custom—and it makes sense to provide the same data in as many formats as possible to maximize the number of share targets your app works with. This sample implementation of `OnDataRequested` provides data in three formats, although for demonstration purposes it doesn't use equivalent data for all three. If you need to perform asynchronous actions, you can call `e.Request.GetDeferral` beforehand and then call `Complete` on the returned `DataRequestDeferral` object when all the work is done.

In the share APIs, images are not represented directly as streams, but rather as `RandomAccessStream`**Reference** objects that wrap streams. You can construct one with one of its three static methods: `CreateFromStream`, `CreateFromFile`, or `CreateFromUri`.

 Always use `HtmlFormatHelper.CreateHtmlFormat` **when passing an HTML string to** `SetHtmlFormat`**!**

Target apps won't be able to process an arbitrary HTML fragment because they expect a specific format returned by `CreateHtmlFormat`. For example, here is the `string` returned by `CreateHtmlFormat` for the simple input of `"<b>Richer</b> content to share"`:

```
Version:1.0
StartHTML:00000097
EndHTML:00000216
StartFragment:00000153
EndFragment:00000183
<!DOCTYPE><HTML><HEAD></HEAD><BODY><!—StartFragment —><b>Richer</b>
content to share<!—EndFragment —></BODY></HTML>
```

With this handler for `DataRequested` in place, Figure 19.8 demonstrates the appearance of the Share pane after the user invokes the Share charm.

Figure 19.9 demonstrates how three different share targets handle the data being shared. The Mail app uses the title for the email message subject and the URL for the message body. It ignores the text and HTML, although if no URL were shared, it would use the HTML for the body instead. If there were no HTML or if the HTML was invalid, it would use the plain text. The People app acts the same way (when posting to Facebook) although it doesn't do anything with the title. And Rowi, a Twitter app, displays the plain text *and* the URL!

FIGURE 19.8   The Share pane shows the title and description set by the handler of the `DataRequested` event.

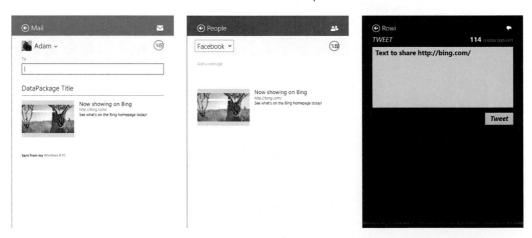

FIGURE 19.9   Three share targets handle the same data package in slightly different ways.

You can programmatically show the Share pane as follows:

```
DataTransferManager.ShowShareUI();
```

With this, you could, for example, provide your own button that encourages users to share their latest score after playing your game.

In addition to the built-in formats, you can share data in a custom format using DataPackage's generic SetData or SetDataProvider methods. (The former accepts the data as a generic object, whereas the latter accepts a delegate that provides the data when invoked by the target.) The first parameter of both of these methods is a string ID identifying the format. In fact, the various methods such as SetText, SetHtml, and so forth, are shortcuts for calling SetData with the appropriate ID. The IDs for the six built-in formats are represented by properties on the static StandardDataFormats class and have the following values:

→ StandardDataFormats.Bitmap: "Bitmap"

→ StandardDataFormats.Html: "HTML Format"

→ StandardDataFormats.Rtf: "Rich Text Format"

→ StandardDataFormats.StorageItems: "Shell IDList Array"

→ StandardDataFormats.Text: "Text"

→ StandardDataFormats.Uri: "UniformResourceLocatorW"

As for your own custom formats, they are good only if other apps are built to receive such data. Therefore, you should stick to standard IDs (and therefore standard representations) that are widely used. Conventions are bound to emerge over time for representations of people, places, movies, and so on, perhaps based on schemas such as what is shared at http://schema.org.

Being a Share Target

Apps that are appropriate share targets are more rare than apps that are appropriate share sources. However, any app involved with publishing, storing, or transforming data—even something silly such as adding speech bubbles to photos—can be a good share target.

Being a share target is more involved than being a share source. To be able to receive content, an app must declare itself as a share target in the package manifest for specific formats and/or file types.

Much like the search contract, the easiest way to support the share target contract is to right-click on your project in Visual Studio, select **Add, New Item...**, then choose **Share Target Contract** from the list. Unless you change its name, this adds a Page called ShareTargetPage1.xaml to your app. It also adds "Share Target" to the list of supported declarations to your package manifest, claiming to support both text and URI data formats, as shown in Figure 19.10. You can modify which formats you want to support here, and/or list extensions for file types you want to support.

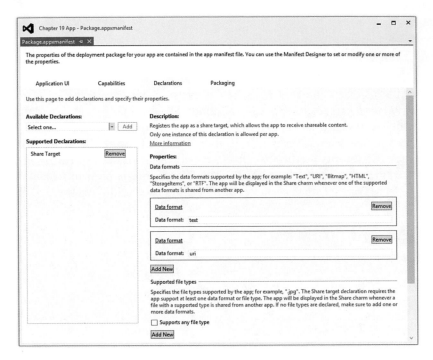

FIGURE 19.10   The auto-generated share target contract makes your app support receiving text and URIs by default.

The generated Page is used to fill in the Share pane once the user selects your app as the share target. In this situation, your app gets activated specifically for the sharing action, so this is enabled by the following code that gets automatically added to App.xaml.cs:

```
/// <summary>
/// Invoked when the app is activated as the target of a sharing operation.
/// </summary>
/// <param name="args">Details about the activation request.</param>
protected override void OnShareTargetActivated(
  ShareTargetActivatedEventArgs args)
{
  var shareTargetPage = new Chapter19.ShareTargetPage1();
  shareTargetPage.Activate(args);
}
```

If you run your app at least once (to get it deployed) after following these steps, and then invoke the Share charm from a *different* app (such as the share source shown earlier), you see the result in Figures 19.11 and 19.12. Your app is automatically added to the list of available targets as long as the data to share is in a format your app claims to handle.

FIGURE 19.11   The Share pane lists your app if it supports the share target contract for any of the available data formats.

FIGURE 19.12   When your app is selected, the auto-generated `ShareTargetPage1` is hosted inside the Share pane.

In Figure 19.12, the top part of the Share pane is provided by Windows, but it is based on your app's display name, small logo, and background color in your package manifest.

ShareTargetPage1 is a simple page that doesn't do much. It displays some information from the data package, has a TextBox for hypothetically adding a comment to the shared data, and a "Share" Button that doesn't do anything other than report that it completes the action so the pane automatically dismisses.

The data package is exposed to the target app via the ShareTargetActivated EventArgs instance initially passed to OnShareTargetActivated. It has a ShareOperation property (of type ShareOperation) with a Data property that reveals the available formats and provides methods (GetTextAsync, GetHtmlFormatAsync, and so on) for retrieving the data. When you start processing the data, you should call ShareOperation's ReportStarted method, and when you're done, you should call its ReportCompleted method. The latter is what makes the Share pane automatically dismiss. Although if the user dismisses the pane while you're still doing work, Windows will still let you complete your task. If completing your task involves a background task, call ReportSubmittedBackgroundTask instead.

 When getting HTML-formatted data via GetHtmlFormatAsync, **be sure to pass it to** HtmlFormatHelper.GetStaticFragment **in order to get a plain HTML fragment!**

This is because the share source is (or should be) passing a specially formatted string that was returned from HtmlFormatHelper. CreateHtmlFormat.

Notice that the list of share targets in Figure 9.11 contains links to specific actions that can be performed by the Mail app. These are called *quick links*, and any app can provide them. To do this, you can create a QuickLink object (which has properties such as Id, Title, and Thumbnail) and pass it to an overload of ShareOperation. ReportCompleted when you complete a share operation as the share target. This, of course, means that you can provide a quick link to Windows only if the user has previously shared something for your app. The idea is that the QuickLink you provide is supposed to represent the action just performed, because if the user did it once, then she is likely to want to do it again.

If you are later invoked via a quick link, the ShareOperation object given to you has its QuickLinkId property properly filled out so you can take the appropriate action. If your quick link doesn't make sense to persist after it is invoked, you can call ShareOperation. RemoveThisQuickLink to prevent it from appearing in the list in the future.

Devices

You can think of the Devices pane shown by invoking the Devices charm much like the Share pane. The current app is the *source* that has content to send to a *target* device. The pane enables the user to choose a target device appropriate for whatever content is available to send.

Only Windows-certified devices such as printers, screens, speakers, and receivers can be exposed via this mechanism as target devices. However, with a little work, any app can be a *source* for registered devices. There are two things that an app can do to become a source (ignoring projecting the screen, which is automatically supported for all apps, including the desktop): support printing and support streaming content with Play To.

Printing

Supporting printing in your app is straightforward. With a little interaction with a `PrintManager` class and the use of a XAML-specific `PrintDocument` class that knows how to print any `UIElement`, you can integrate with the built-in print—and print preview—functionality accessible through the Devices charm. Note that you must opt into this support. The Windows team chose not to enable every app to be automatically printable, because the results are likely to not be great without explicit support from the app.

Listing 19.1 demonstrates the code needed to supply the print manager with a simple two-page document that can be previewed and printed. Although the content supplied to the print manager should often match what's on-screen, or be a print-friendly reformatting of the content on-screen, this actually provides arbitrary XAML content that has nothing to do with the current (blank) page. This is done for demonstration purposes, just to emphasize the flexibility you have with printing.

LISTING 19.1   `MainPage.xaml.cs:` Supporting Print and Print Preview

```
using System;
using Windows.Graphics.Printing;
using Windows.UI;
using Windows.UI.Core;
using Windows.UI.Xaml.Controls;
using Windows.UI.Xaml.Media;
using Windows.UI.Xaml.Printing;

namespace Chapter19
{
  public sealed partial class MainPage : Page
  {
    // Supports printing pages, where each page is a UIElement
    PrintDocument doc = new PrintDocument();

    public MainPage()
    {
      InitializeComponent();

      // Attach handlers to relevant events
      doc.GetPreviewPage += OnGetPreviewPage;
      doc.AddPages += OnAddPages;

      PrintManager printManager = PrintManager.GetForCurrentView();
      printManager.PrintTaskRequested += OnPrintTaskRequested;
```

LISTING 19.1   Continued

```csharp
  }

// Prepare the print preview pages
void OnGetPreviewPage(object sender, GetPreviewPageEventArgs e)
{
  this.doc.SetPreviewPageCount(2, PreviewPageCountType.Final);
  if (e.PageNumber == 1)
  {
    this.doc.SetPreviewPage(1, new Viewbox { Child = new Button {
      Content = "PAGE 1!", Background = new SolidColorBrush(Colors.Red) } });
  }
  else
  {
    this.doc.SetPreviewPage(2, new Viewbox { Child = new Button {
      Content = "PAGE 2!", Background = new SolidColorBrush(Colors.Red) } });
  }
}

// Prepare the real pages
void OnAddPages(object sender, AddPagesEventArgs e)
{
  this.doc.AddPage(new Viewbox { Child = new Button {
    Content = "PAGE 1!", Background = new SolidColorBrush(Colors.Red) } });
  this.doc.AddPage(new Viewbox { Child = new Button {
    Content = "PAGE 2!", Background = new SolidColorBrush(Colors.Red) } });
  this.doc.AddPagesComplete();
}

// Prepare and perform the printing
void OnPrintTaskRequested(PrintManager sender,
                          PrintTaskRequestedEventArgs args)
{
  // This gets invoked as soon as the Devices pane is shown
  PrintTask task = args.Request.CreatePrintTask("Document Title",
    async (taskArgs) =>
    {
      // This is invoked on a background thread when the Print
      // button is clicked
      var deferral = taskArgs.GetDeferral();
      await this.Dispatcher.RunAsync(CoreDispatcherPriority.Normal, () =>
      {
        // This must run on the main thread
        taskArgs.SetSource(doc.DocumentSource);
        deferral.Complete();
```

LISTING 19.1   Continued

```
        });
      });
    }
  }
}
```

Although `PrintDocument` exposes methods for adding preview pages and "real" pages, this must be called inside relevant events: `GetPreviewPage` and `AddPages`. Similarly, initializing the *print task* must be done from a `PrintTaskRequested` event on the `PrintManager` object. All of this is set up inside `MainPage`'s constructor. Be careful where you attach (and/or detach) handlers to these events in a multi-`Page` app to make sure the right thing happens regardless of which `Page` is currently on the screen.

For print preview, you can tell the print manager how many pages exist with a call to `PrintDocument`'s `SetPreviewPageCount` method, but only once `OnGetPreviewPage` is already being called requesting a preview of the first page. This implementation creates two preview pages, with each one containing a simple `Button` in a `Viewbox` (so it scales to uniformly fill the space on the page). This XAML content happens to be identical to the XAML content used for the real pages, but this doesn't have to be the case. For example, you can choose to do something different because it's significantly faster than producing the real page.

 Treat a print preview as required, not optional!

The Printing pane shows a print preview regardless. If you don't provide one, it shows a `ProgressRing` indefinitely, and that makes your app appear to be broken.

The handler for the `AddPages` event is similar to the handler for the `GetPreviewPage` event, except all pages should be added at once, followed by a call to `AddPagesComplete`. The handler for `PrintTaskRequested` is more complicated, however. This event is raised as soon as the Devices charm is invoked, although typically all that is done by a handler at that point is call `CreatePrintTask`. The rest of the logic is in a delegate passed to `CreatePrintTask` that gets invoked when the user clicks the Print button (after selecting a printer and changing any options).

The job of the delegate is to hand the *document source* to the print manager. This is exposed via the `DocumentSource` property on `PrintDocument`, which is a UI-technology-agnostic Windows Runtime object, unlike the XAML-specific `PrintDocument`. The document source is given to the print manager by a call to `SetSource` on the argument passed to the delegate. To complicate matters, however, this delegate gets invoked on a background thread, but accessing the `DocumentSource` property must be done on the main thread. Therefore, this code uses the typical `Dispatcher` trick to marshal back to the main thread, but it must use a deferral so the caller of the delegate knows to wait until the marshaled code completes.

The handling of `PrintManager`'s `PrintTaskRequested` method and the call to
`CreatePrintTask` is what prompts the Devices pane to show printers, as seen in Figure
19.13. Once a printer is selected, Figure 19.14 shows the print preview rendering the
content created inside `OnGetPreviewPage`. After the Print button is clicked and printing
completes, the user gets a notification about the new file as shown in Figure 19.15 if the
Microsoft XPS Document Writer is selected as the printer (because it prints to a file). If the
user taps the notification and opens the document in the Windows Reader app, he or she
can see the two-page document as shown in Figure 19.16 (in snapped mode).

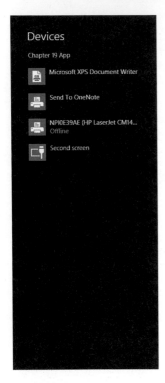

FIGURE 19.13   Handling `PrintTaskRequested` and calling `CreatePrintTask` makes Windows
show target printers for your app.

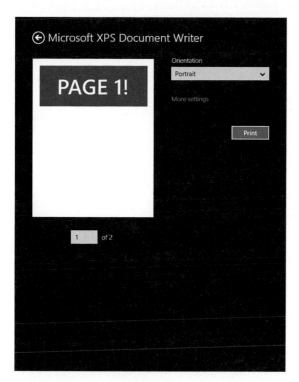

FIGURE 19.14   The print preview experience shows the rendered XAML passed to
PrintDocument's SetPreviewPage method.

FIGURE 19.15   The notification that appears once printing to a file completes

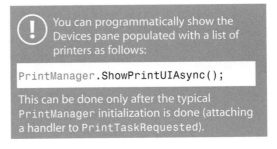

FIGURE 19.16   The final document, as seen in the Windows Reader app

There are a number of additional events you can handle in order to customize the experience further. For example, PrintDocument exposes a Paginate event that enables you to update your content in response to user settings changes that affect pagination (such as page size or orientation), PrintTask exposes a Completed event so you can see whether the printing finished successfully, and so on.

> (!) You can programmatically show the Devices pane populated with a list of printers as follows:
>
> ```
> PrintManager.ShowPrintUIAsync();
> ```
>
> This can be done only after the typical PrintManager initialization is done (attaching a handler to PrintTaskRequested).

You can also customize the printing options in three basic ways: changing default options, configuring which options are displayed, and adding your own custom options.

Changing Default Options

Once you create a PrintTask inside the handler for PrintTaskRequested, you can override its default options via its Options property of type PrintTaskOptions. For example, the following addition changes the default page orientation to landscape instead of portrait:

```
void OnPrintTaskRequested(PrintManager sender, PrintTaskRequestedEventArgs args)
{
  // This gets invoked as soon as the Devices pane is shown
  PrintTask task = args.Request.CreatePrintTask("Document Title",
    async (taskArgs) =>
    {
      …
    });

  task.Options.Orientation = PrintOrientation.Landscape;
}
```

Configuring Displayed Options

If you pass the `PrintTaskOptions` object to
`PrintTaskOptionDetails.GetFromPrintTaskOptions`, you get back a
`PrintTaskOptionDetails` instance that can be used to completely customize which
options are displayed inside the printing pane. You can add, remove, and reorder them.
The following change clears the default list of options and adds four specific ones:

```
void OnPrintTaskRequested(PrintManager sender, PrintTaskRequestedEventArgs args)
{
  // This gets invoked as soon as the Devices pane is shown
  PrintTask task = args.Request.CreatePrintTask("Document Title",
    async (taskArgs) =>
    {
      …
    });

  PrintTaskOptionDetails details =
    PrintTaskOptionDetails.GetFromPrintTaskOptions(task.Options);
  details.DisplayedOptions.Clear();
  details.DisplayedOptions.Add(StandardPrintTaskOptions.Copies);
  details.DisplayedOptions.Add(StandardPrintTaskOptions.PrintQuality);
  details.DisplayedOptions.Add(StandardPrintTaskOptions.HolePunch);
  details.DisplayedOptions.Add(StandardPrintTaskOptions.MediaSize);
}
```

Note that not all printers support all options, and unsupported ones are ignored. For
example, out of these four chosen options, the Microsoft XPS Document Writer displays
only the `MediaSize` one.

Adding Custom Options

`PrintTaskOptionDetails` supports exposing custom options that make sense only to your
app. For example, the Calendar app could support printing modes of Day, Week, or
Month, independently of the current display on the screen.

The following code adds two custom options. One can be set to freeform text, whereas the other must be set to a value from a predefined list:

```
void OnPrintTaskRequested(PrintManager sender, PrintTaskRequestedEventArgs args)
{
  // This gets invoked as soon as the Devices pane is shown
  PrintTask task = args.Request.CreatePrintTask("Document Title",
    async (taskArgs) =>
    {
      ...
    });

  PrintTaskOptionDetails details =
    PrintTaskOptionDetails.GetFromPrintTaskOptions(task.Options);
  details.DisplayedOptions.Clear();
  details.DisplayedOptions.Add(StandardPrintTaskOptions.MediaSize);

  // A custom text option
  PrintCustomTextOptionDetails option1 = details.CreateTextOption(
    "CustomId1", "Header");
  details.DisplayedOptions.Add("CustomId1");

  // A custom list option
  PrintCustomItemListOptionDetails option2 = details.CreateItemListOption(
    "CustomId2", "Contents");
  option2.AddItem("customItemId1", "As Seen on Screen");
  option2.AddItem("customItemId2", "Summary View");
  option2.AddItem("customItemId3", "Full Details");
  option2.AddItem("customItemId4", "Multiple Columns");
  details.DisplayedOptions.Add("CustomId2");

  // Handle options changes
  details.OptionChanged += OnOptionChanged;
}
```

The IDs you choose are used to understand the user's selection when the OptionChanged event is raised with a specific ID and value. You should act upon your custom settings in the handler for OptionChanged (whose implementation is not shown in this example). The result of adding these two custom options is shown in Figure 19.17.

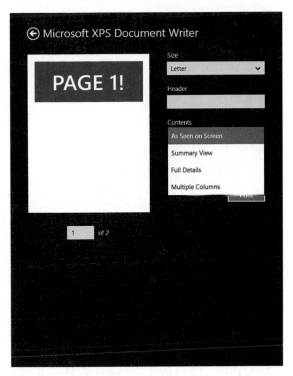

FIGURE 19.17   Two custom options are shown when printing from the Devices pane.

Play To

With the Play To feature, you can stream images, audio, and video from your app to any compatible device, such as TVs and audio receivers. The device must be on the same local, private network with sharing enabled (typically done when first connecting to a private network). On a public network or one without sharing enabled, you can manually add the target device from the Devices section of the PC Settings app. When an app supports Play To and compatible devices arc available, they appear on the Devices pane (potentially alongside printers).

To support this in your app, you work with a *Play To manager* in much the same way you interact with the print manager. When the user invokes the Devices charm, `PlayToManager`'s `SourceRequested` event is raised, so you must attach a handler as follows:

```
PlayToManager playToManager = PlayToManager.GetForCurrentView();
playToManager.SourceRequested += OnSourceRequested;
```

The job of the handler is to hand a *Play To source* to the Play To manager. Much like `PrintDocument`'s `DocumentSource` property that exposes a document source, three `UIElements` expose a `PlayToSource` property (of type `PlayToSource`). These elements are `Image`, `MediaElement`, and `MediaPlayer` (which exposes the underlying `MediaElement` property).

Therefore, you can send an audio/video file from a MediaElement named mediaElement to the Play To device as follows:

```
void OnSourceRequested(PlayToManager sender, PlayToSourceRequestedEventArgs args)
{
  // This is invoked on a background thread when the Devices pane is shown
  var deferral = args.SourceRequest.GetDeferral();
  var handler = this.Dispatcher.RunAsync(CoreDispatcherPriority.Normal, () =>
  {
    // This must run on the main thread
    args.SourceRequest.SetSource(mediaElement.PlayToSource);
    deferral.Complete();
  });
}
```

This is the same pattern as printing, including the marshaling from a background thread to the main thread in order to access MediaElement's PlayToSource property. Doing this with an Image looks identical; replace mediaElement with an appropriate Image variable.

That's all there is to it! Finding a compatible device is the hard part; writing the code is the easy part. Documentation sometimes mentions a "Play To contract," but nothing needs to be done with the package manifest.

You can programmatically show the Play To user interface as follows:

```
PrintManager.ShowPlayToUI();
```

A few more features exist for customizing the experience a bit more. For example, you can stream a whole playlist (or a slideshow of images) by chaining multiple PlayToSources together. This is done with PlayToSource's Next property, which can be set to another PlayToSource. Through PlayToSource's Connection property, you can discover the current state of the Play To connection (Connected, Rendering, or Disconnected). You can also attach handlers to events for state changes, errors, or when the next PlayToSource is transferred for the playlist/slideshow scenario. This enables you to customize what you show in your app in response to what is happening on the other device.

Don't have a fancy TV that supports Play To? It's okay, because you can still test Play To as long as you have a second computer on the same local network (with the same sharing requirements described earlier). Here's what you must do on the second computer:

1. Launch Windows Media Player.
2. In its **Library** view, open the **Stream** menu, and then check the **Allow remote control of my Player...** option. Leave Windows Media Player open.
3. In the **Devices and Printers** control panel, click **Add a device.** Your Windows Media Player instance should appear as a **Digital media player.** Add it.
4. On the first computer, you should now be able to select this as a Play To target.

Settings

Any app can integrate with the Settings pane shown by the Settings charm. The pane enables you to add custom links to its list. The goal, much like with the other charms, is to make it easy for all apps to expose a consistent mechanism for exposing settings so users know how to find them.

Documentation sometimes refers to a "Settings contract" for integrating with the Settings pane, but you don't need do anything special in your package manifest. You simply need to handle SettingPane's CommandsRequested event as follows:

```
SettingsPane.GetForCurrentView().CommandsRequested += OnCommandsRequested;
```

Then you can add links from within the event handler as follows:

```
void OnCommandsRequested(SettingsPane sender,
                         SettingsPaneCommandsRequestedEventArgs e)
{
  e.Request.ApplicationCommands.Add(new SettingsCommand(1, "#1", OnCommand));
  e.Request.ApplicationCommands.Add(new SettingsCommand(2, "#2", OnCommand));
  e.Request.ApplicationCommands.Add(new SettingsCommand(3, "#3", OnCommand));
  e.Request.ApplicationCommands.Add(new SettingsCommand(4, "#4", OnCommand));
  e.Request.ApplicationCommands.Add(new SettingsCommand(5, "#5", OnCommand));
  e.Request.ApplicationCommands.Add(new SettingsCommand(6, "#6", OnCommand));
  e.Request.ApplicationCommands.Add(new SettingsCommand(7, "#7", OnCommand));
  e.Request.ApplicationCommands.Add(new SettingsCommand(8, "#8", OnCommand));
  // Adding any more throws an exception!
}
```

You can add up to eight links. Each one has an ID (of type object), a string label, and a callback that is invoked when the link is clicked. Figure 19.18 shows the resultant Settings pane.

You can programmatically show the Settings pane as follows:

```
SettingsPane.Show();
```

You can provide a separate callback for each command, or you can use the same one (as done in the preceding code) and distinguish which command was invoked via its ID. For example:

```
void OnCommand(IUICommand command)
{
  int id = (int)command.Id;
  switch (id)
  {
    case 1:
      …
  }
}
```

FIGURE 19.18 The maximum eight app-specific links are added to the Settings pane, along with the ever-present Permissions link.

When one of the links is clicked, you can do whatever you'd like, but the convention is to show a new piece of UI that mimics the Settings pane. Unlike when your app is a share target, you cannot inject custom UI into the pane itself. When one of the links is clicked, the Settings pane closes.

The following XAML is for a user control (a simple custom control) that mimics a Settings pane with custom content. You can add one to your project by selecting **User Control** from the **Add New Item** dialog in Visual Studio, and then replacing its XAML content with something like this:

```
<UserControl x:Class="Chapter19.CustomSettingsPane"
  xmlns="http://schemas.microsoft.com/winfx/2006/xaml/presentation"
  xmlns:x="http://schemas.microsoft.com/winfx/2006/xaml">
  <Popup Name="popup" IsLightDismissEnabled="True" Closed="Popup_Closed"
      HorizontalAlignment="Right" Width="345">
    <Popup.Transitions>
      <TransitionCollection>
        <PaneThemeTransition/>
      </TransitionCollection>
    </Popup.Transitions>
```

```
<Grid Name="grid" Background="Brown" Width="345">
  <StackPanel VerticalAlignment="Top" Margin="21,30,0,0">
    <!— The header, with a back button and title —>
    <StackPanel Orientation="Horizontal">
      <Button Style="{StaticResource SnappedBackButtonStyle}"
        Click="BackButton_Click"/>
      <TextBlock Text="Custom Settings" FontWeight="Normal"
        Style="{StaticResource SubheaderTextStyle}" Margin="-2,-2,0,0"/>
    </StackPanel>
    <!— Placeholder content for configuring settings —>
    <StackPanel Margin="13,0,0,0">
      <ToggleSwitch Header="One"/>
      <ToggleSwitch Header="Two"/>
      <ToggleSwitch Header="Three"/>
    </StackPanel>
  </StackPanel>
</Grid>
</Popup>
</UserControl>
```

The key to making this act like a "pane" is the use of a right-aligned `Popup` with its light dismiss behavior enabled. Furthermore, the use of `PaneThemeTransition` provides the same entrance and exit animation used by the panes shown by the charms bar. This control features a back `Button` for returning back to the real Settings pane, because clicking one of its links is what shows this custom pane. It uses the more compact **Snapped**BackButtonStyle, which is standard for such panes. It looks just like the ones in Figure 19.9.

The following C# is the code-behind for this `CustomSettingsPane` control:

```
using Windows.UI.ApplicationSettings;
using Windows.UI.Popups;
using Windows.UI.Xaml;
using Windows.UI.Xaml.Controls;

namespace Chapter19
{
  public sealed partial class CustomSettingsPane : UserControl
  {
    public CustomSettingsPane()
    {
      InitializeComponent();

      // Detach the Popup so the PaneThemeTransition kicks in next time
      this.Content = null;
```

```
    // Keep the pane's height equal to the screen height
    this.LayoutUpdated += (sender, e) => this.grid.Height = this.ActualHeight;
  }

  public void Show(IUICommand command)
  {
    // Reattach and open the popup
    this.Content = this.popup;
    this.popup.IsOpen = true;

    // Potentially change the contents based on the chosen command
    …
  }

  void Popup_Closed(object sender, object e)
  {
    // Detach the Popup so the PaneThemeTransition kicks in next time
    this.Content = null;
  }

  void BackButton_Click(object sender, RoutedEventArgs e)
  {
    // Go "back" to the Settings pane
    SettingsPane.Show();
  }
 }
}
```

Recall that PaneThemeTransition kicks in only for an element's *initial* entrance, so this code must detach the Popup from the element tree and reattach it each time it gets shown in order for the animation to occur. The control's LayoutUpdated event is handled to ensure that the pane background stretches to fill the screen's height, which doesn't happen automatically because the host Popup doesn't stretch.

Notice the nifty trick for implementing the back Button's behavior. This doesn't do a real back navigation as with Pages in a Frame, but BackButton_Click is able to simulate it by programmatically showing the Settings pane.

A Page can therefore declare an instance of CustomSettingsPane as follows:

```
<Page … xmlns:local="using:Chapter19">
  <Grid Background="{StaticResource ApplicationPageBackgroundThemeBrush}">
    <local:CustomSettingsPane x:Name="settingsPane"/>
    …
  </Grid>
</Page>
```

and show it whenever one of the app's custom settings links is invoked:

```
void OnCommand(IUICommand command)
{
  this.settingsPane.Show(command);
}
```

The resultant custom pane is shown in Figure 19.19.

FIGURE 19.19   The `CustomSettingsPane` user control acts like another page of the Settings pane.

> `CustomSettingsPane` implements the light-dismiss behavior that is standard for settings UI, but there are other guidelines you should follow when implementing your own. Settings should be simple, concise, and get applied instantly. In other words, there should not be any OK or Apply `Button` for committing the changes. In Figure 19.19, toggling the `ToggleSwitches` should be enough.

Summary

Integrating with Windows 8 charms is a great way to differentiate your apps from others, and can even help users spread the word about your app. Even more to the point, as users become accustomed to using these charms to search, share, print, stream, and adjust settings, they will be frustrated by apps that do not follow these conventions.

Sometimes it might still make sense to have your own button or link for some of these concepts, but you can just programmatically show the relevant pane when your own user interface element is invoked. One notable exception to using charms can happen with search. If the primary purpose of your app is search (such as the Bing app), then it's best to have your own search experience directly in your app. Also note that the Search pane isn't appropriate for "Find on page" functionality because the pane is designed to navigate the user to a different (search results) page. The Internet Explorer app uses its own AppBar-like UI for "Find on page" when the user presses Ctrl+F.

As a user of Windows 8, you should be aware of the following handy keyboard shortcuts related to the charms and their panes:

Windows+C: Show the charms bar

Windows+Q: Show the Search pane in its default mode (in-app search if the current app supports it, otherwise it defaults to searching for apps)

Windows+W: Show the Search pane, defaulted to searching settings

Windows+F: Show the Search pane, defaulted to searching files

Windows+H: Show the Share pane

Windows+K: Show the Devices pane

Windows+P: Show the "Second screen" (projection) part of the Devices pane

Windows+I: Show the Settings pane

Chapter 20

EXTENSIONS

This chapter examines the extensions that enable an app to integrate more deeply with Windows. Extensions are more than just API calls. Each one of these requires a declaration on the Declarations tab in your package manifest. Although extensions are *not* contracts, they have many similarities. For example, extensions leveraged by your app are not listed in the Windows Store as potentially unwanted features like capabilities. The use of some extensions requires capabilities, but many don't require any.

Account Picture Provider

Any app—even one with no capabilities—has the power to change the current user's account picture. (The user is prompted before the change is made.) This is done with the `Windows.System.UserProfile.UserInformation` class. It contains several methods for getting information about the current user (`GetDisplayName`, `GetAccountPicture`, `GetFirstName`, `GetLastName`, and so on). It even defines an `AccountPictureChanged` event, just in case you use the picture within your user interface and need to refresh it. Most importantly for this topic, it also defines four methods for setting the account picture:

→ **SetAccountPictureAsync**—Sets the picture to a passed-in `StorageFile`.

→ **SetAccountPictureFromStreamAsync**—Sets the picture to a passed-in `RandomAccessStream` instead.

→ **SetAccountPicturesAsync**—Simultaneously sets a small picture, large picture, and even a video from three passed-in StorageFiles. (You can set a subset of these, but you must at least include a large picture or video.)

→ **SetAccountPicturesFromStreamAsync**—Simultaneously sets the three versions with passed-in RandomAccessStreams instead.

The following code sets the account picture to a JPEG file chosen by the user via the file picker:

```
async Task SetAccountPicture()
{
  // Get a JPEG from the user
  FileOpenPicker picker = new FileOpenPicker();
  picker.FileTypeFilter.Add(".jpg");
  picker.FileTypeFilter.Add(".jpeg");
  StorageFile file = await picker.PickSingleFileAsync();
  if (file != null)
  {
    SetAccountPictureResult result =
      await UserInformation.SetAccountPictureAsync(file);
    if (result == SetAccountPictureResult.Success)
    {
      // Congratulations! This is your new account picture.
    }
  }
}
```

There are a number of ways the operation can fail, indicated by the returned SetAccountPictureResult enumeration, such as a file that is too large. The user also has a way to disable all changes to the account picture, which causes the call to return SetAccountPictureResult.ChangeDisabled.

Just because an app *can* change the user's account picture doesn't mean it should, of course. If this makes sense for your app, perhaps because it's an image-effects app, you should declare it as an *account picture provider* in the package manifest. When you add this to the declarations list, Windows places a link to your app inside the relevant part of the PC Settings app, as shown in Figure 20.1.

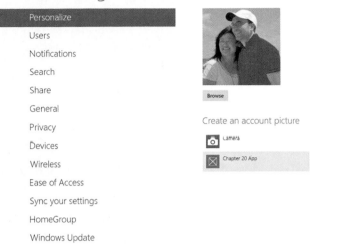

FIGURE 20.1 Your app is added to the "Create an account picture" list when you add the Account Picture Provider declaration to your package manifest.

When your app is activated in this fashion, it is a *protocol* activation. You can detect this condition as follows by overriding the OnActivated method in App.xaml.cs:

```
protected override void OnActivated(IActivatedEventArgs args)
{
  if (args.Kind == ActivationKind.Protocol)
  {
    ProtocolActivatedEventArgs protocolArgs = (ProtocolActivatedEventArgs)args;
    if (protocolArgs.Uri.Scheme == "ms-accountpictureprovider")
    {
      // The user just picked this app via the "Create an account picture" link.
      // Initialize the app appropriately for setting it.
      …
    }
  }
}
```

There is no specific On*XXX*Activated method for this type of activation, which is why the generic OnActivated must be used. There are multiple reasons for an app to receive an activation of type Protocol, so the ProtocolActivatedEventArgs.Uri must be checked to determine what happened. The actual URI (ms-accountpictureprovider:///) doesn't point to anything; it is used to distinguish the action that provoked the activation.

AutoPlay Content and AutoPlay Device

An app with an *AutoPlay content* declaration can be listed as a choice for the user to launch when he or she inserts new content, such as a CD, DVD, or Blu-ray disc. This situation can even be triggered when content is shared between two PCs via a tap-and-go gesture (leveraging Near Field Communication). If you add AutoPlay Content to the declarations list in your package manifest, you'll notice that you must explicitly define at least one *launch action*. Each launch action consists of three pieces of data:

→ **Content event**—The name of a predefined AutoPlay event that you want to handle. A list of these is available at http://bit.ly/StSRHf.

→ **Action display name**—The text that is displayed to the user inside the AutoPlay UI.

→ **verb**—An ID that that your code can use if you need to distinguish between multiple launch actions for the same event.

There are a number of specific AutoPlay events, such as `ShowPicturesOnArrival`, `PlayMusicFilesOnArrival`, `PlayVideoFilesOnArrival`, `HandleDVDBurningOnArrival`. There's also a fallback event if all else fails: `UnknownContentOnArrival`. Figure 20.2 shows what happens if you add the following launch action to your package manifest and then insert a disc with no recognizable media:

→ Content event: **`UnknownContentOnArrival`**

→ Action display name: **`Browse the files with this app, please!`**

→ verb: **`browse`**

Adding launch actions for certain events requires you to add the Removable Storage capability to your app. But don't worry; Visual Studio refuses to build your project and prompts you to add the capability if it is missing.

When your app is activated via this mechanism, it is a *file* activation. That means that you must override the `OnFileActivated` method in `App.xaml.cs`; the generic `OnActivated` method is not called. For this example, you can do this as follows:

```
protected override void OnFileActivated(FileActivatedEventArgs args)
{
  if (args.Verb == "browse") // Our only specified verb
  {
    foreach (IStorageItem item in args.Files)
    {
      // args.Files is a collection of relevant StorageFiles and StorageFolders
      …
    }
  }
}
```

The initial AutoPlay notification

The AutoPlay user interface that appears when the notification is tapped

FIGURE 20.2   Your app is added to the AutoPlay user interface when you add the AutoPlay Content declaration to your package manifest with an appropriate launch action.

If you add two launch actions for the same event, as shown in Figure 20.3, then you get two links in the relevant AutoPlay user interface, as shown in Figure 20.4.

FIGURE 20.3   Defining two launch actions for the same event: a "browse" action and a "play" action

FIGURE 20.4   Having two launch actions for the same event means two links in the AutoPlay user interface.

The AutoPlay Device declaration works the same way as AutoPlay Content—it's just meant for the subset of AutoPlay events that correspond to attaching a device, such as a digital camera. These events have names such as `WPD\ImageSource`, `WPD\AudioSource`, and `WPD\VideoSource`. (WPD stands for Windows Portable Devices.)

Contact Picker

Apps can use the Windows contact picker to get information about one or more of the user's contacts. This works a lot like the file picker and doesn't require any special capability or contract to be implemented. You just need the user to explicitly choose the contact(s). You can use it as follows:

```
// Get a contact from the user
ContactPicker picker = new ContactPicker();
ContactInformation info = await picker.PickSingleContactAsync();
```

`ContactPicker` also defines a `PickMultipleContactsAsync` method for getting a collection of `ContactInformation`s.

`ContactInformation` exposes the contact's thumbnail photo, name, phone numbers, email addresses, locations, instant message accounts, as well as custom fields. If you require only a subset of the information (as is usually the case), then you should add field names to `ContactPicker`'s `DesiredFields` property to restrict the information that is obtained. This is a collection of `strings`, but static `KnownContentField` properties make it so you don't need to know the exact `string` representation of each standard piece of information. The following addition grabs only the email address of the chosen contact:

```
ContactPicker picker = new ContactPicker();
picker.DesiredFields.Add(KnownContactField.Email);
ContactInformation info = await picker.PickSingleContactAsync();
```

`ContactPicker` also exposes a `CommitButtonText` property for customizing the label on the OK button, and a `SelectionMode` property that provides a hint to the UI that you're interested only in certain fields. This can potentially affect the display, depending on the source of the data.

Although the common case is, by far, to pick contacts from the People app, the contact picker enables other apps to plug in and provide their own notion of contacts. That's where the Contact Picker declaration comes in. If you add this to the list of declarations in your package manifest, then your app appears as a choice in the contact picker, as shown in Figure 20.5.

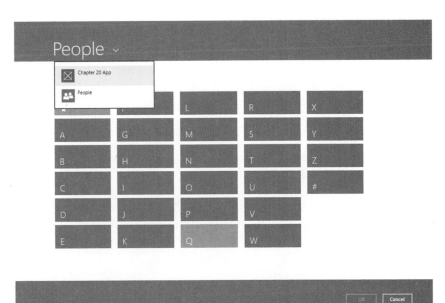

FIGURE 20.5 Your app is added to the contact picker's list of apps when you add the Contact Picker declaration to your package manifest.

When your app is activated in this fashion, it is a *contact picker* activation. You can detect this condition as follows by overriding the OnActivated method in App.xaml.cs:

```
protected async override void OnActivated(IActivatedEventArgs args)
{
  if (args.Kind == ActivationKind.ContactPicker)
  {
    // The user just picked this app in the contact picker,
    // so show appropriate UI and pass along the args
    ContactPickerActivatedEventArgs pickerArgs =
      (ContactPickerActivatedEventArgs)args;

    …
  }
}
```

The user interface you display in this condition is hosted inside the contact picker and gets most of the screen's real estate (the white region in Figure 20.5). In this user interface, you should provide a way to enable the user to select contact(s), and then pass the data to the ContactPickerUI property on ContactPickerActivatedEventArgs.

ContactPickerUI contains AddContact, RemoveContact, and ContainsContact methods and even a ContactRemoved event to make it easy to manage the selection. The event is necessary because the user can remove previously selected contacts from the bottom portion of the screen that is outside the control of your app. For example, the following code adds a simple contact to the current selection:

```
Contact contact = new Contact { Name = "Adam Nathan", Thumbnail = … };
contact.Fields.Add(
  new ContactField("someone@example.com", ContactFieldType.Email));
pickerArgs.ContactPickerUI.AddContact("contactId", contact);
```

From the ContactPickerUI object, you can also examine the DesiredFields specified by the user as well as the desired SelectionMode, because both of these can affect how you display your contacts. The People app adjusts its display to show the most important desired field, although it ignores the SelectionMode property.

File Type Associations

You can add any number of File Type Associations declarations to your package manifest, one per file type. With each one, you have a few pieces of information to fill out:

➔ **Display name**—Text used to describe the type of file in Control Panel.

➔ **Logo**—An image used for file icons in the Windows desktop. If you don't specify one, your app's small logo is used.

➔ **Info tip**—Text used for the icon's tooltip in the Windows desktop.

→ **Name**—An all-lowercase ID used by Windows that should never change, even if you update the display name in a future version of your app.

→ **Edit flags**—You can decide whether downloaded files of this type are safe to automatically open. The choices are "Open is safe" or "Always unsafe."

→ **Supported file types**—You can specify one or more file extensions for the same logical file type, such as having both .jpg and .jpeg for a JPEG file. With each file type, you must specify the content type (a MIME type) and the file type (the extension, beginning with a period).

If you add a File Type Associations declaration to your package manifest with the following values then create a new file.adam file, you'll see the result shown in Figure 20.6 inside File Explorer (the program formerly known as Windows Explorer):

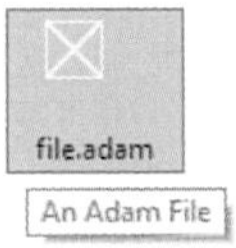

FIGURE 20.6   Viewing a custom file in File Explorer

→ Name: **adam**

→ Info tip: **An Adam File**

→ Supported file types: Content type=**application/adam**; File type=**.adam**

Even if the app's small icon weren't white-on-transparent, it's still not a great choice for a file icon because it doesn't get scaled. Therefore, you should not only specify an image file (and include it in your project), but you should leverage resource qualifier support to supply multiple sizes: 16x16, 32x32, 48x48, and 256x256. This is done with the target-size resource qualifier. If you specify a logo of Assets/logo.png in your package manifest, then you should include the following files in your project:

→ Assets/logo.**targetsize-16**.jpg

→ Assets/logo.**targetsize-32**.jpg

→ Assets/logo.**targetsize-48**.jpg

→ Assets/logo.**targetsize-256**.jpg

If the file is double-clicked in File Explorer, your app gets a file activation, just like in the AutoPlay example. This time, however, the verb is "open." The following code handles this:

```
protected override void OnFileActivated(FileActivatedEventArgs args)
{
  if (args.Verb == "open")
  {
    foreach (IStorageItem file in args.Files)
```

```
    {
      // args.Files contains each StorageFile being opened
      ...
    }
  }
}
```

If you add a file extension already being handled by other apps (such as `.jpg`), then
the user gets a notification the next time he or she attempts to open a file of that type,
shown in Figure 20.7. Your app is also added to the list of choices, also shown in
Figure 20.7.

The initial notification   The "Choose default program…" dialog

FIGURE 20.7   Windows handles multiple apps wanting to handle the same file type gracefully.

Protocol

With the Protocol declaration, you can handle URI protocols such as `mailto` or
completely custom ones. This is basically the URL equivalent to File Type Associations.
With each one you add to your package manifest, you can specify the following
information:

→ **Display name**—Text used to describe the protocol.

→ **Logo**—An image used for icons in the Windows desktop, just like with the File Type
Associations setting. If you don't specify one, your app's small logo is used.

→ **Name**—The URI scheme without any colons or slashes, such as `mailto`.

If you add a Protocol declaration with Name set to adam (and the other values blank), then you can type a URL like adam://blah in Internet Explorer and you'll get a prompt like the one shown in Figure 20.8 before launching your app.

From desktop Internet Explorer

Did you mean to switch apps?
This website is trying to open "Chapter 20 App".

Yes   No

From the Internet Explorer app

FIGURE 20.8   Getting prompted before launching an app for a custom URI scheme

When invoked in this way, your app gets a protocol activation, just like in the Account Picture Provider. This time, however, the Uri reveals the exact URL being invoked:

```
protected override void OnActivated(IActivatedEventArgs args)
{
  if (args.Kind == ActivationKind.Protocol)
  {
    ProtocolActivatedEventArgs protocolArgs = (ProtocolActivatedEventArgs)args;
    // Act upon protocolArgs.Uri
    …
  }
}
```

If you want Windows to consider your app as a Web browser, you can declare that you handle the http (and https) protocol.

Background Tasks

Background tasks enable an app to run custom code in response to certain system events or at timed intervals, even if it isn't running. If you want to play audio in the background, a lot of support exists specifically for this. Therefore, we first look at background audio and then look at every other kind of background task.

Background Audio

As explained in Chapter 12, "Audio and Video," if you switch away from your app while
it plays an audio file, the audio instantly fades out and pauses. When you switch back, it
fades back in and unpauses. If you want the audio to continue playing while your app is
offscreen, you need to do three simple things:

→ Set the `AudioCategory` appropriately on the `MediaElement` playing the audio.

→ Add an appropriate Background Tasks declaration to your package manifest.

→ Handle a few `MediaControl` events.

Setting the `AudioCategory`

`MediaElement`'s `AudioCategory` property can be set to influence how Windows treats the
audio. To enable audio to play in the background, you must set `AudioCategory` to either
`BackgroundCapableMedia` or `Communications`. (`Communications` is higher-priority, but it is
appropriate only for real-time chat apps.) The following code does this for a user-selected
MP3 file that gets automatically played by setting it as the source for a `MediaElement`
named `mediaElement`:

```
IRandomAccessStream stream;

async Task PlayUserSelectedMusic()
{
  // Get an MP3 file from the user
  FileOpenPicker picker = new FileOpenPicker();
  picker.FileTypeFilter.Add(".mp3");
  picker.SuggestedStartLocation = PickerLocationId.MusicLibrary;
  StorageFile file = await picker.PickSingleFileAsync();
  if (file != null)
  {
    this.stream = await file.OpenAsync(FileAccessMode.Read);
    this.mediaElement.SetSource(this.stream, "audio/mp3");
    this.mediaElement.AudioCategory = AudioCategory.BackgroundCapableMedia;
  }
}

void MediaElement_MediaOpened(object sender, RoutedEventArgs e)
{
  this.stream.Dispose();
}
```

Adding the Background Tasks Declaration

When you add a Background Tasks declaration to your package manifest, you must fill
out two pieces of information: the supported task type(s) and the entry point. For the
supported task type(s), select the Audio option. For the entry point, you can put a

dummy value when the background task is background audio. Although Visual Studio enforces that you must put *something* for this (or the HTML-specific start page option), the actual value is unused in this case.

Handling MediaControl Events

The final thing you must do to enable background audio is add support for the *media transport controls*. This is the user interface that enables the user to interact with the audio regardless of whether the source app is on the screen. The volume control morphs into this user interface when background audio exists, so the user summons it by changing the current volume.

To support the media transport controls, you must handle four events on a static MediaControl class from the Windows.Media namespace. This can be done as follows:

```csharp
MediaControl.PlayPauseTogglePressed += OnPlayPauseTogglePressed;
MediaControl.PlayPressed += OnPlayPressed;
MediaControl.PausePressed += OnPausePressed;
MediaControl.StopPressed += OnStopPressed;

async Task OnPlayPauseTogglePressed(object sender, object e)
{
  // This is invoked on a background thread
  await this.Dispatcher.RunAsync(CoreDispatcherPriority.Normal, () =>
  {
    // This must run on the main thread
    if (this.mediaElement.CurrentState == MediaElementState.Playing)
    {
      this.mediaElement.Pause();
    }
    else
    {
      this.mediaElement.Play();
    }
  });
}

async Task OnPlayPressed(object sender, object e)
{
  // This is invoked on a background thread
  await this.Dispatcher.RunAsync(CoreDispatcherPriority.Normal, () =>
  {
    // This must run on the main thread
    this.mediaElement.Play();
  });
}
```

```
async Task OnPausePressed(object sender, object e)
{
  // This is invoked on a background thread
  await this.Dispatcher.RunAsync(CoreDispatcherPriority.Normal, () =>
  {
    // This must run on the main thread
    this.mediaElement.Pause();
  });
}

async Task OnStopPressed(object sender, object e)
{
  // This is invoked on a background thread
  await this.Dispatcher.RunAsync(CoreDispatcherPriority.Normal, () =>
  {
    // This must run on the main thread
    this.mediaElement.Stop();
  });
}
```

Although not required, you should also set some properties on MediaControl to improve its display:

```
MediaControl.TrackName = "The Track";
MediaControl.ArtistName = "The Artist";
MediaControl.AlbumArt = new Uri("ms-appx:///Assets/AlbumArt.png");
```

Of course, you can often get the real track and artist names from file metadata.

With all these steps taken, background audio not only works, but the volume control gets the additional media transport controls while the audio is playing. This is shown in Figure 20.9.

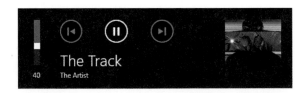

The volume control with
no background audio

The volume control with added media transport controls
when background audio is active

FIGURE 20.9   When background audio is working, media transport controls are automatically shown alongside the volume control.

In Figure 20.9, the previous track and next track buttons are disabled, but you can enable them by handling MediaControl's PreviousTrackPressed and NextTrackPressed events. One neat thing about supporting MediaControl is that it makes your app automatically work with hardware media buttons on remote controls, keyboards, or any other

 While your app plays background audio, it will not get suspended!

Therefore, be sure to act responsibly in this situation to avoid excessively draining the device's battery. If your app gets muted or if the audio stops, then the normal suspension rules apply once again.

relevant peripherals. In fact, of the four required events, only PlayPauseTogglePressed is invoked by the on-screen media transport controls. The rest are for supporting hardware buttons. MediaControl has a long list of additional events that you can handle for even deeper integration with hardware buttons (RewindPressed, FastForwardPressed, RecordPressed, and so on).

Custom Background Tasks

For any type of background task other than playing audio, you have more work to do. You must create a class that implements an interface called IBackgroundTask, register the task, choose a trigger, and potentially do a little more.

Implementing IBackgroundTask

IBackgroundTask is a simple interface with a single Run method. The following dummy implementation does nothing other than show how to report progress and support cancellation, which are two features that can be leveraged by your app when it runs in the foreground:

```
public sealed class CustomBackgroundTask : IBackgroundTask
{
  bool isCanceled;

  public void Run(IBackgroundTaskInstance taskInstance)
  {
    // Support cancellation
    taskInstance.Canceled += (sender, reason) => this.isCanceled = true;

    for (uint progress = 0; progress <= 100; progress++)
    {
      if (this.isCanceled)
        break;

      // Send progress information
      taskInstance.Progress = progress;
    }
  }
}
```

To perform asynchronous work, you must follow the typical deferral pattern initiated by calling `GetDeferral` on the passed-in `IBackgroundTaskInstance`. Note that your background task is hosted specially and runs in a different process than the rest of your app. Its execution is independent of whatever your app is doing at the time.

Registering the Task

As with background audio, you must add two pieces of information to the package manifest: the supported task type(s) and the entry point. For the supported task type(s), select the relevant type, such as "System event" or "Timer." (These choices are discussed in a moment.) For the entry point, put the namespace-qualified type name of your class that implements `IBackgroundTask`, such as `Chapter20.CustomBackgroundTask`.

You must also write some registration code that you typically run every time your app runs. The following helper method does this work for any task whose information is passed in:

```csharp
static BackgroundTaskRegistration RegisterBackgroundTask(string name,
  string entryPoint, IBackgroundTrigger trigger,
  IBackgroundCondition[] conditions)
{
  // If it's already registered, be sure to return the existing task
  // to avoid registering the same task multiple times
  foreach (BackgroundTaskRegistration task in
          BackgroundTaskRegistration.AllTasks.Values)
  {
    if (task.Name == name)
      return task;
  }

  // Register and return a new task
  BackgroundTaskBuilder builder = new BackgroundTaskBuilder {
    Name = name, TaskEntryPoint = entryPoint };

  // Specify what triggers the task
  builder.SetTrigger(trigger);

  // Add any conditions
  if (conditions != null)
  {
    foreach (IBackgroundCondition condition in conditions)
    {
      builder.AddCondition(condition);
    }
  }

  return builder.Register();
}
```

The code must first check whether the task has been registered to avoid registering it multiple times. If it is registered, it returns the previously registered instance. If this is the first time, it constructs a custom background task with a `BackgroundTaskBuilder`. In addition to a name and an entry point (the same namespace-qualified task class name), the task must be given a trigger that determines when it runs. It can also be given any number of conditions that restrict when it runs further. Triggers and conditions are discussed in a moment.

 Don't register your background task multiple times!

A background task can be registered multiple times, which is why it's important to guard against that. It can negatively impact the performance of your task, or even its correctness.

 If your background task is a one-time activity or has a limited timeframe in which it is useful, you can unregister it with `BackgroundTaskBuilder`'s `Unregister` method when the time is right.

Leveraging Background Work from the Foreground

Windows doesn't do anything with the progress reported by a background task or whatever results it produces, but your app can. The `BackgroundTaskRegistration` object (returned by our `RegisterBackgroundTask` helper) exposes two events: `Progress` and `Completed`. Your app's initialization code might do something like the following:

```
BackgroundTaskRegistration task = RegisterBackgroundTask("My Task",
  "Chapter20.CustomBackgroundTask", trigger, null);
task.Progress += OnProgress;
task.Completed += OnCompleted;
```

If your app happens to be running in the foreground while your background task reports progress and/or completes, these events get raised instantly. If either of these conditions happens while your app is suspended, then the events are raised when your app resumes.

No data gets passed directly from the background task to the foreground app, but you can write both sides such that they agree upon a place to look for any necessary data. For example, you can use local app settings or app files.

Triggers

Every background task must be given a single trigger that determines what causes it to run. There are six kinds of triggers: `TimeTrigger`, `MaintenanceTrigger`, `SystemTrigger`, `PushNotificationTrigger`, and the limited-use `NetworkOperatorHotspotAuthenticationTrigger` and `NetworkOperatorNotificationTrigger`.

`TimeTrigger` and `MaintenanceTrigger` both enable a background task to run at a regular interval. In their constructors, you specify the interval in terms of the number of minutes and a Boolean that determines whether the task should be executed only once (when true) or if it should continuously be invoked until the task is unregistered (when false). For example:

```
MaintenanceTrigger trigger =
  new MaintenanceTrigger(freshnessTime: 30, oneShot: false);
BackgroundTaskRegistration task = RegisterBackgroundTask("My Task",
 "Chapter20.CustomBackgroundTask", trigger, null);
```

Regardless of which you use, you must choose "Timer" as the task type in your package manifest.

So what's the difference between TimeTrigger and MaintenanceTrigger? MaintenanceTrigger causes the task to be invoked only while the PC is on AC power, whereas TimeTrigger runs the task regardless. To help conserve battery power, Windows doesn't allow just any app to use a TimeTrigger, however. It has to be an app that the user has added to the lock screen. That's because presumably the user cares about frequent updates for such apps. Note that for either type of trigger, Windows doesn't invoke the task *exactly* on the requested interval. It claims to do so only within 15 minutes of the scheduled interval.

SystemTrigger covers a number of different events, and you choose the specific one with a value from the SystemTriggerType enumeration. For example:

```
SystemTrigger trigger = new SystemTrigger(
  triggerType: SystemTriggerType.NetworkStateChange, oneShot: false);
BackgroundTaskRegistration task = RegisterBackgroundTask("My Task",
 "Chapter20.CustomBackgroundTask", trigger, null);
```

Some trigger types require the app to be added to the lock screen, whereas others don't. Here's the full list:

→ **TimeZoneChange**

→ **SmsReceived**

→ **LockScreenApplicationAdded** and **LockScreenApplicationRemoved**

→ **InternetAvailable** and **NetworkStateChange**. The latter includes changes in network cost as well as connectivity.

→ **OnlineIdConnectedStateChange**, for when the user's Microsoft account changes.

→ **ServicingComplete**, for when an app has been updated.

→ **UserPresent** and **UserAway** (lock screen app only)

→ **ControlChannelReset** (lock screen app only)

→ **SessionConnected** (lock screen app only)

Be sure to select "System event" for the task type in your package manifest when you use a SystemTrigger.

Conditions

To help preserve battery life, you can further restrict when your background task runs by applying any number of extra conditions. Each condition is an instance of SystemCondition constructed with a SystemConditionType enumeration value that describes it. For example:

```
IBackgroundCondition[] conditions = new IBackgroundCondition[] {
  new SystemCondition(SystemConditionType.InternetAvailable),
  new SystemCondition(SystemConditionType.UserPresent);
};
BackgroundTaskRegistration task = RegisterBackgroundTask("My Task",
  "Chapter20.CustomBackgroundTask", trigger, conditions);
```

The values of SystemConditionType are:

→ **UserPresent** and **UserNotPresent**

→ **InternetAvailable** and **InternetNotAvailable**

→ **SessionConnected** and **SessionDisconnected**

Summary

Extensions enable an app to do some powerful things that you might not expect. Some of this power, such as file type associations, is even able to impact the desktop experience.

Although you can do a lot with background tasks, there are some other options for keeping your app looking up-to-date, such as using live tiles or scheduled notifications. These are explained in the final chapter of this book.

A few more extensions exist that aren't examined in this chapter:

→ **Camera Settings**—Enables an app to add custom options (such as special effects) to the Camera app. Meant for developers who make cameras (independent hardware vendors or original equipment manufacturers).

→ **Print Task Settings**—Enables an app to replace the default print settings with a custom user interface (and code that communicates directly with the printer).

→ **Game Explorer**—Enables an app to specify a Game Definition File that contains metadata such as the game's rating in various rating systems (ESRB, PEGI, and so on). This enables the Family Safety feature in Windows to properly control access to a game.

→ **Certificates**—Enables an app to install digital certificates. The main reason for this is to authenticate a user to web services over SSL.

Chapter 21

SENSORS AND OTHER DEVICES

This chapter shows how to interact with the large number of sensors and other devices that are standard on Windows 8 tablets. Of course, you must not assume that any of these devices are available to your app given that Windows 8 also runs on traditional desktops. Not only that, but sensitive devices—the ones that provide location and proximity data—can be disabled for your app at any time via the Permissions link on the Settings charm.

Accelerometer

Several times a second, the accelerometer reports the direction and magnitude of the total force applied to the device. This force is expressed with three values—X, Y, and Z—where X is horizontal, Y is vertical, and Z is perpendicular to the screen, as shown in Figure 21.1.

z

FIGURE 21.1   The three accelerometer dimensions, relative to the screen

The magnitude of each value is a multi-plier of g (the gravitational force on the surface of Earth). Each value is restricted to a range from -2 to 2. If the device rests flat on a table with the screen up, the values reported for X and Y are roughly zero, and the value of Z is roughly -1 (1 g into the screen toward the ground). That's because the only force applied to the device in this situa-tion is gravity. By shifting the device's angle and orientation and keeping it roughly still, the values of X, Y, and Z reveal which way is down in the real world thanks to the ever-present force of gravity. When you abruptly move or shake the device, the X, Y, and Z values are able to reveal this activity as well.

> **The accelerometer's Y axis grows in the opposite direction compared to normal UI coordinates!**
>
> As shown in Figure 21.1, the Y axis grows upward rather than downward.

> Regardless of how you contort your device, the X, Y, and Z axes used for the accelerometer data remain fixed to it. For example, the Y axis always points toward the top edge of the screen.

To get the accelerometer data, you call the static `Accelerometer.GetDefault` method and attach a handler to its `ReadingChanged` event. You can also get the current reading on demand by calling its `GetCurrentReading` method. Both of these techniques provide you with an `AccelerometerReading` class with four simple properties: `AccelerationX`, `AccelerationY`, `AccelerationZ` (all doubles), and `Timestamp` (a `DateTimeOffset`). The physical accelerometer is always running, but data is reported to your app only while you have a `ReadingChanged` event handler attached.

> **Be sure to handle the case when** `Accelerometer.GetDefault` **returns** `null`**!**
>
> This is what happens when the current PC has no accelerometer. And like all the sensors, your app can easily run on PCs without one.

To get the best performance and battery life, it's good to detach your `ReadingChanged` handler when you don't need the data. You can also adjust `Accelerometer`'s `ReportInterval` property by setting it to a larger number of milliseconds than its default refresh rate (revealed by its `MinimumReportInterval` property).

Tossing Motion

The following handler for `Accelerometer`'s `ReadingChanged` event contains a simple algorithm for detecting a tossing motion, such as flipping a coin in the air:

```
// Process data coming from the accelerometer
void OnReadingChanged(Accelerometer sender,
                      AccelerometerReadingChangedEventArgs e)
{
  // We want the threshold to be negative, so
  // forward motion is up and out of the screen
  double threshold = -1;

  // Only pay attention to large-enough magnitudes in the Z dimension
  if (Math.Abs(e.Reading.AccelerationZ) < Math.Abs(threshold))
    return;

  // See if the force is in the same direction as the threshold
  // (forward throwing motion)
  if (e.Reading.AccelerationZ * threshold > 0)
  {
    // Forward acceleration
    this.acceleratingQuicklyForwardTime = e.Reading.Timestamp;
  }
  else if (e.Reading.Timestamp - this.acceleratingQuicklyForwardTime
          < TimeSpan.FromSeconds(.2))
  {
    // This is large backward force shortly after the forward force.
    // Time to invoke the tossing action!

    this.acceleratingQuicklyForwardTime = DateTimeOffset.MinValue;

    // We're on a different thread, so transition to the UI thread
    await this.Dispatcher.RunAsync(CoreDispatcherPriority.Normal, () =>
    {
      // A toss happened! React appropriately.
      …
    });
  }
}
```

Only two properties of `AccelerometerReading` are examined: `AccelerationZ` and `Timestamp`. The algorithm is as follows: If the app detects a strong forward force followed quickly by a strong backward force, it considers it a toss.

Notice that the threshold is negative, which seems to contradict the description of the Z axis in Figure 22.1. That's because when you hold a device flat and accelerate it upward, it "feels heavier" in the opposite direction, causing the value of `e.Reading.AccelerationZ` to *decrease*. You experience the same sensation when going up in a fast-moving elevator. The same behavior applies to either direction in any dimension. This is the difference between measuring g-forces (what accelerometers do) versus actually measuring acceleration.

The accelerometer's ReadingChanged **event is raised on a non-UI thread!**

This is great for processing the data without creating a bottleneck on the UI thread, but it does mean that you must explicitly transition to the UI thread before performing any work that requires it. This is true for other sensor events covered in this chapter as well.

Because of hardware variations between different devices, apps that use the accelerometer should often enable the user to adjust or otherwise calibrate the interpretation of the raw data.

Shake Detection

A common use of the accelerometer is to detect when the user shakes the device. This is not trivial to detect from the raw data, however, especially if you want the recognition of the gesture to feel the same as shake detection done by other apps. (In the past, I've implemented this logic by detecting if at least two out of the three acceleration values are sufficiently different from previously-recorded values. Of course, "sufficiently different" can be hard to judge.) Fortunately, `Accelerometer` has a built-in `Shaken` event that tells you when a standard shake has occurred. `AccelerometerShakenEventArgs` exposes nothing other than a `Timestamp` property.

Gyrometer

Whereas an accelerometer detects linear motion, a gyrometer reports *angular* motion. You can get this data with a `Gyrometer` class that looks almost identical to `Accelerometer`. You get an instance by calling `Gyrometer.GetDefault`, you can attach a handler to its `ReadingChanged` event (or call its `GetCurrentReading` method for data on demand), and you can adjust its `ReportInterval`. The only difference (other than the lack of a `Shaken` event) is that GyrometerReading's properties are **AngularVelocity**X, **AngularVelocity**Y, **AngularVelocity**Z, and `Timestamp`.

Inclinometer

The inclinometer is a bit harder to understand, and you probably don't need to use it unless you write a flight simulator. It measures *pitch*, *roll*, and *yaw*, which maps to an airplane's elevator, aileron, and rudder inputs, respectively.

The shape of the `Inclinometer` API looks like `Gyrometer`. You get an instance by calling `Inclinometer.GetDefault`, you can attach a handler to its `ReadingChanged` event (or call its `GetCurrentReading` method), and you can adjust its `ReportInterval`. `InclinometerReading`'s properties are `PitchDegrees`, `RollDegrees`, `YawDegrees`, and `Timestamp`.

Compass

The compass sensor follows the same pattern as the others. The `Compass` class has identical members to `Inclinometer` and `Gyrometer`, except the readings returned are of type `CompassReading`. `CompassReading` exposes three properties:

→ **HeadingMagneticNorth**—A `double` representing the magnetic-north heading in degrees.

→ **HeadingTrueNorth**—A nullable `double` representing the true-north heading in degrees. This can't always be determined, so the property is `null` in such cases.

→ **Timestamp**—The date and time that the measurement was taken; a `DateTimeOffset`, like all the other `Timestamp` properties.

Light Sensor

With the ambient light sensor, you can automatically dim, brighten, or otherwise adjust your app's content based on the surrounding lighting conditions. (If you do this, please make it optional, otherwise you will annoy users like me!)

The light sensor once again follows the same pattern as the others. The class is called `LightSensor` and the readings returned are of type `LightSensorReading`. This has two properties: `IlluminanceInLux` and `Timestamp`. `IlluminanceInLux` measures the amount of light in lux units.

Orientation

Chapter 4, "Layout," describes how you can detect orientation changes with the static `DisplayProperties.OrientationChanged` event. This enables you to detect landscape, landscape-flipped, portrait, and portrait-flipped orientations. There are two orientation-related sensor APIs, however, that expose richer data: `SimpleOrientationSensor` and `OrientationSensor`.

SimpleOrientationSensor

`SimpleOrientationSensor` is much simpler to use than `OrientationSensor`, and its APIs are a bit simpler than the other sensors, too. Besides its `GetDefault` method, it exposes only a `GetCurrentOrientation` method and an `OrientationChanged` event. The device's current orientation is reported via a member of the `SimpleOrientation` enumeration:

→ **NotRotated** (the same as *landscape*: horizontal and upright, like a laptop screen)

→ **Rotated180DegreesCounterclockwise** (the same as *landscape-flipped*: horizontal and upright, but upside down)

→ **Rotated270DegreesCounterclockwise** (the same as *portrait*: vertical and upright, with the hardware Start button on the left)

→ **Rotated90DegreesCounterclockwise** (the same as *portrait-flipped*: vertical and upright, with the hardware Start button on the right)

→ **Faceup** (lying flat on a horizontal surface, screen up)

→ **Facedown** (lying flat on a horizontal surface, screen down)

OrientationSensor

The full `OrientationSensor` class is like a combination of the accelerometer, gyrometer, and compass. It reveals a 3x3 *rotation matrix* and a *quaternion*. This class has the same surface area as most of the other sensor classes: `GetDefault` and `GetCurrentReading` methods, a `ReadingChanged` event, and `ReportInterval` plus `MinimumReportInterval` properties. The `OrientationSensorReading` class that reveals the data exposes two properties besides `Timestamp`: `RotationMatrix` and `Quaternion`.

Location

With the `Geolocator` class—and the Location capability—you can retrieve the PC's geographic location. This information can come from a GPS device, or from an algorithm that uses Wi-Fi triangulation and the current IP address if no GPS device exists.

To get the current location, you create an instance of `Geolocator` and call `GetGeopositionAsync`:

```
Geolocator locator = new Geolocator();
Geoposition position = await locator.GetGeopositionAsync();
```

The returned `Geoposition` object contains two properties: `Coordinate` and `CivicAddress`.

`Coordinate`, of type `Geocoordinate`, exposes the following properties:

→ **Latitude** and **Longitude**—doubles specified in degrees.

→ **Accuracy**—The accuracy of the latitude and longitude information, specified in meters.

→ **Altitude**—A nullable `double` specified in meters. (Nullable because this information might not be available.)

→ **AltitudeAccuracy**—The accuracy of the altitude, specified in meters.

→ **Speed**—A nullable `double` specified in meters per second, if the user is moving.

→ **Heading**—A nullable `double` that reveals the direction of any motion, specified in degrees relative to true north.

→ **Timestamp**—The date and time that the measurement was taken.

`CivicAddress` attempts to map the precise location to an address. It exposes the following properties, all `strings` except for the last one:

→ **City**

→ **State** (which could also be the province, if applicable)

→ **PostalCode**

→ **Country** (the two-letter ISO-3166 country code)

→ **Timestamp**

If some of these can't be determined, they are left as empty `strings`. When running this on an older laptop, the only piece of information you might get is the `Country`.

Getting the user's location once might be acceptable for some scenarios, but most location-based apps want to track the user's location as he or she moves. You can do this by handling `Geolocator`'s `PositionChanged` event. Handlers are given a `PositionChangedEventArgs` object with a `Position` property of type `Geoposition`, the same class already described. You can control how frequently updates are provided by changing `Geolocator`'s `ReportInterval` and/or `MovementThreshold` properties. If you require high accuracy at the expense of battery life, you can change its `DesiredAccuracy` property from `Default` to `High`.

`Geolocator` also exposes a `LocationStatus` property with a corresponding `StatusChanged` event. This property tells you whether the location provider is still initializing, ready, disabled, and so on.

Proximity

All official Windows 8 tablets have a Near Field Communication (NFC) chip, which can communicate with another NFC chip up to about 4cm away. Because of this close range, the two devices are meant to be tapped together to trigger a custom action on one or both devices. This gesture is often referred to as *tap and go*.

NFC is mostly associated with making payments from a smartphone by tapping a special reader, but there are several "proximity" scenarios enabled by NFC. You can tap two NFC-enabled devices together to enable to send/receive a simple message. You can tap the devices together as a simple way to bootstrap a normal WiFi or Bluetooth network connection between two instances of your app. (Even better, your app doesn't need to be running or installed on the second device! If your app isn't running, the second user is invited to launch it. If your app isn't installed, the second user is offered a link to it in the Windows Store!) You can even tap a little card or sticker with an unpowered NFC chip inside to receive a message from it. These are sometimes called *NFC tags*. To use the proximity APIs discussed in this section, your app must have the Proximity capability.

> 💡 By supporting the Share charm, you can support proximity-based sharing without doing any extra work (and without requiring the Proximity capability)! The user can select "someone nearby" on the Share pane and let Windows automatically use proximity as the mechanism for sharing without your app knowing what happened.

Sending and Receiving Messages

To receive a message from an NFC tag or device when it is tapped on your local device, you attach a callback to `ProximityDevice`:

```
// Receive an NFC message
ProximityDevice device = ProximityDevice.GetDefault();
long id = device.SubscribeForMessage("WindowsUri", OnMessageReceived);
```

In the rare case you don't want to use the default proximity device, you can enumerate available devices and select one by its `string` ID via other static `ProximityDevice` methods.

The first parameter to `SubscribeForMessage` describes the type of message you want to handle. The list of possible types is documented at http://bit.ly/S6hHGz, although you can append a period and a subtype to some to create your own custom types. In this case, the code is handling URI messages. The returned ID can be passed to `ProximityDevice.StopSubscribingForMessage`, although calling this is optional.

The callback looks as follows:

```
void OnMessageReceived(ProximityDevice sender, ProximityMessage message)
{
  string uriString = message.DataAsString;
  // Use the URI
  …
}
```

You can either get the message as a `string` via `ProximityMessage`'s `DataAsString` property, or as an `IBuffer` via its `Data` property. You can copy an `IBuffer` to a byte array with the `ToArray` extension method defined in the `System.Runtime.InteropServices.WindowsRuntime` extension method.

To send a message, you can call one of the publishing methods on `ProximityDevice`:

```
// Send an NFC message
ProximityDevice device = ProximityDevice.GetDefault();
long id = device.PublishUriMessage(new Uri("http://pixelwinks.com"));
```

Once you do this, any later tap and go gestures send the message. Alternatively, you can call `PublishMessage` with a `string` message and `string` message type, or `PublishBinaryMessage` with an `IBuffer` message and a `string` message type.

Finding and Communicating with a Peer Device

To connect to a nearby peer device and initiate a network connection, you can use the following code:

```
ProximityDevice device = ProximityDevice.GetDefault();
// Handle tap from peer:
PeerFinder.TriggeredConnectionStateChanged += OnConnectionStateChanged;
PeerFinder.Start(); // Call Stop when done
```

Windows chooses the best available option for the connection, although you can exclude specific options by setting static `PeerFinder` properties such as `AllowBluetooth` and `AllowWiFiDirect` to false.

The event handler can look as follows:

```
void OnConnectionStateChanged(object sender,
                              TriggeredConnectionStateChangedEventArgs args)
{
  switch (args.State)
  {
    case TriggeredConnectState.Connecting:
      // This instance of the app is the "server" or "host"
      this.isClient = false;
      break;
    case TriggeredConnectState.Listening:
      // This instance of the app is the "client"
      this.isClient = true;
      break;
    case TriggeredConnectState.Completed:
      // The connection is complete, so start communicating
      StreamSocket socket = args.Socket;
      if (this.isClient)
      {
        socket.InputStream.AsStreamForRead().ReadAsync(…);
        …
      }
      else
      {
        socket.OutputStream.AsStreamForWrite().WriteAsync(…);
        …
      }
      break;
```

```
      case TriggeredConnectState.Failed:
        …
        break;
      case TriggeredConnectState.Canceled:
        …
        break;
      case TriggeredConnectState.PeerFound:
        // Could show an optional message
        …
        break;
  }
}
```

This handler gets called more than once in both instances of the app. The one chosen as the "server" gets called first with `TriggeredConnectState.Connecting`, and the one chosen as the "client" gets called first with `TriggeredConnectState.Listening`. When subsequently called with `TriggeredConnectState.Completed`, both sides can communicate with each other via a socket. This code uses the `AsStreamForRead` and `AsStreamForWrite` extension methods to communicate by reading from/writing to a standard .NET stream.

Summary

Despite there being a long list of sensors to take advantage of, they are all simple to use. The trick is not how to get the raw data, but rather how to devise suitable algorithms that operate on the data! Unlike in Windows Phone, none of these sensors require a capability. Only the sensitive devices—location and proximity—do.

Chapter 22

THINKING OUTSIDE THE APP: LIVE TILES, TOAST NOTIFICATIONS, AND THE LOCK SCREEN

Windows 8 provides apps opportunities to impact the user's experience even when they are not occupying the screen. This chapter examines these three opportunities. You might be surprised how easy they are to use! Live tiles enable you to have a rich presence on the Start screen, toast notifications enable you to alert the user and make your app a click away (even while the user is working on the Windows desktop), and the lock screen provides some extensibility points that make it possible to give the user important status updates.

Live Tiles

Chapter 1, "Anatomy of a Windows Store App," shows how to customize your tile in a few basic ways and optionally support a wide tile. All of the choices are static, however. Now, you can see how to turn your tile into a dynamic *live tile*, which can update in a number of rich ways at any point in time. You can even support *secondary tiles* that can provide users with even more information right on the Start screen, and can also serve as helpful shortcuts into specific areas in your app.

Tile Templates

Your live tile cannot contain arbitrary XAML (or HTML). Its appearance is tightly controlled by an XML template. With such a template, you choose one of several predefined layouts and, depending on the choice, can specify a few lines of text and a few images. Although this means your customization possibilities are limited, it also means that it's easy to give your app a live tile with a standard look-and-feel, including animations.

For example, the following method can be invoked at any time to update an app's tile:

```
void UpdateTile()
{
  // This is the tile template
  string xmlString = @"
<tile>
  <visual>
    <binding template='TileSquareBlock'>
      <text id='1'>Big</text>
      <text id='2'>Little</text>
    </binding>
  </visual>
</tile>";

  // Load the content into an XML document
  XmlDocument document = new XmlDocument();
  document.LoadXml(xmlString);

  // Create a tile notification and send it
  TileNotification notification = new TileNotification(document);
  TileUpdateManager.CreateTileUpdaterForApplication().Update(notification);
}
```

Here, the chosen template is called `TileSquareBlock`. This template expects two pieces of text. The one with an `id` of 1 appears on the top in a large font, and the one with an `id` of 2 appears underneath in a small font. The call to `CreateTileUpdaterForApplication` returns a `TileUpdater` instance that exposes a variety of interesting behaviors. For now, we call its `Update` method to perform the update.

Figure 22.1 shows how an app's tile changes after the call to `UpdateTile` is made. The yellow comes from the background color chosen in the package manifest, which wasn't previously seen because the tile logo has no transparency. The icon shown in the resultant live tile is not just a shrunken version of the logo; it is the small logo specified in the package manifest. The text in this, and other, examples is dark gray because "Dark" is chosen as the foreground text color in the package manifest so it shows up nicely on the yellow background.

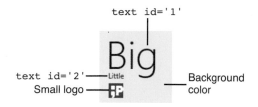

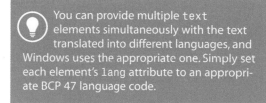

Before tile notification   After tile notification

FIGURE 22.1   Transitioning from a static tile to a live tile

After the call to UpdateTile is made, the visual update to the tile animates in the next time the user views the tile. This type of update to a tile is called a *local notification*. There are other ways to update your tile, and these ways are covered in the upcoming "Updates"

> You can provide multiple text elements simultaneously with the text translated into different languages, and Windows uses the appropriate one. Simply set each element's lang attribute to an appropriate BCP 47 language code.

section. For now, we look at all the different types of templates. There are two main categories: templates for (normal) square tiles and templates for wide tiles.

Square Tile Templates

We can subdivide the square tile templates into static ones that don't move after their initial entrance animation, and "peek" ones that periodically animate between two different regions. Figure 22.2 displays all the static square templates. The ones with text expect 1–4 text elements with ids of 1, 2, 3, and 4, respectively. The one with an image expects an image element with an id of 1. When used with a right-to-left language, the alignment of text is flipped accordingly.

The following template is used to create the image-based tile:

```
<tile>
  <visual>
    <binding template="TileSquareImage">
      <image id="1" src="Assets/tileImage.jpg" alt="A description"/>
    </binding>
  </visual>
</tile>
```

In this case, the implicit ms-appx URI requires that the image is packaged along with the app in an Assets folder. The URI can alternatively fetch an image from the Web (http or https) *if* the app has the "Internet (Client)" capability. It can also fetch an image from local storage using an ms-appdata URI. And, of course, it can use an explicit ms-appx URI, such as ms-appx:///Assets/tileImage.jpg.

The alt text is not used in a tooltip for the image, but it is used by assistive technologies such as screen readers.

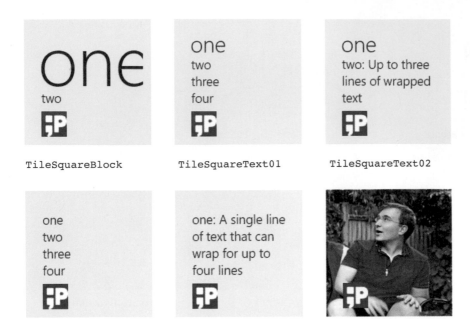

TileSquareBlock   TileSquareText01   TileSquareText02

TileSquareText03   TileSquareText04   TileSquareImage

FIGURE 22.2   Each of the static square live tile templates

On an image element, you can set addImageQuery="true" to make Windows automatically append a query string that specifies several resource qualifiers (in a slightly different syntax than what was introduced in Chapter 11, "Images"). For example, http://pixelwinks.com/tileImage.jpg can become http://pixelwinks.com/tileImage.jpg**?ms-scale=100&ms-contrast=standard&ms-lang=en-US**. This enables a Web server to serve different variations of an image based on characteristics of the current device.

Tile images can be at most 1024x1024 pixels!

They also must be no more than 200 KB, and must be a PNG, JPEG, or GIF.

If you don't want your app's small logo to appear in the corner of your live tile, you can mark the binding element in your tile template with branding="name" to show its name instead, or branding="none" to show nothing. With branding="none", you can fit one more line of tile template text than what is demonstrated in the examples in this chapter.

The other type of square tile templates—peek templates—are not square at all. They expect 1–4 pieces of text (with ids from 1–4) and one image (with an id of 1). The image is placed above the text, and the tile periodically slides between the image filling the square region and the text-based area filling the square region. These templates are visualized in Figure 22.3, as if you could see the whole surface simultaneously. Note that the small logo (if shown) remains stationary, so it appears over the image when the image is shown.

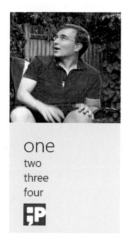

TileSquarePeekImageAndText01

TileSquarePeekImageAndText02

TileSquarePeekImageAndText03   TileSquarePeekImageAndText04

FIGURE 22.3   Each of the "peek" square live tile templates

The TileSquarePeekImageAndText04 template is used by the People app's square tile (when the user shrinks its wide tile).

If using XML strings inside your code leaves a bad taste in your mouth, there are two other options. One is to use the `TileUpdateManager.GetTemplateContent` method, which requires a value of the `TileTemplateType` enumeration that lists all possible templates. This returns an `XmlDocument`, which you can modify before constructing a `TileNotification` with it. The other option is to use the `NotificationsExtensions` project that is included in the Windows SDK sample at `http://bit.ly/I8Bpga`. This includes a `TileContentFactory` class that exposes a static method for creating each type of template, such as `CreateTileSquarePeekImageAndText04`. This returns an object with simple properties to set, and a `CreateNotification` method that returns the necessary `TileNotification` instance.

Wide Tile Templates

To take advantage of all the extra space, many more templates exist for wide live tiles. These can be divided into three categories: text-only templates, templates that use images, and "peek" templates. Figure 22.4 shows all the text-only templates. They indicate which `id` belongs to each piece of text; from 1 all the way to 8 (or 10 if the `binding` is marked with `branding="none"`). `TileWideBlockAndText01` is used by the Calendar app, and `TileWideText01` is used by the Finance app.

Recall that for an app to support a wide tile, it needs only to provide a wide logo in its package manifest. Because a user can toggle between an app's wide tile and square tile at any time, any update to a wide tile should include a corresponding update to the square version as well. This is a matter of including two `bindings` in your tile XML, one for the square tile and one for the wide tile:

```
<tile>
  <visual>
    <!-- For the square tile -->
    <binding template="TileSquareText04">
      <text id="1">one: A single line of text that can wrap.</text>
    </binding>
    <!-- For the wide tile -->
    <binding template="TileWideText03">
      <text id="1">one: A single line of text that can wrap.</text>
    </binding>
  </visual>
</tile>
```

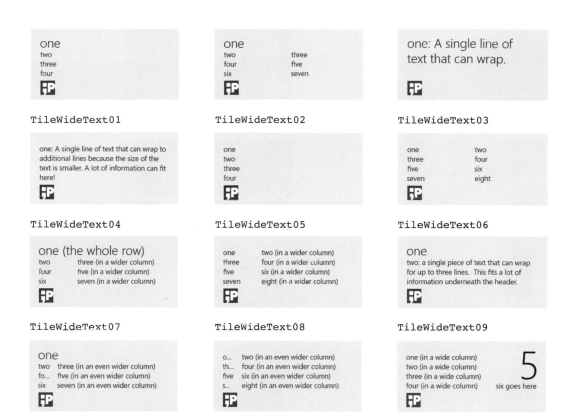

FIGURE 22.4   Each of the text-only wide live tile templates

Figure 22.5 shows the image-based templates for wide live tiles.

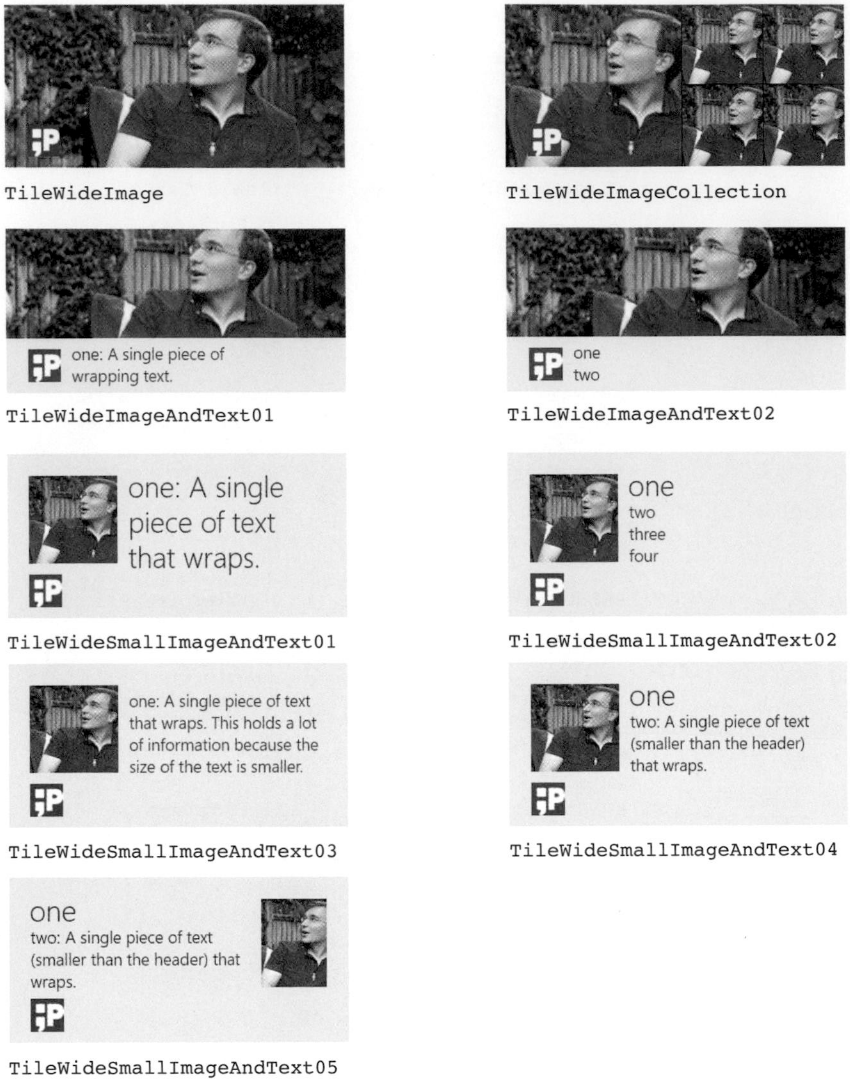

`TileWideImage`

`TileWideImageCollection`

`TileWideImageAndText01`

`TileWideImageAndText02`

`TileWideSmallImageAndText01`

`TileWideSmallImageAndText02`

`TileWideSmallImageAndText03`

`TileWideSmallImageAndText04`

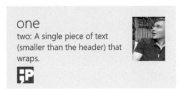

`TileWideSmallImageAndText05`

FIGURE 22.5 Each of the static wide live tile templates that use images

`TileWideImageAndText01` is a popular template and used by Bing apps, such as News and Sports. `TileWideImageCollection` is recognizable as the template used by the People app. It supports five different images, with ids from 1–5, where 1 gets the large display. Note that the regions are not *quite* square, but the uniform scaling and centered cropping does a good job of displaying the images in a reasonable fashion.

Figure 22.6 illustrates all the peek templates for wide live tiles, which animate between the upper rectangular region and the lower one. These consist of six basic templates with a single image on top, two extra templates with a single image on top, and the original six templates with an image collection on top instead. It's unclear why the single-image variety gets two extra templates: `TileWidePeekImageAndText01` and `TileWidePeekImageAndText02`. To make matters more confusing, `TileWidePeekImageAndText01` looks no different than `TileWidePeekImage04`!

TileWidePeekImage01

TileWidePeekImage02

TileWidePeekImage03

TileWidePeekImage04

TileWidePeekImage05

TileWidePeekImage06

TileWidePeekImageAndText01

TileWidePeekImageAndText02

TileWidePeekImageCollection01

TileWidePeekImageCollection02

TileWidePeekImageCollection03

TileWidePeekImageCollection04

TileWidePeekImageCollection05

TileWidePeekImageCollection06

FIGURE 22.6   Each of the "peek" wide live tile templates

Updates

You have four options for updating a live tile:

→ Local

→ Scheduled

→ Periodic

→ Push

Local

This is what has already been shown: calling `TileUpdater`'s `Update` method at any time. By default, local updates never expire.

Scheduled

To schedule an update for a specific date and time, you call `TileUpdater`'s `AddToSchedule` method rather than `Update`. `AddToSchedule` requires a **Scheduled**`TileNotification` object, which is like `TileNotification` but must be constructed with a `DateTimeOffset` representing the delivery time (along with the `XmlDocument` defining the content). To cancel a pending update, you can call `TileUpdater`'s `RemoveFromSchedule` method.

By default, scheduled updates expire three days after they are delivered. As always, you can override this by setting `ExpirationTime` appropriately.

Periodic

By calling `TileUpdater`'s `StartPeriodicUpdate` method, you can specify a `Uri` that points to a place to fetch tile XML along with a recurrence. Windows updates the tile according to this schedule, regardless of whether your app is running. With an overload of `StartPeriodicUpdate`, you can also specify a starting time other than the default of "right now."

The `Uri` presumably points to a website under your control. Because it's generated in code, you are able to customize it in order to serve custom tile content based on the user's

Regardless of which approach(es) you use to update a live tile, you can set an expiration date with `TileNotification`'s `ExpirationTime` property (a nullable `DateTimeOffset`). The different types of notifications have different default expiration times.

Instead of only showing the most recent update, you can change the behavior of your live tile to automatically cycle among the five most recent updates. The Photos app does this to provide a slideshow experience, and the People and Sports apps do this to maximize the amount of interesting content shown.

To enable this, call `TileUpdater`'s `EnableNotificationQueue` method and pass true. The tile continues to behave in this fashion, regardless of whether your app is running, until or unless you eventually call `EnableNotificationQueue` again with a value of `false`.

If you want to update any of the queued tile contents in-place, then you should assign `TileNotification`'s (or `ScheduledTileNotification`'s) Tag property to an arbitrary `string` of your choosing. If you perform a new tile update with a tag that matches an existing one in the queue, the existing one gets replaced. This is great for displaying changing values such as stock prices without worrying about stale information being displayed to the user along with the newer information.

identity or preferences. The recurrence for this method is specified with one of the following values from a `PeriodicUpdateRecurrence` enumeration: `HalfHour`, `Hour`, `SixHours`, `TwelveHours`, or `Daily`.

Both overloads of `StartPeriodicUpdate` have a corresponding `StartPeriodicUpdate`**Batch** method that accepts a collection of `Uri`s—up to five. This option makes sense when you use the notification queue to cycle between five pieces of content. You can stop the periodic updates by calling `TileUpdater`'s parameterless `StopPeriodicUpdate` method.

Push

Push notifications, which go through Windows Push Notification Services, can trigger live tile updates, badge updates, toast notifications, and even arbitrary background tasks via `PushNotificationTrigger`. To find out how to set up a service that works with Windows Push Notification Services and how to consume it from your apps, see `http://bit.ly/RSXomc`.

Badges

Tiles, whether "live" or not and whether square or wide, support a numeric or graphical *badge* that overlays status on the bottom-right corner (or bottom-left corner when a right-to-left language is in use). A numeric badge is used by the Mail app to show the number of new messages, and the Store app to show the number of available updates. Graphical badges can be used for some limited additional scenarios, such as showing the user's online status in a chat app.

Applying a badge looks much like updating a tile. The following `UpdateBadge` method places a badge with the number two on the app's tile, with differences from the previous `UpdateTile` method highlighted:

```
void UpdateBadge()
{
  // This is the badge template
  string xmlString = @"<badge value='2'/>";

  // Load the content into an XML document
  XmlDocument document = new XmlDocument();
  document.LoadXml(xmlString);

  // Create a badge notification and send it
  BadgeNotification notification = new BadgeNotification(document);
  BadgeUpdateManager.CreateBadgeUpdaterForApplication().Update(notification);
}
```

This produces the result shown in Figure 22.7.

FIGURE 22.7   A numeric "2" badge applied to a tile

The number must be greater than or equal to one. Trying to display a badge with a value of zero, for example, makes the badge disappear altogether. Oddly, any number greater than 99 is forced to be displayed as "99⁺," as shown in Figure 22.8.

FIGURE 22.8   Badge numbers don't go higher than 99.

Graphical badges cannot be an arbitrary picture; you have eleven icons available. To choose one, set badge's value attribute to one of the strings in Figure 22.9 rather than a number. (You can also set the value to none to make the badge disappear, just like setting it to 0.)

| available | unavailable | away | busy | error | attention |

| alert | playing | paused | activity | newmessage |

FIGURE 22.9   All possible values for graphical badges

Badges have many of the bells and whistles that live tiles have. You can set an ExpirationTime on BadgeNotification, and you can use BadgeUpdater's StartPeriodicUpdate/ StopPeriodicUpdate methods for the same type of periodic updates. You also have the same two options for interacting with badges without manipulating XML strings, although the XML is so simple in this case that these other mechanisms don't add much value.

> **(!) The first four graphical badges in Figure 22.9 do not respect the package manifest's foreground text setting!**
>
> Although all the other images have a "light mode" and a "dark mode" to correspond to the two foreground text choices, the four status circles always render with a white border. This makes them not very suitable for light tiles, such as the yellow ones used throughout this section.

Secondary Tiles

As mentioned in Chapter 7, "App Model," an app can have any number of additional tiles known as *secondary tiles*. These are meant to jump to a specific part or mode of the app. For example, the Finance app enables the user to pin individual stocks to the Start screen. The user gets one secondary tile per stock, and clicking one brings up a page populated with data specific to that stock.

An app cannot spam the Start screen with arbitrary secondary tiles; each tile must be added with user consent. You do this with the SecondaryTile class in the Windows.UI.StartScreen namespace. After you construct one, you can set a number of properties (or use an overloaded constructor that sets the same values): Logo, SmallLogo,

WideLogo, ShortName, BackgroundColor, and so on. Most important are the TileId and Arguments properties, because this information gets passed to OnLaunched via LaunchActivatedEventArgs so your app can identify whether a secondary tile (and which secondary tile) was just clicked. You can set these however you like.

After you construct and configure a SecondaryTile instance, you can call its RequestCreateAsync method to prompt the user to pin the tile. For example, the following code presents the user interface shown in Figure 22.10:

```
SecondaryTile tile = new SecondaryTile();

// Set some required properties
tile.TileId = "1";
tile.ShortName = "Short Name";
tile.DisplayName = "Display Name";
tile.Arguments = "args";
tile.Logo = new Uri("ms-appx:///Assets/Logo.png");

// Show the "Pin to Start" user interface
await tile.RequestCreateAsync();
```

All five properties set in this code are required. (Even Arguments must be set to a nonnull and nonempty string, regardless of whether you have any use for this value.) If not set, the values of properties such as BackgroundColor and ForegroundText (which is not the text itself but the Dark or Light choice) are inherited from the app's primary tile.

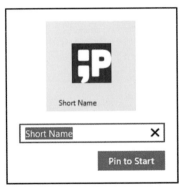

The built-in popup comes complete with a preview and the capability to assign a new "short name" displayed on the tile. If you want to place the popup in a specific location, you can call an overload of RequestCreateAsync that accepts a Point, or one of two overloads of RequestCreateForSelectionAsync that position it relative to a Rect that is supposed to represent a selection.

FIGURE 22.10   Presenting the built-in Pin to Start user interface is easy.

SecondaryTile exposes Request**Delete**Async and Request**Delete**ForSelectionAsync methods that prompt the user to unpin a tile with the user interface shown in Figure 22.11. You must call this on an

FIGURE 22.11   Presenting the built-in "Unpin from Start" user interface is also easy.

instance of SecondaryTile that has a matching TileId. Providing this feature in your app is optional, of course, because users are able to unpin tiles directly from the Start screen.

SecondaryTile also enables enumerating all the secondary tiles you create with its static FindAllAsync method, or checking for the existence of one with its static Exists method that must be passed a tile ID. You can also update a secondary tile's properties by constructing an instance with the right ID and calling its UpdateAsync method.

Secondary tiles can be live tiles and support badges, just like primary tiles. You follow the same procedures described previously, but call TileUpdateManager's CreateTileUpdaterFor**SecondaryTile** method instead of CreateTileUpdaterForApplication, and BadgeUpdateManager's CreateBadgeUpdaterFor**SecondaryTile** method instead of CreateBadgeUpdaterForApplication. Both of these methods must be passed a tile ID.

Toast Notifications

Toast notifications, affectionately called this because they "pop up" like toast in a toaster, are the little messages in rectangles that appear in the upper-right corner of the screen (or upper-left when a right-to-left language is used). Creating and showing a toast notification has many parallels to creating and updating live tiles.

 If your app uses toast notifications, don't forget to set "Toast capable" to "Yes" in the package manifest!

This can be found on the Application UI tab in Visual Studio.

Toast Templates

As with live tiles and badges, toast notifications are defined by simple XML templates. For example, the following method can be invoked at any time to trigger a toast notification, with differences from live tiles and badges highlighted:

```
void SendToast()
{
  // create a string with the toast template xml
  string xmlString = @"
<toast>
  <visual>
    <binding template='ToastText01'>
      <text id='1'>Alert!</text>
    </binding>
  </visual>
</toast>";

  // Load the content into an XML document
```

```
XmlDocument document = new XmlDocument();
document.LoadXml(xmlString);

// Create a toast notification and send it
ToastNotification notification = new ToastNotification(document);
ToastNotificationManager.CreateToastNotifier().Show(notification);
}
```

This produces the result in Figure 22.12. It automatically picks up the colors and small icon from the package manifest.

Here, the chosen template is called ToastText01. It expects a single piece of

FIGURE 22.12   A simple toast notification

text that can wrap. Figure 22.13 demonstrates all eight available templates. Four are text-only, and the other four are the same as the first four with an added image.

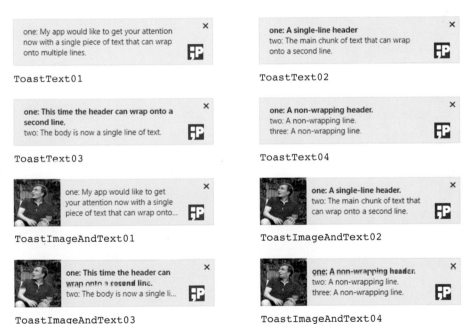

FIGURE 22.13   Each of the toast notification templates

In these templates, the text elements have ids from 1–3 and the image element, if present, has an id of 1. The same rules about image size and formats that apply to live tiles apply to toast notifications as well. As with live tiles, text elements support the lang attribute, and image elements support the addImageQuery attribute. In addition, the two options for avoiding XML manipulation are available for toast notifications: ToastNotificationManager.GetTemplateContent and the NotificationsExtensions project in the Windows SDK.

By default, a toast notification stays on the screen for seven seconds unless the user inter-acts with it. However, by setting the `toast` element's `duration` attribute to `long`, you can make it remain on the screen for *twenty-five seconds*! For example:

```xml
<toast duration="long">
  <visual>
    …
  </visual>
  <audio …/>
</toast>
```

This is meant for situations in which a person is waiting for you to respond, such as in a chat session.

You can customize the audio that gets played by a toast notification by including an `audio` element as a child of the `toast` element in the XML template. For example:

```xml
  <toast>
<visual>
  <binding template="ToastText01">
    <text id="1">Alert!</text>
  </binding>
</visual>
<audio src="ms-winsoundevent:Notification.Mail"/>
</toast>
```

You have only eight sounds to choose from (in addition to the default `ms-winsoundevent:Notification.Default` sound):

→ `ms-winsoundevent:Notification.IM`

→ `ms-winsoundevent:Notification.Mail`

→ `ms-winsoundevent:Notification.Reminder`

→ `ms-winsoundevent:Notification.SMS`

→ `ms-winsoundevent:Notification.Looping.Alarm`

→ `ms-winsoundevent:Notification.Looping.Alarm2`

→ `ms-winsoundevent:Notification.Looping.Call`

→ `ms-winsoundevent:Notification.Looping.Call2`

The sounds with "Looping" in the name support looping *if* the `toast` element's `duration` is set to `long` *and* audio's `loop` attribute is set to `true`. You can also mute the sound altogether by setting audio's `silent` attribute to `true`.

Options for Showing Toast Notifications

Although toast notifications don't have the same kind of periodic option that live tiles have, there are three ways to show one:

→ Local

→ Scheduled

→ Push

As with live tiles, you can refer to http://bit.ly/RSXomc for more information about push notifications. This section examines local and scheduled notifications.

Just like TileNotification, ToastNotification defines an ExpirationTime property, although it's not meaningful due to the short-lived nature of notifications.

Local

This is the approach that has already been shown. In addition to calling ToastNotifier's Show method, you can call its Hide method to hide the toast early, presumably due to some user action inside your app. However, local toast notifications are not the most common kind because toast notifications are generally meant to be shown when your app is *not* already running.

One important issue that hasn't yet been addressed is how you can respond to a user clicking on a toast notification. Doing so switches to your app if it's already running, or launches it otherwise. When your app isn't running, it looks like a regular launch activation, so you can't distinguish between the user clicking the notification or doing a regular launch. For locally shown toast notifications, however, you can attach event handlers to some events on the ToastNotification object: Activated, Dismissed, and Failed. Although the terminology is confusing, the Activated event is raised if the user clicks the notification. In a Dismissed event handler, you can determine why it was dismissed with a value from the ToastDismissalReason passed through ToastDismissedEventArgs. ApplicationHidden means the app called ToastNotifier.Hide, TimedOut means the seven (or twenty-five) seconds elapsed with no interaction, and UserCanceled means that the user clicked the little X button on the notification.

Scheduled

To schedule a notification for a specific date and time, you call ToastNotifier's AddToSchedule method instead of Show. AddToSchedule requires a **Scheduled**ToastNotification object that must be constructed with a DateTimeOffset representing the delivery time (along with the XmlDocument defining the content). If you want to cancel a pending notification, you can call ToastNotifier's RemoveFromSchedule method.

ScheduledToastNotification provides a slick additional feature. Via an overloaded constructor, you can specify a *snooze interval* (a nullable TimeSpan that must be between 60 seconds and 60 minutes) and maximum snooze count (a uint from 1–5). This enables you to easily support alarm-style functionality.

The Lock Screen

Using the same techniques already demonstrated for live tiles, an app can easily display status information on the user's lock screen. The lock screen has two regions you can update, with the user's permission. One is a badge that works much like the badge on a live tile, and one is a larger region that can contain text, much like the text on a live tile. The user is able to select up to seven apps that show badges on the lock screen, and only one that shows custom text. This is controlled in the Personalize section of the PC Settings app, shown in Figure 22.14.

Lock screen apps

Choose apps to run in the background and show quick status and notifications, even when your screen is locked

Choose an app to display detailed status

FIGURE 22.14   Each of the toast notification templates

To enable your app to be selectable as a lock screen app, you must set "Lock screen notifications" to "Badge" in your package manifest, and you must assign a 24x24 badge logo. This logo is not only used for badges on the lock screen, but they are shown in the PC Settings user interface in Figure 22.14. By convention, they should be white-on-transparent, although the app in this chapter uses a red and white icon so it stands out.

To enable your app to be selectable as the one-and-only lock screen app that shows detailed status, you must change "Lock screen notifications" in your package manifest from "Badge" to "Badge and Tile Text."

The amazing thing about the two lock screen regions is that if your app already supports badges and a wide live tile, you don't need to do anything else! If the user designates your app as a lock screen app, then any badge update—numeric or graphical—gets echoed on the lock screen. If the user designates your app as the lock screen app that can display detailed status, then updating your wide live tile automatically updates the detailed region on the lock screen. This is pictured in Figure 22.15.

There are a few limitations to note. The text area works only with a wide tile template; square tile templates are ignored. Furthermore, if the template contains images, these are ignored (but accompanying text is still shown). This lock screen region also doesn't perform periodic rotation of notifications or any animations. It simply shows the most recent text. Also, for some reason, the numeric badge doesn't show 99+ for numbers greater than 99. It shows 99 instead.

Wide tile template

Badge template

FIGURE 22.15   Each of the toast notification templates

Rather than passively hoping that the user adds your app to the lock screen, you can prompt the user to add your app by calling `BackgroundExecutionManager`. `RequestAccessAsync`. This presents a standard dialog that gives the user the choice to allow or deny the action. An app is allowed to make this request only once. After that, calls to RequestAccessAsync are ignored (unless the reason the user decided against allowing it is that all seven spots on the lock screen were already filled).

Secondary tiles can also be added to the lock screen separately from the app. To make it eligible to become a lock screen badge, you must set `SecondaryTile`'s `LockScreenBadgeLogo` property to an appropriate `Uri`. To make it eligible to become the provider of the lock screen's detailed status, you must set `SecondaryTile`'s `LockScreenDisplayBadgeAndTileText` property to `true`.

As mentioned in Chapter 20, "Extensions," lock screen apps have additional triggers available to them for running background tasks. Not only that, but their background tasks are given more CPU cycles to do their work0 and a higher allowance of network data usage.

Summary

With live tiles, toast notifications, and lock screen features, your apps can integrate nicely with Windows without any special capabilities required. All these mechanisms still keep the user in control, however. A user can "turn off" a live tile, decide whether it should be wide or square, or even completely unpin a tile from the Start screen. A user can also disable toast notifications (completely or app-by-app) and notification sounds from within the PC Settings app. And a user can decide which apps, if any, get one of the coveted spots on the lock screen.

INDEX

Symbols and Numbers

A

E

G

M

N

T

X

Y

Z

UNLEASHED

Unleashed takes you beyond the basics, providing an exhaustive, technically sophisticated reference for professionals who need to exploit a technology to its fullest potential. It's the best resource for practical advice from the experts, and the most in-depth coverage of the latest technologies.

informit.com/unleashed

Windows 8 Apps with HTML5 and JavaScript Unleashed
ISBN-13: 9780672336058

OTHER UNLEASHED TITLES

Windows Phone 7.5 Unleashed
ISBN-13: 9780672333484

ASP.NET Dynamic Data Unleashed
ISBN-13: 9780672335655

Microsoft System Center 2012 Unleashed
ISBN-13: 9780672336126

System Center 2012 Configuration Manager (SCCM) Unleashed
ISBN-13: 9780672334375

Windows Server 2012 Unleashed
ISBN-13: 9780672336225

Microsoft Exchange Server 2013 Unleashed
ISBN-13: 9780672336119

MVVM Unleashed
ISBN-13: 9780672334382

System Center 2012 Operations Manager Unleashed
ISBN-13: 9780672335914

Microsoft Dynamics CRM 2011 Unleashed
ISBN-13: 9780672335389

SharePoint Designer 2010 Unleashed
ISBN-13: 9780672331053

ASP.NET 4.0 Unleashed
ISBN-13: 9780672331121

Silverlight 4 Unleashed
ISBN-13: 9780672333361

C# 5.0 Unleashed
ISBN-13: 9780672336904

Microsoft Visual Studio 2012 Unleashed
ISBN-13: 9780672336256

SAMS

informit.com/sams

Try Safari Books Online FREE for 15 days

Get online access to Thousands of Books and Videos

Feed your brain

Gain unlimited access to thousands of books and videos about technology, digital media and professional development from O'Reilly Media, Addison-Wesley, Microsoft Press, Cisco Press, McGraw Hill, Wiley, WROX, Prentice Hall, Que, Sams, Apress, Adobe Press and other top publishers.

See it, believe it

Watch hundreds of expert-led instructional videos on today's hottest topics.

WAIT, THERE'S MORE!

Gain a competitive edge

Be first to learn about the newest technologies and subjects with Rough Cuts pre-published manuscripts and new technology overviews in Short Cuts.

Accelerate your project

Copy and paste code, create smart searches that let you know when new books about your favorite topics are available, and customize your library with favorites, highlights, tags, notes, mash-ups and more.

* Available to new subscribers only. Discount applies to the Safari Library and is valid for first 12 consecutive monthly billing cycles. Safari Library is not available in all countries.

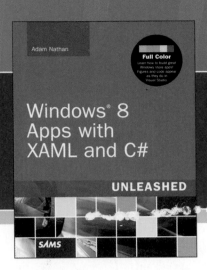

Windows® 8 Apps with XAML and C# UNLEASHED

Adam Nathan

Full Color
Learn how to build great Windows store apps! Figures and code appear as they do in Visual Studio

SAMS

FREE
Online Edition

 Safari
Books Online

Your purchase of **Windows® 8 Apps with XAML and C# Unleashed** includes access to a free online edition for 45 days through the **Safari Books Online** subscription service. Nearly every Sams book is available online through **Safari Books Online**, along with thousands of books and videos from publishers such as Addison-Wesley Professional, Cisco Press, Exam Cram, IBM Press, O'Reilly Media, Prentice Hall, Que, and VMware Press.

Safari Books Online is a digital library providing searchable, on-demand access to thousands of technology, digital media, and professional development books and videos from leading publishers. With one monthly or yearly subscription price, you get unlimited access to learning tools and information on topics including mobile app and software development, tips and tricks on using your favorite gadgets, networking, project management, graphic design, and much more.

Activate your FREE Online Edition at
informit.com/safarifree

STEP 1:   Enter the coupon code: QUBDWFA.

STEP 2:   New Safari users, complete the brief registration form.
Safari subscribers, just log in.

If you have difficulty registering on Safari or accessing the online edition,
please e-mail customer-service@safaribooksonline.com